CONSUMER PROTECTION LAW

To Elizabeth with love from Geraint.
To Catherine with love from Steve.

Consumer Protection Law

GERAINT G. HOWELLS
Department of Law, University of Sheffield

STEPHEN WEATHERILL
Department of Law, University of Nottingham

Dartmouth

Aldershot • Brookfield USA • Singapore • Sydney

Published by
Dartmouth Publishing Company Limited
Gower House
Croft Road
Aldershot
Hants GU11 3HR
England

Dartmouth Publishing Company
Old Post Road
Brookfield
Vermont 05036
USA

British Library Cataloguing in Publication Data
Howells, Geraint G.
  Consumer Protection Law
  I. Title II. Weatherill, Stephen
  344.10371

Library of Congress Cataloging-in-Publication Data
Howells, Geraint G.
    Consumer protection law / Geraint G. Howells, Stephen
Weatherill.
      p.   cm.
    Includes bibliographical references.
    ISBN 1-85521-729-5 (hbk.). – ISBN 1-85521-733-3 (pbk.)
    1. Consumer protection–Law and legislation–Great Britain.
  2. Consumer protection–Great Britain. I. Weatherill, Stephen,
  1963-   . II. Title.
  KD2204.H69   1995
  343.41'071–dc20
  [344.10371]   95-30983
                                                                   CIP

ISBN 1 85521 729 5 (Hbk)
ISBN 1 85521 733 3 (Pbk)

Printed in Great Britain at the University Press, Cambridge

Contents

Table of Cases

Table of Statutes and Statutory Instruments

Preface

Elements of consumer protection may be traced back through the centuries, but as a field of academic legal study, consumer protection is still a relatively young subject. We believe it is an area of law which warrants more research and we hope that our book will encourage students to explore this subject. We find the subject particularly interesting because of its position at the interface between the social and commercial life of states and their citizens and hope our enthusiasm can be passed on to the reader.

Although consumer law is potentially a very broad subject we have essentially limited our scope to the general law relating to the marketing and supply of consumer goods and services. We have largely avoided discussing specific problems relating to particular product and service sectors, such as financial services, package holiday or timeshare contracts, but of course we felt bound to give credit contracts a special treatment. This is a similar approach to most consumer law textbooks. There are perhaps three distinctive features of this book to which we should draw the reader's attention. First, we see consumer law and competition law as closely interlinked. Although constrained by space, we seek to give more than a passing nod in the direction of competition law as well as, of course, exploring the limits of competition in the market as a consumer protection technique. Second, we consider EC law as central to an understanding of UK consumer law, not as a footnote to domestic law. The impact of EC directives on consumer law alone seems to justify this approach. Third, as consumer law is a modern subject, which is a response (in part) to new marketing and sales techniques which give rise to similar problems in many economies, we believe a global comparative approach is useful and have used comparative examples to illustrate different regulatory techniques at appropriate points in the text.

This book is longer than most of the consumer law textbooks currently in use. We believe the topic justifies this length of treatment at degree level. We hope it is written in an accessible manner which can provide a solid base for all students and a springboard for the more industrious.

We would like to thank the publishers for keeping our price competitive. Indeed we should like to thank our publisher, John Irwin, for having faith in this project. Thanks should also go to the following who commented on parts of the text: John Adams, Graham Battersby, Robert Bradgate, Richard Bragg, Peter Cartwright, Tim Jones, Hans Micklitz, Iain Ramsay, Catherine Redgwell, Graham Stephenson and Chris Willett. Special thanks should go to Julie Prescott who expeditiously and efficiently turned our manuscript into camera ready copy and put up with our requests for alterations and amendments. We both have Brunel University on our C.V., and are happy to acknowledge with gratitude the many insights into consumer law and policy that have been provided by Geoffrey Woodroffe, Professor of Law, in that University. Finally thanks to our families. Geraint would like to thank his wife, Elizabeth, for her understanding, his daughter Laura for giving him opportunities to be distracted from the computer and his new daughter Bethan, whose arrival during the final stages of the manuscript's preparation certainly distracted her father. Stephen thanks his Law Department for the grant of study leave; Catherine and his mother for their support; and Hull City for thoughtfully avoiding a promotion challenge that would have interrupted the completion of the book.

The book is a joint work and of course the authors take joint responsibility for the final product. It may interest some readers to know who took main responsibility for each chapter; Geraint Howells took main responsibility for Chapters 3-8, 11, 13, 16-7 and Stephen Weatherill took the lead in Chapters 1-2, 9-10, 12, 14-5.

The text attempts to state the law as of 1st January 1995, but it has been possible to include several developments which occurred up until June 1995.

We would welcome any comments on the scope and approach of the book.

GERAINT HOWELLS
STEPHEN WEATHERILL

1 The Map of Consumer Protection Law

1.1 INTRODUCTION – THE NATURE OF THE LAW OF CONSUMER PROTECTION

1.1.1 Markets and Consumers

It may be useful to begin with a model of an economic system which is as alluring as it is unrealistic. Producers have to sell their goods to consumers in order to survive. They will only be able to sell to consumers what consumers want to buy. Consumer preference will dictate what is made available. Producers compete. Consumers choose. The 'invisible hand' of producers behaving in response to consumer preference organises the market. The survival instinct among producers which is instilled by the mechanism of competition will ensure an efficient allocation of resources. Given the stimulus of competition, resources will not be wasted. Production will stand in equilibrium with consumption. Viewed from this perspective, the market economy is a self–organising system.

A society based on this model of 'perfect competition' in the market should secure the best of all possible worlds for the consumer. The consumer, indeed, is dominant. He or she exercises the power of commercial life or death over suppliers in the shape of his or her purchasing decisions. The consumer will be supplied according to his or her preference and, for society generally, there will be no waste of resources. From the consumer standpoint, we might characterise a 'perfect' market as one where there is no such thing as an unsafe product or even a poor quality product. There are simply products of different types from which the consumer can choose. Increased demand will in theory lead to an increase in price, but a corresponding increase in supply will quickly restore equilibrium between supply and demand.

By contrast, in the absence of competition, inefficiency will prevail. Consumers will not be able to express their preference by sending messages via choice among competing products or services. Items may be produced which are not wanted, because the absence of competitive process obstructs the transmission of messages.

Competition in the market seems inherently desirable. That is a perception, however, which may serve as a starting point, but as no more than that.

1.1.2 Markets and their Practical Operation

It is easy to draw on individual experience to realise that this perfect system breaks down. Consumers have a voice which is much louder in theory than in practice. Consumers often simply do not know the nature of the products which are on offer. They want to buy the 'best' product, yet may be unable to make an informed choice. What does the consumer know about the qualities of the individual video or drug which is on offer? The perfectly operating market system makes assumptions about informed stimuli delivered from the 'demand-side', the consumer, which are unrealistic and becoming ever more unrealistic in an era of bewildering technological advance. Such lack of information affects the message sent by consumer purchase to producer. It undermines faith in the ability of the unregulated market to operate as a perfect market which will deliver the best possible outcome for the consumer. Losing customers is the ultimate sanction against failure to meet consumer demand, yet the efficacy of that sanction is impaired in modern market conditions.

Nevertheless markets are flexible and may be capable of adjusting themselves. In a simple, small market lack of information might not prove a serious problem. Word will get around about variations between quality of products and the relative reliability of suppliers. In complex market conditions, however, this control over supplier behaviour becomes erratic, since information is transmitted haphazardly. For the average consumer, the purchase of expensive products which turn out not to meet consumer aspirations cannot simply be written off to experience. Nor is it comforting to expect that the seller of a dangerous drug or poisonous wine will not build up a loyal client base. At the other extreme, cheaper goods are typically sold by small traders, perhaps moving around markets or car–boot sales, who will frequently be untraceable by consumers and who will not be concerned to build up repeat custom. True, markets for information may grow up alongside markets for products.[1] In the United Kingdom the obvious example lies in the Consumers Association's publication *Which?* Such support improves the consumer/supplier dialogue, but does not constitute a complete 'perfection' of the market. It cannot be comprehensive. In some markets, consumers are not even aware that they are underinformed, so the growth of a market for information provision will not readily help.

Absence of 'perfection' on the 'demand-side' may be accompanied by flaws on the 'supply-side'. In some markets, choice will be restricted by the existence of only a limited number of suppliers. The notion that rival

---

1   For pathbreaking analysis, G. Stigler, 'The Economics of Information' (1961) 69 *Journal of Political Economy* 213.

suppliers must dance to the consumer's tune is false where the consumer's influence is thwarted because of a lack of competition. Such problems may arise because some or all of the relevant firms have decided to forego the unpredictable outcomes of competition in favour of collusion. Such a cartel will rob the free market of its defining competitive edge and deprive the consumer of choice. Some markets are structurally incapable of delivering competition. With a monopoly supplier, there is no competition at all and the consumer's position is grossly weakened.

More fundamental scepticism may exist as to whether the market system really is in the consumer interest. The supplier/consumer relationship assumes a transfer of wealth, not its redistribution. If one wished to adjust the position of individuals in society rather than simply treat them as consumers within the economy, then it would not be deemed appropriate to leave the market to its own devices. Such an approach would prompt an interest in adjusting the market. Wealth maximisation would be subordinated to wealth distribution.

Consumer demand is itself a controversial notion. Some observers doubt whether a defensible notion of demand can realistically exist in a modern economy which is so far removed from undistorted individual choice. For some commentators, firms are able to manipulate demand through strategies such as product promotion, on which much money is invested in the modern economy.[2] The notion of 'false consciousness' describes a situation where consumers in the modern economy cannot really know what they want.[3]

This account has not yet drawn on the role of law. Markets can doubtless develop autonomously as a privately organised system. But today the pattern of the market can no longer be realistically assessed without taking account of the degree of intensity of public intervention. The modern market is characterised by centuries of State involvement which affects the simple process of private economic relations between supplier and consumer. This arises directly where the State takes on the role of supplier, as it has in many areas where mixed economies have developed. Moreover, outside such relationships, private economic arrangements are significantly affected by a mass of statutory interventions in the market which have accumulated over many years. The 'simple' consumer/supplier relationship cannot be pursued without reference to the place of the State in the market. At a rather

---

2   Cf J.K. Galbraith, *The Affluent Society* (Deutsch, 1985); R. Unger, *False Necessity: Anti–Necessitarian Social Theory in the Service of Radical Democracy* (Cambridge University Press, 1987).

3   Eg D. Kennedy, 'Distributive and Paternalist Motives in Contract and Tort Law, with special reference to Compulsory Terms and Unequal Bargaining Power' (1981–82) 41 *Maryland Law Rev* 563.

straightforward level, it is assumed that legal consequences flow from a consumer transaction and that in the event of, for example, breach of promise, remedies in law are available. The State provides the framework for the vindication of such rights. This is uncontroversial. The modern debate is not about whether or not the State should have a role; the difficult questions revolve around the appropriate intensity of State participation in the economy and in society.

1.1.3 Law and Markets – The Scope of this Book

The law of the market economy has a wide scope. It covers law which sustains, promotes, curtails and adjusts the structure of a free market. In many cases it is based on political perceptions of the nature of the market economy. Within an overall political acceptance of the desirability of a market economy, there are many nuances of approach towards the way that market should be permitted to operate, with law used to achieve such adjustments. However, an accumulation of legal rules introduced by governments of different political complexions in the UK over many years has left the law of the economy in a patchwork state.

Consumer protection law can be understood only against such backgrounds.[4] The consumer's place in the economy and in society attracts differing interpretations. For most people, probably no theory feels intuitively completely correct or completely incorrect. Different perspectives contain their own truths. The law is affected by choices made about the identity of the consumer and the role he or she is supposed to play in the economy and in society. Consumer protection law has a range of possible rationales, some of which may conflict. The modern law has grown by accretion. The law now protects the consumer from a lot of different things in a lot of different ways and, as the law of market regulation has accumulated over the centuries since the days of the aleconner and obligatory cheap corn supply,[5] for a lot of different reasons. Consumer protection law is susceptible to neither neat nor narrow definition. Its scope is open-ended. Defining the 'consumer' is an endemic problem in shaping the law which will be encountered on a number of occasions in the course of this book. Whether one chooses the label 'consumer law', 'trading law' or 'the law of trade

---

4   For a wide selection of sources, see I. Ramsay, *Consumer Protection Text and Materials* (Weidenfeld, 1989). Cf T. Bourgoignie, *Elements pour une theorie de la Consommation* (Story-Scientia, 1988); J. Goldring, 'Consumer Law and Legal Theory: Reflections of a Common Lawyer' (1990) 13 *JCP* 113.

5   A. Ogus, 'Regulatory law: some lessons from the past' (1992) 12 *Legal Studies* 1.

practices' is not of central importance; it is however critical to appreciate that, irrespective of labels, the map of consumer protection law has fuzzy edges and one should know what lies beyond, including paths to other areas of law and the bridges to other academic disciplines such as economics and politics. This book tries to provide a full awareness of this breadth and ambiguity. Operating on the basis that the law of consumer protection is an aspect of the law of the economy, its objective is to show where the law of the economy which is not treated in depth within the confines of this book fits into the overall pattern. To some extent we present all law affecting the market as, directly or indirectly, law which affects the consumer interest, although choices have necessarily been made about the depth of the examination provided.

Accordingly the book examines the range of legal rules which offer support for the consumer, typically regarded as under informed and in a weaker position than the supplier. It seems that inequality of economic power between consumer and supplier is the key to scepticism about the modern unregulated market as an adequate defender of the consumer interest. The identification of inequality is but a starting point. It is, after all, an inequality which seems endemic to modern society. It cannot be removed. The shaping of consumer policy depends on pinning down the specific consequences of that inequality which are susceptible to legal control. It is critically important to appreciate that simply because some things go wrong for some consumers, nonetheless it is vital to examine precisely how and why the law might intervene in the market. Take the car boot sale, mentioned above. Should the consumer be protected from the risk of buying a faulty product? Not on one view, since the consumer who chooses to buy in such an environment ought to be alert to the risks. On the other hand, not all consumers *are* alert, leading one to consider a policy which assumes a rather high level of consumer gullibility. Thus the shaping of consumer policy may depend on what kind of consumer is being protected.[6] Then, the policy maker needs to identify where the problem lies and how best it can be resolved. Is the issue the inadequacy of private law rights enjoyed by the consumer? If so, it may be appropriate to adjust the pattern of private law (Chapters 3–9). Inadequacy may refer to securing compensation for the consumer and/or to preventing a recurrence of the practices at issue. Is the problem that those rights cannot effectively be enforced? If so, questions of improving access to justice come to the fore (Chapter 17). If the matter is seen to require regulatory intervention separate from the private law relationships that

---

6   Cf overview by T. Wilhelmsson, 'Consumer images in East and West', in H–W. Micklitz (ed.), *Legal Unity or Legal Diversity* (forthcoming).

comprise a consumer transaction, then techniques of public law require consideration (Chapters 10–14).

Both private law and public law contribute to this core aspect of consumer protection. Here, however, is an illustration of the open–ended nature of consumer protection law. If intervention follows from economic inequality, then it cannot be confined solely to the consumer/supplier relationship. There are similar reasons for intervening to protect the small trader dealing with a large trader. It will be seen that consumer protection law spills over into the wider field of trade practices law. This book also contains an examination of the law designed to address problems on the 'supply-side', usually termed 'competition law' but correctly included within the sphere of consumer law as a contribution to the better functioning of the market. Chapter 15 examines the problems caused by diminution in competition and in consumer choice on the supply-side. Legal measures are directed in some respects at curing such weaknesses on the supply-side, for example, by forbidding collaboration between competitors which restricts consumer choice, save in exceptional circumstances. In other respects the law acquiesces in such weaknesses but seeks to curtail their most damaging consequences. This may be observed in monopoly law, where the existence of economic dominance may be tolerated, but its exercise controlled.

The market in which the consumer is active today is not merely a national market. The process of market integration in the European Community has advanced rapidly over recent years so that the Community is an increasingly important source of consumer protection law (Chapter 2). More widely still, international institutions, such as those established under the GATT and the United Nations,[7] have a role to play in the pattern of consumer protection. At a more subtle level, problems faced by consumers and markets have many similarities the world over. Discussion of the desirable scope and methods of consumer protection is improved by an awareness of comparative legal perspectives, which are also reflected in this book.

The book also draws in elements of the political debate. A perception of the false consciousness of the consumer leads to a legal response which is less than respectful of individual consumer freedoms expressed through market transactions. More broadly, if one believes that markets are not just, one will not be reluctant to interfere with them. This view locates the rationale for consumer protection beyond the economic sphere of mere market failure. At the other end of the political spectrum, the book does not neglect the argument that markets are or should be sacred and that limits

---

7   Cf D.Harland, 'Implementing the principles of the United Nations Guidelines for Consumer Protection' (1991) 33 *Journal of the Indian Law Institute* 189.

must be placed on the capacity of the State to intervene in them and so undermine private economic freedom.

Ultimately this book is based on the belief that consumer law is not simply a matter of plugging a few gaps in the market system. Consumer law raises issues which are central to the determination of how our society views the citizen.

1.2 THE PLACE OF PRIVATE LAW

The competitive free market allows the consumer to respond to a disappointing purchase by switching to another supplier. The law here has no role to play. However, such disappointment may be of a form that is capable of conversion into a legal remedy against the trader (whether or not the consumer also decides to use another supplier next time). Where what is supplied fails to conform to consumer expectation, English law may offer a remedy, whether in contract or in tort, enforced through the courts.

Contract protects consumer expectations engendered through the bargaining process. By providing a sanction in the event of failure to fulfil those expectations, the law acts to secure the enforceability of expressed consumer preference. Tort law operates beyond the realm of obligations agreed between producer and consumer. Even in the absence of agreement, tort imposes certain obligations on producers and distributors of goods.

The conferral of such individual legal rights on consumers offers a more direct protection of consumer demand than the more indirect and, in practice, greatly obscured sanction of commercial failure caused by withdrawal of custom. Failure to conform to agreed (contract) or required (tort) standards will result in legal liability. This protects the consumer and sharpens the message to the producer about the need to use resources in an efficient manner. Private law gives the consumer autonomy to act in the belief that he or she holds rights protected by law that can be asserted without the need to rely on an intermediary.

Current market practice assumes that private economic relations involve the possibility of State support, at the very least in the shape of providing for the enforcement of private law rights. These rights comprise, as a minimum, the obligations agreed between the parties. However, the consumer/supplier relationship under the private law today encompasses more than simple agreement, since both the courts and Parliament have extended the legal implications of the consumer/supplier relationship. Viewed from this perspective, the law provides a method of creating as well as fulfilling consumer expectations and of imposing liability on defaulting suppliers. This should support the trader's incentive to satisfy consumer preference and should improve the operation of the market.

The account that follows in Parts 3 and 4 of this Chapter surveys some modern developments in the scope of contract and tort law. Private law has been shaped and bolstered by the judges and by Parliament to adjust the pattern of market relations and, sometimes directly, sometimes indirectly, to protect the consumer. This has done much to create a discernible framework of consumer protection law within the private law. However, it will be shown that some markets require public regulation, for reasons associated with the inadequacies of private law to achieve a free and fair market. This is examined in Parts 7 to 9 of this Chapter. It is a theme of this book, however, that the mixture of rationales and methods for intervention in consumer transactions today embraces such a range of (in places) conflicting aims that a simple objective account of what is at stake may misleadingly suggest that the development of the law has been a precise science. This is far from the truth. The best that can be done is to identify the several trends that comprise modern consumer protection law: trends such as identification of market failure and of, distinctively, a mistrust of the fairness of the market mechanism; also trends that embrace the fortification of consumer rights in private law and that move beyond the private law into the sphere of creating regulatory regimes directed at controlling practices likely to damage the consumer interest. Consumer lawyers must indeed possess a wide field of vision.[8]

1.3 CONTRACT LAW AND ITS FUNCTION IN THE MARKET ECONOMY

1.3.1 The Function of the Law of Contract – Efficiency of Exchange

Put simply, contract law provides security for the recipient of a promise who has given something in return for that promise. However, the purpose of a contract in a market economy deserves closer scrutiny. In many respects, contracts are the lifeblood of a market economy. Simple one–off, over–the–table transactions are not the stuff of modern commerce, nor have they been since the Industrial Revolution. Rather, complex linked deals are the norm. Contracts allow long term planning. Contract law provides security for those who act in reliance on the deals struck. Commerce revolves around promises made and promises fulfilled and, if not fulfilled, made good in other ways, backed by law.

---

8   For such an overview, see I. Ramsay, 'Consumer Law and Structures of Thought: a Comment' (1993) 16 *JCP* 79.

The law has long enshrined a notion of the efficiency of exchange. Contract law seeks to promote bargains, because bargains constitute wealth–creating transfers. A simple example will help to make the point, although its apparent simplicity is unpicked below. If A has an item worth 100 to him, which is worth 200 to B, they will exchange it at 150 (assuming there are no other bidders) and both are better off as a result. Overall, society generally is better off as a result of a transaction beneficial to both A and B which prejudices no third party. The process of exchange ensures the efficient allocation of resources. This model makes a number of assumptions that are probed further below. However, it serves as a basic theoretical demonstration of the advantages of economic exchange. Indeed, on a theoretical model, it does not matter where initial entitlements to property lie. The market will secure the most efficient outcome; via a process of exchange, resources will reach the hands of the person who most values them – the so–called 'Coase Theorem'.[9]

Contract law enforces bargains and thereby induces parties to conclude contracts in the first place. Without law to back up promises and provide sanctions for reneging, deals would be short term only. Firms would not be able to plan ahead, aware that default by their contracting parties will be remedied. Contract law facilitates the operation of the market economy. Indeed in a complex commercial world, where transactions typically relate one to another as part of a long term pattern, contract law may be seen as the cement which holds the whole structure together.

At the commercial level, there is much to be said for the view that contract law should reflect business expectation. It should seek to achieve certainty and predictability in its operation. Litigation should not be a spin of the roulette wheel or else it will be needlessly encouraged, leading to waste of money and disruption of planning.

From this perspective, the function of contract and contract law is therefore to facilitate commercial exchange. Taken to a logical extreme, this seems to dictate that the law should unquestioningly serve the parties' wishes. Deals are struck to maximise both parties' wealth – why else? – and it is not the function of courts to interfere. Courts enforce contracts. The role of the judges is therefore rigidly confined to upholding contracts, as a reflection of the will of the parties and the interest of society in facilitating commerce. On this basis, the legislature too should maintain a strictly non–interventionist stance. This is the very core of 'freedom of contract'. The parties are free to deal; the role of law is not to interfere with that freedom, but simply to protect the deals struck.

Most of the time, of course, contract law is a shadowy concept in the

---

9   R. Coase, 'The Problem of Social Cost' (1960) 3 *J Law & Econ* 1.

background once commercial relationships are afoot. Parties co–operate in the conduct of their commercial affairs, eager to avoid the costs, disruptions and potential harm to commercial reputation consequent on litigation.[10] In the words of an anonymous Wisconsin businessman; 'You can settle any dispute if you keep the lawyers and accountants out of it. They just do not understand the give-and-take needed in business'.[11] In practice contracts are adjusted during their lifecycle. Perhaps in response to such stimuli, some recent developments in English contract law manifest a greater readiness to uphold agreed contractual renegotiation than had previously been the norm.[12]

1.3.2 Limitations of the Law of Contract

The simple transaction between A and B mentioned above deserves closer scrutiny. The transaction seems efficient in the sense of wealth–creating; it seems appropriate to offer legal protection for the deal struck. However, some of the unstated assumptions require examination. The model assumes A and B are equally informed about the nature of the product and other background information relevant to the transaction. This will often not hold true. In an extreme case, informational imbalance may inhibit the conclusion of the deal. Legal intervention to ensure disclosure may be appropriate to improve the operation of the market. For example, in a market where goods of different quality are available at prices varying from 100 to 500, but where the consumer is completely unable to distinguish between goods on the basis of quality, the result will be consumer unwillingness to pay at the higher end of the price scale. As a result, sellers will simply withdraw better quality goods from that market. The process will continue; bad will drive out good. Legal intervention is justified as a means of correcting problems

---

10   Famous empirical studies include S. Macaulay, 'Non–contractual relations in Business: A Preliminary Study' (1963) 28 *Am Soc Rev* 55; H. Beale and A. Dugdale, 'Contracts between Businessmen: Planning and the use of contractual remedies' (1975) 2 *Br J of Law and Soc* 45. Cf I. Macneil, 'Contracts: Adjustment of Long–term Economic Relations under Classical, Neoclassical and Relational Contract Law' (1977–78) 72 *Northwestern Univ LR* 854.

11   Macaulay *op. cit.* 61. Cf also the more recent account of D. Campbell and D. Harris, 'Flexibility in long–term contractual relationships: the Role of Co–operation' (1993) 20 *JLS* 166.

12   Eg *Williams v Roffey* [1991] 1 QB 1.

caused by such intransparency.[13] This is an illustration of 'market failure' as a rationale for adding public intervention to the basic pattern of the market allied to private law.

On the A 100/ B 200 model, if A is simply more skilled at negotiating than B (in general or because of special knowledge relevant to the transaction in question), A may be able to push the price above 150, which benefits both parties equally, towards 200, which then gives A the lion's share of the advantage. From the point of view of wealth maximisation, that may be irrelevant: as long as the transfer occurs, society is better off and it does not matter whether one party gains more than the other. We might also consider it proper to allow A to reap the rewards of his or her skill, which would dictate that, as a matter of policy, the law would not interfere. Such a non-interventionist stance might be further supported by the perception that A will have a reduced incentive to develop such skills unless allowed to profit from them; A's inhibited motivation might damage society's broader interests. However, depending on one's perception of the importance of fairness and the distribution of wealth, legal controls may be considered appropriate to protect B, the individual who is liable to be exploited. It might be judged that a pattern of wealth maximisation alone should be subordinated to a pattern of wealth distribution.

A further assumption underlying the A/B model is that the transaction does not affect third parties. That is unrealistic in most deals of any commercial significance. Transactions typically have implications affecting more than simply the contracting parties. Where A and B conclude a contract that will make both better off, but will prejudice a third party X, then the simple assumption that the deal is desirable and deserves non-interventionist legal respect requires more careful inquiry. From an economic perspective we might assume that, where A and B can compensate X and still ensure that everyone is better off, the deal is desirable judged against the overall interests of society and can and should proceed.[14] Achieving that compensatory transfer is problematic. For the lawyer, the introduction of X complicates the pattern, since the legal rights of X will frequently be difficult to identify. The simple suffering of economic harm caused by the conduct of others is not of itself a cause of action at law. Tort law recognises only a more restricted

---

13 G. Akerlof, 'The Market for Lemons: Qualitative Uncertainty and the Market Mechanism' (1970) 84 *Q J Econ* 488.

14 In law and economics jargon, 'Kaldor-Hicks' efficiency refers to a situation where A/B/C *et al.* are better off and, although X(s) are worse off, the aggregate losses of X(s) are smaller than the aggregate gains of A/B/C *et al.* This is in contrast to a situation where A/B/C are better off and no one is worse off, which is known as 'Pareto efficient'.

range of liability. Even where X has a legal right, its effective vindication through legal proceedings or threat thereof will not be cost–free. The pattern becomes all the more complex and all the more prone to shelter A and B from accounting for the full costs of their actions where there are multiple Xs. Where the impact of harm is diffused and the victims are not deemed sufficiently proximate to the actors, the chances of those suffering loss being able to establish the violation of a right under English tort law are reduced. Even if a legal right has been infringed, the smaller the loss suffered by individuals, the weaker the incentive to pursue the path of legal redress. 'Transaction costs' affect the process; in fact, the `Coase Theorem'[15] operates in its pure form only in the absence of transaction costs, which will be rare indeed. A and B may therefore behave in a way that will benefit their own interests, but prejudice those of third parties, yet they may not bear the costs imposed on those third parties. Precisely the same observations may be made about the activities of a single person, C, which, equally, might benefit C while imposing costs on third parties for which C might not be held to account. The overall balance between A and B's (or C's) advantages and X's costs might still favour the former, in which case there might be reasons for simply allowing the deal or the activity (because of the maximisation of wealth that follows) or for allowing it but on terms which ensure that X has an opportunity to secure compensation from A and B or C (because of concern about the distribution of wealth). Where the overall balance shows that the advantages to the parties are outweighed by the disadvantages felt generally, then the market has failed to deliver an efficient outcome. Legal intervention to remedy this outcome might therefore be appropriate.[16] Specifically, A and B (or C) could be subjected to some form of control; they would then find limitations placed by law on their freedom to choose how to behave.[17]

Finally, the A/ B contract may maximise wealth, but it assumes existing allocations of that wealth. G may value the item at 300; but if G can pay no more than 50, G will not be able to acquire the item. Contract law is not involved in obligatory altruism. Through the application of other legal instruments, the State may involve itself more generally in such explicit

---

15 Note 9 above.
16 For an attempt to identify criteria relevant in deciding whether to leave regulation of conduct to the private law or to introduce administrative control, see S. Shavell, 'Liability for Harm versus Regulation of Safety' (1984) 13 *J Legal Studies* 357.
17 See Chapter 1.8 below on the range of regulatory techniques.

wealth distribution. In this direction, and distinct from contract law, lie tax law and welfare law.[18]

This is by no means a comprehensive account of the limitations of the value of contractual freedom in the market nor of the types of legal response that may follow.[19] Its purpose is to illustrate the complexities of the ramifications of an apparently simple transaction in the modern economy. These nuances dictate a need for a rather sophisticated pattern of law, embracing both private and public law. At stake are elements of the correction of market failure and, additionally, the achievement of fairness to consumers (*inter alia*) as the economically weaker parties. Consumer protection law has a wide range of forms and objectives.

What follows is an exploration of the potential of the private law in this direction, followed by an examination of public intervention. It bears repetition that the patterns described below represent the accumulation of centuries of activity and any peculiarities exposed should be assessed in that spirit.

1.3.3 Freedom of Contract

Freedom of contract was presented above as a cornerstone of wealth maximisation and, accordingly, as a notion demanding respect under the law. In its heyday, freedom of contract carried a flavour which transcended the economy. It is not uncommon to find powerful assertions by 19th–century English judges concerning the individualist nature of contract and the role of the law in protecting and enforcing such bargains once they were freely arrived at. Judges would not question the content of a bargain once it had met the required form for enforcement as a contract under English law. The judge would have no interest in whether the bargain seemed fair or unfair, as long as it represented an agreed exchange. Thus deception would be a basis for judicial intervention, but plain foolishness would not, nor would an apparently remarkably low or high price. The consequence for parties contemplating entry into a contract was clear; they should take scrupulous care to look out for their own interests. They should satisfy themselves that

---

18 For descriptions and prescriptions of the role of contract law in wealth distribution, see A. Kronman, 'Contract Law and Distributive Justice' (1980) 89 *Yale Law J* 472; H. Collins, 'Distributive Justice through Contracts' [1992] *Current Legal Problems* 49; R. Brownsword, G. Howells and T. Wilhelmsson, *Welfarism in Contract Law* (Dartmouth, 1995).

19 For a recent treatment at more length and in more depth, see M. Trebilcock, *The Limits of Freedom of Contract* (Harvard University Press, 1993).

the deal was beneficial to them because, once the contract was concluded, it would then be fruitless to ask a court to absolve them of any obligations for which they had lost enthusiasm or whose scope they had misperceived.[20] *Caveat emptor* – let the buyer beware – was an assertion of individual responsibility.

A famous high-water mark in the notion of judicial *laissez–faire* was the observation of Sir George Jessel MR in 1875 that

> '[I]f there is one thing which more than another public policy requires it is that men of full age and competent understanding shall have the utmost liberty of contracting, and that their contracts entered into freely and voluntarily shall be held sacred and shall be enforced by Courts of Justice.'[21]

He resisted arguments that a contract assigning patents should be declared void on public policy grounds. He commented that the public policy doctrine controlled the enforceability of contracts to commit a crime or to perform immoral acts, but that he 'should be sorry to extend it much further'. He ruled in favour of the enforceability of the contract in question.

The religious imagery chosen by Sir George Jessel is a striking illustration of the belief that such notions transcend 'ordinary' law and are instead part of some higher set of norms which confer power on the individual citizen with which the State should not interfere.

The belief in individualism was a central tenet of the common law of contract during the 19th century; as a corollary there was a suspicion of collectivism as a suppression of the freedom of the individual. A vivid manifestation of this stance is found in the common law's reluctance to recognise the collective nature and purpose of trade unions. Unions in the 19th century were consistently seen through the lens of the restraint of trade doctrine as a distortion of the 'proper' individual contractual relationship, and not as a legitimate reaction to the relative impotence of individual workers in their relationships with employers.[22] The actions of unions and unionists were capable of incurring tortious liability, *inter alia*, where they interfered with contractual relationships, most notably between employer and employee and employer and supplier or customer. Present too were the perils of criminal liability. The intervention of statute was necessary to decriminalise

---

20   Eg *Smith v Hughes* (1871) LR 6 QB 597.
21   *Printing and Numerical Registering Co v Sampson* (1875) LR 19 Eq 462, 465.
22   For a critical account, see Lord Wedderburn, *The Worker and the Law* (Penguin Books, 1986), esp. Chs. 1, 7.

the strike[23] and to protect the organisation of collective action from a liability at common law that would have wrecked the trade union as an institution.[24] The liability of individuals engaging in industrial action has ebbed and flowed through the 20th century. For most of its duration, common law liabilities have been extended by the judiciary while until 1979 Parliament typically responded by extending statutory immunities. Since 1979, however, the labour market policies of successive Conservative administrations, expressed through a series of Acts, have brought a curtailment of the immunities enjoyed by both unions and individuals.[25]

The labour market has similarities to the product market. Many of the reasons why individual employees cannot effectively bargain with employers can readily be transplanted to explain why consumers cannot effectively bargain with suppliers. However, consumers have not banded together in unions in the ways adopted by workers. The consumer interest is more diffuse than that of workers in the same factory or the same trade. The consumer 'strike' – a boycott - is very difficult to organise. Even if successfully pursued, boycotts can generate tortious liability for the participants, for which there is no statutory immunity. The law of defamation might also impede the pursuit of a consumer campaign against a particular trader. Consumer representative organisations play a role in expressing the voice of the consumer, but their political impact is limited and their membership relatively small. Furthermore, English law's preference for individuals surfaces at the procedural level, where individual actions are the norm and collective or representative actions very much the exception.[26] In many cases of consumer detriment, individual loss suffered will be small even though one producer may in aggregate have caused significant harm. The requirement that each individual consumer pursue his or her own claim separately operates severely to restrict consumer redress and the control of producers through the operation of the private law.

Accordingly there is no 'collective consumer law' which is analogous to the development of collective labour organisation and collective labour law. The impediments to creating such a pattern out of the diffuse interests of consumers provides a rationale for public intervention to achieve the

---

23 This was (loosely) the effect achieved by the Conspiracy and Protection of Property Act 1875.

24 Most notably, the House of Lords ruling on union liability in *Taff Vale Railway Company v ASRS* [1901] AC 426, leading to the protection of the Trade Disputes Act 1906.

25 For a thorough account, see P. Davies and M. Freedland, *Labour Legislation and Public Policy* (Clarendon Press, 1993).

26 Part 1.6 of this Chapter; more generally, Chapters 16 and 17.

protection for the consumer which cannot be achieved by the operation of the market. Discussion of such techniques follows in this Chapter, beginning in Part 1.7 below. However, further examination of the scope of the private law is called for. The labour law analogy offers further illumination. The contract of employment remains the cornerstone of the employer/worker relationship, yet modern law has moved far beyond the 19th–century *laissez–faire* stance. Built into an essentially contractual relationship are elements such as an employee's right not to be unfairly dismissed, established by statute,[27] and a right to be treated with respect by an employer, developed by the judiciary.[28] These rights are enjoyed by a worker independently of the package that has been negotiated with the employer. The law of the contract of employment has distinctive features departing from the model of 'pure' contractual freedom in the direction of employee protection. Much the same has occurred in relation to the law of the consumer contract. The notion of respect for the parties' bargain as the sole source of legal rights and obligations has declined. In part this flows from a realisation that the notion of contractual freedom, which underpins judicial non–interventionism, is no longer necessarily realistic in the modern consumer transaction where the relationship between parties is typically economically imbalanced in favour of the supplier. Consumer contract law now embraces rights and obligations inserted into the relationship by judicial activism and by statutory intervention. The law thus encompasses considerably more than the parties' agreement.

1.3.4 The Decline of a Common Set of 'Contract Law' Principles

It would be misleading to assume that the connected themes of individualism, freedom of contract and judicial non–interventionism in the parties' bargain have lost their relevance to 20th-century commerce. The rationales which underpinned the 19th–century perspective largely hold true today in the commercial sphere, at least where the parties negotiate at arms length, sustained by more or less equal economic strength. In commercial transactions, the need to encourage and protect long–term planning continues to dictate a rigid law of contract, which enforces bargains and does not judge their merits.[29]

Moreover, the value of contract–as–exchange is still firmly part of the consumer perspective of the role of the market. Like commercial parties, a

---

27   Now contained in the Employment Protection (Consolidation) Act 1978.
28   Eg *Woods v W.M. Car Services* [1982] ICR 693.
29   Although even here legislative intervention has occurred; cf. Chapter 9.3 below.

consumer choosing between two products can also use the law of contract to plan ahead by extracting guarantees about the durability of the product. The consumer does not know for sure which of two brands of washing machine will last the longer, since he or she is no expert. But he or she can buy the product plus a promise about durability, secure in the knowledge that the law will protect the promise bought in the event of default. The consumer will have a legal entitlement to compensation should the product fail to meet the promised standard of durability. In this manner the private law is capable of filling the information gap which afflicts the consumer. It protects, and thereby induces, planning.

However, the overall picture of contract law as a means of establishing a long–term framework for a commercial relationship does not accord with the reality of many consumer transactions. For the consumer, deals will frequently lack the long-term relational flavour which characterises much commercial dealing. Nor will the terms have been settled as a result of often protracted arms length negotiation between teams of sharp lawyers. Consumer purchases may be financially on a small–scale as far as the supplier is concerned, although they may loom large for the budget of an individual consumer. Consumer purchases are frequently concluded on the basis of standard-form contracts, which the consumer will almost never have read nor will ever read. Negotiation on price or conditions is hardly typical of the average purchase of, for example, a video recorder or a train ticket.

Absence of effective negotiation and agreement may spur an instinctive interest in intervention in such deals. However, the point should be taken that the mere fact that the context of the consumer transaction differs from that of the commercial transaction is not of itself a cause for criticism or intervention. The case of the standard-form contract is instructive. Such a contract might suggest itself as an instrument for the supplier to oppress the ill–informed consumer. That may occur. Yet the standard–form contract is not the irredeemable evil it is sometimes portrayed. It would be in the interest of neither consumer nor trader to sit down and hammer out terms for each and every transaction, quill pens doubtless in hand. The modern consumer economy is based on the standard–form contract because its use is efficient, reducing time and money which would otherwise be spent on negotiating. Business can plan on the basis of its standard terms and pass on cost savings via the price. The consumer stands to benefit from the use of standard-form contracts, although there are counterbalancing costs. The standard–form contract tends to enhance the power of the supplier who will have a greater awareness of the content of the contract. The consumer will typically be under informed and may 'accept' peculiarly disadvantageous terms. The notion that free will, a bargain and an agreement lie at the heart of a consumer contract is rather distorted by the prevalence of standard-form contracts which often go largely unread. This analysis suggests that the use of standard-form contracts may be desirable in principle, but that they might generate justifications for regulation where 'freedom of contract' has effectively converted big firms into legislators in the market.[30]

In modern economic conditions, the supplier/consumer relationship is typically imbalanced in favour of the supplier. The supplier knows more about the product or service. The more complex the subject matter, the less likely that the consumer will be capable of making any kind of informed judgement about quality or even safety. The supplier is more familiar with the nature of the transaction and the standard form involved; it is his or her job to conclude such transactions, whereas it may be an uncommon, even intimidating, experience for the consumer. The observation about imbalance need not form a point of criticism. It is simply an observation that there is little congruence between the large–scale commercial contract and the average consumer purchase. Contracts vary. They may have certain common features relating to the notion of an exchange between the two sides to a transaction, but there is an immense gulf in expectations between the major commercial deal and the small–scale consumer contract. Building the Channel Tunnel and buying a loaf of bread both involve 'contracts', but is it really useful to give them both the same label?

This throws up a central question in the modern law of contract: is it realistic or desirable to attempt to maintain a common set of contractual principles applicable to all bargains, or should one accept that different types of contract attract different types of legal response? If 'contracts' have infinite variety, then it may be unhelpful to think of a unified law of contract. Worse, it may be positively damaging to treat unlike contracts alike by seeking solutions drawn from some spurious set of common rules, whereas the variety of situations which may arise should instead be judged in the light of a more sensitive and nuanced legal structure. Simply put, is there a law of contract or a law of contracts? That is a question which invites a description of the modern law, but one must also adopt a prescriptive focus; *should* there be a fragmentation of the law of contract into discrete compartments? More fundamentally still, it is important to appreciate that contract law is simply part of the wider law of obligations, and that that wider law too varies in its application depending on the subject matter at issue. Some commentators have sought to describe and/or to prescribe a fresh (or, for some, rediscovered) approach to the basis of the law of obligations that no longer

---

30   For a classic analysis see F. Kessler, 'Contracts of Adhesion – Some Thoughts About Freedom of Contract' (1943) 43 *Col L Rev* 629. Cf the vigorous argument for intervention of D. Slawson, 'Standard Form Contracts and Democratic Control of Lawmaking Power' (1970–71) 84 *Harvard L Rev* 529. Cf also the influential analysis of Arthur Leff, 'Contract as Thing' (1970) 19 *American Univ LR* 131. A collection of relevant materials is found in Ramsay n. 4 above Ch. 4.

places significant weight on special legal rules arising from the defining fact of a bargain struck between the parties.[31]

It is possible to cast doubt on the viability or desirability of freedom of contract in the realm of consumer contracts. Such 'freedom' as may exist is greatly attenuated by the features of a mass production economy. The expectation in commercial contract law that the courts will do no more than act as conscientious protectors of the parties' negotiated bargain has no necessary place in the absence of such negotiation. That perception then provides an intellectual invitation to rethink the nature and purpose of the law in consumer contracts. It points towards the adoption of a legal approach which is more prone to controlling the substance of deals rather than simply enforcing them once they display the requisite legal form. It suggests a possible role for the law in adjudicating on the 'fairness' of a deal, rather than simply regarding agreements as sacred and entitled to unquestioning legal protection.

At this point in our attempt to develop a control function for the law of consumer contracts, it is appropriate to observe that the stumbling block of 19th–century judicial non–interventionism may not have been such a substantial obstacle after all. Sir George Jessel's dictum venerating contractual liberty as sacred provides a memorable 19th–century soundbite, but the extent to which it faithfully represented the law even at that time has been questioned. Professor Atiyah, in particular, has cogently demonstrated that the strength of the dam which supposedly held back interventionism has been exaggerated.[32] This thesis holds that it was the prevalent acceptance of the economic virtue of contractual freedom that shaped contract law theory throughout the 19th–century. Historical patterns were touched on by Lord Diplock in *Schroeder Music Publishing Co Ltd v Macaulay*.[33] He described the general 19th–century rule of non–interventionism in contracts, which permits only specific and exceptional instances of intervention, against a background of a pre–existing readiness to tests contracts generally against a standard of unconscionability. He appears to envisage that theories about freedom of trade had been absorbed by the judiciary during the 19th–century and had caused a shift in the law. So the 'hands-off' judicial approach had not existed since time immemorial: it was a reflection of the times.

---

31   Contrast G. Gilmore, *The Death of Contract* (Ohio State University Press, 1974) with C. Fried, *Contract as Promise* (Harvard University Press, 1981). Cf P. Atiyah, *Essays on Contract* (Oxford University Press, 1988).

32   Esp P. Atiyah, *The Rise and Fall of Freedom of Contract* (Oxford University Press, 1979). Cf J. Gordley, *Philosophical Origins of Modern Contract Doctrine* (Oxford University Press, 1991).

33   [1974] 3 All ER 616, 623. The substance of the case is discussed below at 1.3.6.

Throughout the 20th–century, incursions into contractual freedom have grown, largely as the result of a perception that contractual freedom is neither reflective of nor desirable in the modern mixed economy. State interventionism in the market and in setting norms for private relationships and wide–ranging (if erratic) judicial activism have contributed enormously to this decline in the centrality of the autonomy of the parties. In recent years, some have developed the view that the wheel has turned full circle – or that the wheel should be turned full circle – and that individual autonomy should be reclaimed as part of an insistence on free choice in the market. Reduction in interventionist legislation has refocused the law of contract on the parties' bargain; reduced State participation in the market has enhanced the importance and breadth of dealings with private suppliers. Protection of tenants, employees and consumers has been curtailed; public monopoly supply of water and energy is no longer the norm. This is further elaborated in Part 1.9.3 of this Chapter. The pattern is erratic. The influence of EC membership has in several areas opposed the policy preferences of successive Conservative governments in power in the UK since 1979. For example, control of unfair terms in consumer contracts in the UK is stronger now than it was 15 years ago.[34] However, the challenge to public intervention and the consequent re–emphasis on individual agreements represents a major feature of the pattern of legal development in recent years.[35]

1.3.5 Control of Contracts – The Bargaining Phase

One approach to adjusting contract law in the light of the diminution in effective negotiation which characterises modern consumer contracts would involve a more sceptical examination of the process of decision making in consumer contracts. One need not deny that the law of contract is and should be uniformly based on an idea of individual autonomy. However one might be able to find elements in the supplier/consumer relationship which do not conform to that paradigm. The consumer is often not really negotiating freely or with full knowledge about the bargain. One could then use the law to improve the transparency of the bargaining process and to control outcomes which are not deemed to be the product of proper contractual freedom.

In English law, both common law and statute display features which correspond to this perception. It is notorious that consumers will not read all

---

[34]   Chapter 9.

[35]   For a valuable overview, see P. Atiyah, 'Freedom of Contract and the New Right' in *Essays on Contract* (Oxford University Press, 1986).

the small-print on a document. This may be viewed as 'reality' departing from the 'theory' of free bargaining. Old cases show that the common law accepted, even perpetuated, the gulf between theory and practice. A brief consideration of case law is justified in order to elucidate these issues, although more specific discussion is provided in Chapter 9. *Thompson v London Midland and Scottish Railway Co*[36] arose out of an excursion taken by Mrs Thompson in Lancashire in the course of which she was injured as a result of the defendant's negligence as she was trying to disembark from a train. The ticket included a notice that it was issued subject to conditions shown in the company's timetables. In the timetable could be found a term excluding liability for injury 'however caused'. The timetables were not on display. They cost sixpence each. Mrs Thompson, moreover, could not read. The Court of Appeal held that, irrespective of whether any inquiries had actually been made by this consumer about the nature of the conditions in the timetable, she was bound under the contract by the conditions to which the ticket had laid a trail. The railway company had brought the conditions sufficiently to the notice of the consumer and was thereby protected from liability in damages.

Latterly the common law has responded more actively to the absence of negotiation about, agreement on, or even awareness of, terms in such situations. Decisions in recent years show that failure to bring unusually onerous clauses adequately to the attention of the consumer will result in their exclusion from the binding terms of the agreement. *Thornton v Shoe Lane Parking*[37] involved a claim for compensation for injury suffered in the defendant's car park by Mr Thornton, 'a freelance trumpeter of the highest quality'.[38] The consumer received a ticket from an automatic machine on arrival at the car park. The ticket referred to conditions displayed on the premises, one of which excluded liability for such an event. The plaintiff knew nothing of this. The Court of Appeal decided that the defendants had not done enough to bring the clause to the attention of the consumer and that therefore it was not binding. The consumer's claim for damages succeeded. The approach in this case examines what the trader has or has not done with more rigour than was apparent in *Thompson* and takes more explicit and sympathetic account of the consumer's lack of knowledge. Lord Denning quite explicitly remarked on the 'fiction' of negotiation about such conditions, even in the days when an actual person may have supplied the ticket to a

---

36   [1930] 1 KB 41.
37   [1971] 2 QB 163.
38   As we learn from the characteristically memorable first sentence of Lord Denning MR's judgement.

consumer. The perception of a 'fiction' applied with all the more force where a machine had dispensed the ticket.

An important recent case which emphasises transparency outwith the sphere of the exclusion clause and even outwith the consumer context is *Interfoto Picture Library Ltd v Stiletto Visual Programmes Ltd.*[39] The case concerned the enforceability of a clause included in printed conditions accompanying photographic transparencies owned by Interfoto and provided for the use of Stiletto. The clause in question required a fee to be paid in the event that the transparencies were retained longer than 14 days. Stiletto forgot they held the transparencies and were billed for £3,783.50 in accordance with the clause. This was an exorbitant rate, according to the judges of the Court of Appeal before whom Stiletto sought to show that the clause should not be held enforceable as part of the contract. Stiletto succeeded in defeating Interfoto's claim for the full sum apparently due under the clause. The Court of Appeal held that a particularly onerous or unusual contractual condition, which would not generally be known to the other party, would not be enforceable unless the party seeking to rely on that condition could show that it had fairly been brought to the other party's attention. This test was not met and Interfoto accordingly could not rely on the clause.

The modern trend exemplified by *Thornton v Shoe Lane Parking* and *Interfoto v Stiletto* appears to derive from judicial scepticism about the realistic nature of the 'agreement' struck, especially where a standard form is used. These decisions are not necessarily in conflict with the principle expressed several decades earlier in *Thompson*. It remains true that if the trader has done enough in the opinion of the court to bring the terms to the attention of the consumer, then those terms bind even if the consumer does not actually know of them. That issue is a question of fact to be determined on the facts of the individual case. However, a great deal more is now expected of the trader. It will be rarer for the consumer to be bound at common law by terms of which he or she is ignorant, especially when those terms are presented in standard form and a fortiori where those terms are out of the ordinary. In this sense, active disclosure of terms may be a precondition to their enforceability, thus motivating the supplier to adopt a more open strategy.

The common law has in this way been moulded to enhance the openness of negotiation. This ought to improve market transparency. Statutory intervention provides a number of examples of explicitly imposed requirements to disclose information. The use of defined forms is a favoured technique for alerting the consumer to the need to be aware of the nature and

---

[39]   [1988] 2 WLR 615, [1988] 1 All ER 348.

possible consequences of the transaction into which he or she is entering. English contract law normally leaves it to the parties to choose how they will record their agreement. Any document will do. Oral contracts are in principle enforceable. However, in defined circumstances, statutory rules stipulate the use of particular forms. Chapter 7, dealing with consumer credit, provides an account of the elaborate rituals that surround the conclusion of defined transactions in that field. Part of the objective of such intervention is to warn the consumer to be on his or her guard; another objective is to supply more specific and detailed information to the consumer of credit. The assumption is plainly that the private law, even stimulated by modern judicial activism, does not yield a market that is sufficiently transparent to permit informed, efficient decisions to be taken. The capacity of disclosure rules and rules stipulating the use of particular forms to bridge the information gap and effectively to cure market failure is examined critically below in Part 1.8.3 of this Chapter.

1.3.6 Control of Contracts – The Substance

An objective of legal intervention in the bargaining phase, discussed above, is the improvement of transparency in order better to inform the consumer. A distinct technique may involve the acceptance of clauses as part of the contract, but their subjection to some broader check. Contracts, once entered into, might be reviewed more openly by the courts against some standard of fairness. This could be justified in pursuit of consumer protection as a reflection of the unfair imbalance which characterises the pre–contractual bargaining phase, especially, perhaps, where standard–term contracts are employed. Consumers might be thought in danger of exploitation. Plainly the nature of the control would require careful elaboration. However, the critical policy breakthrough would involve recognition that the bargain, once struck, is not then immune from intervention. It is an approach which involves public inquiry into the fairness of private decisions, not least on the basis that the private decision is reached only under distorted conditions.

English common law of contract has *not* taken this approach. The English judiciary has not been prepared to claim a general common law jurisdiction to inspect the fairness of bargains.[40] English law enforces promises once they have satisfied the 'tests of enforceability', traditionally the

---

40   Lord Denning sought to develop such a doctrine in *Lloyds Bank v Bundy* [1975] QB 326, at least where inequality of bargaining power is present, but this has not found favour in the House of Lords; cf *National Westminster Bank v Morgan* [1985] AC 686. Cf J. Cartwright, *Unequal Bargaining* (OUP, 1991).

three requirements of agreement, consideration and the intention of the parties to create legal relations, and provided they are not affected by a fairly narrow range of vitiating factors, such as misrepresentation or duress. A 'fairness' check has no direct role to play.

There are isolated areas in which a species of fairness is employed to control a bargain. The restraint of trade doctrine, for example, involves control over employment and related contracts which is based on an assessment of fairness in the public interest and in the interest of the parties. In *A. Schroeder Music Publishing Co Ltd v Macaulay*[41] the House of Lords held that an agreement entered into by a young unknown song–writer on the standard terms of a publishing company was unenforceable. Lord Reid doubted that the contract had been 'moulded by any pressure of negotiation'.[42] Had the economic imbalance between the parties not precluded the opportunity for real negotiation, his approach would have been significantly different and less prone to intervene.[43] There is nothing in the speeches in the House of Lords which disputes the competitive nature of the market. There were, presumably, a number of publishing companies willing to offer terms to young and unknown writers.[44] Yet all such deals would occur against a background of significant inequality of bargaining power. The decision seems to be based on the notion that it was not a *fair* market, at least from the perspective of the writer and, more broadly, the public interest in enjoying the fruits of the composer's work, and that the deal should therefore be controlled. The strictness and length of the restraint were judged unjustified. The publishers could, presumably, have concluded an enforceable contract with the composer, provided the terms were less restrictive, even in the absence of full negotiation. It seems, then, that there is some threshold to intervention in contracts in restraint of trade that the courts themselves fix.

Lord Diplock in *Schroeder v Macaulay* was careful to observe that the contract in question, one in restraint of trade, 'fell within one of those *limited* categories of contractual promises in respect of which the courts still retain the power to relieve the promisor of his legal duty to fulfil them'.[45] The

---

[41]   [1974] 3 All ER 616.

[42]   *Ibid* p. 622.

[43]   Macaulay, the composer of 'Love Grows where my Rosemary goes', was treated more favourably than George Michael, whose canon is rather better known and, partly for that reason, whose bargaining power is rather stronger. The contract in *Panayiotou v Sony Ltd* [1994] 1 All ER 755 was held enforceable.

[44]   For criticism of the decision from this and other perspectives, M. Trebilcock, 'The Doctrine of Inequality of Bargaining Power' (1976) 26 *Univ Toronto LJ* 359.

[45]   623c, emphasis added.

common law asserts no *general* jurisdiction to set aside 'unfair' contracts. The sentiments of Sir George Jessel maintain their grip.[46] The typical consumer contract would be immune from the type of inquiry undertaken in a restraint of trade case such as *Schroeder v Macaulay*. To this extent, the common law seems to possess an inherent respect for agreements and for markets.

Statutory intervention has made some limited incursion into the notion that the law is simply the agreement of the parties. Consumer credit legislation confers powers on the courts to interfere with extortionate credit bargains.[47] The power is necessarily flexible, but it is also plainly intended that it should not be used lightly. This has proved to be the case and, in practice, very few instances of the reopening of agreements have occurred. Reasons for this infrequent interventionism doubtless lie in part in the narrow scope of the statutory rules, but probably also in the natural reluctance of a judge trained in the common law of contract to engage in assessment of the relative worth of the two sides to a bargain.

The Unfair Contract Terms Act 1977 invalidates some clauses absolutely and subjects others to a judicially–applied test of reasonableness. The Act is of central importance to the assessment of the development of a distinctive law of consumer contracts. However, it also demonstrates the fuzzy edges of the law of consumer protection, for the Act is capable of controlling (some) terms in (some) commercial contracts.[48] In fact, the Unfair Contract Terms Act 1977, as all students quickly learn, is a statute burdened by a thoroughly misleading name. 'Unfairness' is an unsatisfactorily abbreviated summary of its control mechanism. Moreover, although contract terms are not its only concern (for it also applies to some non–contractual notices), not all contract terms are affected by it, only the limited category of exclusion and analogous clauses.[49] Nonetheless, the Unfair Contract Terms Act 1977 represents a significant statutory modification of the common law of contract in the direction of intervention in the bargain.

Cases such as *Thompson and Thornton* (see above) would be potentially affected by the Act. The issues of incorporation of terms would continue to be addressed in the same way. The common law of incorporation is not affected by the Act; if a term is not shown to be part of the contract, it cannot be enforced within the contract.[50] However, once an exclusion clause

---

46   See above 1.3.3.
47   Sections 137–140 Consumer Credit Act 1974. See Chapter 7.12 below.
48   For more detailed discussion, see Chapter 9.
49   Chapter 9.6.3 below.
50   Chapter 9.2 below.

is shown to form part of the contract and to protect the party wishing to rely on it,[51] the Act ensures that there is still scope for legal inquiry into its enforceability. The clause will be void in defined circumstances. That in *Thompson*, which excluded liability for personal injury, would indeed now be void.[52] Other clauses are tested against a judicially applied test of reasonableness.[53]

The 1977 Act applies only to exclusion and cognate clauses. A broader control of unfair terms is exercised under the EC's Directive on Unfair Terms in Consumer Contracts.[54] All contract terms, not only exclusion clauses, are subject to control. A term covered by the Directive shall be regarded as unfair if, contrary to the requirement of good faith, it causes a significant imbalance in the parties' rights and obligations arising under the contract, to the detriment of the consumer. An Annex to the Directive provides an indicative and non–exhaustive list of the terms which may be regarded as unfair.

Although the Directive is broader than the 1977 Act in its coverage of all terms, not simply exclusion clauses, it is nonetheless narrower in applying only to terms that have not been individually negotiated. Individually negotiated terms are *not* controlled by the Directive, although it does not preclude their control under national law.[55] The thrust of the Directive is to regulate terms drafted in advance whose nature the consumer has been unable to influence. It seems to be assumed that in such deals the consumer will be less well informed than in others where he or she has been more actively involved in negotiation. Moreover, unlike the Unfair Contract Terms Act, the Directive is confined to consumer contracts alone. This aspect means that it constitutes a major development towards a distinctive law of consumer contracts.

1.3.7 Implication of Terms into Contracts

Legislative intervention is not only concerned to eliminate (some) unfair terms from consumer contracts, but also to add terms into contracts independently of negotiation between the parties. Under the Sale of Goods

---

51   On interpretation, Chapter 9.2 below.
52   On special rules relating to transport, see *Chitty on Contracts* (Sweet and Maxwell, 1989).
53   Chapter 9.6.1 below.
54   Dir. 93/13 OJ 1993 L95/29, Chapter 9 below.
55   In fact, in the UK, the UCTA does exercise control over individually negotiated terms in defined circumstances, Chapter 9 below.

Act 1979, for example, certain terms are implied into defined contracts. The terms offer protection to the buyer quite independently of negotiation between the parties. Products must correspond to description; they must be of satisfactory quality; they must be fit for any purpose which has been agreed.[56] The supply of a defective product is effectively rendered a breach of contract by these requirements (which are examined at length in Chapter 4).

It might initially be felt that such terms are implied on the basis that they replicate what would have been agreed had the parties in the market actively negotiated on these matters. In the past, there may have been some validity in that interpretation. Its logical corollary would be that the parties could agree to exclude the terms should they see fit, which indeed was the position until 1973. However since 1973, the character of these terms as imposed by law (and not as the product anticipated to follow from bargaining) has been demonstrated by the legal rule that, in defined transactions, the terms cannot validly be excluded even if the parties agree on such exclusion.[57] These implied terms therefore reflect State-imposed minimum standards for the transaction, divorced from individual will. Consumers cannot bargain away such protection, wittingly or unwittingly.

The law is not static. The process of legislative adjustment of the content of the contract remains under continuing review. Although the terms mentioned above are implied independently of agreement by the parties, there must be a contract in the first place to which the terms can attach. The implied terms under the Sale of Goods Act therefore apply only to the consumer/retailer relationship, which is contractual, and not to the consumer/manufacturer relationship which is not contractual, save in exceptional circumstances.[58] Yet it can cogently be submitted that in modern conditions it is really the manufacturer who is responsible for the quality of the product. The retailer is frequently a mere conduit. Legislative reform is therefore mooted to adjust the common law to reflect more faithfully the practice of production and marketing. The Department of Trade and Industry published a Consultative Document in 1992 which proposed that legislation should be introduced to render the implied terms enforceable outwith the contract. The EC Commission published a 'Green Paper' in November 1993 which was similarly motivated. These proposals are examined further in Chapter 4. Such potential developments lend further weight to the view that

---

56 Ss.13,14 Sale of Goods Act 1979.
57 Initially the Supply of Goods (Implied Terms) Act 1973, now contained in s.6 Unfair Contract Terms Act 1977; see Chapter 9 below.
58 Chapter 4.2.2 below.

the private law of consumer protection has acquired its own distinctive flavour.

1.3.8   Questions about the Modern Function of Consumer Contract Law

The Unfair Contract Terms Act 1977 and the Sale of Goods Act 1979 are leading examples of modern statutes that put aside freedom of contract as an inadequate reflection of the reality of the circumstances in which the transaction is concluded. State regulation of the bargain is seen as an appropriate response to the economic imbalance between supplier and consumer. The market is affected by such legislative intervention. The message transmitted by consumers to supplier and producer is supplemented by a message added by the State, namely, that in contracts subject to the Acts there are certain minimum quality levels which must be adhered to and certain standards of fairness which must be met, at least in the specific context of the types of clause controlled by the Unfair Contract Terms Act and now, more broadly, under the EC Directive on Unfair Terms in Consumer Contracts.

Beyond such relatively piecemeal massaging of the tradition of judicial non–interventionism, it might be possible to construct a much more radical stance which would disengage consumer contract law entirely from the notion of freedom of contract and instead present entry into and enforcement of (some) contracts as a type of 'privilege' available only on fulfilment of certain preconditions.[59] That involves substantial reconceptualisation of the law in this area and a deconstruction of the law of contract into a law of contracts.

These interventions largely reflect the notion that it is not contracting per se which stimulates a need for legal control, but rather the presence of an imbalance between the parties which causes prejudice. The emphasis is thus on protection of consumers, not of business parties. There are grey areas. Commercial relationships too can be profoundly imbalanced. The Unfair Contract Terms Act 1977 has limited application even to commercial deals[60]; the Sale of Goods Act 1979 does not operate exclusively in the area

---

59   Cf some of the recategorisation of familiar material by H. Collins, *The Law of Contract* (Butterworths, 1993). Cf also T. Wilhelmsson, *Critical studies in private law: a treatise on need-rational principles in modern law* (Kluwer, 1992); J. Adams and R. Brownsword, *Understanding Contract Law* (Fontana, 1994).

60   Chapter 9.

of consumer contracts.[61] The consumer transaction receives especially intensive control points to a fragmentation in the law of contract. Therefore it is a question of increasing importance whether this represents a patchwork of alterations to the core principle of freedom of contract or whether freedom of contract no longer reflects the nature of contract law applicable to the consumer. It has already been suggested in this account that one may doubt whether there are any 'general principles' of contract law at all.

Judicial and legislative intervention may be directed at the realisation of conceptions of social justice. Consumer protection is but part of this field of inquiry into the limitations of contractual freedom as a basis for delivering a fair distribution of resources, a perception that invites attempts to adapt the law to a more overt control function. Other types of relationship provide further evidence of the fragmentation of the law of contract into a law of contracts. The law of landlord and tenant and the law of employee protection are nominally based on contract law and the core relationship at stake is contractual, but the legal techniques involved have drifted far from *laissez-faire* commercial contract law as normally understood. Independently of the content of the agreement, tenants and employees, like consumers, enjoy legal rights against landlords, employers and suppliers respectively.

This touches on politically contentious areas. The desirability of the development of rights for such groups, beyond the protection they are able to secure from the market, has been increasingly questioned. The principal concern of successive Conservative administrations since 1979 has been the damage done to market flexibility by such intervention. For example, protecting workers or tenants by law may deter the willingness of providers of jobs or accommodation to make them available in the first place. Setting minimum standards in consumer transactions deprives the consumer of choice. This has prompted a rigorous scrutiny of such interventionist laws under a general policy umbrella of deregulation. At this end of the spectrum rests the view that the State should not interfere with the inherent freedom and self–operability of the market.[62] It is precisely here that some have seen the modern (re–)rise of individualist contract law, for in so far as special legal protection is rolled back, what remains is what the market can deliver; what can be negotiated under a contract.

This policy debate is increasingly a battleground in the EC, where Social Policy has developed as the most prominent flashpoint. At the EC level, there is an additional choice. The UK doubts the desirability, *inter alia*, of common labour standards across the whole Community and urges instead competition between different national regimes, in a market where companies

---

61   Chapter 4.
62   Chapter 1.9 below.

would vote with their feet. The Treaty on European Union enshrines this unstable agreement to disagree on the evenness of the EC playing field.[63] It is an issue of regulatory philosophy that is sure to be reopened in 1996, the planned date for the next intergovernmental conference at which Treaty revision will be considered.[64]

It may be a matter of personal taste whether one views this as contract law in a phase of adjustment or whether the stretching of these 'principles' into wholly heterogeneous situations really means that discourse about contract law 'principles' now obscures the practical abandonment of common principles. For consumer law in particular, there remains no consensus on whether the topic is a discrete area of law with its own distinctive rationales or whether it is simply an assortment of existing principles of contract (and other) law defined as consumer law only because they happen to apply in some circumstances to consumers. There is a pressing need to establish coherence between the distinct rationales that offer themselves as bases for intervention.[65] The divergence of approach tends to surface where new initiatives designed to protect consumers as a group are proposed. For example, at EC level, some greeted the notion of special protection for consumers against unfair contractual terms as an alarming challenge to the integrity of private law; others welcomed such protection precisely because of its recognition that consumers need special treatment.[66] Others again worried that consumers alone were offered protection that ought to have been extended to other economically weak parties.[67]

Whichever style of categorisation is preferred, modern consumer contract law operates in a manner quite distinct from the classic (and rather exaggerated) notions of individual freedom to contract and legal non–interventionism. Both judicial and legislative developments have combined to establish a pattern of control over the supplier/consumer relationship.

---

[63]   Further below, Chapter 1.9.3.

[64]   Art.N(2) Treaty on European Union.

[65]   Cf in this direction G. Howells, 'Contract Law: The Challenge for the Critical Consumer Lawyer' in T. Wilhelmsson (ed.), *Perspectives of Critical Contract Law* (Dartmouth, 1993).

[66]   Cf Chapter 9.4.1 below; from the former perspective, see especially Brandner and Ulmer (1991) 28 *CMLRev* 647. For an explanation of what is at stake for the German lawyer, cf N. Reich, 'Diverse Approaches to Consumer Protection Philosophy' (1991–92) 14 *JCP* 257, esp. 264–7.

[67]   Eg H. Collins, 'Good Faith in European Contract Law' (1994) 14 *Oxford JLS* 229.

1.4 TORT LAW AND THE CONSUMER

Tort law is largely the product of the judges, although a statutory overlay has recently increased in importance. Over the course of this century, the ability of the consumer to proceed in tort against traders with whom he or she has no contractual relationship has in many respects been enhanced. Tort law, whether judge made or statutorily developed, blurs further the simplicity of freedom of contract and the notion that private parties have autonomy to fix the limits of liability incurred for their actions.

The very existence of tort law is a recognition that obligations agreed between contracting parties are an inadequate expression of legal responsibility in modern society. As a matter of policy, tort law imposes certain duties on individuals to compensate other individuals in the event that loss is suffered. This notion of 'fairness beyond the bargain' is already part of contract law in the shape of statutory intervention to place certain core implied terms in consumer (and other) contracts, but tort law takes the scope of such obligations beyond the contractual network. The ebb and flow of the imposition of liability in tort reflect shifting judicial conceptions of the appropriate place for loss to be borne in the absence of a pre–existing contractual arrangement agreeing allocation of responsibility. Study of those judicial choices is itself a fascinating field of inquiry.[68] The flexible and value-laden standards of negligence liability provide many insights into judicial conceptions of loss bearing in particular and fairness in society in general.[69] Choices made in courts about whose shoulders shall bear loss affect the whole climate of commercial activity. Tort law thus assumes an indirect regulatory function.

For the consumer, tort law offers some legal protection beyond the contractual network. It is the tort of negligence which has been most prominent. This allows the consumer to seek compensation outwith the narrow contractual relationship for loss suffered as a result of the supply of an unsafe product. Claims against a manufacturer are possible. The position of the consumer was strengthened still further by the extension of liability for the supply of a defective product secured by Part I of the Consumer Protection Act 1987, which implements the EC Product Liability Directive. As a corollary to the enhanced position of the consumer plaintiff, the defendant trader is exposed to wider potential liability and, in theory, should be induced to take more care to avoid causing loss to the consumer. Tort law affects the balance; to some extent, tort law *is* the balance.

---

68 For a recent critical account, see J. Conaghan and W. Mansell, *The Wrongs of Tort* (Pluto Press, 1993).

69 Eg P. Cane, *Atiyah's Accidents, Compensation and the Law* (Butterworths, 1993).

For the English tort lawyer, a Scottish case, *Donoghue v Stevenson*,[70] is the most famous breakthrough in favour of the consumer. It was held that a consumer could sue a manufacturer, with whom he or she had no contractual relationship, for compensation for physical injury or property damage suffered as a result of the negligent supply of a product. The manufacturer owes the consumer the famous 'duty of care' elaborated by Lord Atkin in this case. Subsequent case law has achieved a steady widening in the scope of this duty and potential liability, to the advantage of the consumer.[71]

Negligence liability is limited by the requirement that the plaintiff demonstrates fault on the part of the defendant trader. The requirement of 'fault' allows an element of judicial assessment of whether the risks of the conduct are outweighed by the potential benefits. Activities conferring benefits on society in general may be judged compatible with the standard required by negligence law, even where harm is foreseeably inflicted on an individual or individuals. `The purpose to be served, if sufficiently important, justifies the assumption of abnormal risk'.[72] A consumer might be badly injured, even killed, by a drug; yet in negligence law this does not automatically mean that the supplier is a tortfeasor. A calculation of the countervailing benefits of the supply of the drug would be required under traditional negligence law. Here lies tort law's regulatory flavour; the law demands a cost-benefit analysis of particular types of conduct. Statute has intervened to impose additional potential liabilities on parties involved in the manufacture and supply of goods. Part I of the Consumer Protection Act 1987 was introduced to implement the EC's Product Liability Directive, based on Article 100 EC. This is formally concerned with the equalisation of competitive conditions in the EC,[73] but by setting common rules on liability for the supply of defective products, its effect, in the UK at least, was to establish a significant new source of consumer protection. In implementation of the Directive, Part I of the Act introduced a regime which appeared to be a radical departure from standard negligence law and to offer a much more extensive protection to the consumer of unsafe goods. It seemed to impose liability for loss caused by products in a defective condition, irrespective of the conduct of the supplier. In fact, on closer inspection, the Act is notable in places for its obscurity. Defining 'defective' for these purposes is

---

70   [1932] AC 562.
71   Chapter 6.2.3.2.
72   Per Asquith LJ in *Daborn v Bath Tramways* [1946] 2 All ER 333, 336. Cf, for instance, *Watt v Hertfordshire CC* [1954] 1 WLR 835; *Bolam v Friern Hospital* [1957] 1 WLR 582.
73   Chapter 2.3.3.

problematic,[74] while the availability of shelter from liability for unforeseeable defects dilutes the legal standard.[75] Remarkably the substance of the Directive seems to date to have remained litigation free, in the UK at least. However, its role in buttressing the private law of consumer protection cannot be discounted.[76]

The consumer who is injured by a product has opportunities to sue in tort which are broader than those available in contract. However, the consumer's ability to use the law of tort to secure compensation for loss suffered as a result of quality deficiencies in a product, rather than lack of safety, is much restricted. Quality failings are normally remedied through the law of contract, which provides only restricted opportunities for the consumer, especially in the light of the rules of privity that typically confine the consumer to a claim against the retailer alone.[77]

Tort law depends on judicial attitudes. In the tort of negligence, at least, liability in negligence for inflicting economic loss is imposed only exceptionally.[78] The current judicial attitude in the UK is that the tort of negligence has a limited function to play in the area of economic loss; moreover, if advances in protection are to be put in place, it lies with Parliament not the judiciary to act. In 1990, Lord Oliver in *Murphy v Brentwood DC* declared that:

> '...I do not think that it is right for the courts not simply to expand existing principles but to create at large new principles in order to fulfil a social need in an area of consumer protection which has already been perceived by the legislature but for which, presumably advisedly, it has not thought it necessary to provide'[79]

Judicial activism ebbs and flows over time. There are wide variations in judicial readiness to 'adjust' the law, Lord Denning being the most famously innovative judge active in post War Britain. However, if Lord Oliver's remarks are representative of a general trend, negligence law in the hands of judges appears to be entering a quiet period, at least in relation to economic

---

74 Chapter 6.2.3.3.3.

75 In more depth, Chapter 6.2.3.3.3.

76 For discussion of the current state of product liability law in the UK, see J. Stapleton, *Product Liability* (Butterworths, 1994). For a global comparative survey, see G. Howells, *Comparative Product Liability* (Dartmouth, 1993).

77 See Chapter 4 for reform in the area of Consumer Guarantees.

78 Cf R. Bernstein, *Economic Loss* (Longman, 1993).

79 [1990] 2 All ER 908, 938.

loss.[80] Even though much of the above description has been of judges reshaping the 19th–century law of commerce to match the 20th–century consumer society, it appears that there are limits to the dynamic evolution of the common law.[81] One should be aware of the risk of overstating the coherence of the relationship developed by judges between liability arising in contract and in tort, but, in relation to economic loss at least, there is the suggestion of a recent resurgence in the importance of contract law and the acceptance of obligations by agreement; similarly, a decline in the importance of tort law and the readiness of judges to impose obligations inspired by a more general sense of (extra–contractual) social responsibility.[82]

1.5   THE COSTS OF CONSUMER PROTECTION THROUGH PRIVATE LAW

1.5.1 Costs of Intervention in the Common Law of Contract

Whether contract or tort is involved, the imposition of obligations on traders to compensate consumers is not cost–free. For example, the requirement that goods are of satisfactory quality, violation of which permits a consumer claim for breach of contract, plainly sets minimum standards. These will be reflected in price. One can interpret the satisfactory quality requirement as a State–imposed restriction on the consumer's choice to buy at a lower price a product whose quality is less than 'satisfactory'. The restriction of consumer choice can be defended by reference to the perception that (most) consumers cannot really choose effectively in an unregulated market. Denying choice to buy a product of unsatisfactory quality is today uncontroversial, not least because this aspect of the Sale of Goods Act has been in force for almost a century, until 1994 in the guise of 'merchantable', rather than satisfactory,

---

80   On the respective roles of Parliament and the courts in developing liability rules, comparable judicial reluctance is manifested in *Cambridge Water Co Ltd v Eastern Counties Leather* [1994] 1 All ER 53.

81   See, generally and famously, on this issue, G. Calabresi, *A Common Law for the Age of Statutes* (Harvard University Press, 1982).

82   The ruling in *Junior Books Ltd v Veitchi Co Ltd* [1983] 1 AC 520 had seemed to indicate an increasing readiness to allow tort claims in situations which were one (and, perhaps, subsequently more) step(s) removed from contractual relationships. *Murphy* n.79 does not overrule *Junior Books*, but is noticeably more cautious on the development of a broader scope of negligence liability for economic loss. For fuller discussion, see Bernstein n.78 above.

quality. However, it is always necessary and often much more controversial to test against a cost/benefit calculation more novel, deeper forms of intervention designed to protect the consumer.

The phenomenon of the exclusion clause is controlled by the Unfair Contract Terms Act 1977. It may initially seem inconceivable that there can be any benefit to a consumer in a clause which excludes the supplier's liability and causes loss to fall on the consumer. Yet the Act outlaws only a small number of exclusion clauses,[83] leaving others to be assessed against a reasonableness test. The consumer remains able to 'choose' to bear the loss. This is explicable when it is appreciated that exclusion clauses perform the very valuable function of allocating risk. A party who accepts a contractual term which, by excluding the other party's liability, makes it clear that he or she will bear that loss may plan accordingly. He or she may take out insurance against the loss at issue or may simply run the risk. The other party will need no insurance against that risk, nor need to plan to cover the cost of its occurrence. The result should be that the assumption of risk through the placement of the exclusion clause is reflected in the price. Put simply, you pay less if you are willing to exclude the other party from specified liability. This function of conscious, planned risk allocation via an exclusion clause dictates that, in the commercial sphere at least, courts should not interfere.[84]

In *Thompson*,[85] an element in the Court of Appeal's finding that the exclusion clause had been adequately brought to the notice of the consumer lay in the price of the excursion ticket, which was much lower than that of a standard ticket. This remains entirely valid as an observation on the function of exclusion clauses in favour of a supplier in offering the consumer the choice of a riskier journey at a lower price. It holds less water in a situation where the consumer was in fact unaware of the circumstances and was not making an informed choice. The Unfair Contract Terms Act 1977 permits control of exclusion clauses in (mainly) consumer contracts, but here too the apparent costs of exclusion clauses should be weighed against possible benefits. At least where consumers are adequately informed about the risks at stake, there are reasons in favour of permitting them to choose between protection from loss, for which a premium will doubtless be payable, and the risk of loss expressed in exclusion of supplier liability, for which a lower price should in theory be offered. The attempt to conserve consumer choice is reflected in the Unfair Contract Terms Act 1977. Schedule 2 contains a

---

83   Chapter 9.5 below.

84   This is the very strong message of the House of Lords's decision in *Photo Productions v Securicor* Chapter 9.2 below, a case involving commercial parties.

85   Note 36 above.

non-exhaustive list of guidelines to be employed in the application of the reasonableness test.[86] Account should be taken of 'alternative means by which the customer's requirements could have been met'. Regard should be had to 'whether the customer knew or ought reasonably to have known of the existence and extent of the term'. The strong impression is that the further the situation departs from 'take it or leave it!' at the time of contracting, the more likely that the term will be thought reasonable. *Woodman v Photo Trade Processing*,[87] a decision which has gained more prominence than most County Court decisions, provides a valuable illustration of how the Act may operate in practice. The plaintiff took photographs of a friend's wedding to be developed by the defendant. They were ruined, but, in accordance with a notice displayed on the premises, the defendant offered Woodman only the cost of a new film as compensation. This limitation of liability was found to be unreasonable and Woodman was awarded £75. Subsequently it has become common practice for suppliers in this trade and others to offer varying ceilings of compensation for any damage caused, depending on the price paid by the consumer. The consumer can choose to buy more protection. Whether the terms are reasonable or not remains a question of fact, but the supplier is likely to be in a stronger position the greater the level of disclosure made and choice offered.[88]

1.5.2 Costing Tort Law

Obligations imposed by tort law are not cost-free. A system which makes fault–free producers strictly liable for harm caused by the supply of unsafe products may seem determinedly pro–consumer. What if the consequence is that producers adopt a very cautious attitude to the marketing of new products for fear that innovation, which has unforeseen and unforeseeable implications, may prove financially catastrophic? Consumers might then be protected at the cost of having innovation stifled. It may then be submitted that society would be better advised to permit producers protection from liability where they can show that they were pursuing innovation which unforeseeably went wrong. Such a calculation of rather intangible and

---

[86]   Strictly Schedule 2 applies only to contracts controlled by ss.6 & 7, but it has been used more broadly; see Chapter 9.6.1.1.

[87]   *Which?* July 1981. Reprinted in C.J. Miller and B.W. Harvey, *Consumer and Trading Law Cases and Materials* (Butterworths, 1985) p. 245 and in Ramsay n.4 above p. 107.

[88]   On implications of disclosure rules, see especially discussion of the work of George Priest in Chapter 4.

hypothetical costs and benefits dogged the negotiation of the EC's Product Liability Directive, subsequently implemented in the UK by Part I of the Consumer Protection Act 1987.[89] It was a wrangle that was never satisfactorily resolved. The Directive, as adopted, allowed States to choose whether or not to include a defence of this type, the so–called 'development risk' defence which, according to the Directive, protects a producer from liability where 'the state of technical and scientific knowledge at the time when he put the product into circulation was not such as to enable the existence of the defect to be discovered'.[90] The UK decided that it would opt to dilute strict liability in this way.[91]

Recent years have witnessed a ferocious debate in the USA about what some have identified as a 'crisis' in product liability law. There have been trends towards remarkably high awards in some areas and steep rises in the price of insurance. Some commentators have identified a declining commercial incentive to innovate and, as a result, impaired consumer choice. This has prompted proposals that the consumer interest would be served by a tort system that moves towards less, not more, generosity to plaintiffs.[92]

The implications of such choices may be wide–ranging. Under a fault–based regime, a manufacturer of a new and, in the majority of cases, beneficial drug which has catastrophic but wholly unforeseeable side–effects will probably escape liability for the loss caused. There would be no fault. Those injured will have no claim at common law other than a contractual action against the retailer which will be of practical utility only where that retailer is sufficiently large. Worse, English law holds that there is no claim in contract at all where the drug has been supplied by the National Health Service.[93] Loss would lie where it fell, with the consumer. The replacement of fault–based liability by a strict liability system combined with the development risk defence would probably rarely have an impact on the outcome. The manufacturer will be protected by the defence; loss will lie where it falls. A 'pure' strict liability system, on the other hand, will allow a successful claim by any consumer able to show that the defendant has supplied the drug which caused the harm. Loss will be shifted on to the trader. This latter outcome may seem instinctively correct. The manufacturer took the profits and should bear the loss. A connected observation is that the manufacturer is in the best position to take precautions against the supply of

---

89   Chapter 6.

90   Article 7(e) Dir.

91   It is not clear whether the UK has implemented this provision properly in the 1987 Act (section 4(1)(e)), Chapter 6.2.3.3.3 below.

92   The debate is tracked more closely in Chapter 6.

93   *Pfizer v Ministry of Health* [1965] 1 All ER 450.

unsafe goods and should therefore be given the strongest possible incentive so to do. Such arguments point in the direction of a strict liability system. Moreover, the manufacturer can buy insurance cover against liability, though this, of course, will be reflected in the price. In this way, loss suffered by a minority of unfortunate consumers will be compensated by a premium paid by all purchasers of the product. This may instinctively seem fair. Yet prices will rise, reducing consumer choice about risk-taking. Innovation may also be stifled by a rigid liability regime. Increasing insurance premiums and/or the costs of settling consumer claims may drive smaller firms out of the market, leaving supply in the hands of a few large firms and pushing the market structure towards oligopoly. In short, there are real choices to be made about the priorities of consumer protection and consumer choice in the market and the preceding description is only a simple framework.[94] Where does society feel most comfortable about loss falling? That perception will then be translated into legal rules, whether devised by the judiciary or the legislature.

The choice between strict liability and fault-based liability may thus involve a cost benefit calculation containing many nuances. Some of the considerations are political, others economic, but all must be absorbed and balanced by anyone with an interest in shaping consumer policy.[95]

The capacity of the tort system to provide an efficient method for compensating injury has come under attack in recent decades. Criticism has led to radical change in some parts of the world. The tort system generates some rather haphazard outcomes. A fault–based system can often mean that an unlucky few consumers bear loss through no fault of their own. On the other hand, strict liability places the loss indirectly on all consumers through higher prices, though even then the plaintiff must show that the product has caused his or her loss. Causation is always a problematic element in the consumer's claim in tort. Producer insolvency acts as a further potential hindrance to the consumer's claim. The result is that some instances of loss will fall through the net and go uncompensated. Some observers have gone further and commented on how tort law protects only certain kinds of interests, certain types of loss. It certainly does not operate as a comprehensive method for protecting the unfortunate in society.[96]

Consequently more direct State intervention has been proposed. In New Zealand, for example, it has not been possible to bring a tort action to secure

---

94   Cf G. Howells (ed.), *Product Liability, Insurance and the Pharmaceutical Industry: An Anglo–American comparison* (Fulbright Papers: Manchester University Press, 1991).

95   Cf Stapleton, Howells n.76 above.

96   Cf J. Stapleton, *Disease and the Compensation Debate* (OUP, 1986).

compensation for most personal injuries since 1974.[97] There is instead a State-run benefits system. Accidental injury is compensated, irrespective of the identity of the party who has inflicted the loss, but the matter has been taken out of the private and into the public domain. To take the example of the supply of a drug with unforeseen side effects, the availability of an award of compensation to a victim would no longer hinge on the behaviour of the manufacturer or supplier or on the condition of the product. The State system would compensate the victim for the loss suffered. The system appeals on grounds of fairness, but attracts criticism for the diminished incentives it creates for accident prevention (although evidence of the capacity of fault-based tort systems effectively to deter harm is equivocal).[98] Much more generally, it is possible to locate the range of activities of a modern Welfare State in a context which sees private law as inappropriate to the types of difficulties which may arise for the individual.

Nevertheless, for all the criticism it has received, the liability system survives in the UK as a key component of the law of consumer protection. Fluctuations in the scope of negligence liability remain at the heart of the private law of consumer protection. For the law of consumer protection in the UK and in the EC, however, the Product Liability Directive has opened up new areas of inquiry.[99]

1.6 REDRESS AND ACCESS TO JUSTICE

Legislative adjustment of what might be termed the common law of consumer protection improves the position of the consumer and, in perhaps a rather imprecise way, helps to make more effective the market mechanism based on consumer/supplier dialogue. It helps to prevent the trader from escaping the brutal consequences of failing to satisfy the consumer. Yet there are gaps in that control. Common law contract and tort, even supplemented by statutory enhancement of rights, do not cover every instance of consumer loss. The result is that the market does not operate perfectly and resources may be wasted. This invites consideration of public regulation of the market

---

[97]   For an extended (and positive) account by a former Prime Minister of New Zealand, see Sir Geoffrey Palmer, 'New Zealand's Accident Compensation Scheme: Twenty Years On' (1994) XLIV *Univ of Toronto Law J* 223. For a briefer contrast with English law, see J. Miller, 'No–fault compensation in New Zealand' (1993) 3 *Consumer Policy Review* 73. Chapter 6 of this book explores these issues further.

[98]   Cf D. Dewees and M. Trebilcock, 'The Efficiency of the Tort System and its Alternatives: a Review of the Empirical Evidence' (1992) 30 *Osgoode Hall LJ* 58.

[99]   More fully, discussed in Chapter 6.

divorced from the private supplier/consumer relationship. Study of this phenomenon begins below in Part 1.7.

The case for public controls becomes all the stronger when account is taken of practical difficulties which confront consumers seeking to enforce legal rights, however generous those rights may seem on paper. Access to justice is examined at length in Chapter 17, but an overview of the issues is appropriate at this point. Such problems deepen our understanding that an effective consumer protection programme cannot be constructed from the operation of the private law alone.

Most fundamental of all is consumer ignorance of the law. Attractive though rights may look on paper, they will play a major role in the consumer/supplier relationship only where a sufficient number of consumers are aware of them. The retailer is liable for the quality of a product by virtue of the statutory terms implied in contracts concluded with the consumer. The manufacturer has no such contractual liability, although statutory reform may alter that.[100] Yet few consumers will not have been confronted by retailers who, at least as an opening gambit, suggest that the consumer's complaint should be directed elsewhere, higher up the supply chain. In fact, paradoxically, the more sophisticated and nuanced consumer protection law is on paper, the greater the risk that consumers will be confused by it and alienated from it in practice. Legal rights should be easy to grasp and to use. Lack of understanding of the law among consumers plainly defeats much of the purpose of the law. It should not be left out of account that ignorance of and/or disinterest in the nuances of consumer law among practising lawyers, perhaps even combined with antipathy to consumer disputes as trivial complaints, are yet a further impediment to its practical impact.[101]

In part this leads to the charge that consumer protection law is, or has become, law for the middle class, at least (or especially) in its private law manifestations. The middle class complains about purchases, whereas poorer sections of society worry about being able to make purchases in the first place. It hardly matters whether a product is of satisfactory quality if you cannot afford it. The middle class understands the law and can either use it or threaten to use it; poorer sections of society are doubtful about its relevance to their needs. The allegation that consumer law is middle class law is not without foundation. If it is true that adjustment of the private law is of disproportionate assistance to already affluent members of society, then a stronger commitment to public law regulation may be appropriate.

---

[100] Consumer Guarantees, Chapter 4.

[101] Further discussed at Chapter 17.2.2 particularly in connection with the work of Macaulay.

Even where the consumer is aware, however dimly, that a legal point has arisen, it is a practical truth that literally the last thing that the typical disgruntled consumer will do is to initiate litigation against a trader. Court proceedings take time and cost money, even if they are ultimately successful. Naturally, if they are lost the consumer may be greatly out of pocket and obliged to pay his or her own costs and those of the other (winning) side. In practice, the cost of formal resort to law typically excludes the middle class as much as poorer members of society. Moreover, courts are intimidating to the average citizen. Consequently there will be a strong consumer preference to avoid legal proceedings. Frequently consumers write off loss to experience, occasionally perhaps after attempting to complain. The majority of consumers do nothing which will immediately affect the supplier's pocket. This is particularly likely to be the case in the event of small scale loss incurred as a result of a disappointing purchase. The rational consumer will not invoke the law. This may provoke the reaction that, if the loss written off is small scale, then the problem cannot be very serious and need not concern policy makers. That may be complacent. An accumulation of a large number of small scale losses all caused by the same supplier represents in aggregate a large problem. Yet the unrealistic expectation of the common law that each individual must pursue his or her own claim will conceal that large problem. This generates an inefficient market which is not subject to effective correction.

Where action is actively pursued by the consumer, informal settlement will be preferred, where feasible. This preference will to some extent be shared by the trader. The small trader, especially, will be almost as reluctant as the consumer to embark on the perilous seas of litigation from which it is notorious that lawyers normally emerge the real and (sometimes) only winners. Nonetheless the risk remains that traders, typically with more resources at their disposal than consumers, will be able to use consumer reluctance to litigate as a method for fobbing off the vindication of consumer rights.

The range of possible responses that can be envisaged is examined at length in Chapter 17. First and foremost consumer education has a valuable role to play. This could profitably begin in schools. The capacity of the consumer to pursue an individual action could be enhanced by facilitating recourse to law. There is no need to abandon the effort to improve the structure of the private law; quite the contrary. Nor should one abandon attempts to improve consumer access to justice. Developments in the small claims procedure provide welcome examples of steps in this direction. More vigorous progress towards class/representative actions under English law would be valuable.[102] In the context of the internal market, attention also needs to be devoted to handling cross–border complaints.[103] Ultimately, however, the case for at least some public intervention seems unanswerable and it is to these issues that the discussion now turns.

1.7 RATIONALES FOR PUBLIC INTERVENTION

It is not difficult to construct a powerful argument that a legal system based on individual action by 'consumer' against 'trader' bears no useful relation to an economy of mass production and extended distribution and marketing chains. The pursuit of such distinct goals as the correction of market failure and fairness within a market order cannot be fully achieved under a system based purely on private law.

Contract and tort law both have limitations in sharpening the messages expressed by consumers about producer behaviour. The common law of contract is based on the doctrine of privity of contract. Accordingly, the consumer may sue the party to whom he or she paid money for the item – and no one else. As a corollary, the consumer who has not bought the product, for example the recipient of a gift, has no rights in contract at all. Since modern marketing typically puts the consumer at several removes from the manufacturer, the contractual claim brought by a consumer against the manufacturer of a faulty product is a rarity. Tort law partially fills these gaps, taking legal responsibility for manufacture and marketing into wider realms than are recognised by the artificially confined law of contract. However, tort law too has limitations, its focus being on inadequate *safety*, not inadequate *quality*. Where a product fails to achieve suitable quality standards, the claim lies only in contract. Moreover, whereas liability for breach of contract is strict, negligence liability depends on fault on the part of the defendant. The fact that a consumer has been harmed is not of itself enough to ensure the success of a claim, although the Consumer Protection Act 1987 has improved the consumer's position.[104] Tort law fundamentally protects only certain kinds of interest. Accordingly, contract and tort law offer protection to the consumer, but both have gaps in the framework of that protection. Inefficient behaviour may not be corrected.

Contract and tort are also limited in their capacity to deliver fair outcomes. Contract, classically, is in any event concerned with no such thing. It has latterly moved more in the direction of controls reflecting notions of

---

102 Chapter 17.3.
103 Cf the European Commission's Access to Justice Green Paper, Chapter 17.9.3.
104 Chapter 1.4 above, Chapter 6 below.

fairness, but this aspect remains relatively unsophisticated and is in any event not undisputed.[105] Tort law is more allied with ideas of social fairness. However, as judge–made law, it remains erratic and unpredictable in its scope.

Such qualifications to the role of tort and contract in securing an efficient and fair market are greatly deepened by the practical problems of securing access to justice. The reluctance of consumers to go to court and the absence of effective recourse to representative actions together shelter producers from the consequences of their failure to fulfil consumer demand and expectation, while also denying consumers the practical enjoyment of legal rights.

The perception that private law rights are often hazily understood by consumers and that their pursuit is frequently neglected sharpens the policy perception that an effective programme of consumer protection in the modern market must embrace public law too. For the benefit of consumers, for the benefit of fair and honest traders who find themselves exposed to dishonest competition, and in the public interest generally in an efficient market system, action to improve the operation of the market can be justified.

1.8 CHOICES BETWEEN FORMS OF PUBLIC REGULATION

Intervention may take many different forms.[106] The popularity of various forms of regulation has risen and fallen over time. Regulatory agencies may assume very different shapes,[107] while rationales for interventions have varied. The distinctive notions of intervention to correct market failure and the non–economic motivation of fairness have enjoyed fluctuating levels of attraction. Political fashion has changed. After several decades in which the pattern of market regulation gradually intensified, in recent years there has been a growing scepticism about the worth of the regulatory impulse. This scepticism is associated with the policies of successive Conservative governments since Mrs Thatcher became Prime Minister in 1979. However, there is nothing new about the perception that policymakers should be aware that regulation may produce winners and losers, and that a cost–benefit calculation should be performed. The courts too are perfectly aware of the

---

105 Chapter 1.3.4 above.

106 For an important recent investigation, see A. I. Ogus, *Regulation: Legal Form and Economic Theory* (OUP, 1994). Cf also the materials and commentary provided by Ramsay n.4 above.

107 Cf the several examples studied in R. Baldwin and C. McCrudden, *Regulation and Public Law* (Weidenfeld and Nicolson, 1987). Also Ch.3 in Ramsay n.4 above.

trade-offs at stake. In *Tesco Supermarkets Ltd v Nattrass*, Lord Diplock discussed the scope of the defence that reasonable precautions have been taken, available to a trader accused of an offence under the Trade Descriptions Act 1968. He was moved to comment that:

> 'If considerations of cost and business practicability did not play a part in determining what employers carrying on such businesses could reasonably be expected to do to prevent the commission of an offence under the Act, the price to the public of the protection afforded to a minority of consumers might well be an increase in the cost of goods and services to consumers generally'.[108]

The result of tensions from decade to decade concerning the role of consumer policy is a patchwork of controls which must be assessed with an awareness of the melting pot of the history of consumer protection. Attempts to identify what individual initiatives are 'for' and how they fit coherently into a wider framework will, on occasion, aim at producing a master–plan that does not exist. Consumer protection law *is* a patchwork. However, this does not detract from the importance and value of attempting to construct a rigorous and transparent cost–benefit analysis to justify regulatory intervention – as long as one is aware, first, that quantification of costs and benefits may reflect subjective value judgements and, second, that it is perfectly possible and not uncommon to make the political judgement that justice requires that an overall cost be placed on society generally in support of a disadvantaged minority.

1.8.1 Quality Standards/Bans

An obvious intervention in the market is the imposition of minimum quality or safety standards, backed by bans on non–conforming products or services. Infringement of these standards could attract penalties in the form of fines or even, ultimately, imprisonment. Enforcement responsibilities would typically be placed in the hands of public authorities who would enjoy powers of investigation, prosecution and seizure of offending items. Such agencies tend to develop a flexible strategy for enforcement. Prosecution and conviction may be relatively easy to achieve, not least because regulatory offences arising in the field of consumer protection are typically strict liability offences. However, formal prosecution is often seen to serve a limited purpose and is commonly used only against rogue traders. If the objective is

---

[108] [1971] 2 All ER 127, 151h. For deeper discussion, see Chapter 14.2.

to achieve a basic quality or safety level, the enforcement officer will typically prefer to act by persuasion, guidance and co–operation. Where the officer considers that the trader wishes to comply, it is normal to devise an appropriate strategy so that there is no call to invoke costly formal proceedings. This co–operative pattern is underpinned in the UK by a tradition of local enforcement. Trading standards officers operating at local level get to know 'their' traders and establish a modus vivendi. It should also be pointed out that the nature of the standard which is legally required will also affect the climate of enforcement; very precise rules leave little room for doubt, whereas vaguer notions such as 'reasonable safety' invite flexibility.

The law of consumer protection provides several illustrations of this type of regulatory offence. It is formally a sub species of the criminal law, although the objective of correcting market failure lends it a flavour that is distinct from the normal run of the criminal law. The philosophy and practice of the regulatory offence are considered more fully in Chapter 14. Consumer safety law provides an example of this style of intervention: products must meet specified safety standards; supply of an unsafe product attracts penalties, normally fines, possibly imprisonment. Trading standards authorities possess a range of powers which may be exercised against traders and against the goods themselves.

Apart from incurring criminal liability, supply of an unsafe good will equally represent a breach of contractual terms, most pertinently the implied term of satisfactory quality under the Sale of Goods Act 1979. The consumer will be able to sue the retailer for any loss suffered. Tort law may also provide a potential course of action for the consumer. In this way precisely the same incident may attract both criminal and civil consequences. The purpose of the two regimes is distinct. The imposition of criminal liability is motivated by the perception that, first, informational imbalance impedes the capacity of the consumer to avoid unsafe products; and, secondly, that the private law cannot adequately secure the market from the supply of unsafe goods. The several reasons for this are suggested above, ranging from the consumer's potential difficulty in shaping a claim in contract or tort against the relevant defendant trader, to the consumer's reluctance even to bother with the pursuit of a legal action where costs appear capable of outweighing benefits. Any fine imposed is payable into public funds. By contrast, the consumer who pursues a private action, albeit supported by a statutorily implied term, is suing for compensation for his or her own loss. Damages are then directed into the pocket of the consumer.[109]

---

[109] But compare the role of the compensation order in bridging the gap between criminal penalty and consumer compensation; Chapter 14.3.4.

In some exceptional circumstances, statute may provide that a criminal offence also forms the basis for a liability in tort for breach of statutory duty. Section 41 of the Consumer Protection Act 1987 provides an example. This is additional to criminal liability arising and any separate claim in tort or contract. However, there is no evidence that the provision has yet exerted any significant practical impact.

The use of misleading trade descriptions has also led to the creation of the regulatory offence. The pattern of the Trade Descriptions Act 1968 has much in common with that of the law governing consumer safety (and is examined in Chapter 10). The application of a misleading trade description may similarly attract consequences on two levels, criminal and civil. The false claim may attract criminal liability under the Trade Descriptions Act 1968. Here too the perception is that the market plus the private law are inadequate to secure protection for consumers and for honest traders against parties dealing on a dishonest basis. The same mischief can also frequently be converted into an action for breach of contract and/or the basis for a claim in tort by an individual consumer who is misled, although the Act is not tied to the private law and may impose criminal liability where no contractual or tortious liability would be at stake.

The type of standard properly set by the law has come under close scrutiny in recent years. Whereas legal standards tended in the past to be detailed and prescriptive, it has become increasingly popular to prefer broadly phrased, target performance standards. This is particularly noticeable in the Consumer Protection Act 1987. In the field of consumer safety, the 1987 Act has shifted the focus of control towards a general standard requiring reasonable safety, which is applicable 'horizontally', across a whole range of products.[110] The general standard will be elaborated in individual product sectors as appropriate, *inter alia* by standards set by private bodies. This emphasis on the general duty has replaced the pre–1987 focus of the law which was directed at the regulation of individual product types in individual instruments, often in rather precise and detailed depth. Part III of the Consumer Protection Act 1987 introduces a general and flexible offence in the field of misleading pricing. This replaces the narrower offence contained in s.11 of the Trade Descriptions Act 1968.[111] The application of the prohibition against misleading price indications is amplified by a Code of Practice. The pattern of food safety law, examined in Chapter 13, displays comparable characteristics by constructing a general statutory framework amplified by more specific secondary legislation and soft law. It does *not*, however, establish a single general offence of supplying

---

[110]   Definitional issues arise; Chapter 12.5.1.
[111]   Chapter 10.5.

unsafe food. The notion of a general duty to trade fairly has also come under consideration in recent years although the UK has not yet adopted such a measure.[112]

The motivations for this shift in regulatory policy are several.[113] It allows more flexibility to enforcement agencies and to traders. Typically the amplification of the broadly-phrased legal standard is achieved by private standards-setting bodies which are likely to have more expertise than public agencies. The past practice of detailed standards attracted criticism for its tendency to ossify practice and deter innovation.

This is an aspect of regulatory technique where the approaches of the EC and the UK are complementary. The EC adopted a 'New Approach' on technical harmonisation in 1985,[114] which pledged that, as far as possible, the past (and notorious) tendency of EC measures to lay down detailed and rigid rules will be abandoned.[115] In its place comes a broader, more flexible type of harmonised standard. Manufacturers enjoy choice about how to achieve the stipulated level, thereby providing them with the opportunity and the incentive to innovate. The Toy Safety Directive,[116] a typical New Approach measure, establishes the requirement that toys shall be safe, which means that they shall comply with 'essential safety requirements' amplified in an Annex to the Directive. Conformity with European standards is one method of demonstrating conformity with these essential safety requirements. In this way the Community standard of safety is linked to private standards (although it remains the case that safety, as defined in the Directive, is the standard that must be met; the Community has not delegated the basic task of setting the legal standard to the private sector). A second method of demonstrating conformity involves securing type approval for a model which, although not complying with recognised standards, is nonetheless certified as safe. Since the legal requirement has been shorn of its rigidity, producers have leeway to innovate. In this way, the basic notion that the public authorities will set standards, rather than simply leaving them to the market, is preserved. Non–conforming products may not be sold. However,

---

112   Chapter 16.5.4. Cf Sir Gordon Borrie, 'Trading Malpractices and Legislative Policy' (1991) 107 *LQR* 559; P. Circus, 'Should there be a general duty to trade fairly?' (1988) 6 *Trading Law* 238; Miller and Harvey n.87 above Ch.10, 'Aspects of the duty to trade fairly'.

113   Cf Ogus note 106 above, Ch.8.

114   OJ 1985 C136/1.

115   For an account of the New Approach in the light of the weaknesses which it addressed, see J. Pelkmans, 'The New Approach to Technical Harmonisation and Standardisation' (1987) 25 *JCMS* 249.

116   Directive 88/378 OJ 1988 L187/1.

the type of standard at issue is significantly altered, as is the freedom of action of traders subjected to the legal regime.

1.8.2 Regulating Traders

1.8.2.1 Registration and Licensing

Minimum standards plus a ban on non-conforming products comprise a relatively common form of public regulation, typically enforced *ex post facto*. In such circumstances, the sanction, most commonly a fine, is judged an adequate deterrence against the public being put at risk. Any trader is able to enter the field, but, once active, must comply with the regulatory standards. By contrast, in some sectors, it is considered inadvisable simply to permit all traders unrestricted access to the market, with only the back-up of sanctions in the event that the goods or services on offer fail to reach the statutory requirements. In such circumstances, regulatory controls may be directed at the trader him or herself.[117] The intensity of control may vary. Traders may be forced merely to register; they may require a licence; and/or they may be authorised to enter the market only after showing evidence of competence through some form of qualification. A supervisory agency will have to be established whose functions may vary from the mere maintenance of a register at one end of the regulatory spectrum to the imposition of training requirements and examination procedures at the other.

This type of control is more intrusive than simply setting a basic minimum standard for goods or services. Its benefits include the probability of greater security that goods or services below the required standard will not be released on to the market, because of the element of pre–authorization. The technique of registration and (a stricter control) licensing allows channels of supervision over a trade which can be exercised by public authorities. The public body is better placed to exercise control than in a system where standards are simply laid down and where any individual may, unannounced, choose to begin to trade. Typically, sanctions would be imposed for trading without a licence or without having registered, irrespective of evidence of any harm caused.

1.8.2.2 Costs of Regulation

However, more intrusive regulation involves costs. Endowing an agency with

---

[117]   Cf Ogus note 106 above Ch.10.

expertise may involve a substantial resource commitment.[118] Furthermore, there is the less tangible damage done to the flexibility of the market. Rules such as these amount to barriers to market entry. They impede competition, for any would-be entrant must scale the barriers, which may be rather low in the case of mere registration, but which can be much higher if the trader is required to hold qualifications. Those inside the system have an incentive to raise barriers to those outside, for example by persuading the licensing authority to impose entry qualifications. Setting standards may protect the consumer from unscrupulous traders, but those very standards also deprive the consumer of choice among traders adopting different practices. Of course, impeding competition is the very rationale for intervention: it has been determined that the market should not be a free–for–all. But it is always essential to analyse with care the benefits of securing a certain level of protection as against the costs of removing the possibility of (some) competition. This is a further expression of an endemic problem in consumer policy making: where does unfair competition which is liable to mislead shade into fair but fierce competition which maximises consumer choice?

Examples of the phenomenon of controlling market entry are numerous. The power to manufacture or to sell some products is controlled. Retailing alcoholic drinks on premises open to the public cannot be undertaken unless the individual concerned has first obtained a licence.[119] Appropriate authorisation must be secured.[120] The manufacture and sale of drugs and medicines have been subjected to regulatory control for many centuries. Innovative research and development in this area are vital for society, but so is control over both the manufacture of products that may cause enormous harm to consumers and the availability of goods that may fall into the wrong hands.[121] Part of the rationale for such close scrutiny lies in the perception

---

118   On this and other aspects, see S. Breyer, *Regulation and its Reform* (Harvard University Press, 1982).

119   A justices' licence under the Licensing Act 1964.

120   So must appropriate beer supplies, a market where entry is restricted not only by public intervention, but also by a market structure which places a great deal of power in the hands of relatively few suppliers. Hence the interest of competition authorities in the beer supply market; in the UK, cf MMC report *The Supply of Beer* Cm 651 (1989) and its consequences, summarised in R. Whish, *Competition Law* (Butterworths, 1993), pp. 576–7; in the EC, cf Case C–234/89 *Stergios Delimitis v Henninger Brau* [1991] ECR I–935, followed by Commission Notice OJ 1992 C121/2.

121   L. Hancher, *Regulating for Competition* (Clarendon Press, 1990) and, on recent developments at EC level, P. Deboyser, 'Recent Developments in the Community Law Relating To Medicinal Products' (1994) 2 *Consum LJ* 213. Surveying the policy

that consumers are under informed and that supply decisions cannot be left to the unregulated market.

Examples of registration and licensing in specific sectors will be encountered below. For instance, the Consumer Credit Act 1974, which requires that a licence be obtained to carry on a consumer credit, consumer hire or ancillary credit business, is examined at length in Chapter 11. Numerically, this is a very significant control regime, since some 150,000 consumer credit licences are in existence. The Food Safety Act 1990 introduced registration requirements for premises used as a food business, a less rigorous (and cheaper) means of control.

The style of control varies. Within consumer credit licensing, there is continuing debate about the proper substantive and personal scope of the regime. The Director General of Fair Trading and the Government have exchanged differing views. This debate about intensity of regulation is also tracked in Chapter 11.[122] It is probably not generally appreciated that estate agents are not required to hold a licence as a precondition to entering the market, although statutory powers exist whereby orders can forbid individuals from pursuing activities as an estate agent.[123] The benefits of market flexibility and open competition available as a result of the absence of prior licensing requirements must be judged alongside the cost of the risk that unscrupulous or incompetent traders may take advantage of unsupervised market entry to harm the unwary consumer.[124]

In a trade regulated by a licensing system, unacceptable performance, however defined, can ultimately result in the revocation of the licence. The State, through its appointed regulatory agency, thus directly determines the trader's commercial life or death. This confers very effective control powers on the regulator, able to revoke a licence or, more creatively, to improve standards by persuasion or veiled threat. It is possible to describe this system as an attempt to replicate the results that would be reached were the market operating 'perfectly', where inadequate performance would be commercially fatal and would necessarily cut short the survival of the supplier of unwanted goods or services. This description is partly accurate, although public intervention cannot properly mimic the market because it is fed by different

---

issues, E. Kaufer, 'The Regulation of New Product Development in the Drug Industry' in G. Majone (ed.), *Deregulation or Re-regulation?* (Pinter, 1990). See also (1989) 12 *JCP* Issue 3, Special Issue.

[122] Chapter 11.1.

[123] Estate Agents Act 1979. See J. Murdoch, *Law of Estate Agency and Auctions* (Estates Gazette Ltd., 3rd ed, 1994).

[124] Cf research into the trade by M. Clarke, D. Smith and M. McConville, *Slippery Customers: Estate Agents, the Public and Regulation* (Blackstone, 1994). The slippery customers of the title are both estate agents and their customers.

stimuli: there is no invisible guiding hand. However, a pure market failure explanation seems inadequate to account for some modern manifestations of licensing requirements. Fairness is one element in the scope of consumer credit regulation, examined in Chapter 11. Unfair exploitation of poor consumers by suppliers of credit has stimulated intervention, even though one may also identify market failure rationales, such as under–information, at work in such circumstances.

1.8.2.3 Professions

Establishing regulatory agencies is costly. In many areas the State has been tempted to pass on the job to professional bodies and so reduce its direct costs. Another advantage is that the profession is likely to have a level of expertise and understanding of what is at stake that cannot be matched by a public agency without major expenditure. This is loosely described as self–regulation, a nuanced phenomenon requiring rather tighter definition (provided below at 1.8.4). Patterns vary according to the level of State control. The State may simply withdraw from the field and allow completely unrestricted market entry; alternatively, it may continue to require that market entrants meet specific qualification requirements, but delegate the task of devising and defining those thresholds to the industry itself. These are distinctive types of self-regulation/deregulation.

In fact, in a number of areas private bodies pre date State interest. Many 'professions' have organised their own affairs over many years, even centuries, and the State may have come to endow their activities with statutory protection. The phenomenon of the profession deserves further, brief consideration. The term instinctively seems to imply a 'special' kind of job, to which entry is restricted by rigorous qualifications requirements. Remarkably, the lawyer can offer little that is more precise. There is no crisp dividing line between what can or should be termed a profession and what can or should not. The notion of 'professional' seems to involve an element of State recognition of and protection for the status achieved and the expertise provided, but the pattern varies. This is reflected in the sociological discussion of the phenomenon of the profession.[125] By common consent, doctors and lawyers are 'professionals'; rat catchers and buskers probably are not. Yet all work for a living by providing a service to others. The distinguishing features seem to be qualification requirements which are prerequisites to market entry and standards of conduct post-entry, typically

---

[125] Eg T. Johnson, *Professions and Power* (Macmillan, 1972).

laid down and elaborated by the industry, but endowed with statutory effect. This leaves grey areas: plumbers? taxi drivers?

The absence of precise legal categorisation of the professional means that each occupation must be treated individually in an appraisal of the legal regime applying to those wishing to be active in it. 'Professional' status suggests State recognition; the professions have carved out a privileged place for their market in the State structure. In so far as that involves rules governing entry, a degree of inflexibility is the hallmark of the market for professional services. The perceived benefits of regulation – warranty of quality provided to the consumer and fair competition between suppliers – must be weighed against the costs. Precisely these issues have come to the fore in recent years at national level where awareness of the anti–competitive effects of professional rules has risen.[126] State scrutiny of the insulation from open competition offered to the professions has intensified, in some areas drawing a response from professional bodies designed to maintain their sheltered position.[127]

The impact of European market integration has intensified the re–examination of the nature and purpose of professional rules. The expanding cross–border market for services has brought EC law of free movement into play as a means of challenging professional rules which act as entry barriers.[128] In *Commission v France, Italy, Greece*[129] the European Court found incompatible with Article 59 EC national rules that made the provision of services by tourist guides subject to the possession of a licence, itself dependent on a particular qualification. Such rules tended to force visiting tour parties to use local guides (in practice the only people holding the required licence) rather than guides from their home State. The Court considered that in this case the competitive market was capable of serving consumer interests and that State–imposed entry barriers could not be justified. EC law supplies an increasingly significant deregulatory impulse. Nevertheless, EC law recognises certain interests which justify the maintenance of restrictive rules; it is not a charter for a deregulatory free–for–all. For example, it would not leave choice between doctors to the market, since qualification requirements are justified. Areas of lawful restrictions to market integration have prompted the development of

---

126   For some discussion in the context of the legal profession, see R. Abel, 'Between Market and State: The Legal Profession in Turmoil' (1989) 52 *MLR* 285.

127   A. Gamble, *The Free Economy and the Strong State* (Macmillan, 1988); M. Brazier, J. Lovecy, M. Moran and M. Potton, 'Falling from a Tightrope: Doctors and Lawyers between the Market and the State' (1993) XLI *Political Studies* 197.

128   S. Weatherill and P. Beaumont, *EC Law* (Penguin Books, 1993), Ch.19.

129   Cases C–154/89, C–180/89 and C–198/89 [1991] ECR I–659, 709, 727.

Community rules on professional qualifications – a classic instance of re–regulation at Community level designed to achieve the liberalisation of the Community–wide market. Following the 'New Approach' to technical harmonisation,[130] recent Community activity has shifted away from the establishment of rather rigid and typically rather limited profession–specific rules towards general 'horizontal' measures establishing looser common Community rules and laced with more mutual recognition.[131] Generally, this has projected into the Community arena the central question of the function of rules of professional qualifications.[132]

It should finally be added that action can be taken against particular traders who have proved to be a menace to a free and fair market by issuing a 'cease and desist' order under Part III of the Fair Trading Act 1973. This is a court order, although the preparatory work of investigation is performed by the Office of Fair Trading. The order may be made against a trader who has engaged in a persistent course of conduct detrimental to consumers, contravening either the civil or the criminal law or both. It does not matter that violations have not been recorded in formal litigation. An order may be issued where, for example, there is an accumulation of evidence of breaches of contract, none of which has been pursued in legal action by a consumer. In the light of the frequency with which many small–scale breaches of contract do indeed go unchallenged in formal legal proceedings, the 'cease and desist' order provides an interesting illustration of the capacity of public regulation on an *ad hoc* basis to fill a gap caused by the practical weaknesses in the pattern of the private law.[133]

1.8.3 Consumer Information

1.8.3.1 Policy

A further technique lies in intervention designed to improve consumer information.[134] The Trade Descriptions Act 1968, examined in Chapter 10, has a role to play in suppressing misleading description. However, the law

---

130 1.8.1 above.
131 Directive 89/48 on a general system for the recognition of higher–education diplomas OJ 1989 L19/16; Directive 92/51 on a second general system for the recognition of professional education and training OJ 1992 L209/25.
132 Cf A.C. Oosterman–Meulenbeld, 'Quality Regulation on Professional Health Care Practice in the European Community' [1993/1] *LIEI* 61.
133 For more extended examination, see Chapter 16.
134 A. Ogus note 106 above Ch.7

can operate more positively. By requiring particular types of information to be made available to consumers, the law serves to bridge the information gap, permitting the consumer to choose between different types of product in an informed manner. The technique avoids the objection to the setting of minimum standards that the State is thereby taking away from the market the decision about what will and will not be available. Information disclosure addresses the market failings of informational imbalance, but then leaves the market to set its own quality levels. This technique is also usually cheaper to enforce.

The technique of information disclosure has become popular in recent years and is especially apparent at EC level. The notion that the consumer, duly informed and thereby protected, is able to participate fairly and effectively in the market has assumed the status of a guiding principle of policy.[135] The European Court considers that the suppression of information to consumers may itself infringe Article 30. In *GB–INNO v CCL*[136] the Court held that a Luxembourg law controlling the provision by a trader of information about prices was capable of impeding trade in goods from States where no such control was imposed. It declared that 'under Community law concerning consumer protection the provision of information to the consumer is considered one of the principal requirements'. The restrictive law was incompatible with Article 30 EC.

EC rules in this area are in part motivated by the process of securing the integration of the market.[137] For all systems, a powerful rationale for such intervention lies in the perception that consumer information reduces the imbalance of knowledge between consumer and trader which is the hallmark of the modern economy. The market is corrected by information disclosure in the sense that it becomes more efficient and competitive. Consumers are enabled to transmit messages to suppliers which reflect 'real' preferences, undistorted by the lack of transparency. Suppliers are thereby enabled to compete with each other more fairly and efficiently.

1.8.3.2 Examples of Informational Intervention

In the area of consumer credit, information disclosure has played a major role in the development of legal control of the market. This may be observed

---

[135] S. Weatherill, 'The Role of the Informed Consumer in European Community Law and Policy' (1994) 2 *Consum LJ* 49.

[136] Case C–362/88 [1990] ECR I–667.

[137] Chapter 2.

in both UK law and in the pattern of EC rules. Directive 87/102,[138] amended by Directive 90/88,[139] approximates national provisions concerning consumer credit. As Directives made under Article 100a, market integration serves as their formal constitutional justification.[140] The Community measures take as their principal objective the maximisation of the consumer's awareness of the costs of credit. In this vein, the Preamble to the Directive declares that 'the consumer should receive adequate information on the conditions and cost of credit and on his obligations.' Article 3 is concerned to ensure that an advertisement displayed at business premises involving an offer of credit in which figures relating to costs are indicated shall include 'a statement of the annual percentage rate of charge'. Other provisions serve to improve the transparency of the transaction, though the measures leave the cost of credit largely unaffected. The substance of the bargain is thus largely untouched by this measure, but the process of making the bargain is controlled.

Existing law in the UK had already adopted the technique of information disclosure as a means of achieving consumer protection in this area. The Consumer Credit Act 1974 is also largely concerned with the transparency and fairness of the bargaining process, rather than the content of the bargain. Absorption of the EC rules was relatively unproblematic. The current pattern of the law is examined in more depth in Chapter 11.

A further example of transparency lies in the requirement that a trader who advertises goods for sale must make it plain that those goods are being sold in the course of a business. The perceived mischief was that traders were pretending to be private sellers, for example, by advertising in classified columns of newspapers – a particularly popular trick among second-hand car dealers. Consumers might be induced to enter into a contract without being properly aware of its commercial nature. The intervention requires disclosure, so that consumers are put on their guard, without in any way directly affecting the content of any bargain that may be struck.[141] Equally, such intervention is a means of improving the market by promoting fair competition between traders, for, without such laws, open and honest trading would be undermined.

---

[138] OJ 1987 L42/48.

[139] OJ 1990 L61/14.

[140] Chapter 2.3.3.

[141] Business Advertisements (Disclosure) Order 1977 No.1918. It is of course necessary to determine the scope of acting 'in the course of a business' which on occasion has caused difficulties; cf Chapters 3, 9.6.2.

A particularly subtle form of information disclosure was contained in the Consumer Guarantees Bill.[142] Although this Bill, initially sponsored in 1990 by the National Consumer Council and pursued as a Private Members' Bill, did not become law, it deserves brief consideration for the regulatory technique it envisaged. Manufacturers of specified products would have been obliged to make clear whether or not such products were accompanied by a guarantee of at least one year's duration. There was no substantive obligation to offer a guarantee, which remained a private market decision. Rather, there was simply an obligation to inform the consumer of the manufacturer's stance – guarantee or no guarantee. The idea was plainly to assist informed consumer choice in the area of guarantees, which is notorious for its complexity, but without intervening directly in the substance of any deal. Subtle though the scheme appeared, it lacked governmental support and accordingly failed.

1.8.3.3 A Case Study – Upholstered Furniture

The regulation of upholstered furniture in the UK provides a useful illustration of the choices to be made. The perceived problem was not upholstered furniture as such, but the polyurethane foams they contained. Such foam is cheap, but relatively flammable in comparison with older types of stuffing and, once ignited, it gives off great heat and toxic fumes. Once a fire starts, the presence of the foam rapidly accelerates the process, making escape difficult and typically taking oxygen from the atmosphere with the result that victims die of asphyxia. Consideration of regulatory intervention was prompted in Parliament by regular pressure by a London Labour MP Ronald W. Brown, parliamentary adviser to the Furniture, Timber and Allied Trades Union.[143] Awareness of the degree of danger grew and was doubtless further stimulated by high profile disasters such as the Manchester Woolworths fire of May 1979 where ten people died in circumstances where burning foam acted as a contributory factor. Misperception of the risk by the under informed consumer was likely to persist. The need for intervention in the market to set standards governing the flammability of upholstered furniture was accepted by the government.

However, it was not prepared to ban the foam altogether. No adequate alternative was available and a complete ban would have removed consumer opportunity to choose relatively cheap, albeit riskier, furniture. After a

---

142 Examined in Chapter 4.2.3.2.

143 Eg 859 H.C Deb. 2058–2070 (13 July 1973); 928 H.C. Deb. 494 (WQ) (22 March 1977).

period of consultation, the regulations were made in May 1980 as the Upholstered Furniture (Safety) Regulations 1980.[144] The aim was to make furniture covering resistant to ignition in the home. Two tests were introduced, known as the cigarette test and the match test. Furniture was exposed to a heat source of the described type; if it underwent progressive combustion within a specific period, then it failed the test. After a transitional period, the rules were fixed in 1982 in a way that involved significantly different consequences depending on which of the two tests was failed. Failing the cigarette test meant that the furniture could not be marketed, but failing the match test meant only that the furniture had to have red–edged, triangular labels attached to it warning against the careless use of matches. The Minister, Sally Oppenheim, explained this to the House of Commons as a means of delivering 'reasonable protection of consumers against avoidable hazards, as well as against an unreasonable limitation of choice and an unacceptable rise in the price of furniture.'[145] The industry had pressed for mere self–regulation, whereas other sources had demanded stricter intervention. Strong comments were made in Parliament criticising the choice of minimum standards backed by a ban (the cigarette test) in one case and information disclosure (the match test) in the other.

Why was conformity with the cigarette test, but not the match test, made mandatory? The Minister stated that the insidious smouldering cigarette, which could cause a fire once the household had retired to bed, was a greater danger than the match, since any blaze it caused would be capable of immediate detection and extinction.[146] The Minister added the justification that technology was insufficiently advanced to provide an alternative, cheap fabric which would pass the match test. Resistance to a match flame is not as readily achievable as resistance to a smouldering cigarette. It appears that pressure from the furniture industry was a major element in diluting the consequences of failing the match test.[147] It is naturally common for an industry to devote large resources in order to influence regulatory decisions affecting its interests.[148]

---

[144] SI No 725.

[145] Debate at 985 H.C. Deb. 834–892 (22 May 1980); quote at 835.

[146] 983 H.C. Deb. 376 (WQ) 28 April 1980.

[147] Comments in this vein appear in the Parliamentary debates; and cf Henry Swain, chief architect of Nottinghamshire County Council and closely involved with such furniture, *Architects Journal* May 1985, 'Fire: the Road from Fairfield'.

[148] Cf. Part 1.9 below on agency capture and the broader issue of public choice. For a US perspective, cf. P. Quirk, *Industry Influence in Federal Regulatory Agencies* (Princeton, 1981).

Further regulations were made in 1983 – the Upholstered Furniture (Safety) (Amendment) Regulations 1983.[149] These provided that even furniture passing the test had to bear a (green–edged) label. Furniture failing the cigarette test continued to be banned. Furniture failing only the match test could be sold, but had to bear a warning label. The regulations also included specific and more stringent controls over children's furniture.[150] Here again there was fierce Commons debate about whether the proper balance had been struck.[151] The Minister at the time, Sir Gerard Vaughan, declared:

> 'Customer purchasing power is tremendously effective. I hope that customers will look out for furniture with a safety label and ask traders why they do not stock more of that furniture. In that way we shall increase the incentives for the industry to produce such furniture.'[152]

This is a striking assertion of the role of information disclosure regulation in pushing the market towards a pattern where consumers can send messages to producers about their wants and thereby secure an efficient allocation of resources. It has been echoed in a number of other sectors, touching both safety and economic interests. For example, the Director General of Fair Trading has applauded the Consumer Credit Act for its endorsement of 'freedom of contract within a framework of rules designed to ensure openness; consumer protection is attained in large part through measures to ensure that full and truthful information about credit contracts is available to consumers'.[153] Such comments assume a rather active consumer. They also assume a consumer who can process information rather skilfully. If that does not happen, then the information imbalance is not cured; incentives to attend to desired levels of safety will not be transmitted to suppliers. The market will continue to fail.

For upholstered furniture, what was obviously at stake was a cost/benefit analysis, balancing the risks to consumers against the protection of traders, and embracing perceptions of the advantages of different forms of intervention. Consumer choice was a major consideration for the government. But passing the legislation was part of the hurly burly of the British political process, in which the choices and values at stake were not

---

149   SI No. 519.
150   Replacing the Children's Furniture (Safety) Order 1982 which, as required under the Consumer Safety Act, expired after 12 months; cf Chapter 12.2 below on temporary measures in the field of consumer safety.
151   40 H.C. Debs. 306–319 (29 March 1983).
152   *Ibid* 317–318.
153   *Consumer credit deregulation* (OFT, 1994), examined in Chapter 11.

laid bare in a transparent, scientific manner. The issues were hotly disputed, predominantly along party political lines. In debate, it was argued that the speed of a fire caused by a match (rather than a cigarette) should require tighter, not looser, control; also that allowing the trade to avoid a mandatory match test because of the absence of adequate alternative technology hardly induced it to invest in a search for an alternative. In any event the government made its choice between regulatory techniques.[154]

The law is currently contained in the Furniture and Furnishings (Fire) (Safety) Regulations 1988 which revoke those of 1980 and 1983.[155] These Regulations adjust the detail of the pattern discussed above, but retain the technique of mandatory labelling as a means of informing the consumer.

As suggested above, the technique of 'informational intervention' assumes the ability of consumers effectively to digest and act upon the information given.[156] If the consumer is not competent to 'process' the information provided, then the intervention is ineffective as a means of market correction. This comment applies to warnings designed to inform about safety risks; it applies equally to accumulations of small print designed to alert consumers to threats to their economic interests. Information provision must be carefully judged. Warning labels must neither under inform nor (less often considered) over inform.[157] Worse, such laws, if effective on paper but not in practice, are open to criticism as a mere sham designed to legitimate the continued supply of unsafe goods or unfair practices against which consumers are not able to take proper precautions. A further twist is that informational intervention will typically inform some consumers but not all. What of consumers who cannot read? What of consumers who cannot read English? Choices have to be made about whether the provision of information is satisfactory. Scepticism about the value of information disclosure in curing market failure and in protecting the consumer would induce one to pause briefly to consider improving the delivery of the message before moving on (if still unsatisfied and if willing to

---

154 On the US experience, cf P. Linneman, 'The Effects of Consumer Safety Standards: the 1973 Mattress Flammability Standard' (1980) 23 *Jnl Law and Econ* 461.

155 S.I. No.1324.

156 For a rather sceptical perspective on the efficacy of disclosure laws, see R. Cranston, *Consumers and the Law* (Weidenfeld and Nicolson, 1984), Ch.9. Cf also W. Whitford, 'The Functions of Disclosure Regulation in Consumer Transactions' (1973) 2 *Wisconsin L Rev* 400.

157 The furniture industry criticised the labels originally proposed as 'too frightening and would lead to people who had started to buy furniture to pay instead for a package holiday'; debate of 22 May 1980, note 145 above, col 838.

accept curtailment of consumer choice) to the imposition of minimum standards and a ban.

1.8.3.4 Doorstep Selling

'Doorstep selling' provides a final, useful case study in choices between regulatory techniques. Such choices are in some circumstances complementary, but in others competing. 'Doorstep selling' refers to sales methods which involve the seller arriving on the doorstep and there trying to persuade the consumer to buy a product or a service. The discussion may be instigated by the trader without any invitation by the consumer. It typically takes place away from business premises. In some circumstances it may be that the practice is beneficial to consumers, particularly, for example, if they are geographically isolated. However, the perceived risk is that the consumer may be caught unawares and may enter into a contract to which he or she would not have agreed in a 'normal' business environment. Doorstep sellers have accumulated a rather bad reputation for deceitful, pressure tactics; the familiar sign, 'No Hawkers!', is a legacy of such days. Many jurisdictions have developed controls over this selling technique. In 1974 the UK introduced statutory requirements that doorstep callers selling on credit must possess a licence; it also banned unsolicited doorstep selling of money loans. Furthermore consumers were given a 'cooling off' period after the conclusion of defined agreements involving the supply of credit, within which a right of cancellation could be exercised. More general protection is now available as a result of EC Directive 85/577, the 'Doorstep Selling' Directive, which addresses the legal protection of 'the consumer in respect of contracts negotiated away from business premises'.[158] It too requires a 'cooling off' period, giving the consumer a minimum of seven days in which to withdraw from a contract concluded in the circumstances defined by the Directive.[159] Other provisions in the Directive oblige traders to provide consumers with notice in writing of their right of cancellation. It is very much a device of consumer information. The transaction may be concluded and enforced on whatever terms the parties may agree, but the consumer is to be supported in the pre- and post-bargaining phase. This is consumer choice in the free market, but with account taken of the 'surprise element' in such deals, as the Directive's Preamble describes it.[160]

---

[158]   OJ 1985 L372/31. See Chapter 8.

[159]   Articles 1–3.

[160]   Italy's failure to implement this Directive gave rise to the European Court's regrettable decision that consumers derive no directly effective rights under an

It is important to appreciate that Community law does not forbid doorstep selling. It recognises the potential harm to the consumer interest that may result from its use, but chooses to regulate it by supporting the informed consumer. Consumer choice is maintained, but the law attempts to secure transparency in that choice.[161] National contract law is affected by the Directive; contracts covered are enforceable, but the consumer receives support in the pre–contractual phase and the opportunity to escape from the deal for seven days after the agreement which, under the normal English common law of contract, would be regarded as the conclusive moment of contract formation.

The Directive is built on the assumption that the selling technique in question need not be forbidden completely, but it recognises that an alternative view may be taken. Article 8 states that the Directive 'shall not prevent Member States from adopting or maintaining more favourable provisions to protect consumers in the field which it covers.' It is therefore open to Member States to choose to intervene in the market with a ban rather than the more limited EC preference for informational intervention. On this model of minimum harmonisation, regulatory diversity within the EC is tolerated, notwithstanding the obstruction this represents to the pursuit of a uniform cross–border marketing campaign.[162]

In the UK the Directive was duly implemented in the Consumer Protection (Cancellation of Contracts Concluded away from Business Premises) Regulations 1987.[163] Contracts are unenforceable unless they provide written notice of the right to cancel within seven days. These Regulations follow the Directive and do not impose stricter rules. As a matter of law, the Regulations must be interpreted to conform to the Directive in the event of ambiguity,[164] but no problems of interpretation have arisen in the UK.

Doorstep selling is examined in more detail in Chapter 8. It will be appreciated that some of the concerns about the capacity of the technique to induce consumers to enter into deals without adequate information apply with all the more force to traders relying on modern technological advances

---

unimplemented Directive against private suppliers: Case C–91/92 *Dori v Recreb*: Chapter 2.4.3.

[161] Cf discussion of the work of Ison in Chapter 7.8, doubting whether effective consumer protection can be achieved short of a ban on the practice.

[162] The European Court found that a French rule banning such practices was compatible with EC law given its contribution to consumer protection: Case 329/87 *Buet v Ministere Public* [1989] ECR 1235.

[163] S.I. No. 2117. See Chapter 8.

[164] Case 14/83 *Von Colson* [1984] ECR 1891; Case C–106/89 *Marleasing* [1990] ECR I–4135. Chapter 2.4.2.

to sell goods or services without any physical contact with the consumer. Mailshots, fax, telephone and television are all part of modern marketing and selling. Such practices are not limited to national markets. Indeed they are peculiarly suited to cross–border trade. Regulation of such 'distant selling' is also examined in more detail in Chapter 8.

1.8.4 Self–regulation

Public regulation is costly not only in the inflexibility it may bring to markets, in the reduction in consumer choice and the inefficiency it may induce among those sheltering behind regulatory barriers, but also in the cost of establishing institutions and buying the expertise to devise appropriate standards. From the perspective of reducing costs, there is accordingly an incentive to prefer self–regulation.

Self–regulation is a phrase which may encompass a range of distinctive techniques. It is possible to eliminate State involvement entirely in the conduct of trade. Any regulation that then occurs is purely private, perhaps the product of the activities of a trade association. The market order reigns, subject to the possibility that rules agreed between firms may attract the interest of the competition authorities.[165] Such State withdrawal may occur on the explicit or implicit understanding that, if the market generally or the industry's own self–regulation in particular proves ineffective (however this is judged), then the State will intervene. There are other types of 'self–regulation' which do not involve such a depth of State withdrawal. The State may set standards, but leave it to the industry itself to police compliance. Alternatively, the State may require that standards be set by the industry, then check the adequacy of those standards, and leave policing compliance to the industry. Self–regulation, in its several manifestations, has both costs and benefits.[166]

Where rule–setting and/or policing is performed through a trade association, costs are incurred by the industry not by the State. If the system is well respected within the industry, it will be observed with a minimum of fuss. A co–operative atmosphere generates willing and argument-free adherence. Compliance rates in such situations may be higher than in a system imposed from outside involving confrontational enforcement, where co–operation may be patchy or grudging.

---

165 Chapter 15, especially 15.2 on cartels and restrictive practices.
166 For a lengthy, and in a number of respects sceptical, discussion, see R. Cranston, *Consumers and the Law* (Weidenfeld and Nicolson, 1984) Part I.

In several sectors, privately generated Codes of Practice have assumed a significant role in consumer protection.[167] This is an aspect of self–regulation. Codes of Practice are typically an expression of the industry's own commitments, not necessarily driven by State compulsion. Codes may establish levels of best practice which extend beyond legal requirements. For example, there is no common law obligation for a supplier to repair a defective product. The standard remedies are rejection of the goods and/or damages,[168] whereas codes typically provide for repair. Such commitments are doubtless useful marketing ploys. As such they may engage the contractual responsibility of parties to the Code towards buyers.[169] However, the creation of formal legal enforceability is normally neither the purpose nor the principal perceived role of codes. In so far as they offer effective protection of existing rights and, indeed, the promise of enhanced rights, Codes of Practice are also very much to the benefit of the consumer.

Arbitration procedures in the event of dispute are common features of Codes. It may be in the interest of trader and consumer to resolve disagreement through quick and cheap arbitration cures. Nonetheless there is a risk that a consumer may feel dissatisfied about his or her treatment at the hands of the industry. This suggests that access to the ordinary courts ought to remain open even where the consumer has agreed to waive such recourse. Statutory intervention has in fact secured this protection for the consumer.[170]

The costs of self–regulation are in some ways the reverse of the benefits. If independent scrutiny is lacking, there is a risk that checking compliance may be less than rigorous. Even subconsciously, the industry may come to regard the Code as a cosy arrangement, largely for its own benefit rather than that of consumers. It is also possible that Codes may breed anti–competitive cartels.[171] Moreover, there is no effective method of securing enforcement of a Code against those who choose not to join the body through which supervision is practised or, indeed, against traders expelled from that body. The Code is not automatically applicable throughout the industry: rogue traders can opt out or cheerfully accept exclusion.

Such problems may lead to a recognition that some statutory overlay to a purely private Code is required. Membership of a private body may be made mandatory by the State, while the detailed arrangements for admission and conduct are left in the hands of the private body. This pushes private

---

167   Cf R. Lowe and G. Woodroffe, *Consumer Law and Practice* (Sweet and Maxwell, 1991), Ch.9 and Appx. 1; Miller and Harvey n.87 above, Ch.9.
168   Chapter 4.1.5.
169   Chapter 4.2.2.
170   Consumer Arbitration Agreements Act 1988, Chapter 17.
171   Note 165 above.

industry arrangements into a twilight world between market and State – as was previously observed in relation to the connected phenomenon of professional qualifications.[172] This method may be a means of ensuring the delivery of common standards across the board. It also confers on those within the industry an immunity from competition. There are ambiguous consequences for the consumer, torn between State protection and choice in the market.

The EC has played a part in the shift from 'pure' self–regulation to administrative support. For example, in the UK advertising was regulated for many years by the industry itself. Initiatives at EC level brought change. Since the majority of Member States could not accept that public controls over misleading advertising should be entirely excluded, the Directive on Misleading Advertising required the insertion of a role for public authorities.[173] This was implemented into the UK's system by giving the Director General of Fair Trading power to take action against misleading advertising.[174]

1.9 STATE REGULATION AND INDIVIDUAL FREEDOM

1.9.1 The Costs and Benefits of Regulation

It bears repetition that in all these circumstances regulation cannot be costless. Where the State chooses to set standards of any type, it is interfering with the 'pure' market system based on supplier and consumer dialogue. Costs involved in setting minimum standards, for example, involve higher prices, depressed consumer choice and the erection of entry barriers which circumscribe market flexibility. Honest traders might rightly claim protection from dishonest rivals, but there is less justification in claiming protection from fair, if fierce, competition. Techniques such as minimum standards and licensing may all be attacked from these perspectives. Moreover, in all these instances there will be a need to establish regulatory agencies which determine where minima should be fixed and how unfair competition should be distinguished from its fair but fierce cousin. Regulatory institutions are expensive and their judgements will rarely prove controversy-free. Studies suggest a risk that agencies may be 'captured' and deliver decisions reflective of the interests being regulated rather than the

---

[172] 1.8.2.3 above. Cf also the increasing list of Ombuds, considered in Chapter 17.
[173] Directive 84/450.
[174] Chapter 10.6.

broader public interest they are designed to serve.[175] Beyond the more limited notion of capture, 'public choice' analysis is devoted to the idea that impartial and efficient decision making cannot be delivered by public agencies. The State is a corporate enterprise, 'selling' laws to buyers (whether it recognises it or not).[176] Powerful interest groups will be able to manipulate the process in order to secure regulation that suits their interests at the expense of less effectively represented groups, of which consumers may be a prime example.[177] The messages of such analysis include an insistence on suspicion of the motivation for lawmaking and an awareness that regulatory failure should be taken every bit as seriously as market failure.[178]

This is not to concede that State decisions are not justifiable or worthwhile on a cost/benefit analysis. Many of the preceding pages have been devoted to a demonstration of rationales for intervention. The market is far from 'perfect'; perfection is unobtainable and, in some circumstances, undesirable. The law has a range of functions in achieving adjustments dedicated to improving the operation of the market and addressing questions of fairness. However, some of the severe economic and political critiques of regulation over recent years have had the salutary effect of forcing some hard looks at rationales for intervention. Perhaps there had been a tendency to assume that the costs of market failure justify intervention, without an adequate appreciation that intervention too may bring costs. After the onslaught of public choice analysis and the sustained deregulatory rhetoric and, to a lesser degree, practice of successive British governments (discussed below), such comfortable assumptions are long buried.

1.9.2 Constitutional Limitations on Regulation

Some analysts have endeavoured to adopt a constitutional perspective in addressing the cost/benefit assessment relevant to intervention. Consumer choice is a political matter. State intervention can be viewed as hostile to

---

175 Eg A. Peacock (ed.), *The Regulation Game* (Blackwell, 1984).
176 A major influence is J. Buchanan, see eg *Liberty, Markets and State* (Brighton, 1986). For discussion at length, see papers collected at (1988) 74 *Virginia Law Review* 167. Also important is S. Peltzman, 'Towards a more general theory of regulation' (1976) 19 *Jnl Law and Econ* 211.
177 Cf M. Trebilcock, 'Winners and Losers in the Modern Regulatory System: Must the Consumer always lose?' (1975) 13 *Osgoode Hall LJ* 618.
178 Further, P. Farber and P. Frickey, *Law and Public Choice: A Critical Introduction* (1991); Ogus n.106 above, Ch.4.

individual freedom. At a rather simple level this has been plain in recent years in political observations about the superiority of the Western free market over the State-run economies of Eastern Europe. Competition was able to do what the State could not. 'Socialism collapsed because it literally could not produce the goods' according to Peter Lilley, then Secretary of State for Trade and Industry, in a June 1991 speech. Free competition and minimal State intervention has a flavour of not only economic efficiency, but also individual rights and democratic freedom. Discussion of competitive markets and non–intervention by the State thus inevitably invites consideration of political ideology, which may be reflected in legal rules.

The advisability of restricting consumer choice through legal intervention in the market should be a matter of interest to anyone involved in consumer policy. However British legal thinking would typically assume that the basic decision to intervene or not ultimately forms part of the assessment made by the policymaker on whom legislative competence has been conferred by statute. Once the law has been duly passed, there is no legal test to govern the constitutionality of intervention. Constructing a framework to test the validity and permissible scope of State intervention to curtail economic freedoms would form the analytical starting point for consumer lawyers in some European jurisdictions and in some quarters in North America, but in the UK such notions are unfamiliar.

Some strands of political thinking have attempted to identify a coherent framework for protecting the liberty of the individual from State intervention. The competitive market, led by the expression of consumer preference, is a form of economic enfranchisement of the citizen, and incursions require justification from both the economic and the political perspective. Such analysis would set limits on the scope of State choices taken on behalf of consumers and citizens generally. In a system which operates on the basis of judicially enforceable constitutional limits on State power, such perceptions may be transformed into legal controls over competence to legislate for the economy. In such a regime, consumer protection laws (*inter alia*) which diminish individual choice (*inter alia*) may be susceptible to constitutional review. They may be invalidated if they trespass on a constitutionally protected domain. For the British observer, that is plainly a point of comparative legal interest, but not one that will instinctively suggest itself as fertile material for litigation strategies. In the future, however, it might become a point of very direct interest in so far as the EC is developing into a system characterised by such constitutional limitations to legislative power. EC law is part of the legal system in the UK and it imports a form of constitutional review unfamiliar to the traditions of constitutional law centred on Parliamentary sovereignty. This is becoming part of the currency of the House of Lords which is beginning to decide cases that manifest acceptance of obligations derived from EC law to review laws duly passed by

Parliament. In *EOC v Secretary of State for Employment* threshold provisions of the Employment Protection (Consolidation) Act 1978 were declared incompatible with EC equality law.[179] In making an order in such terms, their Lordships denied that this was a case of domestic judges explicitly declaring the UK in breach of the EC Treaty; however, constitutional sensitivity notwithstanding, this was the practical effect.

EC law imposes restrictions on regulatory competence based on principles that include proportionality, protection of legitimate expectations and protection of fundamental rights.[180] These principles control both EC acts and national acts within the sphere of EC law.[181] The entry into force of the Treaty on European Union on 1 November 1993 provided the Court with the opportunity, not as yet activated, to test acts against the principle of subsidiarity contained in Article 3b. Obscure though Article 3b seems in detail,[182] at a general level it seems to offer scope for judging the comparative efficiency of regulatory action taken at Community and/or at national level. Furthermore, it seems that EC law enshrines a notion of freedom of expression which may be capable of conversion into a legal instrument for challenging laws that impede commercial free speech – notably, advertising. In *ERT v Dimotiki* the Court interpreted the scope of the freedom to provide services 'in the light of the general principle of freedom of expression embodied in Article 10 of the European Convention on Human Rights'.[183] In that case State restrictions on broadcasting had to be justified with reference to the Convention mediated through the 'general principles' of Community law. No adequate justification was forthcoming.

It is worthwhile to consider briefly whether such principles could be deployed to challenge Community rules imposing restrictions on the advertising of tobacco products. Directive 89/622,[184] amended and extended

---

179   [1994] 1 All ER 910, applying the *Factortame* rulings.

180   S. Weatherill and P. Beaumont, *EC Law* (Penguin Books, 1993) Ch.8.

181   On the EC as a constitutional legal order supervised by the Court, see E. Stein, 'Lawyers, Judges and the Making of a Transnational Constitution' (1981) 75 *Amer J Intl L* 1; J. Weiler, 'The Transformation of Europe' (1991) 100 *Yale LJ* 2403; F. Jacobs, 'Is the Court of Justice of the European Communities a Constitutional Court?' in D. Curtin and D. O'Keeffe (eds.), *Constitutional Adjudication in European Community and National Law* (Butterworths (Ireland), 1992); K. Lenaerts, 'Constitutionalism and the Many Faces of Federalism' (1990) 38 *AJCL* 25.

182   Cf. divergent views on its scope and justiciability expressed *passim* in D. O'Keeffe and P. Twomey, *Legal Issues of the Maastricht Treaty* (Chancery, 1994).

183   Case C–260/89 [1991] ECR I-2925.

184   OJ 1989 L359/1.

by Directive 92/41,[185] is based on Article 100a[186] and concerns the labelling of tobacco products, which are required to carry a range of specified warnings. The issue is sensitive. Further initiatives have been proposed, including a complete ban on advertising, except within tobacco retail outlets,[187] but remain blocked due to the absence of an adequate majority in Council.[188] Were such rules to be adopted, it would seem open in principle to dissenting States, and perhaps private parties,[189] to seek annulment of such intervention as action beyond the competence of the EC and/or as an infringement of rights of expression within the market. True, such a submission would by no means be assured of success. On the first aspect, questions of competence are tricky,[190] but in the past the Court has never ruled EC acts unlawful for lack of Community competence. On the second aspect, the European Convention on Human Rights (and therefore, indirectly, the EC legal order) envisages limitations on freedom of expression in accordance with what is 'necessary in a democratic society'.[191] The scope of commercial free speech is little developed in either European Community or European human rights law.[192] This is in contrast to the relatively sophisticated understanding of its potential scope in North America, where it has been a focus for heated controversy about the nature of constitutional freedom in the commercial context.[193] In Canada precisely this type of constitutional challenge to advertising restrictions has been pursued by

---

[185] OJ 1992 L158.

[186] Chapter 2.3.3.

[187] OJ 1991 C167/3, amended OJ 1992 C129/5.

[188] Qualified majority voting is the rule under Article 100a.

[189] Subject to showing sufficient standing under Art.173 EC; see Weatherill and Beaumont n.180 above, pp. 197–212.

[190] Doubts have been expressed whether measures confining advertising of tobacco products are properly based on Art.100a, given their contribution to improving health, but no litigation has been pursued on the point. Cf K. Bradley, 'Legal Developments in the European Parliament' (1992) 12 *YEL* 505, 520. See Chapter 2 generally on the scope of EC competence.

[191] Article 10 ECHR.

[192] In relation to the European Convention, cf *Markt Intern and Beerman v Germany* ECHR Series A No.165: no violation of Art.10, decided on President's casting vote.

[193] For a flavour of this debate, see A. Hutchinson, 'Money Talk: Against Constitutionalising (Commercial) Speech' (1990) 17 *Canadian Business Law Journal* 2 and comment following in the same issue of the journal by R.J. Sharpe, D.A. Strauss and D. Cohen.

tobacco companies, with an (as yet) uncertain outcome.[194] However, for present purposes, it suffices to make the point that constitutional review of market regulatory laws in the EC may become more prominent in coming years. To this extent, the application of the theories of regulation discussed here may come to form part of the armoury of even the practising English commercial lawyer.[195]

1.9.3 Political Perspectives and Recent British Practice

Some political and economic analysts have endeavoured to create a framework for testing the democratic and constitutional legitimacy of some aspects of legal intervention in the market. In recent years Hayek, an economist with legal and political bents, has been an influential source of such thinking. Hayek's writing emphasises the efficiency of spontaneous order in the market.[196] The market has an inherent capacity for self-correction and will deliver outcomes superior to a programme of public intervention. This is not to advocate a law–free market; quite the contrary. Hayek is an enthusiastic supporter of the common law, believing it to incorporate tendencies of flexibility and self–correction comparable to the virtues which he attributes to the market mechanism more generally. His criticism is directed at State intervention to 'adjust' the operation of the market in the (alleged) public interest. Such legislation cannot be as 'informed' as the directions chosen by the market system and must therefore yield inferior results. Intervention, with an appeal to social justice, is no more than an attempt by the few, able to exercise transient power, to wrest extra benefits for themselves at the expense of wealth maximisation for the whole

---

194 *RJR Macdonald Inc et al v Canada*, Supreme Court hearing, late 1994. For a brief comment, see I. Ramsay (1994) 2 *Consum LJ* CS62.

195 German commentators, in particular, are more accustomed to such notions of (loosely) economic constitutional law and are already well advanced in developing frameworks of analysis at EC level. For a valuable survey of what this may involve, see C. Joerges, 'European Economic Law, the Nation–State and the Maastricht Treaty' in R. Dehousse (ed), *Europe After Maastricht* (Law Books in Europe, 1994). For historical background, see D. Gerber, 'Constitutionalising the Economy: German Neo–liberalism, Competition Law and the "New" Europe' (1994) 42 *Amer J Comp Law* 25.

196 Naturally, it is difficult (and unfair) to seek to distil the essence of extensive writing into a few short paragraphs. Hayek's principal insights are contained in his three volume work *Law, Legislation and Liberty* (Routledge and Kegan Paul, 1973, 1976, 1979).

of Society.[197] Such views are firmly rooted in an agenda designed to maximise individual freedom in society by limiting the role of the State.[198]

Such perspectives are capable of translation into a legally enforceable set of norms against which legislation may be tested. On this model, constitutional limitations would be set on the role of the State both in the market and in society; or, as a corollary, individual freedoms in the market and in society would be constitutionally protected from State interference.[199] Hayek devoted considerable energy to developing precisely this type of constitutional framework. Recent years have witnessed a rise in scholarship that, for all its distinctive points of emphasis, is loosely connected by a shared antipathy to State intervention in the market. The public choice school, mentioned above, is marked by the special vitriol it reserves for the motivations that underpin lawmaking and lawmakers.[200] In the competition/anti trust law field, the Chicago School has developed related perceptions of the damage done by an interventionist policy which intrudes on private decisions guided by the order of the market. The Chicago School has accordingly called for a retreat in the application of competition law and has succeeded to a significant degree in its quest to emphasise the primacy of market decisions in the US.[201] Competition law has comprised only one, albeit high-profile, area of debate. In North America, too, Hayek's approval of the efficiency of the common law, combined with distrust of public intrusion into private rights, has been matched by the Law–and–Economics school associated with, among others, Richard Posner, who has written that 'Statutory or constitutional as distinct from common law fields are less likely to promote efficiency'.[202] Atiyah, among other critics, has questioned precisely what is envisaged in this context by the common law, which is after

---

[197] Hence the chosen title of Volume 2 of Hayek's three volumes, *The Mirage of Social Justice.*

[198] Cf *inter alia* R. Nozick, *Anarchy, State and Utopia* (Blackwell, 1974); M. Friedman, *Capitalism and Freedom* (University of Chicago Press, 1962). The pathway back to John Stuart Mill's 1859 work *On Liberty* (Routledge, 1991), does not deviate significantly.

[199] For general discussion, see M. Loughlin, *Public Law and Political Theory* (Clarendon Press, 1992); on Hayek especially, pp. 84–104. Cf also A. Ogus, 'Law and Spontaneous Order: Hayek's Contribution to Legal Theory' (1989) 16 *Jnl Law and Society* 393.

[200] 1.9.1 above.

[201] Cf eg R. Bork, *The Antitrust Paradox* (Basic Books, 1978). For an overview, see T. Frazer, *Monopoly, Competition and the Law* (Harvester Wheatsheaf, 1992).

[202] R. Posner, *Economic Analysis of Law* (Little, Brown and Co, 1986), p. 21.

all hardly a monolith.[203] Others have accepted the value of the analytical framework demanded by the Law–and–Economics school, but shudder to adopt its prescriptions without the leavening influence of other insights into the role of law in society.[204] It is here that this book takes its stand, proud to accept the wide range of influences in the melting pot of consumer law and practice.

In Europe, it may be thought an irony that the Hayek thesis and its cousins have had their deepest influence in the UK where legal tradition does not readily accommodate the process of constitutionalisation elaborated by Hayek. The policies of the Conservative administrations in power since 1979, initially under the leadership of Margaret Thatcher, were transparently shaped by an awareness of the Hayek description of the ills of intervention and his prescription of the virtue of removing regulation.[205] In the light of the pressures and compromises that characterise modern politics and lawmaking, it would certainly be unrealistic to suppose that a precise match between the Hayek analysis and the record of the Thatcher administrations could be demonstrated. Nonetheless the influence of thinking that intervention in the market is damaging to its efficient operation and to the liberty of the individual is splashed over a range of policies.

The drive to curtail the role of the State has been manifested by several key policy initiatives which had much to do with the reduction of the participation of the State in the economy. Given the absence of a written constitution in the UK, these were achieved through specific legislative and administrative initiatives rather than any formal restructuring of the constitution. Indeed, the very absence of explicit constitutional constraint facilitated the execution of a remarkably radical policy. Nonetheless, some commentators have identified in these shifts a broader pattern which amounts in aggregate to a change in the relationship between private and public sectors in the UK which is of a dimension of constitutional significance.[206]

---

203 Cf Ch.7 in his *Essays on Contract* (OUP, 1988).

204 For an entertaining overview, see J. Ziegel, 'What can the Economic Analysis of Law teach Commercial and Consumer Law Scholars?', Ch.12 in R. Cranston and R. Goode (eds.), *Commercial and Consumer Law: National and International Dimensions* (OUP, 1993).

205 Loughlin n.199 above provides a great deal of relevant material. Cf A. Barron and C. Scott, 'The Citizens Charter Programme' (1992) 55 *MLR* 526.

206 C. Graham and T. Prosser, *Privatising public enterprises: constitutions, the state and regulation in comparative perspective* (OUP, 1991). For comparative work, see M. Moran and T. Prosser (eds.), *Privatisation and Regulatory Change in Europe* (Open University Press, 1994). See also T. Daintith and M. Sah, 'Privatisation and the Economic Neutrality of the Constitution' [1993] *Public Law* 465.

Part of the policy was directed at closer scrutiny of regulatory intervention in the economy. A deregulation programme was directed at reviewing a range of interventions in the market with a view to repealing the accumulation of regulations. The flavour of the programme is readily judged by the titles chosen for a White Paper of 1985, 'Lifting the Burden'[207] and a further White Paper in 1986, 'Building Businesses ... Not Barriers'.[208] Drawing up, administering and complying with regulations were perceived to cost business a great deal of money. This is transparently correct. What is at stake is judging the balance between such costs and the benefits that may accrue. The policy of the Thatcher administrations seems to have involved a heavier emphasis on the costs of regulation as an incursion into commercial freedom than had previously been the norm. Much comment was directed at the need for balance between consumer and trader, with the location of that balance shifting towards the trader as regulatory intervention was trimmed. So the 1985 White Paper declared that 'the scales are still tipped too far against business'.[209] The 1986 White Paper was determined 'to alter the balance while avoiding a free for all'.[210] Close attention was paid to 'costs of compliance' and it became part of governmental policy that compliance cost assessment should accompany all proposals for new measures.[211] The UK had some success in exporting the procedure of compliance cost assessment to the EC, although it remains unclear whether in Brussels the same relative values were put on costs and benefits in the substantive application of cost compliance testing.

The phrase 'Victorian values' was bandied around with some lack of discrimination in the political discourse of the 1980s. It was used both as praise and as criticism. However, in embracing the virtue of contractual freedom in the market (and the connected value of individual responsibility in society), there was a reassertion of much of the flavour of 19th–century *laissez–faire* commercial law. Some deregulation was achieved; probably more significantly, new initiatives to regulate were regarded with scepticism and many were blocked.

Consumer policy was one element in the programme, but only a relatively small element. The whole range of State intervention came under scrutiny. Employment protection laws were examined. It was, broadly, perceived that intervention to protect workers was damaging to market flexibility. Lack of employer flexibility, it was argued, was likely to reduce

---

[207]   Cmnd. 9571.
[208]   Cmnd. 9794.
[209]   1.7.
[210]   1.6.
[211]   Cf Ogus n.106 above pp. 162–5, revealing US origins.

the number of jobs made available in the first place. In vogue was the view that 'regulations cost jobs' and that decision making on the scope of benefits enjoyed by workers should belong in the private sector. Employment protection laws were trimmed to enhance such market flexibility. For example, the law against unfair dismissal survived, but its scope of application was curtailed. In most circumstances, employees are able to claim only after completing a defined period of continuous service. This was raised progressively through the 1980s from six months, to one year and by the mid–1990s stood at two years.[212] In the EC, the UK doggedly opposed new legislation in the field. This policy reached its logical culmination at Maastricht, where negotiations on enhanced EC Social Policy competence reached an impasse in the face of the UK's implacable opposition. The solution chosen was the creation of a special pattern in a Protocol which envisaged extended social policy making among the other eleven Member States, with the UK excluded.[213] It was commented above that this compromise fragmentation cannot be thought likely to endure in its current form beyond the next round of Treaty revision, planned for 1996.[214]

The legal protection of tenants was similarly scrutinised. It was supposed that protection of those in private rented accommodation was likely to inhibit new accommodation coming on to the market. From this perspective, loosening regulatory controls would stimulate supply and return flexibility and choice to the market. Accordingly, aspects of protection of tenure were trimmed, most notably in the Housing Act 1988.[215]

The emphasis on deregulation persists under John Major. In early 1994 a Deregulation and Contracting Out Bill was published, accompanied by Ministerial commitments to slash away at red tape perceived to inhibit business flexibility. The Deregulation and Contracting Act was passed in late 1994. Specific instances of deregulation within the Act are rather esoteric. They include procedural aspects of competition investigations, betting on Sundays (which is liberalised) and control of knackers' yards.[216] The real impact of the Act cannot be judged by its specific terms, which in themselves do not match up to triumphant ministerial claims to have cut swathes through the field of regulatory intervention. The true potential lies in Chapter 1 of Part 1 of the Act, sections 1–6. This confers a power on Ministers to make

---

212 S.64(1)(a) Employment Protection Consolidation Act 1978 as amended.
213 For a comprehensive account, R. Nielsen and E. Szyszczak, *The Social Dimension of the European Community* (Handelshojskolens Forlag, 1993).
214 1.3.8 above.
215 Cf on law and policy M. Davey, *Residential Rents* (Sweet and Maxwell, 1990).
216 Sections 7–12, 20, 31 respectively.

orders to amend or repeal enactments that impose a burden[217] affecting any person in the carrying on of any trade, business or profession. The Deregulation and Contracting Out Act has been drafted in order to provide a basis for future adjustment of the regulatory climate in a wide range of fields without the need for the government to plan specific primary legislation.

The debate about regulatory reform is by no means new, but rather an old debate reinvigorated. It has long been perceived that a policy raising legal requirements for entry to and/or performance in markets may have ambiguous consequences for consumers. Supply may be choked off or may grow outside the law (in black markets) as traders seek to evade costs and consumers seek to maximise choice.[218] The key to the policy shift in the UK since 1979 has been a greater readiness to find that the costs of intervention outweigh the benefits. For all the insistence on the use of cost–benefit analysis, the strong impression persists that market solutions are viewed as inherently preferable. The consequences of this should be fully appreciated; they bridge the gap between the initial discussion in this Chapter of the private law and the ensuing examination of public law. In so far as public controls are eliminated, the law of consumer protection shifts back towards the law of contract and tort. Atiyah, writing in 1979, made this point powerfully in the following terms:

> 'Freedom of contract naturally suits the strong, and is disadvantageous to the weak. When there is a return to free collective bargaining, then the result will usually be an increase in earnings differentials... though American political thinkers may argue that greater economic equality cannot be merely assumed to be a principle of justice, but needs to be justified,[219] there is little sign that this is an acceptable position in England.'[220]

There is no need to labour the point, for it will be immediately apparent that this invites consideration of the extent to which the shifts of the last 16 years in the political map of the UK have affected the roles of the private and public law of consumer protection and, therefore, the position of the consumer in society.[221] Probably not high on Atiyah's 1979 agenda were the implications of the EC for freedom of contract. This source has exerted an

---

217 That word again! cf text at note 207 above.
218 Cf the work of Cayne and Trebilcock, published in 1973, in relation to regulation of the supply of consumer credit, referred to in Chapter 7.3.
219 A footnote reference is here made, *inter alia*, to Nozick n.198 above, pp. 232–3.
220 In *The Rise and Fall of Freedom of Contract* note 32 above, pp. 648–9.
221 Cf P. Atiyah, *Introduction to the Law of Contract* (OUP, 1989), Ch.1.

increasing influence on the domestic scene, in a number of areas operating in a quite different way from that which would have been chosen by the British government acting alone. Chapter 9, dealing with Unfair Terms, provides a particularly revealing illustration of the role of the EC in challenging notions of freedom of contract in a more radical fashion than has been the norm in the UK.

'Deregulation' is a broad notion. It has not simply been a matter of cutting back on the scope of regulation, but also of changing its style. Standards–setting is a long-standing component of regulatory policy. As examined above in Part 1.8.1, a preference was instituted for broad performance standards in place of strict and specific ones. The State did not withdraw from the task of setting quality standards (in some areas), but it was more prone to allow flexibility to the private sector in determining how to achieve the required levels. This was an area where the UK adjusted its policy hand in hand with the EC.

A further aspect of the UK's policy involved a reduction in State ownership. The policy of selling assets in the public sector to the private sector is normally but loosely described as 'privatisation'. Like deregulation and self–regulation, privatisation is best seen as an umbrella term embracing several distinctive elements of policy.[222] The programme of transfer of assets from State to private sector is part of the process. This has embraced, for example, telecommunications, gas and water supply.[223] In budgetary terms alone, this has been highly significant, with the government receiving tens of billions of pounds as a result of such sales. In part, the programme was motivated by economic expectations of realising greater efficiency in the private sector, which ought to operate to the advantage of the consumer.[224] This economic assumption was plainly accompanied by the political perception that the State ought to withdraw from the market and offer enhanced freedom to private actors. Here again is an area where private contractual freedom, with all its limitations, has regained a prominence previously buried under the prevalence of State supply.

Privatisation as such does not necessarily yield a more competitive market. Where a monopoly is transferred from public into private hands, the same considerations discussed in Chapter 15.3 damage consumer welfare. In some circumstances attempts have been made to inject competition into the

---

222   Summarised in Ogus note 106 above, pp. 287–94. Cf D. Bos, 'Privatisation in Europe: A Comparison of Approaches' (1993) 9 *Oxford Rev of Economic Policy* 95.

223   For a collection of essays surveying several sectors, M. Bishop, J. Kay and C. Mayer, *Privatisation and Economic Performance* (OUP, 1994).

224   Cf. J. Winward, 'Privatisation and Domestic Consumers', Ch.12 in Bishop *et al* n.223 above.

market, although the privatisation programme has attracted criticism from some commentators for missing opportunities in some sectors.[225] In some instances, rightly or wrongly, the Government has deemed the fostering of competition to be impossible or undesirable. Accordingly, a feature of the privatisation programme has been the creation of new agencies designed to supervise the privatised monopoly. These have assumed a bewildering number of guises.[226] Transparency has not been helped by the proliferation of odd acronyms designating these agencies – OFFER, OFTEL, OFWAT and so on.[227] Price control and quality standards have been imposed by the regulator, in part as compensation for the absence of competition which in theory would have ensured such controls.[228]

Even in areas that in principle remained within the province of the public sector, fresh emphasis was placed on the contractual nature of supply relationships. 'Contracting–out' of public services became highly voguish. This policy was further developed in Part II of the Deregulation and Contracting Act 1994. In the National Health Service, an 'internal market' was created within which the distinct functions of buyers and sellers were supposed to be disentangled from the pre–existing bureaucratic maze, a process which demanded a significant degree of legal rethinking.[229] The health service reforms, most of all, were fiercely controversial, with objection taken to the basic notion that a market could or should be instituted for the supply of such services.[230] The supposed rise of consumers' private market

---

[225] See M. Bishop, J. Kay. C. Mayer, *The Regulatory Challenge* (OUP, 1995). This is especially the message of the book's Introduction.

[226] For a collection of relevant essays, see Bishop *et al* n.225 above.

[227] Supervising the electricity, telecommunications and water industries respectively. See the Competition and Service (Utilities) Act 1992. For valuable legal perspectives in overview, see J. McEldowney, 'Law and Regulation: Current Issues and Future Directions' in Bishop *et al* n.225 above. See also N. Lewis and P. Birkinshaw, *When Citizens Complain* (Open University Press, 1993), esp. Ch.9; P. Craig, *Administrative Law* (Sweet and Maxwell, 3rd ed, 1994), pp. 229–42; B. Harvey and D. Parry, *The Law of Consumer Protection and Fair Trading*, (Butterworths, 1992), Ch.4; J. Ernst, *Whose Utility? The Social Impact of Public Utility Privatisation and Regulation in Britain* (Open University Press, 1994). Cf also the several contributions in (1992) *Consumer Policy Review*, Issue 1, Special Issue.

[228] Cf Chapter 15.

[229] Cf eg I. Harden, *The Contracting State* (Open University, 1992); M. Freedland, 'Government by Contract and Public Law' [1994] *Public Law* 86; P. Craig, *Administrative Law* n.227 above, Ch.3.

[230] See D. Hughes, 'The Reorganisation of the National Health Service: the Rhetoric and Reality of the Internal Market' (1991) 54 *MLR* 88.

freedoms was conspicuously associated with the rhetoric surrounding the Citizens' Charter, in which John Major invested much political capital.[231] In areas of public ownership too, consumer choice in a market order was to prevail.

1.9.4 Consumers and Society

Questioning the place of the State in the market has been a fertile field for theorists in recent years, although examining the operational utility of some of the theories espoused remains an underdeveloped aspect of the debate. We believe, in writing this book, that the construction of theoretical underpinnings is vital in drawing the map of consumer protection. A great many social and political assumptions are embedded in the choice between these different forms of intervention. 'Consumer choice' may be taken as a slogan of freedom from the unduly interventionist State; by contrast, it may be taken as the abandonment of the bewildered consumer to the uncaring mass market. More subtly, consumer choice may free *some* consumers from unwanted mollycoddling, while subjecting others to exploitation. We welcome the recent emphasis on rigour in analysis of costs and benefits. We are saddened by the impression that it is no longer politically fashionable to concede that wealth maximisation might cheerfully be subordinated to wealth distribution in the cause of contributing by legal regulation to a more just market and a more harmonious society. Consumer law, we repeat,[232] is part of shaping a society.

---

231 Cm. 1599 (1991). Cf Barron and Scott n.205 above.
232 1.1 above.

2 European Community Consumer Policy

2.1 THE DEVELOPMENT OF THE EUROPEAN COMMUNITY AND ITS LEGAL ORDER

2.1.1 National and International Markets

Much of the discussion presented in Chapter 1 of this book has examined the operation of markets and evaluated their capacity to deliver effective consumer protection. Discussion of the limitations of markets can be pursued in relation to the legal regulation of any market. Problems of the type exposed in Chapter 1 affect the operation of all markets whatever their territorial scope. Accordingly, legal intervention may be considered at national level, but also at transnational level. As the process of market integration in Europe develops, it is increasingly to Europe that one must look for a layer of consumer policy making which is additional to national law making.[1]

It lies far beyond the scope of this Chapter to provide an examination of the modern European Union that is remotely comprehensive. Other sources must be consulted for a deeper examination of the history of the process of European integration[2] and the contribution of the new legal order to that evolution.[3] Assuming here that the reader is familiar with the basic constitutional and institutional building blocks of the Union, there follows an exposition of the pattern of development of the European Community from the consumer perspective.

---

1   T. Bourgoignie and D. Trubek, *Consumer Law, Common Markets and Federalism*, (Walter de Gruyter, 1986); G. Woodroffe (ed), *Consumer Law in the EEC* (Sweet and Maxwell and Centre for Consumer Law Research, 1984); N. Reich, *Europäisches Verbraucherrecht* (Nomos Verlagsgesellschaft, 1993); V. Kendall, *EC Consumer Law* (Wiley Chancery Law, 1994).

2   J. Pinder, *European Community: The Building of a Union* (OUP, 1991); A. Williams, *The European Community* (Blackwell, 1992), M. Wise and R. Gibb, *From Single Market to Social Europe* (Longman, 1993).

3   J. Steiner, *Textbook on EC Law* (Blackstone Press, 4th ed, 1994). J. Shaw, *European Community Law* (Macmillan, 1993), S. Weatherill and P. Beaumont, *EC Law* (Penguin Books, 1993), D. Wyatt and A. Dashwood, *European Community Law* (Sweet and Maxwell, 3rd ed, 1993).

2.1.2 A Brief History of the European Community Pre–Maastricht

The Treaty of Paris led to the founding in 1952 of the first of the three European Communities, the European Coal and Steel Community. In 1958, the Treaties of Rome created the European Economic Community and EURATOM (the European Atomic Energy Community). The breadth of the EEC ensured that it was by far the most important of the three Communities. It was concerned with economic integration across all sectors, but in no small measure was also motivated by the desire to achieve a political restructuring of the European continent. To give effect to its ambitions it was built on a Treaty which contained clearly expressed legal rules designed to achieve integration and regulation. It possessed its own institutions which were competent to adopt legislation in those areas where power had been transferred to it from national level by the Treaties. Economic integration was to be achieved through the application of legal rules.

The original six Member States were France, Germany, Italy, Belgium, the Netherlands and Luxembourg. 1973 saw the first Accessions, those of the United Kingdom, Ireland and Denmark. Greece joined in 1981. Spain and Portugal brought the number to 12 in 1986. The start of 1995 heralded the entry of Austria, Finland and Sweden, bringing total membership to 15.

Outside the core 15 lie further rings. The European Economic Area (EEA) came into being at the start of 1994 and now comprises the 15 plus Iceland and Norway. The EEA is based on a body of law that is in many respects comparable to, though not so ambitious as, the EC system. It is frequently viewed as a 'training ground' for potential members; in fact, Austria, Finland and Sweden spent one year (1994) in the EEA before moving to full membership at the start of 1995. Switzerland occupies a special, partially detached position, having decided by referendum in 1992 not to join the EEA. The majority of States in the former Soviet bloc have concluded Association Agreements with the EC and several have applied for membership. Both economically and politically, these countries diverge significantly from the Community norm, but Hungary, Poland and the Czech Republic, in particular, are hopeful of proving themselves ready to join by 2000. This brief survey demonstrates that the influence of the EC now spreads far beyond its core membership of 15.

The text of the original Treaty of Rome remained unamended in any significant respects until 1987 when the Single European Act came into force. It added several new competences to the Community's armoury and also made important institutional adjustments, notably in the raising of the Parliament's profile. Of prime importance was the insertion of a new provision into the Treaty, Article 100a. This permitted the adoption by qualified majority vote of measures required to secure the completion of the internal market by the end of 1992. This emphasised the commitment of the

Member States to deepen yet further the process of integration, explicitly at the economic level, but inevitably also involving a political dimension.

2.1.3 From European Community to European Union

In December 1991, the 12 Member States agreed a major revision to the structure of the Community. This was contained in the Treaty on European Union agreed at Maastricht in the Netherlands. Aspects of this next stage were rather ambitious and were fiercely opposed by some shades of opinion in most Member States. However, ratification was secured in all 12 Member States after almost two years of vigorous debate and the Treaty came into force on 1 November 1993. The Treaty on European Union amended important aspects of what was the EEC Treaty and renamed the EEC the 'EC', the European Community. The Treaty on European Union also introduced two new areas outside the parameters of existing EC integration where the Member States committed themselves to work in co–operation: Foreign and Security Policy[4] and Justice and Home Affairs.[5] There is now a European Union which is built on three 'pillars'; the pre–Maastricht pattern of the European Communities (comprising the E(E)C, the Coal and Steel Community and EURATOM) represents only one of these three pillars. The EC retains its institutionally and constitutionally distinctive character. It seems that the two new pillars, essentially intergovernmental in character, will not yield directly effective or supreme laws. For this reason, this Chapter and this book remain focused on *Community* law and not on Union law.[6] The three–pillar pattern renders the shape of 'Union law', in so far as it may properly be said to exist, rather opaque.

The European Community post–Maastricht has altered its shape in a number of substantial respects: there is an enhancement of the Community's competences; the status of Citizenship of the Union is created; and adjustments are made to the legislative procedure which strengthen the position of the Parliament. Perhaps the centrepiece is the insertion into the EC Treaty of detailed provisions designed to lead to Economic and Monetary Union. The planned establishment of a single currency by the start of 1999, as envisaged by the Treaty, now seems less secure in the wake of turbulence on the international money markets.

---

4   Title V, Art.J TEU.

5   Title VI, Art.K TEU.

6   Although the Justice and Home Affairs intergovernmental pillar may provide a forum for developing effective access to justice; see Chapter 17.

2.1.4 The Nature of Economic Integration

The integration movement was powered in the early post–war years by individuals with a political commitment to a species of federal Europe.[7] Explicit political integration was, however, largely eschewed in the original Treaty in favour of economic integration. The lack of clarity in the precise location of the balance between the Community's political and economic ambitions remains its major flashpoint. In any event, according to Article 2 of the Treaty, the Community aims to establish a 'common market' involving the free circulation of the factors of production. In the EC it is customary to regard the 'four freedoms' as the cornerstone of the notion of the common market; that is, the free movement of goods, persons, services and capital. Free movement is achieved by dismantling impediments to internal trade within the area. Additionally, in common markets States lose independence over trade policy at their external borders. There will be a common external commercial policy and also a degree of common policy making for the internal area.

Economic theory suggests that there is a 'virtuous circle' in economic integration.[8] As borders are removed there is increased competition, yielding wider consumer choice. There should be higher quality goods and services available; producers must achieve this in order to survive in the fiercer competitive environment. Integration should also permit firms to realise economies of scale. Their production runs will be longer, which allows more efficient use to be made of plant. This should yield lower prices which will be passed on to the consumer by producers eager for the business which will ensure survival. The market will be reshaped for and by businesses that are able to restructure operations to the European level, for example through the conclusion of distribution deals or, more radically, through merger or takeover.

Common market theory places the consumer as the ultimate beneficiary of the whole process, albeit as a passive recipient of the advantages of cross–border commercial activity. From this perspective, economic integration in Europe is in itself a form of consumer policy.

2.1.5 From Common Market to Internal Market

The development of the common market in Europe had considerable momentum in the early years, but progress had become very sluggish by the

---

7   Eg Jean Monnet, Robert Schuman, Paul–Henri Spaak. Cf. Pinder note 2 above.
8   For a classic exposition of the economic objectives of the EC, see D. Swann, *The Economics of the Common Market* (Penguin, 7th ed, 1992).

early 1980s. Much trade was free, but there were significant impediments to the completion of a common market. Consequently the Commission imaginatively sought to reinvigorate the whole process by establishing the '1992' programme – the task of securing the completion of the Community's internal market by the end of 1992.

The 1992 project was first explained in detail in the Commission's White Paper of 1985;[9] this covers the economic and political advantages of completing the internal market and sets out a programme of legislative action required to achieve that end. In paragraph 12 it declared that:

> 'The reason for getting rid entirely of physical and other controls between Member States is not one of theology or appearance, but the hard practical fact that the maintenance of any internal frontier controls will perpetuate the costs and disadvantages of a divided market...'

Legally, the project was defined in a provision newly inserted into the Treaty in 1987 by the Single European Act. This was originally Article 8a EEC, although it was renumbered Article 7a EC from 1 November 1993 (as a result of the Treaty on European Union amendments). It provides that:

> 'The Community shall adopt measures with the aim of progressively establishing the internal market over a period expiring on 31 December 1992... The internal market shall comprise an area without internal frontiers in which the free movement of goods, persons, services and capital is ensured in accordance with the provisions of this Treaty.'

The completion of this 'area without internal frontiers' was closely tied to the Treaty amendments of the Single European Act. Article 100a, mentioned above, was also introduced by the Single European Act with effect from 1987. Its purpose was to give a very practical thrust to the legislative programme through the removal of the national veto over Community legislative action in the field of harmonisation of laws. This shift in Council voting rules to qualified majority was required so that the political expression of commitment to deepening the integrative process could take practical effect.

Many of the economic virtues identified as resulting from the completion of the internal market are no different from those expected to flow from the creation of a common market. It has always been a moot point precisely how much less ambitious the internal market is than the common market. Does the internal market policy, for example, abandon the commitment to Community–wide regulatory strategies that has long been associated with the

---

9   COM (85) 310.

common market, or does it simply readjust short–term priorities? However, in the internal market, as in the common market, the consumer is envisaged as the ultimate beneficiary of the more efficiently functioning market.

At the end of 1992, it was vividly apparent that the consumer was in a better position. The completion of the internal market in accordance with the Treaty had in principle established the right of private consumers to move freely across borders and to return home with whatever they pleased for their private consumption. Although in the past consumers had typically been regarded as the passive beneficiaries of free trade through enhanced choice, they are increasingly able actively to enjoy the benefits of an integrated market. The Court too has made plain its view that the consumer has the right to treat the Community as border free and to 'travel freely to the territory of another Member State to shop under the same conditions as the local population'.[10] Some of the possible legal implications of using Community policy to encourage active cross–border shopping are discussed below.[11]

2.1.6 The Role of the European Court of Justice

Critical to the rapid development of the integrative process has been the contribution of the European Court of Justice. Its interpretation of the Treaty injected enormous vitality into the whole process. The Court was not prepared to regard the Treaty as 'traditional' international law, with the result that the EC legal order quickly developed a character of its own. In 1991 the Court acclaimed what is in many respects its own creation as the 'constitutional charter of a Community based on the rule of law'.[12] The legal rules governing integration were interpreted actively in accordance with what the European Court viewed as the spirit of the Treaty. The waning of national economies and the growth of a European economy were accelerated by the Court's frequent preference, in cases of doubt, to interpret the law in a manner conducive to integration. The *Cassis de Dijon* decision, examined below at 2.2.2, provides a classic illustration of this jurisprudential trend. On the constitutional plane, the Court insisted that EC law could be enforced at national level – the principle of direct effect[13] – and that it must be applied by national courts in preference to any conflicting national law – the

---

[10] Case C–362/88 *GB–INNO–BM v Confederation du Commerce Luxembourgeois* [1990] ECR I–667.

[11] 2.3.5. below.

[12] *Opinion 1/91* [1991] ECR I–6079.

[13] Case 26/62 *Van Gend en Loos* [1963] ECR 1.

principle of supremacy.[14] The Court reasoned that, without such principles, the system envisaged by the Treaty simply would not work. In consequence the prosecution of the integrative process did not simply rest with the relevant Community institution, the Commission, challenging defaulting Member States before the European Court. The enforcement of the law was additionally put in the hands of individuals who were able to enforce rights to enjoy the fruits of integration by challenging public authorities in national courts. In this sense, the conferral of individual rights through the notion of direct effect had both a policing and a democratising function. The Article 177 preliminary reference procedure allowed the European Court to oversee and guide the development of the law at national level. In effect it co–opted national courts into the job of enhancing the objectives of the EC.

2.2 COMMUNITY TRADE LAW

2.2.1 'Negative Law' and the Consumer Interest

The pursuit of economic integration through law requires a framework for controlling and, where appropriate, prohibiting national rules which obstruct free trade. Several core provisions of the EC Treaty operate as a restriction on national legislative action which may have an effect hostile to cross–border trade. These provisions are termed 'negative' in that their effect is to strike down national measures where they conflict with the 'greater good' of market integration, subject only to narrowly defined exceptions.

Article 30 is the principal provision designed to achieve the free movement of goods. It provides that:

> 'Quantitative restrictions on imports and all measures having equivalent effect shall, without prejudice to the following provisions, be prohibited between Member States.'

More helpfully and more broadly, Article 30 has been interpreted by the Court to prohibit:

> 'all trading rules enacted by Member States which are capable of hindering, directly or indirectly, actually or potentially, intra–Community trade.'[15]

---

14   Case 6/64 *Costa v ENEL* [1964] ECR 585.
15   Case 8/74 *Dassonville* [1974] ECR 837.

This is the renowned *Dassonville* formula, the key to its application being the *effect* of a measure. Once a measure is shown to affect trade between Member States, it is susceptible to challenge via Article 30. It is the breadth of the formula which is remarkable although, in its November 1993 ruling in *Keck*, the Court slightly curtailed its outer margins in ruling that there is no actual or potential, direct or indirect, barrier to inter–State trade such as would allow the invocation of Article 30 where national laws apply to all traders active on the national territory and affect in the same way in law and in fact the marketing of national products and those originating in other Member States.[16]

The Treaty contains a narrow list of exceptions to Article 30 in Article 36. This envisages trade barriers 'justified on grounds of public morality, public policy or public security; the protection of health and life of humans, animals or plants...'Article 36 adds that '[s]uch prohibitions or restrictions shall not, however, constitute a means of arbitrary discrimination or a disguised restriction on trade between Member States.' The Court has followed a consistent line whereby the scope of derogation from the basic principle of free movement is construed narrowly. This approach serves to advance the overall cause of welding national markets into a single European market.

Article 30's application in the area of goods has a parallel in Article 59 in the area of services. Article 59 has also been interpreted by the European Court as an instrument for controlling national measures that inhibit suppliers of services from treating the wider market as integrated.

The economic advantages of the free movement of goods and services are the advantages of the common/internal market as a whole.[17] The process should deepen competition among producers and suppliers and thereby enhance consumer choice. The application of Community 'negative law' to sweep away obstructive national law serves the consumer interest in the sense that it contributes to the integrative process of which the consumer is theoretically the ultimate beneficiary. There is a consumer interest in free trade and in deregulating national markets within the wider European market.

In summary, national rules which impede consumer choice in the integrating market are in jeopardy. The Court has condemned national laws which 'crystallise given consumer habits so as to consolidate an advantage acquired by national industries concerned to comply with them.'[18] Laws

---

16   Cases C–267 and 268/91 *Keck and Mithouard* [1993] ECR I–6097. For comment on the extent to which this ruling curtails the scope of Art.30, see L. Gormley [1994] *Euro Bus L Rev* 63; N. Reich (1994) 31 *CMLRev* 459; D. Chalmers (1994) 19 *ELRev* 385.

17   2.1.4 above.

18   Case 170/78 *Commission v United Kingdom* [1980] ECR 417; Case 178/84 *Commission v Germany* [1987] ECR 1227.

which protect domestic producers from competition confine consumer choice in a manner hostile to the basic expectations of market integration.

2.2.2 The Ruling in *Cassis de Dijon*

The '*Dassonville* formula' for Article 30 plainly applies to border controls and discrimination against imported goods, but it is much broader and is also capable of catching national technical rules and standards. Such measures do not discriminate against imports and in many cases were introduced long before the EC came into existence and were not designed to interfere with cross—border trade at all. However, it is their *effect* which is critical. Litigation involving Cassis de Dijon, a French blackcurrant liqueur, provided the Court with the opportunity to establish how Article 30 applies to national technical rules which do not discriminate according to nationality, but which nevertheless have an effect hostile to market integration.[19]

The Court's ruling concerning the importation of French Cassis de Dijon into Germany provides a famous example of the application of Article 30 to open up the market to secure enhanced consumer choice. German law imposed restrictions on the marketing of weak alcoholic drink, supposedly as an aspect of consumer health protection. The Court was unable to identify in this measure any coherent policy serving the consumer interest. The German measure simply denied the German consumer the opportunity to try a product made according to a different tradition. The national rule fell foul of Article 30 as unlawful State suppression of consumer choice.

It should be fully appreciated that in the Cassis de Dijon ruling the Court was dealing with two competing aspects of the consumer interest. On the one hand, Article 30 represented the consumer interest in market integration and enhanced choice. On the other hand, the challenged German measure was itself presented as a means of consumer protection; it therefore represented the consumer interest in regulation at national level. The Court was choosing in effect between different perceptions of where the consumer interest lay. In *Cassis de Dijon* itself, the resolution was quite straightforward because the German law was a thoroughly unmeritorious method of (alleged) consumer protection. In fact, the real protection enjoyed under the German law was that of German producers able to monopolise consumer choice. In other cases, the balance between consumer choice in the wider market and consumer protection at national level may be finer. This balancing task projects EC trade law into the realms of difficult decisions about what is best for the consumer; decisions that some have viewed as involving a risk that

---

19   *Cassis de Dijon* is more formally known as Case 120/78 *Rewe Zentrale v Bundesmonopolverwaltung für Branntwein* [1979] ECR 649.

choices made in the context of free trade law may undermine national standards of consumer protection. This is a key issue in assessing the scope of EC law and policy and is discussed further below.[20]

The *Cassis de Dijon* ruling provides a strong impetus in favour of free trade between Member States in traditional products. It enshrines a principle of 'mutual recognition'. This holds that if a product is fit for the market of one Member State, then it should be considered fit for the markets of all other Member States. Only exceptionally may products which are satisfactory in their country of origin be excluded from the market of the State to which they are exported. This exceptional restriction on free trade was explained by the Court in *Cassis de Dijon* in the following terms;

> '[o]bstacles to movement in the Community resulting from disparities between the national laws in question must be accepted in so far as those provisions may be recognised as being necessary in order to satisfy mandatory requirements relating in particular to the effectiveness of fiscal supervision, the protection of public health, the fairness of commercial transactions and the defence of the consumer.'

The final phrase in this observation draws attention to the point that consumer protection is explicitly recognised as a 'mandatory requirement' which may be successfully advanced as a reason for maintaining a national law which inhibits cross–border trade. However the impetus towards free trade is strong and powerful reasons must be shown by the State to justify rules which subordinate consumer choice and free trade to national 'mandatory requirements'. Germany failed to defend its law in the *Cassis* case itself.

2.2.3 *Cassis de Dijon* – the Subsequent Case Law

In a large body of case law the *Cassis de Dijon* principle has been employed to sweep away national rules which hinder the free movement of goods, resulting in wider consumer choice. Not infrequently, as in *Cassis* itself, the national rule found to be incompatible with EC law has ostensibly been a measure of consumer protection.

Walter Rau v De Smedt provides a good example of the application of the '*Cassis* principle'.[21] The case concerned the compatibility with Article 30 of a Belgian law requiring margarine to be marketed in cube–shaped blocks.

---

20 Comparable issues arise in international trade law under the GATT; L. Kleftodimou, 'Protecting the consumer under GATT' *Consum LJ* forthcoming.
21 Case 261/81 [1982] ECR 3961.

The Court accepted that such a rule impeded the importation into Belgium of margarine marketed in different ways in other Member States. Consumer choice in Belgium was hampered and, as the Court observed and as economic theory dictates, margarine cost more in Belgium under this regime than in neighbouring States. The Belgian law was presented as a measure of consumer protection: the packaging requirement allegedly made margarine readily identifiable on the shelf and distinct from butter. The Court was unpersuaded that this consideration should override the consumer interest in a competitive cross–border market and enhanced choice. It did not exclude the possibility of national initiatives taken to protect consumers, but the rule at issue was too rigid:

> 'It cannot be reasonably denied that in principle legislation designed to prevent butter and margarine from being confused in the mind of the consumer is justified. However...... Consumers may in fact be protected just as effectively by other measures, for example by rules on labelling, which hinder the free movement of goods less.'

It is fairly common for the Court to find a restrictive national rule to be incompatible with Article 30 because it represents a disproportionate intervention in the market. The Court has frequently held unlawful stricter measures which suppress products where information provision might have sufficed to achieve consumer protection. These are cases which demonstrate the principle that even where the *end* of consumer protection may provide a justification for a trade–restrictive measure, the *means* employed must be the least restrictive of trade still capable of meeting the end in view.[22] States must regulate with an eye to the wider demands of an integrated market. In the famous 'Beer Purity' case, *Commission v Germany*,[23] the Court ruled against German regulations which had the effect of excluding from the German market beers brewed according to different styles in other Member States. This application of Article 30 enhanced the choice of the German drinker. The Court was quite explicit in its view of the availability of consumer information as a regulatory technique which is less restrictive of trade than rules that stipulate permitted and non–permitted ingredients. The Court commented that 'even where... beers are sold on draught' information may be provided 'on the casks or the beer taps.' The intended result is that the (informed) consumer is then enabled to exercise choice in accordance with his or her own (informed) preferences, rather than have that choice confined by governmental intervention.

---

22   Cf S. Weatherill, 'The Role of the Informed Consumer in European Community Law and Policy' (1994) 2 *Consum LJ* 49.

23   Case 178/84 [1987] ECR 1227.

The same formula has been increasingly applied by the Court to Article 59 where similar economic issues arise and where it has accordingly developed a similar legal formula involving a trade off between the advantages of market integration and the merits of the challenged national rule. For example, it has held that tourists should be able to choose guides who know their needs and their language instead of being supplied only with guides licensed by the host State.[24] As explained in Chapter 1, this is part of a process whereby EC law serves to deregulate national markets made rigid by (often long standing) technical rules.[25]

2.2.4 The Scope for Defending National Rules that Obstruct Trade

National rules which do not impede cross–border trade within the meaning of the *Dassonville/Keck* test[26] are not susceptible to challenge under EC trade law. However, even where the rule exerts an impact on trade adequate in principle to trigger Articles 30 or 59, the rule is not automatically unlawful. EC law recognises that not all national technical rules are unlawful, even though they may impede trade between Member States. In a minority of cases, national rules have been found to meet the 'mandatory requirements' test. In such circumstances, free trade and consumer choice do not prevail over national choices concerning market regulation.

National rules which restricted the marketing of strong alcoholic drink were ruled compatible with Article 30 in *Aragonesa de Publicidad Exterior SA (APESA) v Departamento de Sanidad y Seguridad Social de la Generalitat de Cataluna (DSSC)*.[27] Even though such rules affected the sales of such drink from other Member States, the Court was persuaded that the benefits of consumer choice should not prevail over the consumer interest in public health protection set by the regulating body at national level. Thus EC law does not create a wholly deregulated 'free for all' in the market.[28] This ruling provides a neat contrast to the Court's entirely understandable scepticism in the *Cassis de Dijon* case that controlling the supply of *weak* alcoholic drink could form part of a coherent policy of public health protection.

---

24 Cases C–154/89, C–180/89 and C–198/89 *Commission v France, Italy, Greece* [1991] ECR I–659, 709, 727.

25 Chapter 1.8.2.3.

26 2.2.1 above.

27 Cases C–1, C–176/90 [1991] ECR I–4151.

28 S. Weatherill, '1992 and Consumer Law: Can Free Trade be Reconciled with Effective Protection?' (1988) 6 *Trading Law* 75.

In the services sector, the Court has similarly found that Article 59 EC does not provide a means for eliminating *all* national rules shown to obstruct trade. It remains open to Member States to show justification, provided that it is recognised by Community law. *Customs and Excise Commissioners v Schindler*[29] involved a challenge to restrictions imposed by British authorities on invitations to participate in German lotteries posted from the Netherlands to British residents. The European Court found this to be an obstruction to the integration of the market for such services. However, it was prepared to accept that such national rules are capable of justification. The UK explained that its rules were designed to prevent crime, to ensure honest treatment of gamblers and to avoid the stimulation of demand in the gambling sector which may have damaging social consequences if taken to excess. The European Court conceded that the law governing the free movement of services does not preclude such national rules 'in view of the concerns of social policy and of the prevention of fraud.'[30]

2.2.5 The Sensitivity of the Court's Role in Shaping the Consumer Interest in EC Law

There are cases which lie very close to the dividing line between lawful and unlawful national measures. In settling these 'hard cases', the Court is obliged to develop its own conception of how far national authorities should be permitted to intervene in the market to protect the consumer where that intervention will affect the broader interests of market integration. The Court finds itself forced to judge the legitimacy of distinctive national philosophies of consumer protection in an integrating market. This is especially apparent where national measures designed to protect the economic interests of consumers are at stake.

Where the Court prefers free trade over national consumer protection, it exposes itself to the criticism that it is using the law of market integration to diminish national standards of protection. That risk, however, is inherent in the *Cassis de Dijon* formula. The crucial point rests in the scope of the national justifications that the Court is prepared to acknowledge as capable of overriding the impetus of integration through law.

National rules designed to protect consumers' economic interests, such as those which address deceptive marketing practices, may impede trade where they differ State by State. The impediment arises where the use of a technique employed in State A is forbidden in State B, which forces the trader to pursue a different strategy especially for State B. Where that

---

29 Case C–275/92 [1994] ECR I–1039.
30 Para. [63] of the ruling.

happens, the importer into State B is forced to adapt and is therefore at a disadvantage compared to State B's own traders. This is sufficient to trigger Article 30 in accordance with the *Dassonville* formula, refined in *Keck*.[31] The obstructive effect on trade requires the Court to scrutinise the national rules from the perspective of the *Cassis de Dijon* formula and to balance the consumer interest in an integrated market against the consumer interest in protection at national level. National rules are based on notions of deception which may be relative: 'hard sell' in one State may be 'unfair sell' in another. The Court's jurisprudence provides a window on distinct national views on the methods which traders should and should not be allowed to use in seeking to drum up business. The Court must then evaluate what level of protection may be provided at national level consistently with the demands of the law of market integration.

Schutzverband gegen Unwesen in der Wirtschaft v Y. Rocher GmbH[32] displays a policy preference in favour of a free market in information allied to a free market in goods. German law prohibited advertisements in which individual prices were compared, except where the comparison was not eye catching. Rocher showed that the rule inhibited its ability to construct an integrated marketing strategy because it could not export to Germany techniques used elsewhere in States with more liberal laws. The European Court focused on the fact that German law controlled eye catching advertisements whether or not they were true. The law thus suppressed the supply of accurate information to the consumer. The Court's ruling leaves no room for doubt that such a restriction cannot find justification under Community law. German law will have to be liberalised.

Verband Sozialer Wettbewerb eV v Clinique Laboratories SNC[33] involved a challenge to a German law that prohibited the use of the name 'Clinique' for cosmetics, because of an alleged risk that consumers would be misled into believing the products had medicinal properties. This rule was held to impede trade in goods marketed in other Member States under the 'Clinique' name. Article 30 was thus relevant; the *Keck* threshold was crossed. It fell to Germany to show justification for the rule. Germany was unable to do this to the Court's satisfaction. The Court was not persuaded that there was sufficient likelihood of consumer confusion for a barrier to trade to be justified.

The decisions in *Rocher* and in *Clinique* relax the grip of national laws which seem to regard consumers as more gullible than the European Court will acknowledge. Yet other cases suggest a greater readiness on the part of

---

[31]   2.2.1 above.
[32]   Case C–126/91 judgment of 18 May 1993.
[33]   Case C–315/92 [1994] ECR I–317.

the Court to accept that a free flow of marketing practices may not be achieved by virtue of the application of Article 30.

Oosthoek's Uitgeversmaatschappij[34] involved rules imposed in the Netherlands which controlled the offer of free gifts as an inducement to purchase encyclopaedias. Sellers from outside the Netherlands who were accustomed to using such marketing methods were forced to alter their strategy for the Dutch market, thus impeding integration.[35] The Court conceded that the banned marketing techniques could result in consumers being misled. It ruled that it was accordingly possible to justify the Dutch rules as measures necessary to prevent deception and to enhance consumer protection and fair trading. Similarly, in *Buet v Ministere Public*[36] the Court held that a French law which prohibited 'doorstep selling' of educational material was not incompatible with Article 30 in view of its contribution to the protection of consumers from pressure selling tactics.[37]

By way of a concluding example, the controversial nature of the Court's use of the *Cassis de Dijon* formula is memorably encapsulated in a single case where Court and Advocate General adopted diametrically opposed views on the desirability of achieving consumer choice through the abolition of national regulatory measures. In *Drei Glocken v Centro–Sud* the Court followed its *Cassis* approach in holding unlawful Italian technical rules governing the composition of pasta.[38] It held that it was incompatible with Article 30 to prohibit the sale in Italy of imported pasta made from common wheat or from a mixture of common wheat and durum wheat. The result was market integration and consumer choice; the Italian consumer did not *have* to buy unfamiliar imported types of pasta, but could do so if he or she chose.

However, the Advocate General in the case reached precisely the opposite conclusion. He would have held the Italian law lawful and would thus have perpetuated market segregation. He was concerned that the Italian consumer would be confused by the appearance on the market of unfamiliar pasta products. He presented a vigorous view that labelling products would not have been enough to provide adequate information to the consumer steeped in the history and culture of pasta. The Advocate General would thus

---

34   Case 286/81 [1982] ECR 4575.
35   This seems enough to cross the *Keck* threshold for the invocation of Art.30, 2.2.1 above, especially in light of the *Clinique* ruling. See especially [15] of the ruling in *Oosthoek*.
36   Case 328/87 [1989] ECR 1235.
37   Nor was the legislation pre–empted by the 'Doorstep Selling' Directive (Dir.85/577 OJ 1985 L372/31 on the protection of the consumer in respect of contracts negotiated away from business premises), for that Directive is 'minimum' in character. See further Chapter 1.8.3.4, and, on the detailed law of doorstep selling, Chapter 8.
38   Case 407/85 [1988] ECR 4233.

have ruled out market liberalisation until the Community had introduced legislation to clarify the area.

It is rare for an Advocate General's Opinion to find absolutely no favour with the Court, which subsequently delivers the authoritative ruling in the case. This emphasises how sensitive and delicate the balance may be between free trade and national market regulation in Article 30 cases.

2.2.6 From Negative to Positive

The Advocate General's Opinion in *Drei Glocken v Centro–Sud* that legislation was needed to harmonise national laws and to open up the market was rejected by the Court. However, the disagreement highlights the need to discuss the function of Community legislation, rather than primary Treaty provisions, in developing EC consumer policy.

Some national laws, although not many and not those in *Cassis de Dijon* nor *Drei Glocken*, will survive the application of 'negative law' under Articles 30 and 59 and persist in obstructing market integration. The classic constitutional response of the EC to areas where 'negative law' is insufficient to integrate the market is harmonisation; that is, 'positive' action by the Community to introduce its own regulatory rules applicable throughout the Community. Positive Community action may be required in order to advance market integration. Common Community rules may be needed to replace national rules obstructive of trade where those national rules are held lawful. More generally, a large integrated market may require an integrated structure of regulation. Harmonisation from this perspective is the Community's response to market failure.[39] However, the following section examines the difficulties which confront the translation of this notion of a need for 'positive' Community consumer policy making into a practical set of legal rules.

2.3 THE SHAPING OF EC CONSUMER POLICY UNDER THE TREATY

2.3.1 The Gap in the Treaty

Economic theory holds that market integration is itself ultimately in the consumer interest. The intensification of competition should serve the consumer by increasing the available choice of goods and services, thereby inducing improvements in their quality and reduction in their price. As

---

[39] Chapter 1.

explained, EC 'negative law' is an indirect form of consumer policy in its capacity to remove national impediments to integration.

However, one would look in vain in the Treaty as it existed prior to 1 November 1993 for a direct expression of the consumer interest. The consumer was mentioned only in Articles 39, 40, 85(3), 86 and 100a and each of those references was tangential only. In contrast to competition policy, for example, which was elaborated within the Treaty, consumer policy lacked independent identity. Prior to the entry into force of the Treaty on European Union on 1 November 1993, examined in 2.3.5 below, the Treaty offered no catalogue of consumer rights or interests which existed independently of the general notion that the consumer will benefit from the process of market integration.

This is of some constitutional significance. The European Community is not omnicompetent. It has powers only where they are conferred by its Treaty. Therefore the absence of a specific Community competence to legislate in the consumer interest represented a severe impediment to the possibility of moving beyond 'negative' law to a 'positive' Community consumer policy.

Accordingly, perhaps it would be tempting to suppose that the creation of an integrated Community market would require the sort of Community-wide regulation which is needed to support any market, whatever its territorial scope. Perhaps it would also be tempting to apply the theoretical analysis based on market failure presented in Chapter 1 to the European market as well as to the national market. However, constitutionally, the perceived need to regulate the market has not been the driving force of Community consumer policy making. Pre–Maastricht, market integration occupied the dominant constitutional position, with consumer protection evolving as a by–product.

The constitutional gap in Community consumer policy was filled by the Treaty on European Union which established a competence for the Community in the area of consumer policy (see 2.3.5 below). However, the potential impact of that new provision can be assessed only with an awareness of the erratic and indirect evolution of EC consumer policy before 1 November 1993.

2.3.2 The Development of Soft Law

The starting point in the evolution of a Community consumer protection policy is found in the Council Resolution of 14 April 1975 on a preliminary programme for a Community consumer protection and information policy.[40]

---

40   OJ 1975 C92/1.

This was the first attempt to provide a systematic framework for the development of Community consumer policy, although it was necessarily undertaken against the constitutional background of an absence of specific legal base. The Annex to the Resolution, a 'Preliminary Programme of the European Economic Community for a Consumer Protection and Information Policy', offered at Point 3 a statement of five basic rights:

(a) the right to protection of health and safety,
(b) the right to protection of economic interests,
(c) the right of redress,
(d) the right to information and education,
(e) the right of representation (the right to be heard).

The Annex observed that in the modern market economy the balance has shifted away from the consumer in favour of the supplier. This imbalance has deepened the need to improve information about rights among consumers and to provide information to support freer choice.

The first Resolution was followed in 1981 by a second along largely the same lines.[41] The third programme was presented in 1986 by which time the Community had fixed its goal of completing the internal market by the end of 1992,[42] a policy objective which heavily influenced the document. The 1992 internal market policy also informed the next document, the Council Resolution of 9 November 1989 on future priorities for relaunching consumer protection policy.[43]

On 3 May 1990 the Commission published a Three-year Action Plan of Consumer Policy in the EEC (1990–92).[44] Part A of the paper provided a brief overview under the title *Consolidation of Progress*; Part B provided a *Three Year Action Plan*, to end on 31 December 1992. There were four main areas of focus selected 'because of their importance in building the consumer confidence necessary to support the implementation of the internal market': consumer representation, consumer information, consumer safety and consumer transactions.

In June 1992, the Council agreed a Resolution on future priorities for the development of consumer protection policy.[45] The second Three Year Action Plan was published in July 1993 under the subtitle 'Placing the Single Market at the service of European consumers'.[46] This plan was located in the

---

41   OJ 1981 C133/1.
42   OJ 1986 C167/1.
43   OJ 1989 C 294/1.
44   COM (90) 98.
45   OJ 1992 C186/1.
46   COM (93) 378.

context of both the completion of the internal market and the agreement (though not at the time yet the ratification) of the Treaty on European Union. However, such resolutions and plans do not constitute formal Community legal acts; they cannot remedy the absence of an explicit Treaty base for EC consumer policy making.

2.3.3 Legislative Action Relevant to the Consumer

None of the above means that there is no Community legislation of significant interest to the consumer. It means, however, that Community 'consumer policy' has been developed indirectly, driven by the process of market integration, not market regulation. Where laws differ State by State, the creation of an integrated market is impeded. Some such disparities between national laws will be unlawful, as in the landmark *Cassis de Dijon* ruling and many others subsequently. Some national laws will nevertheless be justifiable and remain in place as lawful trade barriers.[47] The classic EC response is the harmonisation of such laws in order to establish a common Community rule. In this way Community laws come into existence in order to integrate the market, although their incidental effect is additionally to regulate it.

The original Treaty of Rome may have lacked a title devoted to consumer protection, but the Community has always enjoyed explicit competence to pursue legislation designed to approximate national provisions which directly affect the establishment or functioning of the common market. This was found in Article 100. As explained above, a further provision, Article 100a, was inserted into the Treaty by the Single European Act in 1987 in order to accelerate the process of law making needed to achieve a completed internal market by the end of 1992. Article 100a permits the adoption of harmonisation legislation in the areas to which it refers by qualified majority voting in Council. States may be outvoted and bound by legislation with which they disagree.[48]

Where divergences in national consumer protection laws affect market integration, the Community has in several areas acted to put in place its own consumer protection laws.[49] Such laws contribute to the equalisation of competitive conditions in the market. These are then implemented at national

---

47   Cf. cases at notes 35–37 above.

48   Article 100a(4) envisages the possibility of an application to the Commission for permission to apply non–conforming rules.

49   For recent discussion, see M. Goyens, 'Consumer Protection in a Single European Market: What Challenge for the EC Agenda?' (1992) 29 *CMLRev* 71; X. Lewis, 'The Protection of Consumers in European Community Law' (1992) 12 *YEL* 139.

level and become part of the fabric of consumer protection in the Community generally and in each individual Member State.

The body of what can indirectly be termed EC consumer protection legislation touches both private law and public law. It covers both protection of the safety of consumers and their economic interests. The following list identifies the most high–profile measures and provides a representative cross–section of Community activity;

1. Council Directive of 25 July 1985 on the approximation of the laws, regulations and administrative provisions of the Member States concerning liability for defective products.[50]
2. Council Directive of 23 June 1990 on package travel, package holidays and package tours.[51]
3. Council Directive of 5 April 1993 on unfair terms in consumer contracts.[52]
4. Council Directive of 3 May 1988 on the approximation of the laws of the Members States concerning the safety of toys.[53]
5. Council Directive of 29 June 1992 on General Product Safety.[54]
6. Council Directive of 10 September 1984 relating to the approximation of the laws regulations and administrative provisions of the Members States concerning misleading advertising.[55]
7. Council Directive of 20 December 1985 to protect the consumer in respect of contracts negotiated away from business premises.[56]
8. Council Directive of 22 December 1986 for the approximation of the laws, regulations and administrative provision of the Members States concerning consumer credit; Council Directive of 22 February 1990 amending Directive 87/102/EEC for the approximation of the laws, regulations and administrative provisions of the Member States concerning consumer credit.[57]
9. Directive of the Parliament and Council of 26 October 1994 on the protection of purchasers in respect of certain aspects of contracts

---

[50]   Dir 85/374 OJ 1985 L210/29. See Chapter 6.
[51]   Dir.90/314 OJ 1990 L158/59. Implemented in the UK by the Package Travel, Package Holidays and Package Tours Regulations 1992, S.I 1992/3288.
[52]   Dir 93/13 OJ 1993 L95/29. See Chapter 9.
[53]   Dir 88/378 OJ 1988 L187/1. See Chapter 12.
[54]   Dir.92/59 OJ 1992 L228/24. See Chapter 12.
[55]   Dir. 84/450 OJ 1984 L250/17. See Chapter 10.
[56]   Dir.85/577 OJ 1985 L372/31. See Chapter 8.
[57]   Dir 87/102 OJ L 42/48; Dir 90/88 OJ 1990 L61/14. See Chapter 7.

relating to the purchase of the right to use immovable properties on a timeshare basis.[58]

All these measures were adopted on the basis of either Article 100 or 100a of the Treaty. None is a measure of EC 'consumer protection law' in a formal, constitutional sense. However, all significantly affect national consumer law and all are examined at length at appropriate points in this book.[59]

The Member States of the EC are under an obligation to implement these Directives in their domestic legal orders.[60] The EC Treaty envisages that Directives will become part of national law through national implementing measures. The UK has done this in respect of all the above measures. Each is part of domestic law, although the national implementing measures do not stand alone; they must be interpreted in the light of the Directives.[61] Accordingly, the pattern of EC law is part of the pattern of law in the UK. EC law is part of English law by virtue (on the traditional model) of the European Communities Act 1972. EC law must not be placed in a setting external to domestic law. The controls over the market exercised as a result of these EC initiatives have been discussed several times in Chapter 1 at the level of policy and will be seen to permeate the book's treatment of the substantive law of consumer protection.

In practice, the constitutional genesis of Community consumer protection law is not of immediate importance in the application of laws in the UK. These laws, initially in the shape of Directives, become domestic consumer protection law and must be enforced as effectively as law emanating from a purely domestic source. The fact that a Directive is formally designed to integrate the market does not lessen its impact, often profound, on the relevant domestic law of consumer protection. Directive 85/374, the Product Liability Directive,[62] is concerned with harmonisation of national laws. Because Article 1 provides that 'the producer shall be liable for damage caused by a defect in his product' it improves the position of the injured consumer in the UK where liability rules have been based on the fault of the producer rather than the defectiveness of the product.[63]

---

58 Dir. 94/47 OJ 1994 L280/83. 2.3.5 below explains the reference to both Parliament and Council in the title of this measure; it is a consequence of the Treaty on European Union.

59 Excepting only those dealing with package travel and timeshare.

60 Arts. 5 and 189 EC.

61 The *Marleasing* principle; see 2.4.2 below.

62 Note 51 above.

63 For further details of this regime, see Chapter 6.

2.3.4 The Risk that EC Legislation may Depress Standards

Concern has been expressed from time to time about the potential risk that EC legislative initiatives may set standards below those prevailing at national level. Were this to happen, free trade would be achieved at the expense of consumer protection. This fear exists alongside the risk (commented on above in 2.2.2) that Community negative law may sweep away national choices concerning market regulation and consumer protection. The allegation that positive Community rules have depressed existing standards is difficult conclusively to rebut or to sustain. Individual sectors must be assessed. A related concern is that, even where standards are not lower, their effective enforcement is severely impeded by the unchecked flow of goods across borders throughout the extensive territory of the Community. This may make it difficult to track down goods that are unsafe, an aspect which raises questions about appropriate strategies of enforcement practice in the internal market.[64] At this stage, the reader should simply be aware that these are real and recurrent points of concern in appraising the impact of EC rules on consumer protection.

Constitutionally, attempts have been made to alleviate such fears. Article 100a, introduced by the Single European Act, includes in Article 100a(3) the admonition that, in making proposals for legislation affecting, *inter alia*, consumer protection, the Commission 'will take as a base a high level of protection.' This proviso is weakened by its reference to a 'base' only; also by the realisation that it is the Council and the Parliament, not the Commission, that ultimately adopt such measures. However, at the very least, Article 100a(3) demonstrates sensitivity to the charge that EC harmonisation law might follow a lowest common denominator.

Fears that standards may be lowered by EC intervention have also been addressed by the frequent use of the 'minimum harmonisation' formula in Article 100 and, especially, Article 100a Directives. The minimum formula establishes a floor of Community regulation below which States may not dip, but it permits States to set stricter rules above that floor mandated by the EC measure. On this model, EC legislative intervention does not totally pre–empt national choices; free trade is placed alongside, not above, national market regulation and consumer protection. For example, the Directive on Unfair Terms in Consumer Contracts, an Article 100a measure,[65] is minimum in character and therefore does not preclude the application of stricter or wider control of unfair terms under national law.[66]

---

64   Cf Chapter 12.6.
65   Note 52 above.
66   Chapter 9.

These techniques have been lent yet further prominence by the Treaty on European Union, to which attention now turns.

2.3.5 The Treaty on European Union and Consumer Protection

As mentioned in the above commentary, the pattern of Community consumer protection policy was altered by the entry into force of the Treaty on European Union on 1 November 1993. The prevailing enforced constitutional connection between consumer protection and market integration, via Articles 100/100a, has been relaxed. For the first time EC competence in the area of consumer protection is established independently of the process of market integration through harmonisation under Articles 100 and 100a.[67] The relevant provision is Article 129a EC, which reads as follows:

1. The Community shall contribute to the attainment of a high level of consumer protection through:
    (a) measures adopted pursuant to Article 100a in the context of the completion of the internal market;
    (b) specific action which supports and supplements the policy pursued by the Member States to protect the health, safety and economic interests of consumers and to provide adequate information to consumers.
2. The Council, acting in accordance with the procedure referred to in Article 189b and after consulting the Economic and Social Committee, shall adopt the specific action referred to in paragraph 1(b).
3. Action adopted pursuant to paragraph 2 shall not prevent any Member State from maintaining or introducing more stringent protective measures. Such measures must be compatible with this Treaty. The Commission shall be notified of them.

The elevation of consumer protection to the status of a Community common policy is confirmed by an addition to Article 3 which now provides that 'the activities of the Community shall include... a contribution to the strengthening of consumer protection.'

For both Article 100a and 129a the legislative procedure involves qualified majority voting in Council and the possibility of a Parliamentary veto. Measures will be the product of both Council and Parliament and will bear reference to both in their title. This explains why the Timeshare

---

[67] See H.–W. Micklitz and S. Weatherill, 'Consumer Policy in the European Community: Before and After Maastricht' (1993) 16 *JCP* 285.

Directive, made after the entry into force of the Treaty on European Union, is a Directive 'of the Parliament and Council',[68] whereas pre–Maastricht Directives are 'Council Directives.'

It will be noted that the first phrase in Article 129a(1) is much firmer in its commitment to high levels of consumer protection than is Article 100a(3), most of all in engaging the Community, not simply the Commission. In addition, it moves beyond Article 100a(3)'s weak notion of taking a high level of protection merely 'as a base'. Moreover, minimum harmonisation is elevated to Treaty status in this area of competence by virtue of Article 129a(3) EC.

The precise impact of this new provision remains unclear since the nature of the specific action envisaged by Article 129a(1)(b) has yet to emerge from practice. However, as a general comment, the opportunity now exists further to develop the role of the EC as a generator of consumer protection law which is autonomous of the law of market integration.[69]

On some views, the step forward for consumer protection in Article 129a is accompanied by a step back in the new Article 3b. Which step is the longer is as yet unclear. Article 3b contains the principle of subsidiarity, which, like the provision on consumer protection, was newly inserted into the Treaty by the Maastricht amendments:

1.   The Community shall act within the limits of the powers conferred upon it by this Treaty and of the objectives assigned to it therein.
2.   In areas which do not fall within its exclusive competence, the Community shall take action, in accordance with the principle of subsidiarity, only if and in so far as the objectives of the proposed action cannot be sufficiently achieved by the Member States and can therefore, by reason of the scale or effects of the proposed action, be better achieved by the Community.
3.   Any action by the Community shall not go beyond what is necessary to achieve the objectives of this Treaty.

This formulation raises more questions than it answers. Some States, especially Germany and the UK, seem prepared to regard it as a basis for trimming Community competence in many areas, including consumer policy making. By contrast, the Economic and Social Committee has criticised the

---

[68]   Note 58 above.
[69]   Consider proposals on Consumer Guarantees examined in Chapter 4.3 from this perspective. In its Green Paper published before the entry into force of the Treaty on European Union, the Commission does not commit itself to use of a specific legal base; either Art. 100a or 129a seem possible contenders. Cf also Chapter 17 dealing with the Green Paper on Access to Justice.

use of subsidiarity as an excuse for undermining Community law making, especially in the consumer policy field, emphasising the risk that the integrated market will be under regulated if initiatives are blocked.[70]

'Subsidiarity' is a slogan for a politically complex debate about how the Community market is most efficiently regulated and, specifically, how competence shall be divided between Community and Member States. The core meaning of Article 3b is elusive. This is primarily because this formulation simply reflects the problem of dividing competences between Community and Member States, instead of attempting directly to address it. Subsidiarity represents a continuation, even an intensification, of the competence debate, not its resolution. Sir Leon Brittan regards it as a method for identifying the 'best level' for regulatory activity in the Community.[71] This rendition is important and helpful, because it brings out the point that subsidiarity is not based on preconceptions about centralisation or decentralisation. Instead it is a matter of *efficiency* – problematic though such a test will doubtless prove in practical application, whether by politicians or by judges.

2.4 COMMUNITY LAW WITHIN THE NATIONAL SYSTEM[72]

2.4.1 The Pattern of Community Law within the National Legal System

It is commonplace that, for members of the European Community, EC law forms part of the national legal order. However, although EC law is national law, not a severable body of law, Community measures and their application at national level raise some special problems of their own, all of which will be observed in this book. Their potential overlap with existing domestic law requires careful attention in implementation and application. The existence of relevant Community law is capable of affecting future domestic initiatives. For instance, any national law measure which is likely to impede trade may need to be tested against the requirements of Community trade law, inviting consideration of the scope of 'negative law' examined earlier in this Chapter. Similarly, any national law likely to impinge on an area already occupied by Community legislation may be legally pre–empted by the Community norm and therefore be unenforceable. Whether such pre–emption occurs depends on a careful examination of the scope of the relevant Community measure.[73]

---

70   OJ 1993 C19/22.

71   [1993] *Public Law* 567, 574.

72   The major textbooks mentioned at n.3 above provide comprehensive treatment of these constitutional issues.

73   Cf the pre–emptive impact of the General Product Safety Directive, Chapter 12.

Minimum harmonisation, whereby Community measures require States to put in place minimum requirements but also permit them to set more protective standards, is increasingly in vogue in Community consumer policy making. Its use will be seen in a number of areas covered by this book.[74]

Measures with a Community origin cannot be interpreted within a purely domestic context. It may be appropriate to seek interpretative assistance from the European Court through the Article 177 preliminary reference procedure. Moreover, measures with a Community origin cannot be enforced within a purely domestic context. The development of Community–wide patterns of consumer protection places demands on enforcement authorities to set up cross–border administrative structures and channels for information sharing. There is a certain logic in the development of Community–wide regulatory strategies in parallel with Community–wide marketing strategies pursued by traders, although the practical details of that process will only evolve fully over time.[75]

2.4.2 The Effect of Directives at National Level

EC law is part of the pattern of domestic law. There is, however, one important constitutional limitation on the impact of EC law at national level which may diminish the vitality of EC consumer protection initiatives. This limitation applies to Directives, which are the most fertile source of EC consumer protection law. According to Article 189 EC, a Directive:

> 'shall be binding, as to the result to be achieved, upon each Member State to which it is addressed, but shall leave to the national authorities the choice of form and methods.'

It is a Treaty violation for a Member State to fail to implement a Directive; such default may lead to proceedings brought by the Commission under Article 169 EC against the State before the European Court in Luxembourg. However, the formulation in Article 189 EC appears to mean that where a Member State fails to implement a Directive properly, the protection envisaged under the Directive is unavailable to the individual before a national court until such time as the appropriate implementing measures are put in place. Such a gap in legal protection would severely weaken the impact of the EC Directive as a legal instrument, especially given that wilful non–implementation or simply delayed implementation, whilst not the norm, nonetheless remains regrettably common.

---

[74] Cf Chapter 9.

[75] Cf Chapter 12.6 for more detailed exploration of practice.

Mindful of the precariousness of the Directive as a source of rights, the European Court has developed its jurisprudence in order to enhance the impact at national level of unimplemented Directives. There are three major elements in the Court's campaign.

First, in the absence of proper implementation, a Directive couched in sufficiently clear terms is capable of being applied directly by national courts against the State. The rationale for this direct effect of Directives lies in the inequity which would follow from permitting a State to plead its own wrongful default in order to escape obligations envisaged under a Directive. Therefore an individual who acts in conformity with a Directive after its deadline for implementation will be able to rely on that Directive before national courts in order successfully to defend a criminal charge based on existing law which has improperly not been amended in the light of the Directive.[76] A State employee who is the victim of discrimination on grounds of sex forbidden by an unimplemented Directive, but not unlawful under national law, is able to rely on the Directive before national courts in proceedings brought against the State as employer.[77] This route is rendered all the more vigorous by the European Court's insistence on a wide definition of 'State' for these purposes.[78] However, its limits lie in the Court's refusal to accept that Directives can be enforced in this way against private parties. According to the Court's ruling in *Marshall*, the private sector employee discriminated against on grounds of sex cannot rely on the Directive in an action before national courts against his or her employer.[79]

Second, in the absence of implementation, national courts are expected to fulfil an obligation to interpret existing national law in order to conform with Community law. Article 5 EC imposes on national authorities, including courts, a duty of fidelity towards the Community. As part of this remarkably flexible obligation, the Court observed in *Marleasing SA v La Comercial Internacional de Alimentacion SA*[80] that:

'... in applying national law, whether the provisions in question were adopted before or after the directive, the national court called upon to interpret it is required to do so, as far as possible, in the light of the wording and the purpose of the directive in order to achieve the result

---

76   Case 148/78 *Pubblico Ministero v Ratti* [1979] ECR 1629.
77   Case 152/84 *Marshall v Southampton Area Health Authority* [1986] ECR 723.
78   Eg Case C–188/89 *Foster v British Gas* [1990] ECR I–3133.
79   Case 152/84 note 77 above; in fact, in this case, the plaintiff was able to rely on the unimplemented Directive because she was employed by the State, widely defined.
80   Case C–106/89 [1990] ECR I–4135.

pursued by the latter and thereby comply with the third paragraph of Article 189 of the Treaty.'[81]

This formula deepens the penetration of Directives into the national legal order even in the absence of implementation. As a form of 'indirect effect', it may be used to reshape national law in the light of a Directive even in proceedings between private parties. Its limitations lie in the demands which it makes on the ingenuity of national judges. The route will be effective especially, and perhaps only, in circumstances where national law exists which is capable of an interpretation consistent with the unimplemented Directive.[82]

Third, failure to implement a Directive may result in the liability of the State to compensate individuals who have suffered loss caused by such non–implementation. The recognition that EC law may require the availability of such a remedy in national legal orders came in the landmark decision in *Francovich and Others v Italian State*.[83] In this case, Italy had failed to implement Directive 80/987, which requires States to set up guarantee funds to compensate workers in the event of employers' insolvency. Lack of clarity in identifying the institutions responsible for payment precluded a finding that the Directive was capable of direct effect. Yet the Court declared that:

'... the full effectiveness of Community provisions would be affected and the protection of the rights they recognise undermined if individuals were not able to recover damages when their rights were infringed by a breach of Community law attributable to a Member State.'

The Court stipulated three requirements that must be met before the State will incur liability. First, the result prescribed must involve the conferral of rights on individuals. Second, the content of the rights must be capable of identification on the basis of Directive. Third, a causal link between the Treaty violation and damage suffered by an individual must be demonstrated.

The *Francovich* ruling has the potential to bypass the complex questions about the scope of the direct effect of Directives. It shifts the focus of the individual's claim away from the identity of the party (private or public) against which rights under the Directive are envisaged towards the State as the party responsible for putting rights in place in the national legal order. In this sense a *Francovich* claim is more direct, although claims based on the direct and indirect effect of Directives are not precluded. *Francovich* extends

---

[81]   The third paragraph of Article 189, referring to the Directive, is extracted above.
[82]   Cf *Duke v GEC Reliance* [1988] 2 WLR 359, [1988] 1 All ER 626.
[83]   Cases C–6 & C–9/90 [1991] ECR I–5357, [1993] 2 CMLR 66.

the protection available to the individual prejudiced by non–implementation of a Directive.

Francovich liability is no universal panacea. Elucidation of the principles on which liability is based is still awaited, though commentators have remarked on its extraordinary scope.[84] The financial consequences could be enormous, calling to mind the spectre of liability in an indeterminate amount to an indeterminate number of plaintiffs. Such fears have led to close confinement of liability for economic loss in English law and in other systems, at least where the harm is not caused deliberately or maliciously.[85] The Italian State's infraction in *Francovich* was plain and had indeed already been recorded in a judgment of the European Court.[86] It is plausible that the Court will choose to confine the scope of liability in subsequent cases, at least in those involving genuine but mistaken attempts to comply with Community law.[87]

Some clarification of the scope of *Francovich* liability in the consumer context may emerge from litigation prompted by Germany's tardy implementation of Directive 90/314, which approximates national laws governing package travel, package holidays and package tours.[88] Compensation is being pursued by a number of holiday makers who claim to have been denied protection envisaged by the unimplemented Directive.[89]

A fundamental practical weakness in the value of the *Francovich* claim lies in its inappropriateness to the 'small–scale' claimant. The individual envisaged as the recipient of rights under a Directive (whether in the field of employment or consumer protection), but whose enjoyment of those rights is thwarted by non–implementation of the Directive, would ideally prefer simply to vindicate those rights in a relatively straightforward action against employer or trader. This, however, is not possible where that employer or trader is not part of the 'State'. The *Francovich* claim for compensation is then a useful second–best, but it is indirect and its scope is uncertain.

---

[84] Discussed by P. Craig, 'Francovich, Remedies and the Scope of Damages Liability' (1993) 109 *LQR* 595; M. Ross, 'Beyond Francovich' (1993) 56 *MLR* 55; J. Steiner, 'From Direct Effects to Francovich' (1993) 18 *ELRev* 3; R. Caranta, 'Government Liability after Francovich' (1993) 52 *CLJ* 272.

[85] Cf Chapter 1.4.

[86] Case 22/87 *Commission v Italy* [1989] ECR 143.

[87] Cf the rather opaque ruling in Case C–128/92 *H. Banks & Co Ltd v British Coal Corporation* [1994] ECR I–1209, where the Court seems to have limited its rulings to the specific facts of the case, which arose out of the European Coal and Steel Treaty.

[88] Note 51 above.

[89] Eg Case C–178/94 *E. Dillenkofer v Bundesminister der Justiz*, one of several references made by Landgericht Bonn. For comment see *EuZW* 14/1994 442.

2.4.3 Absence of Horizontal Direct Effect

The gap in constitutional protection lies in the Court's refusal to acknowledge that wrongfully unimplemented Directives are capable of horizontal direct effect; that is, that they cannot be employed by one private party against another private party, but rather only against the State. Both 'indirect effect' and *Francovich* liability offer limited scope for avoiding the worst consequences for the individual of that gap in enforceability of rights envisaged under a Directive. However, they cannot alter the basic point of the *Marshall* ruling[90] that one private individual cannot rely on a Directive as such in proceedings at national level against another private party.

This is rather damaging for the consumer's interest. In most situations the consumer will wish to rely on rights under a Directive against another private party, usually a trader. If the Directive has been implemented, the consumer can rely on the national implementing measures, which should be interpreted in the light of the Directive. If it has not been implemented, the consumer is denied the protection envisaged under Community law. The consumer may attempt to persuade the national court to interpret existing national law, if any exists, to accord with the Directive. This is a rather uncertain route and depends on national judicial capability and willingness. The consumer may sue the State for compensation. This will be unrealistic in most situations of small–scale individual loss. In practical terms, the consumer's effective protection lies in reliance on the Directive in litigation with the trader, whether as plaintiff or as defendant, yet it is precisely this 'horizontal direct effect' which the European Court is not prepared to admit.

In *Paola Faccini Dori v Recreb srl*, a decision of July 1994,[91] the European Court confirmed its *Marshall* ruling. The litigation in *Dori* arose in the consumer field. The ruling maintains that there is a gap in protection for the consumer wishing to rely on a right envisaged under a Directive against a private party, such as a supplier, where that Directive has not been implemented. Italy had failed to implement the Doorstep Selling Directive in time.[92] On Milan Railway Station, Ms Dori was lured into a contract covered by the Directive by a seller of educational material. Under the Directive, she should have been entitled to claim a right to withdraw from the deal and, having 'cooled–off', she decided that she wished to exercise that right. Under Italian law no such right existed. She was thus bound to the deal unless she was able to plead the Directive before the Italian courts against the supplier, a private party. The matter was referred to the European Court under the Article 177 procedure. The Court adhered to the *Marshall* ruling

---

[90]   Note 77 above.
[91]   Case C–91/92 [1994] ECR I–3325.
[92]   Note 56 above; more fully, Chapter 8.

and held that the Directive could not be directly effective in such circumstances. In maintaining this constitutional barrier to the impact of EC Directives at national level, the Court conformed to the wishes of the majority of Member States whose strong submissions to the Court in *Dori* against horizontal direct effect testified to the sensitivity of this area of law.

That Ms Dori was denied a right which she was supposed to enjoy under a Directive seems to weaken the vigour of EC consumer protection law. The rationale for the Court's stance can be traced back to its reasons for accepting that Directives are capable of direct effect against the State in the first place. Where the State has improperly failed to implement, it should not be able to benefit therefrom; accordingly, Directives may be enforced against it directly before a national court. By contrast, the private trader or employer is not at fault for the absence of implementation and may indeed have no knowledge of the lack of conformity of national law with a Directive. On this reasoning it might seem unfair to allow a private party such as an employee or a consumer to invoke an unimplemented Directive before a national court against another private party. Neither private party is 'at fault'; the State is the culprit for the flawed legal position at national level. This is a strong reason for welcoming the decision in *Francovich* for turning the focus on to the defaulting State.

In refusing to accept that the consumer could enforce the terms of the Directive against her supplier, the Court mentioned the availability to Dori of an action against the State based on *Francovich* principles. This is welcome in theory, but in practice seems rather unrealistic. The prospect of pursuing an action against the Italian State would probably be sufficiently daunting to dissuade the vast majority of consumers from making use of *Francovich*. Consumer rights would go unvindicated; State default would not be penalised.[93] A consumer in such circumstances simply wishes to exercise a right to withdraw from a contract, involving, if necessary, a suitable defence to a claim for breach of contract where he or she refuses to pay sums due under the contract from which withdrawal has occurred. This is the effective method of protecting consumer rights; it is the effective method of securing observance of Directives throughout the territory of the Community; and the

---

93   Cf pre–*Dori* but clearly aware of its imminence, AG Jacobs in Case C–316/93 *Vaneetveld v SA Le Foyer* Opinion of 27 January 1994: 'the possibility for the individual, under *Francovich*, to claim damages against the Member State where a directive has not been correctly implemented is not, in my view, an adequate substitute for the direct enforcement of the directive. It would often require the plaintiff to bring two separate sets of legal proceedings, either simultaneously or successively, one against the private defendant and the other against the public authorities, which would hardly be compatible with the requirements of an effective remedy'. This point was not tackled in the Court's ruling of 3 March 1994 in Case C–316/93, [1994] ECR I–763.

effective method of securing the equality of the individual before Community law, irrespective of nationality. Drawing on such perceptions, horizontal direct effect was powerfully urged upon the Court in *Dori* by its Advocate General, Herr Lenz. However, such recognition of the horizontal direct effect of Directives was rejected by the Court in 1986 in *Marshall* and that rejection was confirmed in *Dori*.

None of these constitutional problems arise provided that the State complies with its obligation to implement Directives within the national legal order. Gratifyingly, the UK's record of implementation of Directives in general and consumer protection Directives in particular is commendable.

3 Private Law and Consumer Protection

3.1 THE PRIVATE LAW BACKGROUND

A consumer lawyer needs to have a thorough understanding of private law, that is the common law (such as contract and tort), personal property law and the law of equity. This book, which concentrates on rules particularly affecting consumers, is long enough without going into these topics in detail. But three famous consumers – Mrs Carlill,[1] Mrs Donoghue[2] and old Mr. Bundy[3] – bear witness to the truth that the consumer lawyer remains ignorant of the traditional private law rules at his peril.

It is particularly important for the consumer lawyer to recognise when the common law has either developed distinctive rules for consumers or applied the law more generously in favour of consumers. For instance, the courts are more likely to treat a pre-contractual statement as a term of the contract (rather than a mere representation) when it is made by a seller to a consumer, because of the seller's special knowledge or skill compared to the other party.[4] Equally the courts have strictly construed the rules on incorporation of terms into contracts, where a term would seriously affect the consumer's interests.[5] However, the type of private law which is usually treated as the core of consumer protection law is legislative in form. Consumer protection has become synonymous with the Sale of Goods Act 1979 and analogous legislation covering other supply contracts, the Consumer Credit Act 1974, the Unfair Contract Terms Act 1977 and the strict liability provisions contained in the Consumer Protection Act 1987.

One of the major criticisms of the private law is that, even if the substantive law were adequate, it would still fail to protect consumers adequately because of the practical difficulties they face in enforcing those rights. Consumers need to be educated so that they can recognise they have legal claims and know how to enforce them. Attempts to overcome these problems by consumer education, legal advice and improved access to justice

---

1   *Carlill v Carbolic Smoke Ball Co* [1893] 1 QB 256.
2   *Donoghue v Stevenson* [1932] AC 562.
3   *Lloyds Bank v Bundy* [1975] QB 326.
4   See *Dick Bently Productions Ltd v Harold Smith (Motors) Ltd* [1965] 2 All ER 65; cf. *Oscar Chess Ltd v Williams* [1957] 1 All ER 325.
5   Eg the cases on exclusion clauses such as *Chapelton v Barry UDC* [1940] 1 KB 532.

through such initiatives as small claims courts and class action procedures are discussed in Chapter 17. Some lawyers have great faith in the ability of the private law to right wrongs.[6] Increasingly, however, consumer lawyers are recognising the limits to the private law.[7] We are sceptical about the effectiveness of the private law in protecting consumers.[8] This is not to say that consumers do not benefit from increased private law rights, but rather that other methods may be more effective and the benefits of private law rights tend to be spread rather unevenly. Thus middle class well educated consumers are usually those with the motivation and resources to utilise their legal rights. Private law rights are more frequently invoked with respect of high value consumer products or where there are significant consequential damages – in other words where the prize is worth fighting for. It is important not to conclude from the fact that the private law may not be greatly helping consumers that it can never be a powerful weapon in their hands. This may well be a question of legal culture. The English common law is firmly rooted in the notion of freedom of contract, and the judiciary which makes and applies laws has a conservative outlook which carries with it a restricted view of the potential of the law to upset market determined outcomes. This applies not only to the way that judges develop the common law, but also to how they interpret statutes.[9] This need not be the case. Thus one can look to the United States and see how the common law was radicalised to provide remedies for consumers who were injured by defective products[10] and to Scandinavia where s.36 of the Contracts Act (which allows the courts to rewrite unfair contracts) has been a powerful weapon in the hands of an activist judiciary.[11]

---

6   See for instance J.A. Jolowicz, 'The Protection of the Consumer and the Purchaser of Goods under English Law' (1969) 32 *MLR* 1.

7   See R. Cranston in *Consumers and the Law* (2nd ed.) (Weidenfeld and Nicolson, 1984) at p.66 where he states that 'the private law is an inadequate tool of consumer protection'.

8   See 1.2–1.6.

9   For example, see the way judges have interpreted the extortionate credit bargain provisions of the Consumer Credit Act 1974, discussed in L. Bently and G. Howells, 'Judicial Treatment of Extortionate Credit Bargains' [1989] Conv. 164. The British judiciary tends to reflect the view of Lord Devlin, who was prepared to accept there was some room for judicial activism (drawing inspiration from the consensus of opinion to develop the law), but no place for judicial dynamism (drawing inspiration from outside the consensus and seeking to make this the consensus): see Lord Devlin, *The Judge*, (Oxford University Press, 1979).

10   See 6.2.1.

11   Also significant is the fact that in the US the juries play a central role in deciding civil cases, while in Scandinavia most consumer cases are dealt with by the

3.2 CLASSIFICATION OF CONSUMER TRANSACTIONS

Consumers enter into a variety of transactions, some categories of which are easily distinguishable – for instance, contracts for goods as compared to contracts for services. Often, however, consumers are unaware of the legal form of their agreement; they are unlikely to know that a credit sale is governed by a different statute than a hire-purchase agreement, and may be indifferent to the distinction. Equally, whether a consumer hires or buys a product may be of no particular moment, with factors swaying the decision one way or the other likely to be other than legal niceties. The legal form of consumer transactions can, however, be significant as it determines which legislation governs the transaction at hand. This is true even though the importance of the distinctions between types of transactions has diminished as the statutory protection afforded consumers in sale transactions has been extended to other categories of transactions. The distinction nevertheless, remains important because, inter alia, a different standard is applied to contracts for services than to contracts for goods; only the Sale of Goods Act 1979 contains a detailed scheme covering the passing of property; the right to reject is lost in different circumstances in sale contracts than under other contracts, sale of goods contracts have special rules on mistake and frustration[12] and there are some differences in the rules relating to exclusion clauses. The reader may wish to reflect whether it is sensible to maintain these different regimes, or whether the rules might not usefully be harmonised as part of a codification exercise to remove or at least reduce the differences.

3.2.1 Sale

During the 19th century a considerable body of case law developed around the buyer/seller relationship. Sir Mackenzie Chalmers was given the task of drafting Sale of Goods legislation which codified the common law position[13] and the Sale of Goods Act appeared on the statute book in 1893. Following

---

Consumer Complaints Boards rather than the ordinary courts. For a discussion and comparison of contract law generally, but also dealing with the question of consumer protection, in the UK and Scandinavia, see R. Brownsword, G. Howells and T. Wilhelmsson (eds), *Welfarism in Contract Law* (Dartmouth, 1993).

12   These are not discussed in this book.

13   Apparently the previous position was altered in some ways by drafting details and amendments made in Parliament: see R. Bradgate and N. Savage, *Commercial Law* (Butterworths, 1991) at p. 142.

more recent recommendations from the Law Commission[14] the Act was amended by the Supply of Goods (Implied Terms) Act 1973, and these and other changes were consolidated in the Sale of Goods Act 1979.[15] This in turn has been recently amended by the Sale and Supply of Goods Act 1994.

S.2(1), Sale of Goods Act 1979 defines a contract of sale as 'a contract by which the seller transfers or agrees to transfer the property in goods to the buyer for a money consideration, called the price.' The two key elements of the definition are the commitment to transfer ownership and the requirement for a money consideration.

The requirement that there must be a commitment to transfer ownership explains why a hire–purchase agreement is not a sale. A hire–purchase agreement involves a hire contract with an option to purchase. Although the option is usually a mere technicality the possibility remains that the consumer could meet his hire obligations and then decide not to exercise his option to purchase and simply return the goods to their owner. By contrast a 'credit sale' is a straightforward sale, with the buyer simply being given time to pay the price. A 'conditional sale' is more like a hire–purchase agreement, since it provides for the payment of the price by instalments, with an agreement that the property will be transferred at some future time, usually when all the instalments have been paid. However, conditional sales remain within the scope of the Sale of Goods Act since there is a commitment to sell and are known as 'agreements to sell'; however, they have been assimilated to hire–purchase contracts for certain purposes.[16]

If the contract is not for a money consideration, it will be one of barter or exchange which is now governed by the Supply of Goods and Services Act 1982. We discuss below the difficult matter of how part exchange contracts should be classified. The lack of a money consideration also means that the Sale of Goods Act 1979 does not cover gifts which are again within the scope of the 1982 Act.[17]

It should be noted that s.61(1), Sale of Goods Act 1979 defines goods as including 'all personal chattels other than things in action and money...; and

---

14 Law Com. No. 24, Scot Law Com. No. 12, *First Report on Exemption Clauses: Amendments to the Sale of Goods Act 1893*, (1969).

15 The Law Reform (Enforcement of Contracts) Act 1954 removed the rule which rendered unenforceable contracts for the sale of goods valued at more than ten pounds which had not been evidenced in writing.

16 See eg s.25(2), Sale of Goods Act 1979 and s.14, Supply of Goods (Implied Terms) Act 1973.

17 The Unsolicited Goods and Services Acts 1971 and 1975 allow a consumer to treat as an unconditional gift goods which are sent to him unsolicited where the sender does not recover them within six months or within 30 days of having a notice served on him by the recipient.

in particular "goods" includes emblements, industrial growing crops, and things attached to or forming part of the land which are agreed to be severed before sale or under the contract of sale.' An interesting point is whether blood comes within the definition of goods. This has become particularly acute in recent times with a number of scares involving blood or blood products contaminated with the HIV virus. In the US the dominant trend is to treat the supply of blood as a service and hence subject to negligence rather than strict liability standards.[18] There are also debates concerning whether software programmes are goods, although a distinction seems to be developing between 'off the shelf discs' which are treated as goods and programmes devised or adapted for a specific purpose which are more readily viewed as having a sizeable service element.

3.2.2 Hire–purchase

S.15, Supply of Goods (Implied Terms) Act 1973, and s.189(1), Consumer Credit Act 1974, both provide a definition of a hire–purchase agreement which requires (a) that the goods are bailed in return for periodic payments, and (b) that the property in the goods will pass if the terms of the agreement are complied with and one of the following occurs: (i) an option to purchase is exercised, (ii) a specified act is performed by a party to the agreement, or (iii) any other specified event happens.

In part the development of hire–purchase was a response to the legal regime which used to exist. The use of hire–purchase side–stepped the requirement, which existed until 1954, that contracts for goods valued at more than ten pounds had to be evidenced in writing; it also avoided the statutory scheme which had been put into place by the Sale of Goods Act 1893. The value to traders of using hire–purchase contracts was greatly enhanced by two decisions at the end of the last century. In *Helby v Matthews*[19] a hirer was held not to be a person who had bought or agreed to buy goods and so could not pass a good title on to a third party by virtue of s.25(1), Sale of Goods Act 1979. *McEntire v Crossley Bros.*[20] decided that a hire–purchase contract did not need to be registered under the Bill of Sales Acts 1878 and 1882 as the hirer has no property over which to grant security.

---

18 See *Hyland Therapeutics v Superior Court* 175 Cal. App. 3d 509, 220 Cal Rptr. 590 (1985): and see discussion in A. Clark, *Product Liability,* (Sweet & Maxwell, 1989) at pp. 61–2.

19 [1895] AC 471.

20 [1895] AC 457.

The common law had implied terms into hire–purchase contracts similar to those implied into sale contracts; these were placed on a statutory footing by the Supply of Goods (Implied Terms) Act 1973. When we consider consumer credit we shall note that various aspects of the credit element of hire–purchase transactions were covered by the Hire–Purchase Acts of 1938 and, particularly, of 1964. This regulation by form caused some creditors to chose other less well regulated forms of credit provision before the Consumer Credit Act 1974 provided a comprehensive regime for regulating consumer credit based on the substance and not the form of the transaction.

3.2.3 Barter or Exchange

An important requirement for there to be a sale of goods is a money consideration. Where instead goods are transferred for other goods, there is a contract of barter and exchange.[21] Part 1 of the Supply of Goods and Services Act 1982 implies terms regarding title, description, quality and fitness into contracts 'for the transfer of goods'. This covers contracts under which a person agrees to transfer the property in goods other than excepted contracts.[22] Excepted contracts include (1) those covered by similar legislation (such as sale, hire–purchase and trading stamps[23]), (2) transfers made by deed, without any consideration other than the presumed consideration imported by the deed, and (3) contracts involving mortgages, pledges, charges or other security.[24]

Esso Petroleum Ltd v Commissioners of Customs and Excise[25] involved a promotion in which coins bearing likenesses of the 1970 English football World Cup squad were given away with every four gallons of petrol. In a case brought by the Customs and Excise to determine whether purchase tax was payable on the coins, the House of Lords held that the coins were not supplied under a contract for the sale of goods since the consideration was not money but the collateral contract of buying the petrol. Professor Atiyah has argued that this was a wrong interpretation because the four gallons of petrol had to be paid for by mean of a cash consideration.[26] Much of the significance of this distinction has now been removed by the enactment of the

---

21   Of course money is sometimes transferred, not for its value as a unit of currency, but for its own collector's value, in which case it could form the basis of a contract of exchange; see *Moss v Hancock* [1899] 2 QB 111.
22   S.1(1), Supply of Goods and Services Act 1982.
23   See Trading Stamps Act 1964.
24   S.1(2), Supply of Goods and Services Act 1982.
25   [1976] 1 All ER 117.
26   P.S. Atiyah, (1976) 39 *MLR* 335.

Supply of Goods and Services Act 1982, but it remains significant because some differences persist, for instance the question of when property passes.

The time of property passing was the crucial issue in the Irish case of *Flynn v Mackin and Mahon*,[27] which raised the interesting question of whether a part–exchange deal was a sale or barter. This involved the purchase of a new car for the buyer's old car and £250. The transaction was held to be one of barter, but it seemed clear that if the parties had fixed a price for the old car then it would have been a sale. In *Aldridge v Johnson*[28] a transfer of barley for bullocks with money covering the difference was held to be a sale as a money value had been given to them. *Bull v Parker*[29] involved the exchange of new riding equipment for old and £2; here no value had been fixed, but the court accepted the value of the new equipment as being £4. If a sale can be found where either the parties have fixed a value on the goods or the value can be readily ascertained, then most consumer part–exchanges will be sales since the price of new consumer durables are fairly standard and the value of the exchanged item can be assumed to be the price of the new item minus the cash element.[30] However, it may be possible to see the part–exchange deal as involving two contracts: a sale of the new goods and an exchange of the part-exchanged goods.

3.2.4 Work and Materials

Whenever goods are supplied, one is in a sense paying for both the raw materials and the skill of the designer and manufacturers of the finished product. In some instances, however, the skill element becomes dominant so that, as was said in *Watson v Buckley Osborne & Co*, the contract 'is really half the rendering of services and in a sense, half the supply of goods'.[31] That case involved a hairdresser applying hair–dye, with the consequence that strict liability for merchantable quality was applied to the goods element. The test seems to be whether the court considers the substance of the contract to be the production of something to be sold (a contract for the sale of goods) or whether the skill and labour are the substance of the contract and the passing of the article is ancillary (a contract for work and materials).

---

27   [1974] IR 101: see C. Canton, (1976) 39 *MLR* 589.
28   (1857) 7 E&B 883.
29   (1842) 2 Dowling N.S. 345.
30   Cf. s.73, Consumer Credit Act 1974 which provides, that where a credit contract is cancelled and goods have been taken in part-exchange, then they should be returned or a part-exchange allowance paid equal to the sum agreed or, failing that, such sum as it would have been reasonable to allow in respect of the part-exchanged goods.
31   [1940] 1 All ER 174 at 180.

Thus contracts to supply a meal[32] and false teeth[33] have been held to be contracts of sale, whilst contracts to paint a picture[34] and print a book[35] have been held to be contracts for work and materials. These tests are of course somewhat arbitrary. The practical consequences of the classification have been much reduced of late, although the distinction retains some residual relevance. Also it should be mentioned that the courts have become more flexible and no longer require that a contract should categorically be classified under one heading or the other. Thus in *Hyundai Heavy Industries Ltd v Papadopoulos*[36] a contract to build a ship was held to be a contract of sale, but it was recognised that it also had some of the characteristics of a building contract.

Again the significance of the distinction between contracts for the sale of goods and other contracts has decreased. The Law Reform (Enforcement of Contracts) Act 1954 removed the requirement that contracts for the sale of goods valued at £10 or more had to be evidenced in writing. Also the implied terms in sale of goods contracts have been extended to the goods element of a contract for work and materials, first by case law[37] and then by statute in the Supply of Goods and Services Act 1982. However the distinction is still relevant in determining the consumer's right to reject goods and terminate the contract, in determining the time when property passes and possibly also in the recovery of advance payments by a consumer who defaults.[38] In a

---

32 *Lockett v A and M Charles Ltd* [1938] 4 All ER 170.

33 *Lee v Griffin* (1861) 1 B & S 272. In this case the Court in fact adopted a different approach. Rather than look at the relative importance of the work and materials element, it considered that all contracts should be viewed as contracts of sale where the purpose is to transfer goods to a consumer which he or she did not previously own. Benjamin's *Sale of Goods* (Sweet & Maxwell, 1992) states at p. 41 that 'It has yet to be appreciated that a decision of this problem can be reached only by adopting one or the other of these equally arbitrary rules'. He then goes on to cite *Deta Nominees Pty Ltd v Viscount Plastic Products Pty Ltd* [1979] V. R. 167, where the Supreme Court of Victoria preferred the approach in *Lee v Griffin* in holding plastic moulding dies made to the customer's specification to be a sale of goods contract.

34 *Robinson v Graves* [1935] 1 KB 579.

35 *Clay v Yates* (1856) 1 H & N 73.

36 [1980] 2 All ER 29.

37 See notably *Young & Marten Ltd v McManus Childs Ltd* [1969] 1 AC 454.

38 These are recoverable in sale of goods contracts, subject to any counterclaim for damages: *Dies v British International Mining etc. Corp.* [1939] 1 KB 724. This was distinguished in *Hyundai Heavy Industries v Papadopoulos* [1980] 2 All ER 29 on the basis that the contract was to manufacture and sell. Since then the Court of Appeal has made a more appropriate distinction on the basis that in *Dies* there was a total failure of consideration, which was not the case in *Hyundai*: see *Royal*

contract for work and materials the goods element is governed by Part I and the service element by Part II, Supply of Goods and Services Act 1982.

3.2.5 Hire

S.6(1), Supply of Goods and Services Act 1982 provides that 'a contract for the hire of goods' means a contract under which one person bails or agrees to bail goods to another by way of hire, other than an excepted contract'. Consumers may sometimes prefer to hire than to buy for several reasons. Generally the repairing obligation under a hire contract remains with the owner. Thus when televisions were first marketed and were less reliable in their performance than their modern counterparts, many consumers preferred to hire and leave the repairing obligation on the rental company. This is a less common reason for renting nowadays, not only because of improved product standards, but also because firms prefer to sell goods and then offer insurance cover against breakdown. These insurance policies also raise important consumer protection issues, with reports that some stores push their own policies rather than the cheaper cover offered by some manufacturers.[39] Renting is also useful when goods are rapidly developing in sophistication. Renters usually have far greater flexibility in upgrading to a newer model than do owners. Also renting may be a cheaper option for a consumer than buying, especially where the goods are only wanted for a short period. This perhaps explains why television rental continues to be popular amongst students! Of course hirers of goods have the same interest as buyers in the quality of goods and Part I, Supply of Goods and Services Act 1982 implies similar terms to those provided for under the Sale of Goods Act 1979.

3.2.6 Service

Too frequently consumer lawyers concentrate on sale of goods law and neglect the large amount of consumer contracts which concern services. Some of these relate to the consumer's health and safety and are therefore of vital importance, although medical negligence has expanded to such an extent that it has now become a topic in its own right. Other service contracts

---

International Ltd v Cannon Film Sales Ltd [1989] 3 All ER 423. See J. Beatson, 'Discharge for Breach: The Position of Instalments, Deposits and Other Payments due before Completion' (1981) 97 *LQR* 389.

39 See Office of Fair Trading Report, *Extended Warranties on Electrical Goods*, (OFT, 1994).

are vital to the consumer's economic interest, such as insurance and banking law. It is important to note that the financial services sectors have often managed to exempt themselves from general consumer protection measures. Again these are areas which merit book–length consideration in their own right. There remain, however, a large number of mainstream consumer service contracts covering, for example, hairdressers, car repairers, plumbers, decorators, electricians and gas–fitters. Generally these types of contracts are unregulated, with self–regulatory controls varying in effectiveness from sector to sector. Some, such as estate agents, travel agents and tour operators, have proved especially troublesome and have been subjected to special regulation.[40]

S.12, Supply of Goods and Services Act 1982 defines a 'contract for the supply of a service' as being one under which a supplier agrees to carry out a service. Part II of the Act implies terms into service contracts, though these are generally less demanding than for goods. For instance, a supplier is only under the implied obligation to carry out the service with reasonable care and skill. Contracts of service and apprenticeships are excluded, but a contract is a contract for the supply of a service, whether or not it also relates to the transfer, bailment or hire of goods. As noted, the goods element is covered by Part I, Supply of Goods and Services Act 1982.

3.3 TOPICS COVERED

We have already noted that we cannot deal with the background private law rules in any detail. Instead we will concentrate on the statutory interventions to protect consumers which have become significant features on the consumer law landscape over the last three decades. Even here, we have had to be selective. We have chosen to look in Chapter 4 at issues of quality, in Chapter 5 at questions surrounding the passing of title and who carries the risk, in Chapter 6 at liability for dangerous goods and services, in Chapter 7 at consumer credit and in Chapter 8 at the rules governing doorstep and distant selling. We have already noted that we do not have space to cover the special rules on mistake and frustration contained in the Sale of Goods Act 1979. Other notable omissions are the rules on when goods should be delivered and on how the price of goods should be calculated absent express agreement. Suffice it to note that the thrust of the statutory rules indicate that, in default of agreement between the parties, goods should be delivered

---

[40] Estate Agents Act 1979 and Package Travel, Package Holidays and Package Tours Regulations, S.I. 1992/3288.

or services performed within a reasonable period of time,[41] and that the buyer must pay a reasonable price.[42]

3.4 DEBATES ON PRIVATE LAW AS A TECHNIQUE OF CONSUMER PROTECTION

When considering chapters 4–8 the reader should continually be reflecting on the themes raised in Chapter 1. It may also be useful to preface these chapters with some further comments about the usefulness (or otherwise) of private law as a technique for protecting consumers. On the whole we tend to be sceptical of the value of private law remedies, at least without procedural reforms to make it easier for consumers to enforce rights. There is a real danger of symbolism without substance. Thus one set of questions which should be asked is whether the objectives being sought are best achieved through private law. For instance, is the quality and safety of goods most likely to be improved through implied terms requiring goods to be of satisfactory quality and imposing liability for defective products? Or would quality and safety be enhanced more effectively through the greater regulation of product standards?

Of course, private law remains essential if the concern is to compensate the individual, rather than the improvement of the position of consumers in general. Consumer groups actively seek to improve consumer private law rights and have had a number of major successes: the introduction of strict liability for products, the replacement of the implied term of merchantable quality with one of satisfactory quality and the establishment of cooling off periods in consumer credit and doorstep contracts. The debate is not so much between private law and public law techniques, but rather about the best way of integrating the two.

So far as private law is concerned, the debates centre on how far economic relationships can and should be reordered by giving consumers minimum contractual rights and inalienable tort rights. In other words to what extent freedom of contract can be restricted to further the goal of social justice, although we would argue that, given the structure of markets, the concept of freedom of choice by consumers is somewhat illusory in many instances. Businesses will inevitably react to the legal framework, possibly by raising prices, possibly by withdrawing from markets. The trick is to get the right balance so that, overall, consumers benefit more from the legal controls than they suffer from reduced choice. Clearly poorer consumers are the most vulnerable to reduced choice as they cannot afford to meet increased

---

41 See, s.29(4), Sale of Goods Act 1979, s.14, Supply of Goods and Services Act 1982.
42 See, s.8(2), Sale of Goods Act 1979, s.15, Supply of Goods and Services Act 1982.

costs, but the question is whether the costs of poor quality goods and services are not even greater.

Most people have their own views on the extent to which the law should protect consumers. As noted in Chapter 1, deregulation is currently in vogue. The truth is that there is remarkably little empirical evidence on the cost of consumer laws. This is particularly so with regard to private law, where the supplier does not usually have direct costs imposed on him (except the occasional requirement to use a prescribed form of contract). Rather the costs of private law regulation are indirect in the sense of meeting damage claims or changing procedures to prevent such claims arising.

4 The Quality of Goods and Services

4.1 IMPLIED TERMS

The Sale of Goods Act 1979 (and analogous legislation covering other supply contracts) imply terms governing the quality of goods supplied.[1] These conditions require that goods correspond with their description, are fit for their purpose and are of satisfactory (formerly merchantable) quality.[2] There is strict liability for breach of these terms; in other words, a seller cannot claim that it was not his or her fault that the term was breached or even that it was impossible for him to prevent the term being breached.[3] This strict liability in relation to the quality of goods should be contrasted with the position in relation to services, where suppliers are only required to carry out the service with reasonable skill and care.[4] These terms are conditions, meaning that breach of them, even to a minor extent, gives the buyer the right to reject the goods and/or claim damages, although restrictions have recently been placed on the non–consumer buyer's right to reject.[5]

4.1.1 Correspondence with Description[6]

In comparison with the implied terms, which mandate minimum quality standards, the requirement that goods comply with their description might

---

1   Reference will be made mainly to sale contracts in the following text, but also where appropriate to corresponding provisions in other statutes. For a discussion of which Acts correspond to which transactions, see Chapter 3. At several points in this chapter we will refer to the recent amendments made by the Sale and Supply of Goods Act 1994.

2   There are also terms implied relating to sale by sample, but we will not consider these save to note the general principle that goods must correspond with both their description and any sample; see, for instance, s.15, Sale of Goods Act 1979. In the consumer context this may be relevant, for instance, in the sale of carpets.

3   *Frost v Aylesbury Dairy Co* [1905] 1 KB 608.

4   S.13, Supply of Goods and Services Act 1982.

5   See 4.1.5.

6   S.13, Sale of Goods Act 1979; ss.3 and 8, Supply of Goods and Services Act 1982; s.9 Supply of Goods (Implied Terms) Act 1973.

appear rather weak. It can, however, be an important source of consumer protection since it is implied in all sales contracts, not merely those where the sale is in the course of a business: in the latter case, only the quality conditions are implied. Also it can apply where the goods fail to conform to the description, even if they are of proper quality and perform the task expected of them. For instance, it would provide redress where a suit described as being 'all wool' is partly synthetic. The description condition can also relate to the quality of goods supplied. Thus an aspect of quality can be made an element of the description itself; the presence of extraneous material may then breach the description condition.[7] In addition, whether goods are fit for their usual purposes may help decide whether they comply with their description.[8]

S.13(1) makes the implication of the term that goods comply with their description dependent on there being a 'contract for the sale of goods by description'. Where the contract concerns future or unascertained goods, it will always be one by description. However, it is more problematic to apply this to contracts of specific goods (ie where the contract relates to particular goods, not goods of a particular kind). Case law originally gave a liberal interpretation to this phrase, as shown by Lord Wright in *Grant v Australian Knitting Mills*[9] stating:

> 'there is a sale by description even though the buyer is buying something displayed before him on the counter: a thing is sold by description, though it is specific, so long as it is sold not merely as a specific thing, but as a thing corresponding to a description'.

This generous interpretation was probably given because, at that time, there had to be a sale by description for the merchantable quality condition (as it then was) to be implied. This is no longer the case, but case law has been confirmed by s.13(3), Sale of Goods Act 1979 which provides 'a sale of

---

7   In *Pinnock Bros v Lewis and Peat Ltd* [1923] 1 KB 690, copra cake was not held to be properly so described because of the presence of castor beans; but cf *Ashington Piggeries v Christopher Hill* [1972] AC 441 where the House of Lords found that herring meal was properly so described despite the presence of dimethylnitrosamine which rendered it unfit for use as mink food.

8   Thus Davies LJ in the Court of Appeal in *Christopher Hill v Ashington Piggeries* [1969] 3 All ER 1496 gave the example of oysters which he suggested may not properly be described as such if they were not fit for human consumption. Similarly in *Toepfer v Continental Grain Co* [1974] Lloyd LR 11 the example of 'new–laid eggs' was used to show that a description of goods can include a statement of their quality.

9   [1936] AC 85 at 100.

goods is not prevented from being a sale by description by reason only that, the goods being exposed for sale or hire, are selected by the buyer'. This is of course the position with regard to supermarket purchases.

S.13 might be considered remarkable for it appears to state that express terms of the contract will also be implied terms. The danger is that too many representations about the product are elevated to the status of terms in reliance on s.13, so that the distinction between contractual terms and representations is obliterated.[10] This is especially dangerous as some of the decisions, although admittedly in commercial contexts, have found the condition breached and rejection possible for very minor breaches of description.[11] The modern approach is to limit the elements of the description covered by the implied condition, with other aspects of the description being treated as warranties or innominate terms. Thus Lord Diplock in *Ashington Piggeries v Christopher Hill*[12] stated:

> 'The description by which unascertained goods are sold is.... confined to those words in the contract which were intended by the parties to identify the kinds of goods supplied.'

More recently, in *Harlingdon & Leinster Enterprises v Christopher Hull Fine Art*,[13] this trend was reinforced when it was said that there could be no sale by description unless that description was so influential as to become an essential term of the contract.

4.1.2 Quality Conditions – Some Common Features

The common law principle of *caveat emptor* (buyer beware) is still to be found in the Sale of Goods Act 1979, 14(1) providing that:

> 'Except as provided by this section and section 15 below and subject to any other enactment, there is no implied term about the quality or fitness for any particular purpose of goods supplied under a contract of sale.'

---

10 See *Beale v Taylor* [1967] 1 WLR 1193.

11 *Arcos Ltd v Ronaasen & Son* [1933] AC 470 (order of half–inch thick staves to make cement barrels was rejected as only 5 per cent met specification although nearly all the rest were good to within one tenth of an inch); *Re Moore & Co and Landauer & Co Ltd* [1921] 2 KB 519 (involved the delivery of the correct number of tins of canned fruit (3000); but rejection allowed as half the cases contained 24 instead of the prescribed 30 tins, despite an arbitrator's finding that the value was unaffected).

12 [1972] AC 441 at 503.

13 [1990] 1 All ER 737.

However, this basic statement of the *caveat emptor* principle has in modern times been highly qualified by the existence of implied terms relating to the fitness and quality of goods.[14] The Sale of Goods Act 1893, which codified the common law, implied conditions of merchantable quality and fitness for purpose. Before examining the particular features of these two implied quality conditions certain features common to both terms will be considered.

4.1.2.1 Limitation to Business Activity

In the 1893 Act the merchantable quality condition was made contingent on the seller dealing in goods of that description, whilst the fitness for purpose condition was implied into contracts where the goods were of a description which it was in the course of the seller's business to supply. These provisions could have been quite narrowly interpreted to exclude sales which were not part of the essential functions of the business, for example sales by a car dealer who sold cuddly toys as a special promotion. The Supply of Goods (Implied Terms) Act 1973 implemented the recommendations of the Law Commission[15] so that the quality conditions were implied wherever there was a sale 'in the course of a business'. This would seem to catch a broader category of transactions, but is still rather vague. The only assistance to interpretation given in the Act is that business includes 'a profession and the activities of any government department (including a Northern Ireland department) or local or public authority'[16] It remains a matter of speculation whether charities are to be treated as businesses, although one suspects that when charities operate on a commercial basis the provisions would apply to them. It is also uncertain whether the provisions catch the 'amateur entrepreneur', for example, someone who makes jewellery and sells it at car boot sales to supplement their normal income.

There is a danger that if the narrow interpretation given by courts in other contexts to the phrase 'in the course of a business' is applied to sale of goods legislation then the position could be similar to that prior to the 1973 amendments. Some sales of goods by businesses might not attract the protection of the implied terms if they do not form an essential element of the business. This narrow interpretation is present in trade description and unfair contract terms legislation, where the courts have only held sales to be in the course of a business if they were an integral part of the business.[17] In those

---

14   See 1.3.7.
15   Law Com 24 and Scot Law Com 12, *Exemption Clauses in Contracts First Report: Amendments to the Sale of Goods Act 1893* (1969).
16   S.61, Sale of Goods Act 1979.
17   See Chapters 9 and 10.

contexts, such an interpretation may have policy justifications – namely not imposing criminal liability for false trade descriptions on private individuals, and extending the absolute ban on the use of certain exclusion clauses to small businesses when making purchases not connected with their own trade or profession. A similar narrow interpretation in the present context would pose a serious threat to consumer protection. Such a step appears unlikely, however, given the view of Lord Wilberforce in *Ashington Piggeries v Christopher Hill*[18] when he said:

> 'I cannot comprehend the rationale of holding that the subsections do not apply if the seller is dealing in the particular goods for the first time... what the Act had in mind was something quite simple and rational: to limit the implied conditions of fitness or quality to persons in the way of business as distinct from private persons'.

4.1.2.2 *'Goods Supplied'*

The implied terms of fitness for purpose and satisfactory quality relate to goods supplied under the contract. The phrase 'goods supplied' has been interpreted widely to include (i) extraneous goods supplied with the goods contracted for, such as the detonator which was included in the supply of coalite in *Wilson v Rickett Cockerell & Co Ltd*,[19] and also (ii) the packaging and containers in which goods are supplied, like the returnable mineral water bottle in *Geddling v Marsh*.[20]

4.1.3 Satisfactory Quality

The implied term that goods comply with their description and the term requiring goods to be fit for a purpose made known by the buyer to the seller (considered below at 4.1.4) are relatively uncontroversial. Everyone can agree that goods should be as described and fit for their purpose, especially where it is clear that the sellers know of the purpose and that their skill or judgment is being relied upon by the buyer. It is more difficult to agree what general standard should be expected of all goods.

---

[18]   [1972] AC 441 at 494.
[19]   [1954] 1 QB 598.
[20]   [1920] 1 KB 688.

Imposing mandatory standards regulating the quality of goods[21] can be criticised as infringing the consumer's freedom to bargain for a reduced price in return for a reduced quality product, or at least an assumption of responsibility for any defects which occur.[22] However, the law has long recognised the desirability of imposing such a right to minimum quality. The common law implied a term that goods should be of 'merchantable quality' and this was codified in the Sale of Goods Act 1893. Merchantable quality was also to be found in the Sale of Goods Act 1979 and analogous legislation for other supply contracts, before the Sale and Supply of Goods Act 1994 reformed the implied term to one of 'satisfactory quality'.

So long as the term was implied only to the extent that the parties had not excluded or modified it, it could be said not to infringe the doctrine of freedom of contract. It could be taken as reflecting the minimum quality condition which would have applied had the parties been forced to agree a term acceptable to both. However, since 1973 the term has been non–excludable in consumer contracts.[23] It cannot be denied that freedom of contract has been restricted, but such restrictions are justified since a seller who supplies goods without basic assurances as to their quality can be assumed to be exploiting the consumer's weak bargaining position or vulnerability, since no right–thinking person would buy goods without such a minimum assurance.[24]

The imposition of this standard ought not to mean that poor consumers will be unable to purchase some goods due to the high minimum standards pricing them out of their range, since price is a relevant factor in determining the appropriate standard. Rather it prevents poor consumers (and others) making bargains which worsen their position. When one agrees the price for goods, it must be assumed that one has certain expectations about their quality which are reflected in the price paid. If the goods fail to reach those minimum standards, then the bargain will unfairly reduce the wealth of the consumer who would have paid too much for the product in terms of the bargain he or she believed they had struck.

A distinction should be drawn between the legally prescribed minimum standards and the higher standards which may be guaranteed, usually by the manufacturer, in separate commercial guarantees, offered as additional protection to that provided by the law. However, statements made in order to promote a product may also be relevant in raising the required legal

---

21   A distinction can perhaps be drawn between quality matters and safety matters; see the discussion of product liability in Chapter 6.

22   Cf 1.5.1 and 1.9.1.

23   See now s.6, Unfair Contract Terms Act 1977: discussed in Chapter 9.

24   See discussion below at 4.2.1.

minimum quality expected of it, if they cause the consumer to expect higher quality.

4.1.3.1 From Merchantable to Satisfactory Quality

The 'merchantable quality' definition was criticised for being unsuitable for consumer transactions since it was based on whether the goods were saleable; goods might still be saleable even if they did not meet consumer expectations. It was also argued that the term simply did not make sense to the general public and, as interpreted, had come to concentrate too heavily on the functional aspects of goods.[25] The sting of some of the criticisms had perhaps already been removed by a number of more pro–consumer interpretations of the term 'merchantable quality', notably in *Rogers v Parish (Scarborough) Ltd*[26] where the court took notice of the consumer's interest in not having a car which merely functioned, but also met his other legitimate expectations concerning its appearance. However, the factors which consumers frequently complain about – such as minor defects, aesthetic flaws and lack of durability – were still only implicit in the definition. The major advantage of the 1994 reforms may prove to be, not the switch from merchantable to satisfactory quality, but rather the clarification of the relevant factors to be taken into account in determining whether that standard has been breached.

In its 1987 *Sale and Supply of Goods*[27] report, the Law Commission considered the merchantable quality condition should be replaced by a new term having two elements: the first part would set out the basic principle; the second would list specific aspects of quality. Three standards were canvassed for the first element (i) a qualitative standard (such as, 'good quality'), (ii) a neutral standard (for instance, 'proper quality') or (ii) a 'full acceptability' standard. In opting for a full acceptability standard, the Law Commission recognised that it was moving away from both the usability test (as laid down by Lord Reid in *Kendall v Lillico*) and the prevailing statutory definition, in favour of the approach of Dixon J in *Australian Knitting Mills v Grant* (these are considered below at 4.1.3.2). Regarding the list of specific aspects of quality, the Law Commission wanted to include fitness for purpose, but to give it less prominence and to include other relevant aspects such as appearance and finish, freedom from minor defects, safety and durability.

---

[25]   See Law Com 160, Scot Law Com 104, *Sale and Supply of Goods*, (1987) at para. 2.9.

[26]   [1987] 2 All ER 232 : see 4.1.3.3 at (iv).

[27]   Law Com 160, Scot Law Com 104 *op. cit.*, at 3.1–3.61.

Reforms along the lines proposed by the Law Commission form the basis of the amendments made by the Sale and Supply of Goods Act 1994[28] to the Sale of Goods Act 1979 and analogous legislation; subject to one significant alteration. The Department of Trade and Industry preferred to use the term 'satisfactory' rather than 'acceptable' quality. 'Satisfactory quality' was considered to be more demanding and favourable to the consumer, It also avoided any possible ambiguity arising from 'acceptable' being used to define the quality demanded and 'acceptance' also being used to determine when the right to reject was lost.[29]

It is hard to assess the significance of the change in terminology. It must be hoped that the courts appreciate that this change is intended to underpin moves to increase consumer protection but, until case law is built up, no one can be sure. Indeed, one of the arguments against change is that the consumer will suffer from uncertainty as the new rules are litigated. Many of those critical of the change also suggest that the law had already developed in the consumer's favour to the position where, in practice, the new rules will have no appreciable impact on the level of protection afforded. A distinction might be drawn here between the law in books and the law in practice. Most consumer complaints get nowhere near the appellate courts, or even the county courts, but rather are settled over the shop counter or by exchange of letters. At this level, even if consumers were aware of their right to have goods of merchantable quality, they might not have been able to comprehend the level of quality that referred to, or might have been easily wrong footed by sellers who put forward their own favourable interpretation of the law. The same possibility exists under the amended law, but consumers may feel more confident that their view of what constitutes 'satisfactory quality' is just as valid as that of the seller.

The problem is that satisfactory is a vague term; more like the qualitative standard which the Law Commission rejected; nevertheless the Law Commission talked about goods having to be of 'good' or 'sound quality' which seems more demanding than merely having to be 'satisfactory'. Satisfactory goods might mean those of quite a good quality; on the other hand the adjective might be applied to goods which only just make the grade. For these reasons it is hard to say whether satisfactory is a more demanding standard than acceptable. On the one hand it could be argued that no one would accept goods which were not satisfactory; on the other hand, consumers do sometimes accept goods they are not satisfied with, or at least not entirely satisfied with.

---

28 On this see G. Howells, *Consumer Contract Legislation – The New Law*, (Blackstone, 1995) Ch. 2.

29 See 4.1.5.2.

The new term refers to goods which a reasonable person would regard as satisfactory. A criticism of the old definition of merchantable quality had been that, by only requiring goods to be as fit 'as it is reasonable to expect', the standard 'expected' could be decreased as quality standards declined and consumers came to expect faults in goods.[30] This reading may have been pessimistic, for whilst one may have differing expectations of the performance of goods, generally one could reasonably expect goods to be produced to the correct specification, so that sellers would, at least, be liable for manufacturing defects. By referring to the objective standard of the reasonable person and by removing the reference to expectation, the new definition should remove any such doubts.

4.1.3.2 Relevance of Cases on Merchantable Quality

Before considering the new term of satisfactory quality in some detail, it is necessary to consider whether the old cases on merchantable quality retain any value. Commercial lawyers who have mastered the nuances of the intricate case law in this area appear reluctant to disregard it, so that the old case law is likely to be used by way of analogy. A good example of this desire to hang on to the past is the way in which the courts treated the 1973 amendment, which defined merchantable quality, and became s.14(6), Sale of Goods Act 1979. Prior to this the case law had shown two trends: one favoured a definition of merchantable quality based on 'acceptability' the other on 'usability'. However, it is fair to say that the two approaches overlapped and that some judges approved both approaches, failing to realise that they were based on different foundations. Representative of the 'acceptability' approach is the dicta of Dixon J in the High Court of Australia in *Australian Knitting Mills Ltd v Grant*[31] where he stated that goods:

> 'should be in such an actual state that a buyer fully acquainted with the facts and, therefore, knowing what hidden defects exist and not being limited to their apparent condition would buy them without abatement of the price obtainable for such goods if in reasonably sound order and condition and without special terms.'

The alternative 'usability' approach is encapsulated in Lord Reid's view expressed in *Kendall v Lillico & Sons Ltd*[32] that lack of merchantable quality meant:

---

30 See Law Com 160, Scot Law Com 104, *op. cit.*, at para 2.11.
31 (1933) 50 CLR 387 at 418.
32 [1969] 2 AC 31 at 77.

'that the goods in the form in which they were tendered were of no use for any purpose for which goods which complied with the description under which these goods were sold would normally be used, and hence were not saleable under that description.'

The usability standard came to be viewed as most suitable in the business context, whilst the acceptability test was viewed as more consumer friendly, which is perhaps ironic as the latter derived from dicta concerned with the saleability of goods and hence reflected the mercantile ancestry of the term. Back in 1969 the Law Commission had proposed a statutory definition of merchantable quality based on the concept of acceptability[33] but this was criticised, resulting in the definition introduced in 1973 being weighted towards the usability approach. Thus the definition provided that:

'Goods of any kind are of merchantable quality within the meaning of subsection (2) above if they are as fit for the purpose or purposes for which goods of that kind are commonly bought as it is reasonable to expect having regard to any description applied to them, the price (if relevant) and all other relevant circumstances.'

One might have thought that once a statutory definition had been provided the old case law could be discarded. This was indeed the view of Mustill LJ in *Rogers v Parish (Scarborough) Ltd*[34] who rejected the notion that parliamentary draftsmen had simply reproduced 'in more felicitous and economical terms the gist of the speeches and judgments previously delivered'. He further stated that the new definition, being 'clear and free from technicality', should be able to solve the majority of cases without reference to the prior intricate case law. By contrast, Lloyd LJ in *Aswan Engineering v Lupdine*[35] took the view that the statutory definition was 'as accurate a representation of Lord Reid's speech in *Kendall v Lillico* as it is possible to compress into one sentence' and relied on previous case law. It may be harder for judges to interpret the 1994 reforms in this way for it is not a matter of applying a definition to an existing term, but rather of replacing the term with a new term. Thus all the old chestnuts (such as the application of the term to minor defects and durability) will have to be looked at afresh. One suspects that, as the essential question remains the same – what is the minimum standard expected of goods? – judges will still seek to rely on existing case law, although perhaps in a more indirect, inspiration seeking, way than in the past.

---

33   Law Com 24, Scot Law Com 12, *op. cit.,* at para. 43.
34   [1987] 2 All ER 232.
35   [1987] 1 All ER 135.

4.1.3.3 Satisfactory Quality – The New Term

It may be useful to set out the implied term of satisfactory quality found in the amended s.14, Sale of Goods Act 1979:[36]

'(2) Where the seller sells goods in the course of a business, there is an implied term that the goods supplied under the contract are of satisfactory quality.

(2A) For the purposes of this Act, goods are of satisfactory quality if they meet the standard that a reasonable person would regard as satisfactory, taking account of any description of the goods, the price (if relevant) and all the other relevant circumstances.

(2B) For the purposes of this Act, the quality of goods includes their state and condition and the following (among others) are in appropriate cases aspects of the quality of goods:

(a) fitness for all the purposes for which goods of the kind in question are commonly supplied,

(b) appearance and finish,

(c) freedom from minor defects,

(d) safety,

(e) durability.'

Some of the factors are the same as those which applied under the old law (description, price and the state and condition of the goods[37]); some are amended (such as which purposes the goods should relate to), while others make explicit what was probably implicit within the old law (appearance and finish, freedom from minor defects, safety and durability). The description of the goods should always be considered when assessing their satisfactory quality, but the other factors only if relevant or in appropriate cases. These may not be the only relevant factors, but they are the ones which give most cause for debate and so will be considered in more detail. For the reasons discussed above, many cases decided under the old law will be considered because similar factors were raised under the old law. Nevertheless, great care should be taken when drawing any conclusions from the old case law since the courts were applying these factors against a different standard – 'merchantable' rather than 'satisfactory' quality.

---

36 Cf ss.4(2),9(2), Supply of Goods and Services Act 1982, and s.10(2), Supply of Goods (Implied Terms) Act 1973.

37 State and condition were also previously considered as aspects of quality, but had not previously been stated as part of the definition of merchantable quality. They were located in s.61,(1) Sale of Goods Act 1979.

(i) Description

The description is clearly relevant in assessing what would amount to satisfactory quality. If goods were described as 'shop–soiled' or second–hand, they would still have to be of satisfactory quality, but the consumer would be expected to put up with some defects which would not be satisfactory if found in perfect new goods.[38] The purposes for which goods are used also interrelates with the description applied to them. Compare mahogany wood and chipboard. The purchaser of chipboard could not complain because it was unsuitable for making a dining room suite, whereas the purchaser of high grade mahogany would rightly by dissatisfied if the wood was not of sufficient quality to be used to make furniture.

The inclusion of description as a factor relevant to the assessment of satisfactory quality leads to the possibility that some aspects of the product's description, which are not sufficiently central to be included within the description for the purposes of s.13, might nevertheless lead to liability for lack of satisfactory quality. In *Harlingdon Ltd & Leinster Enterprises v Christopher Hull Fine Art Ltd*,[39] Slade LJ was keen not to allow plaintiffs in at the back door (through s.14) when the front door (s.13) was closed to them. That case involved a sale between art dealers of a painting which was attributed erroneously to 'Münter'. The reason for not extending liability to such cases is clearly expressed by Nourse LJ who took the view that, because art dealers accepted that the attribution of paintings was an imprecise science, the principle *caveat emptor* should rule; this was especially so as the plaintiffs were in fact experts in German expressionists whilst the defendants were not. That reasoning can be criticised since the satisfactory quality term is implied, even if there was no reliance on the part of the buyer. The dissenting opinion of Stuart–Smith LJ that the merchantable quality term was breached by the description may well prove to be the view which holds sway in the consumer context. It is noteworthy that he applied the words of Mustill LJ in *Rogers v Parish (Scarborough) Ltd*[40] who said 'the description "Range Rover" would conjure up a particular set of expectations'.

---

[38] Cf *Bartlett v Sidney Marcus* [1965] 2 All 753 (buyer of a second hand car, which was usable, could not complain about a defect in the clutch, even if it was more serious than had been thought by the parties at the time of sale).

[39] [1990] 1 ALL ER 737.

[40] [1987] 2 All ER 232.

(ii) Price

The role of price is quite complex, though it should be noted that the statute requires it to be taken into account only *if relevant*. Clearly the fact that goods are reduced in price or are in a sale should not lead one to expect lower quality. Equally, the fact goods are cheap does not excuse their shoddiness. On the other hand, what is satisfactory for economy goods may well be unsatisfactory for superior goods. In other words the issue of price should generally serve to raise expectations above those generally held about that type of product, but should not reduce them. If a seller wants to reduce his liability in return for supplying a product of lower quality, he should do so by adding a description such as 'damaged goods' or 'shop–soiled'. In other words, the price mechanism should not be used a medium for conveying messages about defects in the product quality, as the consumer may fail to appreciate these; however, price can be used to convey messages about superior quality. The consumer who finds cheap goods may consider him or herself fortunate to have discovered good quality goods at bargain prices; those who pay for top quality goods expect something above the ordinary. Thus in *Rogers v Parish (Scarborough) Ltd*[41] Mustill LJ said of a Range Rover: 'The factor of price was also significant. At more than £16,000 this vehicle was, if not at the top end of the scale, well above the level of an ordinary family saloon. The buyer was entitled to value for his money.' Similarly in *Shine v General Guarantee Corp*,[42] a case involving a second hand Fiat X–19, Bush J considered it relevant that the buyer had thought he was purchasing an enthusiast's car, of the mileage shown, at the sort of price cars of that age and condition could expect to fetch. In fact he was buying a car which had been submerged in water for 24 hours, an insurance write–off, which 'no member of the public, knowing the facts, would touch with a barge pole unless they could get a substantially reduced price to reflect the risk they were taking.'

(iii) Fitness for Purpose

Whereas the fitness for purpose term covers specific, perhaps unusual purposes, which the buyer has made the seller aware of, by contrast the satisfactory quality term covers fitness for all the purposes for which goods of the kind in question are commonly supplied. This is an improvement on previous interpretations of the law and follows the Law Commission's recommendations. There had been debate over whether, to be merchantable,

---

41 [1987] 2 All ER 232.
42 [1988] 1 All ER 911.

goods had to be fit for all their common purposes or whether it was sufficient that they were fit for one purpose. The statutory definition had referred to goods having to be 'fit for the *purpose or purposes* for which goods of that kind are commonly bought'. One might have been forgiven for thinking that the reference to purposes in the plural meant that goods had to be fit for all their common purposes. However, in *Aswan Engineering v Lupdine*[43] it was held that goods only had to be fit for one purpose; references to purposes in the plural was to cover goods of high quality which are expected to be fit for purposes over and above those of lower quality goods.

Whatever the rights and wrongs of the position under the old law, that has now changed. What may have been appropriate when goods simply had to be merchantable (and goods fit for *a* purpose would certainly find a buyer) does not necessarily apply when they have to be satisfactory. This may be one area where the change of terminology bites – but note it is a change in terminology supported by a change in the list of relevant factors. Nothing necessarily hangs on the change from merchantable to satisfactory quality. It may still be the case that, on the facts of *Aswan*, the goods would be found to be of satisfactory quality, since they only have to be fit for the purposes for which the goods are *commonly* supplied. *Aswan* involved plastic pails which could not stand the extreme Kuwaiti heat; it may still be found, as a matter of fact, that exposure to Kuwaiti heat was not one of the purposes for which the pails were commonly supplied.

(iv) Appearance, Finish and Freedom from Minor Defects

The Law Commission proposed that the new definition of quality should refer to appearance and finish and freedom from minor defects. It also made the point that these were separate elements. Appearance and finish refer to aesthetic aspects; minor defects refer to minor functional elements. The 1994 amendments do list these aspects separately, but it is useful to consider them jointly for they raise similar issues. Part of the problem with including these as aspects of quality is that, if the goods are found to have breached the implied term, then the potential remedy of rejection of the goods and repudiation of the contract may appear too severe. This may explain why in the past courts have not found minor defects to render goods unmerchantable where the buyer was seeking rejection,[44] which in turn meant that there was no remedy at all for these defects. The prior law had in fact made progress in

---

[43]   [1987] 1 All ER 135.

[44]   See *Millars of Falkirk Ltd v Turpie* 1976 S.L.T. 66, where the complaint involved a leakage from a power steering unit which would cost at most £25 to repair.

recognising these aspects as relevant in determining the quality of goods supplied, Mustill LJ in *Rogers v Parish (Scarborough) Ltd*[45] stating that:

> 'the purpose for which "goods of that kind" are commonly bought....would include in respect of any passenger vehicle not merely the buyer's purpose of driving the car from one place to another but of doing so with the appropriate degree of comfort, ease of handling and reliability and, one might add, of pride in the vehicle's outward and interior appearance.'

The 1994 amendments clarify that appearance and finish and freedom from minor defects are relevant factors, but note that the presence of such a defect will not necessarily render the goods unsatisfactory as they are only to be considered in appropriate cases as part of the overall assessment of the goods' quality. The defect might be so minor as to render it *de minimis*. Thus on the facts of *Millars of Falkirk v Turpie*,[46] a minor defect in a new car, which could cheaply and easily be remedied, might still be found not to render the car unsatisfactory. Equally, a scratch on a kitchen sink might breach the implied term, but a similar scratch on a rain bucket intended for use in the garden might not.

(v) Durability

Like appearance, finish and freedom from minor defects, the question mark over whether durability was a relevant aspect of quality seems to have arisen, not so much from disagreement about the need for goods to be durable, but rather from concern about the remedies which are available should they prove not to be durable. In particular, there was concern not to give a long term right to reject. As we shall see, in sale contracts this risk does not exist since the right to reject is lost after goods have been retained for a reasonable period of time, but it is a possible risk in other contracts where the right to reject is only lost after the buyer has learned of the defect and has affirmed the contract.

There is a theoretical debate as to whether the defect must have been present at the time the goods were delivered or whether there can be liability on the basis that the goods simply did not last as long as they should have done. In practice, if goods wear out too quickly, this will be treated as being due to some defect which must have existed when they were supplied.

The inclusion of durability was a moot point under the previous law, much of the debate actually arising in the context of fitness for purpose and

---

45   [1987] 2 All ER 232 at 237.
46   1976 S.L.T. 66.

whether, to be fit for their purpose, goods had to last for a reasonable time. Nevertheless, the comments have obvious relevance to the debate on satisfactory quality where fitness for purpose is a relevant factor. In *Crowther v Shannon Motors Co*[47] Lord Denning seemed to cast doubt on the judge at first instance's statement that the car had to go for a reasonable time, whereas in *Lambert v Lewis*,[48] Lord Diplock did not doubt that there 'is a continuing warranty that the goods will continue to be fit for that purpose for a reasonable time after delivery.' What a reasonable period of time is of course depends on the nature of the product. Thus the inclusion of durability as a relevant factor removes any uncertainty. It is appropriate to note that there is no obligation in English law for manufacturers and retailers to stock spare parts or provide servicing facilities, although provisions along these lines are found in various codes of practice.

(vi) Safety

It is inconceivable that dangerous goods would be held to be satisfactory, but the inclusion in the statutory list of relevant factors is a useful clarification.

Some more general points can be made about the satisfactory quality term. Like its predecessor, it is independent of any commercial guarantee offered by manufacturers and retailers; thus a defect cannot be disregarded simply because it can be repaired under a commercial guarantee. As Mustill LJ noted in *Rogers v Parish (Scarborough) Ltd*,[49] the commercial guarantee was 'an addition to the buyer's rights, not a subtraction from them, and it may be noted, only a circumscribed addition since it lasts for a limited period and does not compensate the buyer for consequential loss and inconvenience'.

Equally the goods will not fail to be satisfactory if something has to be done to them before use, so long as the buyer can be assumed to know of this requirement. Thus in *Heil v Hedges*,[50] pork chops infected with trichinae were held to be merchantable as they were safe when cooked. In contrast, in *Grant v Australian Knitting Mills Ltd*,[51] underpants with traces of sulphites which caused dermatitis were unmerchantable; although they would have been safe if washed before wearing, one cannot be expected to wash one's underpants before putting them on for the first time! One suspects that goods could be rendered not of satisfactory quality by the instructions supplied with them, although there is no direct authority on this point since the case where

---

[47]　[1975] 1 All ER 139.
[48]　[1981] 1 All ER 1185.
[49]　[1987] 2 All ER 232.
[50]　[1951] 1 TLR 512.
[51]　[1936] AC 85.

the issue was raised restricted its discussion to whether instructions could render goods unfit for a particular purpose.[52]

The satisfactory quality term is implied regardless of whether the buyer relied on the seller's skill and judgment; thus the term is of wider application than the fitness for purpose term. It also applies to latent defects, so long as they were present at the time the goods were delivered. As was graphically stated by Lord Ellenborough in *Gardiner v Gray:*[53] 'The purchaser cannot be supposed to buy goods to lay them on a dunghill'. However, s.14(2)(C), Sale of Goods Act 1979 makes it clear that the satisfactory quality term

> 'does not extend to any matter making the quality of goods unsatisfactory–
> (a) which is specifically drawn to the buyer's attention before the contract is made;
> (b) where the buyer examines the goods before the contract is made, which that examination ought to reveal, or
> (c) in the case of a contract for sale by sample, which would have been apparent on a reasonable examination of the sample.'

The important point to note is that there is no obligation on a consumer to make an inspection. If the consumer chooses to inspect the goods, liability will only be excused for defects which *that* examination ought to have revealed.[54] Thus if the consumer examined the bodywork of the car, this would not prevent the car being held unsatisfactory because of mechanical faults. The effect of any expertise of the consumer on whether defects ought to have been revealed is problematic. If the consumer's expertise allows for a different order of examination then there will be no liability for defects which ought to have been revealed by that examination. If the expert consumer undertakes an examination which would not have revealed a defect to the ordinary consumer, but ought to have revealed it to someone with his or her particular expertise, the position is unclear. Is the standard that of the reasonable average consumer, or is the expertise of the consumer to be taken into account so that what ought to be revealed relates to that particular examination, ie an expert examination?

---

52 Cf *Wormell v RHM Agriculture (East) Ltd* [1987] 3 All ER 75: see 4.1.4.
53 (1815) 4 Camp 144.
54 Note that this was an amendment from the original wording which had referred to *such* rather than *that* examination and had been interpreted to catch a consumer who had only looked at the outside of barrels although he had been offered the opportunity to undertake a more thorough examination; see *Thornett & Fehr v Beers* [1919] 1 KB 486.

A potential trap for the unwary consumer was highlighted by the facts of *R & B Customs Brokers v UDT*[55] This involved the purchase of a car on conditional sale. There was an interlude between the consumer taking possession and the contract being concluded by the finance company signing the agreement. During this time the purchaser became aware that the roof of the car leaked. Did this mean that he was barred from complaining about the defect, given that the relevant date for assessing what examination had been made was the time of contract (not the time the consumer took possession)? In *R & B Custom Brokers Ltd v UDT* the Court of Appeal did not find it necessary to answer this question. However, given the potential consumer detriment from what appears to be the literal reading of the section, it is disappointing that during the recent amendments to the legislation, the opportunity was not taken to clarify the position. The matter is particularly unfair to consumers since when a finance company signs the forms is a factor outside their control; they are only likely to know the contract has been concluded after the event.

4.1.4 Fitness for Purpose

S.14(3), Sale of Goods Act 1979[56] implies a term that goods will be fit for any particular purpose made known by the buyer to the seller:

> 'Where the seller sells goods in the course of a business and the buyer, expressly or by implication, makes known –
> (a) to the seller, or
> (b) where the purchase price or part of it is payable by instalments and the goods were previously sold by a credit–broker to the seller, to that credit–broker, any particular purpose for which goods are being bought, there is an implied condition that the goods supplied under the contract are reasonably fit for that purpose, whether or not that is a purpose for which such goods are commonly supplied, except where the circumstances show that the buyer does not rely on the skill or judgment of the seller or credit–broker.'

Whereas the satisfactory quality condition governs the general expectations of quality, the fitness for purpose condition provides protection for the consumer who has particular demands of the goods which he makes known to the seller and who relies on the seller's skill and judgment to ensure that

---

55 [1988] 1 All ER 847.
56 Cf ss.4(4) and 9(4), Supply of Goods and Services Act 1982 and s.10(3), Supply of Goods (Implied Terms) Act 1973.

the goods possess those qualities. The result of case law and the statutory amendments to the implied condition, which were effected by the Supply of Goods (Implied Terms) Act 1973, have ensured that fitness for purpose does not cover only very specialised particular purposes which were directly brought to the seller's attention, but rather overlaps to a large extent with the satisfactory quality condition.[57] There may be benefit to consumers in this. Judges may be reticent to hold that a product is unsatisfactory, perhaps because they are reluctant to give a wholesale condemnation of it, especially as they may be uncertain as to what standard to expect of various products. By contrast finding a product is unfit for a particular purpose does not require a judgment of the product as a whole, but simply its ability to perform a particular function. In this case the standard expected of the goods (ie the particular purpose to be achieved), has been agreed by the parties and therefore does not need to be imposed by the judge, who simply has to assess whether the purpose can be fulfilled by the goods.

The provision has not been limited to very narrow particular purposes. The particular purpose can be very general, for instance driving a car. Also the condition has been applied to goods with only one purpose: for instance, the hot water bottle in *Priest v Last*.[58] Difficulties sometimes surround the application of the section to situations where the goods are adequate for the general population, but something renders them unfit in relation to a particular purchaser. Generally the seller will not be liable for any particular sensitivities of the purchaser unless they are brought to his attention. This explains why the defendant in *Griffiths v Peter Conway*[59] was not liable when the Harris Tweed coat purchased by the plaintiff caused her to contract dermatitis due to her unusually sensitive skin. In *Manchester Shipping Lines v Rea*,[60] a coal merchant was held to have breached the fitness for purpose condition by supplying coal which was unsuitable for a particular ship. As there is no standard ship, the merchant ought to have checked that the consignment was suitable for that ship. This shows that, while sellers will not be liable for abnormal sensitivities of which they were not aware, they will be liable for supplying goods unsuitable for people with obvious special conditions. For example, a woman who is obviously pregnant should not be given drugs which are dangerous for someone in that condition. In some circumstances where there are different grades of goods, the seller can be expected to make enquiries as to the appropriate product to be supplied. For example, if someone drives to a garage and asks the attendant to fill up their

---

57 This overlap was considered of no moment by the Law Commission: Law Com 160, Scot Law Com 104, *op. cit.* at para. 2.19.

58 [1903] 2 KB 148.

59 [1939] 1 All ER 685.

60 [1922] 2 AC 74.

car, which only runs on unleaded petrol, then leaded petrol would be unfit for the purpose. It does not seem unreasonable to suggest that either the attendant should know the correct grade of petrol for that make of car or should make enquiries of the consumer.

For the fitness for purpose condition to be implied, the buyer must have made known the purpose for which he or she wants the goods. However, this can be made known implicitly by virtue of the circumstances surrounding the transaction. The purchaser must also have relied upon the seller's skill and judgment. However, the courts realise that, in the consumer context, such reliance will seldom be explicit. Rather there will be an implicit expectation 'that the tradesman has selected his stock with skill and judgment.'[61] It is clear from the revised wording of s.14(3) that the burden is clearly on the seller to show that there was no reliance. However, it would still be possible for a seller to argue that it was unreasonable in the circumstances for the buyer to have relied upon him. This might be the case where the seller had refused to vouch for the goods, but had expressed an opinion 'for what it is worth'. Given the restrictions on the use of exclusion clauses, such a possibility would appear desirable, but would not necessarily be immune from attack as an exclusion clause.[62] In any event it should be noted that the buyer will be held to have relied upon the seller's skill and judgment even if the reliance is only partial. Thus if a customer specifies the desired qualities of the goods, but leaves the seller some freedom in the selection of materials, then the fitness for purpose condition is implied.

Where the seller can only supply one particular brand or where the buyer specifically requests a particular brand, it is sometimes suggested that there can be no reliance on the seller's skill and judgment. Thus in *Wren v Holt*,[63] where a customer purchased ale from a tied house, there was considered to be a basis for a finding that he could not have relied upon the seller's skill and judgment. Hopefully a different decision would be reached nowadays, as the burden is clearly on the seller to establish that the buyer did not rely upon him. Where the seller only sells one brand of goods, one may be entitled to expect that he has selected a brand which is fit for its purpose. Where a particular brand is requested, there may be a more arguable case that the buyer relied upon the producer's publicity and marketing, rather than on the seller's skill and judgment in the selection of the product. There may nevertheless be aspects of a product about which the buyer continues to rely on the seller. For instance, when purchasing a glass of beer in a free house, a customer may rely upon his or her own general preference as to which

---

61 Per Lord Wright in *Grant v Australian Knitting Mills* [1936] AC 85.
62 Cf *Smith v Eric Bush* [1989] 2 All ER 514, but see discussion at Law Com 24 and Scot Law Com 12, *op. cit.* at para. 37.
63 [1903] 1 KB 610.

brewery's beer to select, but nevertheless may continue to rely on the landlord to serve it in a proper condition. This partial reliance would seem to bring into play the full scope of the implied condition that the goods are fit for their purpose. Our example may be exceptional in that most goods are pre–packaged, with no opportunity for the retailer to affect their quality. In appropriate circumstances therefore, the request for a particular brand may be evidence which a seller could put forward to persuade the court that the buyer had not relied on his skill and judgment.

It is worth reiterating that breach of the implied conditions is a matter of strict liability. Thus in *Kendall v Lillico*,[64] Lord Reid, whilst noting the illogicality of his own position, nevertheless found that 'an assurance that the goods will be reasonably fit for his purpose covers not only defects which the seller ought to have detected but also defects which are latent in the sense that not even the utmost skill and judgment on the part of the seller would have detected them'. However, the standard does not require goods to perform their functions perfectly: rather they have to be *reasonably* fit for their purpose. In determining the appropriate standard 'the rarity of the unsuitability would be weighed against the gravity of its consequences'.[65] There is also flexibility built into the determination of what the particular purpose of the goods is. Thus clearly whilst a family saloon, sports car, minibus and truck are all bought to be driven, they also have different purposes in relation to their optimum speed, the number of passengers they can carry and the weight they can bear. The Court of Appeal has accepted the principle that goods can be rendered unfit by the provision of inadequate or misleading instructions (and presumably by the failure to supply any instructions), although, on the facts of the case it was held that the instructions were not misleading.[66]

4.1.5 Remedies

Contract terms can be divided into three categories. Conditions give the right to repudiate the contract and/or claim damages. Warranties only ever give rise to a claim in damages, whilst breach of innominate terms (otherwise known as intermediate stipulations) may permit repudiation depending upon the seriousness of the consequences of breach. The implied terms are classed as conditions giving the consumer the right to reject the goods and/or claim damages.[67] The remedies in non–consumer sales contracts have been

64 [1969] 2 AC 31 at 84.
65 Per Lord Pearce in *Kendall v Lillico* [1969] 2 AC 31 at 115.
66 *Wormell v RHM Agriculture (East) Ltd* [1987] 3 All ER 75.
67 See sched. 2, Sale and Supply of Goods Act 1994.

restricted so that rejection is not possible where this is unreasonable,[68] but in consumer sales the automatic remedies of rejection and/or damages remain.

Before considering the scope of the remedies in more detail, it is important to note the remedies which are not available. In sales law, the seller is under no obligation to cure defects by repairing or replacing defective goods. In practice, of course, these remedies are widely used and are commonly provided for in the voluntary guarantees issued by manufacturers. In the debate surrounding whether a right to cure should be introduced into UK law, there is often confusion over what is being proposed. There is a world of difference between allowing consumers to opt for cure and requiring them to accept cure. The categoric right of consumers receiving defective goods to reject them[69] is an important weapon in the consumer's hand which should not be diluted. However, it has been suggested that sellers should be allowed to opt to cure, rather than be forced to accept the consumer's rejection of the goods and repudiation of the contract, where this is reasonable (for example, in the case of a minor and easily repairable defect). At first glance this seems attractive, but in reality few consumers would seek rejection and repudiation for a minor defect. A party normally relies on a minor infraction to withdraw from a contract in the commercial context, where the real reason for wanting to escape is external to the contract itself, for example, commodity price fluctuations. It is sometimes suggested that rejection may be too serious a remedy for minor defects; indeed there is evidence that the courts have failed to find the merchantability condition breached where the remedy being sought for a minor defect is rejection of the goods.[70]

In the consumer context, however, one must ask why a consumer is rejecting for an apparently minor defect? It is very likely that what appears to the outsider as a minor defect in fact has a major impact on the consumer, undermining his or her confidence in the goods. Given that the value of goods, such as a new car, may represent a considerable amount of the consumer's wealth, his or her interest in feeling secure in the purchase deserves protection. Take the facts of *Millars of Falkirk Ltd v Turpie* which concerned a new Ford Granada – an up–market car (even presumably by the standards of solicitors from whose ranks the purchaser came). The defect was a leak in the power steering box, in itself a minor problem only costing £25 (in 1973) to put right. Yet the sellers had attempted repair once – unsuccessfully – and the purchaser, fearing he had a 'lemon', repudiated the contract. Did he overreact? If so, it should not have been beyond the wit of the court to find the car unmerchantable – since presumably we would want

---

68 See s.15A, Sale of Goods Act 1979.
69 Assuming, as we shall see, they act promptly.
70 See *Millars of Falkirk Ltd v Turpie* 1976 SLT 66.

the seller to take some responsibility for this defect – and yet find technical reasons (of which we shall see there are several possibilities) for finding the right to reject lost, leaving the purchaser with a claim in damages. Restricting the right to reject may thus look attractive in theoretical terms, but undermining the clear right to reject will be damaging in the real world everyday practice of enforcing consumer rights, since traders will be able to exploit ambiguity in the definition of what amounts to a minor defect.

In its 1983 Working Paper, the Law Commission had suggested that the seller be given the statutory right to cure where refusal would be unreasonable.[71] Yet it had changed its mind by the time of its Final Report in 1987, believing this to be inappropriate in many commercial transactions[72] and fearing it might weaken the rights of consumers. Certainly requiring consumers to accept cure would weaken their rights; this is a possible criticism of the EC Green Paper on Consumer Guarantees.[73] There is not the same danger in providing consumers with the right to demand cure. Admittedly, unscrupulous traders could deliberately misrepresent the law so that a right to demand cure comes to be treated as a duty to accept cure, but the answer is to educate the public and use fair trading laws to bring errant traders to heel, rather than allow the fear of law breaking to stunt the proper development of the law. There are reasons why consumers may want a right of cure: they may be happy with the goods and want them repaired or they may be happy with the deal they struck and simply wish the defective goods supplied to be replaced by goods of the proper agreed standard. The difficulty is to know how to make the remedy effective in the sense that, if a seller refuses to cure, the consumer is left with a claim for damages and is no better off than at present. Of course, the damages could be altered so that they are increased where cure has been refused, in the same way as an Industrial Tribunal can make a higher award where an employer has refused to reinstate a worker. This is an example of how the civil law has sometimes to be supported by administrative controls on parties who flout it.

4.1.5.1 Rejection

S.11(3), Sale of Goods Act 1979 sets out the remedies for breach of conditions and warranties, but in a rather convoluted manner. Thus a breach

---

71 Law Com WP No. 85 and Scot Law Com Con Memo No. 58, *Sale and Supply of Goods* (1983) at 4.26–4.62.

72 But it did, of course, propose to restrict the right to reject in non–consumer sales to situations where it is reasonable to do so: see Law Com 160, Scot Law Com 104, *op. cit.* Ch. 4.

73 See 4.3.

of warranty is said to give rise to a claim for damages, but not a right to reject the goods and treat the contract as repudiated. It does not say expressly that breach of condition does give the right to reject the goods and treat the contract as repudiated, but this can be implied from the obvious contrast drawn between the remedies for breach of warranty and breach of condition. From this it appears that every rejection gives the consumer the right to treat the contract as repudiated; of course it would be open to the consumer to reject the goods but keep the contract alive by accepting an offer to cure. Yet the wording of an earlier part of the section is more equivocal as it states that breach of a condition *may* give rise to a right to treat the contract as repudiated. Some commentators have drawn the conclusion that English law already knows a right of cure since rejection of the goods need not repudiate the contract; the defect can be remedied by repairing specific goods or replacing goods which were unascertained when the contract was made.[74] However, the case often relied on to support this proposition, *Borrowman, Phillips & Co v Free and Holes*,[75] (and other similar cases) have all involved rejection and re–tender of documents under documentary sales. Any right of cure is unlikely to apply where the goods themselves had been rejected. Certainly any right to re–tender would have to take place before the time for delivery, since buyers can refuse to accept late delivery.[76] In the consumer context, the courts are likely to treat the remedies of rejection and repudiation as inseparable (unless voluntarily separated by the consumer) since the breach of the implied term will be seen as destroying the consumer's confidence in the bargain.[77] The seller may be able indirectly to persuade the consumer to accept an offer to cure in the knowledge that an unreasonable refusal of that offer may be treated as a failure to mitigate and be reflected in a lower award of damages. However, where the nature of the breach is such that the consumer has lost confidence in the seller, then one can anticipate that the courts will be slow to treat such a consumer as having unreasonably turned down an offer to cure.

It may be that only part of a consignment of goods is defective. Can a buyer reject the defective part and retain the remainder? The position used to be that where a buyer accepted all the goods or part of them then, unless the

---

[74] Goode, *Commercial Law,* (Penguin, 1982) pp. 298–301.

[75] (1878) 4 QBD 500.

[76] The time for delivery will be that set by the contract or failing that delivery must take place within a reasonable time: see standard commercial law textbooks for more detailed treatment, eg P. Atiyah, *Sale of Goods* (Pitman, 1990) Ch. 10.

[77] R. Bradgate and F. White, 'Rejection and Termination in Contracts for the Sale of Goods' in *Termination of Contracts*, J. Birds, R. Bradgate and C. Villiers eds. (Chancery, 1995).

contract was severable, the right to reject had been lost.[78] The one exception to this was provided by s.30(4), Sale of Goods Act 1979 which had allowed a buyer to reject goods which did not correspond with the contract description and retain those that did.[79] The Law Commission recommended that a similar right of partial rejection be introduced where part of a consignment was defective,[80] and this has been implemented by the Sale and Supply of Goods Act 1994. This provides for a new s.35A, Sale of Goods Act 1979 which, subject to any contrary intention in the contract, allows a buyer to reject goods which are not in conformity with the contract, whilst retaining others which are unaffected by the breach. However, it also provides that, where the sale is of one or more 'commercial units', then a buyer accepting goods which form part of such a commercial unit is deemed to have accepted all the goods making up the unit.[81] A 'commercial unit' is identified as a unit division which would materially impair the value of the goods or the character of the unit. Thus if the goods supplied were a lampset, comprising a matching base and shade, one of the parts could not be accepted and the other rejected.

4.1.5.2 Acceptance

S.11(4), Sale of Goods Act 1979 provides that:

> 'Where a contract of sale is not severable and the buyer has accepted the goods or part of them, the breach of a condition to be fulfilled by the seller can only be treated as a breach of warranty, and not as a ground for rejecting the goods and treating the contract as repudiated, unless there is an express or implied term of the contract to that effect.'

The loss of the right to reject on acceptance is particularly severe because of the wide range of circumstances in which s.35, Sale of Goods Act 1979 provides that the buyer is deemed to have accepted the goods. There is no equivalent of this rule in legislation governing other types of supply contracts where the loss of the right to reject is governed by the common law concept of affirmation. We shall see that the rejection remedy is generally kept alive for longer in those other contracts than is the case in sale contracts.

However, the rule that acceptance bars rejection does not apply to severable contracts. Thus where goods are delivered in instalments or even if

---

78 S.11(4), Sale of Goods Act 1979.
79 This has now been repealed: see s.3(3), Sale and Supply of Goods Act 1994.
80 Law Com 160, Scot Law Com 104, *op. cit.* at para. 6.9.
81 S.35(7), Sale of Goods Act 1979.

they are delivered at the same time, but can be treated as independent elements, the buyer will be free to accept the fit goods and reject the defective instalments. Indeed, in appropriate circumstances, the consumer may be able to argue that there is not one contract, be it severable or otherwise, but rather a series of individual contracts. The contract itself may expressly or impliedly allow rejection after acceptance.

S.35, Sale of Goods Act 1979 provides for three circumstances in which goods are deemed to have been accepted:

(i) *when the buyer intimates to the seller that he has accepted them.*[82] This intimation may be express or implied. Of particular concern in the consumer context are delivery notes, which consumers are often asked to sign to indicate that they accept the goods. Typically the goods are delivered in a form that prevents the consumer from immediately inspecting their quality and yet an appropriately worded delivery note might have the effect of removing the consumer's right to reject the goods.[83] This was more clearly the case prior to the 1994 amendment to the Sale of Goods Act 1979, since this form of acceptance was not treated as being subject to the proviso in s.34 of the Act that goods cannot be accepted until there has been a reasonable opportunity to examine them. Since the 1994 amendments, acceptance will no longer occur by intimation unless the buyer has had a reasonable opportunity to examine the goods.

(ii) *when the goods have been delivered and the buyer does any act in relation to them which is inconsistent with the ownership of the seller.*[84] This is a confusing provision, since if the buyer has bought the goods, then why should the buyer not behave in a manner inconsistent with the seller's ownership? To make sense of it, one must treat the seller's ownership as being a conditional form of ownership based on the residual interest in the return of goods properly rejected. An example often given of an act which was inconsistent with the seller's ownership is a sub–sale. Even prior to the 1994 amendments, acceptance could not be deemed in this circumstance until there had been a reasonable opportunity to examine the goods. Thus, even if goods are passed directly to a sub–buyer, rejection would be possible if, on examination, they were found to be defective. The amended Act provides that goods are not deemed to be accepted merely because they are delivered to

---

[82] S.35(1)(a), Sale of Goods Act 1979.

[83] It is possible that such a note would be caught by s.13, Unfair Contract Terms Act 1979, which controls exclusions or restrictions on rules of evidence.

[84] S.35(1)(b), Sale of Goods Act 1979.

another under a disposition or sub–sale.[85] This does not state that such a sub–sale or disposition cannot be an act inconsistent with the seller's ownership, but seems to emphasise the point that mere re–sale is not enough and that the actions of the parties must be considered in determining whether acceptance has occurred. The types of situations where acceptance is properly deemed to have occurred on this basis are those where the buyer is unable to return the goods as he or she has incorporated them into other goods in a way which prevents them from being easily removed[86] or where it would be unfair to allow rejection as he or she has used them for longer than necessary for the purpose of testing.[87]

Repairing defective goods could clearly be viewed as an act inconsistent with the seller's ownership when the repair was effected either by the buyer or someone other than the seller. Where the seller is allowed to repair the goods, it is hard to see how this could be inconsistent with his ownership and yet this possibility has been alleged.[88] Clearly a consumer could preserve the right to reject the goods should an attempted repair by the seller prove to be ineffective by expressly stating such a reservation, but it seems wrong to make consumer rights depend upon the consumer having the knowledge and foresight to negotiate with the seller over the intricacies of sales law. Thus, following the recommendations of the Law Commission, the 1994 amendments provide that a buyer is not deemed to have accepted goods merely because he asks for, or agrees to, their repair by or under an arrangement with the seller.[89]

(iii) *when the buyer retains the goods after the lapse of a reasonable time without intimating that he has rejected them.*[90] This is the most controversial of the various forms of deemed acceptance, in part because the case law has on occasions construed a reasonable time very strictly. Thus in *Bernstein v Pamson Motors*,[91] for instance, a reasonable period of time was held to have elapsed after three weeks, during which the consumer had been ill and had only driven the car 142 miles. Rougier J held that the statute removed the right to reject after the goods had been retained for a reasonable period of time, noting that

---

85 S.35(6)(b), Sale of Goods Act 1979.
86 *Mechan & Sons Ltd v Bow, McLachlan & Co Ltd* 1910 SC 785.
87 *Heilbutt v Hickson* (1872) LR 7 CP 438.
88 See Law Com WP No. 85 and Scot Law Com Con Memo No. 58, *op. cit.* at para. 2.56.
89 S.35(6)(a), Sale of Goods Act 1979.
90 S.35(4), Sale of Goods Act 1979.
91 [1987] 2 All ER 220.

there was no qualification that the period of time should be reasonable in relation to the opportunity to discover the defect. Somewhat contradictorily, he then went on to suggest that what is a reasonable time depends upon the facts of the case. He was clearly concerned to promote the 'commercial desirability of [allowing] the seller to close his ledger reasonably soon after the transaction is complete'. However, he also noted the need to consider the nature of the goods and their function from the buyer's point of view, stating that 'the complexity of the intended function is clearly of prime consideration here. What is a reasonable time in relation to a bicycle would hardly suffice for a nuclear submarine.' If one takes the words of the judge at face value, these factors are relevant in determining the ability of the buyer to return the goods, but this seems nonsensical since it takes just as long to return a complex as a simple product (unless it is one where installation and, more importantly, removal take a long time). The difference between the complex and the simple product lies in the time needed to discover defects; the judge was in fact doing what he denied was relevant – taking the possibility of examination into account, albeit (on the facts of the case) not very generously. The amended Sale of Goods Act 1979 now makes it clear that, in determining whether a reasonable time has elapsed, the question of whether a buyer has had a reasonable opportunity to examine the goods is a material factor.[92] Although note that there is no requirement that there must have been an opportunity to examine the goods before the goods can be deemed to have been accepted.

Bradgate and Savage note that the effect of prior case law has been that, where there is a latent defect, the right to reject is lost before the buyer is aware of the defect.[93] This would still be the case after the 1994 amendments since, even if a buyer is given a reasonable opportunity to examine the goods, latent defects would not be discovered. Bradgate and Savage go on to state that this goes against the notion that merchantable quality (as it then was) requires goods to be reasonably durable. However, what it actually does is to admit that durability is a concern, but that rejection is not an appropriate remedy for this manifestation of lack of satisfactory quality. This approach was supported by the Law Commission in its 1987 report, but might perhaps be questioned. In other supply contracts the right to reject is only lost once the buyer is aware of the defect and affirms the contract. Allowance can then be made for any use and enjoyment the consumer has derived from the goods prior to their rejection. This is preferable to relying on damages to ensure

---

92   S.35(5).
93   *Commercial Law*, at p. 221.

justice. Injustice could arise if the goods retain some residual worth even after the durability defect emerges and consumers have to retain goods they are not satisfied with. This is because, in calculating damages, allowance will be made not only for the satisfactory performance the consumer has enjoyed prior to the defect materialising, but also for the subsequent limited utility the consumer can derive from the goods. The burden of making use of the residual utility in the goods should be placed on the seller rather than the consumer: the seller is the one who caused the future performance to be lower than anticipated and can more easily find someone willing to buy goods with reduced performance. The consumer should not be forced to accept goods which are unsatisfactory even if he or she is partially compensated.

4.1.5.3 Affirmation

The rules which provide for the loss of the right to reject on acceptance only apply to contracts of sale. They do not apply to contracts of barter or exchange, contracts for work and materials, hire, nor hire–purchase and (by statute) they do not apply to conditional sales. It is the law's policy to treat hire–purchase and conditional sale transactions in a similar manner.[94]

In contracts other than sale contracts, the right to reject is only lost where the buyer has affirmed the contract, waived the breach or is estopped from relying on his or her right to terminate. Most commonly the courts will look to see if the contract has been affirmed. The important point to note is that affirmation can only take place once the buyer is aware of the defect. Thus, there is in effect a long term right to reject.[95]

In sale contracts, rejection of goods will lead to recovery of the full price paid on the basis that there has been a total failure of consideration. Where the contract is for hire or hire–purchase and the goods have been used for some time prior to rejection, there will not have been a total failure of consideration: therefore, rather than permitting the recovery of the full price, damages will equal the cost of hiring a replacement less the value of the use the hirer has enjoyed.[96] Where the defect is serious and arose early in the hire period this may result in a hirer recovering all, or almost all, of his money. Indeed in *Farnworth Finance Facilities v Attryde*,[97] Lord Denning suggested that the value of the use of the motor cycle for 4,000 miles was offset by the trouble the consumer had suffered. Because of this discretion to do justice by

---

94 S.14, Supply of Goods (Implied Terms) Act 1973.
95 *Farnworth Finance Facilities v Attryde* [1970] 1 WLR 1053.
96 *Charterhouse Credit Ltd v Tolley* [1963] 2 QB 683.
97 [1970] 1 WLR 1053.

fixing the level of damages so as to take into account the value the buyer received from his or her use of the goods prior to rejection, these rules seem preferable to the rule in sales law that acceptance bars rejection. It is unfortunate that the Law Commission came out against any change in the law.[98] The position of contracts for the supply of goods which do not involve an element of hire, but which are nevertheless not subject to the rule that acceptance bars the right to reject (such as conditional sale, barter and exchange and work and materials contracts) is unclear. If goods rejected as unsatisfactory due to lack of durability are treated as giving rise to a total failure of consideration, then injustice could occur. Allowance should be made in appropriate cases for the use and enjoyment the consumer has had of the goods.

4.1.5.4 Damages[99]

The measure of damages for breach of the implied quality conditions is the contractual one of seeking to put the consumer into the position he or she would have occupied had the contract been performed properly. S.53(2), Sale of Goods Act 1979 provides:

> 'the measure of damages for breach of warranty is the estimated loss directly and naturally resulting, in the ordinary course of events, from the breach of warranty'

This is similar to the common law test in *Hadley v Baxendale*.[100] S.53(3) goes on to state that:

> 'In the case of breach of warranty of quality such loss is prima facie the difference between the value of the goods at the time of delivery to the buyer and the value they would have had if they had fulfilled the warranty'.

It is important to note that damages are not restricted merely to the intrinsic reduction in quality of the goods, but also cover consequential losses such as loss of profits which would have been generated from the intended use of the

---

[98]   Law Com 160, Scot Law Com 104, *op. cit.* at 5.1–5.13.

[99]   Space does not allow justice to be done to the complex law of damages: see, for instance, works such as D. Harris, *Remedies in Contract and Tort*, (Weidenfeld and Nicolson, 1988).

[100]   (1854) 9 Exch 341.

goods and more significantly in the consumer context, any personal injury damages.

From the consumer perspective the problem with damages as a remedy is that although they may seem to compensate consumers fully for the difference in value between goods of proper and defective quality, they nevertheless often fail to take into account the incidental costs incurred and the distress and inconvenience caused to consumers. In this respect the judgment in *Bernstein v Pamson Motors Ltd*[101] is enlightened for, although the remedy of rejection was refused, the damages awarded included the plaintiff's cost of making his way home on the day of the breakdown, the loss of a full tank of petrol, £150 for a 'totally spoilt day, comprising nothing but vexation' and compensation for being without a car (until such time as he unreasonably refused a substitute). The problem is that few such cases get to court and settlements rarely take account of these elements; nor indeed are consumers likely to find so sympathetic a judge. Even this relatively generous calculation of damages fails to allow for the disappointment in having made a bad bargain, since no allowance was made for the fact that the consumer had been deprived of the feelings of pride and enjoyment in his new purchase. Damages for loss of enjoyment have been awarded in a few cases, but these have involved contracts whose purpose was for the consumers to enjoy themselves. Thus damages for loss of enjoyment have been awarded for breach of holiday contracts[102] or a contract to take wedding pictures,[103] but the courts have been reluctant to extend this to other contracts where the disappointment resulted simply from the failure to perform the contractual obligations.[104]

4.2 COMMERCIAL GUARANTEES

So far we have considered the quality obligations which are imposed by law on suppliers of goods and services. These can be seen as premised on an 'exploitative' theory, under which suppliers are assumed to be capable and (in some cases) willing to exploit their position to impose unfair terms on consumers and in particular to restrict their obligations in such a way that they do not satisfy the legitimate expectations of consumers. We now turn our attention to the express warranties given with goods. These are the additional warranties voluntarily given, usually by manufacturers, but

---

101 [1987] 2 All ER 220.
102 *Jarvis v Swans Tours Ltd* [1973] QB 233, *Jackson v Horizon Holidays Ltd* [1975] 1 WLR 1468.
103 *Diesen v Samson* 1971 SLT 49.
104 *Woodar Investment Development v Wimpey Construction UK* [1980] 1 WLR 277.

occasionally by retailers. They usually come as part of the overall package of goods and are thus not paid for directly; rather the cost of the guarantee is included in the price of the goods.

There has been a recent trend for manufacturers and retailers to offer extended warranties purchasable by the consumer. These policies give rise to their own problems, especially when they are long term and are underwritten by an insurance policy, for which the premiums may or may not be kept up. The cost of such extended warranties has also been the subject of debate, due to the allegation that some retailers push their own service contracts and leave the consumer ignorant of cheaper contracts offered by manufacturers.[105] In theory this two tier guarantee level – normal guarantee and extended guarantee – should be applauded as it allows consumers to select the level of cover desired, but does not force all consumers to pay for long term guarantees. The danger is that the additional cover is both overpriced and provides only what consumers had come to expect under the normal guarantee. There is also a related issue, namely that consumers may feel bound to take on the extended warranties because the cost of after–sales service is priced artificially high. Although these issues are of, possibly increasing, significance, we will concentrate on the more central issue of guarantees supplied as part of the goods or services package, which we will call 'commercial guarantees'.

4.2.1 Rationale for Regulation

Early regulation of commercial guarantees may have been based on an 'exploitative' theory which tried to prevent manufacturers from using guarantees as a medium to restrict their own obligations, rather than giving additional rights. There may have been some justification for this approach. For instance, the leading US product liability case of *Henningsen v Bloomfield Motors*[106] involved a guarantee for a new car under which the manufacturer agreed to replace defective parts for a short period (90 days or 4,000 miles), but only 'if the part is sent to the factory, transportation charges are prepaid, and if the examination discloses to its satisfaction that the part is defective'. As the Court itself said, it is hard to imagine a greater

---

105   See Office of Fair Trading, *Extended Warranties on Electrical Goods*, (OFT, 1994) which complained of a lack of transparency and competition and questionable selling practices. The Office of Fair Trading is supporting moves for a voluntary code of practice and, failing that, is threatening to make a reference to the Monopoly and Mergers Commission or a recommendation to the President of the Board of Trade that a price marking order should be made.

106   (1960) 161 A 2d 69.

burden on the consumer or a less satisfactory remedy. The Office of Fair Trading in 1986 felt that 'All too often...it seems that guarantees are used merely as a marketing ploy, a source of additional revenue for the supplier, or even a means of diverting consumers' attention from their legal rights.'[107] These problems have largely been overcome through the development of better commercial practice prompted by (i) regulators, (ii) s.5, Unfair Contract Terms Act 1977, which prohibits terms in consumer guarantees excluding loss or damage arising from the fact the goods are defective due to the negligence of someone involved in the manufacture or distribution of the goods[108], and (iii) reg. 4 of the Consumer Transactions (Restrictions on Statements) Order 1976[109] which requires guarantees to carry a notice that the consumer's statutory rights are unaffected. This latter provision also serves the useful ancillary function of bringing the existence of the statutory rights to the buyer's attention.

Commercial guarantees are voluntary in the sense that the manufacturer can decide whether or not to offer such a guarantee.[110] George Priest has argued that there are dangers in mandating too high a level of guarantee.[111] His criticisms are most relevant to legal guarantees which are mandatory, but also apply in a limited way to commercial guarantees, as it is sometimes suggested that where such guarantees are offered they should have a mandatory minimum content. He argues that his 'investment theory' largely both explains and justifies the limitations which are found in commercial guarantees. His argument is that the best level of cover should be fixed by the market rather than be mandatorily imposed. If this level is too high, then there will be little incentive for consumers to allocate resources to avoid defects arising: thus the number of defects will increase and the generality of consumers will be forced to pay for those who either overuse or misuse their products.

Priest's theory might well explain why there are certain exclusions in commercial guarantees, such as those relating to unusual uses or non-consumer uses of goods, and why there are sometimes shorter guarantee

---

[107] Office of Fair Trading, *Consumer Guarantees*, (OFT, 1986) at p.27. More recent findings of the Office of Fair Trading suggest consumer guarantees are less of a problem.

[108] There is no similar provision relating to services.

[109] S.I. 1976/1813.

[110] In some countries, such as Greece, there is a requirement that all consumer durables be accompanied by a guarantee, whilst in France a standard (NFX 5002) is mandated for electrical household appliances and audiovisual equipment.

[111] G. Priest, 'A Theory of the Consumer Product Warranty' (1981) 90 *Yale LJ* 1297; cf W. Whitford, 'Comment on a Theory of the Consumer Product Warranty' (1982) 91 *Yale LJ* 1371.

periods for product parts which might be subject to greater intensity of use by consumers. Yet this free market philosophy only works in a market characterised by perfect information. A third theory in relation to guarantees is the 'signal' theory. This is premised on the idea that a 'guarantee' sends certain signals to consumers about a product's quality. Thus most suppliers would wish to have product guarantees which at least reflected the general level of such guarantees, so as to encourage confidence in their product. However, there are dangers. Manufacturers may realise that consumers are only interested in the central aspects of the guarantee and thus take the opportunity to restrict the application of its less important elements. Even more dangerous is the fact that manufacturers can seek to benefit from the confidence the granting of a guarantee engenders in the consumer, whilst in fact giving nothing or very little beyond what is required by law. This is the thinking behind laws such as the US Magnuson–Moss Warranty – Federal Trade Commission Improvement Act 1975.[112]

The Magnuson–Moss Act requires a clear and conspicuous designation of warranties as either 'full' or 'limited'. Full warranties must meet specified standards. For instance, the guarantee must contain specified information (such as, identifying the warrantor, including his address; providing a statement of the products or parts covered and what the warrantor will do in the event of a defect, when and at whose expense; stating the duration of the warranty; providing details of how the warranty can be invoked and of informal dispute machinery, as well as a statement as to whether this machinery has to be invoked before going to court[113]). Such warranties must not affect the implied warranties and as a minimum must provide for remedy ie repair within a reasonable time and without charge if a consumer product has a defect, if it malfunctions or fails to conform with the written warranty. There is also a so–called lemon provision whereby, after a reasonable number of attempts[114] to remedy defects or malfunctions, the warrantor must allow the consumer to elect either a refund or replacement (without charge) of the product or part; if the replacement of a part is involved, there shall be no charge for its installation.

---

[112] 15 US Code 2301.

[113] In an attempt to reduce consumer enforcement costs, consumers can be required to use informal dispute settlement procedures prior to the courts if those procedures meet the standards imposed by the Federal Trade Commission. That these standards are very strict may be part of the explanation as to why few manufacturers have established such schemes: see I. Ramsay, *Consumer Protection*, (Weidenfeld and Nicolson, 1989) at p. 451.

[114] The Federal Trade Commission can produce rules specifying what constitutes a reasonable number of attempts by the warrantor to remedy a defect or malfunction under different circumstances.

Such provisions help to increase the information provided to consumers as they ensure that the guarantee has some content. However, to be effective there must be either a pre–vetting system, so that warrantors seek permission to use certain words or perhaps display a certain standard mark (although there is a danger of a profusion of such marks) or else protection of designated terms under trade description law. The advantage of such a scheme is that consumers can be educated about the value of looking for products carrying such guarantees and this can stimulate competition. One could even imagine a system of graduated designations depending on just how superior to the legal minimum the guarantee was, though an over complicated system must be avoided.[115] This issue will be returned to in the context of proposed reforms after some of the legal problems relating to the enforceability of guarantees are considered.

4.2.2 Privity and Commercial Guarantees

The doctrine of privity of contract is much criticised, but remains a central feature of the common law. This raises important issues about the enforceability of commercial guarantees which are issued by non–contracting parties. Thus in the typical case, a guarantee is granted by a manufacturer, but the consumer contracts with the retailer. In England, at least, the courts are unwilling to bridge the privity gap through tort law in the absence of any personal injury.[116] Where the manufacturer has expressly made statements concerning the quality of products or service (which induced the consumer's purchase), there may be less justification for allowing manufacturers to hide behind technical privity rules. In fact two situations should perhaps be treated separately: first, where the guarantees are found in advertisements and promotional material and, second, where there is a specific contract document delivered with the goods.

4.2.2.1 Pre–contractual Promotion

American law has generally found manufacturers liable in tort where there has been an express warranty in the absence of privity, even for pure

---

115 See G. Howells and C. Bryant, 'Consumer Guarantees: Competition or Regulation?' (1993) 1 *Consum LJ* 3.
116 See discussion of *Junior Books v Veitchi* [1982] 3 All ER 201 below at 4.2.2.3.

economic losses.[117] In Australia and New Zealand statutory reforms have held manufacturers liable for their promotional material.[118] Recovery in English law is more limited for, under *Hedley Byrne v Heller*[119] economic losses resulting from negligent mis–statements require the parties to be in a special relationship.[120] In *Lambert v Lewis*[121] Stephenson LJ said: `We cannot regard the manufacturer and supplier of an article as putting himself into a special relationship with every distributor who obtains his product and reads what he says or prints about it and so owing him a duty to take reasonable care to give him true information or good advice.' Recent developments relating to the concept of duty of care in the general law of negligence, such as *Caparo Industries Ltd v Dickman*[122] and *Murphy v Brentwood DC*,[123] support this restrictive approach.

4.2.2.2 The Ineffectiveness of Tort Law

This restrictive approach has also prevented tort law from creating a more direct duty on manufacturers not to cause economic loss to consumers by producing substandard, but not dangerous, goods. Even in the high watermark case of economic loss liability – *Junior Books v Veitchi*[124] (where the majority imposed liability for substandard flooring on a nominated subcontractor because of his quasi–contractual relationship with the plaintiff) – the judges nevertheless explicitly denied such a relationship would generally be found in ordinary manufacturer–customer relationships in the absence of contractual privity.

---

[117]   *Randy Knitwear Inc. v American Cyanamid Co* 181 NE 2d 399 (1962); *Seely v White Motor Company* 403 P 2d 145 (1965): see generally J. Phillips, 'Misrepresentation and Products Liability' (1990) 20 *Anglo–Am LR* 327.

[118]   See J. Goldring, L. Maher and J. McKeough, *Consumer Protection Law*, (Federation Press, 1993); S. Todd, 'Consumer Law Reform in New Zealand: the Consumer Guarantees Act 1993' (1994) 2 *Consum LJ* 100.

[119]   [1964] AC 465.

[120]   See generally R. Bradgate, 'Misrepresentation and Product Liability in English Law', (1990) 20 *Anglo–Am LR* 334.

[121]   [1982] AC 225 at 264.

[122]   [1990] 1 All ER 568.

[123]   [1990] 2 All ER 908.

[124]   [1982] 3 All ER 201.

4.2.2.3 Collateral Contract

It may of course be possible to create a separate collateral contract based on advertisements, which was after all what happened in the most famous contract law case of all, *Carlill v Carbollic Smokeball Co*[125] In this situation, a collateral contract was formed to enforce the promise of the warrantor, with the consumer providing the necessary element of consideration by entering into a contract with a third party to purchase the goods manufactured by the warrantor. The difficulty is that the courts tend to be cautious about finding that the necessary intention to create a collateral contract existed.

Thus in certain cases the collateral contract concept can also be used to hold the manufacturer liable for commercial guarantees supplied with the goods. The difficulty may be to show that the consumer knew of the guarantee before making the purchase and that the goods were therefore bought in reliance on the manufacturer's promise. There may also be problems with establishing that the manufacturer intended to be legally bound to purchasers, but presumably the courts would be readily willing to imply such an intention. A recent county court decision took the novel approach of holding the retailer liable for the honouring of the manufacturer's guarantee on the basis that it had formed an express term of the sale contract.[126] The decision has no precedent value and, as it is not fully reported, its reasoning cannot be analysed, but, if correct, must have been based on fairly unique circumstances.

Often a guarantee only becomes valid when the consumer returns a registration card. There are indeed important questions as to whether the consumer should lose his or her guarantee rights simply by failing to perform this task. Returning the card can easily be viewed as involving too much trouble for small purchases or can be accidentally overlooked. The requirement to return the card, as compared to the obligation to provide proof of purchase, seems more closely related to obtaining marketing information than anything which is necessary for the functioning of the guarantee. Nevertheless, if a consumer does provide such information, then this might be viewed as the consideration necessary to create a contract which binds the manufacturer to honour the guarantee. The enforceability of commercial guarantees is therefore not clear cut, but there appears to be little empirical evidence to suggest that manufacturers seek to deny liability on this basis.

---

[125] [1893] 1 QB 256. See too *Wood v Letrik Ltd, The Times*, 12 January 1932.

[126] *Alexander v Comet Group PLC* [1995] CPR 29.

4.2.2.4 Horizontal Privity

Privity also poses a problem in the horizontal direction. In other words subsequent owners of the goods, be they donees or purchasers, do not have any contractual rights against the manufacturer, even assuming the original purchaser can assert such rights. Where goods are bought by someone at the express request of another, the courts might circumvent the privity rule by the use of agency and, possibly might on appropriate facts, be able to stretch a point and find the donor of goods to have acted as the agent of the donee. In any event, such analyses would not assist the subsequent purchaser.

4.2.3 Legal Problems Surrounding the Commercial Guarantee and Reform Proposals

Thus the problems posed by commercial guarantees can be stated to be: concerns over their legal enforceability; ensuring consumers have proper information about the content of the guarantees, and the need to ensure they do not undermine the legal minimum protection provided by mandatory law. Some of the reform proposals relating to commercial guarantees will now be considered.[127]

4.2.3.1 Office of Fair Trading

It has already been noted that, in 1986, the Office of Fair Trading found the position relating to consumer guarantees to be unsatisfactory. It saw its role as one of improving practice through consumer education, developing the provisions on guarantees in codes of practice and as part of their supervisory function under Part III of the Fair Trading Act 1974. Various recommendations were made to those who promoted, issued or sold guarantees. These were that :

- Consumers should be shown and encouraged to study guarantees before making a purchase. Where the consumer pays for the guarantee and has not been able to fully understand its terms, the consumer should be allowed to cancel within a specified period of, say, three days.
- The number of expressions used should be reduced. In most cases 'consumer guarantee' would suffice with 'insurance' being added where the arrangement involves an insurance policy.

---

[127] See generally G. Howells and C. Bryant, *op.cit.*

- Manufacturers and others should avoid giving promises or undertakings unless they are legally enforceable.
- Guarantees should be clear, comprehensive and simple.
- Guarantees should state what is covered, any exclusions or conditions, the name and address of the guarantor, the beneficiary, the nature of the scheme (eg if it is insurance based) and how claims can be made.
- Guarantees should be transferable to subsequent owners (subject to reasonable conditions).
- The original packaging should not be required to make a claim.
- Charges should not be imposed which are likely to deter claims.
- An extension of the guarantee period should normally be allowed where the consumer has lost the use of the product for a significant period.
- Where long term (more than one year) guarantees are concerned there must be satisfactory arrangements to ensure that the guarantee can be enforced throughout its term.

The weakness of these proposals lies in the fact that, whilst they call for a reduction in the number of terms used, they fail to impose any standardised meaning on the use of such terms.

4.2.3.2 National Consumer Council

This weakness was not to be found in the National Consumer Council's report, *Competing in Quality*.[128] This proposed that the term 'guarantee' be restricted to promises given free of charge. These would have to be labelled as 'total guarantees', 'retailers' total guarantees' (where granted by the retailer) or 'limited guarantees'. The influence of the Magnuson–Moss Act is apparent. The proposals respected the voluntary nature of commercial guarantees, but would have required a statement to be made as to whether cars and specified consumer durables carried a 'total guarantee' and, if so, its duration. Although 'limited guarantees' could be given, they would have to be clearly marked as such. A 'total guarantee' would be defined as a guarantee lasting at least 12 months (in the case of motor vehicles 12 months/18,000 miles) which did not involve any unreasonable preconditions, such as completion of a guarantee card, payment of money or a requirement that the product be returned in its original packaging. The guarantor must repair all defects, unless they were shown to have been caused by misuse or failure reasonably to maintain or service the product. The guarantor should not require that the product be serviced by a particular person or that particular parts be used. The Office of Fair Trading would be given powers to

---

[128] (NCC, 1989).

intervene if it considered that the guarantee was made dependent on unreasonable servicing requirements. If the product could not be repaired within five days (three in the case of cars), the consumer should be allowed the free loan of an equivalent item or reimbursement of reasonable expenses. The consumer should have the right of refund or replacement if: (i) the product was not returned within 21 days of notification of the claim; or (ii) the repair was ineffective, or (iii) the product had been under repair for various reasons for 30 days within a 12–month period. It was further proposed that retailers be jointly and severally liable for guarantees given by producers, with a right of indemnity against producer/importers, but that producer/importers would not be liable on a retailer's guarantee.

The National Consumer Council proposals take the provision of consumer information seriously. Consumers can be educated to look for 'total guarantees' and be informed of their meaning, whilst they will be quizzical of a product or service which offers only a 'limited guarantee'. One criticism of the National Consumer Council's proposals was that they did not define 'defect'. Would a guarantor therefore, be able to refuse to repair minor defects or claim that the guarantee did not include durability, so that wear and tear could be used as a defence? In 1990, a Private Member's Consumer Guarantees Bill sought to implement these proposals, as well as those of the Law Commission to reform the implied quality conditions,[129] but the proposals on guarantees were unacceptable to the Government and the Bill failed to reach the statute book.[130]

4.2.3.3 Department of Trade and Industry

The matter of consumer guarantees was raised in the *Department of Trade and Industry Consultation Document on Consumer Guarantees*.[131] The Department rejected the notion of using legislation to require that guarantees be given or to establish the minimum content of guarantees. Perhaps somewhat unrealistically, it preferred to leave the matter to be resolved by market competition. It did, however, have a few positive proposals to resolve some of the legal problems surrounding consumer guarantees. Thus, it proposed that manufacturers should be civilly liable for the performance of

---

[129] The Bill would have replaced merchantable quality with a test of 'satisfactory quality' (instead of 'acceptable quality' as favoured by the Law Commission) and the problem of defining defect in the consumer guarantee provisions would also have been resolved by relating it to the standard of 'satisfactory quality'.

[130] See C. Willett, 'The Unacceptable Face of the Consumer Guarantees Bill', (1991) 54 *MLR* 552.

[131] (DTI, February 1992).

their guarantee to the consumer and that in cases where the manufacturer is based outside the UK the manufacturer's guarantee would be enforceable against the importer.[132] This is a welcome recognition of commercial reality and should cause few problems.

More dramatic, perhaps, is the proposal that retailers should be jointly and severally liable with the manufacturer for the manufacturer's guarantee. In principle, an increased number of defendants is desirable so that insolvency and other chance events preventing the consumer from recovering can be avoided. The law of contribution and the negotiation of contracts can then determine how the losses fall within the commercial chain. Nevertheless there may be some problems with holding retailers jointly liable with manufacturers, particularly small retailers. Part of the problem is that retailers will not be able to control the guarantees given by manufacturers and may even be unaware of their content. If they are to be made liable for them, then there might have to be a provision (as exists under Irish sales of goods legislation) for retailers to disclaim liability for manufacturers' guarantees. Certainly the retailer could not be expected to carry out all the terms of the guarantee; for instance, repairing obligations must be interchangeable with monetary compensation since, apart from the very large electrical outlets and department stores, retailers do not, and cannot be expected to, keep service departments.

The Department of Trade and Industry made it clear that the consumer should not have to choose between his or her rights under the guarantee and his or her statutory rights, and believed there is at least an arguable case that time taken up in pursuing rights under the guarantee should not prejudice the consumer's right to reject under the statutory provisions. It also favoured a measure of damages which covered putting the defect right and compensating for economic losses rather than one which merely compensated for the reduced value of the defective product.

The consultation paper favoured amending the implied terms along the lines eventually enacted in the Sale and Supply of Goods Act 1994. It also proposed breaching privity to make manufacturers, or (in the case of imported goods) importers jointly liable for breach of the implied terms. This proposal, along with those on commercial guarantees, remained unimplemented, but has again been placed firmly on the agenda by a recent European *Green Paper* which deals with both statutory implied terms and guarantees.

---

132   The fact that the importer is the importer into the United Kingdom and not the importer into the European Union might cause some problems under European Law.

4.3   EC GREEN PAPER ON GUARANTEES FOR CONSUMER GOODS AND AFTER–SALES SERVICE

In November 1993 the European Commission issued a *Green Paper on Guarantees for Consumer Goods and After–Sales Services*[133] Provisions on this matter had previously been included in drafts of the Unfair Terms in Consumer Contracts Directive. In the first draft such issues were dealt with in the annex of unfair terms[134] but, in the second draft, in the body of the Directive itself.[135] The Council, however, saw the issues of unfair contact terms and guarantees as distinct and asked the Commission to consider whether harmonisation of national legislation in this area was needed. The *Green Paper* which represents the Commission's initial response, includes a

---

[133]   COM (93) 509.

[134]   OJ 1990 C243/2, Annex, clause (c).

[135]   OJ 1992 C73/7, Art. 6:

'1. The Member States shall take the necessary measures in order to ensure that the consumer is guaranteed, as purchaser under a contract for the sale of goods, the right to receive goods which are in conformity with the contract and are fit for the purpose for which they were sold, and to complain, within an appropriately extensive period, about any intrinsic defects which the goods may contain.

2. For the purpose of exercising these rights, the Member States shall take the necessary measures in order to ensure that the consumer is guaranteed the choice of the following available options :

– the reimbursement of the whole of the purchase price,

– the replacement of the goods,

– the repair of the goods at the seller's expense,

– a reduction in the price if the consumer retains the goods,

and the right to compensation for damage sustained by him which arises out of the contract.

3. In cases where the seller transmits to the consumer the guarantee of the manufacturer of the goods, the Member States shall take the necessary measures in order to ensure that the consumer is guaranteed the right to benefit from the manufacturer's guarantee for a period of 12 months or for the normal life of the goods, where this is less than 12 months, and to enforce payments, either by the seller or by the manufacturer, of the costs incurred by the consumer in obtaining implementation of that guarantee.

4. The Member States shall take the necessary measures in order to ensure that the consumer is guaranteed, as purchaser under a contract for the supply of services, the right

– to be supplied with those services at the agreed time and with all due efficiency,

– to have the supplier's warranty that the supplier has the requisite skill and expertise to supply the services in the manner specified in the foregoing indent.'

thorough survey of national laws on this subject. The diversities highlighted by that study are seen to justifying the need for Community action so that consumers feel confident in crossing borders to purchase goods and services. In addition, the legal position is simplified for businesses and distortions in competition are prevented.[136]

The *Green Paper* considers three issues:

(i)   *Legal guarantees* by which is meant the legal protection offered by the law, such as the implied terms of satisfactory quality and fitness for purpose.
(ii) *Commercial guarantees* offered by guarantors (eg manufacturers or retailers) and subject to the conditions laid down by the guarantor.
(iii) *After–sales service* which is defined to exclude matters covered by the commercial guarantee and hence involves the payment of a fee (the main issue being the availability of spare parts).

The possible solutions proposed by the *Green Paper* for each of these three areas will now be considered.

4.3.1 Legal Guarantees

The Commission appeared reluctant to resolve the problems raised by the legal guarantee by modifying the rules of private international law so that consumers took their own national laws with them when purchasing abroad. Whilst this might encourage consumers to shop abroad, it meant that suppliers would still be faced with the cost of complying with different national laws. Indeed this problem would have been further exacerbated as suppliers would not necessarily know in advance which law applied to a particular transaction. Also, instead of creating a common European

---

136   In this regard the European Court of Justice case of *Alsthom v Sulzer*, Case 339/89, [1991] ECR 120 is illustrative. The Court held that French case law – which presumed manufacturers and traders knew that the goods sold were defective, and hence, in the instant case, rendered a clause limiting liability void – could lead to distortions in competition. In this case, the German sub–contractor had been able to rely on an exclusion clause, but the French shipbuilding company had not been able to rely on such a term. Despite possible distortions to competition, the Court held Arts. 34 and 85 of the Treaty of Rome were not breached since the purpose of the laws was to protect purchasers and not to encourage agreements contrary to Art. 85; also because the laws applied without distinction to all contracts governed by French law and because the parties had a free choice as to which law governed the contract (although this latter point does not always apply to consumer contracts; see 17.9.2.2).

consumer policy, this approach would discriminate against consumers from countries with low levels of consumer protection.

4.3.1.1 Scope of the Proposals

Thus the *Green Paper* shows a preference for minimal harmonisation of the legal guarantee, showing due respect to the subsidiarity principle. It is proposed to limit the benefit of the guarantee to consumers by restricting the guarantee to consumer goods ie those of a type ordinarily intended for private use or consumption. This method of delimiting protection to consumers was preferred to one based on the nature of the purchaser, since the guarantee is viewed as an attribute of the product. It also avoids the inconsistency of different guarantees applying to the same product. Such a move represents a change from the traditional English approach, however, which invokes the same guarantee to all goods supplied in the course of a business. However, in relation to exclusion clauses, it would extend the current scope of protection. The Unfair Contract Terms Act 1977 only entirely prohibits the use of clauses excluding the implied quality conditions where the goods concerned are consumer goods and the purchaser deals as a consumer.[137] The *Green Paper* proposes that the European legal guarantee would be non–excludable for all consumer goods, regardless of the status of the purchaser. One serious weakness with the proposed legal guarantee is that it would only apply to durable goods and to new goods. Whilst the legal guarantee would have to be applied differently to non–durable goods, it should still apply. (Presumably there is thought to be less of a European dimension to non–durable goods.) Equally the exclusion of second–hand goods is a flaw, especially when one considers the number of problems which second–hand cars give rise to. Again there is perceived to be a reduced European dimension to such sales. The harmonisation is described as 'minimal', meaning that Member States should be free to retain or enact more stringent provisions. This would appear to be a necessary safeguard, given the exclusions from its scope outlined above and other respects in which the proposal is less protective of the consumer than current UK law.

4.3.1.2 Defect

The key concept is the definition of defect. A definition based around 'legitimate expectations' is put forward as a synthesis of the laws of the Member States. Trying to find a term which each Member State can relate to

---

[137]　See 9.6.2.

almost inevitably involves a compromise representing the lowest common denominator, which can mean all things to all men. In this context 'legitimate expectations' is probably as good as any other and fits into a pattern of European consumer law which tries to fulfil consumer expectations.[138] However, it could be firmed up by making it clear that matters such as fitness for common purposes, appearance and finish, minor defects, safety and durability are covered. One might also be concerned if the concept was meant to exclude obvious defects where these had not been drawn to the consumer's attention or should have been revealed by the type of examination the consumer had made of the product.

Vendors will be liable for defects existing at the time of delivery and manufacturers for defects existing at the time the goods were placed on the market. Crucially, however, it is proposed that the burden should be on the vendor or manufacturer to prove that the defect did not exist at the relevant time.

4.3.1.3 Remedies

The *Green Paper* sees a fundamental link between the definition of defect and the remedies available. Thus it notes that, in the past, French law defined defects narrowly because the consequences of breach were serious. Thus whilst the *Green Paper* favours a broad definition of defect, it has a restrictive scheme of remedies. This approach is unsatisfactory even in a minimal directive. One of the advantages of the present English law is that the consumer has the right to reject for any breach, however minor (albeit that this right can be lost too easily). Such a right to reject gives the consumer a powerful bargaining advantage, which should not be diluted if the provisions are to be effectively enforced by consumers. The *Green Paper* proposal gives the purchaser the option of four remedies:

(i)   repudiation of the contract,
(ii) reimbursement of part of the price,
(iii) replacement of fungible products,
(iv) repair.

---

138 See the product linability defect standard which refers to 'legitimate expectations' and the Unfair Terms in Consumer Contracts Directive which can viewed as ensuring that consumers' legitimate expectations are satisfied: see R. Brownsword, G. Howells and T. Wilhelmsson, 'Between Market and Welfare: Some Reflections on Article 3 of the EC Directive on Unfair Terms in Consumer Contracts' in *Fairness in Contracting* C. Willett (ed.), (Edward Elgar, forthcoming).

It would be for Member States to determine the provision of damages for consequential losses at the national level.

This would provide United Kingdom consumers with two new remedies of replacement and repair. The problem is that these new remedies are not solely at the option of the consumer, but in some circumstances can be forced on a consumer who would prefer to reject the goods or obtain damages. Thus,

(i)   replacement or repair can be offered instead of repudiation, although the consumer should only be required to tolerate one attempt at repair or replacement;

(ii) any of the other remedies can be offered instead of partial reimbursement;

(iii) repudiation or repair can be offered instead of replacement. The repair must, however, be immediate. Repudiation can only be a substitute for replacement if the latter is not possible or not possible immediately and the consumer is unwilling to wait;

(iv) replacement within the same period as repair can be offered and if neither repair or replacement is possible the contract can be repudiated;

(v)   reimbursement of part of the price can be imposed on a consumer in respect of minor defects, unless the consumer can prove the damage is significant for him or her.

Where suppliers have knowledge of the defect, they will not be able to object to the consumer's choice of remedy.

Whilst there must be some constraint on the right to demand repair and replacement, these proposals leave the supplier with too much discretion. Art. 6 of the second draft Unfair Terms in Consumer Contracts Directive[139] had left the choice of remedy with the consumer. Even though the UK could retain stronger remedies, it would be preferable if the Directive did not include all these options as their sheer complexity and range would tend to confuse the consumer.

4.3.1.4 Liable Parties and Beneficiaries

The *Green Paper* recognises the reality of modern commercial practices by suggesting that the manufacturer be jointly liable with the vendor for the legal guarantee. There would, however, be differences between the obligations of the manufacturer and vendor. Thus manufacturers would, quite rightly, not be liable for any declarations by the vendor. More

---

[139]   OJ 1992 C73/7.

controversially, manufacturers would only be liable to repair and replace goods, although if repair or replacement was not possible they would then be liable for the consumer's direct losses. The rationale behind this is that, since manufacturers cannot control the price, they should not be liable to repay that price. This problem, however, could be dealt with by negotiation between the links in the supply chain. Again if consumers are to be able to use their rights, the keyword must be 'simplicity'. This is also why one should object to the notion of 'quasi–subsidiary' liability, meaning the proposed restriction whereby consumers can only claim against the manufacturer if it is impossible or onerous to sue the vendor. This would include cross–border situations and thus might overcome internal market problems, but overcomplicates the legal guarantee scheme.

It is further suggested that the benefit of guarantee be enjoyed by all subsequent owners of the product, a conclusion which again follows from viewing the guarantee as an attribute of the product. The Netherlands extends the protection to users, but this would only seem to be of value if consequential damages are recoverable.

4.3.1.5 Limitation Periods

The *Green Paper* appears rather confused on the question of limitation periods. Whilst it properly states that no special formality or procedure should be needed to invoke the guarantee, rather disturbingly it recommends a short time limit for submitting claims, presumably a period beginning once the defect was discovered. Provision is also made to suspend time during negotiations. Yet this requirement could mean that consumers who are ignorant or uncertain of their rights lose their claim. The only relevant period should be the limitation period in which claims are brought, currently six years in the UK. There should be resistance to any reduction to a shorter period, especially the six month period common in many civil law countries. The *Green Paper* seems to conflate the notion of a limitation period, with that of a guarantee period. However, questions of the guarantee period really relate to whether the definition of defect includes durability. It is pleasing to note that the *Green Paper* considers that a new guarantee period should begin for replacement goods or in the event of a repair.

4.3.1.6 Links with the Commercial Guarantee

The *Green Paper* properly supports the requirement that commercial guarantees should mention the existence of the legal guarantee. On the question of linkage with the commercial guarantee the issue is raised as to whether the relationship should be based on complementarity (ie both can be invoked) or subsidiarity (ie the legal guarantee can only be invoked if the commercial guarantee has proven unsatisfactory). Since the courts normally only become involved when the commercial guarantee has not assisted the consumer it would be better to view the two guarantees as complementary. In no way should the commercial guarantee be an excuse for providing less protection than that afforded under the legal guarantee.

4.3.2 Commercial Guarantee

The *Green Paper* noted two types of problems related to commercial guarantees: (i) those related to its legal status (legal problems), and (ii) those concerned with implementing commercial guarantees in relation to goods purchased in other Member States (European problems). The *Green Paper* proposed three ways of dealing with these.

(i)   A regulatory and unitary approach whereby both problems are resolved by European legislation. The main objection to this would be that it penalised smaller firms who might not be able to guarantee after–sales service throughout the Community.
(ii) A voluntary approach whereby incentives (such as a 'quality label' or protected designations, or pure self–regulation through Codes of Conduct) are used to encourage suppliers to resolve the legal and/or European problems by self regulation. However, the Commission is concerned that, as a result some of the legal problems may remain unresolved and, moreover, that Member States may therefore feel obliged to legislate in this area in a manner which gives rise to distortions of competition and to barriers to trade.
(iii) The Commission therefore clearly seemed to favour a mandatory legal scheme covering the legal problems, whilst encouraging the European aspects of the guarantee to be handled by voluntary means.

4.3.2.1 Legal Problems

The *Green Paper* rightly states that the commercial guarantee should provide additional rights to the legal guarantee, should mention the existence of the legal guarantee and summarise its content (this last matter will be a useful additional right for UK consumers). The commercial guarantee is to be considered as a contract between the guarantor and the holder of the goods. However, the consumer is only viewed as having a right of action against the manufacturer if other redress avenues have failed. Therefore, if the guarantee provides for complaints to be addressed to the retailer, this must have been attempted and failed. The aim should be to make the redress as simple as possible. This is why, in addition to making manufacturers directly liable, the Irish solution of making retailers liable on manufacturers' guarantees (unless they state the contrary), ought to be adopted. Matters of account between links in the distribution chain should not concern consumers. Concerned that it might be expecting too much for vendors to control all guarantees offered by manufacturers, the Commission appears hesitant to extend liability beyond selective distribution systems. The Commission proposes that the guarantee be valid for anyone in possession of the guarantee document and proof of initial purchase. There are also some proposals relating to form and transparency of commercial guarantees.

The weak link in the proposals relating to legal problems is that the content of the guarantee is left entirely to the supplier's discretion, except that it must go beyond the legal guarantee; it must also contain some fall back provisions which apply if the guarantee is silent on those matters (ie the right to claim repair or replacement for any defect, unless caused by the user, for a period of one year). Whilst manufacturers and retailers should be free to decide whether to give a commercial guarantee, nevertheless the word 'guarantee' conjures up expectations in the mind of the consumer. Thus minimum standards ought to be set which guarantees must satisfy before earning that description. This could be controlled either by awarding a mark, such as the 'Eco–label' system,[140] or by controlling the use of such terms as 'guarantee' by trade description rules. This would raise similar issues to those raised by the Commission's own suggestions relating to 'Euro–guarantees'.

4.3.2.2 Euro–guarantees

The Commission wishes to promote the use of 'European' guarantees, by which it means the common application of guarantee conditions for all goods of the same type and brand throughout the Community and the real possibility of implementing the guarantee wherever the goods are purchased. However, it is stressed that this does not mean that the producer would have to establish an integrated distribution network. Rather it would simply grant the consumer Community–wide access to a system which allows him to invoke the guarantee. The *Green Paper* states that it should include returning the defective goods to the producer at his expense: if this means at the consumer's expense, then this should at least be refundable if the complaint turns out to be justified.

---

[140] For a discussion of the Eco–labelling system see F. Maniet, 'The Eco–label and Consumer Protection in Europe' [1992] *EConsum LJ* 93.

To put such a system into place, the Commission suggests a term such as 'Euro–guarantee' which should be a protected label or designation; it also recommends a prohibition on claims or designations which might lead to confusion with the protected label. Two ways of achieving this are proposed:

(i)   the creation of a labelling system such as exists for the Eco–label[141] or the protection of geographical indications and designations of origin for agricultural products and foodstuffs;[142]
(ii) a system based on the protection of the designation 'Euro–guarantee', whose rules would be worked out in advance. The *Green Paper* is rather vague on this second option, which presumably would involve the use of trade descriptions laws for post–marketing control. This is inferred from the fact that the *Green Paper* states that the first option has the advantage of prior control, but has the disadvantage of involving the setting up of new 'bureaucratic' structures. The latter option could be effective in countries with strong enforcement authorities, but may be subject to abuse in countries with less developed consumer protection authorities.

4.3.3 After–sales Services

The *Green Paper* properly sees after–sales service as a responsibility of the manufacturer and suggests three options. Agreement could be sought on a voluntary basis, with industrial sectors setting minimum commitments for the availability of spare parts. Alternatively there could be a legal requirement that spare parts be available for the normal life span of a product, with appropriate periods being determined by Codes of Practice or standardisation. Finally, one approach is simply to require manufacturers to state on the product label the period for which they commit themselves to stock spare parts. This last method relies on a false belief in the extent to which information alone can create an informed consumer. Reliance on pure self–regulation has the problem that rogue traders can go unpenalised. The regulatory approach, combined with the involvement of both industry and consumer groups in fixing the appropriate periods, appears to be the best way forward. This could also cover the important issue of the price of after–sales service, since high costs discourage repairs which are economically beneficial to the consumer and environmentally friendly to the Community as a whole.

---

141   OJ 1992 L99/1.
142   OJ 1992 L208/1 and 9.

4.4 REFLECTIONS ON THE LAW RELATING TO QUALITY

The rules relating to quality are of great practical significance to consumers. They also provide useful material with which to consider many issues which are central to the study of consumer law, illustrating its rather patchwork and *ad hoc* development. Common law rules have been put into statutory form at different times and with different results depending upon the form of contract. The case for harmonisation and possibly codification clearly needs to be considered. Also the question of whether consumer law should be treated as a special area separate from the influence of commercial law needs to be addressed.

Regarding the substance of the law, we have followed the debate over the extent to which mandatory minimum quality conditions should be laid down or whether businesses should be left free to compete in the market place by offering a range of levels of guarantee. There is also the connected question of the extent to which information provisions can be relied on to inform consumers of the quality of the guarantee they are purchasing and the form in which that information should be provided. Recently, there has been a recognition that the law in this area must be modernised to take on board the consumer perspective. Traditional legal rules, such as the privity rule, are being looked at again to take account of the modern economy in which the consumer more often looks to the manufacturer than the retailer for redress when goods are defective. The final part of the chapter shows that, even in what many traditional English contract lawyers view as the heart of their subject, the influence of European Community law cannot be ignored.

5 Title and Risk

5.1 INTRODUCTION

In this chapter we turn our attention to two aspects of personal property law of concern to consumers. First, have they obtained a good title to the goods bought? Second, when do the goods become their property (with the usual consequence that risk passes to the buyer)? These topics are of great practical concern. For instance, many consumers find themselves involved in disputes relating to title because of competing claims for cars which had been stolen and resold. Consumers also need to understand the rules on the passing of property, for instance, if their supplier goes into liquidation in order to determine who has rights over goods which have been paid for but not supplied prior to liquidation.

The rules relating to title and risk can be highly technical and consumers can easily find themselves on the wrong end of technical legalistic arguments. For example, many consumers would be surprised to find that they may be the party at risk when a piece of furniture they have ordered is destroyed in a warehouse fire. Our treatment of this topic will be shorter than that which is customarily given to it in commercial law texts.[1] We have decided not to go into detail on this topic as it is less directly concerned with creating consumer protection values than some of the other areas considered. Many of the problems facing consumers in this area are the result of the ad hoc development of the law rather than any intent to penalise consumers or ideological refusal to protect them. Indeed many businesses do not stand by their legal rights where this would produce injustice. Also, in relation to the question of who should obtain title to goods the private individual is just as likely to be a wrongfully dispossessed owner seeking to recover his or her car as the purchaser of stolen goods who risks having made a worthless purchase.

The rules of personal property are, nevertheless, an important aspect of consumer law. In addition to the practical relevance of the topic, the rules on title also serve as a good example of how the law has developed without any coherent theoretical basis. We will see later that attempts to reform the law on the basis of clearly formulated principles have proved unsuccessful to-date. However, in the title area, none of the proposals has suggested a fair scheme for allocating, between the innocent original owner and the innocent

---

1   See R. Bradgate and N. Savage, *Commercial Law*, Chs 14–17.

purchaser, the risk of goods being stolen and sold on. Fidelity to legal tradition seems to have prevented substantive justice from being achieved.

5.2 TITLE

The law's dilemma with regard to whether the purchaser of goods from someone other than their true owner should be given a perfect title is well illustrated by the oft–quoted dictum of Lord Denning that:

> 'In the development of our law, two principles have striven for mastery. The first is for the protection of property; no one can give a better title than he himself possesses. The second is for the protection of commercial transactions; the person who takes in good faith and for value without notice should get a good title. The first principle has held sway for a long time, but has been modified by the common law itself and by statute so as to meet the needs of our times.'[2]

The first principle is encapsulated in the Latin maxim *'nemo dat quod non habeat'* (no one can give what he does not have) and represents the common law position which is now found in s.21, Sale of Goods Act 1979. Several inroads into this principle are to be found in ss.21–25, Sale of Goods Act 1979. These rules only apply directly to contracts for the sale of goods, but they are likely to be applied to other contracts since they largely reflect the common law. Other statutes to be considered include the Factors Act 1889 and the Hire–Purchase Act 1964.

One of the problems with formulating legal policy in this area is that one is faced with allocating a loss to one of two equally innocent parties. The typical scenario is that the true owner of goods parts with them to an intermediary, who then sells them on to a purchaser, with the purchaser and true owner left to fight for ownership. The intermediate party might be somebody who stole the goods, or obtained them dishonestly, for example, by passing a forged cheque. But it might equally be someone acting in ignorance, for example, a hirer under a hire–purchase contract who mistakenly believed he or she was free to sell the goods or an agent who acted outside his or her authority.

In such cases the true owner will usually bring an action for conversion against the possessor of the goods, based on the possessor having dealt with the property in a manner so as to deny the true owner's title. Either the *nemo*

---

2   *Bishopsgate Motor Finance Corp. Ltd v Transport Brakes Ltd* [1949] 1 KB 322 at 336–7.

dat rule is applied and the true owner recovers[3] or one of the exceptions is applied and the possessor recovers. Faced with two innocent parties,[4] the temptation is to find a solution which shares the misfortune between them. This aim was judicially expressed by Devlin LJ in *Ingram v Little*. He was frustrated by the lack of pragmatism in the common law which resolved the question of ownership in the instant case by reference to the technical question of whether the initial contract of sale was void or voidable. His Lordship continued:

> 'For the doing of justice the relevant question in this sort of case is not whether the contract was void or voidable, but which of the two innocent parties should suffer for the fraud of a third. The plain answer is that the loss should be divided between them in such proportion as is just in all the circumstances. If it is pure misfortune the loss should be borne equally; if the fault or imprudence of either party has caused or contributed to the loss, it should be borne by that party in the whole or in the greater part.'[5]

When considering this matter, in 1966, the Law Reform Committee rejected the idea of apportionment as impractical. Further it considered that the uncertainty created by such a rule would increase litigation. It thought it would be difficult to establish the fact or extent of parties' 'negligence', especially given the chain of hands through which the goods usually passed. There was obvious suspicion that in many cases the first purchaser lacked good faith, but there would be evidential difficulties in proving this.[6] The Committee's proposed reforms are considered below. For now it is sufficient to note that there is widespread criticism that the exceptions to the *nemo dat* principle have developed without the support of any clear theory. What is clear is that, given the repeal of the 'market overt' exception[7] and the decision

---

3   Note that in a conversion action, credit should be given for any improvements made to the goods: *Greenwood v Bennett* [1973] 1 QB 195. Lord Denning considered that the improver would himself have a cause of action for unjust enrichment: see S. Anderson, 'Unjust Enrichment and the Innocent Purchaser' (1973) 36 *MLR* 89; such a statutory right has indeed now been provided by s.6(1), Torts (Interference with Goods) Act 1977.

4   It is sometimes suggested that the first purchaser is rarely wholly innocent, but usually the goods have passed through several pairs of hands before they reach the party against whom the action for recovery of the property is brought.

5   [1960] 3 All ER 332 at 351–2.

6   Law Reform Committee, *Transfer of Title to Chattels*, (Cmnd 2958, 1966).

7   See 5.2.9.1.

in *National Employers Mutual General Assurance Ltd v Jones*,[8] no title can be passed where the goods have been stolen or lost and have not been given to the original transferee with the (albeit perhaps fraudulently obtained) consent of the true owner.

French and German law favour the purchaser when the true owner parted with possession voluntarily and the US Uniform Commercial Code strongly favours the promotion of commercial activity over property rights by placing the burden of preventing fraudulent transactions on the original owner who, after all, is best placed to control activities in relation to the goods or insure against their loss. Favouring the purchaser seems a sensible policy, since the eventual buyer of the goods does not know and cannot be expected to know, for instance, that goods were being hired under a hire–purchase contract, that an agent had exceeded his authority, that title in goods had been reserved or that they had been bought with a forged cheque or one that would not be honoured. At least the original owner has the opportunity to control actions so as to protect himself from such risks. This type of thinking lies behind many of the exceptions to the *nemo dat* rule, but we shall see that, at other times, the protection of third parties is lost because of terms of contracts made with the true owner of which they could not be aware.

Battersby makes the insightful point that what is needed, perhaps even more than theoretical logic, is practical evidence of how the rules on title and possible reforms thereto will work out in practice.[9] Most importantly the role of insurance needs to be considered: owners of cars and other expensive household goods are likely to be insured, whereas insurance is not normally available against purchasing goods with bad title. But equally before this is assumed to give pat answers the policy of insurers in using subrogation rights and assignment of claims has to be taken into account. Battersby notes that the unattractive, but not wholly irrational, outcome might be different regimes for different types of goods, as indeed already exists for cars in the hire–purchase context.[10]

Equally it might be argued that finance companies do not need as much protection as the purchasers of goods which are technically owned by finance companies under hire–purchase agreements; especially given the fact that finance companies have the ability to vet their potential customers. If the goods are sold, they only lose their security whilst retaining the right to sue the debtor for the amount owing under the loan agreement.

---

8   [1988] 2 All ER 425; see 5.2.7.
9   G. Battersby, (1991) 54 *MLR* 752.
10   See 5.2.8.

5.2.1 Nemo Dat

The basic *nemo dat* principle is set out in s.21(1), Sale of Goods Act 1979 which states:

> 'Subject to this Act, where goods are sold by a person who is not their owner, and who does not sell them under the authority or with the consent of the owner, the buyer acquires no better title to the goods than the seller had, unless the owner of the goods is by his conduct precluded from denying the seller's authority to sell.'

5.2.2 Exceptions in s.21

The next sub–section immediately goes on to provide for exceptions, including where the Factors Acts apply[11] and where the sale takes place under a special common law or statutory power or under a court order.[12] The main section itself contains two exceptions. Thus title will pass where the seller has the consent or authority of the owner to sell the goods; also under general agency principles apparent authority will be sufficient even if the agent has exceeded his or her actual authority. The more extensive protection afforded where goods are purchased from a mercantile agent is discussed below.[13] The section also preserves the common law defence that an owner can be estopped by his conduct from denying the seller's authority to sell.

5.2.3 Estoppel

Estoppel is most easily founded on a representation made by the true owner that the seller is in fact the owner or at least has authority to sell the goods. A classic example is *Eastern Distributors v Goldring*[14] which involved a car purchase. Unfortunately the intending car purchaser did not have a sufficient deposit, although he did own a van. The dealer created a sham transaction whereby it was made to look as if the dealer was the owner of the van with the intention that the money forwarded for its purchase would act as a deposit for the car. Unfortunately only the loan for the van was approved: this meant that the dealer purported to transfer title to the finance company

---

11   S.21(2)(a), Sale of Goods Act 1979.
12   S.21(2)(b), Sale of Goods Act 1979.
13   See 5.2.4.
14   [1957] 2 QB 600.

who then hired it to the customer with the option to purchase. When, later, the question of ownership of the van arose the true owner was estopped by his connivance in signing the forms from denying that the dealer had been in a position to transfer title to the finance company. Similarly in *Shaw v Metropolitan Police Commissioner*[15] the owner would have been estopped by the act of giving his car to another party with a letter stating that the car had been sold to that party and a blank vehicle transfer notification form. However, the contract between that party and the subsequent purchaser provided that property would only pass on payment and this had not happened. Thus the true owner was held not to be estopped since s.21(1) was not held to apply to agreements to sell. In both cases there was a positive representation that the other party owns the goods. It should be possible to raise an estoppel based purely on conduct, but the courts will require more than simply the fact that a party has been allowed to retain possession of the goods.[16]

Despite the sound dictum of Ashurst J in *Lickbarrow v Mason*[17] that 'whenever one of two innocent parties must suffer for the fraud of a third, he who has enabled such person to occasion the loss must sustain it', the courts have been reluctant to allow negligence to be the basis of estoppel. They have required that the true owner owe the purchaser a duty of care, which is a difficult requirement to satisfy in respect of claims for economic loss.[18] *Central Newbury Car Auctions Ltd v Unity Finance Ltd*[19] concerned a swindler who had persuaded a garage to let him take a car and its log book away before the hire–purchase agreement had been confirmed. It was held that no title had passed and that the garage could recover the car. There was, however, a strong dissent from Lord Denning who considered that the garage's behaviour amounted to negligence to the point of recklessness and that an estoppel could be based, not merely on giving possession of the car, but also the recognised means of transferring ownership – the log book. However, the log book is not in fact a document of title to the car, although of course in practice many people ignore (or are ignorant of) the warning on the document which states the keeper may not be the legal owner.[20] In

---

15   [1987] 3 All ER 405.
16   In the Canadian case of *McVicar v Herman* (1958) 13 DLR (2d) 419, there was no estoppel where an employer simply allowed an ex–employee to retain possession of his company car.
17   (1787) 2 TR 63.
18   For the general test see *Caparo Industries v Dickman* [1990] 1 All ER 568.
19   [1957] 1 QB 371.
20   The position is likely to be similar despite log books being replaced by registration documents.

Mercantile Credit v Hamblin,[21] the true owner of a car asked a friend to help her get a loan. She filled out what she thought was an application form, but it was actually a hire–purchase form which allowed the 'friend' to appear as is if he owned the car. It was held that she did owe the subsequent buyer a duty of care (this may be decided differently given the current retrenchment of duty of care situations in the law of negligence), but nevertheless it was held that the duty of care had not been breached since she had known the fraudulent party socially and it had been reasonable for her to rely on him. *Eastern Distributors v Goldring* was distinguished on the basis that, in the instant case, the true owner had not been a party to the fraud.

The reluctance to base liability on negligence is well illustrated by *Moorgate Mercantile Co. Ltd v Twitchings*.[22] This concerned a dispute as to ownership between two finance companies, both of which belonged to HPI Ltd. HPI Ltd is a private company formed to register hire–purchase agreements on cars to which 98 per cent of all finance companies belonged at that time. The true owner of a car was a finance company which belonged to HPI, but which failed to register the car. The hirer offered the car to another company which also belonged to HPI and which bought the car after checking the register and finding no entry. HPI were held not to be agents of the finance companies, so that its answers did not amount to a representation that no finance company had an interest in the car. By a bare majority the House of Lords held there was no duty of care owed by the owner to register with HPI. The majority was swayed by the fact that membership of HPI was voluntary. Whilst it must be right that no one should be forced to register with a private company, unless under specific statutory authority, a distinction could perhaps be drawn so as to impose a duty of care between companies who had chosen to join and participate in the system. Nowadays HPI has changed its rules so that all members are contractually bound to register all agreements and members may well have a contractual claim against other members who fail to register agreements.

5.2.4 Mercantile Agents

S.21(2)(a), Sale of Goods Act 1979 expressly preserves the provisions of the Factors Acts. Factors were central to trade in the 18th and 19th centuries. They sold goods in their own name but on behalf of principals. Ensuring that those trading with factors could do so with confidence was the purpose behind a series of Factors Acts, culminating in the 1889 Act which remains in force today. Strangely, the provisions of the Act do not refer to 'factors';

---

21 [1965] 2 QB 242.
22 [1977] AC 890.

rather the term 'mercantile agent' is used, which is defined as 'a mercantile agent having in the customary course of his business as such agent authority either to sell goods, or to consign goods for the purpose of sale, or to buy goods, or to raise money on the security of goods.'[23]

S.2(1), Factors Act 1889 in effect extends the ability of the mercantile agent to pass good title beyond the limits of normal agency law, as follows:

> 'Where a mercantile agent is, with the consent of the owner, in the possession of goods or the documents of title to goods, any sale, pledge, or other disposition of the goods, made by him when acting in the ordinary course of business of a mercantile agent, shall, subject to the provisions of this Act, be as valid as if he were expressly authorised by the owner of the goods to make the same; provided that the person taking under the disposition acts in good faith, and has not at the time of the disposition notice that the person making the disposition has not authority to make the same.'

Note that there are several elements which need to be satisfied before the provision applies. The agent must be a mercantile agent, as defined by the Act. The agent must be in possession of the goods or documents of title and must have them in his or her possession at the time of sale, etc. The agent must be in possession of them with the consent of the owner (this is rebuttably presumed), although it does not matter if the consent was induced by deceit. The agent must have received them in his or her capacity as a mercantile agent. Thus in *Belvoir Finance Ltd v Harold Cole*[24] the section did not apply when a car hire firm – a mercantile agent for other purposes – sold off cars to pay hire–purchase debts. The buyer must act in good faith.

Most debate has centred upon the meaning to be given to the requirement that the mercantile agent be 'acting in the ordinary course of a business of a mercantile agent'. This could have been restrictively interpreted by looking at the type of work a particular agent or class of agent did and not applying the section if, in the particular transaction, the agent acted for other purposes. However, a broader test was preferred in *Oppenheimer v Attenborough* [1908] 1 KB 221. This case concerned a diamond merchant who pledged gems belonging to the plaintiff, the evidence being that diamond merchants did not have authority to pledge their principal's goods in advance. The true owner lost, however, since the Court of Appeal merely required that the business be conducted in the way that a mercantile agent would have acted if it had been part of his business. This has, rightly, been described as a 'very

---

23 S.1(1), Factors Act 1889.
24 [1969] 2 All ER 904.

bland test';[25] by not requiring the buyer to scrutinise the range of activities undertaken by each mercantile agent, it is also one which promotes commercial activity at the expense of protecting property. Some transactions still fall outside the protection, for instance if they take place outside ordinary hours, or at an unfamiliar place or if they are conducted in an unusual manner.[26] *Pearson v Rose and Young Ltd*[27] concerned the sale of a second hand car, where the registration book had been left in the car accidentally. This meant that the mercantile agent was not deemed to have possession of the registration book since it had been left accidentally and had not been placed in his possession for the purpose of the sale. Thus the sale was treated as the sale of a car without documents, which was not considered to be in the ordinary course of business. In contrast, the sale of a new car without documents has been held to be in the ordinary course of business of a mercantile agent.[28] It has been pointed out that there may be occasions when the sale of a second–hand car without documents can be explained on the basis that it had only been recently acquired and that documentation was being awaited.[29]

5.2.5 Seller with Voidable Title

S.23, Sale of Goods Act 1979 provides that:

> 'When the seller of goods has a voidable title to them, but his title has not been avoided at the time of the sale, the buyer acquires a good title to the goods, provided that he buys them in good faith and without notice of the seller's defect of title.'

This section only allows title to be passed where the initial sale contract is voidable, not void. Thus when a fraud has been perpetrated the question often arises as to whether (i) the fraud amounted to a misrepresentation or non–fundamental mistake, in which case the contract would be voidable, or (ii) whether the mistake went to the root of the contract, in which case it would be void. S.23 would not apply in the latter instance. In cases involving rogues buying cars, the distinction often turns upon whether the vendor intended to contract with the person physically before them (in which case

---

25   M. Bridge, *Personal Property Law*, (Blackstone,1993) at p. 99.
26   See, for example, *De Grooter v Attenborough & Son* (1904) 19 TLR 19, when an agent sent a friend into pawnbrokers.
27   [1951] 1 KB 221.
28   *Astley Industrial Trust Ltd v Miller* [1968] 2 All ER 36.
29   See R. Bradgate and N. Savage, *op. cit.* at p. 294.

the contract would be merely voidable), or whether some special characteristic of the person allegedly before them was of vital concern to them (so that the contract was void). This is often a highly artificial distinction. Thus, in *Ingram v Little*[30] a contract was held void as the old ladies who were selling a car refused to accept a cheque without checking the address of the buyer in the telephone book. His real identity was clearly important to them. In contrast, in *Lewis v Averay*[31] where a rogue claimed to be a well known film star Greene in order to persuade the seller to accept a cheque in payment, the courts held that there was only a voidable contract. Lord Denning doubted whether *Ingram v Little* had been correctly decided. Indeed, it seems unfair to make the position of the subsequent buyer dependent upon a question of the technical interpretation of events which took place prior to the making of an earlier contract.

Given that the contract is voidable and not void, s.23 allows the subsequent seller to pass a good title until such time as the contract is avoided. Normally a contract is avoided by notifying the other party of that fact, which may be impossible where the rogue has disappeared. Thus in *Car and Universal Finance Co. v Caldwell*[32] it was held that a contract could be constructively avoided by notifying the police and the Automobile Association of the loss of a car and asking them to look for it. However, we shall see that the impact of this decision is limited by the fact that it does not affect the ability of a buyer to pass a good title under s.25, Sale of Goods Act 1979.

5.2.6 Sale by Seller in Possession

S.24, Sale of Goods Act 1979 provides that:

> 'Where a person having sold goods continues or is in possession of the goods, or of documents of title to the goods, the delivery or transfer by that person or by a mercantile agent acting for him, of the goods or of the documents of title under any sale, pledge or other disposition thereof, to any person receiving the same in good faith and without notice of the previous sale, has the same effect as if the person making the sale or transfer were expressly authorised by the owner of the goods to make the same.'[33]

---

[30] [1961] 1 QB 31.
[31] [1973] 1 QB 198.
[32] [1965] 1 QB 525.
[33] Both this section and the next (s.25) have their counterparts in ss.8 and 9 of the Factors Act 1889. The latter has similar wording but is slightly broader in that it also

This provision applies where a person who has sold goods continues in possession of them. For example, a buyer might leave a car with a seller whilst arranging insurance, and the seller might then sell the car for a second time. The seller's possession need not be lawful and need not be in the capacity of seller: thus it applied where goods had been transferred to a hire–purchase company and the seller retained possession as agent of the finance company.[34] However, the seller must retain possession. If possession is once lost and then the seller comes back into possession of the goods the section does not apply.[35] For consumers, the important consequence is that the section does not apply, for instance, where the consumer takes goods back to the seller for repair.

5.2.7 Sale by Buyer in Possession

S.25 (1), Sale of Goods Act 1979 provides that:

> 'Where a person having bought or agreed to buy goods obtains, with the consent of the seller, possession of the goods or the documents of title to the goods, the delivery or transfer by that person, or by a mercantile agent acting for him, of the goods or documents of title, under any sale, pledge or other disposition thereof, to any person receiving the same in good faith and without notice of any lien or other right of the original seller in respect of the goods, has the same effect as if the person making the delivery or transfer were a mercantile agent in possession of the goods or documents of title with the consent of the owner.'

The person must have bought or agreed to buy; hence case law has determined that this excludes hire–purchase agreements.[36] S.25(2), Sale of Goods Act 1979 extends this exclusion to conditional sales within the meaning of the Consumer Credit Act 1974, where the purchase price or part of it is payable by instalments.[37] However, it was held in *Newtons of Wembley v Williams*[38] that this section continues to apply even where the buyer obtained consent under a voidable contract which has been avoided; to a large extent this has undermined the value to the true owner of the decision

---

applies to any '*agreement* for sale, pledge or other disposition' (emphasis added). Various reform proposals have recommended abolition of the Factors Acts provisions.

[34] See *Worcester Works Finance Ltd v Cooden Engineering Ltd* [1972] 1 QB 210.

[35] *Mitchell v Jones* (1905) 24 NZLR 932.

[36] *Helby v Matthews* [1895] AC 471.

[37] For the special rules which apply in these cases to motor vehicles , see 5.2.8.

[38] [1965] 1 QB 560.

in *Car and Universal Finance Co. v Caldwell*.[39] In contrast to s.24, s.25 requires that the buyer be in possession of the goods with the consent of the seller. However, since it does not matter whether the consent was obtained by fraud,[40] a fraudster can pass a good title under s. 25.

National Employers Mutual General Insurance Association v Jones[41] raised the interesting question of whether, although the purchaser from a thief cannot pass good title, a subsequent purchaser would be able to invoke s.25. On a literal reading of s.25 this should be possible since possession would have been obtained with the consent of the seller and the owner's consent does not appear to be needed. The only reference to 'owner' is at the end of the section when it is provided that the sale shall have the same effect as if the person were a mercantile agent in possession of the goods with the consent of the owner. This literal interpretation was preferred by Sir Denys Buckley in the Court of Appeal who pointed out that there may be good policy reasons for such a distinction: a purchaser from a thief might be able to discover the vendor's lack of title, but this would be virtually impossible for a subsequent purchaser from a legitimate vendor. However, such a conclusion goes against the basic notion that no one can pass on a better title than they have themselves. The majority in the Court of Appeal refused to allow title to pass, arguing that, as the initial transaction was from a thief, there had therefore been no general property (as opposed to a merely possessory title) to transfer; thus the transactions did not fall within the definition of sale; thus s.25 was excluded.

The House of Lords reached the same conclusion by a different route. Lord Goff surveyed the history of the Act and concluded that the sale by the subsequent seller should pass a perfect title only if he was in possession of the goods or documents of title with the consent of the true owner. If someone other than the true owner, even a thief, sells the goods, they will be able to pass such limited title as they possess (eg mere possessory title), but this will be defeasible by the true owner. The problem lies in the history of the statutory drafting of these provisions. Originally the transaction was deemed to have been as valid as if the vendee had been entrusted by the vendor with the documents. This has been changed; the section now provides that the buyer who obtains possession with the consent of the seller is treated *as if* he had the consent of the owner. Lord Goff was concerned that this change in the statutory wording should not result in the seller being able to pass a greater title than that which he actually had. The problem with Lord Goff's analysis is that, whilst this alteration might have not been intended, it does appear to have been made on a literal reading of the section. Moreover,

---

[39]   [1965] 1 QB 525.

[40]   *Du Jardin v Beadman* [1952] 2 QB 712.

[41]   [1987] 3 All ER 385 (CA), [1988] 2 All ER 425 (HL).

as Sir Denys Buckley shows, there are good reasons for differentiating between the first and subsequent purchasers. The reluctance to do so suggests that the rationale supporting most exceptions to the *nemo dat* rule is the belief that where the true owner has delivered possession of the goods freely, albeit perhaps because of trickery, there is justification for favouring the innocent purchaser who had no opportunity of protecting himself. Such a justification does not exist in *Jones* where the goods were stolen.

Further complications in interpreting s.25 arise because, whereas s.24 talks about the sale by a seller in possession having the same effect as if 'the delivery or transfer were expressly authorised by the owner', s.25 less straightforwardly provides that a sale by a buyer in possession shall have the same effect as if the buyer 'were a mercantile agent in possession of the goods or documents with the consent of the owner'. It might have been possible to construe this provision literally on the basis that it is an 'as if' provision and hence simply say that the sale will be treated as if made by a mercantile agent.[42] The Court of Appeal in *Newtons of Wembley Ltd v Williams*,[43] however, preferred a more restrictive approach, requiring the subsequent seller to act as if he were a mercantile agent even though he was not one! On the facts of *Newtons of Wembley v Williams* this test was satisfied as the car in question was sold at an established car market. However, as mercantile agents are businesses and work from business premises during normal business hours, the section would seem to have limited application to private sales, a fact which can have serious consequences in the consumer context. The Law Reform Committee recommended in 1966 that the law should be changed so as to make it unnecessary for the buyer in possession of goods to have acted, in disposing of them, as if he were a mercantile agent.[44]

5.2.8 Disposition of Motor Vehicle on Hire–purchase or Conditional Sale

Problems arise when a person purchasing a car on hire–purchase sells the car off before the credit is repaid. This may be a fraudulent practice or simply ignorance of the legal situation whereby the finance company is the legal owner of the goods. Purchasers of such cars can easily be deceived into believing that the seller had the right to sell since many people ignore the warning on the registration document that 'The registered keeper is not necessarily the legal owner'. A scheme involving finance companies retaining the registration book and issuing cards to hirers was rejected on

---

42 Cf *Langmead v Thyer Rubber Co.* [1947] SASR 29.
43 [1965] 1 QB 560.
44 *Twelfth Report, op. cit.,* at pp. 9–12.

administrative grounds; instead, Part III of the Hire–Purchase Act 1964 applies to situations when a motor vehicle is bailed on hire–purchase or agreed to be sold under a conditional sale agreement. The consequences of any subsequent disposition depend upon whether it is to a private purchaser or to a trade or finance purchaser.

Where the disposition is to a private purchaser then, provided the purchaser acts in good faith with no notice of the hire–purchase or conditional sale agreement, that disposition shall have effect as if the creditor's title to the vehicle had been vested in the debtor immediately before that disposition.[45] Note that the buyer only obtains as good a title as the creditor had and so the buyer's claim can be defeated by anyone with a better title than the creditor – for example, a true owner where none of the *nemo dat* exceptions apply. The notion of a private purchaser is wider than that of a private individual and includes anyone who is not a trade or finance purchaser. Thus it covers anyone who does not carry on a business, which, wholly or partly, consists of purchasing motor vehicles with the intention of selling them or providing finance by purchasing vehicles to let out under hire–purchase or conditional sale agreements. Trade and finance purchasers are not protected even if they buy a car for private purposes. The reason for the distinction is that trade and finance purchasers are expected to use HPI – the industry voluntary scheme for registering hire–purchase agreements. This underlines the rough justice of the decision in *Moorgate Mercantile Co. v Twitchings,*[46] which held that there was no duty of care requiring a finance company to register a hire–purchase agreement. Thus a finance company can fail to register a car and yet another trader cannot obtain a perfect title even if the register has been checked.[47] Individuals can use HPI through motoring organisations and the Cabx.

Individuals can still lose out where a car purchased by them was subject to a hire–purchase or conditional sale agreement if: (i) the first private purchaser did not act in good faith, (ii) there was no disposition by the original bailor; for instance, if the car was stolen or (iii) there was a break in the chain of title between the first private purchaser and the person claiming title in the goods. The private purchaser is assisted by the burden of proof being placed on the finance company and by a series of presumptions in relation to the above matters which could otherwise defeat the purchaser's claim.

---

45   S.27(2), Hire–Purchase Act 1964.
46   [1977] AC 890; see 5.2.3
47   But consider the possibility of a contractual action between members: see 5.2.3.

5.2.9 Reforms

The above description of the law indicates a need for reform in this area in terms of the development of sound principles. Indeed, three significant sets of relevant proposals have been put forward: the 1966 Twelfth Report of the Law Reform Committee on *Transfer of Title to Chattels*;[48] Professor Diamond's 1989 report for the Department of Trade and Industry, *A Review of Securities in Property*, and the Department of Transport's own 1994 Consultation document, *Transfer of Title*. All three reform proposals recommend giving greater protection to the innocent purchaser; in other words preferring the encouragement of commercial activity over property rights. Yet we will begin by looking at a recent actual reform which went in the opposite direction by removing the one exception to the *nemo dat* rule which allowed the purchaser of stolen goods to obtain a good title.

5.2.9.1 Market Overt

The Sale of Goods (Amendment) Act 1994 abolished the doctrine of market overt which had been found in s.22, Sale of Goods Act 1979.[49] This had provided that, where goods were sold in market overt, according to the usage of the market, the buyer acquired a good title to the goods provided they were bought in good faith and without notice of any defect or want of title on the part of the seller. Market overt covered any open public market established by Royal Charter, statute or long established custom. The doctrine was anachronistic and surrounded by anomalies. Thus every ground floor shop in the City of London was deemed to be market overt, whereas the Welsh had abolished the doctrine as long ago as 1542.[50] Also the sale had to have taken place between sunrise and sunset. In *Reid v Metropolitan Police Commissioner*,[51] no market overt title was acquired as the sale took place in the 'half–light'. The alleged origin of the rule derived from times when public outlets for goods were few and the possibility of moving goods to other districts for sale was limited. Thus the owner of stolen goods could be expected to search the public markets for them; if he or she failed to do so,

---

48   *Op. cit.*
49   See G. Howells, *Consumer Contract Legislation – The New Law*, Ch. 3 (Blackstone, 1995).
50   Laws in Wales Act 1542.
51   [1973] QB 551.

then they could not challenge the title of an innocent purchaser.[52] This did not meet the needs of modern times.

As we shall see, some reform proposals favoured extending the exception in favour of all innocent purchasers buying goods from retail premises in the ordinary course of business. In its consultation document, however, the DTI preferred abolition of the market overt rule and this was enacted in a private member's Bill. The impetus for this reform came in part from fear that stolen works of art were being sold at established markets. There was also some concern that car boot sales were becoming an increasingly popular means of selling on stolen goods. The market overt rule was viewed as providing buyers at such markets with good titles, although many of these markets would probably not have been proper 'market overts'.

5.2.9.2 Law Reform Committee[53]

The Law Reform Committee had also proposed the abolition of the market overt rule, but favoured replacing it with a provision enabling a person who buys goods in good faith by retail at trade premises or at a public auction to acquire a good title.[54] The Committee also proposed that, where a party had been deceived into parting with the possession of goods on the basis of the mistaken identity of the other contracting party, such contracts should always be voidable. The decision in *Car and Universal Finance v Caldwell*[55] should be overturned so as to require notification to the other contracting party for rescission to be effective.

5.2.9.3 Diamond

In his submissions to the 1966 Law Reform Committee, Aubrey Diamond had argued that any innocent purchaser who had acted reasonably should be able to retain what he had bought. When he produced his own Report in 1989, Diamond had become less extreme, but still favoured the innocent purchaser more than the present law does. He considered that there should be a general principle that applied wherever the owner of goods has entrusted

---

52 Cf B. Davenport, (1994) *LQR* 165 who considers that the DTI consultation paper inaccurately describes it as an anachronism from medieval law, but does not elaborate.

53 *Op.cit.* on which see, critically, P. Atiyah, (1966) 23 *MLR* 541; cf A. Diamond, (1966) 23 *MLR* 413.

54 But see the powerful dissent by Lord Donovan on this recommendation.

55 [1965] 1 QB 525.

them to, or acquiesced in their possession by, another person, to the effect that a disposition by the possessor in favour of an innocent party would confer good title on the purchaser, to the extent that the owner could have conferred title.[56] Although normally this rule would only apply where the disposition was in the ordinary course of business of the possessor, this caveat would not apply to sales of consumer goods. *Car and Universal Finance Ltd v Caldwell* would also be reversed: it would not be sufficient even that the seller had been notified that the title had been avoided. The innocent purchaser would be protected until the dispossessed owner had repossessed the goods. Such proposals would seem to simplify and rationalise the law. The fact that they do favour the innocent purchaser may be a proper course (given the role of insurance), although of course one would wish to see empirical evidence of the consequences of such a change in the law. Nonetheless, they stop short of ever allowing the innocent purchaser of stolen goods to obtain a good title.

5.2.9.4 DTI[57]

The DTI proposed a change in the law broadly similar to the general principle proposed by Prof. Diamond. The paper is rather brief and its quality as a consultation document was roundly condemned by one former Law Commissioner,[58] who, in the course of his criticisms, notes that the proposals would mean that one could be deprived of goods lent to another and that sale or return would become a gamble. These simple points illustrate the problem that, in trying to balance the advantage of commerce against the protection of property, the law is faced with many permutations of different equities. The abolition of market overt apart, law reform currently seems to be favouring the protection of the innocent purchaser. One wonders whether a regime could not be devised which does justice between the parties rather than impose an all or nothing solution. Even if normally the innocent purchaser should retain possession of the goods, does this apply equally to goods of unique or sentimental value? Perhaps the solution could be for the goods to pass to the innocent purchaser, but with the court having the additional power to order that they be transferred at fair value to the original

---

56   These are Prof. Diamond's preferred reforms. As a minimum reform he proposed that the buyers of goods sold in the course of the seller's business should take free of any security interest: *A Review of Security Interests in Property* (DTI, 1989).The bulk of the report concerned a system of priorities where security interests existed in chattels (but these proposals have subsequently been rejected by the DTI).

57   *Transfer of Title: Sections 21–25 of the Sale of Goods Act 1979*, (June, 1994).

58   B. Davenport, *op. cit.*

owner where he or she can show a sentimental or unique interest in the specific goods which is greater than that of the innocent purchaser.

5.3 DUTY TO PASS GOOD TITLE

The above discussion has involved the battle for ownership between the true owner of goods and a subsequent purchaser. It should be remembered that the buyer of goods who receives a defective title does have rights against his seller under s.12, Sale of Goods Act 1979. In the consumer context, the problem is that often these rights cannot be enforced as the seller is a rogue who has disappeared or a trader who has become insolvent. S.12 implies a condition that the seller must have the right to sell and, in the case of an agreement to sell, must have such a right at the time when the property is to pass.[59] Note that the seller need not have title at the time the contract is made, but should have it when property is to pass. A difficult issue surrounds the question of whether a defect in title at the moment when property should pass can be cured by the seller subsequently acquiring title. This was the scenario in *Butterworth v Kingsway Motors Ltd*[60] where damages were awarded because the claim had been made before the title was 'fed', but the position if the claim had been made later was left open. The obligation to pass a good title under s.12 is non–excludable[61] but the seller can make it clear that he or she can only transfer a limited title.[62]

S.11(4), Sale of Goods Act 1979, which provides that the right to reject is lost once goods have been accepted, does not apply to s.12. Combined with the rule that the buyer can recover any expenses incurred[63] and that no allowance is made for the buyer's use of the goods, this seems to put the luckless intermediate seller of stolen goods in an unjust position. The rule that no allowance is made for the buyer's use of the goods derives from the

---

59 There are also warranties (which only give rise to a claim in damages) that the goods are free of any charges and encumbrances and that buyers will enjoy quiet possession of the goods. Equivalent provisions are found in s.8, Supply of Goods (Implied Terms) Act 1973 (hire–purchase agreements) and ss. 2 and 7, Supply of Goods and Services Act 1982 (contracts for work and materials etc. and hire).

60 [1954] 2 All ER 694.

61 S.6(1), Unfair Contract Terms Act 1977.

62 S.12 (3), Sale of Goods Act 1979.

63 See *Warman v Southern Counties Car Finance Corpn. Ltd* [1949] 2 KB 576 where the purchaser under a hire–purchase agreement recovered his instalment payments, insurance premiums, the cost of minor repairs made to the car as well as the cost of defending the claim of the true owner.

case of *Rowland v Divall*[64] and has been subject to much criticism. In its defence it has been pointed out that since the subsequent buyer in the case had bought the car concerned for resale, not for use, it would have been harsh to have made an allowance for use.[65] Equally the point has been made that the consumer should be compensated for any bother caused. Also, if prices have increased in the meantime, the consumer may find himself faced with having to pay more than the purchase price to buy replacement goods.[66] Reforms providing for an allowance for use have been proposed by both the Law Reform Committee[67] and the Law Commission.[68] In its report on the *Sale and Supply of Goods*,[69] however, the Law Commission changed its mind, partly because it wondered whether the seller of goods who had no right to sell them had any right to benefit from the fact that the other party had used the goods, and also because of the practical difficulties of valuing use and enjoyment. The issue has been raised for discussion again by the DTI's 1994 consultation document on the transfer of title.

5.4 PASSING OF PROPERTY

The Sale of Goods Act 1979 treats property as meaning ownership, that is, the seller's title. It is important to note that there are different degrees of ownership. At one extreme the seller may have a full perfect title in the goods, whilst at the other extreme even a thief has a possessory title which is good against everyone except those with a better title.

Locating the exact moment at which property passes is important because, in sale of goods contracts, risk prima facie passes with property.[70] Thus the purchaser of a new car may be blissfully unaware that, between purchase and delivery, the law may place risk on the consumer, so that it is the consumer's loss should the car be accidentally destroyed in the interim. Also the purchasers of goods by mail order may find themselves at risk for any damage suffered by the goods in transit. Admittedly few traders would

---

[64]   [1923] 2 KB 500.

[65]   G. Treitel, *Law of Contract*, (8th ed.) (Stevens, 1987) at p. 929–931. Cf *Butterworth v Kingsway Motors Ltd* [1954] 1 WLR 1286 where a purchaser was able to recover the purchase price despite having bought the car for personal use and having used it for nearly a year.

[66]   R. Cranston, *Consumers and the Law* , (Weidenfeld and Nicolson, 1984) at p. 161.

[67]   *Op. cit.*

[68]   Law Com WP 65, (1975) and Law Com 121, *Pecuniary Restitution on Breach of Contract*, (1983) and Law Com WP 85, *Sale and Supply of Goods* (1983).

[69]   Law Com 160, Scot Law Com 104, (1987).

[70]   S.20, Sale of Goods Act 1979.

stand by their strict legal rights, but sale of goods law can be criticised for placing the consumer in this legally vulnerable position. In terms of these rules, consumers are more likely to lose out when a company supplying them becomes insolvent. If property has not passed to the consumer, then the company's creditors can claim the goods back, despite the fact that the consumer may have paid for them. Additional importance in locating the moment property passes results from the fact that, if property in goods has passed to a consumer who fails to take delivery, then the seller can sue for the price rather than be limited to a claim for damages.[71]

Before looking at the rules which govern the transfer of property, it is important to note that only the Sale of Goods Act 1979 has specific provisions governing this matter. Supply contracts governed by other legislation are still covered by the common law, although in most cases this will be similar to the position under the Sale of Goods Act 1979.

The Sale of Goods Act 1979 draws an important distinction in this context between specific goods and unascertained goods. Specific goods are goods identified and agreed on at the time of sale.[72] For instance, if a second–hand car was being sold, it would have to be specific as the contract could not refer to another identical item. A particular individualised item would also be specific goods, such as a dishwasher which was reduced because it was scratched. Unascertained goods are not defined by the Act, but can be taken to be all other goods. For example, a contract which specifies a type of new car but leaves the seller free to decide which particular unit to supply will be a contract for unascertained goods.

The basic philosophy of the Sale of Goods Act 1979 is to leave the parties free to determine at what time property should pass.[73] However, the fact that no property in unascertained goods can pass until they have become ascertained can be a cause of injustice.[74] If the supplier becomes insolvent, purchasers will have no property claim over the goods they have ordered and probably paid for.[75] Also no property in future goods can be transferred until the goods have come into existence.[76]

---

[71]   S.49, Sale of Goods Act 1979.
[72]   S.61(2), Sale of Goods Act 1979.
[73]   S.17, Sale of Goods Act 1979.
[74]   S.16, Sale of Goods Act 1979.
[75]   See *Re London Wine (Shippers) Co*, (1986) PCC 121 (wine purchased and stored but no appropriation to individual contracts and company free to sell stock and satisfy customers from other available sources) and *Re Goldcorp Exchange Ltd* [1994] 2 All ER 806. The latter involved purchasers buying an interest in gold rather than wine and was an appeal to the Privy Council from the New Zealand Court of Appeal. The New Zealand Court had circumvented the property problem by holding that the money paid to the company was held on trust for the customers. This has been held

The parties are free to agree when property should pass. Otherwise the Sale of Goods Act 1979 provides a regime which applies unless there is a contrary intention. Absent such an express or implied intention, s.18 lays down five 'rules'. For specific goods the general rule is that, where the contract is unconditional, property passes when the contract is made and it is immaterial whether payment and/or delivery are postponed. Rules 2 and 3 spell out two exceptions which are implicit in rule 1. Rule 2 provides that, where the seller is bound to do something to the goods to put them in a deliverable state, property does not pass until that is done and the buyer has notice that it has been done. Similarly, rule 3 provides that, where the seller is bound to weigh, measure, test or do some other thing with reference to the goods for the purpose of ascertaining their price, property can only pass when that has been done; once again the buyer must have notice that it has been done. Rule 4 governs the particular problem of when goods are delivered for approval or on a sale or return basis. In such circumstances, property passes to the buyer either (i) when he or she signifies approval or acceptance to the seller or does any other act adopting the transaction, or (ii) by the expiration of any period fixed for the return of the goods or, absent any fixed period, by the expiration of a reasonable time.

It has already been stated that property in unascertained goods can only pass once they have become ascertained. Just as there is no definition of unascertained goods, so there is no definition of what ascertainment involves, but it would seem to require no more than identification of the goods by the seller. More crucial is the provision in rule 5 that property passes under contracts for the sale of unascertained or future goods when they are 'unconditionally appropriated to the contract' either by the seller with the assent of the buyer, or by the buyer with the assent of the seller. Where, under the contract, the seller delivers the goods to the buyer (or to a carrier or other bailee or custodian for the purpose of transmission to the buyer), without reserving the right of disposal, he or she is taken to have unconditionally appropriated the goods to the contract.[77] Otherwise the statute does not define 'unconditional appropriation', but case law suggests it

---

possible by the United Kingdom courts (see *Re Kayford Ltd* [1975] 1 All ER 604), but on the facts of this case this was not found to be possible as there was nothing to constrain the way the company dealt with the money. Cf *Re Stapylton Fletcher Ltd* [1995] 1 All ER 192 where Paul Barker QC managed to avoid the decision in *Re London Wine (Shippers) Co* by finding wine had been ascertained when it was put in store with the wine of other customers and not mingled with trading stock. Property then passed on the basis of common intention rather than on the basis of s.18 r.5, Sale of Goods Act 1979 (see below).

[76] S.5(3), Sale of Goods Act 1979.

[77] Rule 5(2), s.18, Sale of Goods Act 1979.

involves the seller doing the last act he or she has to perform before property can be transferred. For example, it might not be sufficient merely to allocate goods to specific customers by putting labels on them; on the other hand goods would be considered to be unconditionally appropriated if an invoice had been drawn up identifying particular items.[78] The undefined nature of this concept gives the courts a good deal of discretion which one might anticipate their using in the consumer's favour, where injustice would otherwise occur. A similar discretion is to be found in the requirement that not only must one party unconditionally appropriate the goods, but the other party must assent to this. The statute makes it clear that this assent may be express or implied. However, does a buyer assent to a seller unconditionally appropriating goods when the seller despatches them by mail order? Such assent was found to exist in a different context in a commercial case,[79] but the courts may be slower to recognise such a right in the consumer mail order contract case because the consequences would be to put the consumer at risk for any damage to the goods in transit.

---

78   *Henry Lennox (Industrial Engines) Ltd v Grahame Puttick Ltd* [1984] 2 All ER 152.

79   *Badische Anilin and Soda Fabrik v Basle Chemical Works* [1898] AC 2000.

6 Product and Service Liability

6.1 THE NATURE OF THE DEBATE

6.1.1 Product and Service Liability Distinguished

The topics of product and service liability are concerned with the damage which products or services cause to persons or property (other than the defective product itself). Product and service liability are traditionally seen as being concerned with tort liability, where the duty of care has imposed obligations on businesses to protect consumers from physical damage to their person or property. By contrast, the purpose of contract law is to protect the economic interests of the consumer; as such, it is more concerned with defects in the quality of the product or service itself. The boundaries, however, are not clear cut. In contract consequential damages are recoverable, whilst in tort it is a moot point whether economic loss or damage caused by one part of the defective product to other parts can be recovered.[1]

Although concerned with essentially the same problems – how to raise consumer safety standards and how to compensate consumers who have suffered accidents – product and service liability have tended to be treated separately. There has been a greater willingness to move towards imposing strict liability for products than services.[2] This bifurcation is unfortunate. Many accidents arise out of the provision of products in the course of a service, and sometimes it is unclear whether an accident has arisen because of a fault in the product or the way the service provider has used the product. Take a car repair. There may be a dispute as to whether an accident has been caused by the replacement part or the way it was installed, particularly if the manufacturer complains that the product was used inappropriately. It is by no means self-evident that a lower standard should apply to service providers than to the supplier of goods.[3]

The general justification for subjecting services to a lower standard of liability than products is that outcomes cannot be guaranteed. Thus whilst

---

1 See 6.2.3.3.5.
2 For some of the policy debates surrounding the choice of standard, see 1.4 and 1.5.2.
3 See J. Stapleton, *Product Liability*, (Butterworths, 1994) pp. 323–36.

service providers can be expected to take care to try to achieve the desired result, a successful outcome cannot be assured.[4] For instance, where the service involves an interrelationship between the service provider and the subject of the service, the outcome often cannot be predicted. Certainly those who provide medical or health care services are aware that individuals react differently to treatment. Equally it is understood that garments can sometimes react idiosyncratically to chemicals applied to clean or treat them, while car mechanics and domestic engineers warn that very occasionally their repair may or may not work depending upon the response of the particular product to the attempted repair.

To reject strict liability for services may be to misunderstand the debate. Since many services are now automated, a certain consistency of outcome can be predicted and expected. Strict liability does not necessarily mean blaming the service provider and imposing liability every time a service fails to produce the desired result. For instance, the simple failure of a technique would not attract liability (other than possible contractual liability) unless it had caused actual damage. Where services do cause damage, either due to some error or for reasons unknown, then the same risk-spreading rationales can be invoked to justify liability as have been used in the context of products. To take a medical example, whether a patient is treated with drugs or operated on may be a matter of patient or doctor preference. It seems absurd that the law can protect the patient against unknown risks associated with the drug, but not the unknown risks associated with the operation. The operation does not have to cure the patient, but it should not make his position worse (except, possibly, to the extent of risks which were accepted as inherent within the procedure).

Much of the controversy surrounding service liability stems from the fact that it includes high risk areas such as medical negligence. Not only does this

---

4   A service provider could however guarantee the outcome and attract liability in contract for that promise. This was alleged in *Thake v Maurice* [1986] 1 All ER 497 where it was claimed that the doctor had guaranteed the permanent sterilisation of Mr Thake, a railwayman who already had five children. However the majority of the Court of Appeal held this was not the effect of their conversations with the doctor since 'in medical science all things, or nearly all things, are uncertain ... that knowledge is part of the general experience of mankind.'. Mr Thake had become fertile again by the process known as 'spontaneous recanalisation' and the doctor was held liable in tort for his failure to warn of this possibility. However in *Greaves & Co (Contractors) Ltd v Baynham Meikle & Partners* [1975] 1 WLR 1095, engineers were found to have warranted that a warehouse would be fit for its intended purpose. Lane LJ stressed that this did not mean that all professionals would be taken to warrant the successful outcome of their endeavours, merely that the facts of the case justified the implication of a warranty.

mean that powerful pressure groups campaign against extensions of service liability, but also that courts and legislatures are hesitant to impose what may turn out to be a potentially wide and burdensome liability. As we shall see, hard cases such as medical negligence, and its counterpart in the products sphere – pharmaceutical liability – point up the problems of using the private law to strike an appropriate balance between compensation for those injured and the sensible development of activities which are clearly socially justifiable and economically useful.[5] The danger is that, if these areas are treated as special cases and dealt with separately under administrative or insurance based schemes then, rather than heralding a more general reform of the law, the excuse will be made that, as the most serious problems have been solved, little need be done in other areas.

6.1.2 The Move towards Strict Liability

The trend to impose stricter standards in the area of products (and, to a lesser extent, in service) liability will become evident. Thus it is often stated that the European Product Liability Directive[6] introduced 'strict liability' into Europe. This followed the lead given by the US, which had known strict products liability since at least 1963.[7] However, the term 'strict liability' is often misunderstood. It does not equate with absolute liability, for defences are normally available. Indeed, most of the strict liability tests are formulated using a defectiveness standard which places some of the risks on to the product/service user. Thus imposing strict liability does not necessarily make the producer the insurer of all harm caused by the product.

The term 'strict liability' covers a range of liability systems of varying degrees of strictness. In theory, whereas fault-based systems judge the behaviour of producers and suppliers against some objective standard of what should reasonably be expected of them, strict liability judges the end product (or service) against objective criteria. It is not a sufficient excuse that the failure to meet the objective standard can be explained away on reasonable grounds. The objective criteria are usually based on a consumer expectation or risk:utility analysis.

The EC Product Liability Directive essentially adopts a consumer expectation standard. This can be seen as less objective than a risk:utility analysis, since it turns on the subjective appreciations of consumers as a body. Broadly, however, the two standards can be seen as being fairly

---

5   Cf discussion at 1.5.2.

6   374/85/EEC, OJ 1985 L210/29.

7   See the decision in *Greenman v Yuba Power Products* 377 P 2d 897 (1963) (Supreme Court of California) and s.402A Restatement (Second) of Torts (1965).

similar as consumer expectations tend to be based on a rough–and–ready balancing of risks and benefits. Equally these standards need not produce results very different from those arrived at in negligence, for both consumer expectations and the risk:utility calculations have to take into account what can be expected of producers. Thus it was stated in the Supreme Court of Washington that: 'In considering the reasonable expectations of the ordinary consumer, a number of factors must be considered including the relative cost of the product, the gravity of the potential harm from the claimed defect and the cost and feasibility of eliminating or minimising the risk'.[8]

What, then, is the difference between a negligence and a strict liability regime? The answer is, partly, that under the former one judges the actions of the various agents in the light of circumstances appertaining at the time the action occurred. Under the latter one *usually* judges the product by the standards existing at the time of the accident or possibly even at the time of trial. Thus, the time frame of the assessment is the essential element in a strict liability regime. However, the word usually is emphasised for strict liability regimes can also contain 'state of the art' or 'development risks' defences which undermine this principle.

The terms 'state of the art' and 'development risks' are often used interchangeably, but we prefer to distinguish them as being two separate though related defences. We understand the 'state of the art' defence to refer to the plea that the product should not be found defective since it offered the level of safety considered adequate at the time it was marketed. Thus, whereas a car without front seat belts might be considered defective today, a car so produced in the 1950s would not be held defective for failing to include a safety device which had not become standard, or even common, at that date. Though known of, the danger was accepted. 'Development risks', on the other hand, are those which were not known of at the time of marketing, but if they had been known about would have prevented the product from being marketed according to the standards of safety current at the time of marketing. For example, the drug diethylstilbestrol (DES) gave rise to vaginal, cervical and genital cancer in the offspring of mothers who ingested the drug as a miscarriage preventative. This unfortunate side effect had a latency period of ten to twenty years. Clearly the risk was not known of when the product was marketed; equally it was a risk which would never have been considered acceptable judged against the standards in place at the time of marketing. Where producers are not held liable for such risks, the defence is known as the 'development risks defence'. The inclusion of these defences often provokes criticism from consumer groups for they can be viewed as undermining the rationales of risk spreading and loss distribution which underpin strict product liability. However, these defences do provide

---

8   *Seattle First National Bank v Tabert* 542 P 2d 774 at 779 (1975).

mechanisms through which legal systems can fine tune the degree of 'strictness' within a liability regime and hence determine the exact manner in which risks are allocated between producer and consumer.[9]

Another hallmark of strict liability regimes is that they tend to channel liability towards the person best placed to control the product and insure the risk involved. In most cases[10] we shall see that this is the producer. This is recognition that in modern conditions where mass produced, pre–packaged goods are the norm, the consumer looks to the producer (rather than the retailer) for guarantees regarding the safety of goods. This contrasts with the position both under the law of contract, which traditionally has imposed liabilities only on contracting parties, and with the law of tort, which imposes liability on the party at fault regardless of their place in the production chain. In the area of service liability, no similar move has occurred to trace liability back to the person who develops dangerous ways of providing services rather than the actual provider of the service. Thus when the European Commission issued a draft European Service Liability Directive (since withdrawn) imposing liability on the 'supplier of services', the one and only extension was that, in some circumstances franchisers would have been jointly and severally liable with their franchisees. Of course, the network of links in the service sector is different in nature from that in the retail goods sector, as services are not physically passed between the parties in the same way. On the other hand, intellectual property rights are owned in techniques and processes used in the provision of services. It is therefore interesting to note that, outside the specific area of franchising, no attempt has been made to bring those who may be the true source of the danger within specific service liability regimes, although they may, of course, be subject to negligence liability.

6.1.3 The Nature of Defects

In relation to products, eight possible types of defect/damage can be isolated – a categorisation offered simply to help elucidate the issues involved in this complicated area. There may well be overlaps between the categories, as when a design defect also involves a development risks defect.

(i) Manufacturing defects concern defects caused by an error in the

---

9   See N. Terry, 'State of the Art Evidence: From Logical Construct to Judicial Retrenchment', (1991) 20 *Anglo–Am Law Rev* 285.

10 In the European Product Liability Directive other policies dictated the additional placing of liability on 'own–branders' and importers into the Community, with lesser obligations being placed on suppliers.

production process or by the use of defective raw materials. Courts are more likely to impose liabilities for this type of defect than any other. This is partly because it is easier for them when an objective standard exists against which the defective product can be judged (the perfect product), and also because it can be presumed that the flaw arose from somewhere within the production and distribution chain. Moreover the consequences of imposing liability can be less severe, since there is no question of requiring the product to be redesigned or permanently withdrawn from the market. The faulty product or batch must simply be withdrawn and any damage remedied.

(ii)   Design defects are the most serious of all since defective design threatens the continued existence of a product, at least in the form in which it is currently marketed. Courts are understandably hesitant about condemning the design of products, because many of these cases involve a complicated balancing of risks and benefits – safety versus access to innovative/useful/attractive consumer products and pharmaceuticals.[11] An added complication is that the more safety features that are built into the design, the higher the cost of the product. This can penalise lower-income consumers, who lose access to goods in order that higher-income consumers can buy themselves greater safety.

(iii) Warning defects are closely related to design defects. While the product design itself may not be inherently defective, the product can be rendered defective by the lack of a warning. Warning defects arise where a product contains an acceptable risk, but is rendered defective by the failure of the producer to inform the consumer of that risk. Courts may be more willing to find a product defective on the grounds of failure to warn than for defective design, since this is less judgmental. The danger is that, if too many warnings are given, their impact is lost, either because the more important warnings are obscured amongst the others or because warnings become so commonplace that they are not taken seriously.

(iv)   Instruction defects are similar to warning defects in that they concern the information provided to the consumer, but differ in that the defect is not a failure to warn of an inherent danger in the product. Instead the defect involves the creation of danger by the failure to inform the consumer of how to use a product safely. The mutually exclusive nature of warning and instruction defects is well illustrated by an example borrowed from Dillard and Hart[12] who describe a new toothpaste which permanently discolours teeth if used more than twice a day. They

---

[11]   See 1.5.2.

[12]   H.C. Dillard and H. Hart, 'Product Liability; Directions for Use and Failure to Warn' (1955) 41 Virginia LR 145.

suggest that an instruction such as 'For Best Results Use Twice Daily' or even 'Do Not Use More Than Twice Daily' would not be sufficient to avoid liability. There is a need both for instructions on to how to use the product and for a warning of the dangers involved if these instructions are not complied with.

(v) Development risks defects are those which only come to light after the product has been marketed. Whether these defects are covered by the liability regime is a touchstone by which to test how 'strict' liability is under any particular regime.

(vi) State of the art defects are elements of a product which, although acceptable when marketed, have subsequently become less acceptable. This is not because they now pose greater danger, but rather because safer alternatives or replacements have emerged or because the need for the product has been reduced in some other way. Liability is less likely to be imposed for state of the art than for development risks defects.

(vii) Post–marketing defects concern the failures to warn of dangers, to recall products or to take other remedial action once a danger has been discovered. Even fault-based systems can use this as a means of compensating for development risks if the producer does not act responsibly once such risks are discovered. What is required will of course depend upon the nature and extent of the danger concerned.

(viii) System damage, a term coined by Børge Dahl,[13] covers risks which are inherent within a product, whose marketing is nevertheless considered justifiable. Examples might be the risk of being cut by a sharp knife or, more contentiously, the risk of contracting cancer from smoking cigarettes. Since the product is of an acceptable standard, we call this 'system damage' rather than 'system defect'. If liability is imposed for system damage, then the legal regime will be approaching the position where the producer becomes the insurer of his products.

These types of damage find their counterparts in relation to services, though some of the terms might be expressed differently. Thus instead of manufacturing defects, one might talk in terms of service component defects. These would cover the use of defective materials or even incompetent staff. Rather than design defects one would talk of process defects, where the complaint would relate to the actual technique or process used. Of course there are some cases which straddle the boundary of service component and process defects. For example, damage caused by the decision of a service supplier to use a particular technique or process in a particular case may either be put down to an error by the individual concerned (service

---

13   B. Dahl, 'Product Liability in Denmark' in *Product Liability in Europe*, (Kluwer–Harrap, 1975).

component defect) or be blamed on the actual process (process defect) depending on just how maverick the individual's judgement is considered to be. Warning defects are commonplace in the service sector, where consumers frequently complain that they were not being told of relevant dangers, for example, risks associated with an operation or with a dry–cleaning process that can damage sensitive materials. Information defects are not usually related to a failure to inform the consumer on how to perform the service, for this is normally done by the professional concerned. The information defect will arise from a failure to tell the consumer how to behave after the service has been performed, for example the need to watch out for danger signs that a repair has not worked properly, or to use the product at less than full capacity for a certain period of time after repair. Development risk, state of the art and post–marketing defects can equally apply to services as to products. System damage also results from services, for example, the risk that an attempted repair could actually damage the object being repaired or the risk of side effects from operations.

6.1.4 Rationales for Strict Liability

There are several justifications for imposing strict liability.[14] In terms of compensation it is viewed as a means of spreading the risks attached to the use of a product or service across all users, rather than letting the risk lie where it falls on the unfortunate victims. So in a sense strict liability imposes a compulsory form of insurance, with the premium being borne by the producer. In theory the producer should be able to reflect this cost in the price of the product. Placing the risk on the producer, even in the absence of fault, is considered justifiable as the producer is involved in a profit–making venture and should be responsible for damage resulting therefrom.[15] The producer is often also the person best placed to obtain insurance. Few individuals are likely to voluntarily take out first-party insurance, while some high risk individuals may have difficulty finding insurers willing to write policies to cover them. Another advantage of strict liability is that it internalises all the costs of the activity concerned. Making the producers of products and suppliers of services liable for any relevant damage caused should force the price up to such a level that the product or service is only consumed to the optimum degree. However, there are some commentators who believe that it threatens the liberty and autonomy of commercial agents

---

14   See J. Montgomery and D. Owen, 'Reflections on the Theory and Administration of Strict Tort Liability for Defective Products' (1976) 27 *SCLRev* 803; also see 1.5.2.

15   See, D. Beyleveld and R. Brownsword, 'Impossibility, Irrationality and Strict Product Liability' (1991) 20 *Anglo–Am L Rev* 257 and J. Stapleton, *op. cit.*, Ch. 8.

to hold them liable for damage where they are not at fault.[16] Even many of those who accept the theory of strict liability are sometimes reluctant to apply the principle when faced with a concrete case involving an innocent defendant. This, perhaps, partially explains why state of the art or development risks defences seem inevitably to 'sneak' into product liability regimes.

6.2 PRODUCT LIABILITY

Before considering the product liability law of the UK, it is instructive to note the general trend in Western legal systems towards strict products liability. It is worthwhile studying US law because it has influenced the adoption of similar principles elsewhere. Also the number and size of awards to victims of product related accidents in the US brought into sharp focus the debate on how far liability rules could be relied upon to perform the social function of compensating accident victims, without threatening the viability of manufacturing industry. A brief consideration of other European legal systems will illustrate that the introduction of strict liability in the European Product Liability Directive was not a bolt out of the blue, but rather reflected a general trend within European civil law.

6.2.1 United States[17]

The need for strict product liability is arguably greatest in countries, such as the US, where there is minimal public health provision and where sizeable portions of the population are without health insurance. Here it performs the very basic function of at least ensuring that the victim's medical costs are recovered. Certainly from an early time the US courts were receptive to arguments extending liability for defective products. Manufacturers were held liable for breach of express[18] and implied warranties[19], even in the

---

16   See D. Owen, 'Products Liability Principles of Justice' (1991) 20 *Anglo–Am L Rev* 238.

17   See G. Howells, *Comparative Product Liability*, (Dartmouth, 1993) Chs 12–13. Of course it should be remembered that there is no such thing as one US law on products liability because each state has its own rules, as do the Federal courts. Indeed in 1987 Michigan, North Carolina, Virginia and the District of Columbia were reported not to recognise strict product liability actions: see R. Bieman, 'Strict Products Liability: An Overview of State Law' (1987) 10 *J Prod Liab* 111.

18   *Baxter v Ford Motor Co* 12 P 2d 409 (1932) (Supreme Court of Washington).

absence of privity. Finally, however, in *Greenman v Yuba Power Products*[20] the courts developed a tort of strict liability for product defects independent of contract. S.402 A of the Restatement (Second) of Torts (1965)[21] states:

> '(1) One who sells any product in a defective condition unreasonably dangerous to the user or consumer or to his property is subject to liability for physical harm thereby caused to the ultimate user or consumer, or to his property.......'

In order to avoid placing too great a burden on high risk socially desirable products, comment K to the section provides that, in the case of an unavoidably unsafe product, 'such a product, properly prepared and accompanied by proper directions and warning, is not defective, nor is it unreasonably dangerous'.

The Restatement left open the question of how defect should be defined. Some courts have adopted a consumer expectation test, but for reasons considered below, most prefer a more objective risk:utility analysis[22] or at least a two pronged test, such as that proposed in *Barker v Lull Engineering Co Ltd*[23] In Barker it was stated that a plaintiff would win his case if he demonstrated either that the product:

> 'failed to perform as safely as an ordinary consumer would expect when used in an intended or reasonably foreseeable manner or... if the plaintiff proves that the product's design proximately caused his injury and the defendant fails to prove ... that on balance the benefits of the challenged design outweigh the risk of danger inherent in such design.'[24]

During the 1970s and 1980s many commentators talked in terms of the United States experiencing product liability crises, with insurance cover for high–risk products becoming outrageously expensive or simply unobtainable.

---

[19]   *Henningsen v Bloomfield Motors* 161 A 2d 69 (1960) (Supreme Court of New Jersey).

[20]   377 P 2d 897 (1963) (Supreme Court of California).

[21]   This is a non–binding, but highly influential, text of the American Law Institute which tries to reflect court practice throughout the states.

[22]   In *Phillips v Kimwood Machine Co* 525 P 2d 1033 (1974) (Supreme Court of Oregon) it was said that: 'A dangerously defective article would be one which a reasonable person would not put into the stream of commerce if he had knowledge of its harmful character. The test therefore is whether the seller would be negligent if he sold the article knowing of the risk involved.'

[23]   573 P 2d 443 (1978) (Supreme Court of California).

[24]   *Ibid.* at 452.

It may be questioned whether such crises really occurred. A few cases caught the headlines when firms were forced into bankruptcy, but they had involved the marketing of very dangerous and clearly defective products.[25] Equally, whilst the US tends to award higher damages than most other countries, and in particular has strong punitive damage laws, most of the $1M+ awards were for very seriously injured consumers. The Presidential Task Force set up to consider the problem came to no firm conclusions on whether tort law was contributing to the perceived crisis. It did however find that the tort system created uncertainty which caused insurers to 'panic–price' their premiums to cover themselves against the uncertainties in the law.[26] It additionally found that high premiums were also due to poor manufacturing practices and to insurers trying to compensate for poor returns on their investments during times of low interest rates.

The US experience was used by some to argue against Europe placing similar burdens on its industry through the adoption of strict liability, or at least to argue that the development risks defence should be included. However, comparisons with the US can be misleading. First, American consumers tend to be more litigious than their counterparts in the UK. This is explained, in part, by the greater access to the courts because of the contingency fee system (where clients pay no fee, but the lawyer obtains a percentage of any award of damages); and perhaps more importantly by there being no liability on the part of the plaintiff to pay the other side's costs if the case is lost. Second, damages in the US are higher than in the UK. There are various possible reasons for this – the high cost of health care, the greater availability of punitive damages and, perhaps most importantly, the fact that (unlike in the UK), damages are awarded by a jury which can be swayed by emotional arguments to award victims large amounts. A jury may also be tempted to take into account that up to 40 per cent of the damages may go to the lawyer by way of contingency fees. Third, courts in the US have also relaxed causation rules. Thus even if a plaintiff cannot identify the exact brand of a product which injured him or her, he or she can sue any producer of the same product and recover damages in proportion to that manufacturer's share of the market.[27]

---

25   Eg A.H. Robins filed for bankruptcy following litigation over the Dalkon intrauterine device.

26   Final Report, Interagency Task Force on Product Liability (Department of Commerce, 1977).

27   See *Sindell v Abbott Laboratories* 607 P 2d 924. There are of course some limitations to this rule, notably that a substantial share of the market must be joined as defendants. Defendants can also escape liability if they prove that their product could not have been the one which caused the damage, eg if it was not sold in the plaintiff's locality or was of a different appearance to that remembered by the plaintiff.

However, some US commentators have noted a turn in the tide in favour of defendants. At the doctrinal level this is illustrated by the debate played out in the Supreme Court of New Jersey, which eventually decided that the unknowability of the defect was a factor to be taken into account in assessing whether a product was defective – in other words the development risk defence was accepted.[28] Empirical evidence also suggests that in recent years plaintiffs are faring less well at the trial court level.[29] In addition, whereas attempts to legislate for limits on tort liability at the Federal level have been unsuccessful, at state level many reforms have been introduced. The American Law Institute is also looking at the possibility of reforming s.402A of the Restatement (Second) of Torts (1965) so that there is a negligence standard for design defects.[30]

6.2.2 Europe

Many European legal systems were developing stricter product liability laws even before the 1985 Directive. This trend was not limited to the area of pharmaceuticals, in which the Scandinavian countries had developed insurance based solutions to the product liability problem and in relation to which Germany had passed a specific Act. In Spain, the Consumer Protection Act 1984 was passed in response to a disaster involving contaminated cooking oil. This extended a form of strict liability to a range of products including pharmaceuticals, but also covering foodstuffs, hygiene and cleaning products, cosmetics, health, gas and electricity services, home appliances, lifts, means of transport, motor vehicles, toys and other products for children.

The general civil law had also been developing to meet the problem posed by individuals injured by defective products. This is perhaps most clearly seen in countries such as France, Belgium and Luxembourg where problems of privity were sidestepped by the creation of an 'action directe' between the consumer purchaser and higher links in the distribution chain.[31] Consequential damages caused by hidden defects (vice cachée) were allowed to be recovered, by presuming the seller of a defective product to have known

---

28 *Feldman v Lederle Laboratories* 479 A 2d 374 (1974) (Supreme Court of New Jersey), disagreeing in this respect with the decision in *Beshada v John–Mansville Products Corpn.* 447 A 2d 539 (1982) (Supreme Court of New Jersey).

29 J. Henderson and T. Eisenberg, 'The Quiet Revolution in Products Liability: an Empirical Study of Legal Change' (1990) 36 UCLA 479.

30 See K. Ross and H. Bowbeer, 'American Product Liability Law Undergoing Revision' (1994) 2 *Consum LJ* 96.

31 See G. Howells, *op. cit.*, Ch. 7.

of the defect and hence to have acted in bad faith, with the result that consequential damages were available and exclusion clauses rendered void.[32] In Austria, contract law has been developed to protect consumers by accepting the notion of contracts having protective effects for third parties.[33]

Equally, however, the inclination of many countries was to reject contract as a way of resolving product liability disputes in favour of tort laws. This underlines the law's increasing recognition that the person responsible for the quality and safety of products is the producer, rather than the retailer with whom the consumer has a contractual nexus. A good example of tort law aimed explicitly at the manufacturer is the French case law based on art. 1384.1 of the Civil Code which, *inter alia*, makes a person liable for things in their keeping. Goldman was concerned that the product user was being unfairly made the insurer of the product's quality.[34] He therefore drew a distinction, which has been accepted by the courts, between 'garde de la structure' (the product's design) and 'garde du comportement' (how the product is used). Whilst the user was responsible for damage caused by the latter, the manufacturer remained liable for the 'garde de la structure'.

Germany is the country which has most strongly rejected an extension of contract in product liability in favour of stronger tort laws.[35] The so–called 'chicken–pest' case saw a reversal of the burden of proof being introduced for manufacturing defects, which was later extended to design defects and recently to warning defects (but not to post–marketing warnings). Germany was seriously affected by the Thalidomide (or Contergan as it was known in Germany) tragedy and as a result passed the Medicines Act 1976, which arguably introduced a form of strict liability for drugs by making pharmaceutical companies liable for harmful effects which go beyond a measure defensible according to medical science and for damage which occurred as a consequence of labelling or instructions for use not corresponding to the findings of medical science.

---

[32] In France this is an irrebuttable presumption, but in Belgium there are limited grounds on which a defendant can rebut this presumption.

[33] This was based on academic writings such as that of F. Bydlinski, 'Vertragliche Sorgfaltspflichten zugunsten Dritter' (1960) 82 *JB* 359.

[34] *La détermination de gardien responsable du fait des choses inanimées*, (Sirey, 1947).

[35] See G. Howells, *op. cit.*, Ch. 8.

6.2.3 United Kingdom

6.2.3.1 Product Liability and Contract Law

One tends to associate product liability with tortious liability. Nevertheless, before the adoption of strict products liability, US contract law was manipulated to provide remedies to consumers against manufacturers. We have also seen that a similar approach was taken in continental Europe, notably in France. In the UK contractual claims can be significant in product liability actions since consequential damages are recoverable; also a claim in contract has the advantage over a claim in negligence that liability is strict – if a term is breached, it is no defence that the person in default exercised all reasonable care not to break the contract (unless of course the term was phrased to require only the exercise of reasonable care). Also in contracts for the sale or supply of goods, the consumer benefits, *inter alia*, from the terms of satisfactory quality and fitness for purpose being implied. Thus the consumer's contractual rights remain a powerful weapon if the other party to the contract is worth suing. They are of no use, however, if someone other than the injured party bought the defective goods or if the supplier cannot be sued, eg is not traceable or is bankrupt.

The UK has failed to break free from the shackles of the privity doctrine in the manner achieved by the US and French courts. Thus in *Daniels and Daniels v White and Tabard*,[36] Mr. Daniels purchased lemonade from a publican for his wife and himself. The lemonade contained carbolic acid. Whilst Mr. Daniels could sue the publican in contract, his wife had no contractual remedies as she was not party to the contract (there was also found to be no breach by the manufacturer of its duty of care in negligence). Thus only one consumer could recover, and only against the publican and not the manufacturers who had been the source of the contamination. Of course, the manufacturer could eventually be held liable in contract by virtue of the parties in the distribution chain suing back up the line, a process, however, that is circuitous and wasteful in terms of litigation costs. Moreover, where the risk falls will, to some extent, be arbitrary depending upon the terms of the supply contracts between the links in the chain and whether a link is broken, for example, by the bankruptcy of a distributor.

There have been several attempts to circumvent privity.[37] Thus, in *Lockett v A. M. Charles Ltd*[38] – a decision which showed very progressive views on sexual equality for its time – a husband and wife ordered a meal

---

[36] [1938] 4 All ER 258.
[37] Cf. discussion in relation to privity and commercial guarantees concerning the quality of goods at 4.2.2.
[38] [1938] 4 All ER 170.

and the wife was made ill by eating the whitebait. It was held that she had a contract with the hotel, for the inference must be that when two or more people order food, even if they are man and wife, each is making him or herself liable to pay for the food they order. Such reasoning would not have helped Mrs Daniels, however, as her husband had taken the lemonade bottle home to be consumed.

Another important technique used to trace liability back to the manufacturer in contract is that of 'collateral contract', where the manufacturer is held liable for a promise made. The consumer's consideration is deemed to be the entering into a contract with some other party to buy the manufacturer's goods. Consideration is provided to the manufacturer in the form of the benefit from increased sales. A classic example of this was the seminal case of *Carlill v Carbolic Smoke Ball Co,*[39] in which the smoke ball company was held liable to pay to Mrs Carlill the £100 it had promised in its advertisement to anyone catching influenza after using its smoke balls. She had purchased these from a chemist and was therefore not in a direct contractual relationship with the manufacturer. This collateral contract approach can self–evidently only impose liability for express and not implied warranties. Of course it is rare that a manufacturer will make specific claims about the safety of his products. One novel case where liability was imposed on the manufacturer for a false safety claim arose in Denmark and involved a 'Trumf' pressure cooker. The advertisement offered a 5,000 kroner reward to the first person succeeding in exploding a 'Trumf' pressure cooker which incorporated a fully automatic safety device. Rather ironically, the advertisement had earlier stated that the 70,000 housewives using the 'Trumf' could take comfort in the fact that the pressure cooker which had exploded the week before was not a 'Trumf'.[40]

In the UK, it would seem that fundamental changes in the privity rule will have to be made by the legislature.[41] It is therefore interesting to note that in its consultation document on 'Consumer Guarantees', the Department of Trade and Industry has proposed not only that manufacturers and retailers should be jointly and severally liable for the manufacturer's guarantee, but also that manufacturers and importers should be jointly and severally liable with the retailer for the satisfactory quality of goods under the Sale of Goods Act. In breaching the privity rule which currently prevents manufacturers from being liable for breach of the implied quality conditions, this would represent a remarkable advance. We have already discussed the potential

---

[39]   [1893] 1 QB 256.

[40]   See G. Howells, *op. cit.*, pp. 162–3.

[41]   But there are some signs of the courts relaxing privity by allowing third party assignees to recover damages: see *Darlington Borough Council v Wiltshier Northern Ltd, The Times,* 4 July 1994.

impact of this in relation to substandard goods.[42] In relation to unsafe goods there will be less impact, for the same result has been largely achieved by the introduction of a form of strict liability in tort. It will, still be relevant, however, for some defences available in tort may not apply in contract.

6.2.3.2 Negligence

Every law student knows of the infamous case of *Donoghue v Stevenson*,[43] involving the snail in a ginger beer bottle. Not only was the judgment of Lord Atkin in that case later to be regarded as laying down a general test for establishing negligence, at least where physical damage is concerned, but it was also a product liability case which established that:

> 'a manufacturer of products, which he sell in such a form as to show that he intended them to reach the ultimate consumer in the form in which they left him with no reasonable possibility of intermediate examination, and with the knowledge that the absence of reasonable care in the preparation or putting up of the products will result in an injury to the consumer's life or property, owes a duty of care to the consumer to take that reasonable care.'[44]

Thus manufacturers could be liable in tort for defective products, but only if they were at fault.[45] The fault requirement would seem to exclude system damage and state of the art or development risk defects from the scope of negligence liability. This is because there is no liability for acceptable risks and because the actions of the producer are judged at the time of marketing, with no hindsight knowledge being imputed.[46]

It is with regard to manufacturing defects that the negligence standard has been most effective in imposing liability on producers. This was not always true. For instance, in *Daniels and Daniels v White Ltd and Tabard*[47] there was no finding of negligence because the manufacturers were held to have fulfilled their duty of care by providing a good system of work and

---

42   See 4.2.3.3.

43   [1932] AC 562.

44   *Ibid.* at 599.

45   However, other links in the distribution chain can be held liable if their failure to take reasonable care caused injury: see the liability of the retailer in *Fisher v Harrods Ltd* [1966] Lloyd's Rep 500.

46   However, we will see that the courts have been quite stringent in their consideration of what knowledge can be expected of the defendant.

47   [1938] 4 All ER 258.

adequate supervision: it was not their negligence which had caused the carbolic acid to get into the lemonade bottle! A more consumer friendly approach seems to have been taken by the Court of Appeal in *Hill v James Crowe (Cases) Ltd*[48] where it was decided either that the manufacturer's system was deficient or that an employee, for whom the manufacturer was vicariously liable, had failed to implement the system properly. Of course, the accident could have arisen without anyone being at fault, but the courts have created an almost automatic presumption that manufacturing defects are the result of the fault of someone within the scope of the manufacturer's control. The injured party is unlikely to be able to pinpoint the exact cause of the defect, however, as all the relevant activity took place within the privacy of the defendant's factory. To counter this information inequality, consumers are greatly assisted by the dictum of Lord Wright in *Grant v Australian Knitting Mills*[49] that the injured party 'is not required to lay his finger on the exact person in all the chain who was responsible, or to specify what he did wrong'. Negligence is found as a matter of inference from the existence of the defect taken in conjunction with all known circumstances.

Design defects are the most complex cases. They involve the court assessing the producer's conduct in the light of the dangers posed by the product and the benefits it brings to society. Of course this assessment is objective so that a producer cannot claim his inexperience as an excuse; equally, specialist producers are held to the standard of expertise they profess to possess.[50] The key feature which distinguishes assessment of design in negligence and strict liability is the time-frame within which the assessment is made. In negligence, producer's actions are judged by the standard to be expected at the time the product was marketed. However, the courts have shown themselves to be quite demanding, requiring that manufacturers establish efficient procedures to monitor developments in scientific knowledge[51] and that, once knowledge is in their domain, they utilise it to the fullest extent.[52]

---

[48]   [1978] 1 All ER 812.

[49]   [1936] AC 85 at 101.

[50]   See *Stokes v GKN (Bolts and Nuts) Ltd* [1968] 1 WLR 1778 at 1783.

[51]   *Vacwell v B.D. H. Chemicals Ltd* [1971] 1 QB 88 (liability for failure to take account of the explosive qualities of boron tribromide when it comes into contact with water – even though this was not mentioned in the four modern texts which the defendants had consulted, including the standard work on the industrial hazards of chemicals).

[52]   *IBA v EMI (Electric) Ltd and BIIC Construction Ltd* (1981) 14 BLR 1 (liability for failure to take account of the effects of accumulations of ice on steel television masts).

If a product breaches safety regulations there may be a civil action for breach of statutory duty, though these rarely occur in practice.[53] Non–compliance with industry standards will normally be evidence of negligence, although an occasional departure from a standard practice may be justified.[54] Conversely, compliance with a regulatory standard will generally be evidence that a defendant behaved reasonably.[55]

In *Wright v Dunlop Rubber Co Ltd*[56] manufacturers were held liable for continuing to supply an antioxidant even after discovering that it had carcinogenic properties and for failing to warn of the danger to customers who had already bought the chemical. A duty to warn existing purchasers was also found in *Walton and Walton v British Leyland UK Ltd*[57] where British Leyland had decided not to recall its Allegro cars to make an adjustment to the wheels, but rather preferred to avoid adverse publicity by waiting until the cars were being serviced to make the adjustment. This was considered to be an inadequate response and the company was held liable for the death and serious injuries caused by a wheel coming off.

6.2.3.3 Consumer Protection Act 1987[58]

The UK had the honour of being the first Member State to implement the Product Liability Directive. Only two other countries (Italy and Greece) managed to implement the Directive within the permitted time limit, with France still failing to enact implementing legislation. However, as we shall see, some aspects of the implementing legislation can be criticised for not conforming to the wording of the Directive, thus giving UK consumers less protection than they ought to enjoy.[59] Where this occurs, however, the

---

[53] S.41(1), Consumer Protection Act 1987; see 12.2.

[54] *Brown v Rolls Royce* [1960] 1 All ER 577.

[55] *Albery & Budden v BP Oil Ltd & Shell UK Ltd* (1980) 124 *SJ* 376.

[56] (1972) 13 KIR 255.

[57] 12 July 1978, unreported.

[58] See G. Howells, *op.cit.*, Ch. 6; A Clark, Product Liability, (Sweet & Maxwell, 1989) and J. Stapleton, *op. cit.* Reform proposals along these lines had been proposed by the Law Commission in Law Com 82, Scot Law Com 45, *Report on Liability for Defective Products*, (Cmnd 6831, 1977) and by Pearson, *Royal Commission on Civil Liability and Compensation for Personal Injury*, (Cmnd 7054, 1978). It is interesting to note that both these reports came out against the inclusion of the development risks defence.

[59] Art. 169 enforcement proceedings were started against the UK, but no action has yet been brought before the European Court of Justice, although it is understood that the Commission does intend to press the matter.

consumer may be able to invoke EC law to obtain the level of protection which should have been afforded under the Directive.[60] This task may be assisted by s.1, Consumer Protection Act 1987 which states that its provisions should be construed so as to comply with the Product Liability Directive.[61] Before considering the detail of the Consumer Protection Act 1987, it is important to remember that the Directive expressly states that it shall be without prejudice to existing laws in Member States.[62] In the UK it is likely that the implied quality conditions will continue to be invoked where a contractual nexus exists between the injured party and the supplier of the defective product. In fact, many practitioners believe that 'strict liability' will simply be used as an additional action to those which already exist in contract and negligence.[63]

6.2.3.3.1 Product: The scope of part I of the Consumer Protection Act 1987, which implements the Product Liability Directive, is delineated by reference to the definition of a 'product'. Product is defined as meaning any goods or electricity, including products comprised in other products either as components, raw materials or otherwise.[64] However, there is an express exclusion for game or other agricultural produce which has not undergone an industrial process.[65] This exclusion can be considered wider than that allowed under the Directive, which defines 'primary agricultural produce' as produce of the soil, stock–farming or fisheries which has not undergone initial processing. It would seem possible that agricultural products could be subjected to initial processing of a 'non–industrial' nature. However, the question of whether the UK's implementation infringes the Directive is uncertain, for the preamble to the Directive does refer to such products that 'have undergone a processing of an industrial nature'. Member States had the option of including primary agricultural produce and game within the scope of their domestic legislation, but to date only Luxembourg has chosen to do so. The reason for the exemption is probably due to the politically powerful farming lobby, which argues that the industry is already well regulated and that defects can be caused by natural conditions beyond the producer's control. These arguments do not pass muster. Many other industries, such as

---

60   See 2.4.2.
61   This reflects the jurisprudence of the European Court of Justice, see 2.4.2.
62   Art. 13.
63   See I. Dodds–Smith, 'The Impact of Product Liability on Pharmaceutical Companies' in *Product Liability, Insurance and the Pharmaceutical Industry*, G. Howells (ed) (MUP, 1991).
64   S.1(2), Consumer Protection Act 1987.
65   S.2(4), Consumer Protection Act 1987.

the pharmaceutical industry, are well regulated, but even the best regulation cannot prevent some consumers from being injured by products. The argument about natural conditions causing defects loses much of its force when one realises that there is no liability for defects occurring after the product has left the producer's control, so there would be no liability for products damaged in storage after they leave the farm. If natural conditions do make primary agricultural produce dangerous (for example, irradiation from nuclear power plants affecting crops), then the loss spreading risk allocation rationales for strict products liability apply with particular force to protect the unfortunate victims who are thereby injured.

6.2.3.3.2 Persons Liable: The Act channels liability primarily towards three economic agents: producers, own–branders and importers. Producers are persons who manufacture products, or win or abstract a substance. Where the product has not been manufactured, won or abstracted, but its essential elements are attributable to an industrial or other process, then producers are persons who carry out that process.[66] Channelling liability towards producers is a recognition that, because they are usually larger in size and more likely to be able to control the quality of the product than retailers, they are therefore better able to insure against the product liability risk.

Own–branders are persons who, by putting their name on the product or by using a trademark or other distinguishing mark, have held themselves out to be the producer.[67] Own–brand names are increasingly common amongst large retailers. Extending liability to them recognises both that they will generally have a substantial influence over the quality of goods they receive from their suppliers, and also that they will be large enough concerns to carry the product liability burden. It is uncertain whether own–branders are singled out as a target of liability because of their economic strength, or simply because they may disguise the fact that the goods were manufactured by someone else. An interesting question is whether chains which 'own–brand' products can escape liability by expressly stating on the packaging that they did not produce it. In such circumstances it could be argued that they have not held themselves out to be the producer of the product. However, it could equally be argued that placing their name on or using a trademark or other distinguishing mark in relation to the product is irrebuttable evidence that they do hold themselves out as the producer. It is not clear whether it was foreseen that own–branders would avoid liability in this manner. If it were permitted, one would hope that any exculpatory statement would have to be given due prominence to be effective, so that the

---

[66] Ss.2(2)(a) and 1(2), Consumer Protection Act 1987.
[67] S.2(2)(b), Consumer Protection Act 1987.

sensible policy of equating the economically powerful own–brander with the producer is not undermined too easily.

The right to sue may be illusory for consumers if it can only be exercised against some distant foreign entity. Therefore the Directive provides for the right to sue the importer of goods into the single market. Provision for this is also found in s.2(2)(c) of the Consumer Protection Act 1987. However, it is important to note that the right can only be exercised against the first importer into a Member State, who may not be the actual importer into the UK. Such a rule makes sense to European legislators concerned to promote the concept of a single market, but it may still leave British consumers having to litigate overseas, albeit with the assistance of the Brussels Convention of 1968 on Jurisdiction and the Enforcement of Judgements in Civil and Commercial Matters.[68]

Although primary liability falls on the above–mentioned persons, suppliers can be liable in certain circumstances. The Act defines supplier widely to cover not only the supplier to the injured party, but also others in the supply chain, including those who supplied defective component parts.[69] A supplier will be liable if the injured person requests assistance to identify one or more of the individuals having primary liability and the supplier fails within a reasonable period to comply with that request or to identify his or her own supplier. The request must be made within a reasonable period of the damage having occurred[70] and at a time when it was not practicable for the injured person to identify all those persons with primary liability.

6.2.3.3.3 Liability: S.2, Consumer Protection Act 1987 imposes liability for damage caused wholly or partly by a defect in a product. Whilst the requirement to prove negligence no longer exists, the plaintiff must still establish that the product was defective and that the defect caused his or her injury.

Causation is likely to be a major stumbling block in product liability cases. Defendants may not wish to rely on technical defences relating to whether their product was or was not defective, but may prefer to deny that their product was the cause of the injury. Particularly where the product is alleged to have caused the plaintiff to contract a disease, it may be difficult for the plaintiff to show that the illness was caused by the product rather than other genetic or environmental factors. The suggestion in *McGhee v National Coal Board*[71] that the plaintiff could be assisted in such cases by

---

68   See 17.9.2.1.
69   S.2(3), Consumer Protection Act 1987.
70   This restriction does not appear in the Directive.
71   [1973] 1 WLR 1.

the burden of proof being reversed and placed on the defendants was emphatically rejected in *Wilsher v Essex Area Health Authority*.[72]

The choice of defectiveness standard is a key issue in any liability regime. S.3(1), Consumer Protection Act 1987 provides:

> 'there is a defect in a product ... if the safety of the product is not such as persons generally are entitled to expect; and for those purposes 'safety' in relation to a product, shall include safety with respect to products comprised in that product and safety in the context of risk of damage to property, as well as in the context of risks of death or personal injury.'

S.3(2) continues to provide that:

> 'in determining .... what persons generally are entitled to expect in relation to a product all the circumstances shall be taken into account, including –
> (a) the manner in which, and purposes for which, the product has been marketed, its get–up, the use of any mark in relation to the product and any instructions for or warnings with respect to, doing or refraining from doing anything with or in relation to the product,
> (b) what might reasonably be expected to be done with or in relation to the product; and
> (c) the time when the product was supplied by its producer to another, and nothing in this section shall require a defect to be inferred from the fact alone that the safety of a product which is supplied after that time is greater than the safety of the product in question.'

This defectiveness standard is a variant on the consumer expectation standard, which has been widely rejected in the US. One problem that has arisen with this standard is as to how it could be applied to obvious dangers, for surely (it is argued) consumers cannot expect an obviously dangerous product to be safe? More generally, it can be criticised for being an essentially norm–reflecting standard, which simply forces consumers to accept the prevailing expectations of safety without imposing any more demanding standards. The level of safety which consumers expect is to some extent physchologically conditioned. Consumers tend to be concerned about short term gains (such as increased speed or lower prices) and frequently consider safety as a more remote concern. This is encouraged by the typical, and understandable, human desire to believe that someone other than ourself will be the unfortunate victim of an accident. Consumers also tend to overvalue large risks (like the possibility a plane might crash) and

---

[72]   [1988] 2 WLR 557.

undervalue smaller long term risks (such as consumption of high cholesterol foods).[73] A more positive interpretation is that the standard is not actually based on what consumers actually expect, but rather on what they should be entitled to expect.

There is also the problem of knowing how the standard is to be applied to vulnerable groups such as children, old people and the handicapped. Presumably the court will take into account the manner and purposes for which the product was marketed, so that if it is clearly targeted at vulnerable groups, it will have to be rendered safe for their uses. Persons generally would expect this, even if they themselves did not require the same protection.

With such an open textured defectiveness standard, much is left to judicial interpretation – a particular problem in a standard applied throughout the European Union. There is an obvious danger that courts in different legal systems will apply the test in an inconsistent manner as a result of their various legal traditions and the socio economic conditions which influence their expectations of safety.

A common problem in product liability cases is the extent to which producers are liable when the product has been misused in a foreseeable manner. By taking into account what might reasonably be expected to be done with or in relation to a product, the Act seems to strike a balance. Blatant misuses (such as drying a cat in a microwave) could not reasonably be expected, but some uses might be expected other than those for which the product was specifically marketed. There is regrettably no express reference to children or other vulnerable groups, but all the circumstance must be taken into account. Thus if erasers were marketed which looked and smelled like fruit, then it should be possible to argue that they were defective: producers might reasonably expect that small children might put them in their mouths and attempt to eat them.

The 'state of the art defence'[74] is actually contained within the definition of defect itself, for by taking into account the time at which the product was supplied, the court must judge the product against the standard of safety which would have been expected at that time. This is reinforced when the section goes on to say that a defect should not be inferred simply because a safer product was subsequently supplied. This accords with the existing position under negligence law, but it does not mean that the fact that a

---

[73] See F.P. Hubbard, 'Reasonable Human Expectations: A Normative Model for Imposing Strict Liability for Defective Products' (1978) 29 *Mercer L Rev* 465 and D. Burley, 'Risk Assessment and Responsibility for Injuries Associated with Medicines' in G. Howells (ed), *op. cit.*

[74] See 6.1.2 for an explanation of how we differentiate the state of the art and development risks defence.

product is subsequently modified to make it safer cannot be used as evidence that such modifications could have been made at the time it was originally supplied. It simply provides that defectiveness cannot be inferred from the mere fact that modifications have subsequently taken place.

The Act also contains a 'development risks' defence. The Directive gave Member States the option of removing this defence, but once again only Luxembourg has taken this up. Some development risks may also be caught by the special pharmaceutical liability regime which applies in Germany.[75] Grave doubts have, however, been expressed as to whether the UK's version of the defence correctly implements the Directive. S.4(1)(e), Consumer Protection Act 1987 provides that it is a defence for the producer to show:

> 'that the state of scientific and technical knowledge at the relevant time was not such that a producer of products of the same description as the product in question might be expected to have discovered the defect if it had existed in his products while they were under his control.'

Art.7(e) of the Directive had provided a defence if the producer proved:

> 'that the state of scientific and technical knowledge at the time when he put the product into circulation was not such as to enable the existence of the defect to be discovered.'

In fact the House of Lords had passed an amendment to bring the defence into line with the wording of the Directive. Under the Lords' amendment, the defence would have applied if 'the state of scientific and technical knowledge at the relevant time was not such as to enable the existence of the defect to be discovered'. However, during the passage of the Bill the 1987 General Election was called and their Lordships were forced to accept the reinstatement of the original Government wording as the price for not seeing the Bill fail for lack of time before the dissolution of Parliament.

There are two respects in which the UK's development risks defence appears to be more generous to producers than that contained in the Directive. First, it introduces the concept of expectancy, whereas the Directive is concerned with 'the plain unvarnished concept of discoverability'.[76] Second, it does not test discoverability against stringent objective criteria, but rather judges producers by the standards of producers of similar products – implying that there are different standards to be expected of different producers. This seems to smack of a very weak negligence type liability. Some commentators argue that the UK has

---

75   See 6.2.2.
76   See Baroness Burton of Coventry, HL Debs. Vol. 485, Col. 849, 9 March 1987.

correctly implemented the defence, for the defence only makes sense if reasonable expectations are taken into account.[77] In many ways the defence sits uneasily within a strict liability regime. The European Commission recognised this and did not want the defence, but had to accept it because otherwise a number of Member States would have resisted the notion of strict liability. In these circumstances the Commission drafted a very narrow defence which would only seem to exclude those risks which are unable to be discovered. Thus risks would be caught by the Directive (even if they had not been discovered) if the state of scientific and technical knowledge was such that they could have been discovered, although the discoverability of the defect was not realised until someone later made the connection between the knowledge which existed and the risk caused by the product. The narrower interpretation of the defence may not be based on logical legal reasoning, but it is perhaps the correct one, given that the defence has no logical place in a strict liability regime and is simply the result of political compromise.

Given the choice of a consumer expectation standard, the inclusion of state of the art and (a broad) development risks defence, it might be argued that the new strict liability standard differs little from the previous negligence liability regime.[78] Perhaps the most significant change has been with regard to the burden of proof. Whereas in a negligence liability regime the burden was on the plaintiff to show that the producer had behaved unreasonably in marketing a defective product, under the new product liability law the burden is placed on the defendant to establish that the state of scientific and technical knowledge affords him a defence. Given the consumer's probable lack of scientific and technical knowledge and the cost of obtaining it, this may be a significant reform. On the other hand producers may find it fairly easy to put forward some evidence to suggest that they could not have had the relevant knowledge and thus effectively force the injured party to disprove their expert evidence. It may be that the courts should be allowed to appoint an expert or automatically grant legal aid whenever the development risks defence is invoked.[79]

6.2.3.3.4 *Defences:* In addition to the development risks defence there are several other defences specifically provided for in the Consumer Protection Act 1987. For all of them it is important to remember that the burden is on

---

[77] See C. Newdick, 'The Development Risks Defence of the Consumer Protection Act 1987' (1988) *Camb LJ* 455 and 'Risk, Uncertainty and Knowledge in the Development Risks Defence' (1991) 20 *Anglo–Am L Rev* 309.

[78] See J. Stapleton, 'Products Liability Reform – Real or Illusory' (1986) 6 *OJLS* 392; C. Newdick, 'The Future of Negligence in Product Liability' (1987) 104 *LQR* 288.

[79] This latter idea has been advanced by the National Consumer Council; see 17.3.1.6.1.

the defendant to establish the defence. Thus it is a defence to establish that the defect is attributable to compliance with any requirement imposed by or under any enactment or with any Community obligation.[80] This defence is actually narrower than it might at first appear since it only relates to statutory standards; compliance with voluntary standards, such as those of the BSI, would not be an automatic defence. Also for the defence to apply, there must have been no way in which the defect could have been avoided and the enactment complied with. As most standards seek to promote safety, this will rarely be the case. Equally, most standards do not require that the product must conform to a specific form, but rather leave an element of discretion to the producer by providing for a range of criteria within which the product must fall. For instance, regulations might provide for maximum and minimum toleration's of substances or temperatures. Only if no way exists for a safe product to be made within that range can the defence apply.

It is also a defence for the defendant to show that he or she never supplied the product.[81] This would protect defendants who have goods stolen from them, as well as ensuring that producers are not responsible for counterfeit goods. It would not, however, protect a producer who, knowing goods are defective, decides not to market them, but finds that they have subsequently been marketed in error by his employees.

There is no liability if the defect did not exist at the time the product was supplied.[82] Thus producers are not liable for subsequent deterioration due to poor storage. They are, however, liable for defects which materialise after supply, so long as they existed at the time of supply. Defendants will also be able to raise a defence if the only supply of the product to another was otherwise than in the course of a business and without a view to profit.[83] It would, however, not exempt goods supplied free as part of a promotional campaign. Like all attempts to exclude non–business liability such exclusions raise problems in borderline cases, such as, for instance, whether or not charities are included.

There is also a specific defence for producers of component parts. Such producers can raise a defence if the defect constituted a defect in a subsequent product and was attributable to the design of the subsequent product or to compliance with instructions provided by the producer of the subsequent product.[84]

---

[80] S.4(1)(a), Consumer Protection Act 1987.
[81] S.4(1)(b), Consumer Protection Act 1987.
[82] S.4(1)(d), Consumer Protection Act 1987.
[83] S.4(1)(c), Consumer Protection Act 1987.
[84] S.4(1)(f), Consumer Protection Act 1987.

There are several other possible defences. Thus a defendant can plead contributory negligence[85] and probably *volenti non fit injuria*, although there is a prohibition on exclusions of liability under the Act.[86] The Act also provides for a three year limitation period from the date the action accrued or, if later, the date of knowledge, ie the date the plaintiff (or someone in whom the right of action had previously been vested) should have known that he had a right of action worth pursuing against an identifiable defendant.[87] There is also a longstop barring actions ten years after the product was supplied by a producer, own–brander or importer. Whilst such a long–stop may be acceptable as a trade–off for the inclusion of the development risks defence, it is less acceptable when that defence is permitted. It does, however, provide a limit to the period for which product records need to be kept. Finally, it should be remembered that the Act's provisions only came into force on 1 March 1988 and so do not apply to products supplied before that date.

6.2.3.3.5 Damages: Injured parties can claim damages for personal injury and death under the same heads as apply in negligence actions. Thus damages can be claimed for both economic losses (like loss of wages) and non–economic losses (such as pain and suffering and loss of amenity). The Directive allowed Member States the option of placing a limit on damages resulting from personal injury and death caused by identical items with the same defect of not less than 70M ECU. This option has been invoked by countries which traditionally combine strict liability with a ceiling on damages (countries such as Germany, Spain and Portugal), but was not taken advantage of by the UK, where such limitations would run counter to the common law tradition.

There are some limitations on the type of property damage recoverable. First, the property damage must exceed £275.[88] The preamble to the Directive states that the aim of this limitation is to avoid litigation in an excessive number of cases. In the UK if that figure is exceeded, then the whole amount of property damage is recoverable. This is different from the position adopted in other European countries where the £275 (or equivalent) is treated like an insurance policy excess and deducted from any claim. The UK approach seems preferable, for otherwise small amounts of property damage could be litigated (ie if £276 of damage was suffered, a claim could be brought for £1). Once litigation takes place then there would seem to be

---

85   S.6(4), Consumer Protection Act 1987.
86   S.7, Consumer Protection Act 1987.
87   See now s.11A, Limitation Act 1980.
88   S.5(4), Consumer Protection Act 1987.

no reason not to allow full recovery. To take more cases out of the scope of the Directive, a better approach would be to raise the threshold, rather than making litigation less attractive by making the amounts recoverable smaller. Second, the Directive does not apply to loss or damage to the product itself or to the whole or any part of any product which has been supplied with the product comprised in it.[89] It could be objected that this restriction is drawn too widely. The Directive talks of 'damage to, or destruction of, any item of property other than the defective product itself'. It might be suggested that, as a component part is a product in its own right then any damage it causes to the end product could be recovered under the Directive, although it is clearly not recoverable under the Act. This argumentation smacks of the complex structure theory which has been rejected in negligence,[90] and has also not been included within the scope of implementing laws in other European countries. It would, however, make sense to permit such recovery. At present when a car is damaged by a defective component, the recovery of damages depends upon whether the component is the original or a replacement: only in the latter instance can the damage be recovered from the producer of the component part. Third, the damaged property (note that this restriction does not apply to the defective product which caused the damage) must have been ordinarily intended for private use, occupation or consumption and also actually have been intended by the plaintiff for his or her own private use, occupation or consumption.[91]

It is unclear which test of remoteness of damage would apply. One would imagine that in torts of strict liability, the defendant would be liable for all direct consequences of his tortious actions, without there being any requirement of foreseeability. However, in a recent case of liability in nuisance and *Rylands v Fletcher*, the House of Lords imposed a foreseeability test of remoteness in respect of torts of strict liability.[92] One suspects that, especially given the inclusion of the development risks defence, the courts will be tempted to apply the test of reasonable foreseeability to liability under the Consumer Protection Act 1987. Matters of foreseeability, which cannot be used as a defence to an allegation of defectiveness under the Act, might then be invoked to avoid liability on the basis that the damage was too remote. This would further undermine the strictness of the product liability regime under the Consumer Protection Act 1987.

---

89 S.5(2), Consumer Protection Act 1987.
90 See *Murphy v Brentwood District Council* [1990] 2 All ER 908.
91 S.5(3), Consumer Protection Act 1987.
92 *Cambridge Water Co Ltd v Eastern Counties Leather Plc* [1994] 1 All ER 53. This was in fact a case of historic pollution which could not have been predicted as being classed as pollution at the time it occurred ie a development risk.

6.3 SERVICE LIABILITY

6.3.1 Negligence

Whilst the notion (if not the reality) of strict liability has become commonplace in products liability discussions, the same cannot be said of service liability where the legal mind set is still firmly wedded to the principle of fault liability. In tort, suppliers of services will typically be held to be under a duty of care to protect the safety of their customers and to ensure that they do not damage the goods they perform their services on. However the standard of care is only the negligence standard of taking reasonable care.

The standard of care was classically expounded by McNair J in *Bolam v Friern Hospital Management Committee*[93] where the learned judge stated:

'The test is the standard of the ordinary skilled man exercising and professing to have that special skill. A man need not possess the highest expert skill ... it is sufficient if he exercises the ordinary skill of a competent man exercising that particular art.'[94]

The judge went on to consider the relevance of common practice when assessing a professional's conduct:

'A doctor is not guilty of negligence if he has acted in accordance with a practice accepted as proper by a responsible body of medical men skilled in that particular art ... Putting it the other way round, a doctor is not negligent, if he is acting in accordance with such a practice, merely because there is a body of opinion that takes the contrary view. At the same time, that does not mean that a medical man can obstinately and pig–headedly carry on with some old technique if it has been proved to be contrary to what is really substantially the whole of informed medical opinion.'[95]

Someone who 'professes to exercise a special skill must exercise the ordinary skill of his speciality'.[96] Indeed the judges will assess the reasonableness of an actor's conduct in the light of the post he or she holds rather than by the qualities of the individual concerned.[97] Many of the principles in this area

---

[93] [1957] 2 All ER 118.
[94] *Ibid.* at 121.
[95] *Ibid.* at 122.
[96] *Maynard v West Midlands Regional Area Health Authority* [1985] 1 All ER 635.
[97] *Wilsher v Essex Area Health Authority* [1986] 3 All ER 801.

involve medical negligence cases (which is becoming a specialist subject in its own right), but they have also been applied to other service providers.[98] The standard reflecting test applied in cases of professional negligence can be criticised from a consumer perspective.[99] Although it is interesting to note that the courts have been more willing to challenge doctors' views as to whether patients should have been more fully informed of the risks associated with their treatment.[100] This might just be an instance of judges being more confident to assess actions in relation to non–disclosure than in relation to diagnosis and treatment, just as judges are more willing to find liability for failure to warn than for a design defect. On the other hand, it could be interpreted more broadly as an example of how judges are prepared to challenge unacceptable practices even if approved by a body of professional opinion.[101] The negligence standard ought not to provide a defence to a doctor who fails to keep pace with changes in professional practice. Some cases have appeared unduly lenient. Thus in *Crawford v Board of Governors of Charing Cross Hospital*[102] a doctor was not liable for failing to adjust his practice following an article published in the Lancet six months previously, while in *Whiteford v Hunter*[103] it was not found to be negligent to fail to use equipment common in other countries but rare in the UK.

Once negligence is established, the plaintiff still needs to prove that the negligence caused the damage complained of. As with product liability,[104] the requirement to prove causation is likely to be a real problem for consumers. The objection is not that causation should not have to be proven, but rather that the present rules are too restrictive and formalistic to allow plaintiffs a fair chance. Causation must be proven on the balance of

---

[98]   See A. Dugdale and K. Stanton, *Professional Negligence*, (Butterworths, 1989).

[99]   For an interesting and lively critique of how the courts deal with professionals, see M. Joseph, *Lawyers Can Seriously Damage Your Health*, (Michael Joseph, 1984).

[100]   In *Sidaway v Bethlem Royal Hospital Governors* [1985] 1 All ER 643 at 663 Lord Bridge said: 'But, even in a case where, as here, no expert witness in the relevant medical field condemns the non–disclosure as being in conflict with accepted and responsible medical practice, I am of opinion that the judge might in certain circumstances come to the conclusion that disclosure of a particular risk was so obviously necessary to an informed choice on the part of the patient that no reasonably prudent medical man would fail to make it.'

[101]   J. Montrose, 'Is Negligence an Ethical or Sociological Concept?' (1958) 21 *MLR* 259: see *Lloyd's Bank Ltd v E.B. Savory & Co* [1933] AC 201 (bank found liable despite following a practice which was adopted by all other banks).

[102]   *The Times*, 8 December 1953.

[103]   [1950] WN 553.

[104]   See 6.2.3.3.3.

probabilities and this is taken to mean that there was a 51 per cent chance that the defendant caused the damage. Yet in many cases there are several possible explanations for a plaintiff's injuries, with the defendant's negligence being just one. The defendant is more likely than the plaintiff to be able to explain the actual cause of the damage, as he or she would have controlled the process which caused the injury; yet the burden is placed on the plaintiff. This seems wrong given that the plaintiff is innocent and the defendant is at fault.

6.3.2 Supply of Goods and Services Act 1982[105]

The Supply of Goods and Services Act 1982 implies into contracts for the supply of a service (which includes contracts where goods are also supplied) a term 'that the supplier will carry out the service with reasonable care and skill'.[106] The section only implies this term when the supplier is acting in the course of a business.

This seems to be a codification of the common law position and also imports into the contractual context the negligence case law concerning what amounts to reasonable care and skill.[107] From a consumer perspective, the term may be less favourable than similar terms implied into consumer contracts in Australia (by s.74, Federal Trade Practices Act 1974[108]) and in Ireland (by s.39 of the Irish Sale of Goods and Supply of Services Act 1980). S.74 of the Australian Act talks about 'due skill and care' while s.39(b) of the Irish Act provides for 'due skill, care and diligence'.[109] 'Due skill' might be considered more demanding than 'reasonable care and skill'.

The Irish law also implies a term 'that the supplier has the necessary skill to render the service', whereas under English law if a consumer discovers that a supplier lacks the necessary skills to perform the task he or she will probably have to wait to see if the task is actually performed negligently. There is unlikely to be a term implied that the supplier possesses the necessary skills, especially given the possibility that the supplier might subcontract the work to a competent person. One exception to this may be where a supplier must possess a licence or other qualifications. Where the supplier falsely represents him or herself as having a special status (for

---

105   See G. Woodroffe, *Goods and Services – The New Law*, (Sweet & Maxwell, 1982).
106   S.13, Supply of Goods and Services Act 1982.
107   See Woodroffe, *op. cit.* at p. 104.
108   See N. Palmer and F. Rose, 'Implied Terms in Consumer Transactions – The Australian Approach' (1977) 26 *ICLQ* 169 at 185–190.
109   Adding speed of performance to the quality aspects.

example, being a member of a trade association), then the contract could be rescinded, and damages claimed, for misrepresentation.

Under the Australian Act, where the consumer makes known the 'particular purpose for which the services are required or the result that he desires the services to achieve', there is then 'an implied warranty that the services supplied ... will be reasonably fit for that purpose and are of such a nature and quality that they might reasonably be expected to achieve that result'. We have noted earlier in this chapter that in English contract law, while it is possible to promise that a service will achieve a particular outcome, this will only be found to be so where an intention to give such an express promise can be established.[110]

The Supply of Goods and Services Act 1982 clearly stopped short of making the suppliers of services strictly liable. Would that have been such a drastic step? Surely dry–cleaners can be held liable for clothes they damage, even if negligence cannot be shown. Even in the most contentious area of medical negligence, which probably would have to be subject to a specific regime, strict liability would not make doctors liable for the failure of medical treatment. Liability would only be imposed where the doctor's actions made a patient worse, for example, through failure to diagnose or improper performance of the treatment, the difference being that the doctor need not be found to be at fault. The move away from a system which requires one party to blame the other should help in the process of achieving settlements, if professionals can be made to feel that their professional conduct is not being questioned. After all, there may be many explanations for why things go wrong besides professional error.

6.3.3 Draft Directive on the Liability of Suppliers of Services[111]

The European Commission published a draft Directive on Service Liability in 1991. Although the Commission's second three year action plan on consumer policy[112] mentions the need to adopt such a Directive, the Commission has announced that the project will be abandoned in favour of a more sectoral approach. Why did this happen? The Commission is notoriously more cautious in relation to services than products, mainly because the single market justifications for European legislative activity in this area are less obvious. The draft Service Liability Directive was in reality a victim of the current vogue of invoking subsidiarity as a ground for not

---

[110] See note 4.

[111] OJ 1991 C 12/8. See Th. Bourgoignie, 'Liability of Suppliers of Services in the European Community : the Draft Council Directive' [1991] *E Consum LJ* 3.

[112] COM (93) 378 final.

legislating at the European level. There were also powerful pressure groups in the service sector countering suggestions that legislation was needed in respect of services. In particular, the medical and architectural professions lobbied hard to be removed from the scope of any Service Liability Directive. The irony is that it is in these specific areas that the Commission may well now direct their attention in order to achieve sectoral solutions.

The features of the now obsolete draft Directive are nevertheless worth mentioning in outline. They illustrate the more hesitant approach of legislators to services than products – even those who wish to do something to help consumers in this area. The draft Directive was based on fault liability. However, the injured party would have been assisted by a reversal of the burden of proof and by the fact that, when assessing fault, account would have been taken of the behaviour of the supplier of the service, who 'in normal and reasonably foreseeable conditions, shall ensure the safety which may reasonably be expected'.[113] This would seem to be a rather limited obligation to ensure safety, as emphasised by the fact that a party was not at fault merely because 'a better service existed or might have existed at the moment of performance or subsequently'.[114] The reversal of the burden of proof would have assisted consumers, but might have been undermined by art.5 of the draft Directive which required the injured person to prove damage as well as the causal relationship between that damage and the performance of the service. In order to establish such a causal relationship, the injured party would doubtless have had to show what exactly in the performance of the service had caused the damage. In practice, this might have amounted to having to prove how the supplier was at fault in the provision of the service – the very element for which the draft Directive had intended to place the burden of proof on the defendant.

6.4 ALTERNATIVES

Improving the common law rules may only be a partial solution to the question of accident compensation for consumers.[115] Most solutions fail to address the basic problem that private litigation is a very expensive way of providing compensation. It is also very arbitrary since it requires the consumer to bring him or herself within what are sometimes technical and narrow grounds for recovery. Not only must there be a ground for recovery, but in addition the consumer must have evidence to establish the claim and

---

[113] Art.1(3) COM (93) 378 final.
[114] Art.1(4) COM (93) 378 final.
[115] See 1.6.

also be fortunate in having a readily suable and solvent defendant. Some countries have sought to avoid the dangers of the private litigation system.

6.4.1 Scandinavia[116]

Scandinavian countries have adopted an insurance based solution. In Sweden, for example, there are insurance based schemes covering injuries caused both by pharmaceuticals and medical accidents. Although these schemes are alternatives to the court, in practice they are more generous, making private law largely redundant within the area of their operation. The theory behind the schemes is to base liability on causation rather than proof of fault or defectiveness, with the advantage that defendants can admit liability without having to concede culpability. Causation is also given a more relaxed interpretation than under the general law. However, much of the schemes' success might be due to the fact that businesses only have to meet moderate costs for financing them. With the nation's social insurance covering a large proportion of the injured person's economic losses, the insurance schemes only have to provide a top–up element.

6.4.2 New Zealand[117]

The most radical reform has been in New Zealand, where the Accident Compensation Act 1982 essentially abolished common law actions for death or personal injury. Instead those who suffer 'personal injury by accident' in New Zealand recover economic losses in the form of periodic payments of up to 80 per cent of the person's previous salary, subject to a maximum ceiling which is pitched at a fairly high level. Non–economic losses are paid as a lump sum. Despite criticisms by academics[118] and challenges to it by the present Conservative Government, the New Zealand scheme remains a model of what a sensible accident compensation scheme might look like.

The challenge would be to introduce a similar scheme in a larger country with a less homogenous society than exists in New Zealand. This is unlikely to happen because of the number of powerful interest groups which have a vested interest in keeping the present system in place – lawyers, insurers, expert witnesses and also possibly those with a privileged position under the existing regime (for example, workers who benefit from workers'

---

116 G. Howells, *op. cit.*, Ch. 9.

117 G. Howells, *op. cit.*, Ch. 16.

118 See R. Miller, 'The Future of New Zealand's Accident Compensation Scheme' (1989) 11 *U Hawaii Law Rev* 1.

compensation schemes and also possibly now consumers who benefit from strict liability regimes).

7 Consumer Credit: Private Law

7.1 INTRODUCTION

The consumer credit industry is an important sector of the economy and one which has a direct impact on the economic health of the nation.[1] Until the early 1970s consumer credit regulation had two explicit aims – to protect consumers and ensure the amount of consumer credit did not have deleterious effects on the general economic health of the nation.[2] Strands of this latter policy remained until 1982, when the practice of requiring minimum down–payments and maximum repayment periods was discontinued.[3] Whilst no longer an explicit policy of the law, the link between consumer credit regulation and the wider economy remains.[4] However, this chapter will concentrate upon the consumer protection aspects of consumer credit and, more particularly, upon the private law remedies available to consumers. Chapter 11 considers the public law regulatory controls on consumer credit.

Consumer credit law is today based around the Consumer Credit Act 1974, which resulted from the Crowther Royal Commission on Consumer Credit.[5] The EC has also enacted Directives approximating the laws,

---

1   See I. Ramsay, 'Credit, Class and the Normalisation of Debt Default' in *Aspects of Credit and Debt*, G. Howells, I. Crow and M. Moroney (eds), (Sweet & Maxwell, 1993) at p. 64 and Crowther, *Consumer Credit* (Cmnd 4596, 1971).

2   This latter function was performed by Control Orders made by the Board of Trade under the Emergency Laws (Re-enactments and Repeals) Act 1964. These laid down minimum deposits for credit contracts and minimum advance payments under hire contracts and in that way allowed consumer expenditure to be controlled.

3   Control of Hiring and Hire-Purchase and Credit Sale Agreements (Revocation) Order 1982 No. 1034.

4   The cautious attitude of lenders, as reflected in the Bankers' Code of Practice, is perhaps one reason why it has taken so long to struggle out of recession in the 1990s. Such caution was a reaction to the criticisms levelled at the industry when the size of the debt problem became apparent. A study by the Policy Studies Institute found that approximately 600,000 households in the UK had problem debts, with the national average debt being £620: R. Berthoud and E. Kempson, *Credit and Debt in Britain: First Findings*, (Policy Studies Institute, 1990).

5   See Crowther, *op. cit.*

regulations and administrative provisions concerning consumer credit.[6] In fact, however, these are not as wide ranging as the Consumer Credit Act 1974, and did not require major amendments to the UK law. The Directives place an emphasis on information provisions, but also contain, inter alia, rules requiring the supervision of creditors, restricting creditor remedies, allowing for a rebate if credit is repaid ahead of time and introducing a limited form of connected lender liability for the quality of goods supplied. We shall see that existing UK law contained these features and more. As the Directive is a minimal harmonisation directive, there is no need to repeal more stringent provisions contained in the Consumer Credit Act 1974.[7]

7.2 HISTORY OF CONSUMER CREDIT[8]

Some form of credit has probably always had (and always will have) a place in human society: some of the oldest records which survive from Mesopotamia are of credit transactions. Of course usury was for a long time condemned by religion and hence the state. However, over time as society became more complex and credit became a necessary lubricant for the consumer market, controls on lending were relaxed. The earliest forms of consumer credit seem to be tradesman's credit, pawnbroking and moneylending. Tradesman's credit from the shopkeeper or the itinerant peddler grew in the 17th– and 18th–centuries, when economic reality dictated that sellers had goods to sell but consumers did not have the money to pay for them (at least not immediately). Pawnbroking became an important form of credit in late 16th–century London. It was widely used by the poor, with clothing being a common item to pawn.[9] By contrast professional moneylending, as opposed to casual lending between friends and families, seems to have been the source of credit used by impecunious middle and upper–class consumers.

---

6   87/102/EEC OJ 1987 L 42/48. This was amended by Directive 90/88/EEC OJ 1990 L 61/14, which introduced a common method for calculating the annual percentage rate (APR), see 7.4.5. Member States which already had a method of calculating the APR can retain their national systems during a transitional period. Harmonisation of the method of calculating the APR is a particular problem for France.

7   For discussion of minimal harmonisation see 2.3.4.

8   See Crowther, *op. cit.* at pp 31–49.

9   In 1572 a bill was drafted which would have set up state–financed pawnshops loaning at 6 per cent to prevent the poor from being exploited. Similar systems operated on the continent, such as the *mont de piété* in France: see G. Howells and M. Moroney, 'Social Lending in Europe' in G. Howells *et al.*, *op. cit.*

Pawnbroking was first regulated in 1603 and a comprehensive consolidating statute was passed in 1872, which remained in force with minor amendments until replaced by the Consumer Credit Act 1974. The Bills of Sale Acts from 1854 to 1891 regulated moneylending which involved chattel mortgages,[10] but it was not until the 1900 and 1927 Moneylenders Acts that a comprehensive system of regulation of moneylending was established, with exemption given to those 'bona fide carrying on the business of banking'. This caused many businesses to apply for certificates to be banks in order to be exempted from the Moneylenders Acts. That many of these businesses were not banks in the accepted sense highlights a problem endemic in attempts to regulate any business activity: the ability of businesses to alter their legal form or the nature of their trading activities in order to circumvent regulation.

Various types of credit also evolved to meet the needs of particular times. Thus the advent of expensive but popular consumer durables gave birth to the hire–purchase transaction, initiated in the 1860s by the Singer Sewing Machine Company. Later it became commonplace to buy expensive consumer goods such as cars on hire–purchase. Hire–purchase was encouraged by two judicial decisions which increased its appeal to lenders. *Helby v Matthews*[11] decided that, as the hirer under a hire–purchase agreement had not bought or agreed to buy goods, he could not pass a perfect title to a third party by virtue of s.25(2), Sale of Goods Act 1979. *McEntire v Crossley Bros*[12] held that hire–purchase contracts did not fall foul of the Bills of Sale Acts requirement to register security interests, as the hirer had no property over which to grant security. Various malpractices involving hire–purchase contracts soon became apparent. Most notable was the practice of 'snatching back' of goods, whereby the agreement was terminated and the goods repossessed on the pretext of a minor irregularity when perhaps almost all the instalments had been paid. Hire–purchase contracts thus came to be highly regulated. First by the Hire–Purchase Act 1938 and later by the Hire–Purchase Acts 1954 and 1964 (which were consolidated in the Hire–Purchase Act 1965) and the Advertisements (Hire–Purchase) Act 1967. The increased regulation of hire–purchase contracts caused some companies to change to rental agreements as a means of circumventing regulation.[13] This resulted in the Crowther Committee recommending that hire contracts be brought within the scope of credit legislation.

---

10 The Bills of Sales Acts 1878–1882 (as amended) remain in force.
11 [1895] AC 471.
12 [1895] AC 457.
13 This was commented upon by Mr. Justice Sachs in *Galbraith v Mitchenall Estates Ltd* [1964] 2 All ER 653 at 659.

There is an interesting contrast between the regulation of hire–purchase transactions and moneylending. Whereas the scope of moneylending legislation was defined by the nature of the lender, hire–purchase legislation referred to the nature of the agreement. However, both approaches were easily circumvented by either changing the status of the lender or the form of the agreement. We shall see that one of the advances made in the Consumer Credit Act 1974 was to regulate according to the substance of the agreement.

There has always been a certain amount of self–help credit. Indeed in earlier times building societies had their origins as self–help associations. Recently the credit union, a financial co–operative, has seen something of a resurgence, but remains a marginal player.[14] Several forms of commercial consumer credit grew out of the self–help movement. Thus check clubs[15] gave way to check trading companies, under which traders gave consumers checks they could cash at specified shops and pay for by instalments to their door–to–door collector. Akin to this was the 'Scotch Drapery' or tallyman system, where itinerant traders would supply goods such as clothing and bedding on instalment credit which they would collect on the doorstep. Check and tally trading have always been most common in the North of England where they remain an important source of working class credit. A recent study has shown the importance of weekly doorstep collected credit to the working class economy.[16]Another important source of consumer credit, widely but not exclusively used by the working classes, are mail order catalogues.[17]

---

14 See R. Berthoud and T. Hinton, *Credit Unions in the United Kingdom*, (Policy Studies Institute, 1989); G. Howells and G. Griffiths, 'Britain's Best Kept Secret – An Analysis of Credit Unions as an Alternative Source of Credit', (1991) *JCP* 443; G. Howells and G. Griffiths, 'Slumbering Giant or White Elephant – Do Credit Unions have a Role in the United Kingdom Credit Market', (1991) 42 *NILQ* 199; G. Griffiths and G. Howells, 'Credit Unions in the United Kingdom and Possible Legislative Reforms to the Credit Unions Act 1979' in G. Howells *et al.*, *op. cit.*

15 Members would save periodic amounts and make withdrawals in turn until they had received their share of the total money.

16 See K. Rowlingson, *Moneylenders and their Clients*, (Policy Studies Institute, 1994). This study showed the importance of both money loans and loans connected with purchases from the trader.

17 Crowther had some concerns about how mail order catalogues should be regulated in relation to price disclosure. Conducting most of their business on credit they did not have, or advertise, cash prices; *Crowther, op. cit.,* pp. 96–9 and 266–7. As with interest–free credit offers, the problem is that consumers who do not take advantage of the credit offer are penalised. Crowther recommended that a prominent statement should be made that no discount is given for cash.

Given the prominence of the High Street banks in today's consumer credit market, it may perhaps come as a surprise to learn that for a long time banks were reluctant to enter the personal finance market, preferring merely to provide overdrafts to those more affluent members of society who had bank accounts. It was as late as 1958 when the banks entered the personal finance market with the Midland Bank leading the way with a Personal Loans Scheme. More recent times have seen banks achieve a deeper penetration of the consumer market.[18]

The credit card has become an important source of consumer credit with an estimated 38 per cent of the adult population possessing a credit or charge card.[19] Recently banks have started issuing cards known as EFTPOS[20] cards, which in many respects provide (absent the credit facility) the same function as credit cards and give rise to similar consumer protection problems. Yet they are not treated as instances of connected lending between the card issuer and the supplier and so escape some of the consumer protection provisions contained in the Consumer Credit Act 1974.[21] The lack of protection of consumers from the dangers of modern technology illustrates how consumer law has simply tended to react to industry innovation. There has been no framework within which consumers could influence from the outset the way in which they wish business practices to develop.

7.3 LAW REFORM

A distinction can be drawn between two types of credit: credit for need and credit for convenience. Typically lower waged people borrow to make ends meet, whilst the more affluent borrow to increase their purchasing power of consumer durables. However, whilst there may be two basic reasons for borrowing, there are – as the preceding brief history of consumer credit law

---

18   The Policy Studies Institute estimates that eight out of ten adults have a current account with a bank or building society: R. Berthoud and E. Kempson, *Credit and Debt: The PSI Report* (Policy Studies Institute, 1992). This was confirmed in a subsequent study of debtors; see I. Crow, G. Howells, M. Moroney, 'Credit and Debt: Choices for Poorer Consumers' in G. Howells *et al., op. cit.* at p.31.

19   R. Berthoud and E. Kempson (1992), *op. cit.* In the terminology of the Act, credit cards are credit–tokens: see s.14, Consumer Credit Act 1974.

20   This stands for 'Electronic Fund Transfer at Point of Sale'.

21   S.187(3A), Consumer Credit Act 1974. This means that the card issuer is not jointly liable with the supplier of goods for their quality; see 7.11. Also if the card cannot be used for credit and hence is not a credit–token, the consumer will not benefit from the protection the Act affords consumers when credit–tokens are lost or misused; see 7.16.

illustrates – multifarious forms of credit. Traditionally the law has drawn a distinction between a money loan and the provision of goods and services with the assistance of credit. Equally the law has differentiated between renting and buying on credit. Whilst these divisions make sense for some purposes, they frequently have more to do with chance and the choice of legal form than with any fundamental economic distinctions relating to the nature of the transaction being entered into. This is the important insight which the Crowther Committee provided in its 1971 critique of the law. The Committee found seven broad types of defects in the law:

(i) Regulation of transactions according to their form instead of according to their substance and function.
(ii) The failure to distinguish consumer from commercial transactions.
(iii) The artificial separation of the law relating to lending from the law relating to security for loans.
(iv) The absence of any rational policy in relation to third party rights.
(v) Excessive technicality.
(vi) Lack of consistent policy in relation to sanctions for breach of statutory provisions.
(vii) Overall, the irrelevance of credit law to present day requirements, and the resultant failure to provide just solutions to common problems.

Crowther recommended the enactment of a Lending and Security Act to provide for a proper and fair means of granting and enforcing chattel mortgages and to deal with those credit practices which need to be regulated for both commercial and consumer transactions.[22] Consumer protection measures would be contained in a Consumer Sale and Loan Act. In its White Paper, *Reform of the Law on Consumer Credit,*[23] the Government accepted the need for a Consumer Credit Bill, but were not convinced of the need for a radical reform of the law relating to security interests.[24] The Consumer Credit Act 1974 was the result.[25]

At one level the legislation should be judged by how well it deals with the technical problem of regulating a complex and fast changing industry which

---

[22] Eg penalty clauses.

[23] (Cmnd 5427, 1973).

[24] This has recently been re-examined by Prof. Diamond, but again no action has been forthcoming: see A. Diamond, 'A Review of Security Interests in Property' (HMSO, 1989).

[25] Limitations of space prevent the text going into fine detail on the Consumer Credit Act 1974, in particular it should be noted there is no discussion of the rules on security or pawnbroking. For a more detailed discussion by one of the present authors, see G. Howells, *Consumer Debt,* (Sweet & Maxwell, 1993).

is comprehensible to the industry and consumer advisers and which also prevents the creation of loopholes in consumer protection. However, a substantive evaluation of the legislation requires some understanding of what its functions ought to be. Crowther saw three primary tasks for consumer credit legislation:[26]

(i)   Redressing bargaining inequality by means such as disclosure requirements, prohibiting false and misleading information, providing a floor of consumer rights and controlling harsh terms.
(ii) Controlling trading malpractices through a licensing system and criminal and civil sanctions.
(iii) Regulating the remedies for default.[27]

These goals should be borne in mind when considering the success of the Consumer Credit Act 1974. It is also of interest to note Crowther's views on the balance which should be achieved in consumer protection measures. Thus whilst advocating loss spreading (by placing the loss on the business where there are two relatively innocent parties), Crowther thought this policy should be tempered by (i) the realisation that if this went too far, then good consumers would end up subsidising bad consumers, and (ii) the probability that if creditor remedies were restricted too much they would resort to extrajudicial (perhaps illegal) measures of self–help. This argument finds echoes in the work of Cayne and Trebilcock, who argue that consumer protection laws can be exclusionary (with lenders refusing to supply credit) or degenerative (leading to the creation of black markets).[28]

A review of the Consumer Credit Act 1974 was recently carried out by the former Director General of Fair Trading (hereafter Director General), Sir Bryan Carsberg, as part of the Government's deregulation initiative. Whilst proposing some amendments, the Act was basically given a clean bill of health. Carsberg particularly applauded the essentially non–interventionist form of the consumer credit legislation, stating:

> 'Perhaps the greatest strength of the Act is that it does not seek to meet its objectives through interventionist action such as interest rate–capping or direct control of the substance of contracts. Rather, it explicitly endorses freedom of contract within a framework of rules designed to ensure

---

26   *Op. cit.* at pp. 234–5.
27   It should perhaps be noted that the Government considered that another purpose of the reform was 'to release the credit industry from existing outdated restrictions': *Reform of the Law on Consumer Credit, op. cit.*, at p. 6.
28   D. Cayne and M. Trebilcock, 'Market Considerations in the Formulation of Consumer Protection Policy' (1973) 23 *UTLJ* 396.

openness: consumer protection is attained in large part through measures to ensure that full and truthful information about credit contracts is available to consumers.'[29]

7.4 STRUCTURE OF THE CONSUMER CREDIT ACT 1974

To understand consumer credit law one needs a firm grasp of the terminology and structure of the Consumer Credit Act 1974. The Act has two features which can help users to comprehend what is necessarily a complex piece of legislation. Section 189 gathers together all the relevant definitions. It is in effect an index for the Act. Schedule 2 provides examples and descriptions of how the draftsmen considered the Act should apply in particular circumstances.[30]

7.4.1 Regulated Agreements

The Consumer Credit Act 1974 only applies to regulated agreements, save for the extortionate credit bargain provisions which apply to all credit bargains. For an agreement to be regulated, the debtor or hirer[31] must be an individual. This therefore means that the scope of the Act extends beyond private consumers to partnerships, but not to corporations (which have a separate corporate legal personality). The intention was to bring small businesses within the scope of the Act, but this test works rather arbitrarily:

---

29   *Consumer Credit Deregulation* (Office of Fair Trading, 1994) at p. 6.

30   It has been alleged that Example 21 is erroneous in describing a cheque guarantee card as providing credit. Dobson argues that the mistake lies in describing the consumer as being 'free' to withdraw the whole balance and then use the cheque card again in a transaction which the bank is bound to honour. Dobson correctly notes that the consumer may be physically – but not legally – free to do so; see P. Dobson, 'The Cheque Card as a Consumer Credit Agreement' [1987] *JBL* 126. Professor Goode has raised similar doubts about examples 16 and 18 which relate to the complicated definitions of multiple agreements; see R. Goode, *Consumer Credit Law*, (Butterworths, 1989) at pp. 155–6. Although regrettable, such inconsistencies should not pose a problem for s.188(3), Consumer Credit Act 1974 clearly states that, in the case of a conflict between Schedule 2 and any other provisions of the Act, the latter shall prevail.

31   The parties to a credit agreement are described as the creditor and debtor and the parties to a hire agreement as the owner and hirer. Although the parties to a hire-purchase agreement are formally in a hire relationship, the Act treats such contracts as credit rather than hire contracts.

whether or not a small business is incorporated does not necessarily reflect the need of the trader for protection. The test can, however, be justified on the basis that, where a trader is not trading as a body corporate it is difficult for the other trader to know in what capacity, private or professional, the person is contracting. Therefore it is better to extend the requirements and protection of the Consumer Credit Act 1974 to all such individuals. However, Sir Bryan Carsberg, until recently the Director General, has proposed that business lending be excluded from the scope of the detailed provisions in the Consumer Credit Act 1974, although firms lending to businesses should still be required to be licensed under the Act.[32] He thought that businesses should satisfy themselves as to the value of contracts they enter into and are more able than consumers to seek independent advice. It is also hoped that the removal of such contracts from the scope of the Act will increase the flexibility of lending and leasing contracts which can be offered to businesses.[33]

Regulated agreements cover both 'consumer credit agreements' and 'consumer hire agreements'. A consumer credit agreement is a 'personal credit agreement' for credit not exceeding £15,000.[34] The notion of a threshold, which can be changed by statutory instrument, was introduced because it was felt that if the amount of credit granted exceeded a certain figure, consumers were in less need of protection. This policy might be questioned. Borrowing large amounts may simply reflect greater need. In some ways the policy of the former hire–purchase legislation was more sensible in linking regulation to the total price of the goods purchased, rather than the amount of credit extended. Take the example of two consumers buying a £20,000 car. The richer of the two is able to put down a sizeable deposit of £10,000 and thus bring him or herself within the protective scope of the Consumer Credit Act 1974, as only £10,000 credit will be extended. The less well–off consumer who can only put down a £2,000 deposit will not be protected as the credit advanced will be more than £15,000. When calculating the amount of credit advanced, it is necessary to deduct any deposit and any element of the total charge for credit.[35] The fact the limit is set as low as £15,000 is

---

[32] *Consumer Credit Deregulation, op. cit.*, Chs 4 and 9.

[33] It had previously been suggested that the UK Government would use the opportunity of implementing the EEC Consumer Credit Directive 87/102/EEC OJ 1987 L42/48 to exclude contracts both where credit is extended for purely business purposes and where the creditor acts as a private individual.

[34] S. 8(2), Consumer Credit Act 1974. The Director General has proposed that this figure be increased to £25,000; see *Consumer Credit Deregulation, op. cit.*, Ch. 10.

[35] The elements included as part of the total charge for credit are calculated on the basis of the Consumer Credit (Total Charge for Credit) Regulations 1980, S.I. 1980/51, but

becoming something of a problem, especially as this excludes many timeshare contracts, which give rise to many consumer protection problems.[36]

The Act plugs an obvious loophole which might have existed in relation to running–account credit. Creditors might have been tempted to fix a credit limit in excess of £15,000 (even though realistically that amount of credit would never be extended) in order to render the agreement unregulated. The credit limit is defined as the maximum debit balance allowed on an account, excluding any temporary arrangements.[37] S.10(3), Consumer Credit Act 1974 prevents this abuse by providing that running-account credit agreements will be regulated even if the credit limit exceeds £15,000 if:

(i)   the debtor cannot withdraw more that £15,000 at any one time; or
(ii) the total charge for credit increases or harsher terms come into force if more credit than a specified figure below £15,000 is withdrawn; or
(iii) it was not probable that more than £15,000 would be borrowed.

The Consumer Credit Act 1974 also applies to hire contracts. Consumer hire agreements will be regulated if they are capable of subsisting for three months and do not require payments in excess of £15,000.

Of course agreements will not be regulated if they are exempt agreements. The categories of exempt agreements will be considered shortly, but before the exemptions can be understood, it is necessary to introduce some terms which the Act uses. This terminology is also needed to understand the substantive provisions considered later in the chapter.

7.4.2 Terminology

Three sets of terms must be understood to make sense of the Consumer Credit Act 1974. These are important not only to be able to assess whether an agreement falls into one of the categories of exempt agreements but also because they allow the Act to fine tune the application of its principles to the different types of consumer credit. The three sets of terms are described below.

---

essentially consist of all interest and other necessary expenses connected with the loan.

[36] See the Timeshare Act 1992 and Timeshare Directive 94/47/EEC, OJ 1994, L 280/83.

[37] S.10(2), Consumer Credit Act 1974.

7.4.2.1 Fixed–Sum and Running–Account Credit [38]

Running–account credit is any facility under which a debtor is able to receive from the creditor or a third party cash, goods or services up to a credit limit. Any credit which is not running–account credit is treated as fixed–sum credit.

7.4.2.2 Restricted–Use and Unrestricted–Use Credit [39]

Restricted–use credit covers agreements:

(i)   to finance a transaction between the debtor and creditor (for example, where a shopkeeper supplies goods under a conditional sale agreement);
(ii) to finance a transaction between the debtor and a supplier other than a creditor (for example, where a double glazing company introduces a customer to a finance house and the finance company pays the money direct to the glazing company);[40]
(iii) to re–finance an existing indebtedness owed to the creditor or another person.

An agreement will not be a restricted–use agreement if the credit is provided in such a way that the debtor is free to choose how the money is spent, even if using it in certain ways would be a breach of the agreement. Any agreement which is not a restricted–use agreement is an unrestricted–use agreement.

7.4.2.3 Debtor–Creditor–Supplier and Debtor–Creditor Agreements [41]

This is perhaps the most important distinction in the Act in that it seeks to differentiate pure money loans from loans which are explicitly connected to the purchase of goods and services. Debtor–creditor–supplier agreements would cover purchases made with a credit card and also those made with the assistance of a loan from a company associated with the seller. For example, a car might be purchased with the assistance of a hire–purchase agreement

---

[38]   S.10, Consumer Credit Act 1974.
[39]   S.11, Consumer Credit Act 1974.
[40]   Since the identity of the supplier need not be known in advance, agreements entered into using a credit card are covered.
[41]   Ss.12–13, Consumer Credit Act 1974.

made with a company whose forms are provided by the car dealer. The Act defines debtor–creditor–supplier agreements as:

(i)   restricted–use credit agreements financing a transaction between the debtor and creditor;[42]
(ii) restricted–use credit agreements financing a transaction between the debtor and a supplier other than the creditor, *if* the creditor has pre–existing relations with the supplier *or* enters into the agreement in contemplation of future arrangements;[43]
(iii) unrestricted–use credit agreements, but only *if* the agreement is made under pre–existing arrangements between the creditor and supplier *and* there is knowledge that the credit is to be used to finance a transaction between the debtor and supplier. This is an anti–avoidance device. It prevents money being given to the debtor (so that technically it is not restricted–use credit as the debtor can apply it for any purpose) when in

---

[42]   Note this means that there can be only two parties to a debtor–creditor–supplier agreement with the creditor and supplier being the same person.

[43]   S.187(2), Consumer Credit Act 1974 provides that 'A consumer credit agreement shall be treated as entered into in contemplation of future arrangements between a creditor and supplier if it is entered into in the expectation that arrangements will subsequently be made between ... [them] ... for the supply of cash, goods and services (or any of them) to be financed by the consumer credit agreement.' Goode suggests that this is narrower than might first be thought since the future transactions referred to must be financed by *the* (meaning *that)* agreement. Thus whilst a credit card used with a supplier who is not yet formally within the card scheme might be covered, it would not, it is suggested, apply where creditor or supplier come together for a trial transaction with a view to making the arrangement permanent (R. Goode (1989), *op. cit.* at p. 147. It would be unfortunate if the definition of a debtor–creditor–supplier agreement were limited in this way. The courts may wish to invoke the mischief rule of interpretation and read into the Act the more generous condition that the future arrangements referred to be financed by the *type of* consumer credit agreement involved in the instant agreement. The point about credit cards being covered (despite the identity of the supplier not being known at the time the credit agreement is made) is dealt with in s.11(3), Consumer Credit Act 1974. This provides that an agreement can be of the restricted–use credit type (and therefore potentially a debtor–creditor–supplier credit agreement) even if the identity of the supplier is not known at the time the agreement is made. This is perhaps further evidence that s.187(2) should be given a broader interpretation, since the object of the narrow interpretation is provided for elsewhere in the Act.

reality the creditor knows it is being used to finance a transaction with a supplier with whom the creditor has pre–existing relations.[44]

Debtor–creditor–supplier agreements falling under category (i) are known as two party debtor–creditor–supplier agreements since the creditor and the supplier are the same person. Agreements which come within categories (ii) and (iii) are called three party debtor–creditor–supplier agreements since three distinct parties are involved.

Agreements which are not debtor–creditor–supplier agreements are debtor–creditor agreements. Rather than leave this as a residual category, the Act spells out which agreements are debtor–creditor, namely:

(i)   restricted–use credit agreements financing transactions with a supplier other than the creditor, not made under pre–existing arrangements or in contemplation of future arrangements;
(ii) unrestricted–use credit agreements not made under pre–existing arrangements with the knowledge that the credit is to be used to finance a transaction between the debtor and supplier;
(iii) any refinancing agreements.

7.4.3 Exempt Agreements[45]

Certain categories of consumer credit agreements are exempted from the provisions of the Consumer Credit Act 1974, save for the extortionate credit bargain provisions. These can be divided into three groups based on (i) the nature of the creditor, (ii) the number of repayments and (iii) the charge for credit.

7.4.3.1 Nature of the Creditor

The exemptions based on the nature of the creditor involve contracts relating to the purchase of land or agreements which are secured on land and certain ancillary transactions. Local authorities have a block exemption when they

---

44   Note it is not sufficient when the credit is for unrestricted–use that future arrangements be contemplated, there must be pre–existing arrangements.

45   See s.16, Consumer Credit Act 1974 and Consumer Credit (Exempt Agreements) (No.2) Order 1985, S.I. 1985/757 (as amended).

enter into such contracts.[46] Other lenders can apply for exemption to the Secretary of State who can make an order exempting them.[47]

7.4.3.2 Number of Repayments

The two most important types of agreement exempted on the basis of the number of instalments are debtor–creditor–supplier agreements for fixed-sum credit (which require no more than four repayments payable within 12 months of the agreement being made) and running–account debtor–creditor-supplier agreements where the balance has to be paid in one instalment when it falls due.[48] The former covers everyday credit such as the newspaper or milk bill which is settled periodically. Such arrangements are probably not viewed as credit since individuals simply pay at set intervals for goods which are regularly supplied and where payment on delivery would be inconvenient to both parties. The latter ground for exemption draws attention to the difference between a charge card, which falls within the exemption, and a credit card which does not. Charge cards, such as American Express, fall within the exemption since the monthly bill must be paid in full, whereas credit cards such as Access and Visa, give the customer the option of repaying in full or paying a sum equal to or greater than the minimum repayment (which is typically 5 per cent of the outstanding balance) and carrying the balance on to the next month.[49]

7.4.3.3 Charge for Credit

Debtor–creditor agreements are exempt on the basis of their low charge for credit if the annual percentage rate charged does not exceed 13 per cent or, if it is higher, one per cent above the highest rate published by the London and Scottish clearing banks in operation during the twenty–eight days prior to the agreement being made. Crowther considered that much of the rationale for protection disappears when the charge for credit is low, but astutely pointed

---

[46] Building societies formerly enjoyed an automatic exemption, but now they must apply for it.

[47] Consumer Credit (Exempt Agreements) (No. 2) Order 1985, S.I. 1985/757 (as amended).

[48] NB: These exemptions do not apply to agreements financing the purchase of land, nor to most pledges nor, most importantly, to conditional sale and hire–purchase agreements.

[49] In such a case interest is normally charged on the full amount credited to the account, but if the balance is paid in full no charge is normally made.

out that this exemption cannot extend to low cost debtor–creditor–supplier agreements for the seller could then hide interest charges by inflating the cash price.[50]

Certain consumer credit agreements with a foreign element are exempt. Also exempt are consumer hire agreements entered into by statutory gas, electricity and water undertakings for the hire of metering equipment.

7.4.3.4 Limited Exemptions

'Non–commercial agreements'[51] and 'small agreements'[52] provide a half–way house between regulated and exempt agreements. They are exempt from various provisions, notably those relating to formalities and the cancellation provisions. Non–commercial agreements are also exempt from the connected lender provisions contained in s.75, Consumer Credit Act 1974.[53]

A 'non–commercial agreement' is a consumer credit or consumer hire agreement which is not made by the creditor or owner in the course of a business carried on by themselves. The business need not be a consumer credit business. Thus a loan made by an employer, for instance, would not be classed as a non–commercial agreement as it would be made in the course of a business.

Small agreements are consumer credit agreements (other than hire-purchase and conditional sale agreements) for credit not exceeding £50 and consumer hire–agreements not requiring payments of more than £50.[54] The Act tries to prevent creditors from gaining the exemptions which apply to small agreements by simply breaking a larger transaction down into a series of smaller transactions. It seeks to achieve this by disapplying the small agreement exemptions to agreements made at or about the same time between the same parties or their associates where it appears probable that there would have been a single agreement but for the desire to avoid the operation of provisions of the Act.

Of course, consumer credit contracts may contain more than one type of credit agreement. The Act makes provision for multiple agreements and provides that the different parts of an agreement will be treated as separate

---

50   *Crowther, op. cit.* at pp. 244–5.
51   S.189(1), Consumer Credit Act 1974.
52   S.17(1), Consumer Credit Act 1974.
53   These would in any event probably not apply to small agreements as s.75 only applies where the cash price exceeds £100.
54   It has been proposed to raise this limit to £150; see *Consumer Credit Deregulation, op. cit.*, at p. 112.

agreements for the purposes of the Act. The Act should apply to each agreement in the appropriate manner.[55]

7.4.4 Credit Tokens[56]

Cards, checks, vouchers, coupons, stamps, forms, booklets or other documents are credit tokens if given to an individual by a person carrying on a consumer credit business, if that person undertakes on production of the card etc. to supply cash, goods or services or to pay a third party for these things in return for payment to him by the individual. Thus credit cards are, in the language of the Consumer Credit Act 1974, credit tokens. A credit–token agreement is a regulated agreement for the provision of credit in connection with the use of the token.

Credit cards were just emerging at the time of the Crowther report and it is in relation to them that the Consumer Credit Act 1974 provisions have sometimes proven to be difficult to apply. This illustrates the law's difficulty in keeping pace with technological developments and changing commercial practices.

7.4.5 APR

The 'APR' or annual percentage rate is required to be disclosed in agreement documents, quotations and most advertisements for credit. Whereas the use of 'flat' interest rates can be misleading, the APR seeks to give a fairer basis of comparison, by taking into account the length of the loan period and the size and rate of repayments. Calculation of the rate is complicated and subject to debate surrounding, *inter alia*, the preferential treatment of overdrafts, what account should be taken of fees and other charges on running account credit and the notional balance which should be assumed on such accounts. In fact the Consumer Credit (Total Charge for Credit) Regulations 1980[57] provide three methods of calculating the APR and the Government has produced 15 volumes of tables to assist in the calculation of the APR. The Director General's report on *Consumer Credit Deregulation* suggested that the calculation of the APR could be simplified by just retaining the general formula contained in the Regulations, which should be amended in line with the simpler formula contained in annex II of the EC 'APR Directive'.

---

[55] S.18, Consumer Credit Act 1974.

[56] S.14, Consumer Credit Act 1974

[57] S.I. 1980/51.

In the same report the Director General made various other recommendations relating to the use of APRs, for instance, that it should not be necessary to disclose the APR for loans of less than £150. It is said to be inappropriate to require disclosure of the APR for small loans as the fixed administrative costs leading to high APRs on such loans give a misleading indication of the value of such credit. Whilst it is true that the APRs for such loans can appear exaggerated due to the fixed administrative costs, the APR does nevertheless indicate the true cost of such loans, even if the value of the loan to the individual might better be judged by the total interest payable or the size of the repayments. There seems little justification for not providing the APR as well as the other information so the consumer can make an informed choice. Studies show that the majority of consumers have an awareness of APRs, but that even where they consider it they take other factors into account as well when deciding from whom to borrow.[58] This indicates that the APR can be a useful comparator. Although more consumer education is still needed, there is little danger that consumers will be confused by apparently exaggerated APRs for small loans.

7.5 FORMALITIES AND COPY PROVISIONS

An important policy of the Consumer Credit Act 1974 is to make consumers better informed so that they enter into prudent credit contracts suited to their needs and circumstances. This policy partly explains the regulation of advertisements and quotations which are discussed in Chapter 11. There is some scepticism about the value of disclosure provisions as a means of assisting consumer behaviour; indeed some commentators believe that the duties to supply copies of the contract and information on default are of more significance. Ramsay considers these provide 'a "contract synopsis"' – a comprehensible summary of the central aspects of the contract which may be referred to during performance and in the event of dispute'.[59] Copy provisions therefore have two functions: warning the consumer of the full

---

[58] I. Crow, G. Howells and M. Moroney, *op. cit.* and *Consumers' Appreciation of Annual Percentage Rates* (Office of Fair Trading, 1994).

[59] I. Ramsay, *Consumer Protection*, (Weidenfeld and Nicolson, 1989) at p. 332. Note ss.77–79, Consumer Credit Act 1974 also impose obligations on creditors and hirers to provide information during the course of agreements, other than non–commercial agreements. On making a written request and payment of a fee (currently 50p) the debtor or hirer is entitled to a copy of the executed agreement and a statement of account, provided that a month has passed since any previous request relating to the same agreement. Also in relation to running account agreements (other than small or non–commercial agreements), the creditor must send the debtor a periodic statement.

extent of the commitments being entered into and providing a permanent record of the agreement by reference to which any disputes can be adjudicated.

7.5.1 Precontract Controls

The Consumer Credit Act 1974 provides for controls over precontractual documentation. Thus s.55 permits regulations to be made prescribing pre–contractual information which must be disclosed, however, no such regulations have been made.

S.58, Consumer Credit Act 1974 provides that where an agreement is secured on land[60] a copy of the unexecuted agreement indicating the debtor or hirer's right to withdraw, together with copies of other documents referred to, should be given[61] to the debtor or hirer seven days before the actual unexecuted agreement is sent. These seven days, together with the shorter of either seven days from the sending of the actual unexecuted agreement or the date on which the unexecuted agreement is returned signed, are known as the 'consideration period'. The creditor or owner must refrain from approaching the debtor or hirer during this period, except in response to a specific request to do so which was made after the commencement of the consideration period. The rationale for this extra protection for agreements secured on land is partly that they are not cancellable. Yet as not all consumer credit or hire agreements are cancellable, and as a far wider range of agreements are subject to s.58, the section also seems to take note of the particular need for consumers to reflect on the risks they undertake when entering into contracts secured by property.[62]

7.5.2 Form of the Agreement

S.61, Consumer Credit Act 1974 provides that regulated agreements must be

---

[60] Other than remortgages and bridging loans.

[61] In the Consumer Credit Act 1974 'given' means delivered (although not necessarily personally) or sent by post; see s.189(1).

[62] One criticism of this provision is that it can lead to the consumer being given three copies of the agreement (one prior to the commencement of the consideration period, another on signing the unexecuted agreement and a further copy of the executed agreement). In such cases the Director General has proposed that there is no need for the consumer to receive the second copy of the unexecuted agreement; see *Consumer Credit Deregulation, op. cit.*, at p. 58.

in the prescribed form;[63] must be signed by the debtor or hirer[64] and by or on behalf of the creditor or owner; must contain all the terms of the agreement other than implied terms and be readily legible.[65] All the information relating to financial and related particulars should be gathered together at one point in the document and not be interspersed throughout it, thus reducing the chance of the consumer being misled by devious presentation of the figures. The APR must be given no less prominence than other financial information.[66] Where the regulations place some prescribed information in capitals, this must also be given prominence in the document either by using capitals, underlining or by large or bold print. The print must be readily distinguishable against the colour of the paper. A signature box must be provided for the debtor or hirer, with the creditor or owner signing outside the box.

7.5.3 Copy Provisions

The debtor or hirer must always receive one copy of the agreement and all documents referred to in it. Whether the debtor or hirer should receive an additional copy depends upon whether the agreement becomes executed upon their signature.[67] If the debtor or hirer's signature executes the agreement, only one copy need be supplied. This will not usually be the case for creditors and owners do not normally sign the agreement before the debtor or hirer. Where the debtor or hirer's signature does not execute the agreement, the debtor or hirer must be given a copy of the agreement when it is either presented for signature or sent to them. A copy of the executed agreement,

---

63 Meaning that it must comply with the Consumer Credit (Agreements) Regulations 1983, S.I. 1983/1553.

64 Note the debtor or hirer must sign personally. It would not be sufficient to sign a blank form and allow the details to be filled in later; see *Eastern Distributors Ltd v Goldring (Murphy, Third Party)* [1957] 2 QB 600 .

65 Note that there is no requirement that the language be easily comprehensible although reg. 6, Unfair Terms in Consumer Contract Regulations 1994, S.I. 1994/3159, implementing the EC Unfair Contract Terms Directive OJ 1993 L95/29 does require that terms in consumer contracts be drafted in plain, intelligible language.

66 Note that, in advertisements, the APR must be given greater prominence; see 11.4.1.

67 The copy provisions are to be found in ss. 62–64 of the Consumer Credit Act 1974 and Consumer Credit (Cancellation Notices and Copies of Documents) Regulations 1983, S.I. 1983/1557.

after signature by the creditor or owner, must then be given to the debtor or hirer within seven days of the agreement being concluded.[68]

Special provisions relate to cancellable agreements[69] which require that where a second copy is needed this must be sent by post. Where no second copy is required, a notice of cancellation must be sent by post within seven days of the conclusion of the agreement. The Act attempts to alert consumers to the right of cancellation by the copies of the agreement and notices having to contain a box with information on the right of cancellation, how and when that right is exercisable and the name and address of a person on whom notice of cancellation may be served. In addition, the second copy or notice of cancellation rights must contain a cancellation form which the debtor or hirer can use to facilitate cancelling the agreement.

7.5.4 Enforcement of Improperly Executed Agreements

If the form and content of an agreement or notice are incorrect or the copy or notice provisions have not been complied with, then the agreement is said to be 'improperly executed'. This means that it is only enforceable against the debtor or hirer by order of the court.[70] Enforcement includes retaking goods or land to which a regulated agreement relates.[71]

A general weakness of the enforcement powers of the Consumer Credit Act 1974 is evident in the rule contained in s.170(1) that a breach of any requirement made by or under the Act shall incur no civil or criminal sanction as being such a breach, except to the extent (if any) expressly provided for by or under the Act.[72] Thus save for exceptional cases, such as protected goods under hire–purchase contracts,[73] if a contract is enforced without a court order, there is no effective sanction save for reporting the matter to the licensing authorities. This is unless some breach of the debtor or hirer's legal rights can be established, such as an action for breach of the implied warranty of quiet possession[74] or an action in trespass or conversion.

---

[68] S.189(1), Consumer Credit Act 1974 provides that 'give' means to deliver or send by post.

[69] See 7.8.

[70] S.65, Consumer Credit Act 1974. Note the agreement is not void or illegal – merely not enforceable. Thus the consumer can still sue on the agreement if goods or services supplied are defective.

[71] S.65 (2),Consumer Credit Act 1974.

[72] This is perhaps a reaction against some of the technical defences which were raised by debtors under the previous laws: see *Crowther, op. cit.* at pp. 310–13.

[73] See 7.13.3.

[74] Eg s.12(2)(b), Sale of Goods Act 1979.

Where the only illegality is the enforcement of the contract in breach of the Act, the suggestion has been made that a mandatory injunction could be applied for to restore the status quo.[75] Nevertheless, the sanctions for infringing the Act's provisions remain weak and at best obscure.

A further weakness in the regulatory regime established by the Consumer Credit Act 1974 is that the requirement to obtain a court order (or where appropriate an order by the Director General) before taking certain steps is waved if the debtor or hirer consents at the time the action is taken. The consent must be at the time the action is taken and so a clause given advanced consent could not, for instance, be included in the credit agreement.[76]

However, assuming reputable creditors would only enforce the agreement after obtaining a court order, it is important to consider the court's powers. The court can dismiss an application to enforce the agreement, but only if it considers it just to do so. In making this assessment, the court must take into account the degree of culpability, the prejudice caused and its own powers to do justice.[77] These include both the specific power to make an enforcement order which reduces or discharges a sum payable by the debtor, hirer or their surety in order to compensate for the prejudice suffered,[78] and the court's general powers to impose conditions on or suspend the operation of orders, or its powers to amend agreements.[79]

There are three circumstances in which the court cannot make an enforcement order.

1. Where a document in the prescribed form has not been signed by both parties. Where a debtor or hirer signed a document containing all the prescribed terms, even if it was not in the prescribed form, then the court has the discretion to allow the agreement to be enforced, but can direct that it is to have effect as if it did not include a term omitted from the document signed by the debtor or hirer.[80]

2. If any of the copy provisions have not been complied with and the creditor or owner has not given the debtor or hirer a copy of the executed

---

[75] R. Lowe and G. Woodroffe, *Consumer Law and Practice*, 3rd ed., (Sweet & Maxwell, 1991) at p. 323. Indeed s.170(3), Consumer Credit Act 1974 expressly states that s.170(1) does not prevent the grant of an injunction or the making of an order of certiorari, mandamus or prohibition.

[76] S.173(3), Consumer Credit Act 1974.

[77] S.127, Consumer Credit Act 1974.

[78] S.127(2), Consumer Credit Act 1974.

[79] Ss.135–6, Consumer Credit Act 1974.

[80] Ss.127(3)(5), Consumer Credit Act 1974. The prescribed terms are to be found in sched. 6 of the Consumer Credit (Agreements) Regulations 1983, S.I. 1983/1553.

agreement and any documents referred to in it prior to the commencement of proceedings.[81] This is not very protective, however, since a creditor or owner only has to provide the relevant documents at any time prior to the commencement of proceedings and an enforcement order can be made.

3. Where a notice of cancellation rights has not been provided.[82] This is the most significant of the restrictions on the court's powers to enforce improperly executed agreements and emphasises the importance of the cancellation provisions.

A final comment should perhaps be made on the emphasis placed by the Consumer Credit Act 1974 on the duties to supply copy documents and cancellation notices.[83] Criticisms have been made that such rules do not really help lower–income groups and ethnic minorities, many of whom are either unable to comprehend the document and/or simply fail to retain it for future reference. Of course the better educated and more articulate consumers will take advantage of consumer protection measures more often than disadvantaged groups. This does not mean that the well–educated or rich do not deserve protection. It may mean that, in addition to information provisions other consumers may need to be protected by other means – such as licensing provisions, controls over terms, controls on creditor remedies and the creation of alternative forms of social credit. Techniques such as bringing all the financial information together in one place and the use of a cancellation form attempt to make the provisions as consumer friendly as practicable. Of course, being given a copy of the agreement does not help to improve its terms (except to the limited extent that creditors may be too embarrassed to put unconscionable terms down on paper) which is why it is important that consumers be given time to reflect on the commitments they are entering into. However, as we shall see the cancellation provisions do not apply to all credit contracts.

7.6 WITHDRAWAL

Consumers frequently enter into credit agreements which they later regret. It is worth remembering that, on ordinary contract principles, a consumer can revoke an offer at any time until it has been accepted by the other party. Thus, as in most instances it is the consumer who fills in the application form and waits to hear if the creditor accepts the offer, the consumer is free to

---

[81] S.127(4)(a), Consumer Credit Act 1974.

[82] S.127(4)(b), Consumer Credit Act 1974.

[83] Cf discussion of information provisions at 1.8.3.

revoke his or her offer until the time of acceptance. It is as well to remember that the basic common law rules provide that acceptance is completed when posted (assuming the post to be an acceptable means of communication) so that any revocation would have to reach the other party before that time.

The Consumer Credit Act 1974 improves the position of the consumer who wishes to withdraw his or her offer to enter into a regulated consumer credit or consumer hire agreement[84] by extending the range of persons on whom notice of withdrawal can be served. In addition to the creditor or owner, notice can also be given to those persons deemed to be their agent. This can be either a credit broker or supplier who was a negotiator in antecedent negotiations or, most importantly, to any person who, in the course of a business, acted on behalf of the debtor or hirer in any negotiations for the agreement. Thus, if a solicitor arranges a loan, it is sufficient to communicate notice of withdrawal to him or her. Notice of withdrawal, must in accordance with general contract principles, be communicated to the other party and if posted only becomes effective on receipt. The notice can be oral or written and need not state that it is a notice of withdrawal, so long as it indicates an intention to withdraw from a prospective regulated agreement.

Withdrawal from a regulated agreement will have the same effects as if the agreement had been cancelled.[85] Consumers are further protected by the provision, in s.59, Consumer Credit Act 1974, which makes agreements void to the extent that they seek to bind a person to enter into a prospective regulated agreement.

7.7 RESCISSION AND REPUDIATION

Where a debtor or hirer is no longer able to withdraw from a contract, they may wish to consider whether there are any circumstances, such as misrepresentation, which might allow them to rescind the contract, or if there has been any breach of contract which would allow them to repudiate it. The Act again extends consumer protection by allowing notice of rescission to be given to the extended category of persons on whom notice of withdrawal could be given.[86]

---

[84] S.57, Consumer Credit Act 1974.

[85] These are more generous to the consumer than the position under general law: see 7.8.3.

[86] S.102, Consumer Credit Act 1974.

7.8 CANCELLATION

Some of the most significant consumer protection measures relate to cancellation rights. The Act gives consumers who enter into certain credit contracts a period of time in which to reflect on the agreement and to cancel it if they do not want to proceed. Typically this will apply to debtor-creditor-supplier agreements entered into in the consumer's home, Cooling–off periods of this type attempt to protect individuals against high–pressure sales techniques and also to provide consumers with information and time to consider whether the product or service suits their needs. Doorstep sales are concluded in circumstances where it was not possible to compare the product or service against those offered by competitors.

Concern to protect consumers, who enter into contracts on the doorstep, is also evidenced by the Consumer Protection (Cancellation of Contracts Concluded away from Business Premises) Regulations.[87] To avoid confusion between those Regulations and the cancellation rules for credit contracts, the former do not apply to contracts which are cancellable under the Consumer Credit Act 1974. Confusion continues to exist between the seven day cooling–off period from the date of the conclusion of the contract in doorstep sales and the cooling–off period in consumer credit contracts. For the latter, the period can range between six and 12 days, or even longer depending upon when the formalities were carried out and upon the efficiency of the postal service. A proposal has been made to harmonise around the seven day period, which means some possible loss of consumer protection as the price for tidying up this area of the law.[88]

Terry Ison has made the provocative suggestion that some type of doorstep selling should be banned altogether, rather than simply be made subject to a cooling–off period.[89] He considers that cooling–off periods, with the requirement for the consumer to give notice of cancellation, can only protect fairly sophisticated consumers. Yet, many of the problems involving doorstep selling result from the targeting of low–income consumers who are unlikely to enforce their rights.[90] Ison therefore suggests a prohibition on itinerant salesmen who sell one type of item on credit terms or who require

---

[87] S.I. 1987/2117: see 8.2.

[88] *Revised Proposals for Legislation on Credit Marketing, op. cit.*, at p. 4; *Consumer Credit Deregulation, op. cit.*, at pp. 62–3.

[89] T. Ison, *Credit Marketing and Consumer Protection*, (Croom Helm, 1979) at pp. 119–120.

[90] It might be objected that this is too paternalist an attitude and underestimates the ability of low–income consumers to look after their own interests. Whilst it is true that many low–income consumers are very astute purchasers, nevertheless they do seem less aware and/or willing to enforce their legal rights.

part–payment in advance.[91] This may seem radical, but we shall see that an outright prohibition on unsolicited marketing of debtor–credit agreements off trade premises already exists and no clear rationale has been given for differentiating between the two regulatory approaches to a fairly similar problem.[92] One problem with prohibitions is that just because the law prohibits a practice does not mean that it ceases. There is a danger that prohibited practices simply go underground. Ison's choice of contracts to be banned resulted from an empirical study of credit practices, which discovered that the incidence of problems experienced varied depending upon the nature of the seller. Nevertheless, it may be particularly difficult to enforce a prohibition which only applies to a class of sellers, because of definitional problems. For instance, an itinerant salesman could easily circumvent the prohibition by giving the appearance of selling more than one type of item. On the other hand, selective prohibition might go some way to meet the objection that a blanket prohibition would simply disadvantage low income consumers by reducing their choice or by forcing them to seek help on the black market. Possibly a more acceptable way of removing creditors who indulge in bad practices would be to strengthen the licensing system.[93] Making the licensing system more proactive would allow the authorities to stamp out bad traders, whilst allowing reputable traders to continue trading and thereby increasing consumer choice and allowing competition on a level playing field.

7.8.1 Cancellable Agreements

For an agreement to be cancellable under the Consumer Credit Act 1974, it must be:

(i) a regulated agreement;
(ii) oral representations must have been made in the presence of the debtor or hirer by a person acting as, or on behalf of, the negotiator. The representations must be oral, not written, and must be made in the presence of the debtor or hirer, so that a telephone conversation would not be sufficient. There is no restriction as to where the oral representations were made – they need not have been made in the consumer's home and could, for instance, be made at the creditor's office. Nor is there any restriction on when they were made – they need not be made at the same time as the contract was signed;

---

91 Ison, *op. cit.*
92 S.49, Consumer Credit Act 1974: see 11.2.3.
93 See 11.1. This may also be a function of a general duty to trade fairly: see 16.5.4.

(iii) the unexecuted agreement must be signed by the debtor or hirer off trade premises; that is, not at the permanent or temporary business premises of the creditor or owner, or of any party to a linked transaction or of the negotiator in antecedent negotiations. A cancellable agreement could be signed at the debtor or hirer's business premises, but normally would be signed at the debtor or hirer's home.[94]

In its 1991 consultation document, *Revised Proposals for Legislation on Credit Marketing*, the Department of Trade and Industry suggested that debtor–creditor–supplier agreements and hire agreements signed on trade premises following face–to–face negotiations should be cancellable.[95] To counter objections that this would harm the consumer interest (as consumers would probably not be allowed to take goods home with them straight away), it was proposed to give consumers the right to contract out of the cancellation rights, although the waiver of such rights would not be allowed as a condition of sale. The cancellation rights would be forfeited if the goods were not returned or were returned in a significantly worse condition. The former Director General, Sir Bryan Carsberg, came out against such an extension, believing that consumers visiting trade premises were not in need of the same protection against spur of the moment decision–making as those who enter agreements in their own home. Indeed, he proposed removing existing cancellation rights where the antecedent negotiations took place on trade premises and the agreement was only cancellable because the consumer subsequently signed the agreement at home.[96]

Certain agreements are exempted from the cancellation provisions notably, (i) non–commercial agreements, (ii) 'small' debtor–creditor–supplier agreements for restricted–use credit, (iii) certain agreements relating to land, (iv) overdraft agreements and (v) debtor–creditor agreements relating to payments to be made in connection with, or arising on, the death of a person.

7.8.2 How and When Can an Agreement be Cancelled?

The debtor or hirer can cancel the agreement at any time after the unexecuted agreement is signed by them up until the end of the fifth day following receipt of the second copy of the agreement or the notice of cancellation.[97] The cancellation period therefore expires five days after the second copy or notice was received and not five days after it was sent. What then is the

---

[94]   S.67, Consumer Credit Act 1974.
[95]   (DTI, 1991) at pp. 3–4.
[96]   *Consumer Credit Deregulation, op. cit.*, at p. 61
[97]   S.68(a), Consumer Credit Act 1974.

position if the notice is lost in the post? Can the cancellation period continue indefinitely? This would appear absurd, but could be the case if the Act were applied strictly. If the creditor or owner is unable to post a replacement copy within the prescribed seven day period, then the replacement cannot properly be said to have been posted 'under' the Act. The courts are unlikely to see any advantage in penalising the genuine creditor or owner in this way, especially as the Act mandates use of the post; rather, they are likely to find that the cancellation period expired at the end of the fifth day following receipt of the replacement copy. Another interesting scenario would arise if the second notice was posted outside the prescribed seven day period. The courts could be equally sympathetic and treat the cancellation period as starting from receipt of the late copy or notice, since it could be argued that the consumer has not been disadvantaged in any way. They may, however, wish to be less lenient in such circumstances for the creditor or owner can be considered in some sense blameworthy. Moreover, since the agreement has not been properly executed, it is unenforceable: as stated previously, failure to comply with the cancellation notice provisions is one of the situations in which the courts are absolutely barred from making an enforcement order. There may also be sound policy grounds for not permitting late copies to be sent. Once the agreement has been running for some time, consumers may find it psychologically harder to cancel an agreement and feel morally bound to honour agreements if they have enjoyed substantial use of the product.

Cancellation can be effected by serving a written notice. This notice can be the form included in the second copy or notice sent to the debtor or hirer, but can be in any form so long as it indicates the intention to cancel the agreement. The written notice must be served on any of the following:

(i)   the creditor or owner,
(ii) any person named in the notice of cancellation rights as being a person on whom such notice can be served,
(iii) the agent of the creditor or owner, who, as with the right of withdrawal, is given an extended definition.[98]

The notice must be served on the other party. It need not be posted, but there is a decided advantage to posting it, for the notice will be deemed to have been served at the time of posting. Therefore a notice of cancellation posted one minute before the expiry of a cooling–off period will be effective, even though it could not possibly have been received within the permitted time.

---

[98]   S.69(6), Consumer Credit Act 1974: see 7.6 for a discussion of those who are deemed to be the agent of the creditor or owner. Note this includes those who are the debtor or hirer's agent, but this category of deemed agent cannot be used for all subsequent functions.

Indeed, it would seem to be effective even if never received. Equally, it would not appear possible to withdraw a notice of cancellation once posted.

7.8.3 Effects of Cancellation

Cancellation has the effect that the agreement and most linked transactions[99] are treated as if they had never been entered into; moreover, any offer by the debtor or hirer or their relative to enter into a linked transaction is withdrawn. Any sums paid are to be repaid on cancellation and any sums which would have become payable cease to be payable.[100] Normally the sums are repayable by the person to whom the money was paid, except in the case of debtor–creditor–supplier agreements for restricted–use credit where the creditor and supplier are jointly liable. The debtor or hirer or (where relevant) their relative, has a lien over goods in their possession supplied under the cancelled agreement, in respect of sums which are repayable.

Where there is a debtor–creditor–supplier agreement for restricted–use credit, a consumer hire agreement or a linked transaction (so that a supply contract is also cancelled), the debtor or hirer is under a duty to return the goods subject to any lien he or she may have over them.[101] The debtor or hirer has a duty to retain possession of the goods and take reasonable care of them for a 21 day period from the date of cancellation. However, this period is extended if a request to deliver the goods was received, which the debtor or hirer has either unreasonably refused or unreasonably failed to comply with. However, the duty is only to deliver the goods to the possessor's own premises; there must have been a written signed request served either before or at the time the goods were collected. The duty to take care of the goods can be brought to an end at any time by delivering them to a person on whom notice of cancellation could have been served (other than to a person who was the deemed agent of the debtor or hirer) or by sending the goods at the debtor or hirer's own expense to such a person. If the goods are sent to the other party, reasonable care must be taken to ensure that they are received by the other party and are not damaged in transit. This presumably requires the use of a reputable carrier under conditions of carriage appropriate for the type of goods involved.

Breach of the duty to return the goods is actionable as a breach of statutory duty. However, in the following four circumstances the duty to return the goods does not apply. Special rules apply both to goods supplied

---

99   Some are saved by the Consumer Credit (Linked Transactions) (Exemptions) Regulations 1983, S.I 1983/1560.

100   S.70, Consumer Credit Act 1974.

101   S.72, Consumer Credit Act 1974.

in emergencies and to goods incorporated into land or some other thing prior to cancellation. Imposing the full effects of cancellation would be particularly unfair on a supplier who had supplied goods in an emergency or where the goods had been incorporated into something else. In such cases it is provided that, where the goods were supplied under a debtor–creditor–supplier agreement for restricted–use credit, only the credit part of the agreement is cancelled, with the debtor having a continued liability to pay for the goods supplied. Also, for obvious reasons, there is no duty to return perishable goods or goods which by their nature are consumed and which were so consumed before cancellation. Although understandable, these provisions could allow consumers a rare opportunity to have their cake without paying for it, although cautious sellers will not supply such goods until the cancellation period has expired.

Where a negotiator[102] agreed to take goods in part exchange under a regulated agreement and the goods have been delivered to him or her, then, unless the goods are returned within ten days of cancellation, in substantially the same condition as when delivered, the debtor or hirer is entitled to a sum equal to the part exchange allowance.[103] The sum will be either that agreed or, if no figure was agreed, then an amount it would have been reasonable to allow. Until repaid the debtor or hirer has a lien on goods supplied under the cancelled agreement.

Unless the cancellation provisions are modified, possible injustices could arise where credit has been advanced under the agreement before cancellation occurs. Debtors might seek to hide behind the rule that any sums payable cease to be payable in order to avoid returning the advance. The Act has special provisions to deal with this situation.[104] If an agreement (other than a debtor–credit–supplier agreement)[105] is cancelled, no interest is payable on amounts repaid within one month of the service of the notice of cancellation or, in the case of credit repayable by instalments, on amounts repaid before the date on which the first instalment is due. The debtor has the option of repaying the whole amount or just a portion without attracting interest on the amount repaid. Repayment can be made to any person on whom notice of cancellation could have been served, except those who had acted on behalf of the debtor. In the case of credit repayable by instalments the debtor, who has not repaid the whole amount outstanding, is still not liable to repay any credit

---

102 S.56(1), Consumer Credit Act 1974 provides that this includes the creditor, owner, credit–broker and suppliers in three–party debtor–creditor–supplier agreements who conduct negotiations with the debtor or hirer.

103 S.73, Consumer Credit Act 1974.

104 S.71, Consumer Credit Act 1974.

105 The problem does not arise in debtor–creditor–supplier agreements as the supplier can repay sums advanced directly to the debtor.

until a written request stating the amount of the remaining instalments is received. The instalments should only include sums in respect of the principal and interest. The creditor must recalculate the instalments as nearly as possible in accordance with the agreement without extending the repayment period.

The rules restricting the manner of rescheduling give rise to some difficult questions of interpretation. For instance, does the repayment period, which must not be extended, refer to a fixed date or to a period of time? If the former, then the instalments may be larger than under the original agreement. Furthermore, should the creditor try to make the instalments as close as possible in size to those under the original agreement, or should the objective be to provide that the APR of the rescheduled agreement is equivalent to that of the original?

No notice need be sent where the credit is repayable otherwise than by instalment. Such agreements continue in force in so far as they relate to the duty to repay the principal and interest.

7.9 TERMINATION

The Consumer Credit Act 1974 gives debtors the right to terminate hire-purchase or conditional-sale agreements[106] and hirers the right to terminate hire agreements.[107] Termination can be effected by giving written notice to anyone entitled or authorised to receive payments. This may be a useful option when the consumer cannot continue to meet his obligations. The effects of termination, however, are only prospective, with the effect that arrears and any contractual liabilities are not affected by it. In addition, unless the contract provides for a lesser amount, on termination of a hire-purchase or conditional sale agreement, the amount paid under the agreement must be made up to half of the total price. Where the total price includes an installation charge, then the amount to be paid is that charge plus one-half of the remainder. The court can order payment of a lesser amount if it considers that it would adequately compensate the creditor for the loss caused by the termination. Thus in some cases the debtor may be well advised to tender a figure below half the total price if the goods still retain sufficient value so that the creditor would be adequately compensated by their return and the amount tendered. The amount payable by the debtor can be increased by the court to take account of loss caused to the creditor resulting from the debtor's breach of the obligation to take reasonable care of the goods. If the debtor wrongfully retains goods after the agreement has been terminated the court

---

[106] Ss.99–100.
[107] S.101.

must order the goods to be returned, unless it considers that, in the circumstances, it would not be just to do so. The court also has powers to make return and transfer orders.[108]

Consumer hire agreements cannot be terminated until 18 months of the agreement have elapsed; the court has no discretion to reduce this period. Notice must be given. The notice period will usually be equal to the shortest payment period under the agreement, unless the agreement provides for a shorter period. In any event the notice period cannot be longer than three months. The right to terminate does not apply if, *inter alia*, (i) the agreement requires payments in excess of £900 each year, or (ii) the agreement relates to goods hired for the hirer's business, which have been selected by the hirer and acquired by the owner at the hirer's request, from a person other than an associate of the owner, or (iii) the goods are let for the purpose of releasing in the course of the hirer's business.

7.10 EARLY SETTLEMENT AND REBATE

Where the debtor has paid a large portion of the total price and the goods still retain some value, then, rather than terminate the agreement, the debtor may find it more beneficial to exercise the right to complete payments ahead of time, take advantage of the statutory rebate for early settlement and then resell the goods or alternatively find a cheaper source of finance.[109] To exercise the statutory right of early repayment,[110] the debtor must give the creditor written notice and tender all amounts payable under the agreement, less the statutory rebate. The debtor can make a written request for the creditor to inform him of the amount which must be paid to discharge his indebtedness.[111]

The rebate is calculated in accordance with Consumer Credit (Rebate on Early Settlement) Regulations.[112] These Regulations are excessively complex, containing five different formulae to calculate the rebate depending upon the repayment provisions and the settlement arrangements. For instance, where credit is repaid by equal instalments the 'rule of 78' applies. This rule derives from the fact that a loan for a year with 12 equal instalments can be analysed as a series of 12 reducing monthly loans: its name results from the fact that the sum of 12 months is 78 (ie

---

[108] See 7.14.2.
[109] Ss.94–7, Consumer Credit Act 1974.
[110] There is a common law right to pay debts ahead of time, but this does not carry with it the advantage of a rebate.
[111] See Consumer Credit (Settlement Information) Regulations 1983, S.I. 1983/1564.
[112] S.I. 1983/1562.

1+2+3+4+5+6+7+8+9+10+11+12 = 78). Although the formulae are complicated, the policy underlying them is to provide a fair balance between creditor and debtor and, in particular, to recognise that the creditor incurs set–up costs and the bulk of administrative expenses at the start of the loan. When Director General, Sir Bryan Carsberg, criticised the 'rule of 78' as being unfair to consumers and proposed that it be replaced by a calculation reflecting the principles of compound interest, which he described as based on an 'actual reducing balance' basis. He was also critical of the present rules which allow the settlement date to be deferred by up to two months to allow the lender to recoup administrative costs. Although the fairness of the principle of allowing the lender to recover 'sunk' costs is not questioned, Carsberg argued that there was no justification for this *ad valorem* charge when administrative costs are roughly the same for all loans irrespective of size. Instead he preferred to allow a settlement fee to be set by the creditor, within a statutory maximum, and to require this figure (or the method of calculation of a figure, within the permitted maximum) to be included in the credit agreement.[113] The former Director General is to be applauded for using the review of consumer credit law – which was inspired by the deregulation initiative – to simplify and enhance consumer protection rather than merely reduce the protection available.

7.11 CONNECTED LENDER LIABILITY

7.11.1 Policy

S.75, Consumer Credit Act 1974 introduced an important consumer protection measure in the form of connected lender liability. This involves making the creditor jointly liable with the supplier for the quality of goods and services. Crowther had set out the rationales for imposing this liability on financiers.[114] Lenders, who offer suppliers business and financial inducements[115] to make misrepresentations about goods or to supply defective goods should not be able to simply walk away from the problems the consumer is left with. Equally a customer in dispute would find it easier if the credit commitments relating to the goods were removed, especially if such goods were sold as a means to help the person produce income, for example knitting machines. Connected lender liability also removes the need

---

[113] *Consumer Credit Deregulation, op. cit.* at pp. 84–92.

[114] *Op. cit.*, at paras 6.6.24–31.

[115] Ramsay suggests that conditions have changed and that nowadays dealers can pressure finance companies to take on risks they would not normally accept in direct lending: see I. Ramsay, *Consumer Protection, op cit.*, at p. 353.

for consumers to have to mobilise their resources and energies to mount a legal action: they can simply default on the loan, wait to be sued and raise s.75 as a defence.

7.11.2 Credit Cards

However, the connected lender liability provisions highlight the fact that Crowther and the subsequent Consumer Credit Act 1974 were a response to the needs of the time and dealt with market conditions as they existed some two decades ago when credit cards were just beginning to be marketed. The connected lender liability rules were principally aimed at the bad marketing practices current at that time. Central heating installations were a particular problem since some suppliers went insolvent before installation, leaving consumers with no heating but large debts. In more recent times one could draw parallels with the double glazing or timeshare industries. In addition to the large number of consumer complaints, the common feature is that the supplier and creditor have close business relations. Indeed s.75 seems to require that there be a close relationship before the connected lender liability bites: thus it only applies to three party debtor–creditor–supplier agreements.

Credit card agreements fall within the scope of s.75[116] and yet there is not the same intimate connection between most credit card companies and the businesses they offer their facilities to.[117] The link between card issuer and supplier has become even more attenuated with the growth in overseas use of cards and with competition rules which require card issuers to honour purchases made by any supplier bearing their card's logo – ie Mastercard or Visa – even if that supplier was recruited by a different merchant acquirer.[118] There is no doubt that many consumers have benefited from the

---

[116] Although note that charge cards, where the balance has to be paid off in one instalment (such as American Express and Diners Club) are not covered as they are exempt agreements. Also note that debit cards, which electronically transfer funds from a current account in a bank, are now also expressly excluded: see s.187(3A), Consumer Credit Act 1974.

[117] Both *Crowther, op.cit.,* at paras 6.12.1–12 and the White Paper *Reform of the Law on Consumer Credit, op cit.,* at para 75 recognised that credit cards would be caught by the provisions, but considered that the same basic conditions applied as when a trader offered hire–purchase or personal loan facilities. Note that s.75 would not apply to hire–purchase agreements since there the goods are first sold to the finance company who then acts as creditor and supplier of the goods.

[118] Typically, when a credit card purchase is made, the supplier sends the voucher to a merchant acquirer who pays him the amount less a Merchant Service Charge (typically 1.6 per cent). The merchant acquirer is in turn reimbursed by the card

protection they derive from having purchased their defective goods or services with the use of a credit card. This has been particularly noticeable in the case of holiday company and airline collapses.[119] But the question remains, whether credit card companies should be forced to act as insurer in this way? It certainly seems to be a rather ad hoc response. Whether a consumer is compensated for a loss depends upon the chance of whether a credit card was used to effect the purchase. It also forces the cost of individual consumer's purchasing choices to be borne by all users of the credit facility. One would guess that the benefits of connected lender liability are more likely to be known of and used by the more educated and prosperous credit card holders. Indeed many poorer consumers will not have access to credit card facilities at all. It might be better to ensure proper compensation is received from suppliers or, where they have become insolvent, from compensation funds. For instance bonding schemes such as that operated in the holiday industry by ABTA and the proposals contained in the EC distant selling Recommendation[120] might provide a fairer way forward. Absent such reforms, one might be tempted to view connected lender liability for credit card companies as a second best solution.

Even if it is considered unfair to impose connected lender liability on all credit card companies, there would be difficulty in differentiating between those lenders who do have a special relationship with the supplier and can therefore legitimately be expected to have responsibility for the quality of goods, and credit supplied by the credit card company. Simply excluding debtor–creditor–supplier agreements which involve a credit token would not

---

issuer minus an Interchange fee (typically 1 per cent) and the issuer then sends a statement to the consumer for payment. For a legal analysis of the relationships created by a credit card, see *Re Charge Card Services Ltd* [1988] 3 All ER 702 (although note that that scheme did not involve a merchant acquirer). *Re Charge Services Ltd* involved a credit card for fuel and the litigation arose when the credit card company went into liquidation. The litigation was between the garages and the company to whom the credit card company had factored its debts. The court found that three separate bilateral contracts were created – between the credit company and supplier, the credit company and cardholder and the cardholder and supplier. The garage's acceptance of payment by the card was an unconditional acceptance of payment of the price; the cardholder was therefore only obliged to repay the credit company, regardless of whether the supplier had been reimbursed.

119 Although it should be noted that some credit card companies are questioning whether they always have liability for travel firm collapses. If the contract was with the travel agent and the agent performed its part of the bargain (for example, by delivering the tickets) it is argued that the supplier has not breached its contract even if the travel company supplying the service subsequently goes out of business.

120 See 8.3.9.

work, for one can easily imagine a proliferation of finance companies issuing cards, as indeed many already do. It may be possible to exclude agreements where the token is capable of obtaining both cash and goods and can be used when purchasing from more than a prescribed number of firms, but this number would have to be sufficiently large so as to exclude retail group cards. It has been suggested that this result is achieved by art. 11(2) (b) of the EC Directive on consumer credit. This article requires that, in order for connected lender liability to apply, 'the grantor of the credit and the supplier of the goods or services have a pre–existing agreement whereunder credit is made available exclusively by that grantor of credit to customers of that supplier for the acquisition of goods and services from that supplier'. It is argued that the word *exclusively* precludes the provision applying to credit cards. Indeed if the provision were given a very literal interpretation, it would require that the creditor only supplied financial services to that particular supplier and no one else. Equally one might interpret it as meaning simply that the credit is provided directly to the supplier – in other words the only requirement is for restricted use credit. What is clear is that art.11 is badly drafted and, perhaps, this supports the view that making such a distinction will inevitably be very difficult. In any event the Office of Fair Trading favours retaining the liability of credit card companies, arguing that they should have some incentive to control those who join their networks and that they are in practice exposed to very little liability due to their right to join suppliers as defendants and claim an indemnity.[121] The claimback procedures of the various international networks should allow the claim to be traced back to the merchant acquirer and eventually to the responsible trader through accounting procedures.[122]

In its *Connected Lender Liability* report the Office of Fair Trading promised to consider whether the liability of credit card issuers should be 'second in line liability' ie only arising when the supplier could not satisfy the claim (which is the basis of connected lender liability under the EC Directive). After consultation this approach was rejected.[123] The Office did, however, propose to help credit card issuers by limiting their liability to the amount of credit loaned and giving them subrogation rights against insurers

---

[121] Ss.75(2) and (5), Consumer Credit Act 1974. It does not apply to debit cards which simply arrange for the electronic transfer of funds from a bank current account: s.187(3A), Consumer Credit Act 1974.

[122] *Connected Lender Liability*, (Office of Fair Trading, 1994).

[123] This was a correct conclusion for second in line liability would reduce the consumer's bargaining position, for it would be uncertain when the consumer had taken sufficient steps against a supplier and could legitimately turn to the creditor. This is particularly true of overseas transactions. Would a consumer have had to have attempted to bring a legal claim in an overseas jurisdiction?

or bond administrators.[124] Once the principle of liability is accepted the limitation of the amount seems no more justifiable for card issuers than any other creditor. The right of subrogation against, for instance, travel industry bonding schemes, does seem fair since it places the burden of default on the industry responsible for the loss.

7.11.3 Section 75

S.75 applies to three-party debtor–creditor–supplier agreements, that is to loans to purchase goods where the creditor and supplier are different persons.[125] The effect of the section is to give the debtor who has any claim against the supplier in respect of a misrepresentation or breach of contract a like claim against the creditor.[126] This section applies even if the transaction may have breached an agreement with the creditor, for example, by exceeding a credit limit.[127]

The importance of s.75 is that it makes creditors liable for breach of implied terms, such as those relating to satisfactory quality and fitness for purpose. The use of the phrase 'like claim' has caused some uncertainty: why was the term 'like' used and not 'identical'? In the Scottish case of *United Dominions Trust Ltd v Taylor*,[128] like claim was very broadly construed; s.75 was used to allow a debtor to rescind a credit contract because of a breach of a term of the supply contract. This seems wrong since at the very least a like claim would appear to refer to a claim under the same contract.[129] The claim would, however, cover consequential damages, such as physical damage caused by dangerous products. To do justice credit

---

[124] See *Connected Lender Liability* (Office of Fair Trading, 1995).

[125] Some credit card companies claim that liability does not attach to them for cards issued prior to the section coming into force on 1 July 1977, and the Office of Fair Trading seems to accept this point (*ibid.*, at p. 30). Therefore the companies are only willing to make *ex gratia* payments up to the amount charged to the account. However, this seems to miss the point that a debtor–creditor–supplier agreement can only come into place when the supplier is identified, namely when the purchase is made – which will be post 1 July 1977. There is clearly a need to distinguish the credit token agreement from the agreements entered into using the credit token.

[126] Unless the parties have agreed otherwise, the creditor has the right to be indemnified by the supplier.

[127] S.75(4), Consumer Credit Act 1974.

[128] 1980 SLT 28.

[129] A misrepresentation concerning the supply contract intended to induce a credit contract could however lead to rescission of the credit contract by virtue of s.56: see 7.11.4

charges incurred when buying defective goods and services ought to be recoverable as consequential damages, at least when goods are rejected.[130] The claim would appear to cover the full extent of the debtor's loss even if only part of the agreement was financed by the debtor–creditor–supplier agreement. This point has become a real issue in the context of time–shares where perhaps only the deposit was paid using debtor–creditor–supplier finance. The debtor may then want to rely on s.75 to rescind the contract for misrepresentations or to repudiate it if there have been serious breaches of contract.

S.75 does not apply to all regulated agreements. In particular it does not apply to non–commercial agreements or to claims relating to a single item to which the supplier has attached a cash price which does not exceed £100 or which is more than £30,000.[131] These restrictions were introduced in the White Paper which preceded the Act, but their rationale was not explained.[132] The purpose of the lower limit would seem to be to serve as a filter. For the sake of efficiency the policy appears to be not to make the creditor liable for minor losses. This may be reasonable, but as some products, such as hi–fis, can be broken down into component parts to which a price of less than £100 could be attached, there is scope for circumvention of the rules. Also goods of low value can give rise to large claims for consequential damages, if for instance they cause personal injury or death. The upper limit presumably reflects the fact that consumers who purchase goods and services of significant value can be expected to make their own

---

130 Of course, the claim would then be a restitutionary claim and although not literally a claim for misrepresentation or breach of contract one suspects the courts would view it as covered by s.75 since it arose out of a breach of contract. Other problems arise with respect to situations where only damages are being claimed for then, if the buyer is awarded damages to put him in the position he or she would have been in had the contract been properly performed, there would seem to be no need to upset the credit part of the transaction. Consumers may well feel aggrieved by this. Other solutions to this problem are discussed by P. Dobson, 'Consumer Credit – a Connected Lender Conundrum' [1981] *JBL* 179. The authors would like to thank Rob Bradgate for helpful discussions on this point.

131 It has been proposed that these figures be changed to £150 and £25,000 respectively: *Consumer Credit Deregulation, op. cit.*, at pp. 113–4. The figure of £25,000 was chosen to bring it into line with the ceiling for regulated agreements, but this misses the point that the regulated agreement ceiling is in relation to credit and the s.75 ceiling is in relation to the price of goods which has traditionally been double the figure used for the ceiling in regulated agreements. To confuse matters more in the second *Connected Lender Liability* report the Director General suggested linking the monetary amount to the amount of credit extended rather than the price of the goods.

132 *Reform of the Law on Consumer Credit, op. cit.*, at para. 78.

inquiries about the provider and not rely on any implicit approval of a creditor. Sensibly, and in contrast to the situation when determining whether an agreement is regulated, the exemption refers to the cash price and not the amount of finance.

7.11.4 S.56

Where an agreement is excluded from s.75, for instance, because the price of the goods falls outside the relevant financial limits (£100–£30,000), the debtor may still be able to make the creditor responsible for the goods or services supplied based on comments made during the negotiations. S.56(2), Consumer Credit Act 1974 provides that certain negotiations with a debtor shall be deemed to be conducted by the negotiator as an agent of the creditor, as well as in his or her actual capacity. At common law the dealer is not held to be the agent of the hire–purchase company.[133]

The negotiator is the person who conducts 'antecedent negotiations' with the debtor or hirer.[134] This includes a credit broker conducting negotiations with a consumer prior to the broker selling the goods to a creditor, who then makes a two–party debtor–creditor–supplier agreement. An example is a car dealer who makes comments about a car before the car forms the basis of a hire–purchase deal between a finance company and the consumer. It also applies to antecedent negotiations made by suppliers who are party to a three–party debtor–creditor–supplier agreement, such as a seller where the purchase is made using a credit card. The antecedent negotiations are taken to commence when the negotiator and the debtor or hirer first enter into communication and include any representations or other dealings between the parties. The breadth of this provision is indicated by the inclusion of advertisements as being an instance when the parties first enter into communication.[135]

Thus, depending on the circumstances, statements made by the negotiator could either be actionable misrepresentations or could form part of the terms of the contract. S.56(2) is thus broader in the scope of contracts it

---

133 *Branwhite v Worcester Works Finance* [1968] 3 All ER 104. This was applied in the context of s.56 in *Mynshul Asset Finance v Clarke (T/A Peacock Hotel)*, unreported, (although it is not clear that it was relevant since s.56 is concerned with someone being deemed an agent, rather than actually being an agent), but was distinguished in *Woodchester Leasing Equipment v Clayton and Clayton* [1994] CL 72 as the thrust of the representations were to persuade the purchaser to lease rather than to buy outright.

134 S.56(1), Consumer Credit Act 1974.

135 S.56(4), Consumer Credit Act 1974.

covers than s.75, which places financial limits on the price of the goods it relates to. S.56(2) also covers statements made by credit–brokers prior to the consumer entering into a two–party debtor–creditor–supplier agreement. Significantly, however, s.56, unlike s.75, does not extend to imposing liability for breach of the implied terms.

S.56(3) renders void agreements which seek to circumvent the provision of the section by making the negotiator the agent of the debtor or hirer or relieving the creditor of liability for the actions of his negotiator.

7.12 EXTORTIONATE CREDIT BARGAINS

7.12.1 Policy

One of the most controversial aspects of credit regulation is the question of whether there should be controls over interest rates. This debate is not about the regulation of high street credit, where the mass of the population might feel that the financial institutions could reduce their interests rates a little. Rather this debate centres on those marginal lenders who lend to low–income, and therefore generally high–risk, borrowers. Many such loans are entered into with doorstep collectors; typically such loans will have an APR of 100-500 per cent. Regulating such transactions gives rise to a moral quandary. The lenders may be able to show that they do not make excessive profits, when the high default rate and high collection costs (often door–to–door collections), are taken into account. Yet frequently such loans force debtors into a spiral of default as they are persuaded to take on roll–over loans to meet their commitments.[136] However, because the regulation of interest rates may have exclusionary or degenerative effects,[137] policy formulations in this area need to be carefully thought through.[138] It is particularly important that reforms which might lead to a reduction in the amount of private sector finance available to poorer sectors of the community should take into account the need to develop social lending[139] and self–help schemes such as credit unions[140] to replace the private sector.

---

[136] For a recent description of moneylending to low income consumers, see K. Rowlingson, *Moneylenders and their Customers, op. cit.*

[137] See 7.3 and D. Cayne and M. Trebilcock, *op. cit.*

[138] See G. Howells, 'Controlling Unjust Credit Transactions: Lessons from a Comparative Analysis' in G. Howells *et al., op. cit.*. See generally 1.5.

[139] See G. Howells, 'Social Fund Budgeting Loans – Social and Civil Justice?' (1990) *CJQ* 9.

[140] See reference in note 14.

Most legal systems have some form of control on credit rates charged. The debate has largely centred on how stringent the controls should be and on whether the technique of control should involve an unconscionability standard (perhaps backed up by a presumption that loans above a certain level are unconscionable) or whether there should be a statutory ceiling on interest rates.[141] Commonwealth countries have tended to follow the unconscionability approach, whilst interest rate ceilings have been a feature of US credit laws and are to be found in France and Germany and other European countries. There is some ambivalence on the part of policymakers as to whether they simply want to protect weak consumers from sharp practices or whether they want the law to have wider redistributive effects by challenging market–determined outcomes.

In the UK the Moneylenders Act 1927 allowed the courts to re–open transactions which were harsh and unconscionable. There had been a *prima facie* presumption that interest rates in excess of 48 per cent were excessive and the transaction was therefore harsh and unconscionable. Crowther supported controls on credit costs saying that 'there is a level of cost above which it becomes socially harmful to make loans available at all'.[142] Yet, because of a fear that the maximum would become the norm and the problem of setting a maximum figure for loans of differing sizes and durations, Crowther preferred extending the provisions of the Moneylenders Act and imposing strict licensing controls rather than the introduction of ceilings. In the White Paper which followed, the Government came out in favour of extending the powers to re–open harsh and unconscionable agreements to all credit agreements, but did not favour the use of a presumption because of the wide variety of agreements involved.[143]

7.12.2 Present Controls

The present controls on extortionate credit bargains are to be found in ss.137–140, Consumer Credit Act 1974.[144] The Act gives the courts the power to re–open extortionate credit bargains. These are agreements requiring the debtor or hirer to make payments which are 'grossly exorbitant' or 'otherwise contravene principles of fair dealing'. These provisions apply to all credit agreements and not just regulated agreements.

---

141 See G. Howells, 'Controlling Unjust Credit Transactions: Lessons from a Comparative Analysis' in G. Howells *et al.*, *op. cit.*

142 *Op. cit.* at p. 275.

143 *Op. cit.* at pp. 19–20.

144 It should not be forgotten than common law doctrines such as unconscionability, undue influence and economic duress may also be relevant.

There is no level above which the interest rate is presumed to be exorbitant. The court is, however, directed to have regard to relevant circumstances and in particular to:

(i)   interest rates prevailing at the time the agreement was made;
(ii) the debtor's age, experience, business capacity and state of health and the degree and nature of any financial pressure he was under when making the credit bargain;
(iii) the degree of risk the creditor accepted having regard to any security, the creditor's relationship to the debtor and any colourable cash price quoted in relation to goods or services included in the credit bargain.

It is generally accepted that the extortionate credit bargain provisions have proved to be rather ineffectual and are in need of reform. There are only five reported instances of the courts reopening credit agreements.[145] This may underestimate the impact of the provisions. Creditors may have modified their charges so as not to fall foul of the provisions, while the threat of invoking the provisions may help in negotiations with creditors. There are, however, several reasons to suspect that empirical observations would not reveal the provisions having a strong influence on the conduct of creditors.

Firstly, the drafting of the provisions indicates a greater concern for procedural than substantive justice. Thus the charging of 'grossly exorbitant' interest is simply viewed as one way of contravening the principles of fair dealing. However, procedural unfairness might not be enough by itself. In *Woodstead Finance v Petrou*[146] it was not held to be sufficient that the principles of fair dealing had been breached: there must also be a 'manifest disadvantage'. This seemed erroneously to import a requirement of the doctrine of undue influence into the statutory provisions.

Secondly, the courts have declined to use the extortionate credit bargain provisions to challenge the market and have accepted its fragmentation into different sectors.[147] The courts have analysed the credit market as consisting

---

145   Two of these cases involved unsecured loans: *Barcabe v Edwards* [1983] CCLR 11 (100 per cent reduced to 40 per cent); *Shahabini v Gyachi*, unreported, 1988 (156 per cent reduced to 15 per cent, increased on appeal to 30 per cent). Three involved secure loans: *Devogate v Jarvis*, unreported, 1987 (39 per cent reduced to 30 per cent); *Prestonwell Ltd v Capon*, unreported, 1988 (42 per cent reduced to 21 per cent) and *Castle Phillips & Co v Wilkinson* [1992] CCLR 83 (4 per cent per month reduced to 20 per cent per annum).

146   *The Times*, 23 January, 1986.

147   See *Davies v Directloans* [1986] 1 WLR 823 where Nugee QC divided the market into banks, building societies, finance houses and secondary finance associations and accepted evidence of the interest charged in each.

of a number of markets for different categories of loan which tend to reflect different levels of risk. Therefore, the interest rates charged to high–risk or 'marginal' debtors are only compared to similar rates charged to equally high–risk or 'marginal' debtors.

Thirdly, the courts have tended to accept the creditor's assessment of risk involved. Despite being directed to consider the value of security, the risk in *Ketley v Scott*[148] was described as 'considerable' and that in *Davies v Directloans*[149] to be of a 'high degree', despite the fact that the loans amounted to only 85 per cent and 83 per cent of the value of the respective securities. The courts have also been unsympathetic to the plight of debtors. Thus in *Wills v Wood*[150] the fact that the borrower was an old lady was not considered relevant as she was not an 'unworldly recluse' and in *Ketley v Scott*[151] a protected tenant, who was trying to purchase a house was not said to be under 'real' pressure as the transaction was of a speculative nature and there was no question of him being left homeless.

Fourthly, perhaps, the biggest weakness of the extortionate credit bargain provisions is that the sanctions lack teeth. The interest rates charged must be grossly exorbitant to justify reopening agreements; the court then has power to reduce the amount to that which is 'fairly due and reasonable'. In such cases, the courts have not been particularly harsh in their treatment of creditors, usually allowing interest to be charged at the top end of the range which would be reasonable.[152] Even if the courts were tougher in their interpretation of what is fairly due and reasonable, simply to allow creditors to charge what would have been appropriate in the first place remains a weak sanction.

Finally, the courts have the discretion whether or not to reopen an extortionate credit bargain. According to some judicial utterances the courts would not have been prepared to reopen agreements, even if the bargain had been found to be extortionate, because of some fraud on the debtor's part. Again one sees the impact of equitable doctrines – such as 'he who comes to equity must come with clean hands' – on the statutory provision. Although there is some justification for the basic principle, it needs to be applied carefully and the naïve must not be confused with the truly fraudulent. For instance, one case involved a couple who stated 'we thought it was very funny to buy a house without having money'.[153] Although the debtors had

---

148   (1981) ICR 241.

149   [1986] 1 WLR 823.

150   *The Times*, 24 March, 1984.

151   (1981) ICR 241.

152   See cases cited in note 145.

153   *First National Securities v Bertrand* (1980) CCLR 5.

some commercial motivation in entering the agreement, they also seem to be just the sort of people the law needs to protect from creditors and themselves.

7.12.3 Possible Reforms

In 1991, in a report entitled *Unjust Credit Transactions*,[154] Sir Gordon Borrie, the then Director General, singled out secured loans made to 'non-status borrowers' and unsecured roll–over or top–up loans as the forms of credit whose cost gave most cause for concern. The report proposed changes to the extortionate credit bargain provisions, recommending that the concept of 'extortionate credit bargain' be replaced by that of 'unjust credit transaction'. Reference to 'grossly exorbitant' payments would be changed to 'excessive' payments. The test of whether an agreement contravened ordinary principles of fair dealing would be replaced by one similar to that used for determining credit licence applications, namely whether the transaction involved business activity which was deceitful or oppressive or otherwise unfair or improper (whether unlawful or not). Also it was proposed that a new factor to be taken into account would be 'the lender's care and responsibility in making the loan, including steps taken to find out and check the borrower's credit–worthiness and ability to meet the full terms of the agreement.' This proposal reflected concern that during the boom in the late 1980s some sectors of the credit industry had not adopted responsible lending policies. It was further suggested that courts be allowed to reopen agreements on their own motion and that the Director General or local authority trading standards officers should be allowed to seek declarations that a particular transaction, or aspect of a transaction, should be deemed to be unjust. The report has been welcomed by the Department of Trade and Industry which has promised primary legislation to implement the proposals when Parliamentary time permits. On one matter the Department disagreed with the report; it preferred that payments should have to be 'grossly excessive', rather than merely 'excessive', in order to prevent too many cases being brought. The Department also proposed to place in regulations the specific factors to be taken into account when determining the justness of the transaction; the intention being to increase flexibility by making it easier to amend the factors to deal with future developments. These amendments are still awaited.

Will these reforms improve the position of consumers? Many of the changes in nomenclature may turn out to be purely symbolic and lacking in substance. For instance, will the judiciary really read into the alteration from 'grossly exorbitant' to 'grossly excessive' any significant change in policy?

---

[154]   (Office of Fair Trading, 1991).

These provisions will typically be applied in the lower courts where judges often adjudicate on the basis of their instinct rather than according to legal niceties. Many of the most valuable reforms – for instance, bringing the definition of unjust conduct into line with that used for licensing and requiring lenders to check the circumstances of potential borrowers – have more to do with procedure than substance. The report rejected the idea of interest rate ceilings and even the notion of a presumptive threshold.[155] However, one suspects that the traditional conservatism of the British judiciary will not be overcome unless it is given more positive encouragement to intervene. This would best be achieved by providing a presumption of unjustness so that courts are alerted to the suspicion that a charge might be too high. How the presumptive figure should be arrived at will generate much debate with opinions differing depending upon whether people are concerned to outlaw some forms of credit because they are expensive *per se*, or whether they simply want to ensure the market is working efficiently and stamp out bad practices.[156] Using a presumptive figure would not have the drawback of inflexibility, which is a major criticism of interest rate ceilings. Special licences could be granted to creditors regularly operating above the presumptive figure; alternatively, creditors could have loans at higher rates authorised by a body such as the Director General.[157]

7.13 CREDITOR REMEDIES

Lending is a risky business and creditors are obviously keen to have contractual rights which they can enforce to secure their position should the agreement go wrong. The law has an interest in ensuring that these rights are not used unfairly or oppressively against debtors in straightened

---

155 Note that as well as the question of the complexity of establishing thresholds, the Office of Fair Trading was concerned that such thresholds could not be introduced without there being a strong social lending sector: see *ibid* at 41.

156 See G. Howells, 'Controlling unjust credit transactions: lessons from a comparative analysis' *op. cit.* at pp. 101–8. Agreements above the presumptive threshold could be scrutinised closely and the circumstances surrounding their conclusion eg agressive (but legal) selling practices can be taken into account to an extent which would not normally be permitted in a legal system which typically leaves the parties free to decide what bargains they strike.

157 Whether such exemptions should be allowed perhaps leads one back to seeking out the underlying purpose of this type of legislation. If a licence or authorisation must be sought, then at least the creditor can be forced to justify his charges and some considered attention can be paid to the pros and cons of allowing a certain type of credit or a particular transaction.

circumstances. Terry Ison has suggested that, in debtor–creditor–supplier type situations, the sanction for non–payment should be limited to repossession of the goods and an adverse credit report.[158] Ison thought such an approach to be justified since as the court system was not able to handle claims by consumers effectively, then it should not be given over to the enforcement of retailer claims. Several beneficial side effects were seen as flowing from the abolition of debt recovery. Creditors would have a greater interest in viewing the goods supplied as security which would provide an incentive not to sell shoddy goods. Lenders would be more careful in their lending policy and would, for instance, obtain credit reports and require significant down payments. There would most likely be a switch from sales financing to loan financing where the consumer was a marginal credit risk. This would make the cost of credit more transparent and also provide a space for the consumer to contemplate the wisdom of the transaction as they went to another place to negotiate a loan. Similar views had been put to the Crowther Committee by Ison. Whilst the Committee appreciated his reasoning, it nevertheless felt unable to go along with such drastic restrictions on creditors' remedies.[159]

7.13.1 Requirement of Notice

7.13.1.1 Non–Breach Situations

The policy of the Consumer Credit Act 1974 is to require the debtor or hirer to give at least seven days notice before terminating the agreement or enforcing terms with serious consequences for the debtor or hirer. S.76, Consumer Credit Act 1974 requires the creditor or owner to give notice before seeking to enforce a term which allows him to:

(i)   demand early repayment of a sum;
(ii) recover possession of goods or land; or
(iii) treat any right conferred on the debtor or hirer as terminated, restricted or deferred.

S.76 does not apply where there has been a breach of the agreement.

S.98, Consumer Credit Act 1974 provides for a notice requirement where the debtor or hirer wishes to terminate the agreement otherwise than by reason of breach of the agreement. In practice the most significant provisions are those on default notices contained in s.87, Consumer Credit

---

[158]   T. Ison, *op. cit.* at pp. 284–90.
[159]   *Op. cit.* at pp. 30–5.

Act 1974. However, ss.76 and 98 are needed to prevent contracts from being drafted in such a way that events which might normally be considered breaches of contract are in fact not construed as such, but nevertheless cause similar consequences to flow. A useful comparison can be drawn with the common law which will strike down penalty clauses resulting from a breach,[160] but is seemingly powerless when similar results arise in non breach situations. Thus a minimum payments clause under a hire–purchase contract has been upheld when a hirer exercised his right to terminate the agreement, rather than be in breach and permit the owner to terminate for breach.[161]

7.13.1.2 Default Notices

S.87 requires a default notice to be served on the debtor or hirer before the creditor or owner can, by reason of any breach by the debtor or hirer:

(i)   terminate the agreement,
(ii) demand earlier payment,
(iii) recover possession of any goods or land,
(iv) treat any right conferred on the debtor or hirer as terminated, restricted or deferred, or
(v)   enforce any security.

The default notice must be in the prescribed form.[162] This notice is in fact one of the most useful consumer information provisions as it provides

---

[160] *Dunlop Pneumatic Tyres Co Ltd v New Garages Motor Co* [1915] AC 79.

[161] *Associated Distributors v Hall* [1938] 2 KB 83. This was followed by the Court of Appeal in *Campbell Discount Co Ltd v Bridge* [1961] 2 All ER 97. However, the House of Lords (*Bridge v Campbell Discounts Co Ltd* [1962] 1 ALL ER 385) avoided having to follow *Hall* by finding that a letter, written by the defaulter (in which he said he was sorry that he could not keep up repayments) was not an exercise of his right to terminate the agreement, but rather a breach of the agreement. The minimum payments clause was then held to be a penalty clause. Lord Denning (at 399) would have been prepared to go further and grant relief whatever the reason for terminating the hiring in order the avoid equity committing itself to the absurd paradox that 'It will grant relief to a man who breaks his contract but will penalise the man who keeps it.' Note that the amounts involved took the contract outside the controls in the Hire–Purchase Act 1938.

[162] See Consumer Credit (Enforcement, Default and Termination Notices) Regulations 1983, S.I. 1983/1561.

consumers with relevant and timely information. Two particularly useful statements which must be contained in default notices are:

> 'IF YOU ARE NOT SURE WHAT TO DO, YOU SHOULD GET HELP AS SOON AS POSSIBLE, FOR EXAMPLE YOU SHOULD CONTACT A SOLICITOR, YOUR LOCAL TRADING STANDARDS DEPARTMENT OR YOUR NEAREST CITIZENS' ADVICE BUREAU'.

> 'IF YOU HAVE DIFFICULTY IN PAYING ANY SUM OWING UNDER THE AGREEMENT YOU CAN APPLY TO THE COURT WHICH MAY MAKE AN ORDER ALLOWING YOU OR YOUR SURETY MORE TIME'.[163]

The default notice must state the nature of the alleged breach. If the breach is capable of remedy, it must specify what action is required to remedy it; if the breach is irremediable, it must specify the compensation demanded for the breach. It must also state the consequences of failing to comply with the notice. The debtor must be informed of a date (at least seven days after service of the notice) by which time the necessary actions must be taken or the compensation paid. Within this period the creditor or owner can take no action which requires the service of a default notice.[164] If the breach is remedied or the compensation paid, then the breach is treated as if it had not occurred. It is only in relation to s.87 notice that the debtor or hirer has the right to rectify matters. There is no corresponding right where the creditor or owner seeks to enforce a right or terminate an agreement in a non–breach situation, and yet, as we have seen, whether an action of the debtor or hirer amounts to a breach can often depend on how the contract was worded. For instance, a debtor who defaults may be in breach or, alternatively, the agreement could state that non–payment makes the whole of the outstanding balance payable.

We have already noted that a general weakness with the enforcement powers of the Consumer Credit Act 1974 is the provision, in s.170(1), that there is no sanction for breach of requirements laid down in the Act, except to the extent expressly provided for. This weakness is well illustrated by the fact that no such sanctions are provided for failing to comply with the default notice procedure (or indeed the procedures required by ss.76 and 98). Is there then no redress when the notice procedures are not followed? The answer is

---

[163] This refers to the possibility that the court will make a time order, a subject considered at 7.14.1.

[164] Ss.76, 87 and 98 of the Consumer Credit Act 1974 do not prevent a creditor from treating the right to draw upon credit as being restricted or deferred and taking steps to that end (eg placing a stop on a credit card or bank account).

no, unless relief can be found in common law provisions. Any redress available to the consumer is therefore the result of accident rather than planning. In *Eshun v Moorgate Mercantile Co Ltd*[165] where goods were recovered without a notice being served (as required under the former Hire–Purchase Act 1965) an action for wrongful retaking of possession was successful. What is the position if, instead of the goods being repossessed, the creditor invokes an accelerated payments clause and the debtor has paid money to the creditor? A. Hill–Smith has suggested that this may be recoverable on the basis that the money was had and received by the creditor on the basis of a mistake of law.[166] It is unfortunate that the Consumer Credit Act 1974 did not contain more explicit sanctions for non–compliance, which could have reflected consumer protection values rather than rely on the *ad hoc* solutions provided by the common law.

There are some instances where the Consumer Credit Act 1974 does provide for severe sanctions for creditors who do not comply with the proper procedures for enforcing their rights. These are considered in the next paragraphs.

7.13.2 Breach of Statutory Duty

S.92, Consumer Credit Act 1974 provides for an action for breach of statutory duty in two situations when goods or land are recovered without a court order. This action arises when either (i) a creditor or owner enters premises to take possession of goods under a regulated hire–purchase, conditional sale or consumer hire agreement, or (ii) a creditor under a conditional sale agreement seeks to recover possession of land from the debtor. It is important to remember the general rule, to be found in s.173(3), Consumer Credit Act 1974, that the need for a court order can be ignored if the debtor or owner gives consent to the doing of such actions at the time they are actually undertaken.

---

165 [1971] 1 WLR 722: this seems to have been on the basis of conversion, although it has been suggested that an alternative basis could be that the goods were returned under a mistake of law. The courts have taken the view that all back payments are recoverable, but it may be doubted whether this approach would be followed where the debtor had benefited from considerable enjoyment from the goods for a substantial period of time.

166 *Consumer Credit: Law and Practice*, (Sweet & Maxwell, 1985) at pp. 179–80.

7.13.3 Protected Goods

There are very severe sanctions laid down in ss.90–91, Consumer Credit Act 1974 if a creditor under a hire–purchase or conditional sale agreement seeks to recover possession of 'protected goods' without a court order.[167] Goods are protected if:

(i)   the debtor is in breach of a regulated hire–purchase or conditional sale agreement, and
(ii) the property in the goods remains with the creditor, and
(iii) the debtor has paid one third of the total price of the goods.

Where the creditor was required to install the goods and the agreement provided for a specified installation charge, then goods are only protected once that charge and a third of the remaining total price have been paid. As an anti–avoidance measure, once a third of the total price of any goods has been paid then that condition is held to be satisfied as regards any subsequent agreement which relates to the same goods.

There are severe consequences if protected goods are wrongfully repossessed. The agreement is terminated[168] (if it were not already) and the debtor is released from all liabilities under the agreement and can recover all sums paid under the agreement. These consequences are intended to deter creditors from repossessing 'protected goods', for the debtor is in effect given free use of the goods up until the time of termination and the creditor risks being left with goods which have deteriorated in value. However, in practice some creditors will continue to 'snatch back' goods if their residual value is greater than the amount to be refunded. The debtor cannot require that the goods be returned,[169] nor for that matter can the creditor bring the agreement back to life by restoring the goods.[170]

---

167 Although once again it is sufficient that the debtor consents to the taking of the goods at the time they are repossessed.

168 Note that the whole of the agreement is terminated even if the protected goods only formed part of the subject matter of the agreement.

169 Cf *Carr v James Broderick & Co Ltd* [1942] 2 KB 275 where it was held that the property was and always had been with the hire–purchase company. The hirer was not given a right of possession. The Act merely provided that a hirer could only properly be deprived of possession by an action brought in the courts.

170 Cf *Capital Finance Co Ltd v Bray* [1964] 1 WLR 323 where it was held that there would have to be a new agreement to reinstate the hire–purchase agreement. The mere fact that the hirer had used the car was not sufficient to demonstrate such agreement.

The prohibition only relates to recovering possession of goods *from* the debtor. It does not apply if the goods have been abandoned[171] or are recovered from a third party to whom they have been wrongfully sold. However, the section would seem to prevent the creditor recovering goods from a third party to whom the debtor had entrusted the goods, for example, a mechanic repairing protected goods.[172]

7.13.4 Consumer Hire

S.132, Consumer Credit Act 1974 provides relief to hirers where the owner has repossessed goods forming the subject matter of a regulated consumer hire–agreement without having obtained a court order. The provisions aim to prevent hirers from being forced to maintain payments even after the goods have been repossessed. It seeks to do justice where the repossessor would otherwise receive a substantial windfall profit in circumstances where significant payments had already been received.

Where goods have been wrongfully recovered the hirer can apply to court for an order that the whole or part of any sum paid under the agreement should be repaid and that obligations to pay further sums in respect of the goods should cease. Such applications can be granted in full or in part, according to what the court considers to be just, having regard to the extent of the enjoyment of the goods by the hirer. The court may make similar provisions whenever it makes an order for the delivery of goods back to the owner.

7.14 POWERS OF THE COURT

The Consumer Credit Act 1974 gives the court some very important powers to assist it to do justice between the parties. It should be mentioned at the outset that these are additional to the court's inherent equitable power to grant relief against forfeiture. This equitable relief has been widely invoked with regard to mortgages to prevent mortgagees from unfairly exercising their equity of redemption. The courts have been circumspect about extending such relief to agreements relating to personal property, though the

---

[171] *Bentinck Ltd v Cromwell Engineering* [1971] 1 QB 324 (decided under Hire–Purchase Act 1965).

[172] *F C Finance Ltd v Francis* (1970) 114 SJ 568 (decided under Hire–Purchase Act 1965).

application of the principle to such cases does appear to have been accepted.[173]

7.14.1 Time Orders

If it appears just to do so, s.129, Consumer Credit Act 1974 gives a court the power to make a time order in the following circumstances:

(i) on application for an enforcement order;
(ii) on an application by the debtor or hirer after he or she has been served with a default notice or a notice under ss.76 and 98, Consumer Credit Act 1974; and
(iii) in any action brought by a creditor or owner to enforce a regulated agreement or any security, or to recover possession of any goods or land relating to a regulated agreement.

Under a time order the court can reschedule the payments under the agreement and, in order to do justice, provide for the payment of such instalments at such times as it considers reasonable. This allows for instalments to be reduced and the repayment period extended. When deciding the size and rate of repayments, the court must have regard to the means of the debtor or hirer. In some cases, a time order was used to reduce the interest rate payable under the agreement.[174] However, a time order was held to be inappropriate if the debtor's offer did not even meet the accruing interest charges and if there was no realistic prospect of the debtor's financial position improving.[175] With respect to non-monetary defaults, such as a failure to take reasonable care of goods, the court can specify a period of time for the debtor to put matters right; if the breach is remedied, it is treated as if it had never occurred. This period of time is known as the 'protective period' during which the creditor or owner cannot take any action which requires the serving of a default notice or invoke any secondary provision

---

173 *Stockloser v Johnson* [1954] 1 QB 376: the scope of the court's jurisdiction remains uncertain. Does the creditor have to have acted unconscionably? Does it apply to hire contracts? Is the court only able to give the debtor more time, or can it order payment to be returned and future payments to be ignored?

174 *Cedar Holdings Ltd v Jenkins* [1988] CCLR 34 and *Cedar Holdings Ltd v Thompson* [1993] CCLR 7, but in *J & J Securities v Lee* [1994] CCLR 44 these were not followed. In *Southern and District Finance v Barnes, The Times*, 19 April 1995 Leggatt LJ in the Court of Appeal held that the interest rate could be varied where it was just to do so.

175 *First National Bank v Syed* [1991] 2 All ER 250.

which becomes operative on the breach. The protective period has effect without prejudice to anything done by the creditor or owner prior to its commencement, so that goods which have been repossessed cannot be ordered to be returned. This protective period only applies to non–monetary breaches. Thus, although instalments might have been rescheduled, there is nothing to prevent the creditor or owner invoking other rights, such as the right to repossess goods. The debtor or hirer would then have to ask the court to use its general powers to suspend orders or impose conditions under s.135, Consumer Credit Act 1974.

7.14.2 Return and Transfer Orders

S.133, Consumer Credit Act 1974 gives the court the power to make 'return' or 'transfer' orders during proceedings relating to hire–purchase or conditional sale agreements for an enforcement or time order or in any action brought by the creditor to recover possession of the goods.

A return order, as its name suggests, requires the goods be returned to the creditor. Such an order is usually suspended and can be made conditional on the creditor returning any surplus on sale to the debtor.[176] An order could be for the immediate return of the goods, but this would be of little practical significance since, on payment of the total price of the goods at any time before they enter the possession of the creditor, the debtor can claim the goods.[177]

A transfer order provides for title in part of the goods to be transferred to the debtor, with the remainder of the goods being returned to the creditor. Limits are placed on the value of the goods which can be transferred to the debtor. These limits are intended to compensate the creditor for having to accept the goods back. The maximum value of goods which can be transferred to the debtor equals the amounts which have been paid under the agreement less one–third of the unpaid balance. Where the agreement does not specify the value of individual goods forming part of the agreement, then the court determines which portion of the total price it is reasonable to allocate to the goods being transferred.

7.14.3 Conditional and Suspended Orders

In any order relating to a regulated agreement, s.135, Consumer Credit Act 1974 allows the court (i) to make the operation of any term of the order

---

[176] The court would use its powers under s.135, Consumer Credit Act 1974.

[177] S.133(4), Consumer Credit Act 1974.

conditional on the doing of specified acts by any of the parties, or (ii) to suspend the operation of any term, either until such time as the court subsequently directs or until the occurrence of a specified act or omission. There are some limits to these powers. For instance, a court cannot suspend the operation of a term requiring a person to deliver up goods, unless it is satisfied that they are in that person's possession. Also the power to suspend a term of the order cannot be used to extend the period for which a hirer is entitled to possess goods under a hire agreement.

7.15 APPROPRIATION OF PAYMENTS

Where a debtor or hirer has more than one regulated agreement with a creditor or owner, it can be important to know how payments have been appropriated between the agreements. On this question may hang determinations such as which goods are 'protected', whether a transfer order can be made (or how much can be transferred) and how much refund, if any, is appropriate under consumer hire agreements where the owner has repossessed the goods. S.81, Consumer Credit Act 1974 gives the debtor the right to appropriate sums between agreements as he or she sees fit. However, where the debtor fails to specify how the sums are to be appropriated, the Act provides a default procedure where one of the agreements is a hire–purchase, conditional sale or consumer hire agreement or an agreement for which security is provided. This default procedure provides that sums should be appropriated to the agreements proportionately to the sums due under them. However, if the default procedure does not apply, then the matter is covered by the common law which leaves it to the creditor to decide how to appropriate payments.

7.16 LOST, STOLEN OR MISUSED CREDIT CARDS

The advent of the plastic revolution has brought many benefits to consumers, but has also introduced many new dangers of financial risk through the unauthorised use of cards. The Consumer Credit Act 1974 contains some protection against such risks. First, a debtor is not liable under a credit token agreement for the use made of the credit token unless he or she has accepted it.[178] Acceptance occurs on signing the token or a receipt for it or when the token is first used. Second, even after acceptance, liability for misuse of the token can be avoided by giving oral or written notice to the creditor that it is liable to be misused. Indeed, there will be no liability at all if the credit token

---

[178] S.66, Consumer Credit Act 1974.

agreement failed to specify the name, address and telephone number of a person on whom such notice can be served.[179] If the credit token is misused by someone who acquired it with the debtor's consent, then there is unlimited liability until such time as the creditor is notified of the possibility of misuse, even if the person has used the card in an unauthorised manner. In other cases, such as where a card is lost or stolen, the maximum liability a debtor can incur for misuse of the card will be £50 (or the credit limit if lower). Charge cards, being exempt from the Act, are also excluded from this protection. It is a matter of some concern that debit cards too are not subject to such a limitation of liability, although a similar limit is contained in the Banking Code of Practice.

7.17 CONCLUSION

There is no doubting the complexity of consumer credit law. Although with hindsight some features of the Consumer Credit Act 1974 could be simplified, the law in this area will inevitably be complex, given the need to make rules watertight so that businesses cannot evade regulation simply by adopting new trading forms. The Consumer Credit Act 1974 was a brave attempt to regulate the substance rather than the form of credit agreements. Nevertheless the Act's limitations are illustrated by the problems it experiences in handling the issues raised by credit cards and EFTPOS cards. Consumer law has once again been shown to be one step behind commercial practice.

Surprisingly there seems to be a general consensus, even amongst the credit industry, about the need to regulate consumer credit. The Director General's report, *Consumer Credit Deregulation*, found little enthusiasm from the credit industry for dismantling the general regulatory structure. This perhaps reflects the 'dangerous' nature of consumer credit. It is a product whose value consumers find difficult to understand and which they can easily use excessively, often without any obvious warning signs until matters have spiralled out of control. The industry's acceptance of the Consumer Credit Act 1974 may also be due to the fact that the Act controls the form of the agreement and restricts some remedies, but leaves the parties largely free to determine its core terms, such as interest rates, security and guarantees. Thus it seeks to ensure fairness in market transactions without questioning whether the market mechanism is appropriate. The extent to which consumer law can bring about redistributive effects is clearly a central theme which readers need to consider.[180]

---

[179] Ss.83–84, Consumer Credit Act 1974.
[180] See 1.3.8.

If consumer credit law is complex, is it too complex to be of use to consumers? Few consumers will be able to know the way the law applies to them in detail. This need not, however, prevent the law being useful to them. There are several things which can be done to allow consumers to enjoy the benefits of laws which are too complex for the majority to understand fully. First, it is important to draw consumers' attention to their rights in ways that are easily comprehensible. Statements in agreement documentation explaining consumer rights in simple prescribed language are an easy way to achieve this. Second, consumer education should not be neglected. What is the use of informing consumers of the APR if they do not know how to interpret that information? Third, consumers should be able to invoke their rights with the minimum of formality. The provision of a form in the actual credit agreement itself to facilitate cancellation is an example of how legal remedies can be made accessible to consumers. Fourth, it is important that there are properly trained and funded advisers to whom consumers can turn once they recognise they have a problem which the law might be able to assist them with.[181] Fifth, the market cannot be regulated by simple reliance on the initiative of consumers to invoke their private law rights. This emphasises the necessity for private law rights to be complemented by the public law controls on the credit market which are considered in Chapter 11.

---

[181] On the problem of funding these services, see G. Howells, 'Funding Money Advice Services' in *The Changing Shape of the Legal Profession*, J. Shapland and R. Le Grys (eds) (Sheffield Institute for the Study of the Legal Profession, 1994).

8 Doorstep and Distance Selling

8.1 DOORSTEP AND DISTANT SELLING – POLICY REASONS FOR INTERVENTION

Most consumer transactions take place between a consumer and trader in a retail outlet. In such cases the consumer will have had the opportunity to see the product and to compare it with other products on sale. Typically the product will be taken away immediately the purchase is complete or arrangements will be made for its delivery. The consumer will have met the supplier and visited the trading premises and will therefore be in a position to make some assessment of the character of the supplier of the goods or service. Two methods of selling – doorstep and distant selling – do not fit the typical consumer sale model described above and give rise to particular consumer protection issues. Both have been the subject of scrutiny by the European Community legislators.

Doorstep selling has been the subject of a community Directive,[1] which has been implemented in the UK by the Consumer Protection (Cancellation of Contracts Concluded away from Business Premises) Regulations 1987.[2] Distant selling potentially raises more complex issues and so far has only been the subject of draft Directives[3] and a Recommendation,[4] although there are some national law provisions which touch on this issue.

Although many laws seek to protect the consumer from unfair selling and marketing practices, there are particular reasons for singling out doorstep and distant selling for special treatment. These two selling techniques are at different ends of the marketing spectrum. Doorstep sales depend on cold selling of a highly personalised form to consumers in the comfort of their own home. Distant selling on the other hand can be highly depersonalised through mailshots, faxes, catalogues and even television,

---

1   Council Directive of 20 December 1985 to protect the consumer in respect of contracts negotiated away from business premises: 85/577/EEC, OJ 1985 L372/31.
2   S.I. 1987/2117.
3   OJ 1992 C156/14 and OJ 1993 C308/18. See also Commission discussion papers COM (92) 11 and COM (93) 396. The latest version is that of the French Presidency Doc 12365/94 CONSOM 67.
4   Commission Recommendation of 7 April 1992, OJ 1992 L156/21.

although it can also be more personalised, when, for example, it is undertaken by telephone.

8.1.1 Restriction on Consumer Choice

One justification for intervention which is common to both doorstep and distant selling technique is that they have the potential to restrict consumer choice. This is particularly so in the context of doorstep selling. A salesperson may knock on the door and persuade a consumer to buy a product which they had never thought they needed or even possibly knew existed before the trader called. In these circumstances the consumer has no time to compare the product offered with those of its competitors. The problem of the consumer's restricted opportunity to compare products and services also applies to some forms of distant selling (eg television selling), but not to others. For instance, goods in catalogues can be compared with High Street equivalents. Difficulties arise when the goods are not available in the High Street for then a consumer at a distance is always faced with uncertainty as to the quality of the goods. Even if there is a description, photograph or television display of the goods this cannot be equated with actually being able to see and handle the goods.

8.1.2 Lack of Knowledge About the Supplier

In both doorstep and distant selling there can be a problem arising from the consumer's lack of knowledge of the character of the seller. This is most acute in distant selling where at its most extreme the order (and money) can be posted off to an anonymous postal box number. The problem also exists in relation to doorstep selling for, although the consumer has met a representative of the supplier, he or she will not have seen the supplier's trading premises.

8.1.3 Coercion

Another reason for intervening in doorstep selling, which does not apply to distant selling, is that consumers often feel coerced to sign contracts for goods they do not really want simply because they are in their own home. This may be because the salesperson harangues them to such an extent that it seems easier to sign than to argue, or possibly because when 'entertaining' in their own home, people find it difficult to be discourteous and insist that they do not want the product or service. One might suggest that consumers should not be so weak and gullible, but it is surprising how many normally sensible people have regretted entering contracts signed in their home on the spur of the moment. The problem is even more acute with vulnerable consumers, such as the elderly.

8.1.4 Privacy

Some of the marketing techniques adopted by distant selling companies give rise to issues of privacy, since they use databases to target their marketing. The consumer's privacy is also affected in doorstep selling, perhaps in an even more direct way, but (short of banning such selling techniques)[5] there is little that can be done to prevent this traditional way of selling. Also with doorstep selling there is less incidence of data being used to target particular individuals; more commonly, areas having a certain social structure will be canvassed.

8.2 DOORSTEP SELLING[6]

Doorstep selling has a trade association, the Direct Selling Association, which has a Code of Practice, but it is also subject to statutory regulation. The Consumer Protection (Cancellation of Contracts Concluded Away from Business Premises) Regulations 1987[7] came into force on 1 July 1988. These provide consumers with a seven–day cooling–off period within which they can cancel contracts governed by the Regulations.[8] This period allows consumers to compare the bargain they have struck with other possibilities. It also gives them the chance to withdraw from agreements they have entered into as the result of undue pressure. Dangers still exist when contracting with doorstep traders about whom little is known. For instance, there is no compensation fund to protect pre–payments or to underwrite guarantees about the quality of such goods.

---

5   As is the case with debtor–creditor credit agreements: see s. 49, Consumer Credit Act 1974 discussed at 11.2.3.

6   A. Hill–Smith, (1988) 85, 21, *LSGaz* 37–38, 41.

7   S.I. 1987/2117.

8   The rational for this type of consumer protection device has already been discussed in the context of consumer credit contracts: see 7.8.

8.2.1 Scope of the Regulations

The Regulations apply to contracts made for the supply of goods and services by a trader to a consumer in four circumstances:[9]

(i) During an unsolicited visit by a trader to the consumer's home or place of work. A visit is only solicited if it is expressly requested by the consumer, but does include a request made after an unsolicited telephone call from a trader, during which the trader indicates a willingness to visit the consumer.[10]

(ii) In the circumstances mentioned in (i), even if the consumer had requested the visit, so long as the goods or services concerned are different from those to which the request related and provided that, when the visit was requested, the consumer did not and could not reasonably have known that the supply of those other goods or services formed part of the trader's business activities. This is to catch 'bait and switch' tactics where a trader claims to be selling one commodity, but is really more interested in catching the consumer's attention to sell other products and services.

(iii) Excursions organised by traders away from their permanent or temporary business premises. Thus excursions to a conference centre or hotel would be caught, whereas those organised to a factory shop would not be covered.

(iv) Contracts are also covered if they are not made by the consumer in the above circumstances, but an offer was made on such occasions. This is included to plug a possible loophole which could exist if offers are accepted by the trader on business premises and therefore the contracts concluded on business premises, but only in a strictly formal sense.

There are various 'excepted contracts':

(i) Various contracts for the sale of land, construction or extension of buildings and related finance. Contracts for the supply of goods to be incorporated into land and for the repair or improvement of property are included so long as they are not financed by a loan secured on land.

(ii) Contracts for food, drink and other goods intended for current consumption by use in the household and supplied by regular roundsmen (eg the milk or newspaper delivered to the home) would not be included.

---

9   Reg. 3(1).
10   Reg. 3(3).

(iii) Contracts entered into after a consumer had an opportunity to read the terms of the contract in a trader's catalogue, prior to the trader's representative calling. The contract or catalogue must, however, have contained or been accompanied by a prominent notice giving the consumer the right to return the goods supplied within seven days of receipt or otherwise cancel the contract within that period without incurring liability. Consumers remain responsible for damage due to their failure to take reasonable care of the goods in their possession.

(iv) Contracts of insurance, investment agreements and agreements for the making of deposits in respect of which regulations have been made under s.34, Banking Act 1987.

(v) Credit agreements (other than hire–purchase or conditional sale agreements) for credit not exceeding £35 and any other contract under which the consumer makes total payments not exceeding £35.

8.2.2 Notice

The Regulations provide that the contract shall be unenforceable unless the consumer is given a written notice of his or her right to cancel the contract within seven days.[11] The notice should contain the information about the trader, a statement of the right to cancel (and that the cancellation form provided can be used) and the name and address of a person on whom notice of cancellation can be served.[12] The notice should be legible and, if incorporated into the document, be given no less prominence than other information except the heading, names of the contract parties and anything inserted in handwriting. The notice must be dated and delivered when the contract is made or when the consumer makes an offer (if the contract would have been cancellable had it been concluded at the time the offer was made).

8.2.3 Cancellation

The consumer can cancel the contract within seven days from when it was made. Notice of cancellation can be served on the trader or anyone specified in the cancellation notice as a person on whom notice can be served. The cancellation notice can be used to effect the cancellation but any written notice will suffice so long as it indicates the consumer's intention to cancel the contract. A notice of cancellation sent by post is deemed to have been served at the time of posting regardless of whether it is actually received.

---

11   Reg. 4.
12   On information provision, 1.8.3.

This is similar to the position regarding cancellation of consumer credit contracts under the Consumer Credit Act 1974; the consequences of cancellation are also provided for in a similar manner.[13]

One point is worth noting in relation to four problem categories of goods, namely, perishable goods, consumable goods which have been consumed prior to cancellation, goods supplied in an emergency and goods which have been incorporated in land or other things. As under the Consumer Credit Act 1974 there is no duty to return such goods. The Consumer Credit Act 1974 plugs the possible loophole created in respect of goods supplied in an emergency and goods which have been incorporated in land or other things by cancelling the credit element but continuing the obligation to pay. However, it allows the consumer to have perishable and consumable goods without paying for them. The Doorstep Regulations are stricter requiring the consumer to pay for all four categories of goods and for services provided in connection with their supply. This weakens the protection for these types of goods, although other elements of such contracts may be cancellable.

It has already been noted that the cooling–off period is a technique familiar to UK consumer law in the context of consumer credit. As the rules are slightly different under both sets of legislation, there was a need to decide which legislation should cover a cancellable contract caught by both provisions. The approach adopted was to withdraw from the scope of the Doorstep Regulations those contracts which are also cancellable under the Consumer Credit Act 1974. There was a problem, however, since the cancellation provisions under the Consumer Credit Act 1974 do not apply to agreements for less than £50. This threshold was too high for the Doorstep Regulations which had a threshold of £35, as dictated by the EC Directive. Therefore the Consumer Credit Act 1974 was amended so that, for agreements cancellable under the Consumer Credit Act 1974 and to which the Doorstep Regulations also apply, the threshold is £35 and not £50.[14]

Problems may still arise because the cancellation period is calculated differently under the Consumer Credit Act 1974 than under the Doorstep Regulations. Under the latter the consumer must have not less than seven days from the making of the contract to cancel it. However, under the Consumer Credit Act 1974 the cancellation period runs out at the end of the fifth day following the day on which the consumer received the second statutory copy of the contract or notice of cancellation. This second copy or notice must always be posted within seven days of the contract being made. Thus a more generous cancellation period is possible than that provided for under the Doorstep Regulations. This need not be a problem, though the period could be for less than seven days in which case there is a question

---

13   See 7.8.
14   S. 74(2A), Consumer Credit Act 1974.

mark over whether the Doorstep Regulations correctly implement the Directive which requires a seven–day cooling–off period from receipt of the notice of cancellation rights. As the second copy or notice must be posted, the earliest it will arrive at the consumer's address is the day after the contract was made at the earliest. For example, if a contract is concluded at 3 p.m. on a Monday afternoon where the second copy or notice is posted at 4 p.m. that day, it should arrive the next day. The consumer then has until the end of the fifth day following receipt of the notice to cancel the contract, namely until midnight on Sunday – some 15 hours short of a full seven days.

The Department of Trade and Industry's view appears to be that the cooling–off period for regulated credit agreements signed off trade premises amounts in all normal circumstances to at least the seven days specified in the Directive. There is perhaps an understandable desire not to have to amend primary legislation unnecessarily or to have too many conflicting systems, especially when any consumer injustice is likely to be minimal and when, in most cases, consumers will be better off under the UK law than under the protection demanded by the Directive. There are proposals to bring the consumer credit cancellation period laws into line with those contained in the EC Doorstep Directive and EC Consumer Credit Directive – namely seven days from the signing of the agreement. When this occurs, all consumers will be granted seven days, but the net result will be reduced protection since many consumers currently benefit from a longer cooling off period where there is a credit element to the contract. However, this may be a price worth paying to simplify the law.[15]

8.3 DISTANT SELLING[16]

Present regulation of distant selling consists of punctuated *ad hoc* legislative interventions directed expressly at distant selling; legislation which regulates distant selling but was not enacted specifically for that purpose (such as the Data Protection Act 1984 and the Consumer Credit Act 1974); a large amount of self–regulatory or 'soft law' by which the industry attempts to

---

15   Office of Fair Trading, *Consumer Credit Deregulation*, (Office of Fair Trading, 1994) at pp. 62–3.

16   See generally R. Bradgate, 'Distant Selling in the United Kingdom and the Proposed E.C. Directive' (1993) 1 *ConsumLJ* 19: G. Howells, 'A Consideration of European Proposals to Regulate Distant Selling' in *Enhancing the Legal Position of the European Consumer*, J. Lonbay (ed) (IEL/BIICL, forthcoming) and for a view in French by the official responsible for European legislation in this area see J. Allix, 'La protection du consommateur en matière de contrats à distance' [1993] *REDC* 95. Also see discussion at 1.8.3.4.

regulate itself and of course the common law. Thus the law has failed to put in place a framework for addressing the consumer protection issues raised in this fast-developing sector.

8.3.1 What is Distant Selling?

Distant selling covers a wide range of trading activities. Some forms are fairly traditional, such as mail order catalogues, mail order advertisements in newspapers, personalised direct mailing and door–to–door distribution of leaflets. Others are of more recent origin. One particularly prevalent practice in recent times has been telephone selling. This has caused a great deal of concern as it is far more intrusive to receive unwanted telephone calls which must be answered than to receive written material which one can choose to read or not. In 1983 the Office of Fair Trading found that 21 per cent of consumers surveyed who owned a telephone had received an unsolicited call, with 17 per cent of these having received five or more calls.[17] More recently, videotex systems allow the customer to view information about products on the television screen and order using a television key pad. Satellite and cable television have also recently introduced shopping programmes and channels where goods are advertised and consumers phone through their orders. It is easy to dismiss some of the more esoteric forms of distant selling as belonging to the world of science fiction. However, by the end of the century we are just as likely to sign an electronic cheque on a computer terminal in our homes as we are nowadays to write a cheque or give our credit card details over the phone. That the last example is now commonplace shows just how quickly new technology allows distant selling to become a regular feature of the consumer's world.

8.3.2 Controls on Solicitation

The Unsolicited Goods and Services Acts 1971 and 1975 provide that in certain circumstances a person who receives unsolicited goods can treat them as an unconditional gift. This arises either (i) when six months have elapsed from when the goods were received and the sender has neither taken repossession of them nor unreasonably been refused permission to do so, or (ii) when 30 days have elapsed from when the recipient sent the sender of the goods notice that they are unsolicited. This is supported by criminal sanctions.

---

17   *Selling by Telephone* (Office of Fair Trading, 1984).

There are some specific prohibitions on distant selling techniques in UK law. Thus the Consumer Credit Act 1974 makes the sending of circulars to minors an offence[18] and prohibits the sending of unsolicited credit tokens.[19] The Financial Services Act 1986 restricts the making of unsolicited calls by personal visit or telephone. Although the making of such calls is not an offence any resulting investment agreement will be rendered unenforceable against the person to whom the call was made.[20]

The Data Protection Act 1984 has a significant impact on distant selling practice. Registered users have to comply with the eight Data Protection Principles set out in schedule 1 of the Act. The First Principle is the most significant in the present context, requiring that personal data be obtained and processed fairly and lawfully. Consent is therefore required before data can be passed on to third parties. In addition, other principles require, *inter alia*, that the purposes for which data is held be specified and that the data should not be used or disclosed in a manner incompatible with such specified purposes. The Act provides a limited exemption for mailing lists held only for the purpose of distributing articles or information, but this exemption is likely to be little used since it requires prior consent, gives the data subject the right to have his or her name removed and only offers limited rights to trade in the data. As most mailers wish to trade their lists they will register under the Act.

The Mailing Preference Service is a voluntary scheme whereby two lists are maintained: the Suppression List includes names and addresses of those individuals who have indicated that they wish to receive less promotional material, whereas the Mailing List covers individuals who have asked to receive information related to special categories of products. Each quarter a Consumer File is sent to mailers who are members of the scheme and they are meant to ensure the current Suppression List is applied to their mailing list. The preferred method is to leave the name on the list, but to apply a suppression marker so that it is not inadvertently added to the list again at a later date. The idea of a similar service for telephone sales has been mooted, but does not presently exist. The Office of Fair Trading has published guidelines for business entitled *Selling by Telephone*.[21]

These matters are also addressed in the British Codes of Advertising Practice and Sales Promotion,[22] which provides guidance on list and

---

[18] S.50.

[19] S.51.

[20] S.56. The Security and Investments Board and the Self–Regulatory Organisations have power to make exemptions from the general regulations: see SIB's Common (Unsolicited Calls) Regulations 1991.

[21] *Op. cit.*

[22] See 10.6.

database practice. The Advertising Association has produced a Code of Practice Covering the use of Personal Data for Advertising and Direct Marketing Purposes. The Direct Marketing Association (DMA)[23] and the Mail Order Traders' Association (MOTA) have Codes of Practice which cover these matters. There is also a National Newspapers Mail Order Protection Scheme (MOPS) Code of Practice, which controls who can advertise mail order goods in national newspapers.

8.3.3 Content of Solicitations

Distant sellers are subject to the general rules on misleading trade descriptions,[24] but also to some specific provisions. Thus the Mail Order Transactions (Information) Order 1976[25] requires that in all written advertisements, circulars or leaflets which invite postal orders requiring payment in advance, there should be a legible description of the name and full business address of the person inviting the order. The Business Advertisements (Disclosure) Order 1977 provides that anyone seeking to sell goods in the course of a business shall not publish or cause to be published an advertisement unless it is reasonably clear from it that the goods are to be sold in the course of a business.[26]

The content of solicitations relating to distant sales is also covered by the self–regulatory codes. Indeed the British Codes of Advertising and Sales Promotion have a special section on distance selling. The Independent Television Code of Practice also contains provisions related specifically to distant selling advertisements and home shopping features. The DMA Code contains rules on solicitations; for example, it requires that any advertisement which could result in the entry into a contractual commitment for goods and services should include a short, simple statement of the essential points of the offer, clearly displayed for the customer to keep. The matter is also covered in the MOTA Code.

---

23 The DMA Code cost the authors £5 to obtain. It was explained that this was charged to everyone who wanted a copy. The authors are a little shocked by this. There are a profusion of codes which are hard to track down and cost money to track down (telephone calls, postage etc.). To add a (not inconsiderable) charge for the Code does little to promote transparency and undermines confidence in self–regulation which appears inaccessible to consumers and their advisers.

24 See Chapter 10.

25 S.I. 1976/1812.

26 S.I. 1977/1918.

8.3.4 Contract Content

The common law does not require contracts to take a particular form, but certain legislation, notably the Consumer Credit Act 1974, does prescribe the form of documents for particular contracts. As already noted the DMA Code does require a short statement of the terms of the offer to be provided; where this cannot be include in the advertisement, but is only possible on an order form, then the statement should be supplied with the goods. The MOTA Code is less stringent simply requiring that the terms of business be so published that they are easily available to all agents and customers.

8.3.5 Right of Withdrawal

The motives for allowing a right of withdrawal in the context of distant selling are more complex than in relation to doorstep selling, where the desire is to allow parties a chance for quiet reflection on a contract struck in the heat of the moment. Removing the danger of rash decision–making certainly plays a part in relation to distant selling, especially where the solicitation is by telephone (which may perhaps be equated to a personal visit) or by an enticing television home shopping feature. This motivation would not explain why the right is extended to mail order sales (for instance, in response to newspaper advertisements or through catalogue sales). Here the policy is far more influenced by a desire to give the consumer an opportunity to assure themselves of the quality of the goods. Thus the right of withdrawal can be seen as an extension of the policy of ensuring that the consumer makes a fully informed choice.

There is no statutory cancellation right applicable to distance sales. However, mail order companies have traditionally allowed consumers to keep goods for a trial period or have offered money–back guarantees. Indeed the MOTA Code recommends that goods should be supplied on not less than 14 days approval. Of course, consumer credit contracts are subject to cooling–off periods, but in the case of consumer credit agreements 'pure' distant sales would be excluded as there is a requirement that there be oral representations made in the presence of the debtor. Certain life insurance contracts are cancellable regardless of whether they are concluded at a distance.[27] Below, we shall see that the introduction of a general cooling–off period is one of the central provisions of the proposed EC Directive on distant selling, but regrettably this will not apply to financial services.

---

[27]   See 75-77, Insurance Companies Act 1982 (and Insurance Companies Regulations 1981, S.I. 1981/1654) and Financial Services (Cancellation) Rules 1989, made under s.51, Financial Services Act, 1986.

8.3.6 Performance

In contracts for the sale and supply of goods and services, where no time for the performance is agreed by the parties, there is an implied term that the goods will be delivered or the service carried out within a reasonable time.[28] In the context of distant sales, these provisions are supplemented by self regulatory rules. Thus the DMA requires that, except in limited circumstances, all advertisements and offers requiring pre–payment should indicate a period for the despatch of the goods of no more than 28 days. The MOPS Code of Practice requires that, subject to certain exceptions, orders be delivered within 28 days and that where this is not possible the customer should be informed of the revised delivery date and offered the option of cancelling the contract. The MOTA Code does not fix a time limit for the satisfaction of orders but does require members to try to ensure as far as possible that goods remain available throughout the life of the catalogue and to notify customers of undue delay, giving them the option to cancel.

8.3.7 Protection of Advance Payments

There is a very real danger to consumers' money in distant selling contracts where pre-payment is required. The danger may consist of fraud, with rogue traders advertising non–existent goods or services, but the greatest danger, however, is the risk of insolvency. This risk is inherent in every transaction requiring a pre–payment, but is exacerbated where consumers are not familiar with the nature of the business they are dealing with, as is frequently the case in distant sales. Companies may be able to reduce the risks to their customers in the event of an insolvency if pre–payments are paid into a separate account and held on trust for the customer.[29] This problem is also tackled by Codes of Practice, most stringently by the MOPS Code of Practice. This Code prohibits 'forward trading' which is the practice under which customer payments are used to purchase goods to satisfy orders. The Code also provides for additional safeguards to be put in place when there is uncertainty about the ability of the advertiser to meet his potential commitments. For instance, this might include (i) where goods advertised are of high value, or (ii) where a large–scale advertising programme is envisaged, or (iii) where there is doubt about an advertiser's solvency. The advertiser might then be required to furnish an indemnity This may take the

---

28 S.29(3), Sale of Goods Act 1979 and s.14, Supply of Goods and Services Act 1982.

29 *Re Kayford Ltd* [1974] 1 WLR 279. Such schemes may run into technical legal problems, however, as there is a requirement to show a sufficient intention to create a trust.

form of a bank guarantee or even the requirement to open a stakeholder account so that the funds are placed in the hands of a trusted third party until the goods are despatched.

8.3.8 Risk

The rules as to when property passes and the related question of who carries the risk of damage to or destruction of goods are considered elsewhere.[30] The result of these rules seems to be that frequently the goods supplied under distant sales contracts will be at the consumer's risk, at least once they are despatched. This harsh rule is alleviated somewhat by the Codes of Practice. Thus the MOTA Code allows the consumer to return goods damaged in transit and obtain a replacement; if no replacement is available the supplier should offer a full refund together with any carriage costs paid.

8.3.9 Draft Directive on Distant Selling[31]

The European Community has shown an interest in regulating distant selling not merely because distant selling is a prevalent practice in the Community, but because of the single market dimensions of distant selling. The single market is intended to help consumers by allowing them to shop wherever in the Community they can find the best deal. Physical constraints mean that cross–border shopping is not a practical possibility for most consumers, save those who live near national borders or when they are on holiday or business trips abroad. Consumers are therefore usually only passive beneficiaries of the single market. They benefit only indirectly from the greater choice and competition resulting from overseas companies being able to establish themselves in their domestic market. Distant selling, especially given the increased use of modern technology, allows the consumer to be an active participant in the single market. A consumer can shop overseas, without leaving their home, simply by using the post, telephone or computer. It is therefore in the Community's interest to foster this sector of the economy so that consumers have the confidence to purchase goods at a distance from any Member State.

Commission Recommendation of 7 April 1992 on distance selling,[32] seeks to promote codes of practice for the protection of consumers in respect of contracts negotiated at a distance. In relation to such contracts, the Codes

---

[30] See 5.4.
[31] See G. Howells, *op. cit.*
[32] OJ 1992 L 156/21.

should have provisions relating to the dissemination of solicitations for custom; the presentation of solicitations; sales promotion; financial security; the right of withdrawal and promoting knowledge of the Code. Recommendations are, however, non–binding and proposals are therefore being made for a Directive which would require Member States to have a floor of consumer protection rights in relation to distant selling, though they would be free to introduce or maintain more stringent measures.[33] One of the most disappointing features of the latest draft of the Directive[34] is that it contains no measures seeking to protect consumers against the risk of bankruptcy. Many consumers will be inhibited from entering into distant sale contracts with overseas suppliers if they are required to make a pre–payment and are unsure as to whether their money is protected in the event of the supplier being fraudulent or insolvent. This protection may in fact exist in many countries, but the advantage of European legislation would be that consumers could be confident that it exists or could seek redress from any Member State which had failed to implement the Directive.[35]

As the final text of the Directive has not yet been settled (and implementation will probably not be required for two years after it has been passed) only a brief outline of its scope and objectives of the Directive is relevant here. The Directive is intended to cover contract between suppliers and consumers which exclusively involve the use of one or more means of communication at a distance. There are several exclusions from the scope of the draft Directive, the most controversial being for financial services.[36] Contracts for supplies of goods for current consumption supplied by roundsmen and contracts for the supply of accommodation, transport, catering and leisure services which are reserved in advance are excluded from the following provisions: (i) those which require information to be provided, (ii) those which give the consumer a seven–day period to withdraw from the contract, and (iii) those which require that goods be supplied within 30 days, unless a different period has been agreed.

Other provisions of the draft Directive give consumers the right to challenge debits made as a result of the fraudulent use of a payment card, prohibit inertia selling and place restrictions on the use of certain means of communication at a distance. In particular, prior consent will be required before consumers are contacted by fax or automatic calling machines.

The draft Directive contains some interesting provisions on redress. In common with many EC directives, there is a provision which requires

---

[33] See 2.3.4
[34] See Doc. 12365/94, CONSOM 67.
[35] See 2.4.2
[36] Mention was made of the need to consider reinforcing consumer protection in respect of distance contracts in the various sectoral directives covering financial services.

Member States to permit public bodies or organisations, recognised under national law as having a legitimate interest in protecting consumers, to take action before courts or administrative bodies. This is similar to the provisions which have led to the Director General of Fair Trading having the right to seek injunctions against misleading advertising[37] and unfair terms.[38] But, it goes further than the Directives which gave rise to those rights of action by requiring Member States to confer upon professional organisations and consumer organisations from other Member States the same rights to act under the same conditions as apply to organisations in their own state. It is unclear how this would apply to the UK if the only body recognised to act is the Director General of Fair Trading. If such a provision is included in the final text, it may exert pressure on the UK to review its policy of not granting standing to consumer organisations to seek injunctions in these types of cases.

8.4 CONCLUSION – THE BALANCING OF INTERESTS

This chapter has looked at two forms of marketing – doorstep and distant selling. In principle there is no reason why consumers should be threatened by either selling technique. Indeed they can be seen as bringing extra choice to consumers, especially those who, for one reason or another (perhaps because of disabilities or family circumstances) do not have easy access to the normal shops. Both techniques, however, have been shown to involve risks of consumers being exploited by disreputable traders. In addition, many forms of distant selling rely on audiovisual communication techniques and electronic payment systems which carry inherent risks even when run by reputable traders. Few people would wish to prohibit doorstep and distant selling,[39] but the consumer's right to safeguards must be recognised. In the long term these safeguards are also essential to traders in these sectors, as they will only flourish if consumers have confidence to buy goods in these unorthodox ways.

---

[37] See 10.6.

[38] See 9.8.

[39] Cf the views of T. Ison discussed at 7.8.

9 Unfair Terms

9.1 RATIONALES FOR CONTROLLING UNFAIR TERMS

In the theoretical caricature of the perfect market, there can be no such thing as a contract term that is unfair. Freely negotiated terms represent the parties' wishes. A term is a term – it cannot be unfair. Both parties have gained from the deal; why else would they have concluded it? To impose legal control over 'unfair' terms involves some value–judgment about the content of a bargain that is divorced from the parties' own perceptions at the time of contracting. Such legal intervention finds its rationale in the imperfections of the market. Realistically, negotiation over terms is not simply a matter of contractual freedom. Many factors obscure the 'purity' of the individual bargain and contribute to the parties' inability to make informed choices.

This suggests that the principal rationale for controlling terms that are 'unfair' lies in the imbalance between supplier and consumer. The capacity of the consumer to bargain over terms which he or she perceives as not being in his or her interest is attenuated in modern economic conditions. Some situations offer the consumer the choice of 'take it or leave it'. More fundamentally still, the consumer may not even know of some conditions. The use of the standard form contract, in particular, may obscure from the consumer the nature of the bargain, especially where terms are buried in small print. In some circumstances, the consumer may be referred for further information about contractual terms to a separate document which is not readily available. This is common practice in the case of tickets.

It remains a theme of this book that the identification of inequality is but a starting point. After all, the inequality at stake here seems incapable of elimination in modern market conditions. The elaboration of a legal response depends on deciding on the specific consequences of inequality which call for control.

However, the shaper of legal policy must be sophisticated. It was explained in Chapter 1 that the initial impression that the standard form contract prevents the consumer from participating actively in contract negotiation may be only part of the picture.[1] Often individual negotiation will be time–consuming and costly, and thus in the interests of neither trader nor consumer. Standard form contracts accelerate the process. In a competitive market, at least, such contracts ought to allow traders to cut costs which should then be passed on to consumers through lower prices. There may be

---

[1]   Chapter 1.3.4.

costs and benefits to intervening in standard form contracts and the law needs to be shaped accordingly.

Should the law catch negotiated contracts too? On the one hand, one might suppose that the presence of negotiation establishes the reality of a freely concluded bargain and that intervention is not required. On the other hand, if one assumes an endemic power imbalance, the fact that the contract was not drawn up in advance, but instead settled between those parties, does not mean that it is truly a reflection of wishes. Negotiation may simply provide the supplier with greater opportunity to exploit his or her superior economic strength. The law must choose its scope for intervention.

The type of term which in English law has aroused most attention is the exclusion clause. Typically, such a term excludes the liability of the supplier for things that go wrong. Consumers may find that they have no effective redress under a contract when they do not get what they expected. The perception is that the exclusion clause requires legal control because the consumer may be unaware of the claims he or she is surrendering by 'agreeing' to a contract containing the clause. As a general perception, it may indeed be true that the phenomenon of exclusion clauses has the capacity to damage the consumer interest. However, exclusion clauses have a function to play which may help the consumer. They help to allocate risk. If a supplier knows where the loss will fall, the price can be fixed accordingly. A consumer prepared to assume risk under a contract may be offered a lower price. Exclusion clauses allocate risk and permit the parties to decide in advance where they will stand if things go wrong. Typically the party bearing the risk can then decide on insurance cover; without an exclusion clause both parties would wastefully need to seek protection. Exclusion clauses may simply be bought and sold; to outlaw them would be to diminish consumer choice. This positive view of the function of the exclusion clause depends on the consumer being adequately informed about the process, which will frequently not be the case. This suggests a need for a legal intervention that is nuanced and, if possible, attuned to the level of information that a consumer has about the clauses on offer.[2]

9.2 JUDICIAL INTERVENTION

In English law, the judicial response to unfair terms has been indirect. The English judiciary has shunned a general jurisdiction to pronounce on the fairness of bargains. Lord Denning's attempt to move the law in such a

---

[2]   See generally D. Yates, *Exclusion Clauses in Contracts* (Sweet and Maxwell, 2nd ed, 1982).

direction in *Lloyds Bank v Bundy*,[3] at least in situations of inequality of bargaining power, has been resisted by the higher courts, not least because of the perception that it is for Parliament, not the courts, to decide where such intervention is proper and what form it should take.[4] This judicial reluctance is to a large extent the corollary of the notion of freedom of contract. The parties determine the bargain; the courts enforce those choices. On this model, fairness is not a matter for the courts. English contract law enforces promises where they represent an agreement, are supported by consideration and where the parties have the intention to create legal relations. Once the deal falls within these parameters, it is enforceable as a contract, unless vitiated, for example, by a misrepresentation or the influence of duress. These are the bounds of the judicial role and they are not necessarily congruent with notions of fairness.

However, elements of fairness may infiltrate judge–made contract law. Chapter 1 of this book demonstrates that the 'hands–off' judicial role is no longer an adequate depiction of modern contract law, in the consumer sphere at least. Elements of fairness permeate the law, even though it is controversial whether these elements are sensibly put together to form a coherent general requirement of fairness as a prerequisite to contracting.[5] The determination of whether a contract has been formed, on what terms and whether it is vitiated may allow an indirect reference to notions adjacent to fairness. The doctrine of economic duress has connections with notions of fairness in dealing. Where an agreement is procured as a result of pressure, the party subjected to that pressure may be able to have it set aside. The problem is the identification of where the margin lies between undue pressure and acceptably tough commercial tactics.[6] It would be unusual to find such issues arising in the context of a consumer transaction. The consumer's problems are more likely to lie in inadequate information and limited choice caused by the nature of the modern market, rather than in duress inflicted by an individual supplier. For similar reasons the role of equitable protection

---

3   [1975] QB 326.

4   Eg Lord Scarman in *National Westminster Bank v Morgan* [1985] AC 686. For discussion see S. Thal, 'The Inequality of Bargaining Power Doctrine' (1988) 8 *Oxford JLS* 17.

5   H. Collins, *The Law of Contract* (Butterworths, 1994) strives in this direction; see further Chapter 1.3 above.

6   Cf. *Pau On v Lau Yiu Long* [1980] AC 614; *Atlas Express Ltd v Kafko Ltd* [1989] QB 833.

against undue influence[7] has a role to play that lies outwith the scope of this book.

The rules of incorporation of terms are capable of being moulded into an indirect method of expressing a view of fairness in the negotiating process. It is possible for judges to exclude 'unfair terms' by use of the rules of incorporation, although one would not expect to see an explicit recognition that this is what was happening. So a term will be part of the contract and enforceable as a term only where sufficient has been done to bring it to the attention of the party against whom it is to be enforced. This seems to occur especially where the judge is of the view that real negotiation and freedom of contract are missing. This may be especially appropriate in relation to standard form contracts and is evident in the robust approach of Lord Denning MR in *Thornton v Shoe Lane Parking*.[8] The more unusual or onerous the term, the more active the steps that are expected of a supplier, on pain of denying enforceability to the term. The most potent recent illustration of this technique in the UK came in *Interfoto v Stiletto*.[9] The Court of Appeal held that a 'particularly onerous or unusual'[10] contractual condition, which would not generally be known to the other party, would not be enforceable unless the party seeking to rely on that condition could show that it had fairly been brought to the other party's attention. This test was not met and Interfoto accordingly could not rely on the clause. The case involved business parties. It is probable that in the consumer context the judiciary would be all the more tempted to adopt such rigorous scrutiny of the enforceability of clauses that are out of the ordinary and/or onerous.[11] This message clearly emerges from the Canadian decision in *Tilden Rent–a–Car v Clendinning*[12] where even the fact that the consumer had signed the printed form did not deter the Ontario Court of Appeal from withholding enforceability from a clause that was 'unusual and onerous'[13] and inconsistent with the true object of the contract. The company had made no attempt to alert the consumer to the clause, even though its booking clerk

---

7   Cf. *National Westminster Bank plc v Morgan* [1985] AC 686; *Barclays Bank plc v O'Brien* [1993] 4 All ER 417; *CIBC Mortgages plc v Pitt* [1993] 4 All ER 433.

8   Chapter 1.3.5.

9   [1988] 2 WLR 615, [1988] 1 All ER 348, Chapter 1.3.5 above.

10   Per Dillon LJ WLR 620e, All ER 352f. Note that a condition need not be both onerous *and* unusual; a condition that is usual in the trade, but onerous, would still require elucidation in so far as the other party would not generally be aware of it.

11   Cf Chapter 1.3 above on the deeper interventionism of consumer contract law in comparison with commercial contract law.

12   (1978) 83 DLR (3d) 400.

13   Dubin JA at 407; semble both elements must be present, contrast n.10 above!

was well aware that he had not read through the form in its entirety as a result of the haste that is normal in car rental.

There is a limit to what judges can do with such rules and there is a limit to what they are prepared to do. In any event this is not a direct check on the fairness of the substance of a bargain, so that although this method may be sufficient to exclude a minor term that is not properly incorporated, it will be useless to tackle a wickedly imbalanced clause which is plainly part of the contract on the rules of incorporation.

A further judicial device used indirectly to control terms, especially exclusion clauses and cognate terms, lies in the insistence that, even where such terms are incorporated, any ambiguity is construed against the party wishing to rely on them. This is the *contra proferentem* rule. For example in *Hollier v Rambler Motors Ltd*[14] a clause excluding liability for 'damage caused by fire to customers' cars on the premises' was held to be ineffective to exclude liability for negligently inflicted fire damage in the absence of explicit reference to negligence. This decision comes close to finding ambiguity where none exists, rather than construing ambiguity in a manner favourable to the party against whom the clause is being enforced.[15] It comes close to rewriting the contract in what the court perceives to be a fairer manner. This trend of intervention disguised as interpretation reached its zenith in the determination of the courts to deny effect even to clearly worded exemption clauses where the result would be to rob the other party of the essence of what he or she was supposed to be receiving under the contract.[16] The *contra proferentem* approach is still a part of English law, but the contortions adopted by the judiciary are now much less marked. Indeed there is explicit recognition that the advent of legislative control renders judicial activism on this scale inappropriate. The courts now feel that they should not strain the process of interpretation of contractual terms in order to avoid what might seem to them to be odd results. *Photo Productions v Securicor* represents a strong statement of judicial deference to the parties' bargain. Lord Diplock commented that 'the reports are full of cases in which what would appear to be very strained constructions have been placed upon exclusion clauses, mainly in what today would be called consumer contracts and contracts of adhesion. ... [A]ny need for this kind of judicial distortion of

---

[14]   [1972] 2 QB 71.

[15]   Cf E. Barendt (1972) 85 *MLR* 644 for an insight into thinking prior to legislative intervention.

[16]   The so-called fundamental breach doctrine exemplified by *Karsales v Wallis* [1956] 1 WLR 936.

the English language has been banished by Parliament's having made these kinds of contracts subject to the Unfair Contract Terms Act 1977.'[17]

The litigation in *Photo Productions v Securicor* involved commercial parties and the House of Lords declined to strain the interpretation of clear words which were 'fairly susceptible of one meaning only'.[18] So the fact that one of Securicor's employees had burned down Photo Productions' factory did not deprive Securicor of the shelter of an appropriately worded exclusion clause. The failure of Photo Productions' claim for over £600,000 in damages does not seem peculiar once one appreciates that the exclusion clause represented the parties' chosen risk allocation, on which depended contract price and purchase of insurance cover. Without the clause, Securicor would have charged more and bought insurance. It was more efficient to let Photo Productions use its intimate knowledge of the condition of its factory to determine how much insurance to buy. The fact of employing Securicor would doubtless have led to a reduction in the cost of that insurance greater than the price paid to Securicor for its services. A decision which disallowed Securicor the protection of the exclusion clause would have defeated the parties' intention at time of contracting.

Absent statutory intervention, the temptation to adopt an activist judicial approach in the consumer sphere might on first impression seem likely to remain on foot, given that full negotiation and openness are less likely to prevail than in the commercial setting. However, as the remarks of Lord Diplock in *Photo Productions v Securicor* indicate, the advent of the Unfair Contract Terms Act 1977 renders it improbable that judges will ever again resort to the past extremes of interpretation. Legislative intervention has reduced the perceived need and, for some, has also cast doubt on the legitimacy of judicial creativity in the field. Nevertheless, it still holds true that instances of genuine ambiguity will be resolved against the party seeking to rely on an exclusion or cognate clause, which will normally operate in the consumer's favour.

9.3 PUBLIC INTERVENTION TO CONTROL UNFAIR TERMS

The common law's indirect methods of controlling unfair terms remain in place. They retain relevance. An unincorporated clause is ineffective and, unfair or not, it will not bind as part of the contract. Therefore consideration

---

17   [1980] AC 827, 851; cf Lord Wilberforce 843.

18   Lord Diplock *ibid*. In similar vein, *Ailsa Craig Fishing Co Ltd v Malvern Fishing Co Ltd* [1983] 1 WLR 964; *George Mitchell (Chesterhall) Ltd v Finney Lock Seeds Ltd* [1983] 3 WLR 163.

of the common law rules logically precedes application of the statutory controls. However, with regard to exclusion clauses, the focus of English law for nearly 20 years has been on a direct form of control of unfairness exercised by the Unfair Contract Terms Act 1977 (commonly known as UCTA). This Act envisages a direct challenge to terms which are indisputably part of the contract between the parties and places in the hands of the judiciary the power to rule (some) terms unenforceable.[19] The availability of this power has reduced the judicial motivation to use indirect routes to attack clauses perceived to be unfair.[20]

The 1977 Act is one of two sources of direct control over unfair terms in English law. The second source lies in the Unfair Terms in Consumer Contracts Regulations 1994.[21]

These Regulations represent the United Kingdom's implementation of the EC's Directive on Unfair Terms in Consumer Contracts,[22] adopted in March 1993 and the deadline for implementation of which was the end of 1994. It applies to all relevant contracts concluded after 31 December 1994. This measure is made under Article 100a EC, which links it to the process of establishing the Community's internal market.[23] Its Preamble explains that disparity between national laws distorts competition between suppliers in the market and that ignorance of the law in other Member States deters consumers from direct purchases in them. The Directive attempts to distil acceptable common principles from diverse national backgrounds and its character as a minimum measure, permitting stricter national rules, is a realistic reflection of that diversity.

As a matter of Community law, the UK's 1994 implementing Regulations must be interpreted in order to conform to the Directive.[24] Accordingly the Regulations cannot be viewed in isolation from the parent Directive. The description below reflects this constitutional relationship by referring in its detailed examination to the 'Regulations/Directive' in order to emphasise the necessary association between the two. Reference is made to the Directive alone, rather than to the implementing Regulations, where comment is directed at its broad structure and policy objectives.

---

19 There are some other specific statutory controls scattered throughout the law. On consumer credit see Chapter 7.12.

20 For evaluation of the Act, see J. Adams and R. Brownsword, 'The Unfair Contract Terms Act: A Decade of Discretion' (1988) 104 *LQR* 94; H. Beale, 'Unfair Contracts in Britain and Europe' (1989) 42 *CLP* 197.

21 S.I. 1994 No. 3159.

22 Dir. 93/13 OJ 1993 L95/29.

23 Chapter 2.3.3.

24 Chapter 2.4.2.

The two sources of control over unfair terms in English law are not coextensive. In some respects the Unfair Contract Terms Act is the more extensive. That the Regulations/Directive exercise a broader control than the Act in other respects means that the implementation of the Directive in the UK has significantly extended the scope of legal intervention. The criteria for control under the Act and the Regulations/Directive have much in common, but they are not identical. This partial duplication creates a rather unhappy pattern, causing confusion among both commercial parties and consumers.[25] It also adds to the costs of compliance by requiring firms to take additional legal advice. The deeper the divergence between the controls envisaged by the two regimes, the trickier the handling of the law will prove to be. The desirable route would be the consolidation of both regimes into a single statute that would reflect the current state of the law controlling unfair contract terms. However, pressures on Parliamentary time precluded this option in the UK, although future consolidation has not been ruled out.

Constitutionally, the result of this double control is as follows. In some areas the Act alone applies. In other areas the Regulations/Directive alone apply. In areas where both the Act and the Regulations implementing the Directive apply, both controls coexist. The Regulations/Directive apply, but so too does the Act. Any controls under the Act that are more stringent or more extensive than the Regulations/Directive may be enforced, provided only that that neither frustrates the achievement of the objectives of the Directive nor conflicts with primary Community law such as the rules governing the free movement of goods under Article 30 EC.[26] The Directive, a minimum measure, does not pre-empt national initiatives which offer more stringent protection,[27] nor does it affect national measures outwith its scope. So, for example, although the Directive does not address individually negotiated terms, it offers no objection to national rules which extend control into that area. Such extended control exists under the Act and is not affected by the implementation of the Directive. Where the scope of the Act and the Regulations/Directive overlaps, but the latter apply a stricter control, the national controls are correspondingly strengthened. However, it is not clear

---

25   Cf brief comment by F. Reynolds (1994) 110 *LQR* 1; R. Bragg (1994) 2 *Consum LJ* 29.

26   The ruling in C–267 and C–268/91 *Keck and Mithouard* renders it highly improbable that Article 30 would affect such evenhanded national laws; Chapter 2.2 above.

27   Article 8 Dir. Contrast the General Product Safety Directive which is not minimum and does pre–empt national rules; Chapter 12.

whether the Regulations/Directive *do* envisage a stricter control test than the Act.[28]

9.4 THE SCOPE OF THE UK AND EC INTERVENTIONS COMPARED AND CONTRASTED

The principal differences between the two regimes lie in three areas. These are explained in this section in advance of a more detailed account of the scope of the law, presented in section 9.5 below.

9.4.1 Types of Contract Covered

The Regulations/Directive catch only unfair terms in contracts 'concluded between a seller or supplier and a consumer'.[29] The Act catches some contracts which are not consumer contracts. On this point, the implementation of the Directive has buttressed English law, but English law is already more ambitious in the scope of contracts covered.

The Act's extension into commercial contracts may readily be explained if one accepts that the primary motivation for control is the fact of economic imbalance. That may apply to the supplier/consumer relationship, but also to the relationship between large and small firms. One would nonetheless expect to see a different type of control over commercial contracts as opposed to consumer contracts, and this is reflected in the Act.[30] The Regulations/Directive do not intrude into the commercial sphere. This does not mean that the rationales for controlling (some) business bargains have been rejected at Community level. In fact the limited scope of the Directive is largely a reflection of its development in the European Commission's Consumer Policy Service, which has limited practical opportunity to move beyond the consumer sphere. Moreover, the ambitions of the Directive dwindled in the face of the political pressures which for a decade delayed the final adoption of a measure affecting only terms in consumer contracts that have not been individually negotiated.[31]

---

[28] 9.6.1.3 below explores the potential in this direction.
[29] Reg. 3(1) / Article 1(1) Dir.
[30] Cf 9.6 below.
[31] The Parliament called for a Directive in the field in 1980 (OJ 1980 C291/35); in 1984 the Commission published a discussion paper (COM (84) 55); in September 1990, the Commission published a proposal (OJ 1990 C243/2), revised in March 1992 (OJ 1992 C73/7). Final adoption was in March 1993. H. Brandner and P. Ulmer offer

9.4.2 Types of Term Covered

The Regulations/Directive catch only terms that have not been individually negotiated. Terms that have been individually negotiated are untouched. Earlier drafts of the Directive had proposed a wider control, but criticism of intervention into terms individually agreed by the parties resulted in the more modest reach of the Directive as finally adopted.[32] The Unfair Contract Terms Act is more ambitious, being capable of catching even negotiated terms. The Act is also broader than the Regulations/Directive because it catches non–contractual notices, not simply contractual terms to which the Regulations/Directive are confined.

With regard to the substance of the term, rather than the manner of its negotiation, the Act is more restricted, being limited to exclusion and cognate terms in contracts. The careful definitions found in the Act of terms caught are absent from the Regulations/Directive. The Regulations/Directive catch all terms in consumer contracts that have not been individually negotiated. On this point the Regulations/Directive are considerably more ambitious than pre–existing controls under English law.

This pattern creates odd overlaps and odd loopholes. A clause such as that held unincorporated in *Interfoto v Stiletto*[33] would, had it been held today to have contractual force, be unassailable under the Act and the Regulations/Directive. The Act would not touch it because it was not an exclusion clause. The Regulations/Directive would not touch it because it did not appear in a consumer contract.

9.4.3 The Control Test

The Unfair Contract Terms Act 1977 invalidates some clauses absolutely and subjects others to a judicially applied test of reasonableness. The Regulations/Directive do not invalidate any clauses automatically – there is no 'blacklist'.[34] A term covered by the Regulations/Directive shall be regarded as unfair if it is a term which 'contrary to the requirement of good

---

critical comment on the 1990 draft at (1991) 28 *CMLRev* 647, which is illuminating especially in the light of subsequent changes made before adoption. Cf. also N. Reich, 'From Contract to Trade Practices Law: Protection of Consumers' Economic Interests by the EC' in T. Wilhelmsson (ed), *Perspectives of Critical Contract Law* (Dartmouth, 1993).

[32] Cf note 31 above; especially critical comments by H. Brandner and P. Ulmer.

[33] Note 9 above.

[34] Earlier drafts of the Directive *did* contain such a blacklist; cf note 31 above.

faith causes a significant imbalance in the parties' rights and obligations arising under the contract, to the detriment of the consumer.'

A question of critical importance is how closely aligned the tests of reasonableness under the Act and unfairness under the Regulations/Directive will prove to be. They are certainly not far apart. They invite consideration of similar aspects of the bargain, such as any imbalance in knowledge between the parties. However, the role of good faith may steer the control originating in the Directive away from the notion of reasonableness. Although the latter is familiar to the English lawyer, the former is foreign.[35] Good faith has a developed meaning in continental European systems, which may come to influence its interpretation under the Directive, which then must transmit into the English legal system. For it should be appreciated that it is not a task for English judges alone to resolve the relationship between the Act's test of reasonableness and the Directive's notion of unfairness. The authoritative source of interpretation for the Directive is the European Court, via the Article 177 preliminary reference procedure. If the European Court develops a distinctive interpretative approach to the control test, any consequent gulf between the Act and the Regulations/Directive will require closing by careful handling at domestic level.[36] Implementation is a continuing process. It is this vital need to be aware of the European Court in the background that dictates the insistence in this Chapter on using the admittedly cumbersome label 'Regulations/Directive'.

There follows a more detailed examination of the scope of legal control over unfair terms. This necessarily requires an elaboration of both the 1977 Act and the Regulations implementing the Directive, which, it bears repetition, must be interpreted in order to conform to the Directive.[37] The explanation is necessarily rendered complicated by the lack of integration between the two systems. Moreover, the lack of practical experience in handling the Directive, whose deadline for implementation expired only at the end of 1994, renders comment in part speculative.

It was explained in Chapter 1 that the less straightforward and accessible consumer protection law becomes on paper, the weaker its practical impact in helping the average consumer. The fact that there are two regimes and a lack of precision within both means that, regrettably, control of unfair terms in the UK is a prime candidate for assessment from that dispiriting perspective. For the proponent of interventionist consumer law, the only consolation in the failure of the UK to consolidate existing law with the controls drawn from the EC Directive lies in the risk that, in the current

---

35 Although it has a developed meaning in the specialist area of insurance contracts.
36 Further below, 9.6.1.3.
37 9.3 above.

deregulatory climate, the process of consolidation would have provided an opportunity to slice away aspects of existing protection which the Directive does not mandate the UK to maintain.[38]

9.5 THE SCOPE OF CONTROL

9.5.1 Exclusion of Liability for Negligence

Section 2 of the Unfair Contract Terms Act deals with attempts to exclude liability for negligence.[39] It catches not only contract terms, but also other notices[40] too. Section 2(1) declares that '[a] person cannot by reference to any contract term or to a notice given to persons generally or to particular persons exclude or restrict his liability for death or personal injury resulting from negligence'. In section 2(2) a more nuanced control is created over exclusion of liability for negligence resulting in other types of harm. Section 2(2) provides that 'In the case of other loss or damage, a person cannot so exclude or restrict his liability for negligence except in so far as the term or notice satisfies the requirement of reasonableness.'

Section 2, like sections 3–7 of the Act, applies only to business liability; private sales are excluded.[41] Business liability is defined in sections 1(3) and 14. The key notions are that it covers liability for breach of obligations or duties arising from things done or to be done by a person in the course of a business (whether his or her own business or another's);[42] or from the occupation of premises used for business purposes of the occupier. For the purposes of section 2, it matters not what status the other party holds. Both business and consumer parties may benefit. By contrast, it will be seen below that in sections 3–7, the status of the other party is critical to the scope of protection; the consumer is more favourably treated than the business person.

The Regulations implementing the Directive operate differently. A term in a contract caught by the regime – that is, a term in a consumer contract that has not been individually negotiated – which excludes liability for negligence is then tested against the notion of unfairness. This is amplified in Schedule 3 to the Regulations, drawn from an Annex to the Directive, which acts as a 'grey list'. In this list for guidance one finds, *inter alia*, precisely the sorts of clauses controlled by section 2 of the Act. The very first term in the

---

38 Cf Chapter 1, especially 1.9.3.
39 Defined in s.1(1).
40 Defined in s.14.
41 Subject to one exception in s.6(4), 9.5.5 below.
42 See 9.6.2 below on 'course of a business'.

list compares with that invalidated by section 2(1). No clause is automatically invalidated by the Regulations/Directive, in contrast to section 2(1) of the Act. Probably most, if not all, courts called on to apply the control envisaged by the Regulations/Directive would find such an exclusion unfair and unenforceable. However, for English law purposes, because the Directive does not pre–empt more stringent measures of national protection, section 2(1)'s rule of invalidity continues properly to be applied, notwithstanding the Community intervention.

9.5.2 Exclusion of Liability for Breach of Contract

Section 3 of the Act imposes a reasonableness test over terms that exclude or restrict a party's liability when in breach of contract. The same reasonableness test is applied to terms that are the basis of an entitlement to render a contractual performance substantially different from that which was reasonably expected or to render no performance at all. A term allowing a holiday company to switch a tourist booked for Spain to Scunthorpe would be controlled by section 3.

Via the Regulations that implement the Directive, such terms are subjected to the unfairness test, provided they appear in consumer contracts and have not been individually negotiated. Several of the terms mentioned in the Schedule to the Regulations/Annex to the Directive would also fall within the scope of section 3 of the Act.[43] However, the Regulations/Directive are wider and catch terms that would escape section 3.

The section 3 control is exercised over a party falling within the defined sphere of business liability who wishes to enforce a term against another contracting party who deals as consumer (defined, 9.6.2 below) or on the other's written standard terms of business (which goes undefined). Here is a hybrid control. Consumer contracts are caught, whether or not they are individually negotiated. Commercial deals are caught,[44] but only where written standard terms of business are concerned. The Act here exercises a broader control than the Regulations/Directive, going beyond the consumer sphere. Even commercial contract law is not unscathed by regulatory intervention.[45]

---

[43] Eg (b), (c), (j), (k).
[44] Subject to an exception for international supply contracts, as defined in s.26.
[45] Cf Chapter 1, especially 1.3.

9.5.3 Indemnity Clauses

Section 4 of the Unfair Contract Terms Act subjects to the reasonableness test terms concerning the enforcement of indemnity clauses by a person with business liability against a person dealing as consumer. This covers indemnification of 'another person (whether a party to the contract or not) in respect of liability that may be incurred by the other for negligence or breach of contract'. The Regulations/Directive subject such standard form terms arising in consumer contracts to the unfairness test.

9.5.4 Guarantees

Section 5 of the Unfair Contract Terms Act invalidates terms, rather than simply putting them to scrutiny against the test of reasonableness. Section 5 covers 'guarantee' of consumer goods and is deliberately widely drawn.[46] 'In the case of goods of a type ordinarily supplied for private use or consumption, where loss or damage arises from the goods proving defective while in consumer use[47] and results from the negligence of a person concerned in the manufacture or distribution of the goods, liability for the loss or damage cannot be excluded or restricted by reference to any contract term or notice contained in or operating by reference to a guarantee of the goods.' Section 5(3) provides that section 5 does not apply as between parties to a contract under or in pursuance of which possession or ownership of the goods passed; in such circumstances other sections, such as sections 2 and 6, would apply. Section 5's main target is the manufacturer's guarantee.

Section 5 is a rather broad provision and is designed to do away with the old habit of presenting the consumer with an apparently attractive 'Guarantee' which, on closer inspection, actually grossly undermines contractual or other rights. It is phrased to catch guarantees whether contractual or not. The Regulations/Directive, by contrast, catch contract terms alone.

9.5.5 Exclusion of Statutorily Implied Terms

Section 6(1) invalidates terms excluding or restricting liability for breach of obligations arising from section 12 of the Sale of Goods Act 1979 and

---

46   On guarantee, s.5(2)(b).
47   Widely defined s.5(2)(a).

section 8 of the Supply of Goods (Implied Terms) Act 1973.[48] These are the implied undertakings as to title. Section 6(1) operates in all types of transaction, consumer or business. Section 6(2) is narrower in its scope, benefiting only a person dealing as a consumer (defined, 9.6.2 below). It invalidates terms excluding or restricting liability for breach of obligations arising from sections 13, 14 or 15 of the Sale of Goods Act 1979 and the corresponding sections of the Supply of Goods (Implied Terms) Act 1973, which are sections 9, 10 or 11. Then, according to section 6(3), exclusion or restriction of precisely these same liabilities is subjected to the reasonableness test where applied against a person dealing otherwise than as a consumer. The distinction between sections 6(2) and 6(3) shows that the consumer receives more extensive shelter from exclusion clauses than the commercial party, but that the Act does not address consumer protection alone. In commercial contracts, one might anticipate that the closer to equality the economic relationship, the more likely that the reasonableness test will be satisfied.[49] This permits account to be taken of the nuances of economic imbalance on a case–by–case basis.

A final twist to section 6 is that it applies not simply to business liabilities within section 1(3), but also to those arising under any contract of sale of goods or hire–purchase agreement.[50] Private sales are caught, although the use of exclusion clauses in such transactions is doubtless uncommon; in any event the statutorily implied terms have a limited role to play in private transactions.[51]

The Regulations/Directive do not catch the commercial contracts over which the Act exercises control because of the EC regime's limitation to consumer contracts. The Regulations/Directive would control such terms where they appear in consumer contracts and have not been individually negotiated with reference to the unfairness test. As explained, in so far as the Act is stricter and broader than the Regulations/Directive, its continued application is not called into question by virtue of the Directive's minimum formulation. The invalidation of exclusion clauses achieved by sections 6(1) and 6(2) remains secure.

---

[48] Exclusion clauses in contracts under which goods pass, but which are not governed by the law of sale of goods or hire purchase, are controlled under s.7 UCTA. S.8 of the Act also inserts a new s.3 into the Misrepresentation Act 1967 dealing with exclusion of liability for misrepresentation.

[49] See further on the reasonableness test, 9.6.1.1 below.

[50] S.6(4) UCTA 1977.

[51] Chapter 4.

9.6 DEFINITIONAL ISSUES

At least three critically important definitional points arise, which in the Unfair Contract Terms Act 1977 are delayed until later sections. First, what is at stake in the application of the apparently vague 'reasonableness' test? Second, who deals as a consumer? Third, what is a clause that 'excludes or restricts liability'? The first two questions have parallels in the Regulations/Directive, although the third does not have a precise equivalent, because all terms, not simply exclusion clauses, are capable of being caught by the Regulations/Directive.

9.6.1 The Control Test

9.6.1.1 The Unfair Contract Terms Act 1977

Section 11 of the Act amplifies the 'reasonableness' test. It is open–ended. The essence of the test is that it depends on the circumstances at the time of contracting. It is for a party claiming that the term or notice satisfies the test to show that it does; this is normally likely to be advantageous to the consumer as the party against whom the term is typically enforced.[52]

Regrettably, the Act chooses not simply to sketch an all–embracing reasonableness test. Section 11 splits up the control. In relation to a contract term, the term 'shall have been a fair and reasonable one to be included having regard to the circumstances which were, or ought reasonably to have been, known to or in the contemplation of the parties when the contract was made.' In the application of the reasonableness test under sections 6 or 7 (only), 'regard shall be had in particular to the matters specified in Schedule 2'. Then, in relation to a notice without contractual effect, section 11 directs that it 'should be fair and reasonable to allow reliance on it, having regard to all the circumstances obtaining when the liability arose or (but for the notice) would have arisen.' Under section 11(4), it is provided that in applying the reasonableness test to a restriction of liability to a specified sum of money, regard shall be had, *inter alia*, to the resources available to the party seeking restriction to meet the liability should it arise and how far it was open to cover himself by insurance.

It is doubtful whether anything useful is served by preferring this set of three rambling subsections[53] over a single, broadly–phrased depiction of

---

[52]   S.11(5).
[53]   Ss.11(1)–11(3).

reasonableness.[54] Such scepticism seems to be shared by the courts. Section 11(2) of the Act restricts the use of the guidelines in Schedule 2 in making a reasonableness assessment to the control exercised by sections 6 and 7, but in practice their impact has been felt more generally.[55] The guidelines for the application of the reasonableness test contained in Schedule 2 are as follows:

(a)   the strength of the bargaining position of the parties relative to each other, taking into account (among other things) alternative means by which the customer's requirements could have been met;
(b)   whether the customer received an inducement to agree to the term, or in accepting it had an opportunity of entering into a similar contract with other persons, but without having to accept a similar term;
(c)   whether the customer knew or ought reasonably to have known of the existence and extent of the term (having regard, among other things, to any custom of the trade and any previous course of dealing between the parties);
(d)   where the term excludes or restricts any relevant liability if some condition is not complied with, whether it was reasonable at the time of the contract to expect that compliance with that condition would be practicable;
(e)   whether the goods were manufactured, processed or adapted to the special order of the customer.

The courts have a wide jurisdiction to make their assessment. These guidelines are not exhaustive. It seems plain that the scope of consumer choice is a central element in the assessment. Suppliers are induced to offer a range of prices. One would suppose that the tighter the exclusion, the lower the price – in a competitive market, at least. Provided a genuine and transparent choice is made available, a supplier is entitled to expect that such marketing techniques will push a court towards a finding that the clauses are reasonable.[56] Guideline (c) also pushes in the direction of greater transparency. The rules of incorporation already dictate a need for openness;[57] even where the term is incorporated on this test, an even greater

---

54   The disjointed pattern is largely attributable to the accretion of legal controls statute–by–statute; UCTA was not the first adventure in this field, although it is the widest–ranging.
55   Cf dicta of Slade LJ in *Phillips Products Ltd v Hyland* [1987] 2 All ER 620, 628.
56   Absence of choice was a factor in the finding of unreasonableness in *Woodman*, 1.5.1 below.
57   Especially *Interfoto v Stiletto* 1.3.5 above.

level of openness may be required by the Act on pain of finding a term unreasonable and unenforceable.

In *Smith v Eric S Bush*, Lord Griffiths commented on the impossibility of drawing up an exhaustive list of relevant factors.[58] This indicates that it is inappropriate to accumulate case law as binding precedent. Abstract points of law are not at stake and the role of the appellate courts is limited.[59] Individual contracts and the circumstances in which they are made vary. However, Lord Griffiths provided a list of matters which should 'always be considered'. These cover comparison of bargaining power; practical opportunity to seek alternative advice; difficulty of the task undertaken in respect of which exclusion of liability is sought; and the practical consequences of the decision on the question of reasonableness. The final factor strongly suggests that the implications of a decision on the cost of insurance should play a part in the reasoning, beyond the specific reference to insurance in section 11(4) in the context of limitation of liability.[60] Plainly the application of the test demands a balancing of several factors and one would seldom find a case in which the pointers are all in one direction.[61]

9.6.1.2 The Regulations/Directive

The control test in the Regulations/Directive provides that a term covered by the regime shall be regarded as unfair if 'contrary to the requirement of good faith [it] causes a significant imbalance in the parties' rights and obligations arising under the contract, to the detriment of the consumer.'[62]

Schedule 2 to the Regulations, reflecting material in the Directive's recitals, directs that:

> 'In making an assessment of good faith, regard shall be had in particular to;
> (a) the strength of the bargaining positions of the parties;
> (b) whether the consumer had an inducement to agree to the term;

---

[58]   [1990] 1 AC 831.

[59]   Cf Lord Bridge in *George Mitchell v Finney Lock* n.18 above; applied by the C.A. in *Phillips Products Ltd v Hyland* [1987] 2 All ER 620.

[60]   See above in this sub–section, 9.6.1.1.

[61]   For illustrations of the practical application of the test, see eg *RW Green v Cade Bros Farms* [1978] 1 Lloyd's Rep 602; *Singer Co Ltd v Tees and Hartlepool Port Authority* [1988] 2 Lloyd's Rep 164; *Smith v Eric S Bush* n.58 above.

[62]   Reg. 4(1), Art. 3(1) Dir.

(c) whether the goods or services were sold or supplied to the special order of the consumer, and
(d) the extent to which the seller or supplier has dealt fairly and equitably with the consumer.'

Schedule 3 to the UK's Regulations, reflecting an Annex to the Directive, provides an indicative and non–exhaustive list of the terms which may be regarded as unfair. This, then, is neither a black nor white but a grey list. Courts may use it as interpretative aid.

Regulation 4(2), reflecting Article 4 of the Directive, provides that unfairness shall be assessed 'taking into account the nature of the goods or services for which the contract was concluded and referring, as at the time of conclusion of the contract, to all the circumstances attending the conclusion of the contract and to all the other terms of the contract or of another contract on which it is dependent'.

Regulation 3(2) provides that:

'In so far as it is in plain, intelligible language, no assessment shall be made of the fairness of any term which:
(a) defines the main subject matter of the contract, or
(b) concerns the adequacy of the price or remuneration, as against the goods or services sold or supplied.'

This is a reworking of a notion that the Directive, in Article 4 and its Preamble, deals with in a regrettably obscure manner. Unfairness does not arise simply where goods or services are overpriced, provided the relevant terms are in plain intelligible language. This represents an important limitation to the regime's scope for checking the fairness of the substance of a bargain. Nonetheless, its precise scope will require elucidation and this is further discussed in Part 9.6.3 below.

Regulation 6, drawn from Article 5, provides that any written term of a contract shall be expressed in plain, intelligible language. Where there is doubt about the meaning of a term, the interpretation most favourable to the consumer shall prevail. Regulation 6 seems close to the *contra proferentem* rule of interpretation in English law.[63] It remains to be seen whether it is stronger.

---

[63]   9.2 above.

9.6.1.3 The Tests Compared and Contrasted[64]

How close is the unfairness test in the Regulations, drawn from the Directive, to the test of reasonableness in the 1977 Act? It is first useful to point out why any divergence is of practical significance. The consequences of any gulf are small where the Act is stricter than or as strict as the Regulations/Directive. It is permissible for English law to apply a control tighter than that under the Directive, for the latter sets only a minimum Community–wide standard. However, the position is different where the Regulations/Directive are seen to be tighter than the Act. It is then necessary to apply that stricter control to terms within the scope of the Regulations/Directive. Control of such terms will accordingly be stricter than that currently exercised under UCTA. If this occurs, the oddity of the bifurcated English mechanism for controlling unfair terms will be sharply exposed. With this practical point in mind, it is appropriate to consider whether the two regimes are indeed distinct, although much comment is necessarily speculative, given that the Directive's deadline for implementation expired only at the end of 1994.

Reasonableness under the Act and unfairness under the Regulations/Directive will frequently yield the same result.[65] The influence of the Act may be observed in the Directive. It is no coincidence that some of the Act's terminology finds its way into the Directive, especially its Preamble. Both invite an appraisal of the bargaining environment as an aspect in assessing substantive fairness. However, perhaps the key point to appreciate is that the authoritative source of interpretation for the Directive is the European Court. It would be a mistake for a national court simply to assimilate the national rules that implement the Directive to existing domestic law. Rather, they must be applied with an eye to their European derivation. Points of interpretative difficulty should be resolved by the European Court, whose authoritative rulings act as a method of securing a common Community–wide approach to the application of the Directive. This justifies the use in this Chapter of the phrase 'Regulations/Directive' as a reminder of that channel.

---

[64]   Cf R. Brownsword and G. Howells, 'The Implementation of the EC Directive on Unfair Terms in Consumer Contracts – Some Unresolved Questions' [1995] *JBL* 243.

[65]   This view is expressed in the DTI Consultation Document on Implementation of October 1993, where it is added that similarity will reduce problems of overlap between Act and Regulations/Directive. However, the DTI's Further Consultation Document of September 1994 is more cautious and explicitly accepts that 'the two tests are not the same.' (p.3)

The possibility of divergence between the European Court's approach to unfairness/good faith and that of the English courts to reasonableness should not be underestimated. The phrase 'good faith', in particular, lacks definition for English lawyers, but has a much more developed meaning in continental legal systems.[66] The European Court is likely to draw on established national traditions and, perhaps, autonomous Community notions in developing what is meant by good faith, which may lead to unfamiliar notions penetrating English law via the medium of the Directive. For example, English law is far less prone to impose pre–contractual obligations of disclosure than some continental European systems.[67] Were the European Court to develop the notion of good faith in the direction of requiring disclosure, on pain of the unenforceability of terms that might have been queried by a consumer had disclosure of relevant background information occurred, then there is potential for a significant change in English law stimulated by the Directive.[68] At this early stage in the life of the Directive and its implementation at national level, comment on its detailed impact is necessarily speculative. However, it is of importance to appreciate that simple application of the reasonableness test familiar from almost two decades of the Unfair Contract Terms Act would be inappropriate in the light of the capacity of the European Court to push the Directive's control test in different and, for English lawyers, unfamiliar directions.

It should also be appreciated that the legal base of the Directive is Article 100a.[69] In formal constitutional terms, this is not a measure of consumer protection, but a measure designed to contribute to the process of market integration by equalising competitive conditions. It is not clear precisely how this will affect the European Court's interpretation of the Directive, but it is at least possible that it will drive that Court into different areas from those which domestic courts have chosen in applying the reasonableness test.

Further speculation is probably superfluous at this stage. Suffice to say that were the control required under the Regulations/Directive to prove more rigorous than that currently applied under English law, then the pattern of domestic control of unfair terms will alter significantly in the areas covered

---

66   J.F. O'Connor, *Good Faith in English Law* (Dartmouth, 1990); H. Collins, 'Good Faith in European Contract Law' (1994) 14 *Oxford JLS* 229.

67   Cf S. Van Erp, 'The Formation of Contracts', Ch.8 in A.S Hartkamp *et al.* (eds), *Towards a European Civil Code* (Martinus Nijhoff, 1994).

68   S. Weatherill, 'Prospects for the development of European private law through Europeanisation in the European Court – the Case of the Directive on Unfair Terms in Consumer Contracts' [1995] *European Review of Private Law*, forthcoming.

69   Chapter 2.3.3.

by the Regulations/Directive and, perhaps, by a kind of legal osmosis, in areas outwith the reach of the new regime as well.

9.6.2 Dealing as a Consumer

Section 12 defines the notion of 'dealing as consumer'. This is the trigger to the control exercised under several sections of the Act (including sections 3, 4 and 6(2)), although it has already been explained in section 5 of this Chapter that the Act has some, though more limited, application even where neither party deals as consumer.

A party to a contract deals as consumer in relation to another party if:

(a) he neither makes the contract in the course of a business nor holds himself out as doing so; and

(b) the other party does make the contract in the course of a business; and

(c) in the case of a contract governed by the law of sale of goods or hire–purchase, or by section 7 of this Act, the goods passing under or in pursuance of the contract are of a type ordinarily supplied for private use or consumption.

The section concludes by declaring that, on a sale by auction or by competitive tender the buyer is not in any circumstances to be regarded as dealing as consumer.[70] Subject to this, it is for those claiming that a party does not deal as consumer to show that he or she does not.[71] This is a valuable protection for the consumer, for it should ensure that 'grey areas', especially likely to arise in determining what is the 'course of a business',[72] are resolved in his or her favour. It is buttressed by the Court of Appeal ruling in *R & B Customs Brokers Co Ltd v United Dominions Trust* which took a surprisingly narrow view of when something occurs in the course of a business.[73] This pushes situations where one party clearly acts commercially, while the other is on the cusp between private and commercial activity, into the sphere of the more intrusive statutory control over

---

[70] S.12(2).

[71] S.12(3).

[72] Cf Chapters 4.1.2.1, 10.2.2 3.

[73] [1988] 1 All ER 847.

business/consumer contracts rather than leaving it subject to the more limited control exercised over business/business contracts.[74]

The Directive is briefer, in the style of drafting typical of Community measures, and this is reflected in the implementing Regulations. Regulation 3 provides that the regime controls contracts between sellers or suppliers and consumers, although it is only terms that have not been individually negotiated that are caught. Regulation 2, drawn from Article 1 of the Directive, provides that consumer means 'a natural person who, in making a contract to which these Regulations apply, is acting for purposes which are outside his business'. Regulation 2 provides that seller means 'a person who sells goods and who, in making a contract to which these Regulations apply, is acting for purposes relating to his business'. Supplier means 'a person who supplies goods or services and who, in making a contract to which these Regulations apply, is acting for purposes relating to his business'.

This notion of 'consumer' appears more limited than the English approach, especially in the light of the decision in *R & B Customs Brokers Co Ltd v United Dominions Trust*.[75] Moreover, in contrast to the Act, the Directive and the implementing Regulations are silent on the burden of proof.[76] However, one should remain aware that the European Court stands as the ultimate arbiter of the proper interpretation of Community acts. It has elsewhere expressed its view of the scope of the notion of 'consumer'.[77] It would be wrong for an English judge to ignore the Community dimension to interpretation in cases within the scope of the Directive. Nonetheless, the minimum character of the Directive means that national law may still exercise control over situations which are not consumer transactions within the Directive.[78] As explained, UCTA does this.

9.6.3 Types of Term

Although the Act, in contrast to the Regulations/Directive, does not catch all contract terms, section 13 is important in providing a wide scope to the types

---

[74] For some commentators this is an undesirable extension; eg Cheshire Fifoot and Furmston's *Law of Contract* (Butterworths, 12th ed, 1991), p. 186. See further Chapter 10.2.2.3, in relation to trade descriptions law.

[75] N.73 above.

[76] For an argument that it should be interpreted to favour the consumer, see Weatherill n.68 above.

[77] Eg Case C–369/89 *Ministère Public v di Pinto* [1991] ECR I–1189.

[78] Cf French law at issue in *di Pinto* n.77 above.

of terms that are caught.[79] Terms that exclude or restrict liability are controlled, but by virtue of section 13 so too are:

(a) making the liability or its enforcement subject to restrictive or onerous conditions;
(b) excluding or restricting any right or remedy in respect of the liability, or subjecting a person to any prejudice in consequence of his pursuing any such right or remedy;
(c) excluding or restricting rules of evidence or procedure.

It is also provided that sections 2 and 5 to 7 control exclusion or restriction of liability by reference to terms and notices which exclude or restrict the relevant obligation or duty. This brings within the scope of the Act an attempt, for example, to deny the existence in the first place of a duty, as opposed to a mere attempted curtailment of that duty.[80] On one view, this extension plugs a potential gap in the Act that could otherwise have been exploited by astute drafting. On another view, it reveals a failure to come to terms with the fundamental question of whether exclusion clauses restrict liability for breach of a duty or define the scope of that duty.[81] The judicial and statutory preference is for the former view,[82] but further litigation may be called for in elucidation of this issue.[83]

The application of the Regulations/Directive to all types of term means that it requires no definition of which terms are and are not caught.[84] The types of term that are conspicuous in the grey list in the Regulations' Schedule 3/the Directive's Annex are those that confer unilateral decision–

---

[79] E. Macdonald, 'Exclusion clauses: the ambit of s.13(1) of the Unfair Contract Terms Act 1977' (1992) 12 *Legal Studies* 277. For a recent broad approach to the reach of s.13, see *Stewart Gill Ltd v Horatio Myer & Co Ltd* [1992] 2 All ER 257.

[80] Cf *Smith v Eric S Bush* [1990] 1 AC 831, [1989] 2 All ER 514; *Phillips Products Ltd v Hyland* [1987] 2 All ER 620.

[81] See B. Coote, *Exception Clauses* (Sweet and Maxwell, 1964).

[82] Especially the House of Lords in *Smith v Eric S. Bush* note 80 above.

[83] Contrast *Phillips v Hyland* n.80 above with *Thompson v T. Lohan Ltd* [1987] 2 All ER 631. Cf N. Palmer, 'Clarifying the Unfair Contract Terms Act 1977' [1986] *Business Law Review* 57; E. Macdonald, 'Mapping the Unfair Contract Terms Act 1977 and the Directive on Unfair Terms in Consumer Contracts' [1994] *JBL* 441.

[84] Subject only to the exclusion under Art.1(2) of the Directive of 'The contractual terms which reflect mandatory statutory or regulatory provisions and the provisions or principles of international conventions to which the Member States or the Community are party, particularly in the transport area.' This appears in adjusted form in Schedule 1 to the Regs.

making powers on the supplier and those that envisage the imposition of obligations on consumers where no corresponding obligations are borne by suppliers.[85] Bringing such terms within the control of UCTA would be difficult, although it might be possible to stretch section 3 in such directions.[86] It is plain that all the terms covered by section 13 of the Unfair Contract Terms Act are capable of falling within the Regulations/Directive, provided they appear in consumer contracts and have not been individually negotiated, but all other types of term are also included. By way of specific example of the broader scope of the Regulations/Directive, section 13(2) of the Act cautions that 'an agreement in writing to submit present or future differences to arbitration' is not to be treated as subject to control,[87] whereas such an agreement would fall within the Regulations/Directive.[88] A term 'requiring any consumer who fails to fulfil his obligation to pay a disproportionately high sum in compensation' is explicitly mentioned in Schedule 3/the Annex,[89] but would escape control under the Act.[90] However, it should be recalled that terms which describe the main subject matter of the contract are not to be tested for unfairness under the Regulations/Directive. Therein lies further fertile ground for the debate about whether clauses restrict liability or define duties.[91]

The Regulations/Directive requires a definition of individual negotiation, for they control only contractual terms which have not been individually negotiated. This notion is explained further in Regulation 3(3), reflecting Article 3(2) of the Directive. A term shall always be regarded as not individually negotiated (and therefore within the scope of the regime) 'where it has been drafted in advance and the consumer has not been able to influence the substance of the term.' Individual negotiation of a term does not preclude the application of the control to the rest of the contract if 'an overall assessment indicates that it is nevertheless a pre–formulated standard

---

[85] Cf. T. Wilhelmsson, 'Control of Unfair terms and Social Values: EC and Nordic Approaches' (1993) 16 *JCP* 435; C. Willett, 'Directive on Unfair Terms in Consumer Contracts' [1994] *Consum LJ* 114.

[86] 9.5.2 above.

[87] Which is not to say that it may not be subject to separate statutory control; Chapter 17.6 on the Consumer Arbitration Act.

[88] Cf. Sched.3/Annex, term (q).

[89] Term (e).

[90] Although it may be the subject of separate control under English law as a penalty clause.

[91] For discussion in this direction, see Brownsword and Howells n.64 above; Macdonald n.83 above.

contract.' It rests with the seller or supplier who claims that a term has been individually negotiated to prove this.

9.7 INSURANCE AND EMPLOYMENT CONTRACTS

The position of the insurance industry is complex and influenced by its determined efforts to isolate itself from control of unfair contract terms. The industry was largely successful in achieving that objective in the Unfair Contract Terms Act, but less so at European level. According to Schedule 1 of the Unfair Contract Terms Act, sections 2 to 4 of the Act do not extend to any contract of insurance.[92] The Regulations/Directive offer no such exclusion. However, as explained above, the Regulations/Directive do not envisage any direct control over the fairness of the price paid for goods or services. The recitals to the Directive explicitly add that this means that, in insurance contracts, 'the terms which clearly define or circumscribe the insured risk and the insurer's liability shall not be subject to such assessment since these restrictions are taken into account in calculating the premium paid by the consumer.' The October 1993 Department of Trade and Industry Consultation Document on Implementation of the Directive proposed the insertion of this provision into the implementing Regulations' Schedule of Exclusions. However, the DTI's Further Consultation Document of September 1994 abandoned this idea, explaining that it added nothing to the basic point that the regime does not address the relationship of price to substance, reflected in Regulation 3(2). Accordingly there is no special provision made for the insurance industry in the Regulations.[93]

Sections 2(1) and 2(2) of the Act do not extend to a contract of employment, except in favour of the employee.[94] The limitation of the scope of the Directive to consumer contracts means that employment contracts are wholly outwith its scope. For the UK, this is confirmed in Schedule 1 to the implementing regulations.

---

[92]   Schedule 1 provides for other exceptions. Briefly summarised, these deal with contracts so far as they relate to the creation or transfer of an interest in land or intellectual property rights, contracts so far as they relate to the formation or dissolution of a company or its constitution, and contracts so far as they relate to the creation or transfer of securities. Terms in such contracts are capable of being caught by the Regulations/Directive, subject to the probability that the Directive applies only to contracts for the supply of goods and services (so not touching the creation or issue of financial securities).

[93]   Cf Brownsword and Howells, n.64 above, on the likely practical operation.

[94]   Sched. 1 of the Act.

9.8 ENFORCEMENT

The Unfair Contract Terms Act operates on the basis of private enforcement in the sense that it is for individual consumers, as plaintiffs or defendants, to make use of it in private contractual disputes. Even though the Act places some burdens of proof on traders, to the consumer advantage, nevertheless the pattern is open to criticism for its obscurity and practical ineffectiveness. This is part of the wider picture of the consumer difficulty in securing effective access to justice, examined in Chapter 17. There is only a small element of public control. The Consumer Transactions (Restrictions on Statements) Order 1976[95] makes it an offence to display certain terms that are void under the Unfair Contract Terms Act.

The extent to which the Directive requires deeper public intervention has been controversial. Article 6 of the Directive requires Member States to provide that unfair terms shall not bind the consumer. The contract shall continue to bind the parties if capable of remaining on foot without the unfair terms. Implemented in Regulation 5, this conforms to the pattern under the 1977 Act and poses no difficulty for English law.

More significantly, Article 7 of the Directive provides that 'Member States shall ensure that, in the interests of consumers and of competitors adequate and effective means exist to prevent the continued use of unfair terms in contracts concluded with consumers by sellers or suppliers'. It is further provided in Article 7(2) that the 'means' referred to shall include 'provisions whereby persons or organisations, having a legitimate interest under national law in protecting consumers, may take action according to the national law concerned before the courts or before competent administrative bodies for a decision as to whether contractual terms drawn up for general use are unfair, so that they can apply appropriate and effective means to prevent the continued use of such terms'.

These rather unclear phrases may require subsequent elucidation of the enforcement obligation which they place on Member States. Their imprecision is attributable to the background diversity between the choices already made by Member States about how to police unfair contract terms in their domestic systems.[96]

For the UK, the Department of Trade and Industry initially proposed a minimalist response based on leaving control in the hands of private litigants before the ordinary courts.[97] Remarkably, with regard to Article 7(2), it was declared that 'UK law at present contains no general provision for

---

[95] SI 1976/1813, as amended by SI 1978/27.
[96] Cf Brownsword and Howells n.64 above.
[97] Consultation Document of October 1993.

representative actions; only a party to a contract may sue under that contract. Thus according to the national law concerned (ie that applying in the UK) this provision can have no effect'. This was fiercely attacked for its failure to provide the effective control required by the Directive.[98] The DTI then had a change of heart.[99] Regulation 8 imposes a duty on the Director General of Fair Trading to consider complaints and the power to seek a court injunction against persons using unfair terms in contracts concluded with consumers.[100] However, no special status is conferred on consumer organisations, which contrasts with practice in several other Member States.[101]

---

[98]   Eg R. Bragg (1994) 2 *Consum LJ* 29, 36–37.

[99]   Further Consultation Document, September 1994.

[100]   The pattern is comparable to that employed in the control of misleading advertising; Chapter 10.6. Cf also Chapter 17.9 which discusses the European Commission's Green Paper on Access to Justice; this airs the possibility of the free movement of injunctions within the Community.

[101]   The Consumers' Association is seeking judicial review of the compatibility with EC law of the decision not to empower consumer organisations.

10 Trade Descriptions

10.1 THE POLICY OF THE LAW OF TRADE DESCRIPTIONS

The suppression of misleading trade descriptions possesses a long history. Hallmarking law has a pedigree going back centuries. The first general statute in the field was the Merchandise Marks Act 1862, replaced by the Merchandise Marks Act 1887. Several statutes of that name followed, the last in 1953. Pressure grew for broader and more sophisticated protection. A Royal Commission was established, yielding the Molony Committee Report on Consumer Protection in 1962.[1] This prepared the ground for what became the Trade Descriptions Act 1968, the starting point for investigation of the current law.

Part of the rationale for such laws lies in the endemic lack of information available to the consumer in the modern marketplace. The perception that the consumer cannot grasp a full awareness of products, especially those that are technologically advanced, has spawned a range of laws requiring labelling and other forms of information disclosure. This technique and some of its manifestations are examined in Chapter 1.[2]

The law studied in this Chapter concerns practices that mislead the consumer. The attachment of a false description to a product distorts the operation of the market, damaging the consumer and the fair trader. In fact, the rationale of protecting fair traders is at least as strong as that of protecting the consumer; the Trade Descriptions Act is firmly part of the wider field of trade practices law. There are limits on the capacity of the market to 'punish' misleading practices. Consumers may decline to revisit dishonest traders, but, for that consumer, the damage may already be done and, given the limited scope for transmission of information, the only way for other consumers to learn is by making the same mistake. The private law has a role to play, but it cannot plug all the gaps. In some cases making a false trade description will be both a crime and a breach of contract and, occasionally, even a tort. However, this will not invariably be so. Some misleading practices may not constitute violations of private law rights. False advertising may be insufficiently precise or formal to generate contractual liability. Even where capable of contractual force, the rules of privity will frequently preclude a consumer bringing an action against an advertiser

---

[1]   Cmnd. 1781.
[2]   1.8.3 above.

unless the item has been bought from him or her.[3] Tort law has a limited role to play in these instances of economic loss.[4] Practical problems of securing effective consumer access to justice add to the inadequacy of private law as a means of deterring misleading trade descriptions.[5] In combination, these factors make the case for public intervention.

The central statute in this area is the Trade Descriptions Act 1968.[6] At stake are also advertising controls, control of misleading prices and misdescriptions of land, found in other enactments and examined below. The 1968 Act is wide–ranging. A Chief Trading Standards Officer, drawing on practical experience, has written that it is the motor trade and the holiday industry which have been especially affected,[7] but the application of the Act is in principle much broader.

The 1968 Act created three main offences. The 'section 1' offence catches the application of a false trade description to any goods or supplying or offering to supply any goods to which a false trade description is applied. This is examined in 10.2 below.

The 'section 14' offence concerns provision of services. It catches the making of a statement concerning the provision of services, knowing it to be false or being reckless in that regard. This offence requires inquiry into the state of mind of the perpetrator, unlike the section 1 offence which concentrates exclusively on the act. Section 14 is examined in 10.3 below.

The 'section 11' offence originally caught offers to supply goods that involved a false indication of price, but proved inadequate for that purpose. This area of law is now covered by Part III of the Consumer Protection Act 1987, studied in 10.5 below.

10.2 FALSE OR MISLEADING DESCRIPTIONS OF GOODS

10.2.1 The Offences

Section 1(1) of the Trade Descriptions Act 1968 provides that;

'Any person who, in the course of a trade or business –

---

3   Chapter 1.3 above.

4   Chapter 1.4.

5   This is mentioned in Chapter 1.6 and examined more fully in Chapter 17.

6   The most comprehensive modern treatment is found in R. Bragg, *Trade Descriptions* (OUP, 1991).

7   D. Roberts, '25 Years of the Trade Descriptions Act 1968' (1994) 13/3 *Trading Law* 193.

(a) applies a false trade description to any goods; or

(b) supplies or offers to supply any goods to which a false trade description is applied ;

shall, subject to the provisions of this Act, be guilty of an offence.'

There are three offences created, one under s.1(1)(a), the core offence of application of a false trade description to goods, and two offences under s.1(1)(b), which catch the supply or offer to supply goods to which a false trade description is applied – not necessarily by the defendant. Contrary to the norm in English criminal law, the prosecution is not required to prove *mens rea* – the guilty mind of the defendant. The absence of any *mens rea* requirement means that, once a false trade description has been applied to an item and continues to be applied, resellers and resuppliers may be guilty of an offence under s1(1)(b).[8] Usually, but not invariably, s1(1)(a) catches dishonest traders, s1(1)(b) careless traders.[9] Formally, however, these are strict liability offences and proof of *mens rea* need not be presented.[10] Nonetheless, the due diligence defence common to a number of consumer protection offences may permit the exoneration of the careful trader.[11] It should also be appreciated that the defendant's mental state will typically affect enforcement practice[12] and, were the matter to proceed to formal conviction, would also be relevant to sentence.[13]

The scope of section 1(1)(b) is widened by section 6, according to which 'A person exposing goods for supply or having goods in his possession for supply shall be deemed to offer to supply them'. This provision is important in taking the scope of the law beyond the rather limited notion of 'offer' in the law of contract formation.[14] The display of goods in shop windows or on shelves falls within the control of the Trade Descriptions Act, even though such displays are not normally viewed as constituting an 'offer' which can be 'accepted' by a customer in a way effective to conclude a contract. This wider reach is important to the effective application of the law in correcting the imperfections of the market. The Act is motivated by policies quite distinct from the law of contract formation. The two systems are therefore properly

---

[8]   The defendant must, however, know of the application of the trade description; *Cottee v Douglas Seaton Ltd.* [1972] 1 WLR 1408, [1972] 3 All ER 750, discussed in 10.2.3 below.

[9]   Cf Lord Lane CJ in *R v Southwood* [1987] 3 All ER 556, 561g.

[10]   For a clear statement in this regard, *Alec Norman Garages Ltd v Phillips* [1985] RTR 164.

[11]   Chapter 14.2 below.

[12]   Chapter 14.3, esp 14.3.5 below.

[13]   Chapter 14.3.4 below.

[14]   Cf *Pharmaceutical Society v Boots* [1952] 2 QB 795.

kept separate, though statutory clarification was probably necessary to ensure that this point was taken by the judiciary.[15]

10.2.2 Course of a Trade or Business

The offence is committed only by a person[16] acting 'in the course of a trade or business...'[17] The House of Lords adopted a perhaps surprisingly narrow notion of dealing in the course of a trade or business in *Davies v Sumner*.[18] Davies was a self-employed courier who transported films and other related material around Wales for the Harlech television company. He owned a car, which he traded in with a misleading odometer reading, thereby obtaining a price far higher than the market value.

Davies was not a car dealer, but the sale of the car was incidental to his work as a courier. The House of Lords was asked to address the question of whether, for the purposes of the statute, Davies was acting in the course of a trade or business when he applied the description. He was not. Lord Keith, delivering the only fully reasoned speech, took the view that a defendant must pursue the trade with some degree of regularity to fall within the scope of the Act. 'Sporadic selling off of pieces of equipment which were no longer required for the purposes of a business' is not caught.[19] Davies had no normal practice of selling cars.[20] Misdescription in the context of one–off sales of used items, or even occasional disposal of items to be replaced, may engage contractual or, less likely, tortious liability, but does not attract criminal liability as a regulatory offence.[21] This decision restricts the scope of the Act, although it does not mean that misdescription in a one–off sale will never be caught. A one–off sale could be caught if that transaction itself constitutes a trade.

---

15   Cf on the notion of dealing in the course of a business, text at notes 22–26 below, where the courts, perhaps unhelpfully, have felt it necessary to align comparably worded criminal and civil law statutory provisions.

16   Normal rules of interpretation dictate that this covers a limited company. S.20 permits prosecution of both a body corporate and, in defined circumstances, an officer thereof. Cf Chapter 14.2.

17   Except for those prosecuted under the by–pass provision, s.23; Chapter 14.2.5 below.

18   [1984] 3 All ER 831.

19   At 834a.

20   Contrast *Havering LB v Stevenson* [1970] 3 All ER 609, where there was sufficient regularity. Cf Bragg n.6 above Ch.2.

21   Although extreme cases may involve offences of obtaining property by deception under the Theft Acts; cf D. Roberts, 'The Use of the Theft Act in Trading Standards Cases' (1992) 9 *Trading Law* 205.

Davies v Sumner was followed in *R and B Customs Brokers Co Ltd v UDT*.[22] That case involved the demarcation under the Unfair Contract Terms Act 1977 ('UCTA') between transactions involving those who deal as consumers and other commercial deals. The latter are still capable of being affected by the Act, but the controls are distinct and, loosely, less intrusive.[23] Dillon LJ took the point that the Trade Descriptions Act is penal whereas UCTA is not; notwithstanding arguments that analogies between the two were therefore inappropriate, he felt driven to a common interpretation of the notion of 'course of business' which appears in both statutes.[24] The Court of Appeal therefore drew on *Davies v Sumner* for a narrow approach to 'course of a business.'[25] A shipping broker and freight forwarding company which had acquired a car on credit terms for only the second or third time lacked the requisite regularity and was therefore not operating in the course of a business (and could accordingly use the Act to invalidate an exclusion clause[26]).

10.2.3 Application of a Trade Description

The notion of 'application' receives elaboration in section 4. According to section 4(1), a person applies a trade description to goods if he;

> '(a) affixes or annexes it to or in any manner marks it on or incorporates it with – (i) the goods themselves, or (ii) anything in, on or with which the goods are supplied; or
> (b) places the goods in, on or with anything which the trade description has been affixed or annexed to, marked on or incorporated with, or places any such thing with the goods; or
> (c) uses the trade description in any manner likely to be taken as referring to the goods. '

Section 4(2) provides that 'an oral statement may amount to the use of a trade description'.

---

22   [1988] 1 All ER 847.
23   Chapter 9.
24   At 853. Also Neill LJ at 859.
25   For criticism, see D. Parry, 'Business or Consumer: a Trap for the Unwary' (1988) 6 *Trading Law* 270. Cf comment by D. Price (1989) 52 *MLR* 245.
26   Had the transaction been within the course of a business, the clause would have stood if reasonable; Chapter 9.5 above.

This seems reasonably broad. In *Roberts v Severn Petroleum*[27] a large pole sign outside a garage displayed the Esso logo and a smaller version of the sign hung over the workshop. The site was in Esso livery. However, no sign appeared on the pumps, which referred only to the star grading of the petrol. The garage was not selling Esso petrol. The High Court ruled that the garage should properly have been convicted of an offence of applying a false trade description.

Repairs effected to a car may amount to the application of a trade description. In *Cottee v Douglas Seaton Ltd*[28] repairs done to a car had subsequently been so carefully covered up that it appeared that the car was completely free from repair work. The High Court considered that a trade description had been applied. Lord Widgery stated that 'an alteration of the goods which causes them to tell a lie about themselves may be a false trade description.' Thus the seller of such a repaired car risks criminal liability, though in fact the case ended in acquittal. The case turned on the sale by a subsequent owner who had not been involved in covering up the repair work and who, moreover, was completely unaware that repairs had been done. An essential ingredient of the offence was missing. Knowledge of the falsity of the trade description is not required for conviction, but knowledge that a trade description is applied to the goods is essential. That was missing in the case.

Buyers as well as sellers may commit the offence. In *Fletcher v Budgen*[29] a car dealer told the owner of a Fiat car brought in for inspection that it was fit for scrap. The dealer knew this was untrue, but the owner, discouraged, sold it to the dealer for £2. After repairs costing about £56, the dealer offered the car for sale at £135. The High Court decided that it was possible to convict a buyer under the Act, not simply a seller. Lord Widgery CJ took account of the normal restrictive approach taken towards criminal statutes; he confessed that, subconsciously, he had always assumed that sellers alone were caught. However he thought that protection was needed against misleading descriptions applied by buyers acting in the course of a trade or business just as much as those applied by sellers. He interpreted the Act accordingly.

In *Fletcher v Sledmore*[30] a car dealer and potential customer visited the defendant, a seller of old cars. The customer asked the defendant about a particular car and was told that it was 'a good little engine'. This was far from the truth. The defendant dealer sold the car to the visiting dealer who then sold it to the customer. The defendant was convicted of applying a false

---

27   [1981] RTR 312
28   Note 8 above.
29   [1974] 2 All ER 1243.
30   [1973] Crim LR 195.

trade description. This decision simply, but clearly, demonstrates that the Act reaches beyond the limitations of contractual relationships.

It is important to be aware that, to a significant extent, the true impact of the Trade Descriptions Act 1968 is not best judged by reading the tiny number of cases that reach the appellate courts, nor even the larger number of decisions on points of fact decided by magistrates. Take *Fletcher v Budgen*.[31] The consumer was unwise, even naive. Why rely on the dealer's comments? It is unlikely that there was no competition in the market; he could have shopped around. Why should resources be devoted to public intervention designed to help consumers so unprepared to look after themselves? – a fortiori where private law remedies for misrepresentation would have been available. *Tesco v Nattrass*, examined at length in Chapter 14,[32] was fought all the way to the House of Lords to establish whether Tesco should have been convicted for displaying packs of washing powder on the shelves at a price one shilling above that advertised on posters.[33] Was such lengthy and expensive litigation justified? Views may differ.[34] However, the real test of the benefit of the Act lies, not in individual cases, but in the more general improvement to the operation of the market resultant on the widespread basis of fair trading instilled by the Act. Its purpose is not to secure a clutch of convictions, but to raise standards.[35]

The trade description must be applied at the time of or before the sale or supply. In *Hall v Wickens Motors Ltd*[36] dealers who had sold a car received a complaint about the steering several weeks later. They informed the buyer that 'there is nothing wrong with the car.' This was far from the truth, but it was held that they had committed no offence. The application of the false description amounts to an offence only where it is associated with the sale or supply of goods. This seems correct. The statute is concerned to eliminate deceptive practices that distort consumer buying decisions. The untruth in *Hall v Wickens Motors Ltd* was not of this type and the customer's apparently ill–judged purchase was thus properly left to the private law.[37]

---

31 Note 29 above.
32 14.2.4 below.
33 They should not have been convicted because they had taken adequate precautions – 14.2.4 below.
34 See further Chapter 14, esp 14.3.4, 14.3.5.
35 Further on enforcement practice, Chapter 14.3.
36 [1972] 1 WLR 1418.
37 A different approach is taken in relation to the misdescription of services, where the supply is not simply a 'one–off' transaction; 10.3.3 below.

10.2.4 Meaning of a Trade Description

Section 2(1) of the 1968 Act provides the following definition of a trade description;

> 'A trade description is an indication, direct or indirect, and by whatever means given, of any of the following matters with respect to any goods or parts of goods, that is to say –
> (a) quantity,[38] size or gauge;
> (b) method of manufacture, production, processing or reconditioning;
> (c) composition;
> (d) fitness for purpose, strength, performance, behaviour or accuracy;
> (e) any physical characteristics not included in the preceding paragraphs;
> (f) testing by any person and results thereof;
> (g) approval by any person or conformity with a type approved by any person;
> (h) place or date of manufacture, production, processing or reconditioning;
> (i) person by whom manufactured, produced, processed or reconditioned;
> (j) other history, including previous ownership or use.'

The list's scope is a great deal more extensive than that of the pre–1968 law.[39] However, the use of this exhaustive, albeit extensive, list (rather than a general, broadly–phrased test) still creates the risk of loopholes through which objectionable practices of a type that ought to be caught by the law might fall. The preference for such a list was motivated by the perceived need for precision in drafting criminal offences. However, more recent trends have introduced some generally worded offences into the law of consumer protection as part of a policy of securing flexibility.[40] Were the Trade Descriptions Act to be redrafted from scratch today, this type of specific list would probably not be employed.[41]

---

[38] Defined in s.2(3) to include length, width, height, area, volume, capacity, weight and number. Note also the concern for quantity accuracy in the Weights and Measures Act 1985.

[39] At length, Bragg n.6 above pp. 22–42.

[40] Chapter 1.8.1.

[41] Chapter 14 discusses more generally whether the use of the criminal law in circumstances of market failure is helpful.

10.2.5 Is the Trade Description False?

According to section 3(1) of the Trade Descriptions Act, 'A false trade description is a trade description which is false to a material degree.'

The scope of the offence is extended by the rest of section 3. Section 3(2) provides that 'A trade description which, though not false, is misleading, that is to say, likely to be taken for such an indication of any of the matters specified in section 2 of this Act as would be false to a material degree, shall be deemed to be a false trade description.' Section 3(3) adds to the scope of the 'trade description' by providing that 'Anything which, though not a trade description, is likely to be taken for an indication of any of those matters and, as such an indication, would be false to a material degree, shall be deemed to be a false trade description'.

Section 3 of the Act allows half–truths or economy with the truth to be caught. It would be fruitless for a trader to deny the falsity of a description that a car has done 50,000 miles by pointing out that it had indeed done 50,000 miles – but also several tens of thousand more miles left unmentioned.[42]

Exhaustive analysis of case law would do little to elucidate what is at heart a question of fact – the falsity of the description. However, illustrations may help.[43] In *Holloway v Cross*[44] a dealer sold a car that had actually done 73,000 miles. The dealer did not know how many miles it had done, but, when asked by the customer, estimated 45,000. The dealer argued that this was no more than an expression of opinion for which he had been asked and not a false trade description. This submission was not successful. It was held that this might fall within section 2, but that that point need not be decided because the comments made were plainly a false trade description within section 3(3).

An example of a more trader–friendly decision is provided by *R v Ford Motor Co Ltd*.[45] A car was sold described as 'new'; in fact it had undergone £50 repairs as a result of an accident suffered in transit. Bridge J held that;

'if the damage which a new car after leaving the factory has sustained is, although perhaps extensive, either superficial in character or limited to certain defined parts of the vehicle which can be simply replaced by new parts, then provided that such damage is in practical terms perfectly repaired so that it can in truth be said after repairs have been effected that

---

42 Cf D. Roberts, 'Trade Descriptions: False by Reason of what it omits' (1988) 6 *Trading Law* 145.

43 More fully, Bragg n.6 above pp. 42–8.

44 [1981] 1 All ER 1012.

45 [1974] 3 All ER 489, [1974] 1 WLR 1220.

the vehicle is as good as new, in our judgment it would not be a false trade description to describe such a vehicle as new.'

The jury had been given a less flexible direction and the conviction was accordingly quashed. By contrast, in *Robertson v Dicicco* description of a car as 'beautiful' when, beneath a gleaming exterior it was badly corroded, resulted in conviction.[46] There is a grey area in which what are close to throwaway comments may attract criminal liability. This suits regulatory policy. The message for the trader is to be cautious in what he or she chooses to throw away. In fact, the different results in *Ford* and *Robertson v Dicicco* are explicable by reference to s.3's avowedly fact–based, non–theoretical standard of falsity 'to a material degree'. The statute makes no attempt to elaborate any sophisticated notion of the level of consumer gullibility in respect of which it seeks to provide protection.[47]

10.2.6 Disclaimers, Odometers and 'Clocking'

Trade descriptions law has been applied to secondhand car dealing with extraordinary frequency. The main points have arisen in relation to odometers, which show the mileage a car has done, and which are therefore also commonly and less technically known as mileometers. All too often they are found to have been altered, to display a lower figure than is accurate. The torrent of case law that has swept through the courts justifies a special section devoted to this particular sector, although the overwhelming impression of such investigation is that it is high time that odometers were made 100 per cent tamper–proof.[48]

The odometer is taken by the courts to amount to a 'trade description, within the Act. The reading is an indication of the car's previous use within s.2(1)(j).[49] If it is false, an offence has prima facie been committed. This has commonly arisen because of the practice of dishonest dealers of 'clocking'; reducing the mileage figures shown on the odometer, thereby allowing the dealer to charge a price inflated above the car's real market value.

---

[46] [1972] RTR 431.
[47] Cf I. Ramsay, *Consumer Protection Text and Materials* (Weidenfeld, 1989), pp. 209–31.
[48] Cf Donaldson LJ's weary opening sentence in *Holloway v Cross* [1981] 1 All ER 1012: 'This is another of the odometer cases.' The writing on the subject too is extensive; for a comprehensive collection of examples from case law and further references to writing, see Bragg n.6 above Ch.3.
[49] *R v Hammertons Cars Ltd* [1976] 1 WLR 1243, [1976] 3 All ER 758.

Naturally most car dealers are honest and are as keen to see such practices stamped out as the consumer.[50] However, all dealers are affected by clocking because, once the car is clocked, it may pass through a number of hands and it will be difficult to discover whether the odometer reading remains accurate. Dealers make the trade description when they put a car on display and may unwittingly commit the s.1(1)(b) offence of supplying or offering to supply goods to which a false trade description is applied. This has no *mens rea* requirement.

A dealer might opt to do nothing, hoping there has been no clocking; then, if it emerges that there has been clocking, seek to rely on the due diligence defence to defeat a prosecution.[51] This is unlikely to succeed in the face of consistent judicial insistence that the defence requires that at least *some* steps be taken.[52] Therefore traders commonly try to avoid potential criminal liability by disclaiming the truth of the reading. This may be an effective means of defeating a prosecution, but the courts have been wary. They have identified the risk that traders may use disclaimers that are deliberately halfhearted and therefore will not effectively prevent the consumer from being misled. Accordingly the message of the case law, broadly summarised, is that a disclaimer must effectively prevent market failure if the trader is to avoid criminal liability under section 1.[53]

In *Norman v Bennett*[54] Lord Widgery CJ accepted that the effect of a false trade description can be neutralised by a contradictory disclaimer. But to be effective the disclaimer must be 'as bold, precise and compelling as the trade description itself'.[55] In *R v Hammertons Cars*[56] Lawton LJ commented that the trader '...must take positive and effective steps to ensure that the customer understands that the mileometer reading is meaningless...'. In essence the trader must ensure that the false statement is disregarded. In law an oral disclaimer may suffice, but it would be imprudent for a trader to rely on this method. Aside from evidential difficulties, the oral disclaimer would often lack the required boldness to overcome the reading on the clock. Worse, the trader planning an oral disclaimer might find that the s.1(1)(b) offence of offering to supply goods to which a false trade description is

---

50 Although, alarmingly, Roberts n.7 above writes that before the Act came into force in 1968, clocking 'was practised by even the highest class of motor dealers'.

51 See Chapter 14.2 on this defence.

52 Cf Chapter 14.2.3.

53 Although if market failure occurs despite the trader having taken real and effective steps to prevent it, then the due diligence defence may still be available; 14.2 below.

54 [1974] 1 WLR 1229, [1974] 3 All ER 351.

55 Precisely these words are used in relation to disclaimers in the Motor Industry's own Code of Practice.

56 [1976] 1 WLR 1243, [1976] 3 All ER 758.

applied has already been committed before any opportunity orally to disclaim occurs.

There is no magic in the type of disclaimer that may be used. At stake is whether the trader has effectively neutralised the false reading so that the buyer is in no way reliant upon it. In *Waltham Forest LBC v TG Wheatley Ltd*[57] a notice in a dealer's office was held ineffective even though it clearly stated that cars were sold subject to an understanding that mileage could not be guaranteed. Lord Widgery explained that[58] 'the purpose of the disclaimer is for it to sit beside, as it were, the false trade description and cancel the other out as soon as its first impression can be made on the purchaser.' The notice in the office was insufficiently proximate to the false descriptions on the cars. A favourite case is *Corfield v Starr*.[59] The trader was convicted despite having displayed alongside a clocked car a notice declaring that 'With deep regret due to the Customer's Protection Act we can no longer verify that the mileage shown on this vehicle is correct'. Doubtless conviction would still have followed even if the trader had cited a statute that actually existed!

In *R v Hammertons Cars*[60] Lawton LJ was conscious of the practical value of avoiding overly–refined discussion of whether the disclaimer is a type of defence, a means of denying the falsity of the description, or a means of preventing the description being 'applied' in the first place. The evidence, he thought, should be looked at as a whole, with the decision lying with the trial court. Ultimately, for Lawton LJ, the question is as follows: 'Has the prosecution proved that the defendant supplied goods to which a false trade description was applied?'

There is much to be said in support of Lawton LJ's emphasis on practicality, but it seems regrettable that the precise legal effect of a disclaimer has not been pinned down. It was held by the Court of Appeal in *R v Southwood* that the disclaimer is not relevant to the offence under s.1(1)(a).[61] The clocker thus cannot evade criminal liability for the application of the false trade description by the use of a disclaimer. Perhaps this seems desirable as an overall policy choice. However, if a disclaimer can prevent a description being applied under s.1, then it is hard to see any strict logic in distinguishing s.1(1)(a) from s.1(1)(b) in this fashion; after all, the neutralising effect of a sufficiently prominent disclaimer is quite unaffected by the history of the clocking that has occurred. In fact, the Court of Appeal

---

57 [1978] RTR 333.
58 At p. 339.
59 [1981] RTR 380.
60 Note 49 above.
61 [1987] 3 All ER 556, applying *Newman v Hackney LBC* [1982] RTR 296. Followed in *Southend BC v White* [1992] 11 Trading LR 65; *R v Shrewsbury Crown Court ex p Venables* [1994] Crim LR 61.

in *Southwood* placed most emphasis on the relevance of the disclaimer to the s.24(1) defence, not the scope of the s.1 offence itself. In sum, it seems that a disclaimer may be used to prevent a s.1(1)(b) (but not s.1(1)(a)) offence occurring in the first place; if ineffective for that purpose, it may still provide a defence to the charge via s.24. The disclaimer seems capable of a dual function.[62]

The Court of Appeal in *Southwood* added that a trader who returns the odometer to zero applies a false trade description. This rejects the argument that 'zeroing' makes it plain that no description is being applied because no one could possibly think that a used car had done no miles. Lord Lane CJ commented that:

> 'The fact that no one was misled or was likely to be misled [by a zeroed odometer] is an irrelevant consideration.'

The trader would have to make more strenuous efforts to alert the customer to the falsity, such as use of a disclaimer, and then (it seems) seek to invoke s.24(1) as a defence to the s.1(1)(b) charge.

10.2.7 Defences and Enforcement

In common with other consumer protection statutes, the Trade Descriptions Act contains defences which mitigate the apparent severity of the main offences which impose strict liability. These may permit exoneration of the careful trader. Given the availability of these defences in several areas of the law (not simply trade descriptions), it is appropriate to consider their nature and purpose separately. This forms part of the subject matter of Chapter 14.

Sections 26–29 of the Trade Descriptions Act 1968 place enforcement responsibilities in the hands of Trading Standards Authorities, operating at local level. In this book, the practice of enforcement of trade descriptions law is also examined separately in Chapter 14, because it has much in common with general practice in consumer protection law.

No civil remedy is created by the Act. According to s.35, a contract for the supply of goods is not void or unenforceable by reason only of the fact that it breaches the Act. In some instances, of course, precisely the same

---

62   Cf Lord Lane CJ in *Wandsworth LBC v Bentley* [1980] RTR 429, *obiter dicta* that the disclaimer prevents a representation being made. Cf *Southend BC v White* and *R v Shrewsbury Crown Court ex p Venables* in the preceding note. In the latter case, semble no misdescription where parties had a mutual understanding that the odometer was quite wrong; see critical comment by C. Dixon (1994) 13 *Trading Law* 297, R. Bragg (1994) 2 *Consum* LJ CS17.

event will be capable of giving rise not only to criminal, but also civil, liability. Misdescription could involve a breach of contract; liability in tort may arise. A trader may have to face both criminal and civil consequences. However, the Act criminalises conduct that is not in breach of private law. The objectives are quite distinct: the existence of the Act is based on the assumptions of the inadequacy of the private law in curing market failure.[63]

10.3 FALSE OR MISLEADING DESCRIPTIONS OF SERVICES

10.3.1 The Offence

Section 14(1) of the Trade Descriptions Act 1968 provides that:

> 'It shall be an offence for any person in the course of any trade or business –
>
> (a) to make a statement which he knows to be false; or
> (b) recklessly to make a statement which is false;
>
> as to any of the following matters, that is to say, –
>
> (i) the provision in the course of any trade or business of any services, accommodation or facilities;
> (ii) the nature of any services, accommodation or facilities provided in the course of any trade or business;
> (iii) the time at which, the manner in which or persons by whom any services, accommodation or facilities are so provided;
> (iv) the examination, approval or evaluation by any person of any services, accommodation or facilities so provided; or
> (v) the location or amenities of any accommodation so provided.'

Several of the elements of s.14 run in parallel to s.1. Both have in common the limitation of liability to the course of trade or business, already examined above in Part 10.2.2.[64] The breadth of s.3 has a (not quite exact) counterpart in s.14(2)(a). 'False' means false to a material degree – s.14(4) echoes s.3(1).

The most striking difference between the s.14 offence and the s.1 offence lies in the mental element required. S.14 is *not* an offence of strict liability. This represented a deliberate choice in 1968. Control of misdescription in the

---

63   In depth, see Chapter 1.
64   S.1 refers to a trade or business; s.14 to any trade or business. No practical differences seem to have followed.

services sector was covered by neither the old Merchandise Marks Acts nor by the Molony Report. S.14 was an innovation, which explains the rather more tentative approach it takes to *mens rea* in contrast to the s.1 strict liability offence applicable to misdescription of goods.[65]

10.3.2 Mens Rea

The presence of a *mens rea* requirement under section 14 leads inevitably to the need for some sophisticated and complex legal reasoning. *Wings Ltd v Ellis*[66] concerned the s.14(1)(a) offence of making a statement known to be false. The case, which reached the House of Lords, arose out of the publication of a holiday brochure including a false statement about the availability of air conditioning in a hotel in Sri Lanka. The company found out the statement was false after it issued the brochure and tried to ensure that corrections were made by all those in receipt of it. However, at least 250,000 brochures had been distributed, so it was scarcely feasible that the company could mount a completely effective campaign. A consumer subsequently read an unamended brochure, booked a holiday and, on returning, complained of the application of a false trade description relating to the accommodation available.

A consumer had been misled; there was a false statement. The House of Lords confirmed the Court of Appeal's decision in *R v Thompson Holidays*[67] that a new statement is made on each occasion that a customer reads a brochure.[68] The defendants knew the statement was false. The problem was that the trader did not know of the falsity when publishing the brochure; but did know when the consumer read it. Furthermore, there was no intent to make a false statement to that particular consumer at that particular time; quite the reverse, in fact. Was the requisite mental element for conviction present?

The House of Lords took the view that conviction was proper, although there are shades of differing emphasis in the speeches. Conviction, Lord Scarman felt, 'advances the legislative purpose embodied in the Act, in that it strikes directly against the false statement irrespective of the reason for, or explanation of its falsity'.[69] Lord Scarman was not deterred by the

---

65 For an explanation in Parliament, see 759 HC Debs 683 (22 February 1968).

66 [1984] 3 All ER 577, [1984] 3 WLR 965. Cf *Yugotours v Wadsley* [1988] Crim LR 623.

67 [1974] 1 All ER 823; not all aspects of that decision were confirmed.

68 Lord Brandon preferred to see a continuing false statement as long as the brochures remained in circulation.

69 At 589j.

submission that this leads to a situation where liability may be imposed, as in this case, without knowledge of the making of the particular statement. He declared that the Trade Descriptions Act 1968 'is not truly a criminal statute. Its purpose is not the enforcement of the criminal law but the maintenance of trading standards. Trading standards, not criminal behaviour, are its concern'.[70]

To this extent, the *mens rea* requirement of s.14 has been interpreted as a lower threshold to conviction than would be the norm in 'proper' criminal statutes.[71] To the submission that this may criminalise the innocent, the answer is that statutory defences are available where a defendant has done everything possible to avoid commission of the defence.[72] Wings Ltd was ill-advised in not advancing such a defence.

S.14(1)(b) creates an offence of recklessly making a statement which is false. According to s.14(2)(b) a statement made regardless of whether it is true or false shall be deemed to be made recklessly, whether or not the person making it had reasons for believing that it might be false.

MFI Warehouses Ltd v Nattrass[73] shows a judicial readiness to follow the rather flexible approach to recklessness intimated by s.14(2)(b). Lord Widgery referred to the distinctive consumer protection flavour of the Trade Descriptions Act and concluded that 'Parliament was minded to place on the advertiser a positive obligation to have regard to whether his advertisement was true or false'.[74] Absence of regard to truth or falsity will suffice; neither dishonesty nor even deliberately closing one's eyes to the truth are required ingredients of the offence.

Both *Wings Ltd v Ellis*, under s.14(1)(a), and *MFI Warehouses Ltd v Nattrass*, under s.14(1)(b), stand as statements of the separation of the regulatory offence from the normal sweep of English criminal law. The nature of the Regulatory Offence is examined more fully in Chapter 14.

10.3.3 Statements About the Future

It will be recalled that under s.1 of the Act a statement made after and unassociated with the sale or supply of goods cannot constitute the application of a misleading trade description. The position is different under s.14, in reflection of the typically ongoing nature of the provision of services

---

70   *Wings Ltd v Ellis* [1984] 3 All ER 577, 587. See further Chapter 14.1 on the policy of the regulatory offence.
71   Chapter 14.1.
72   Chapter 14.2.
73   [1973] 1 All ER 762.
74   At 768b.

in contrast with the 'one-off' sale or supply of goods. In *Breed v Cluett*[75] contracts were exchanged between the defendant builder, Cluett, and buyers of a bungalow which the defendant was still in the process of completing. Three weeks after the exchange of contracts, Cluett told the buyers that the bungalow was covered by the national House–Builders Registration Council 10–year guarantee. Had this been true, it would have meant that the builders bore continuing obligations throughout the guarantee period. However, the claim was untrue and the defendant was found reckless in making the statement. Dorset justices considered s.14 to be limited to statements inducing entry into a contract, which had not occurred here. However, Lord Parker CJ thought it wrong to confine the scope of s.14 in this way and returned the case to the justices with a direction to convict.[76]

As opposed to *Hall v Wickens Motors Ltd*,[77] where it was held that no s.1 offence was committed where a statement was made several weeks after the sale was complete, *Breed v Cluett* was distinguished as a s.14 case where descriptions are caught if applied *in the course* of providing services.

A distinct question arises where a statement relates to the provision of services in the future. In *Beckett v Cohen*[78] a builder, Cohen, agreed to build a garage for a customer within ten days. The garage would be like the customer's neighbour's. The builder ran out of money and did not complete in time. Nor was the garage identical with the neighbour's. Lord Widgery did not decide conclusively that this was the provision of a service, but indicated that he would be surprised if it were not. However, he began his judgment by declaring that 'this is another case in which prosecuting authorities appear to me to be pressing the ambit of the Trade Descriptions Act 1968 to a wholly unacceptable degree'. Lord Widgery stated that s.14 'has no application to statements which amount to a promise in regard to the future, and which therefore at the time when they are made cannot have the character of being either true or false.' S.14 does not catch a promise as to what a provider will do before the contract is completed, where the promise does not relate to an existing fact. This was, he felt, a case correctly belonging in contract law, not criminal law.

There is some force in the submission that the limits of criminality would be overstretched were the criminal law employed in cases of over–optimistic forecasts. Yet it is possible in part to unpick the claim that a promise as to the future cannot be true or false at the time it is made. If x promises to do y within ten days, then the fact of whether y will be done is true or false at the

---

75   [1970] 2 QB 459.
76   Applied in *R v Bevelectric Ltd* (1993) 157 JP 323, discussed by G. Holgate and C. Clayson (1994) 13 Trading Law 55.
77   Note 36 above.
78   [1973] 1 All ER 120

moment the promise is made; it is simply that for ten days we will not know which. The core of the offence, as explained in *Beckett v Cohen*, seems to rest on the need for an existing and presently discoverable fact that is being misrepresented.[79]

If x makes the promise and intends to carry it through, then there is no offence if he fails. By contrast, as was famously observed by Bowen LJ in *Edgington v Fitzmaurice*,[80] 'the state of a man's mind is as much a fact as the state of his digestion'. So to say that one will do y, when at the time one has no intention of doing y, could be a crime, whereas there is no crime if one hopes to do y but simply fails. In *British Airways Board v Taylor*[81] a passenger was told that he had a definite booking on a flight from London to Bermuda. He did not get the promised seat because the airline operated a deliberate commercial policy of overbooking. The House of Lords held that this was a false statement within the scope of s.14 of the Act, not simply a promise as to future conduct.[82] The confirmation of the booking expressed an intention that the airline did not in fact have, for its real intention was to overbook and to jeopardise the passenger's chances of getting a seat.

Although the law does not criminalise over-optimistic forecasts, its application to statements of existing fact may indirectly allow the projection of the law into the future. In *R v Clarksons Holidays*[83] the defendant had made statements about the quality of services available at a hotel in Benidorm. An artist's impression was printed in the brochure. It was not mentioned on that page that construction was still underway. In fact, the hotel had not yet been built and holidaymakers arrived to find it still unfinished and dirty. The conviction of the firm under s.14 was upheld by the Court of Appeal. This was considered to be a statement about existing fact – that the hotel was a going concern – that was untrue. That a representation of existing fact was at stake was sufficient to ground liability.[84] Presumably had it been stated clearly that the hotel 'will be ready', this would not have been an offence, but rather a matter of breach of contract.[85]

---

79 Cf A. White, *Misleading Cases* (OUP, 1991), Ch.9.
80 (1885) 29 Ch D 459, 483.
81 [1976] 1 All ER 65.
82 An acquittal followed for technical reasons associated with transfer of ownership of the airline.
83 (1972) 116 Sol Jo 728.
84 Contrast *R v Sunair Holidays Ltd* [1973] 2 All ER 1233.
85 On quantum, cf *Jarvis v Swan Tours* [1973] 1 QB 233.

10.4 MISDESCRIPTIONS AND INTERESTS IN LAND

The word 'accommodation' within s.14 of the Trade Descriptions Act 1968 seems capable of bringing misdescription of premises let for a short period within the scope of the regulatory offence. However, it does not seem possible to employ the Act more broadly to catch misdescription connected to sale of interests in land. The estate agent who misled was beyond the scope of the regulatory offence. It is difficult to justify protecting the consumer from market failure when he or she buys washing powder,[86] but not when he or she buys a house. This was altered in 1991 with the entry into force of the Property Misdescriptions Act.[87]

Although the Act has been newsworthy predominantly for its impact on estate agency, it is apt to catch other parties involved in sales of interests in land. S.1(1) provides that:

> 'Where a false or misleading statement about a prescribed matter is made in the course of an estate agency business or a property development business, otherwise than in providing conveyancing services, the person by whom the business is carried on shall be guilty of an offence under this section.'

The 'prescribed matter' is 'any matter relating to land which is specified in an order made by the Secretary of State',[88] the relevant order being the Property Misdescriptions (Specified Matters) Order 1992.[89] The list of 33 matters in the Schedule to the Order is fairly broad, covering obvious issues such as location and address, view and proximity to services, but extending much further, for example to easements and to the existence of public or private rights of way.

False means 'false to a material degree'. Misleading, though not false, statements may be caught.[90] Liability is strict, but the normal due diligence defence applies.[91] This defence, common to several statutes creating regulatory offences, is not readily made out. Agents would be ill-advised to

---

[86]   *Tesco v Nattrass* 10.2.3 above.

[87]   For a valuable survey of the law prior to the Act and a critique of the Act, see R. Bragg, 'Regulation of Estate Agents: A Series of Half–hearted Measures?' (1992) 55 *MLR* 368.

[88]   S.1(5)(d).

[89]   SI No 2834. For comment, see A. Samuels, 'Property Misdescriptions Act 1991' (1993) 10 Trading Law 138.

[90]   S.1(5); cf 10.2.5 above under the Trade Descriptions Act.

[91]   S.2.

describe property in accordance with clients' instructions without carrying out their own checks.[92]

The enforcement of the Act is yet another responsibility for local trading standards authorities. The multiplicity of regulatory offences enforced at local level justifies separate treatment of enforcement powers and practice. This is provided in Chapter 14.

The 1991 Act is a valuable measure, but it does not provide the comprehensive coverage of the Trade Descriptions Act 1968 'proper'. There is a strong case for extending its scope to run in parallel to the general offence, as well as a strong case for achieving this as part of a general consolidation of the scattered law of trade descriptions.[93]

10.5 MISLEADING PRICE INDICATIONS

The Trade Description Act 1968 introduced provisions designed to control aspects of practices likely to mislead consumers about prices. These provisions, contained in s.11 of the 1968 Act, were a step forward at the time, but it became apparent that their scope was unduly limited.[94] Traders were able to evade them while still employing practices that were, as a matter of policy, equally objectionable. For example, pricing of services, rather than goods, was excluded. Ingenious attempts by enforcement authorities to stretch s.14 to plug this loophole largely came to grief in the face of a judicial policy of unwillingness to extend the meaning of a statute imposing criminal liability.[95] *Newell v Hicks*[96] involved an advertisement offering a video cassette recorder absolutely free with the purchase of a Renault car. The offer was misleading. The trade–in value of an old car was reduced to take account of the cost of the recorder, so in fact it was not free at all. This was held not to involve potential criminal liability under s.14, since it was not a question of the provision of services, but rather the terms on which the services were provided.[97]

---

[92]   Further on the defence, Chapter 14.2.

[93]   See further 10.7 below.

[94]   For a full account, Bragg n.6 above Ch.4.

[95]   But to address market failure effectively, an active judicial role is important; cf Chapter 14.1 on the possible value of abandoning the use of the criminal law in this area.

[96]   (1983) 128 Sol Jo 63.

[97]   Cf the narrow interpretation of s.14 in *Westminster City Council v Ray Alan (Manshops) Ltd* [1982] 1 WLR 383, [1982] 1 All ER 771. Cf discussion by P. Cartwright (1992) 9 Trading Law 2.

The area of misleading pricing indications is now covered by Part III of the Consumer Protection Act 1987,[98] a prohibition supported by a Code of Practice which fleshes out its scope. In policy terms, Part III of the 1987 Act represents a significant shift in regulatory philosophy. It supplies a good example of the modern trend in legislative consumer protection regulation towards flexible, generally expressed requirements.[99] A general duty allows essential flexibility to enforcement agencies who, in the exercise of control, are constantly 'firing at a moving target'.[100]

Section 20(1) of the Consumer Protection Act 1987 creates an offence in the following terms:

> 'Subject to the following provisions of this Part, a person shall be guilty of an offence if, in the course of any business of his, he gives (by any means whatever) to any consumers[101] an indication which is misleading as to the price at which any goods, services, accommodation or facilities are available (whether generally or from particular persons).'[102]

S.20(2) widens the scope of liability. Giving an indication which later becomes misleading within meaning of s.20(1) is an offence where 'some or all of those consumers might reasonably be expected to rely on the indication at a time after it has become misleading and [the trader has failed] to take all such steps as are reasonable to prevent those consumers from relying on the indication'.

S.21 elaborates the meaning of misleading for the purposes of s.20. 'An indication given to any consumers is misleading as to a price if what is conveyed by the indication, or what those consumers might reasonably be expected to infer from the indication or any omission from it, includes any of the following, that is to say:

(a) that the price is less than in fact it is;
(b) that the applicability of the price does not depend on facts or circumstances on which its applicability does in fact depend;
(c) that the price covers matters in respect of which an additional charge is in fact made;

---

[98] At length, Bragg n.6 above Ch.5.

[99] Cf Chapter 1.8.1.

[100] Sir Gordon Borrie, *The Development of Consumer Law and Policy* (Hamlyn Lectures, Stevens and Sons, 1984) p. 64.

[101] Defined in s.20(6).

[102] The scope of provision of 'services and facilities' and provision of 'accommodation' are amplified by ss.22 and 23. Probably the law would now catch the practice in the *Ray Alan* case, n.97 above.

(d) that a person who in fact has no such expectation –
    (i) expects the price to be increased or reduced (whether or not at a particular time or by a particular amount); or
    (ii) expects the price, or the price as increased or reduced, to be maintained (whether or not for a particular period); or

(e) that the facts or circumstances by reference to which the consumers might reasonably be expected to judge the validity of any relevant comparison made or implied by the indication are not what in fact they are.

S.21(2) offers a parallel list of indications that are misleading to consumers as to a method of determining a price.

The scope of s.21 is broad. It covers the straightforward instance of goods priced on the shelves at 50 for which 60 is charged at the till (point (a) in the list). It also includes cases of goods priced at 50 which, it is stated, will soon rise to 60 where there is no such expectation (point (d) in the list). It also covers subtler cases where goods are priced at 50 which, it is falsely stated, were once priced at 60 or are priced at 60 at a nearby shop (point (e) in the list). S.21(3) is directed specifically at defining relevant comparisons for the purposes of point (e). It should be noted that accurate price comparisons are not suppressed.[103]

The style of the regime established by Part III of the Consumer Protection Act 1987 is significantly affected by the role of Codes of Practice envisaged in s.25. S.25(1) provides that:

> 'The Secretary of State may, after consulting the Director General of Fair Trading and such other persons as the Secretary of State considers it appropriate to consult, by order approve any code of practice issued (whether by the Secretary of State or another person) for the purpose of–
>
> (a) giving practical guidance with respect to any of the requirements of section 20 above; and
>
> (b) promoting what appear to the Secretary of State to be desirable practices as to the circumstances and manner in which any person gives an indication as to the price at which any goods, services, accommodation or facilities are available or indicates any other matter in respect of which any such indication may be misleading.'

---

103 German law of unfair competition has traditionally been much more interventionist and has controlled even accurate comparisons. Such perceived over–regulation of the market has brought German law into frequent collision with EC law of free movement when applied to restrict the development of integrated, cross–border advertising campaigns. See further Chapter 2.2. English law's more permissive stance is more in tune with EC rules.

The legal aspects of Codes of Practice are examined in Chapter 16.3. S.25(2) declares that contravention of an approved Code 'shall not of itself give rise to any criminal or civil liability'. Nevertheless, it is permissible for contravention of, or compliance with, codes to be taken into account in proceedings for an offence under ss.20(1) and (2).

Some of the policy considerations that underpin the use of Codes of Practice are elaborated more fully in Chapter 16.[104] One of several benefits lies in the ability of the Code to provide some specific illustrations of the way in which the law is intended to operate. In a statute, such factual precision runs the risk of rendering the law too rigid or even of offering hostages to fortune but, in a Code, the illustration simply becomes part of the interpretative climate.

In November 1988 the key Code of Practice was approved by the Secretary of State – the *Code of Practice for Traders on Price Indications*.[105] Naturally the Code is influential and is today typically the starting point for both commercial planning and enforcement practice in the pricing field. The Code is especially helpful in its amplification of the scope of legitimate price comparison (both with the same goods or services previously offered or competing goods or services).[106]

S.26 confers a power on the Secretary of State to make regulations. S.26 is a counterpart to s.25, but offers the opportunity to make 'harder' law than the soft law Codes of Practice envisaged by s.25. However, the current policy preference for flexible regulatory regimes dictates a subsidiary role for specific regulations. The same is true of consumer safety law under Part II of the Act, where the same power to make specific regulations may be observed in conjunction with a policy preference to exercise that power sparingly.[107]

Section 24 contains specific defences relevant to Part III. The general due diligence defence in the Consumer Protection Act 1987 is available in relation to s.20(1) offences, which are offences of strict liability. The general defence is examined in Chapter 14.

The above account concerns control of misleading price descriptions. The obligation to disclose prices constitutes a regulatory technique with a separate rationale. It aims to cure a basic imbalance in information flowing from the conditions of the modern market, rather than to address any specific misleading practice.[108] The Price Marking Order 1991 imposes such

---

[104] Chapter 16.3; see also Chapter 1.8.4.
[105] SI 1988 No 2078.
[106] Cf G. Holgate, 'Consumer Protection: Comparisons with other Traders' Prices' (1993) 10 *Trading Law* 22.
[107] Chapter 12.2.
[108] See further Chapter 1.8.3.

obligations,[109] being a measure of particular relevance to shaping a legal framework for 'unit pricing' – prices expressed by reference to units of measurement.

10.6 ADVERTISING

An advertisement that is misleading is perfectly capable of falling within the control of the Trade Descriptions Act 1968. In s.39 advertising is broadly defined to cover catalogues, circulars and price lists. This provision is designed simply to confirm the breadth of the Act's scope. Other standard types of advertising are also perfectly capable of falling foul of the Trade Descriptions Act. If the ingredients explained in 10.2 above are all present, then an advertiser has committed an offence. Advertisements in which a trade description is used in relation to a class of goods are the subject of special treatment in s.5 of the Trade Descriptions Act. An innocent party whose business is publishing advertisements has a special defence under s.25. Misleading pricing in advertisements may fall within the offence created under Part III of the Consumer Protection Act 1987.

The law operates beyond the Trade Descriptions Act, since it is widely perceived that advertisements require a more general type of control. Advertisements may not mislead within the confines of the Act, yet there may still be grounds for public concern. Advertisements have an extraordinary prominence in contemporary culture. In some jurisdictions, advertising regulation has developed into a hotly contested area of public activity.[110] It has been attacked as an intrusion into constitutional rights of (commercial) free expression and as an infringement on the ability of the individual to make his or her own choices free of State intervention. This in turn has prompted spirited defences of the role of the State in correcting market failures and protecting the consumer from the perceived baneful influence of advertising as preference-distorting.[111] Such issues are capable of forming the basis for litigation about the constitutionality of controls over advertising. Some of these issues are explored more fully in Chapter 1 in connection with

---

[109] SI 1991 No 1382, amended 1991 No 1690. This implements relevant EC Directives.
[110] Cf D. Harland, 'The Control of Advertising – a Comparative Overview' (1993) 1 *Competition and Consumer Law Journal* 95. For a description of 16 different jurisdictions, see J. Maxeiner and P. Schotthöfer (eds), *Advertising Law in Europe and North America* (Kluwer, 1992).
[111] For a research agenda, cf I. Ramsay, 'Advertising, Taste Construction, and the Search for an Enlightened Policy: a Critique' (1991) 29 *Osgoode Hall LJ* 573.

the broader issue of the extent to which market regulatory laws may be subject to constitutional review.[112]

For all the occasional furore in the UK about 'shock' advertising techniques,[113] there has been no experience of legal or political debate at such a level of intensity. Self–regulation has a long–standing tradition in the UK. The Advertising Standards Authority is non–statutory and is established by the industry. It has its own Codes of Practice; the British Code of Advertising Practice and the British Code of Sales Promotion Practice, which in early 1995 were consolidated into a single document, the British Code of Advertising and Sales Promotion. Complaints may be lodged with the Authority,[114] which may ask advertisers to withdraw or to amend advertisements that infringe a Code. Reports are published; advertisers are expected to abide by decisions.[115] The core of the Code requires that advertisements be decent, honest and truthful. It will be appreciated that it is the element of decency, in particular, that takes the scope of the Code far beyond the control of the Trade Descriptions Act 1968.[116]

As a result of EC intervention, self–regulation is no longer the exclusive method of control of advertising in the UK. The EC Directive on Misleading Advertising was adopted in 1984.[117] Its legal base was Article 100 which means that it is formally a measure of market integration.[118] Diversity in the law and practice of advertising control State–by–State impedes integration and accordingly Community harmonisation has been pursued.

The UK implemented the Directive by Statutory Instrument in the Control of Misleading Advertisements Regulations 1988.[119]

The substance of the control required by EC law addresses misleading advertising,[120] which is to be suppressed by Member States. The definition of 'misleading' for these purposes is found in Regulation 2(2) of the 1988

---

[112] Chapter 1.9.2.

[113] For good or ill, Benetton, in particular, has attracted attention in this way.

[114] ASA, Brook House, 2–16 Torrington Place, London WC1E 7HN.

[115] On judicial review of decisions, cf *R v ASA, ex parte Vernons* [1992] 1 WLR 1289.

[116] Cf K. Brinkworth, 'The Advertising Standards Authority: Some Recent Developments' (1993) 10 *Trading Law* 66; S. Locke, 'Self–Regulation in Advertising' (1994) 4 *Consumer Policy Review* 111.

[117] Dir. 84/450. For an insight into the flavour of the debate at the time, see P. Thomson, then Director General of the Advertising Standards Authority, 'Self–Regulation in Advertising – Some Observations from the Advertising Standards Authority', Ch.IV in G. Woodroffe (ed), *Consumer Law in the EEC*, (Sweet and Maxwell/CCLR, 1984).

[118] Chapter 2.3.3.

[119] SI 1988 No 915.

[120] Cf Case C–373/90 *Procureur de la République v X* [1992] ECR I–131 for the interpretative assistance of the European Court.

Statutory Instrument, which reflects Articles 2(2) and 3 of the EC Directive. It is the deceptive nature of the advertising that is the key element. It is provided in Regulation 2(2) that:

> '... an advertisement is misleading if in any way, including its presentation, it deceives or is likely to deceive the persons to whom it is addressed or whom it reaches and if, by reason of its deceptive nature, it is likely to affect their economic behaviour or, for those reasons, injures or is likely to injure a competitor of the person whose interests the advertisement seeks to promote.'

The practical impact of the regime naturally depends on the institutional structures set up to police it. Member States have very different traditions. Most of those possessing established control mechanisms employ a more formal system than the UK. This gave rise to difficult debate about the proper structure of the EC Directive. The agreed objective is contained in Article 4(1) of the EC Directive, a provision which obliges Member States to:

> 'ensure that adequate and effective means exist for the control of misleading advertising in the interests of consumers as well as competitors and the general public.'

Legal provisions shall enable persons or organisations regarded under national law as having a legitimate interest in prohibiting misleading advertising to pursue one or both of two stipulated routes: first, the taking of legal action against such advertising and, second, the bringing of such advertising before an administrative authority competent either to decide on complaints or to initiate appropriate legal proceedings. Article 4(2) of the Directive requires courts and administrative authorities to be empowered to take stipulated forms of action, including the making of cessation orders, in the event of offending advertising.

The policy was to permit States the option of retaining administrative structures as adequate regulation in the area. The UK, in particular, was concerned to avoid the imposition of a judicial structure since the Government viewed self–regulation as satisfactory. Article 4(3) of the Directive requires that, where the administrative option is taken, the authorities shall be, *inter alia*, impartial – not dominated by advertisers; also, where the powers are the exclusive preserve of the administrative authority, decisions shall be reasoned and shall be subject to judicial review in the event of impropriety or unreasonableness.

Article 5 of the Directive further illustrates the receptivity of the EC structure to extra–legal enforcement. Article 5 makes it clear that voluntary control of misleading advertising by self-regulatory bodies is not excluded, although proceedings of this nature must be additional to, not in substitution for, the court or administrative route established by Article 4.

The UK chose to implement the Directive at the institutional level by empowering the Director General of Fair Trading, to whom complaints should be made under Regulation 4 of the 1988 Regulations. The Director is empowered by Regulation 5 to apply to a court for an injunction against any person involved in the publication of a misleading advertisement. Litigation in *Director General of Fair Trading v Tobyward Ltd* permitted Hoffman J to discuss the role of the procedure.[121] Complaints about advertisements for a slimming aid marketed by Tobyward were upheld by the ASA, but the advertisements were not discontinued. The ASA referred the matter to the Director General, who sought an injunction. Hoffman J granted it, feeling it proper to 'support the principle of self-regulation'[122] by granting an injunction that would effectively give legal backing to the ASA's finding. He also felt that the interests of consumers demanded the protection of an injunction. The decision is important in instilling respect for ASA rulings and in discouraging advertisers from contesting the decisions of the ASA through litigation.

In essence, the system is self-regulation endowed with statutory backing. It is an interesting method for securing administrative supervision of the market, beyond the private law, but separate from the criminal law.[123] It is perhaps regrettable that the standing of consumer representative organisations to bring proceedings has not been recognised.[124] They are limited to the possibility of complaining to the Director General in the hope that he will take on the matter.

It was mentioned above that the Directive on Misleading Advertising was adopted in 1984 after stiff debate among Member States with different traditions in the field. In fact, the variations in practice prevented agreement on a wider role for EC legislation in the regulation of advertising. The original draft Commission proposal in the field covered misleading, unfair and comparative advertising.[125] The first two types were to be controlled, the third (comparative) liberalised. However, the Directive as finally adopted excluded provisions concerning both unfair and comparative advertising.

---

[121] [1989] 2 All ER 266.

[122] 270g.

[123] For general policy discussion, T. Wilhelmsson, 'Administrative Procedures for the Control of Marketing Practices – Theoretical Rationale and Perspectives' (1992) 15 *JCP* 159.

[124] The same non–recognition marks control of unfair terms; Chapter 9.8.

[125] OJ 1978 C70/4, amended proposal OJ 1979 C194/3.

This reflects the difficulties of hammering out a satisfactory harmonised regime against a background of legal diversity.

Comparative advertising is largely permitted under English law (apart from control under trade mark law), whereas some other systems, including the German, exercise relatively rigorous control.[126] The Commission has periodically attempted to resuscitate its proposals in the area, but has failed to attract sufficient support in Council. Comparative advertising remains unregulated by Community legislation, although some national rules that obstruct its use in cross–border trade have fallen foul of primary Community law.[127] This is a manifestation of the deregulatory impulse of EC trade law.

10.7 REFORM

Why not a consolidated trade descriptions law regime? There is no adequate answer to the question. Consolidation would be welcome.

The motivation in 1968 for confining liability for the newly created offence of misdescription of services to those possessing a (defined and admittedly limited) guilty mind was understandable.[128] More than 25 years later, however, the justification for distinguishing between ss.1 and 14 in this way has been completely eroded. The cause of coherent consumer protection designed to correct market failure would be served by converting s.14 offences into strict liability offences (like those under s.1) in preference to the current 'semi–strict' liability.[129]

Moreover, the law controlling price indications and the description of land could profitably be consolidated into a single, overall regime. This general reform would provide the opportunity to eliminate oddities such as the liability of private individuals under s.23 TDA, exposed in *Olgeirsson v Kitching*.[130]

Consolidation of the law into a general control over misleading trade descriptions, based on the normal pattern of the regulatory offence examined in Chapter 14, would reduce compliance costs for business, enhance effective enforcement and make the law more transparent for consumers.[131]

---

126 Cf note 103 above.
127 See Chapter 2, esp 2.2.5.
128 10.3.1 above.
129 A DTI Communication in 1991 made such a suggestion. In this direction, see P. Cartwright, 'Reforming the Trade Descriptions Act 1968' (1993) 3 *Consumer Policy Review* 34.
130 See Chapter 14.2.5.
131 Advertising controls concerned with aspects other than misdescription would remain separate.

11 Public Regulation of Consumer Credit

The complexities of the Consumer Credit Act 1974 were introduced in Chapter 7 when we discussed how the Act seeks to protect individual consumers through private law mechanisms. In this chapter we focus on the public law regulation of the credit market provided for by the Consumer Credit Act 1974, namely the licensing, advertising and marketing controls and also the controls regulating information held by credit reference agencies.[1] It is worthwhile noting at the outset that the Office of Fair Trading's report on *Consumer Credit Deregulation*[2] found that the system worked fairly well and was supported by the credit industry. While it proposed some changes, notably the abolition of the quotation regulations and the simplification of the advertising regulations,[3] it basically found that the system worked satisfactorily. Industry even welcomed licensing as being 'neither particularly onerous nor costly, yet provid[ing] a measure of reassurance that all those operating in the field of credit and hire have met at least some basic requirements of fitness'.[4]

11.1 LICENSING

Credit is a product about which consumers are very easily confused. It is a product which consumers often seek when they are at their most vulnerable. It is also an industry which in the past has had a bad reputation with regard to its enforcement practices. Hence it is sensible to restrict entry into the industry to those who satisfy certain basic requirements of good character and probity. A licensing system has been adopted.[5] We shall see that a useful by-product of this system is that it provides a fall back mechanism through which the Director General of Fair Trading (hereafter Director General) can ensure that the substantive rights given to consumers are honoured and traders satisfy their obligations. A licence is required to carry on a consumer

---

1 For an overview of techniques and rationales for going beyond the private law regulatory framework, see 1.7-1.8.

2 (Office of Fair Trading, 1994).

3 In addition to the changes to private law regulation discussed in Chapter 7.

4 See *Consumer Credit Deregulation, op. cit.* p.104.

5 See 1.8.2.

credit, consumer hire or ancillary credit business.[6] Ancillary credit businesses include credit brokerage, debt adjusting, debt counselling, debt collecting or operating a credit reference agency.[7] In fact licences are issued to cover various categories – lending money (category A), consumer hire (category B), credit brokerage (category C), debt adjusting and debt counselling (category D), debt collecting (category E) and credit reference agencies (category F).

At present a licence applicant must determine which categories he or she wishes to be licensed for. In practice many applicants apply for all categories just in case they should wish to undertake some business which falls outside their mainstream work. In his deregulation report, the then Director General proposed a simplification so that the licence would cover all aspects, but he would retain the right to show good reason why a particular trader should not carry on a particular type of business, such as debt collecting; alternatively, a trader could specifically request a more limited licence.

The definitions of consumer credit and consumer hire businesses relate to those which enter 'regulated agreements'.[8] Thus, if such a business only ever enters unregulated or exempt agreements, then no licence is needed. However, the same is not true of ancillary credit businesses which must always be licensed regardless of the type of agreements they are involved with. It should be noted that the Act has a general provision which provides that a person should not be treated as carrying on a business of a particular type merely because he or she occasionally enters into transactions of that type.[9] This would remove the need to obtain a licence for that marginal activity.

Nevertheless, the fact that a trader does not need to be licensed does not mean that other provisions of the Consumer Credit Act 1974 do not apply. Equally it should be noted that, whilst the Director General proposed removing most of the Act's controls from business lending agreements, he nevertheless wished to retain the current licensing regime which requires all businesses dealing with individuals (thereby including sole traders and partnerships) to be licensed. As few firms deal exclusively with incorporated associations, this in effect requires almost all businesses to be licensed. It also permits the Director General to use his licensing powers to prevent unfair practices emerging once the regulatory controls of the Consumer Credit Act 1974 are removed from business agreements. These proposed changes can be seen as a sensible realisation that businesses need different forms of regulatory intervention than ordinary consumers. They are more

---

6   Ss.21 and 147, Consumer Credit Act 1974.

7   S.146, Consumer Credit Act 1974.

8   S.189(1), Consumer Credit Act 1974 and see 7.4.1.

9   See *Roy Marshall* (1990) 90 Cr App Rep 73; *Hare v Schurek* [1993] CCLR 47.

often likely to be able to look after their own interests, but the law and enforcement authorities need the power to intercede in those circumstances in which they are as vulnerable as private consumers.

Most consumer credit licences are standard licences issued to named persons, though some group licences have been granted, for example to the Law Society for ancillary credit business carried on by solicitors. The period for which the licence is granted has varied dramatically over the years; initially fixed at three years, it was subsequently increased to ten years in 1979 and to 15 years in 1986. The aim was to reduce the administrative workload of the Office of Fair Trading and to lessen the burden on businesses. It was soon realised, however, that the licence period was too long for the regulators to be able to exercise effective monitoring and control of businesses[10] and in 1991 it was reduced to five years.

There are estimated to be around 150,000 consumer credit licences, with new applications running at around 19,000 a year.[11] The application fee in 1994 was £70 for a sole trader and £175 for anyone else. The licence application procedure is a positive one, which means that the onus is on the applicant to satisfy the Director General that he or she is a fit person to engage in the activities covered by the licence and that the name under which he or she applies is not misleading or otherwise undesirable.[12] When determining a licence application, the Director General can take any relevant circumstances into account, but is particularly directed to consider whether the applicant or his or her past or present employees, agents or associates (or where the applicant is a corporation, the controller of the body corporate or associates) have committed offences of fraud, dishonesty or violence, contravened the Consumer Credit Act 1974 or regulations made under it, carried on discriminatory practices, or engaged in deceitful, oppressive or otherwise improper business practices (whether unlawful or not). The breadth of these powers is quite significant, especially the fact that behaviour can be taken into account even if it is not unlawful.

It is perhaps not an overstatement to suggest that the threat of refusal or withdrawal of a credit licence is the most important weapon in the Director General's fair trading armoury, since almost every trading business needs to

---

10   This is particularly true since the Director General has no powers to seek information from a licensee other than when he or she makes an application under the Act. In *Consumer Credit Deregulation, op. cit.*, p. 102 the Director General proposed that he should be given such powers.

11   *Consumer Credit Deregulation, op. cit.*, p. 94.

12   S.25, Consumer Credit Act 1974; cf the negative procedure under s.3, Estate Agents Act 1979 under which the Director General can make an order prohibiting an unfit person from carrying on estate agency work, but there is no requirement to first obtain a licence.

obtain a consumer credit licence. Director Generals have shown themselves willing to use the threat of withdrawing licences to promote general business standards, not necessarily just those related to the credit aspects of the business.[13] It was very noticeable in the *Consumer Credit Deregulation* report (as on other occasions) that the then Director General frequently drew attention to practices which caused him concern and requested the industry to put its own house in order, with the none too veiled threat that he would invoke his licensing powers should they fail to do so. In one sense licensing is a severe form of regulation, for without it entry to a market is precluded. Nevertheless the Director General made the point that licensing allows him to exert informal pressures which help avoid the need for excessive regulation of particular practices and also prevent the imposition of sanctions where the problem is incompetence or bad management rather than dishonesty.[14]

On application for a credit licence, the Director General can grant the licence, grant it subject to conditions, or refuse the application.[15] During its currency he can vary the licence either on application by the licensee[16] or compulsorily if he would subsequently be minded to grant the licence on different conditions.[17] He also has similar powers to suspend or revoke a licence.[18] Where the Director General is minded to refuse an application, to grant it in different terms from the application, or to vary, suspend or revoke a licence he must inform the applicant of his reasons for that decision and give him or her the opportunity to submit representations in support of his or her application. However, this procedure is not unproblematic for the Director General. As a former Director General has pointed out, the most difficult 'minded to refuse' notices are those based solely on complaints. By their very nature such complaints are based on only one version of events given to the enforcement authorities by discontented consumers. The specific case may have been less memorable to the trader concerned, who deals with a large number of such matters each day and may be unable to remember clearly the incident complained of, and yet still be able to raise sufficient questions and doubts about the complaints to make it impossible for the Office of Fair Trading to make a finding of fact on the issue raised.[19]

As noted, about 19,000 licence applications are made each year, during which time the Office of Fair Trading questions the fitness of around 900

---

13 See for example the action taken against photocopier leasing firms engaged in unfair selling practices, *Bee Line*, 91/4 at p.12.
14 *Consumer Credit Deregulation, op. cit.* at pp. 98-9.
15 S.27, Consumer Credit Act 1974.
16 S.30, Consumer Credit Act 1974.
17 S.31, Consumer Credit Act 1974.
18 S.32, Consumer Credit Act 1974.
19 G. Borrie, 'Licensing Practice under the Consumer Credit Act' [1982] JBL 91.

traders (including existing licensees). Of these 900 cases, 200 will be formally put to adjudicating officers acting on behalf of the Director General to consider whether their licence should be refused, varied or revoked. For the five years 1989–93, the average number of decisions going against the applicant or licensee was 106.[20]

In 1988 the Government proposed removing from the scope of the licensing system ancillary credit and hire traders (those falling within categories C–F) and instead placing them under a negative regime under which they could trade freely until the authorities were alerted to their unfitness to carry on their present range of activities. The Director General was not keen on this proposal and set out his reasons in the *Consumer Credit Deregulation* report.[21] He thought positive licensing had advantages in allowing enforcement authorities to be aware of all traders active in their area, thereby allowing them the opportunity to advise on the legal requirements and hence prevent bad practices occurring. He also noted the practical difficulties his Office had faced when administering the negative scheme under the Estate Agents Act 1979. In addition, moving to a negative scheme would save little money (indeed arguably more money would have to be spent tracking down rogue traders under a negative system). Moreover, as one cannot charge a licence fee under a negative system, the financial burden would have to be met either by increasing the remaining licence fees by 50% or by the Exchequer. The Director General was also keen to retain the full scope of his licensing powers as a lever to establish high standards and promote best practice across the whole credit industry. The most powerful argument against the Government's proposals was that most of the Office's regulatory action was aimed at activities in categories C and E (credit brokerage and debt collection); thus it appeared ludicrous to relax the regulation of the very activities which caused greatest concern.

Unlicensed traders who undertake activities for which a licence is required commit an offence punishable by a £5,000 fine if tried summarily or a fine or up to two years imprisonment if convicted on indictment.[22] The more serious sanction, however, is the unenforceabilty of such agreements without an order from the Director General. This sanction applies to all regulated agreements entered into by unlicensed creditors or owners, other than non–commercial agreements.[23] An incentive is also placed on creditors and owners to monitor their brokers, for any agreements entered into as a result of introductions effected by unlicensed brokers will be unenforceable,

---

[20] *Consumer Credit Deregulation, op. cit.*, p. 94.
[21] *Op. cit.*, pp. 95–99.
[22] S.39, Consumer Credit Act 1974.
[23] S.40(1), Consumer Credit Act 1974.

even if the creditor or owner is licensed.[24] Contracts for the services of ancillary credit businesses will also be unenforceable if the business does not have a licence.[25] When determining whether to make a validating order, the Director General is directed to take all relevant circumstances into account. In the case of an unlicensed trader entering into a regulated agreement[26] or an agreement for the services of an ancillary credit business,[27] the Director General is particularly directed to consider the prejudice caused by the trader's conduct, whether it was likely that a licence would have been granted if one had been applied for and the degree of culpability for the failure to obtain the licence. Where the order is being applied for by a creditor or owner following an introduction by an unlicensed credit broker the Director General is again directed to consider the prejudice caused by the broker's conduct and the degree of culpability on the part of the applicant in facilitating the continuance of an unlicensed business by the credit broker.[28] The Director General has recently pointed out that a validating order is only needed if the agreement has to be enforced through the courts; it is not needed to request or take payments under the terms of the agreement or to accept the *voluntary* surrender of goods.[29] Although intended to counter charges that the law places too great a burden on businesses, this statement also serves to illustrate the ease with which the legal protection afforded to consumers can be circumvented by the trader who takes advantage of the consumer's ignorance of his or her legal rights. This underlines the point that the unenforceability sanction in the Consumer Credit Act 1974 is not very effective.[30]

11.2 SEEKING BUSINESS

11.2.1 Unsolicited Credit Tokens

Certain forms of seeking business are prohibited by the Consumer Credit Act 1974. Thus s.51 makes it an offence to give a credit token to a person who has not asked for it. Credit tokens include such things as trading checks and credit cards. This provision was a response to the marketing practices of

---

[24]   S.149, Consumer Credit Act 1974.
[25]   S.148, Consumer Credit Act 1974.
[26]   S.40, Consumer Credit Act 1974.
[27]   S.148, Consumer Credit Act 1974.
[28]   S.49, Consumer Credit Act 1974.
[29]   *Consumer Credit Deregulation, op. cit.* p. 100.
[30]   These weaknesses have already been considered in relation to the situations where agreements should only be enforceable by court order, see 7.5.4.

some credit card companies who, when credit cards were first launched in the early 1970s, promoted this form of credit by sending unsolicited cards to prospective customers.

11.2.2 Minors

It is also an offence, with a view to financial gain, to send a circular to a minor inviting him or her to borrow money, hire goods, obtain goods or services on credit or apply for advice or information on borrowing money, obtaining credit or hiring goods.[31] In *Alliance & Leicester Building Society v Babbs*[32] there was found to be no intention to obtain financial gain from minors as (i) the circular stated, albeit in regrettable small print, that credit was not available to under 18s, (ii) it was the Society's policy not to lend to minors and (iii) their computers were programmed to prevent money being lent to minors. There is a defence for a person who can prove that he or she did not know and had no reasonable cause to suspect that the person was a minor, but this defence does not apply where the circular is sent to a school or educational establishment for minors.[33] The Department of Trade and Industry's Consultative document *Revised Proposals for Legislation on Credit Marketing*[34] proposed removing this defence, on the basis that the costs it imposed on creditors having to check mailing lists was too high. Instead a new defence was proposed requiring that 'appropriate' precautions be taken to minimise the risk of sending credit circulars to minors and that all 'reasonable' precautions are taken to ensure that any credit circular inadvertently sent to a minor clearly states that the credit is not available to minors.

11.2.3 Canvassing Debtor–Creditor Agreements Off Trade Premises

One of the most restrictive controls on methods of seeking business is that which makes it an offence to canvass off trade premises for debtor–creditor agreements[35] or credit brokerage, debt adjusting or debt counselling services.[36] The aim of these provisions is to protect consumers from being pressured into entering into such contracts in their own home or at social

---

31   S.50(1), Consumer Credit Act 1974.
32   [1993] CCLR 277.
33   S.50(2), Consumer Credit Act 1974.
34   (DTI, 1991).
35   S.49, Consumer Credit Act 1974.
36   S.154, Consumer Credit Act 1974.

gatherings. The definition of 'trade premises' is crucial to the offence. For debtor–creditor agreements this prohibition does not extend to a place where a business is carried on (whether on a permanent or temporary basis) by the creditor, owner, supplier, canvasser or his employer or principal, or the consumer.[37] Where the offence relates to the ancillary credit businesses, then the prohibition does not apply to the permanent or temporary place of business of the ancillary credit business, the canvasser or his employer or principal, or the consumer.[38] Thus the offence can be committed in the consumer's home, unless the consumer runs a business from there; in a public house, unless the landlord is the canvasser; or on the public highway, for instance by approaching customers outside the work's gate or post office.

The offence requires an individual to solicit entry into the relevant agreements by making oral representations during a visit to a place other than a trade premise. Since the oral representations must be made during the course of the visit, telephone canvassing is not caught. For there to be an offence, the visit must have been carried out for the purpose of making such oral representations. Therefore no offence would be committed if such representations were made during a conversation incidental to a social occasion or during the course of collecting repayments under existing loans – unless offering the loan facility was the underlying reason for the visit.

The prohibition does not apply to debtor–creditor–supplier agreements. A common ruse is for a company to sell a service to a family through doorstep selling (family portraits are a common example) and then sell on the account to moneylenders who offer their moneylending services when collecting the payment. This is an attempt to circumvent the prohibition on canvassing debtor–creditor agreements which will not be outside the wording of the prohibition unless there has been a written request to discuss a money loan. It should be noted that the soliciting of an overdraft is excluded from the prohibitions.

No offence will be committed if the visit is carried out in response to a request made on a previous occasion. Thus a company can canvass by mail, advertisements or telephone and make appointments to discuss such agreements in the consumer's home. However, if on that visit an individual is solicited to enter into a debtor–creditor agreement, a separate offence will have been committed unless the request was in writing and signed by or on behalf of the person making it.[39]

---

37   S.48, Consumer Credit Act 1974.
38   S.153, Consumer Credit Act 1974.
39   S.49 (2), Consumer Credit Act 1974: there would appear to be no such offence in relation to soliciting ancillary credit business, where a previous request for a visit, in any form, would appear to be a sufficient defence.

11.3 CONDUCT OF BUSINESS

The Consumer Credit Act 1974 also contains wide powers to make regulations governing the conduct of business, though the only regulations issued to date cover credit reference agencies[40] and pawn records.[41] There are also powers to issue regulations governing the seeking of business by licensees and to require businesses to display prescribed information, but no such regulations have been enacted.

11.4 ADVERTISING AND QUOTATIONS

We have already seen from our study of its private law provisions that the Consumer Credit Act 1974 is less concerned with controlling the content of the agreement than with ensuring that it is transparent and entered into without undue pressure being exerted on the consumer. The requirement to provide copies of the agreement and the prescription of the information which it must contain support this policy. Yet, frequently, once the consumer has reached the stage of signing an agreement, he or she will be psychologically, if not legally, tied into taking credit from that source. Thus it is important that, prior to this stage, the consumer has access to reliable information on alternative credit sources available.

11.4.1 Advertisements

In addition to the law's general controls on advertising,[42] there is a specific prohibition in s.46, Consumer Credit Act 1974 on the conveying of information which is in a material respect false or misleading. There is also a prohibition on advertising restricted–use credit agreements where the person is not holding him or herself out as willing to sell the goods or provide the service for cash, presumably because it is then impossible to calculate the true cost of credit.[43] In addition, there are powers to make regulations governing the form and content of advertisements, breach of which is an offence.[44] 'Advertisement' is defined very broadly by the Act and covers all

---

40   Consumer Credit (Conduct of Business) (Credit References) Regulations 1977, S.I. 1977/330.

41   Consumer Credit (Conduct of Business) (Pawn Records) Regulations 1983, S.I. 1983/1565.

42   See Chapter 10.

43   S.45, Consumer Credit Act 1974.

44   Ss.44 and 167(2), Consumer Credit Act 1974.

forms of advertising, from circulars to television and radio broadcasts. These rules apply to those who indicate that they are willing to provide credit or bail goods, and thus catch a wider category of persons than many of the provisions in the Act: even non–regulated agreements may be caught if they are secured on land. Nor are all of the 'exempt agreements' excluded from the effect of these provisions. However, the provisions do not apply to advertisements for credit which are clearly restricted to corporations or where the credit must exceed £15,000, and there is no requirement that there be security involving land.

The content of the advertisement regulations has been controversial. It took until 1980 for the first set of such regulations to be agreed upon. Those regulations established a tripartite structure where the requirements depended upon whether the advertisement was deemed to be a simple, intermediate or full credit advertisement. This structure has proven complex; with the distinction between full and intermediate advertisements being difficult to discern. Many technical breaches have occurred, even by reputable traders who wished to comply. The present regulations of 1989 amended the original ones and, whilst clarifying their application to brokers and making some simplifications, nevertheless retain the same basic structure, but also introduce the requirement for warnings about the risks associated with secure loans and foreign currency mortgages.[45] With the use of warnings very much in vogue, the Department of Trade and Industry's 1991 *Revised Proposals for Legislation on Credit Marketing* proposed a whole raft of new warnings to be included in credit advertisements,

In the *Consumer Credit Deregulation* report the Director General took a more robust approach. He proposed that a general requirement be retained that all information given should be clear and easily legible. Beyond this, traders should be free simply to advertise in general terms the services they offer. However, where an interest rate or other figure relating to the cost of credit is specified the APR should also be shown and given the same degree of prominence as any given interest rate.[46] Equally where a particular credit product or specific examples of terms are given then information should be supplied about the amount of credit offered (lump sum or credit limit), the number, timing and amount of repayments, the interest rate and the APR, and any other charges and fees.[47] Similar proposals are made in relation to

---

[45] Consumer Credit (Advertisements) Regulations 1989, S.I. 1989/1125.

[46] The present Regulations require that it be given greater prominence, which has given rise to some difficult problems of interpretation; for instance, is it satisfied by merely underlining the APR?

[47] For variable interest rates where this is an initial discounted rate, the APR should also be stated based on the current variable rate, with less prominence and with a

consumer hire advertisements. The Director General accepted the retention of warnings about the consequences of failing to keep up mortgage repayments, but in printed advertisements only. Though promising to undertake further discussions on the question of the use of warnings, he appears to be lukewarm, at best, concerning their effectiveness. This would fit in with his general antipathy to the 'generation ...of small print purely to meet regulatory requirements'.[48]

The Director General's scepticism surrounding the use of warnings may be well founded; indeed, the Regulations would appear to be a case of legislative overkill, although the regulators would contend that the industry had originally favoured that form for the Regulations. Reducing the detailed rules should not cause too many consumer protection problems so long as the Director General is able to make effective use of the broader powers contained in the Act and so long as the detailed rules continue to prevent misleading examples from being given.

11.4.2 Quotations

Similar problems of complexity characterise the Regulations which prescribe the form and content of quotations.[49] It is an offence for traders not to respond to any request – whether written or oral (including those made by telephone) – with a quotation in the prescribed form, unless they are not prepared to do business with the individual making the request. In *Consumer Credit Deregulation*, the Office of Fair Trading took the view that the Regulations were too burdensome, especially as consumers rarely expressly requested a full quotation, but tended instead to inquire about specific terms. It was proposed to abolish the Regulations and in due course to amend s.46, Consumer Credit Act 1974 to make it an offence to provide quotations which are materially false or misleading.

11.5 CREDIT REFERENCE AGENCIES

At the time the Consumer Credit Act 1974 was enacted, the computer age was just dawning. Since then the amount of information stored on computers concerning consumers and in particular their credit record has expanded as has the ability of the credit companies to make use of the data when reaching

---

brief statement as to its applicability, for the period subsequent to the initial rate period.

[48] *Consumer Credit Deregulation, op. cit.* p. 38.

[49] Consumer Credit (Quotations) Regulations 1989, S.I. 1989/1126.

credit–granting decisions. The ethical and policy issues surrounding the collection, storage and use of computer–stored information led to the enactment of the Data Protection Act 1984 and the creation of the Office of the Data Protection Registrar. The Registrar can ensure that the so–called 'data protection principles' contained in the First Schedule to the Act are complied with. These have already caused some debate between the Registrar and the credit industry, in the first place as to whether it was permissible to take into account data held on people other than the applicant for credit who lived at the same address as the applicant: the Data Protection Tribunal held that this was only permissible in respect of family members. Currently there is a debate about whether it can be made a mandatory term of credit contracts that information on the account be passed to credit reference agencies, regardless of whether the account is in arrears.[50]

The Data Protection Act 1984 gives the data subject (the consumer) the right to access data held about him or her and where appropriate to have it corrected or erased. However, this right to access data does not apply where all the data held consists of information which the consumer has a right to access by virtue of s.158, Consumer Credit Act 1974. Any application under the Data Protection Act 1984 is then treated as if it were an application under the Consumer Credit Act 1974.[51]

The Consumer Credit Act 1974 gives the debtor or hirer the right, within 28 days of the termination of negotiations, to make a written request that the creditor, owner or any negotiator inform him or her of any credit reference agency consulted. It is an offence to fail to comply with such a request within seven days. On payment of a £1 fee, the consumer can then apply to the credit reference agency for a copy of his or her file. Within seven working days the agency must provide him or her with a copy or give notice that no file is held. The agency must also inform the consumer of his or her right to give it notice to remove or amend any information which is incorrect and likely to be prejudicial if not amended. Within 28 days of receiving such a notice, the agency must inform the consumer of what steps, if any, it has decided to take. Unless the entry has been removed, the consumer then has 28 days from receiving the notice (56 days from sending the first notice in cases where the agency has failed to respond) to send a further notice requiring that a notice of correction be added to the file. The agency should inform the consumer within a further 28 days if it intends to comply with this request. If the consumer receives no such notice, or if the agency considers it improper to issue the notice of correction, then either party can apply to the

---

50   See G. Howells, 'Data Protection, Confidentiality, Unfair Contract Terms, Consumer Protection and Credit Reference Agencies' [1995] *JBL* 343.

51   Ss.157–160; Consumer Credit (Conduct of Business) (Credit References) Regulations 1977, S.I. 1977/330.

Director General, who will make such order as he thinks fit. There is some evidence that more consumers are becoming aware of their right to inspect credit reference agency files and seek corrections of inaccurate information, though many more probably remain ignorant of these rights. The increased numbers making applications to see their files have caused the credit reference agencies to seek to raise the £1 application fee (which does not cover their costs). Any increase in this fee should be resisted, however, as otherwise consumers will be deterred from invoking this right.

11.6 DEFENCES

Breach of many of the public regulation provisions of the Consumer Credit Act 1974 lead to the commission of offences. S.168 provides a defence to such charges where the person charged can prove:

(i)   that his act or omission was due to a mistake, or to reliance on information supplied to him, or to an act or omission by another person, or to an accident or some other cause beyond his control, and

(ii) that he took all reasonable precautions and exercised all due diligence to avoid such an act or omission by himself or any person under his control.[52]

11.7 PRIVATE VS PUBLIC CONTROLS

The public law controls are intended to prevent problems from arising and to allow authorities to ensure that problems which have arisen are not repeated. Though the relevance of the public law controls may seem rather tenuous to the individual facing a consumer credit problem, many consumers will have benefited from them. The problem is that nobody can quantify the number of individuals who have escaped exploitation by traders refused a credit licence or who have escaped deception by misleading advertisements which might have appeared but for the regulatory controls. Both private and public law controls have their role to play in this sensitive area of consumer protection. However, the lack of consumer education and inadequate access to legal services suggest that the private law cannot by itself assure the consumer of adequate protection against unfair credit practices.

---

[52] For a detailed discussion of the general principles of the defence, see 14.2.

12 Consumer Safety

12.1 RATIONALES FOR CONSUMER SAFETY REGULATION

It is probably the instinctive reaction of a consumer living in a modern Western economy that the State must 'do something' about the risk of unsafe and dangerous goods appearing on the market. The instinctive reaction of the consumer lawyer and policymaker should be to focus much more closely on just why the State should intervene and what form that intervention should take. This reflects the theme, familiar throughout this book, of insisting on convincing rationales for the introduction of laws of consumer protection.

Why should there be laws governing consumer safety? After all, it is presumably not in the interest of any trader wishing to build up a customer base to sell unsafe goods any more than it is in the interest of any consumer to buy them. The mechanism of the market ought to dictate supply of safe goods. Even where an unsafe product slips through the net and causes injury, the private law ought to offer a remedy to the consumer without the need for any regulatory intervention. It is a breach of contract to supply a dangerous product and, even if the required contractual link is missing, the law of tort should fill the gap in consumer protection. Since *Donoghue v Stevenson*[1] it has been plain that manufacturers and other traders in the distribution chain may be liable to pay compensation where harm is suffered by consumers as a result of the supply of an unsafe product. This form of consumer protection has been strengthened by the removal of fault from the test of liability in Part I of the Consumer Protection Act 1987.[2]

Accordingly, the market should serve the consumer interest by dissuading the supply of dangerous products. The private law should complement that dissuasive effect by providing the consumer with a remedy against the trader where the market system breaks down and allows a dangerous product to come into circulation. The rationales for intervening in the market by setting safety standards have been discussed at length in Chapter 1. The modern market operates in a manner which greatly distorts the message about product preference which, on a simplistic analysis, may be communicated from consumer to trader. The consumer is frequently under informed about the nature of goods on offer and will not be able to distinguish between varying levels of safety in products. For these reasons

---

1   [1932] AC 562, Chapter 6.2.3.2.
2   For closer examination of the nuances of Part 1, see Chapter 6.2.3.3.

and others,[3] the market is not a perfect mechanism. Nor does the private law plug all these gaps. Consumer rights arising in contract are limited by the doctrine of privity to a claim against the party from which the item was purchased.[4] Accordingly, the consumer typically has no direct contractual link with the manufacturer; a recipient of a gift typically has no contractual link with anyone at all. This leaves the law of tort as the only means of securing compensation in the event that a consumer suffers injury from a dangerous product, but tort law, negligence in particular, has its own inherent limitations. In claims which fall outside the scope of the Consumer Protection Act 1987, the consumer must show fault on the part of the defendant supplier.[5] Even under the 1987 Act, where liability is in principle triggered by the condition of the product, not the conduct of the trader, there remain hurdles for the consumer to cross, such as the complexity in identifying a defect and the possible availability of defences.[6] Moreover, the consumer is obliged to establish the chain of causation whether the basis of the claim lies in negligence or the 1987 Act. Causation is itself a significant barrier to successful consumer redress.[7] Allied to these weaknesses of the law on paper are weaknesses of the law in practice, which in many ways are even more significant. The time and trouble that must be invested in taking a claim means that most instances of consumer dissatisfaction provoke no complaint at all, and certainly no formal legal proceedings.[8] In isolation, individual consumer loss is typically small and absorbed by the individual, which may mean that a trader 'gets away' with causing a large loss in aggregate. This is especially the case where the loss relates to the quality of the product, but it may also apply in relation to safety. This further weakens the 'message' sent by consumer to trader about real preferences.

In many respects, the use of individual litigation is quite out of line with the realities of mass production and collective consumption. The net result is that market plus the private law emphasis on individual redress do not necessarily prevent the supply of unsafe goods which consumers may not want to buy. The market will operate inefficiently. Consumers may call for protection; honest traders too may call for protection from unscrupulous rivals. Generally the public interest in improving the performance of an imperfect market may call for public intervention to achieve higher standards of safety.

---

3   See more broadly Chapter 1. Cf also P. Asch, *Consumer Safety Regulation: Putting a Price on Life and Limb* (OUP, 1988).

4   Chapter 4.

5   Chapter 6.

6   Chapter 6.2.3.3.3.

7   Chapter 6.2.3.3.3.

8   More broadly, Chapter 17.

The question then turns to the appropriate type of intervention. Immediately it should be recalled that regulation cannot be cost–free. It is always necessary to examine both the benefits of regulating – safer goods – and the costs of regulating – reduction in consumer choice and higher prices where stringent minimum production standards are imposed. Where costs outweigh benefits, regulation need not automatically be excluded,[9] but rationales more sophisticated than a simple cost/benefit calculation will need to be deployed. Chapter 1 explores these issues in more depth.

Chapter 1 also examines choices between forms of regulation.[10] An obvious regulatory response to the problem of unsafe goods lies in the establishment of minimum safety standards. Traders who fall below the minimum by supplying goods which fail to conform commit an offence. Current policy preferences dictate that the standards in question shall be flexible and broadly expressed. The standard expected by law is a rather broad notion of reasonable safety.[11] This regime benefits the consumer by providing a minimum guarantee of safety; however, it costs the consumer by removing the choice to buy less safe goods which, in theory, ought to be cheaper, provided the market is functioning with adequate transparency. It is also a persisting theme that, although honest traders may welcome regulatory intervention to secure protection from unscrupulous rivals, what may seem unscrupulous to an existing operator on the market may from another perspective amount to no more than the onset of fresh competition. Traders already in the market may consciously or unconsciously seek to maintain or even to raise regulatory standards in order to protect their investment from newcomers. From this point of view, minimum standards may serve to reduce competition and consumer choice in the market.

Regulating for a basic safety minimum amounts to the State choosing what can and cannot be bought on behalf of the consumer, rather than allowing the market to make that choice through the supplier/consumer relationship. As explored above, weaknesses in that supplier/consumer relationship provide rationales for State intervention, but this does not remove the intrinsic difficulty in shaping an appropriate minimum safety level chosen by regulatory intervention instead of the market. Rather than setting a minimum standard enforced by a ban on non–conforming products, an alternative method lies in regulation designed to reduce the information gap. Instead of banning less safe goods, it might be possible to require that such goods be labelled in order to display their characteristics. The consumer then retains the choice denied by a minimum standard coupled to a ban, but is able to exercise that choice in a more informed fashion than is normal in

---

9   Cf Asch n.3 above, esp. Ch.4.
10   1.8. Cf Asch n.3 above Part III.
11   12.2 below.

the modern, increasingly complex, market. The case of tobacco products might be evaluated from this perspective.[12] Some very strong tobacco products are banned. Advertising too is allowed only through certain media. However, for most tobacco products there is no ban but rather a requirement that the product's packaging carry a health warning. In the UK, these warnings were for many years attached as a result of a voluntary arrangement between producers and government, but there is an increasingly formal legal basis in the area as a result of the legislative activity of the European Community.[13] It might be noted in passing that the choice between quasi self–regulation and legislative rules is yet a further nuance of the choice between regulatory techniques.[14]

The regulator who chooses informational intervention over a ban must be satisfied that the consumer is capable of absorbing the information. A policy of 'protecting by informing' would go awry if the consumer were unable to identify and act upon the message. Where the consumer cannot readily process the information, the choice between regulatory instruments may swing back towards the minimum standard and the ban on non–complying products. That question remains difficult to resolve in practice. The case of tobacco products again deserves consideration. Some would argue that the risk is such that information cannot be properly absorbed by the consumer and that further restriction on availability is therefore justified. A further complication is provided by the argument that the deterioration in health caused by smoking acts as a burden on the health care system and that accordingly controls over consumption are justified. This aspect has tended to be used as a basis for the employment of a further regulatory technique: the imposition on tobacco products of heavy fiscal burdens.

This provides only a flavour of the debate concerning regulatory techniques. Chapter 1 contains an extended account of the debate about how best to regulate upholstered furniture, where the conflicting pressures for minimum standard plus ban and for informational intervention, preserving choice, resulted in a regime that incorporated both techniques.[15]

---

[12] For a collection of materials, see World Health Organisation, *Legislative Responses to Tobacco Use* (Martinus Nijhoff, 1991).
[13] Especially Directive 89/622 OJ 1989 L359/1. See further Chapter 1.8.3, 1.9.
[14] Chapter 1.8.
[15] Chapter 1.8.3.3.

12.2 THE DEVELOPMENT OF CONSUMER SAFETY LEGISLATION IN THE UK

Prior to 1961 safety regulation in the UK comprised a patchwork of product–specific laws. Individual measures regulated goods such as medicines and fireworks, but there was no single statute capable of imposing obligations relating to safety on producers generally. Severe safety problems could be dealt with only by securing the adoption of new primary legislation, a laborious and cumbersome process. Typically, harm had to occur in order to stimulate a legal response.

These shortcomings were partially addressed in the Consumer Protection Act 1961, the first general statute in the field of consumer safety in the UK. This was innovative in the sense that it was enabling legislation. The Act provided the power for delegated legislation to be made to govern particular product areas which were identified from time to time as requiring specific regulation. Standards could be set to improve the safety of products, backed by criminal sanctions. The flexibility of recourse to secondary rather than primary legislation made it much easier to act once a risk to consumer safety was identified. There was no longer a need to rely on primary legislation.

The structure of enabling legislation was maintained in the Consumer Safety Act 1978. Under this rather more sophisticated statute, four specific types of regulatory instrument were made available: the safety regulation, the prohibition order, the prohibition notice and the notice to warn.

The safety regulation, which was then and still remains (in adjusted form) the most important of these measures, is directed at particular products seen to require specific detailed control. So, for example, safety regulations made under the 1978 Act included measures which established standards, often very specific, which had to be met in the manufacture of products as diverse as gas catalytic heaters, children's hood cords and babies' dummies. Supply of non–complying goods constituted a criminal offence. Supply could also give rise to civil liability under the statute, although this has proved unimportant in practice.[16]

The three new measures introduced in the 1978 Act improved the capacity of the law to deal quickly with newly discovered hazards. The prohibition order involved a general ban on the supply of a particular product. The prohibition notice was served on an individual trader to prevent supply of a particular product. Both could be issued by the Secretary of State with relatively little formality, in contrast to the safety regulation which could be made by the Secretary of State only after consultation. The prohibition order was capable of causing commercial catastrophe for traders in the relevant goods; indeed, the making of such orders in response to

---

[16] This provision is now found in s.41 Consumer Protection Act 1987.

perceived emergencies was frequently highly politicised.[17] The safety regulation was designed as a means of setting standards for the future, whereas prohibition orders and notices were intended as responses to particular problems posed by specific products or specific traders. The fourth of the available measures was the notice to warn which could require a supplier to publish a warning about unsafe goods, but this measure had no practical impact.

The suspension notice was added by the Consumer Safety (Amendment) Act 1986, a statute which was largely directed at improving enforcement powers. The suspension notice prohibited the addressee from supplying the goods for a period of up to six months.[18] It could be made by a trading standards officer having reasonable cause to suspect the contravention of a measure in relation to any goods. The suspension notice enhanced the flexibility of the powers of enforcement, although compensation could be payable where suspected goods turned out to be safe. Powers of seizure were also conferred on trading standards officers, although similar compensation provisions were attached. It was also possible to make an application to a magistrate's court for a forfeiture order against goods. The 1986 Act targeted enforcement more closely at point of first supplier or importer and away from the retail level in order to improve efficient use of scarce resources.[19]

Both the 1961 and the 1978 Acts had the great advantage over the pre–1961 system of allowing rapid action to be taken via secondary legislation on the discovery of a newly identified hazard. The enforcement mechanisms were steadily improved through the 1961, 1978 and, particularly, the 1986 Amendment Act. However, the supply of an unsafe product was not of itself an offence in the absence of pre–existing rules governing that product. The legislation had no impact on producers and suppliers in sectors left uncovered by measures already in place. The only legal constraint on such traders supplying unsafe goods lay in the private law, the inadequacies of which have already been discussed.

A 1984 White Paper on the Safety of Goods[20] commented that a general statutory duty on suppliers to supply safe consumer goods, backed by criminal sanctions;

---

17   Eg the saga of the scented erasers presented in I. Ramsay, *Consumer Protection Cases and Materials* (Weidenfeld, 1989), pp. 478–89.

18   The Act envisages procedures for challenging a suspension notice which should be followed in preference to making an application for judicial review: *R v Birmingham City Council ex parte Ferrero* [1993] 1 All ER 530.

19   Chapter 14 provides a general account of enforcement practice.

20   Cmnd. 9302.

'would induce a greater sense of responsibility on the part of those suppliers who currently regard themselves as unaffected by the legislation [and] would provide wider scope for swift remedial action by enforcement authorities in the case of newly identified dangerous products.'

This perception underlies the Consumer Protection Act 1987, which introduced a general duty to supply only safe goods.[21] This is the principal statute which now governs this field in the UK, although the implementation by Statutory Instrument of the EC Directive on general product safety has significantly altered the pattern of legal control (12.3.3, 12.4 below). The relevant provisions are contained in Part II of the 1987 Act.[22] The innovation for consumer safety regulation introduced by this Act is a 'General Safety Requirement'. Section 10 imposes a duty to supply only safe goods. It is accordingly a criminal offence to supply unsafe goods even in the absence of pre–existing specific regulations applicable to the product category in question. The 1987 Act retains the structure of the 1961 and 1978 Acts whereunder delegated legislation may be made to amplify requirements in particular product categories as appropriate, but shifts the emphasis of control towards the new flexible general duty.

Before making a safety regulation, the Minister is under a duty to consult 'such organisations as appear to him to be representative of interests substantially affected by the proposal' and such other persons as he considers appropriate.[23] The 1987 Act has abolished the Prohibition Order which existed under the 1978 Act. The need to have the capacity to act quickly by making an interim order is covered in the 1987 Act by the 'Expedited Safety Regulation', which is rather wider in scope than the Prohibition Order. Such expedited measures may be made without consultation, but remain in force for no more than twelve months. Typically an emergency may be addressed by a measure made immediately, followed by consultation and a twelve–month period within which occurs calmer reflection on how to tackle the problem for the future. Both the Prohibition Notice and the Notice to Warn remain in place. It is worth adding the explicit point that, in contrast to several jurisdictions around the world, there is no statutory power in the UK to require recall of products.

Consumer Safety regulation has thus reached a position where all producers of consumer goods are subject to the regulatory regime. Specific

---

21 For discussion, see P. Stone, 'Consumer Safety' (1991) 8 *Trading Law* 2.
22 Part I covers product liability and is examined in Chapter 6; Part III covers misleading price indications and is examined in Chapter 10.5.
23 The duty was the subject of successful litigation to quash regulations in *R v Secretary of State for Health, ex parte United States Tobacco* [1992] 1 All ER 212, criticised by B. Schwehr and P. Brown [1991] *Public Law* 163.

areas may still be regulated more tightly and precisely than the general duty through safety regulations. In this way a range of techniques of control beyond the general duty alone may be deployed.

12.3 EUROPEAN COMMUNITY PRODUCT SAFETY LAW

12.3.1 The Growth of EC Product Safety Law

The law of consumer safety has been described earlier in this Chapter as a response to the inadequacies of the market. This book has consistently emphasised that the market is increasingly European; as a reflection of this, the law of consumer safety comprises a combination of domestic and Community provisions.

One aspect of this process is that national consumer safety laws must be applied with regard to the integration of the market. Accordingly, national rules of consumer protection which are capable of impeding trade between Member States must be justified. For example, an insistence that goods comply with *British* standards and an unwillingness to accept imported goods meeting equivalent standards would violate Community law's insistence on mutual recognition of goods. Modern British practice under the legislation mentioned above, in conformity with Community law, is to require compliance with British standards or their equivalent.[24] More positively and directly, Community legislative measures are implemented in the domestic system and become part of the fabric of domestic law. The substance of the law involves a mix of domestic and Community–inspired rules, although the mix may not always be smooth. As well as this substantive mix, the enforcement of the rules involves the creation of an institutional network throughout the European market.[25]

---

[24] S. Weatherill, 'Consumer Safety Legislation in the United Kingdom and Article 30 EEC' (1988) 13 *ELRev* 87.

[25] Several essays in M. Fallon and F. Maniet, *Product Safety and Control Processes in the European Community* (Story Scientia/CDC, 1990) and in B. Stauder, *La Securité des Produits de Consommation* (Schulthess, 1992) examine questions of policy and practice in the development of EC product safety law. For empirical work and critical analysis, cf H–W. Micklitz, *Post Market Control of Consumer Goods* (Nomos, 1990); H–W. Micklitz, T. Roethe and S. Weatherill (eds), *Federalism and Responsibility: a Study on Product Safety Law and Practice in the European Community* (Graham and Trotman, 1994). Also, C. Joerges, 'Paradoxes of Deregulatory Strategies at Community level: the Example of Product Safety Policy' in G. Majone (ed), *Deregulation or Re–regulation* (Pinter, 1990).

European Community consumer safety law has developed out of a rather different perspective from the market failure analysis presented above. As is examined at greater length in Chapter 2, the bulk of EC consumer policy finds its constitutional basis in Articles 100 and 100a of the Treaty, which are directed at the process of market integration. Where national laws differ, they obstruct trade and require harmonisation in order to liberalise the wider market. Accordingly Community consumer laws have developed as part of the quest to create an integrated market. They lack any formal commitment to a process of regulating the market.[26] Yet the effect, if not the formal constitutional intent, of such harmonised laws is to establish a common set of Community consumer safety laws which in turn affect the laws and markets of all twelve Member States.

The content of Community product safety regulation is in many respects comparable to domestic UK laws in the area. At the level of general regulatory philosophy, this is an area where the absorption of Community law into the British system is relatively unproblematic.[27]

12.3.2 Toy Safety

The Toy Safety Directive[28] harmonises laws regulating toy safety throughout the Community. There are Community rules requiring a basic safety level. Only safe toys may be sold; States must admit to their markets toys which are safe. In this sense, the Community rule contributes to both the integration and the regulation of the market.

The Directive provides that toys subject to the regime 'shall satisfy the essential safety requirements', which are performance levels expressed in general terms and amplified in Schedule 2. Safety must be assessed with regard to 'the use of toys in an intended or in a foreseeable way, bearing in mind the normal behaviour of children.' Plainly, a toy may be unsafe if misused where that misuse is foreseeable. The formal legal requirement is conformity with the 'essential safety requirements', but there are two alternative routes open to the manufacturer wishing to show such conformity. One is to produce in accordance with standards – European standards produced by CEN which are adopted as national standards. The other is to conform to an approved model. The manufacturer who does not wish to adhere to the standards may apply for a type approval certificate from an

---

26 This may change in future after the entry into force of the (Maastricht) Treaty on European Union. This establishes in Art.129a a separate EC competence in the sphere of consumer protection; see Chapter 2.3.5.

27 Contrast, for example, the examination of control of unfair terms in Chapter 9.

28 Directive 88/378 OJ 1988 L187.

authorised body. The key is that the manufacturer has a choice of how to conform to the legal requirements, which permits a degree of flexibility and innovation.[29]

The manufacturer must show conformity by attaching a mark originally referred to as the EC mark but now known as the 'CE Marking' as a result of the amendments of Directive 93/68.[30] Because the marking is affixed by the trader and is not pre–checked, it is a statement of conformity and not a guarantee of safety. If toys are found on the market which are CE marked but which do not meet the essential safety requirements, then enforcement action should be taken against them. Such action affects the whole European market and must be managed through Community procedures, considered further below.

The Directive was implemented in the UK as a Statutory Instrument made under the Consumer Protection Act 1987 and the European Communities Act 1972 – the Toys (Safety) Regulations 1989.[31] The Toy Safety Regulations 'shall be treated for all purposes as if they were safety regulations within the meaning of the 1987 Act', subject only to a minor qualification relating to a penalty.[32] The Regulations require that '[t]oys to which these Regulations apply shall satisfy the essential safety requirements'.[33] In accordance with the Directive, provision is also made for the use of the CE marking.[34] It is an offence to supply toys which do not satisfy the essential safety requirements or which do not bear the CE marking.

Digestion of this regime into the English system poses no fundamental difficulty,[35] since, before Community intervention, the safety of toys had already been the subject of regulatory attention in the UK. In fact, regulations governing toy safety were first made under the Consumer Protection Act 1961. The implementation of the Directive has been firmly rooted in this existing structure of control. The Directive required only a relatively technical adjustment to existing rules and, more significantly, the addition of institutional mechanisms to reflect its objective of market

---

29 See Chapter 1.8.1, on the EC's New Approach to technical harmonisation.
30 OJ 1993 L220/1.
31 SI 1989 No 1275. The 1989 Regulations were amended in July 1993 by the Toys (Safety) (Amendment) Regulations, removing the obligation of suppliers of secondhand toys to ensure that toys bear the CE marking and the name and address of the first supplier. Plans to implement Directive 93/68 n.30 above are in preparation.
32 Regulation 15.
33 Regulation 4.
34 Regulation 9.
35 Cf S. Weatherill, 'Toy Safety' in T. Daintith (ed), *Implementing EC Law in the United Kingdom: Structures for Indirect Rule* (Wiley Chancery Law, 1995).

integration. Action taken by enforcement authorities can no longer be regarded as a purely domestic matter.[36]

12.3.3 General Product Safety

The parallel development of domestic and European rules continued with the adoption in 1992 of the General Directive on Product Safety.[37] The Directive largely follows the policy and the substantive pattern of Part II of the Consumer Protection Act 1987. Like Part II, the Directive establishes control over all forms of supply of consumer goods irrespective of product sector,[38] but again it is a flexible notion of control to be elaborated through private standard–making. Whereas Community initiatives were the stimulus for domestic reform of product liability,[39] the reverse influence may be identified in relation to product safety regulation. The General Directive, modelled in significant respects on the UK's domestic regime,[40] will require no significant policy shift in the UK system. In this respect it is in direct contrast to the Product Liability Directive which marks a radical shift in direction for English law.[41] Article 13 of Directive 92/59 asserts that the General Directive applies without prejudice to the Product Liability Directive.

According to Article 1 of the Directive, 'The purpose of the provisions of this Directive is to ensure that products placed on the market are safe.' Article 3(1) provides that 'Producers shall be obliged to place only safe products on the market. '[42] The similarity to the flexible control exercised by

---

36   Further below, 12.6.
37   Directive 92/59/EEC on general product safety OJ 1992 L228/24. For an early discussion of the importance of developments in this field, cf H–W. Micklitz, 'Perspectives on a European Directive on the Safety of Technical Consumer Goods' (1986) 23 *CMLRev* 617. Assessing the Directive as adopted, see G. Argiros, 'The EEC Directive on General Product Safety' [1994/1] *LIEI* 125.
38   Existing sector–specific Community rules governing product safety apply in preference to the general duty: Art 1(2) Dir/Regs.3(c), 4. But note that if particular aspects of the safety of a product are not covered by existing rules, those aspects fall under the general Directive.
39   Chapter 6.
40   Cf discussion in this vein on an earlier draft of the Directive; J.R. Bradgate, 'Product safety: the EEC follows UK lead' (1990) 9 *Trading Law* 2; S. Weatherill, 'A General Duty to supply only safe goods in the Community: some remarks from a British perspective' (1990) 13 *JCP* 79.
41   Chapter 6.
42   Article 3(3) imposes additional obligations on distributors.

Part II of the Consumer Protection Act 1987 is plain; implementing the Directive accordingly presented no fundamental problems of principle for the UK. Practical problems could have been largely avoided too, had the Government chosen to implement the Directive in a statute consolidating the law drawn from the Directive with that already found in Part II of the Consumer Protection Act 1987. The creation of such a single regime would have done much for transparency and predictability. Regrettably, this course was not chosen. The Directive has been implemented in the UK by the General Product Safety Regulations 1994.[43] Made under the European Communities Act 1972, the Regulations came into force on 3 October 1994.[44] Accordingly, consumer safety regulation in the UK is now drawn from two sources: first, the Act and, second, the Regulations which implement the Directive and which must be interpreted so as to conform to it.[45]

12.4 THE POST–1994 PATTERN OF PRODUCT SAFETY LAW

The existence of two sources of product safety law in the UK raises questions of a constitutional nature that are equally of great commercial significance. The two regimes of control are not coextensive. In some respects Part II of the 1987 Act is broader than the Directive; in other respects the opposite is true. In such circumstances the implementation of the Directive has demonstrably extended the scope of legal regulation in the UK.

The criteria for control under both systems is plainly comparable: both are concerned with safety, yet their precise equivalence cannot be guaranteed. The desirable route of consolidation of both regimes into a single

---

43   SI No 2328. See G. Howells, 'The General Duty to Market Safe Products in United Kingdom Law' [1994] *LMCLQ* 479; P. Cartwright, 'Product Safety and Consumer Protection' (1995) 58 *MLR* 222.

44   The Directive stipulates that implementing provisions should be effective from 29 June 1994. Were a person to have been injured by an unsafe product in the intervening three–plus months and to have been able to show that the injury would probably not have occurred had the Directive been implemented, then he or she might be able to claim damages from the State under EC law for failure to implement, as well as from the supplier in contract or tort. Probably this is rather fanciful – but the implications of the *Francovich* ruling, examined at Chapter 2.4.2, are so extensive that any slippage in the implementation of Directives should alert the lawyer to the possibilities of a claim against the State.

45   The *Marleasing* principle of interpretation drawn from Art.5 EC, discussed in Chapter 2.4.2.

statute remains as yet wishful thinking in the face of the pressures of the Parliamentary timetable.

The constitutional relationship between the two systems is as follows.[46] Within areas covered by the Directive, the Directive applies alongside the Act and, to some extent, meshes with it, especially with regard to enforcement. But as a matter of EC law, the Regulations implementing the Directive have precedence over the Act in this sense: goods that are safe within the meaning of the Directive are entitled to be marketed in the UK; the 1987 Act may not be used to block their access. Goods that are unsafe in the sense of not conforming with the Directive must be controlled but, in some circumstances, that will not simply be a national matter, but will require the machinery of the Directive to be engaged. The core point is that the Directive is based on Article 100a and is therefore formally an instrument of market integration. Its philosophy is that there shall be a common Community rule requiring the marketing of only safe goods; such safe goods, wherever made, shall then be freely marketable anywhere on Community territory. This central objective explains why national rules may not be used to control goods that are safe within the meaning of the Community rules. It also explains why, where national action against allegedly unsafe goods *is* taken, that action is not a purely national matter, but must instead be managed within a Community framework.

It is therefore required of national law that it should ensure removal from its market of products that fall below the stipulated safety level; also that it should allow on to its market goods that meet that stipulated safety level. The State may not cut across this basic structure. The General Product Safety Regulations that implement the Directive in the UK faithfully reflect this pattern. Regulation 7 contains the general safety requirement:

> 'No producer shall place a product on the market unless the product is a safe product.'

Regulation 5 is designed to prevent the 1987 Act from cutting across the Directive's requirement that safe goods (within the meaning of the Directive) shall have access to the market. It disables the 1987 Act in areas covered by the Regulations implementing the Directive:

---

46 These issues also have to be tackled in relation to Unfair Terms where again there is dual control – see Chapter 9. However, the pattern examined here is distinct. The Directive on Unfair Terms, as a minimum measure, permits stricter national rules in the field whereas, subject to the authoritative ruling of the European Court, the General Directive does not appear to be minimum in character; accordingly, it pre–empts stricter national controls within its scope of application.

'For the purposes of these Regulations the provisions of section 10 of the 1987 Act are hereby disapplied to the extent that they impose general safety requirements which must be complied with if products are to be (i) placed on the market, offered or agreed to be placed on the market or exposed or possessed to be placed on the market by producers; or (ii) supplied, offered or agreed to be supplied or exposed or possessed to be supplied by distributors.'[47]

Thus the Act and the Regulations are designed not to overlap. Supply of an unsafe product engages one regime or the other, but not both. This is probably the next best solution after the option of consolidating both sources of law into a single statute was rejected.

Assuming that Community rules on safety are at least as high as existing domestic rules, no concerns of policy arise consequent to the addition of the Community layer of safety regulation. True, there are certain practical problems to resolve in aligning the administration of the two regimes, but these are soluble. It is the possibility that the Community standard may be *lower* than the national regime that has stimulated concern. *If* this is the case, then goods that were previously excluded from the British market can no longer be excluded. This possibility has fed fears that Community market integration might be achieved at the expense of national standards of protection.[48] The charge cannot at this stage conclusively be admitted nor rejected, but the reader should bear this underlying policy issue in mind. It is a lurking concern for the development of consumer protection in the internal market.

What follows is a more detailed elaboration of the pattern of consumer safety law. Necessarily it draws on both relevant sources, the 1987 Act and the 1994 Regulations/1992 Directive, although it should be borne in mind that the Regulations envisage that one or other of the regimes will apply, never both.

12.5 DETAILED ASPECTS OF THE LAW

12.5.1 What Types of Product are Covered?

For the Directive, 'product' means 'any product intended for consumers or likely to be used by consumers, supplied whether for consideration or not in the course of a commercial activity and whether new, used or reconditioned.'

---

[47]　In the Regs. the words 'are hereby disapplied' appear at the very end of Reg.5; we have changed their placement to assist clarity.

[48]　Chapter 2, esp 2.3.4.

This is copied in Regulation 2 of the Statutory Instrument, where it is additionally stated that 'a product which is used exclusively in the context of a commercial activity even if it is used for or by a consumer shall not be regarded as a product for the purposes of these Regulations provided always and for the avoidance of doubt this exception shall not extend to the supply of such a product to a consumer'.[49]

Under the Consumer Protection Act 1987, consumer goods are defined as 'any goods which are ordinarily intended for private use or consumption'. There is a range of excluded products:[50]

(a) growing crops or things comprised in land by virtue of being attached to it;
(b) water, food, feeding stuff or fertiliser;
(c) gas which is, is to be or has been supplied by a person authorised to supply it or under section 6, 7 or 8 of the Gas Act 1986 (authorisation of supply of gas through pipes);
(d) aircraft (other than hang–gliders) or motor vehicles;
(e) controlled drugs or licensed medicinal products;
(f) tobacco.

The Directive is inapplicable to second–hand products where they are supplied as antiques; also where they are supplied as products to be repaired or reconditioned prior to being used, provided that the supplier clearly informs the person to whom he supplies the product to that effect. These exclusions are implemented in Regulations 3(a) and 3(b). The exclusion of second–hand products from the 1987 Act is considerably wider in scope than that in the Directive. S.10(4)(c) Consumer Protection Act 1987 provides a defence against a charge of violation of the general safety requirement where it is shown that the terms 'indicated that the goods were not supplied or to be supplied as new goods' where the recipient would acquire an interest in the goods.

12.5.2 Unsafe Products: Offences Committed

For the Directive, Article 2 provides that 'Safe product' means any product which 'does not present any risk or only the minimum risks compatible with the product's use, considered as acceptable and consistent with a high level of protection for the safety and health of persons'. Matters to be taken into

---

49   Note that beyond the scope of consumer safety regulation may lie the Health and Safety at Work Act 1974.

50   S.10(7).

account according to Article 2(b) include the characteristics of the product, its presentation and the categories of consumers at serious risk when using the product, in particular children. This is carried over into Regulation 2 of the UK's Statutory Instrument.

According to s.19 Consumer Protection Act 1987, 'safe', in relation to any goods, means that there is no risk, or no risk apart from one reduced to a minimum, that the goods (or specified activities in relation to them) will (whether immediately or after a definite or indefinite period) cause the death of, or any personal injury to, any person whatsoever.

An offence is committed under s.10 of the Act where a person, acting in the course of a business of his or hers, supplies or offers or agrees to supply or exposes or possesses for supply, any consumer goods which fail to comply with the general safety requirement.[51] S.11(1) empowers the Secretary of State to make safety regulations for the purpose of securing that goods to which the section applies[52] are safe. The same s.19 definition applies and it is an offence to supply in violation of a safety regulation.

Under the Directive it is for Member States to put in place laws which shall ensure that producers and distributors comply with their obligations under the Directive in such a way that products placed on the market are safe.[53] The UK has effectively achieved that in the 1994 Regulations by absorbing the requirements into the regulatory pattern already available under the Consumer Protection Act 1987. Regulations 12 and 13 create offences connected with the supply and/or distribution of goods that fall below the required safety standard. Regulation 11 places enforcement in the hands of local authorities. In practical terms, this means trading standards departments. This follows the same model as is found in the 1987 Act. The powers available to such officers and their practical application are examined in Chapter 14, although issues specific to product safety law and practice in the integrating European market are discussed below in this Chapter at 12.6. The meshing of the Regulations implementing the Directive with the pattern familiar under the 1987 Act is further confirmed by the inclusion in the Regulations of the 'due diligence' defence that also appears in the Consumer Protection Act and other consumer protection statutes.[54] The inclusion of provision for the liability of persons other than the principal offender is also a common feature of consumer protection regulation.[55]

---

[51] It is provided in s.46(5) that '... it shall be immaterial whether the business is a business of dealing in the goods.' 'Supplies' is defined in s.46.

[52] S.11(7); the scope of goods which may be subject to safety regulations is rather broader than those subject to the general requirement.

[53] Article 5.

[54] Reg. 14.

[55] Reg. 15.

Normal aspects of the family of regulatory offences which the General Product Safety Regulations have now joined, these are examined in more depth in Chapter 14.

However, as explained above, even though the two systems share a common regulatory framework, the 1987 Act and the 1994 Regulations implementing the Directive are kept separate in their substantive scope of application.

12.5.3 The Notion of Safety

The notions of 'safe' under the Act and the Directive, as implemented, run in parallel. It is possible that, in future, interpretations given by the European Court will diverge from British judicial practice, a perennial problem where laws deriving from different sources operate in the same field.[56] However, problems seem unlikely or at least likely to be technical only, in contrast to some other areas examined in this book where rather different controls are envisaged under EC law on the one hand and existing domestic law on the other.[57]

For both regimes, potentially dangerous products may still be 'safe' within the legal definition. A hacksaw is plainly capable of inflicting injury, but if designed in a way which minimises the risk in using it, it will be 'safe'. The careful manufacturer will design a product in order to reduce the risk of mishap and will market it with an eye to safe usage, if necessary by attaching appropriate labels and warnings. It seems that products must be safe even if misused where that misuse is reasonably foreseeable. Many similar considerations apply in relation to avoiding civil liability for supplying unsafe products.[58]

The control systems envisage a band of safety which is permissible. That absolute protection from harm is not at stake is reflected in the Directive's provision that 'The feasibility of obtaining higher levels of safety or the availability of other products presenting a lesser degree of risk shall not constitute grounds for considering a product to be unsafe or dangerous'. This is implemented in Regulation 2 of the Statutory Instrument. Products can be less safe than competing items yet still be safe within the legal definition, a manifestation of the concern to maintain consumer choice between varying types of product.

---

[56] Examined in Chapter 2.
[57] Cf particularly the problems of unfair terms, Chapter 9.
[58] Chapter 6.

There is embedded within these definitions of 'safe' a cost/benefit analysis.[59] A product which is moderately risky may be safe where its virtues to society are obvious and significant, yet unsafe if it is equally risky yet of trivial value. Section 10(2)(c) of the 1987 Act explicitly directs consideration to 'the existence of any means by which it would have been reasonable (taking into account the cost, likelihood and extent of any improvement) for the goods to have been made safer.' A floor level of safety must plainly exist below which it is not open to a manufacturer to claim that it would be unreasonable to expect the goods to be made safer. However, above that floor there is scope for development of judicial notions of reasonableness and proportionality in the pursuit of safety.

12.5.4 Accident Data

The accumulation of statistical data about accidents plays an important role in the development of any coherent consumer safety policy. Empirical evidence about where accidents occur should be part of the decision–making process on how to target scarce resources to rule making and to enforcement. Such data may also reveal the desirability of public information campaigns in relation to particular types of risk.

The UK has operated a system for collecting information from hospitals since 1976 called HASS, the Home Accident Surveillance System. However, the United States has a uniquely well–developed system for collecting such data in the Consumer Product Safety Commission.[60] It gathers data primarily from hospital emergency departments, selected from all over the country in order to provide a representative profile. The Commission uses the information gathered to determine priorities as part of a conscious attempt to make objective assessments about risk.

The European Community has moved more slowly into the field of accumulating statistical data about accidents arising from the use of consumer goods. This is in part attributable to the constitutional inhibitions from which it suffers in developing an active consumer policy.[61] The Council established a pilot scheme for an accident information system in

---

59   On how calculations may be made, cf M. Jones–Lee, *The Economics of Safety and Physical Risk* (Blackwell, 1989); Asch n.3 above. The saga of the scented erasers at n.17 above may usefully be read as an antidote to notions that objectivity prevails (quaere whether it *should* prevail.)

60   At more length, G. Howells, *Comparative Consumer Safety Law* (Dartmouth, forthcoming in 1996).

61   Chapter 2.3.

1981,[62] but Member States were able to decide how they would participate and not all chose to become involved.

In 1986 a European Home and Leisure Accident Surveillance System (EHLASS) was established,[63] with data collected over a five–year period from casualty departments of selected hospitals throughout the Community. The data covered all accidents in the home, whether arising from products or behaviour. Evaluation followed as part of a process of establishing priorities for accident prevention. In this instance Member States were obliged to participate.

There was resistance among some Member States to the continuation of the EHLASS project. In 1993, the Council agreed to its continuation for one year only.[64] The Commission pushed with determination to have the scheme placed on a firmer footing,[65] supported by the relevant committee of the European Parliament.[66] The pressure proved successful. A continuation of the scheme was agreed by the Council in 1994 to last until the end of 1997.

12.5.5 The Impact of the 1994 Regulations

In practical terms what difference have the Regulations made to the scope of consumer safety regulation in the UK? *Assuming* that the core safety standard will be applied in the same way as under the 1987 Act,[67] the major impact of the Regulations appears to be as follows.

First and as mentioned above,[68] the new regime has extended the substantive scope of the control, for the Regulations catch secondhand goods. Moreover, a broader range of product sectors are caught. Medicines and food, for example, largely excluded from the 1987 Act, are now subject to the Regulations. Regulation 11(c) makes appropriate provision for placing enforcement in relation to such products in the hands of the agencies normally responsible in such fields.

Second, Regulations 8 and 9, reflecting the Directive, impose more specific obligations on producers and distributors respectively than under the 1987 Act. Regulation 8 requires a producer to provide information to

---

62   Dec. 81/623 OJ 1981 L229/1.
63   Dec. 86/138 OJ 1986 L109/23, subsequently amended, OJ 1990 L296/64. The Decision was stated to be a matter of promoting the consumer protection policy and was therefore based on Art. 235; cf Chapter 2.3.
64   Dec. 93/683 OJ 1993 L319/40.
65   COM (94) 17.
66   Cf PE DOC A 3–173/93, PE DOC A 3–325/94.
67   12.4 above.
68   12.5.1 above.

consumers; also to adopt measures to inform him or herself of risks a product might present and to identify from an illustrative list measures that might be taken. The non–exhaustive list covers marking batches to permit their identification, sample testing of marketed products, investigating complaints and informing distributors of such monitoring. Postmarket control is clearly envisaged and this is likely to prove highly commercially significant.[69] However, although breach of the basic general safety requirement in Regulation 7 is converted into a regulatory offence by Regulation 12, the Regulation 8 requirement seems sanctionless within the Regulations themselves. However, the intention is that it is capable of enforcement by trading standards officers using their conventional powers of issuing a suspension notice prohibiting supply of goods or seeking forfeiture.[70]

Regulation 9 provides that a distributor[71] 'shall act with due care in order to help ensure compliance with the requirements of regulation 7 [the general requirement]'. This general notion seems to lack a penalty in the Regulations, but it too would be enforceable by suspension notice and/or forfeiture. More specifically, Regulation 12 converts into an offence the supply by a distributor of 'products to any person which he knows, or should have presumed, on the basis of the information in his possession and as a professional, are dangerous products'.

Third, the connection with the process of European market integration and regulation means that administrative machinery has been set up to link action taken against unsafe goods at local level with the broader framework of the EC. This is examined further below.

These are the major issues that arise out from the 1994 Regulations.[72] As mentioned, all these comments assume that the safety standard under the Directive, as implemented, is no weaker than that under the 1987 Act. *If* the former turns out to be lower than that previously expected under the latter, then there will indeed be cause for concern about an influx of dangerous goods overwhelming national laws on the tide of market integration. However, this alarming perspective presently seems theoretical only. Of more practical concern may be the point that, even though the standard of safety may be unchanged despite the EC intervention, the establishment of a

---

69   Such action may already be part of business practice as a result of the indirect influence of the private law, especially the concern to avoid liability for supply of defective products; cf Chapter 6.

70   Reg. 11(b). For more detail on enforcement powers, see Chapter 14.3.

71   Defined in Reg. 2 as 'any professional in the supply chain whose activity does not affect the safety properties of a product'.

72   At a more detailed level, section 10(3)(b)(ii) of the 1987 Act is repealed and the Approval of Safety Standards Regulations are revoked; Reg. 6.

border–free market may make it more difficult to enforce the law and, particularly, to monitor dangerous goods that are in free circulation within the Community market. This raises issues of enforcement co–ordination, examined below.

12.6 ENFORCEMENT

Both the 1987 Act and the 1994 Regulations are enforced at local level by, in practice, trading standards officers. The formal powers of the trading standards officer have been mentioned above and are examined in more depth in Chapter 14, being relevant beyond the specific area of consumer safety. Although formal action may be taken against both trader and product, informal enforcement is the norm. Trading standards officers typically regard a prosecution as time–consuming, costly and risky. The outcome may not be clear, especially under the general duty where, in marginal cases, much will depend on the court's own reading of safety expectations. The practical result has tended to be a predominance of informal controls, including guidance to traders. This policy has many benefits for both sides in terms of saved time and money. Only a minority of operators need be dealt with by prosecution and by formal action against their goods. The modern statutory framework confers valuable flexibility on trading standards officers. However, in the majority of cases a co–operative relationship is mutually beneficial to enforcer and trader.

It is explained in Chapter 14 that administrative co–ordination has developed in order to minimise the peculiarities which can arise from local enforcement. The Home Authority principle has been developed by LACOTS, the Local Authorities Co–ordinating Organisation on Trading Standards.[73] This holds that the trader's home authority will normally act as the source of legal interpretation.

The problem becomes all the more acute at European level, where there is a tension between Europe–wide marketing and local or even national enforcement. This is especially problematic where unsafe products, rather than deceptive marketing practices, are at stake, because of the capacity of goods to cause immediate and serious harm to consumers. Therefore, an account of the development of a strategy for co–ordinating enforcement of product safety law at European level belongs here rather than Chapter 14 (which deals with generally applicable issues of enforcement practice).[74]

Disparate interpretations of safety are capable of fragmenting the market where a product is lawfully marketed in one State but prohibited in another.

---

[73] Chapter 14.3.1.
[74] Cf note 25 above for descriptive and prescriptive accounts.

Conversely, if a State allows a product on to its market, expecting it to conform to its own level of safety and then discovering that it does not, consumer safety may be put at risk. In either case, confidence in the viability of the internal market is undermined. Such problems may arise where national laws vary; also where harmonised Community rules have been put in place which are nevertheless subjected to differing interpretations in different Member States.

Increasingly, it is perceived that substantive Community law 'on paper' will not create an internal market without institutional mechanisms being put in place to secure effective and even enforcement of laws throughout the Community. It is precisely this issue which is at the heart of modern strategies for enforcing consumer protection law, national and European, in a market which is also both national and European.

In late 1992 the Sutherland Report was published. Entitled 'The Internal Market after 1992: Meeting the Challenge', it was the report of a committee under the chairmanship of Peter Sutherland, former EC Commissioner, to examine how the internal market might be managed after its deadline for completion at the end of 1992. The emphasis of the report is strongly directed at the future effective application of those laws which had been energetically made at Community level and (in the main) implemented at national level in the run–up to 1992. The Sutherland Report has much to say about the future of enforcement practice; section IV is entitled 'Enforcing the Rules through Partnership'. Its key perception is that, in the internal market, laws are enforced as part of a network of Community responsibilities. It suggests that national authorities have 'Community–wide responsibilities which arise from the fact that their official functions directly affect citizens of all other Member States'.

Specific institutional recognition of the application of laws in the wider market may be found in the two Directives considered above, the Toy Safety Directive[75] and the General Directive.[76] Both merit further consideration as illustrations of the way in which the law operates in an integrated market, where traders are encouraged to treat the market as border–free and in which enforcement authorities too must adopt a strategy which recognises the decline in relevance of the national frontier.

For toys, the 'Safeguard Procedure' envisages the management of situations where toys pose a threat to health or safety, even where they bear the CE marking.[77] Action may be taken at national level against such goods (in the UK, by trading standards officers empowered by the Consumer Protection Act 1987). It is critically important to realise that EC law does

---

[75] 12.3.2 above.
[76] 12.3.3 above.
[77] 12.3.2 above.

not stop action being taken against goods that national agencies believe fail to meet safety standards, even where the toy in question bears the CE marking; quite the contrary, EC law *requires* that unsafe goods be removed from the market.[78] However, since the local or national action taken against CE–marked toys that are believed to be unsafe occurs within a framework of Community market integration, the Commission must be alerted and informed. So, for example, where a suspension notice is issued, the trading standards authority informs the Department of Trade and Industry,[79] which in turn informs the Commission. In this fashion, local and national enforcement is managed within a Community framework.[80]

A similar pattern is established under the General Directive. Where action is taken to restrict the marketing of a product, Member States are to inform the Commission.[81] The only exception covers situations without cross–border implications which, in an integrating market, ought to be few and far between. The UK's Regulations reflect the need to put in place a channel for information transmission. Action taken at local level to prohibit or restrict the supply of any product or to have it forfeit under the Regulations triggers an obligation to notify the DTI,[82] which then passes on relevant information to the Commission in Brussels.[83] The Commission has conferred upon it specified management functions involving consultation and notification. In emergencies the Commission itself may adopt measures through specified procedures, although the threshold criteria are rather restrictive and only rarely likely to be fulfilled.[84]

The Rapid Exchange System (RAPEX) provides for the transmission of information about urgent measures taken at national level because of a 'serious and immediate risk' which a product presents for the safety of consumers. The State informs the Commission, which then transmits details to other Member States; they in turn indicate to the Commission any measures they have taken. The Commission then circulates that information. In the UK the Consumer Safety Unit in the Department of Trade and

---

[78] Art.3 of the Directive, n.28 above.
[79] This obligation is imposed explicitly by Reg.13 of the Toys (Safety) Regs. 1989, n.31 above.
[80] See further Weatherill n.35 above.
[81] Article 7 Dir.
[82] Reg.18 General Product Safety Regs. 1994 n.43 above; Reg.18(2) excludes action in respect of any second–hand product.
[83] An administrative matter not specifically included in the Regs.
[84] Articles 9–11; challenged unsuccessfully by Germany before the European Court, Case C–359/92 *Germany v Commission* [1994] ECR I–3681.

Industry acts as contact point. The System was first set up in 1984[85] and has now been consolidated in the General Directive.

The Safeguard procedures under the Toy Safety Directive (and many others) and the RAPEX system have had teething troubles. They operate erratically. RAPEX, for example, is triggered by a 'serious and immediate risk', but levels of notification vary widely State by State, in part attributable to differing national interpretations. Moreover, the theory of a to and fro of information is not matched fully by practice. A 1993 Commission Report revealed that on average only seven out of (then) twelve Member States comply with their obligation to reply under RAPEX, with 89 days the average time for a reply.[86]

Such discrepancies are only to be expected in the early years of the internal market, but they demonstrate the difficulties in achieving workable integration. The Commission is engaged in the construction of broader networks for information sharing as part of its post–1992 strategy for making the internal market viable in practice.

In tandem with these attempts to manage the market within a framework of structures established by Community rules, there are also 'bottom–up' initiatives to develop cross–border enforcement. Trading standards officers in the UK are beginning to develop links with counterparts in other Member States.[87] The Institute of Trading Standards Administration, the trading standards officers' professional body, has established 'PRODLINK', a database which contains information *inter alia* about dangerous products which are found on the market. Subscribers include British trading standards authorities, but also agencies in Sweden, Norway, the Netherlands and the Republic of Ireland. LACOTS (the Local Authorities Co–ordinating Organisation on Trading Standards) has pursued several routes for enhancing knowledge on how to co–operate across borders. For example, it has published two 'European Directories' which contain a range of factual information concerning relevant authorities throughout the EC.[88] LACOTS presents these booklets with the explicit intent to 'contribute towards the solution of European transborder consumer problems and complaints'. The realisation of this objective seems likely to be a long haul.

---

[85] Dec.84/133 OJ 1984 L70/16.

[86] Commission communication on the handling of urgent situations in the context of implementation of Community rules, COM(93)430.

[87] Cf S. Weatherill 'Reinvigorating the Development of Community Product Safety Policy' (1991) 14 JCP 171–194.

[88] Consumer Product Safety and Consumer Protection Control Bodies, prepared by LACOTS, PO Box 6, 1a Robert Street, Croydon, CR9 1LG.

13 Food Law

13.1 ORIGINS

Controls on food were probably the first form of consumer protection and in England can be traced back to the Assize of Bread and Ale 1266.[1] The early laws were concerned with preventing short weights and measures and with adulteration which allowed sellers to make a profit at the consumer's expense by substituting cheap worthless ingredients for those which should properly have been used. Adulteration can affect both the consumer's economic interests and also potentially his safety interests. In earlier times the laws dealt with specific products. In modern times more general controls on adulteration and consumer protection can be traced back to the Adulteration of Food and Drink Act 1860, whilst the potentially more serious public health aspects were dealt with by the Public Health Act 1875.[2] The consumer protection and public health strands of food regulation were first brought together in the Food Act 1938, with a further consolidation of the law in England and Wales in the Food Act 1984.

However, even before the passing of the Food Act 1984, the Government had announced its intention to review food legislation. In 1985 the Ministry of Agriculture, Fisheries and Food (MAFF) issued a consultation document entitled, *Review of Food Legislation*, carried out other consultation exercises, notably in relation to available defences, and finally issued a White Paper, *Food Safety – Protecting the Consumer*[3] which was the basis for the Food Safety Act 1990. Although the Food Safety Act 1990 was therefore the result of an ongoing review process, its actual timing can perhaps be explained by the large number of food scares which occurred in the late

---

[1] It is interesting that, amongst developing countries the most urgent consumer protection legislation at the moment also relates to food (and medicines) law, see S. Rachagan, 'International Trade and the Third World Consumer: Problems with Double Standards and Dumping' (1993) 1 *Consum LJ* 133.

[2] The consumer protection aspects clearly overlap with legislation on trade descriptions; see Chapter 10. There is also special legislation dealing with weights and measures: for discussion of the Weights and Measures Act 1976, see B. Harvey and D. Parry, *The Law of Consumer Protection and Fair Trading*, 4th ed. (Butterworths, 1992) at pp. 398–415. Equally the public health aspects have links with health and safety laws and of course raise similar questions to those of general product safety; see Chapter 12.

[3] (Cmnd 732, 1989).

1980s concerning, *inter alia* salmonella, listeria, cook–chill foods, bovine spongeform encephalopathy (better known as BSE or 'mad cow disease') and irradiated food. However, it will be seen that, despite its title, the Food Safety Act 1990 does not limit itself to regulating the safety aspects of food, but is also concerned with ensuring that food is of the proper nature, substance and quality and that the consumer is not misled by advertising.

13.2 RATIONALES FOR INTERVENTION

Food is a highly regulated sector. This can be explained by the fact that, as a necessity of life, everyone is forced to consume it. Therefore, there is public pressure to ensure that transactions concerning food are undertaken fairly so that the consumer gets the quality of food expected. There are also serious health risks associated with food. Food interacts with our internal organs and so consumers are obviously concerned about any health risks posed by it. Food can easily become a health risk, as often it is exposed to environmental dangers when growing and can deteriorate if stored improperly or for too long. Risks are also created by food being mishandled by humans during the process of bringing it to the consumer's plate. These risks are increasing in modern times, with new techniques for growing and processing food creating new demands that the food industry be monitored and that consumers be better informed about the nature of the food they eat.

13.3 ENFORCEMENT

The main Government department responsible for food regulation is the Ministry of Agriculture, Fisheries and Food (MAFF). There have been criticisms that the same Government department is responsible for both the interests of producers and consumers of food. To help counter these fears, a Food Safety Directorate has been created so that, within MAFF, food safety functions are separated from food production responsibilities. A consumer panel has also been established so that consumers have a direct means of conveying their opinions on food safety and consumer protection to the Ministry. However, much of the enforcement is carried out at local level by environmental health and trading standards officers. One criticism often made against local enforcement of consumer protection measures is inconsistency of enforcement practices between regions. To counter this, MAFF has issued a Code of Practice under s.40, Food Safety Act 1990 to guide enforcement authorities in the exercise of their functions.[4] The Minister can also issue directions compelling authorities to comply with the Code.[5]

In addition to providing a new regime of offences, the Food Safety Act 1990 has strengthened controls over the food industry by two other procedural reforms. Firstly, enforcement authorities have been given increased powers, with a new emphasis on in–factory enforcement. Secondly, there has been a dramatic tenfold increase in the size of some of the fines for breach of the Act.[6]

13.4 REGULATIONS

The Food Safety Act 1990 is an important piece of consumer protection legislation whose provisions will be considered in detail shortly. Food law is, however, characterised by a superabundance of secondary legislation. The tendency to rely on secondary legislation is understandable, given the bulk of sectoral regulation and the need to amend standards over time with a minimum of formality. Nevertheless, it reduces the amount of Parliamentary control. Although the UK has a good record on consulting consumer groups, reliance on secondary legislation places a great deal of power in the hands of 'expert advisers', who tend to be pro–industry.[7]

The Food Safety Act 1990 continues the tradition of relying on secondary legislation to implement much of the detail by allowing for existing Regulations to continue in force and providing for significant extensions of the regulation making powers.[8] These new regulation making

---

4   See Food Safety Act 1990, Code of Practice No 1: Responsibility for Enforcement of the Food Safety Act 1990; see also Code of Practice No 2: Legal Matters (which deals with handling consumer complaints, powers of entry and the decision whether to prosecute); Code of Practice No 3: Inspection Procedures – General; Code of Practice No 4: Inspection, Detention and Seizure of Suspect Food; Code of Practice No 5: The Use of Improvement Notices; Code of Practice No 6: Prohibition Procedures; Code of Practice No 7: Sampling for Analysis or Examination.

5   S.40(2)(b), Food Safety Act 1990.

6   These fines apply to offences under ss. 7, 8 and 14 (see below).

7   See C. Scott, 'Continuity and Change in British Food Law' (1990) 53 *MLR* 785 at 791 and G. Cannon, *The Politics of Food*, (Century, 1987) .

8   See ss.16–19, Food Safety Act 1990 and for the detail of the legislation see *Butterworth's Law of Food and Drugs* (looseleaf). Scott notes that while there is a general power to make regulations, which must be used to meet the traditional objectives of United Kingdom food law (ie public health and consumer protection),

powers are not limited to 'food'[9] but also cover 'food sources'[10] and 'contact materials'[11] in an attempt to control food production and distribution from the farm to the plate. In response to increased innovation within the food industry, the Act includes powers to regulate 'novel foods'[12] and genetically modified food sources or food derived therefrom.[13] To counter concern about the hygiene standards of some workers involved in the food industry, power was given to require persons involved in a food business to attend a food hygiene training course.[14] A separate provision enables health authorities to provide food hygiene training courses or to contribute towards their cost.[15]

The influence of European law on the food industry has been considerable.[16] With no specific authority to enact the necessary Regulations to implement EC law, the Government previously had to rely on the powers provided by s.2, European Communities Act 1972. S.17, Food Safety Act 1990 now provides Ministers with the express power to meet Community obligations with respect to food, food sources or contact materials.

Local authorities had for a long time complained that their work was hampered by the lack of a register of food premises in their area. New powers have now been given to require the registration of premises used for a food business.[17] Although quite large numbers will be under a duty to register, the procedure is likely to be straightforward and will only involve

---

there are also additional powers which do not have to be justified against these objectives: Scott *op. cit.* at 788.

9   Food is defined as including: (i) drink, (ii) articles and substances of no nutritional value, (iii) chewing gum, and (iv) articles and substances used as ingredients in the preparation of food. The following are expressly excluded: (a) live animals, birds, or live fish which are not used for human consumption whilst alive; (b) fodder and feeding stuffs; and (c) controlled drugs and most medicinal products: see s.1(1),(2) Food Safety Act 1990.

10   Food sources are defined as including 'any growing crop or live animal, bird or fish from which food is intended to be derived': s.1(3), Food Safety Act 1990.

11   Contact materials are defined as covering 'any article or substance which is intended to come into contact with food': s.1(3), Food Safety Act 1990.

12   These are of two types: (i) 'state of the art' products such as new slimming products or the so–called 'improved foods' currently popular in Japan, and (ii) products which may have existed for centuries but which are new to the UK, eg exotic fruits.

13   A good example of which is genetically modified yeast; cf the provisions relating to 'genetically modified organisms' in the Environmental Protection Act 1990.

14   Sched. 1, Para. 5(3), Food Safety Act 1990.

15   S.23, Food Safety Act 1990.

16   See N. Fraselle, 'Consumer Protection and its Integration in Community Policy on Food: General Approach, Principles and Evaluation' (1994) 2 *Consum LJ* 17.

17   S.19(1)(a), Food Safety Act 1990.

revealing such basic information as the business's address, proprietor's name and number of employees. There is unlikely to be a registration charge. The Minister is also given powers (which are unlikely to be widely used) to establish a licensing regime for food business premises if he believes it necessary or expedient to do so to ensure that food complies with food safety requirements or in the interests of public health or to protect or promote the interests of consumers.[18]

The most controversial aspect of the Food Safety Act 1990 was its implicit acceptance of irradiated food. Previously it had only been permitted in limited circumstances, namely in hospitals where patients needed a bacteria free diet. Ironically the word 'irradiation' appears nowhere in the Act, but irradiation can be regulated as a process,[19] labelling Regulations can ensure the fact that the food is irradiated can be drawn to the consumer's attention[20] and it is widely suspected that irradiation plants will be subjected to a licensing regime. Critics of irradiation argue that the process reduces the nutritional value of food and point to the lack of knowledge about the effects of eating irradiated food. Proponents of irradiation claim it increases safety and leads to a longer shelf life and argue that consumers should be given the freedom to decide for themselves whether they want irradiated food. Many, however, took the pragmatic viewpoint that, since it was not technically possible to detect whether food had been irradiated, it was better to legalise the process and hope that producers would comply with the labelling Regulations so that consumers would at least know when they were being offered irradiated food.[21]

13.5 FOOD SAFETY

13.5.1 Rendering Food Injurious to Health

S.7, Food Safety Act 1990 provides for the offence of rendering food injurious to health with intent that it shall be sold for human consumption. The offence can be committed by (i) adding any article or substance to the food, (ii) using any article or substance as an ingredient in the preparation of the food, (iii) abstracting any constituent from the food, or (iv) subjecting the food to any other process or treatment. The section requires a positive act

---

[18] S.19(1)(b), and 19(2), Food Safety Act 1990.
[19] S.16(1)(c), Food Safety Act 1990.
[20] S.16(1)(e), Food Safety Act 1990.
[21] A House of Lords Committee came out in favour of irradiation: see House of Lords, *Report of the European Communities Committee on Irradiation of Foodstuffs*, (4th Rep HL Paper No 13, 1989). See generally Scott, *op. cit.*, at 797–801.

and does not cover omissions to subject the food to a necessary process or treatment.

The Act defines 'injury to health' as 'any impairment, whether permanent or temporary'; it requires that the probable cumulative effect of consuming even ordinary quantities of food of substantially the same composition must be considered.[22] This reference to the cumulative effects of consuming food of certain types is potentially of great significance, given the increased awareness of how health can be injured by even ordinary quantities of products containing ingredients such as cholesterol, alcohol or even salt. Difficult questions of proof and blameworthiness as well as limited resources on the part of enforcement authorities are likely to mean that the provision concerning the cumulative effects of food is unlikely to be used to its full potential.

13.5.2 Food Safety Requirement

The Act also makes it an offence to sell, or deposit or consign to another for the purpose of sale, food which fails to comply with the food safety requirements.[23] This includes food which (i) has been rendered injurious to health; (ii) is unfit for human consumption; or (iii) is so contaminated (whether by extraneous matter or otherwise) that it would not be reasonable to expect it to be used for human consumption.

For the purpose of this section and the following one concerning inspection and seizure, the Food Safety Act 1990 makes the important presumption that if any food is found to breach the food safety requirements then, until the contrary is proved, all food of the same class or description in that batch, lot or consignment will fail those requirements.

Although providing a wider basis for criminal liability than previous laws, the Food Safety Act 1990 failed to include a general safety requirement[24] similar to that provided for most consumer products by Part II of the Consumer Protection Act 1987, but from whose scope food was excluded. Food is now within the scope of the general duty to market only safe products introduced by the General Product Safety Regulations 1994, which implement the European Product Safety Directive.[25]

---

22   S.7(3), Food Safety Act 1990.
23   S.8, Food Safety Act 1990.
24   This was out of step with the current trend to impose general standards: see 1.8.1
25   See 12.5.1.

13.5.3 Inspection and Seizure[26]

Enforcement officers can inspect at all reasonable times food intended for human consumption which has been sold, offered or exposed for sale or is possessed, deposited or consigned for the purpose of sale or preparation for sale. Where the food has been inspected and it appears to the officer that it does not satisfy the food safety requirements, or in the absence of an inspection where it appears that any food is likely to cause food poisoning or any disease communicable to humans, then the enforcement officer has two choices. The officer can either issue a notice that the food is not to be used for human consumption and should not be removed or only moved to a specified place: this gives the officer 21 days to either satisfy himself that the food does satisfy the food safety requirements, in which case the officer must withdraw the notice or, if the officer is not so satisfied, to seize the food and have it dealt with by the magistrates. Alternatively the officer may seize the food immediately and bring the matter before the magistrates for an order for its destruction.

Wherever possible the food should be dealt with by magistrates within two days and in any event in the case of highly perishable food the food should be dealt with by magistrates as soon as possible.[27] If an order is made for destruction of the food, the magistrates must require that any expenses reasonably incurred to achieve this be defrayed by the owner. If, however, the notice is withdrawn or the magistrates refuse to condemn the food, then the enforcement authorities have to pay compensation. Here the Act must strike a balance between the interests of the owner of the food who has been wrongly accused and who may have suffered financial loss as a result and the public interest in limiting the compensation payable by enforcement authorities when they have made a mistake so that the authorities do not become too defensive for fear of jeopardising their limited resources. The Act strikes this balance by limiting any compensation to the depreciation in the value of the food resulting from the officer's actions. Thus the enforcement authorities are not exposed to potentially expensive actions for loss of profit or goodwill, but the owner is still compensated for the loss of or deterioration in quality of the food concerned.

13.5.4 Improvement Notices

S.10, Food Safety Act 1990 provides for the serving of improvement notices on the proprietor of a food business where there are reasonable grounds to

---

[26]   S.9, Food Safety Act 1990.
[27]   See Code of Practice No. 4 *op. cit.* at para. 11.

believe that he or she is not complying with regulations which either:

(i) require, prohibit or regulate the use of any process or treatment in the preparation of food, or
(ii) provide for the observance of hygienic conditions and practices in connection with the carrying out of commercial operations with respect to food or food sources.

This procedure is not, however, suitable where there is an imminent risk to health from a breach of regulations.

The improvement notice must state the grounds for believing that there is non–compliance with Regulations, specify the matters constituting non–compliance, specify the measures the proprietor should take to ensure compliance and specify a time limit of not less than fourteen days for compliance.[28] The proprietor has a right of appeal, details of which (for example, the name and address of the relevant local court) should be contained within notes attached to the improvement notice.

13.5.5 Prohibition Orders[29]

Where a proprietor has been convicted of an offence in connection with the two classes of Regulations for which an improvement notice can be issued then it may be possible for a court to impose a prohibition order. For a prohibition order to be made the court must be convinced that the 'health risk condition' is fulfilled. This requires there to be a risk of injury to health due to either:

(i) the use of any process or treatment,
(ii) the construction of any premises,
(iii) the use of any equipment, or
(iv) the state or condition of any premises or equipment which are used for the purposes of the business.

Where the court finds the relevant regulation breached and the health risk

---

28   Code of Practice No. 5, *op. cit.*, at para. 33 allows for the possibility of the proprietor applying for this time limit to be extended if he or she has a genuine reason for making the request. The Code also states that it is the responsibility of the food authority to make it clear that s.10 allows the proprietor to satisfy the notice by carrying out work of at least equivalent effect to that specified by the officer (at para. 36).

29   S.11, Food Safety Act 1990.

condition satisfied, then it *must* make a prohibition order. The nature of the prohibition varies according to which of the four ways the health risk condition was fulfilled. If it was fulfilled in relation to (i), then the court must prohibit the process or treatment for that particular business; if it was condition (ii) or (iii), then the use of the premises or equipment for that particular business or for a food business 'of the same class or description' must be prohibited; and if it was condition (iv), then the prohibition on using the equipment or premises must extend to their use for any food business.

The consequences of a prohibition order can be severe. Therefore the authorities must issue a certificate lifting the order within three days of their being satisfied that the health risk has abated. A proprietor may apply for such a certificate, in which case the authority must make a decision as soon as is reasonably practicable and, in any event, within fourteen days.

In addition to *mandatory* prohibition orders, the courts also have the *discretion* to issue a personal prohibition order against the proprietor, prohibiting his or her participation in any food business or any food business of a specified class or description. This order is only possible where there has been a conviction under a hygiene regulation,[30] but it is not necessary that the health risk condition be fulfilled. The Act recognises that the proprietor may not be personally responsible for the day to day management of the business or for every outlet it owns. Thus there is the further power to make a prohibition order in respect of the 'manager of a food business', defined to include 'any person who is entrusted by the proprietor with the day to day running of the business.'[31] This allows the sanction to be made against the real culprit without needlessly affecting the general operation of the business.[32] The personal prohibition order prohibits the identified party from participating in the management of any food business or any class or description of food business. Whilst the Act fails to define 'management' a meaning can perhaps be drawn out from the definition of 'manager', though it may still sometimes be difficult to determine whether someone has been *entrusted* with the *day–to–day* management of a business. Too strict an interpretation may prevent the person from obtaining any employment, whereas an excessive leniency may threaten consumer safety. For instance, would a baker subject to the order be allowed to work alone in the bakery

---

30 NB it does not apply where the breach is of a Regulation requiring, prohibiting or regulating the use of any process or treatment in the preparation of food. Breach of such a Regulation can, however, be the basis of a general prohibition order or improvement notice.

31 S.11(11), Food Safety Act 1990.

32 Code of Practice No. 6 *op. cit.* suggests that personal prohibition orders will only be made in extreme circumstances. For a general discussion of these issues, see 14.2.4-5.

department of a supermarket under the overall supervision of a store manager who may know nothing about baking?

13.5.6 Emergency Prohibition Notices and Orders

The ability to issue an emergency prohibition notice is an important new power given to enforcement officers by s.12, Food Safety Act 1990. An emergency prohibition notice can be served by the officer in the same circumstances that give rise to a prohibition order, save that there must be an *imminent* risk of injury to health; also the nature of the emergency makes it self–evident that the proprietor need not have been convicted of an offence under the relevant Regulations. The terms of the emergency prohibition notice parallel those of prohibition orders, with magistrates able to impose an emergency prohibition order containing the same prohibitions. Such an order can be applied for by the enforcement officer, giving one day's notice of his or her intention to do so.

The power to issue emergency prohibition notices places great power in the hands of enforcement officers. This is restricted in two ways. First, the emergency prohibition notice lapses after three days, unless an application is made for an emergency prohibition order. Second, compensation is payable if either no application is made or if the court refuses to make an emergency prohibition order, unless the court declares that it was satisfied that the health risk condition was fulfilled at the time the emergency prohibition notice was served.[33] Note that in this case the amount of compensation is not limited to the loss in value of the food, so that the enforcement authority could potentially be faced with very large claims for damages for loss of profit and reputation. This is perhaps regrettable as it may cause authorities to be reluctant to use what are some of the most effective powers given to them by the Food Safety Act 1990. Emergency prohibition notices and orders cease to have effect after the enforcement authority has issued a certificate indicating satisfaction that sufficient measures have been taken to ensure that the health risk condition is no longer fulfilled. As with prohibition orders, the certificate must be granted within three days of the authority determining that it is deserved; a decision on an application by a proprietor requesting such a certificate should be made as soon as is reasonably practicable and, in any event, within fourteen days.

---

33   Remember that, for the health risk condition to be fulfilled for these purposes the risk of injury to health must have been *imminent*.

13.5.7 Emergency Control Orders[34]

In order to respond to food scares requiring urgent action, the Minister has been given the power to make emergency control orders. These orders can prohibit the carrying out of any commercial operation with respect to any food, food source or contact materials which appear to the Minister to involve an imminent risk of injury to health. The Minster can also give such directions as are necessary and expedient to prevent the carrying out of such operations and can recover reasonable expenses thereby incurred. It is noteworthy that there is no provision for compensation where an emergency control order is made in error. It is interesting to contrast this with the full liability for damages which food authorities are exposed to when their officers serve an emergency prohibition order by mistake. This new power is an important back–up provision, which (although intended to be used infrequently) gives the Government the power to act where traders refuse to take action voluntarily when a risk associated with their food is drawn to their attention.

In relation to these emergency powers, Willet has noted that when traders disagree with the enforcement authorities' assessment of the risk involved, their reaction may well depend upon whether the danger is an isolated occurrence or is inherent in the production process. Thus he contrasts Perrier's withdrawal of water contaminated with benzene (although it was universally acknowledged not to be dangerous) with the defensive attitude of chicken farmers to the risk of salmonella in eggs, where the risk derived from the conditions in which the chickens were kept.[35] It may also have had something to do with protecting a brand name!

13.6 CONSUMER PROTECTION

Under the heading of consumer protection are those measures designed to protect the economic interest of consumers. There are obviously clear overlaps between the food–specific laws contained in the Food Safety Act 1990 and the more general laws governing advertising and trade descriptions.[36]

---

[34] S.13, Food Safety Act 1990.
[35] C. Willet, 'The Law's Role in Emergency Food Control' [1991] *JBL*150.
[36] See Chapter 10.

13.6.1 False or Misleading Descriptions or Advertisements

The Food Safety Act 1990 re-enacts the offence of falsely or misleadingly describing and advertising food,[37] but is wider than the previous provision[38] which required that labels be 'calculated to mislead'. The reference to 'calculated' has been dropped; now any statement need only be 'likely' to mislead.[39] It goes further, however, enabling the Act to catch traders who, while ensuring their advertising and labels are truthful, nevertheless manage to mislead through other means. S.15(3), Food Safety Act 1990 makes it an offence to sell, offer or expose for sale, or have in one's possession for the purpose of sale, any food 'the presentation of which is likely to mislead as to the nature or substance or quality of the food'. The presentation of food includes its shape, appearance and packaging as well as the way it is arranged when exposed for sale, and the setting in which the food is displayed with a view to sale.[40]

It is important to remember that the Labelling of Food Regulations 1984[41] continue in force. These prohibit the misleading presentation of food, prescribe information which must be given with food and impose conditions on the use of claims made with respect to food.

13.6.2 Nature or Substance or Quality

The most commonly used provisions are those in s.14 which make it an offence to sell food not of the nature or substance or quality demanded by the purchaser. The offence can be committed by anyone who sells food for human consumption, but not by someone merely offering to sell food, presumably because of the need for a 'demand' in order to have a standard against which the food can be judged.

The offence involves selling food to the *purchaser's prejudice* and whether that is the case depends upon the *demand* made by the purchaser. The demand provides the standard by which the product is judged; for instance, it will identify the food's grade and type. In *McDonald's Hamburgers v Windle*,[42] an offence was committed when ordinary cola was supplied in response to a demand for diet cola. The purchaser's expectations were affected by the nutritional information notice posted in the store.

---

37 S.15(1)(2), Food Safety Act 1990.
38 S.6, Food Act 1984.
39 The test is whether an ordinary person, not an expert, would be misled.
40 S.53(1) Food Safety Act 1990.
41 S.I. 1984/1305.
42 [1987] *Crim LR* 200.

Prejudice should be judged against the expectations of the ordinary consumer and not those of experts. That explains why no offence was committed in *Collins Arden Products v Barking Borough*[43] when cordial was supplied containing saccharin, despite expert evidence that cordial was an alcoholic drink or a non–alcoholic drink containing sugar to give it a heartening effect. The expert evidence differed from the commonly held understanding of the term. Similarly, a butcher escaped conviction in *Goldup v John Manson*[44] when he sold minced meat with more than 25 per cent fat content, which (according to the public analyst) was the maximum amount of fat which should be allowed. In that case it was relevant that two types of mince were sold and that the meat in question was the cheaper one, with a correspondingly higher fat content.

As the words 'nature', 'substance' and 'quality' are used disjunctively in the Act, a defendant is entitled to know under which head he or she is charged. The three terms do have a degree of overlap and, in relation to older cases, it is important to take care since earlier Acts used the words conjunctively.

Food can be pure and unadulterated and yet not be of the *nature* demanded because it is different from what was demanded. This will again be judged by the expectations of ordinary consumers. Thus in *Riley (Bros) v Hallimond*[45] it was accepted that the description 'butter toffee' implied that it should contain no fats other than butter.

Food is not of the *substance* demanded if it contains extraneous matter, even if it is harmless.[46] However, claims relating to the substance of food are not limited to cases of adulteration:[47] food will not be of the substance demanded if it fails to meet statutory or regulatory standards. Prescribed standards such as those found in texts like the British Pharmacopoeia should normally be followed,[48] but evidence of a lower acceptable commercial standard can be adduced.[49] Where the actual standard required has not been proven, it is sufficient to show that the food is below the lowest possible acceptable standard. Thus a prosecution involving a 'mock salmon cutlet'

---

43   [1943] KB 419.
44   [1982] QB 161.
45   [1927] 44 TLR. 238.
46   *Hall v Owen–Jones and Jones* [1967] 3 All ER 209 (milk containing penicillin).
47   *Few v Robinson* [1921] 3 KB 504, concerning cow milk which did not meet the required standards, but was nevertheless not held to breach the provisions, seems to have been wrong in this respect: such cases are probably better brought under the quality heading.
48   See *Dickens v Randerson* [1901] 1 KB 437.
49   *Boots Cash Chemists v Cowling* (1903) 38 LT 539.

was successful in *Tonkin v Victor Value*[50] by arguing that it should have
contained at least the 35 per cent fish content prescribed by the Fish
Standards (Fish Cakes) Order 1950 – the salmon cutlet implying a superior
quality to the ordinary fish cake. All cases turn on their facts, which explains
why the butcher in *T.W. Lawrence v Burleigh*[51] was convicted for selling
minced meat with 32.7 per cent fat while the butcher in *Goldup*[52] was not
convicted despite his mince having a 35 per cent fat content.

Food is not of the *quality* demanded if there is extraneous matter, even if
it is harmless[53] or if the food is not perfectly constituted. Quality refers to
both the description of the food and its commercial quality. However, whilst
a low price might cause consumers to expect a lower than normal quality of
food, it is submitted that in all cases food should be of satisfactory quality.[54]

13.7 DUE DILIGENCE DEFENCE

S.21(1), Food Safety Act 1990 provides a general defence where a defendant
can prove he or she has taken all reasonable precautions and exercised all
due diligence.[55] In some respects this defence is more generous than that
which preceded it. S.100, Food Act 1984 had a due diligence defence, but
had also required the defendant to prove the commission of the offence was
due to the act or default of another person. There had also been a defence, in
relation to a charge of supplying food not of the nature or substance or
quality demanded, if the presence of extraneous matter was an unavoidable
consequence of the process of collection or preparation. This had been given
a narrow interpretation in *Smedleys Ltd v Breed*[56] where the defendants were

---

50   [1962] 1 All ER 821.
51   (1982) 30 LGR 631.
52   *Op. cit.*
53   See *Barber v Co–op Wholesale Soc Ltd.* (1983) 81 LGR 762 which involved a
     conviction following a green plastic straw being found in a milk bottle. There was no
     evidence that the straw was not sterile.
54   The implied term of satisfactory quality does itself take price into account; see 4.1.3.
55   The details of the due diligence defence are considered at 14.2, for a version of the
     defence applies to a number of consumer protection statutes. It has been argued that
     one effect of the introduction of the defence may be to encourage food manufacturers
     to adopt Hazard Analysis at Critical Control Points (HACCP) type schemes. These
     seek to assess potential hazards by reference to microbiological criteria and to control
     them at critical control points through the types of controls on preparation, conditions,
     temperature and hygiene that are found in the Hygiene (General) Regulations 1970,
     S.I. 1970/1172 : see Scott *op. cit.* at 783.
56   [1974] AC 839. The defence was to be found in s.3(3), Food Act 1984.

held liable because it would have been physically possible to have removed the offending caterpillar, notwithstanding that it had not been detected by state of the art quality controls. In such circumstances the due diligence defence would now be available.

Retailers and others who bought in food, often pre–packaged and with no means of controlling its quality were, however, concerned by the repeal of the 'written warranty defence' which had been provided by s.102, Food Safety Act 1990. This defence applied where the defendant proved he or she:

(i) purchased the goods as an article or substance which could lawfully be sold or dealt with;
(ii) had a written warranty to that effect;
(iii) had no reason to believe at the time of the commission of the alleged offence that it was otherwise; and
(iv) that the goods were, at the time of the alleged offence, in the same state as when he or she purchased them.[57]

The scope of the defence had been restricted somewhat by the decision in *London Borough of Camden v Fine Fare Ltd*[58] that for a large company like Fine Fare to claim that it had no reason to believe that the product had not remained in the same state from the time of purchase until the time of sale, it must have had some system for checking products. However, the duty only extended to checking the continued accuracy of the warranty and did not seek to suggest that the veracity of the original warranty should be queried. It was also significant that the defendant was a large company with the resources and organisation to make whatever checks might be required.

To help meet the concerns of retailers and others, the Government provided for an irrebuttable presumption that the due diligence defence was complied with in certain circumstances. The statutory presumption of due diligence only applies with respect to offences under ss.8, 14 and 15 of the Food Safety Act 1990. To take advantage of the defence, the defendant must have neither prepared the food nor imported it into the UK.[59] To trigger the presumption he or she must also show that the offence was due to the act or default of another who was not under his or her control, or to reliance on

---

57 Obtaining a positive assurance is not normally enough to satisfy the due diligence defence: see *Taylor v Lawrence Fraser* (1977) 121 SJ. 157. The Government was concerned that importers could too easily hide behind a warranty, but to disallow the defence for imports was thought likely to be considered a technical barrier to trade contrary to Article 30 of the Treaty of Rome.
58 2 February 1987 (unreported).
59 Does the exclusion of imports from other EC countries not breach Article 30 of the Treaty of Rome: see 2.2.

information supplied by that person. Additional elements of the defence depend upon the status of the defendant. Those who have not applied their name or mark to the product have only to prove that they did not know and could not reasonably be expected to know at the time of the commission of the alleged offence that their conduct would be unlawful. 'Own-branders' seem, however, to be subjected to a stricter regime and must show that they carried out all reasonable checks on the food or that it was reasonable for them to rely on checks carried out by their suppliers, as well as proving that they did not know and had no reason to suspect that their act or omission would amount to an offence. In practice there may be less difference between the two tests than appears. The requirement that '*non*-own-branders' 'could not reasonably be expected to know' that their conduct would amount to an offence may require them to carry out tests on goods sold, the stringency of such testing depending on the size and resources of the particular defendant and the seriousness of the consequences.

There is much debate about whether the inclusion of a due diligence defence weakens consumer protection by undermining the principle of strict liability or strengthens it by giving businesses an incentive to improve their procedures in order to avoid liability. Certainly the food industry has been very keen to learn what it has to do in order to take advantage of the due diligence defence. The pertinent question might be whether, if the defence did not exist, would they be as keen, more keen or less keen to learn what was required to avoid committing the offences in the first place.

14 The Regulatory Offence

14.1 THE NATURE AND PURPOSE OF STRICT LIABILITY UNDER THE REGULATORY OFFENCE

The prevalence of offences of 'strict liability' in the consumer protection field runs through preceding Chapters. Several offences created in the sphere of consumer protection law impose criminal liability on traders who are responsible for the commission of stipulated acts, without the need for any demonstration that the trader was at fault. The application of a false trade description to goods or the supply or offer for supply of goods to which a false trade description is applied,[1] the supply of an unsafe product[2] and the supply of unsafe food[3] all attract criminal liability even where the trader has neither deliberately, recklessly nor even negligently caused this to happen.

This characteristic concern with the act not the mind distances consumer protection law from the general sweep of English criminal law. Criminal liability is typically not incurred unless not only the perpetration of stipulated acts is established ('*actus reus*'), but also the requisite mental element is proved ('*mens rea*'). Doing an act is not normally deemed a criminal offence independently of inquiry into the actor's state of mind.[4]

The case for and against imposing strict criminal liability is complex and has been investigated elsewhere at a depth that cannot be replicated here.[5] Broadly, the normal insistence that conviction for crime demands a guilty mind rests on the perception that the imposition of criminal liability by the State on an individual is a very serious matter, involving a degree of moral turpitude. It may lead to the infliction of significant penalties, including the individual's loss of liberty. Accordingly, only those guilty in both mind and deed should be punished.

It seems to be assumed that the same objections to the imposition of strict liability do not apply in the law of consumer protection. Several

---

1 Chapter 10.
2 Chapter 12.
3 Chapter 13.
4 A. Ashworth, *Principles of Criminal Law* (OUP, 1991), Ch.5; J.C. Smith and B. Hogan, *Criminal Law* (Butterworths, 1992), pp. 53–91, 99–103.
5 Cf B. Wootton, *Crime and the Criminal Law – Reflections of a Magistrate and Social Scientist* (Stevens, 1963); L. Leigh, *Strict and Vicarious Liability: A Study in Administrative Criminal Law* (Sweet and Maxwell, 1982).

elements combine to lead to this conclusion.[6] The circumstances of the offence are different. Consumer protection offences are not victimless crimes, but the distance between offender and consumer is typically wider than that in crimes of violence or theft. The stigma of conviction under consumer protection laws is not so significant. This seems to form part of a loose notion that infringements of, for example, trade descriptions legislation lie far from the heartland of 'real' criminal law. This is recognised by the customary term used in this field, the 'regulatory offence'.[7]

In *Wings Ltd v Ellis*, a leading case concerning the Trade Descriptions Act,[8] Lord Scarman declared that the Act 'is not truly a criminal statute. Its purpose is not the enforcement of the criminal law but the maintenance of trading standards. Trading standards, not criminal behaviour, are its concern'.[9] This is rather under explained; the dictum assumes a sharp distinction between infractions of trading standards and crime, without elaborating why the two are mutually exclusive. However it must be taken as an important judicial expression of scepticism about the role of the 'true' criminal law in this area. Lord Scarman drew on *Sherras v De Rutzen*[10] for Wright J's well-known dictum that certain statutes (of which, in Lord Scarman's view, the Trade Descriptions Act is one) prohibit acts which 'are not criminal in any real sense, but are acts which in the public interest are prohibited under a penalty'. Therefore, given the subject matter of the 1968 Act, it does not attract 'the presumption recognised by Lord Reid in *Sweet v Parsley*[11] ...as applicable to truly criminal statutes that Parliament did not intend to make criminals of persons who were in no way blameworthy in what they did.'

Apart from justification for strict liability based on the lower level of stigma attached to the (on occasion blameless) offender, the overturning of the normal requirement of *mens rea* is also capable of justification with reference to the effective application of the law. The rationales for public intervention in areas such as food safety, trade descriptions and product safety lie in the need to achieve results that would not be produced by the market operating without regulation – the suppression of unsafe food, misleading trade descriptions and unsafe goods. This objective would be jeopardised by extended refined argument about guilt. At issue is correcting

---

6   Cf Ashworth n.4 above, pp. 135–45; Smith and Hogan n.4 above, Ch.6.
7   Cf A.I. Ogus, *Regulation* (OUP, 1994), Ch.5; I. Ramsay, *Consumer Protection Text and Materials* (Weidenfeld, 1989), Ch.6.
8   [1984] 3 All ER 577, see Chapter 10.3.
9   [1984] 3 All ER 577, 587.
10   [1895] 1 QB 918.
11   [1969] 1 All ER 347 at 349, [1970] AC 132 at 148.

the unsafe or deceptive market.[12] This dictates a preference for addressing (and deterring) the fact of the occurrence of the prohibited act or omission, not the mind of the supplier.

It has been cogently suggested that the pattern of the regulatory offence could be developed much more coherently and with more awareness of its specific functions in curing market failure and achieving consumer protection were it to be formally disconnected from the 'criminal law'.[13] After all, if the justification for employing the regulatory offence is that traders are not really being accused of 'proper crime', but rather of (perhaps unwitting) participation in market failure, then why stigmatise them at all with the label of criminal activity? This analysis has much force and, it is submitted, would do much to align form with practice and perception.

The imposition of strict liability affects and is affected by two further principal characteristics of the regulatory offence. The first is the regulatory defence, which in practical terms mitigates the severity of the basic strict liability offence. The second is the pattern of enforcement, which tends to emphasise co–operation and negotiation in preference to the imposition of formal penalties. These two aspects are considered below.

14.2 THE 'DUE DILIGENCE' DEFENCE

14.2.1 Nature and Purpose of the Defence

Prosecutions for breach of relevant provisions of a number of Acts examined in this book may be met by the defence that the accused has taken, loosely, all reasonable precautions and exercised all due diligence to avoid the commission of the offence; and/or that the commission of the offence is the fault of another. This type of defence is a long–standing feature of trade practices law and may be traced back to the 19th–century Merchandise Marks Acts.[14]

---

[12] Chapter 1.

[13] An important contribution is D. Tench, *Towards a Middle System of Law* (Consumers Association, 1981). Cf, with some sympathy for the Tench view but also some for the deterrent effect of the criminal law, Sir Gordon Borrie, *The Development of Consumer Law and Policy – Bold Spirits and Timorous Souls* (Hamlyn Lectures, Stevens and Sons, 1974), Parts III, VI.

[14] Discussed by A. Painter, 'The Evolution of Statutory Defences' (1982) 1 *Trading Law* 181.

In *Wings Ltd v Ellis* the House of Lords was unmoved by claims that its interpretation of the relevant offence under the Trade Descriptions Act 1968[15] would criminalise the innocent precisely because of the availability of statutory defences. For example, Lord Templeman saw no need to require carelessness as an ingredient of the offence because s.24 permits a defence to the careful trader.[16]

The availability of this defence goes some way to meet the objection to the concept of the strict liability offence that it criminalises the non–blameworthy. It does not wholly meet that objection, for the ingredients of the offence are still committed by an 'innocent' trader who must then seek to bring him– or herself within the scope of the statutory defence. In practical terms this is significant; in the normal run of criminal cases, the prosecution has to prove *mens rea*, whereas, under the strict liability–plus–defence hybrid system, the defendant bears the burden of self–exculpation. Nonetheless the defence does provide a practical means for the innocent trader to seek to avoid incurring criminal penalties. The availability of the defence also recognises that the rationale of inducing traders to take rigorous precautions to avoid committing prohibited acts does not suggest a need to impose criminal liability where the trader shows that he or she has in fact taken all such precautions. Indeed, were criminal liability unavoidable, firms might have a diminished incentive to improve their systems beyond the minimum needed to avoid easily preventable infractions.[17] The 'rational and moral justification' for imposing criminal liability in such circumstances is undermined.[18]

14.2.2 The Defences in Detail

For trade descriptions, the relevant provision is found in section 24 of the Trade Descriptions Act 1968. This provides that:

(1) In any proceedings for an offence under this Act it shall, subject to subsection (2) of this section, be a defence for the person charged to prove –

---

15 Section 14, effectively an offence of 'semi–strict' liability; see Chapter 10.2.3.

16 [1984] 3 All ER 577, 593a.

17 But cf 14.2.3 below on the general impact of the defence on the climate for enforcement. Cf Chapter 13.7 for comment in the context of food law.

18 Cf Lord Diplock in *Tesco Supermarkets Ltd v Nattrass* [1971] 2 All ER 127, 151e, 151h.

(a) that the commission of the offence was due to a mistake or to reliance on information supplied to him or to the act or default of another person, an accident or some other cause beyond his control; and
(b) that he took all reasonable precautions and exercised all due diligence to avoid the commission of such an offence by himself or any person under his control.

(2) If in any case the defence provided by the last foregoing subsection involves the allegation that the commission of the offence was due to the act or default of another person or to reliance on information supplied by another person, the person charged shall not, without leave of the court, be entitled to rely on that defence unless, within a period ending seven clear days before the hearing, he has served on the prosecutor a notice in writing giving such information identifying or assisting in the identification of that other person as was then in his possession.

(3) In any proceedings for an offence under this Act of supplying or offering to supply goods to which a false trade description is applied it shall be a defence for the person charged to prove that he did not know, and could not with reasonable diligence have ascertained, that the goods did not conform to the description or that the description had been applied to the goods.

In relation to specified offences in the field of consumer safety under Part II of the Consumer Protection Act 1987 and in relation to Part III of that Act's offence of misleading pricing, s.39 of the Consumer Protection Act 1987 provides that:

(1) Subject to the following provisions of this section, in proceedings against any person for an offence to which this section applies it shall be a defence for that person to show that he took all reasonable steps and exercised all due diligence to avoid committing the offence.

(2) Where in any proceedings against any person for such an offence the defence provided by subsection (1) above involves an allegation that the commission of the offence was due –
(a) to the act or default of another; or
(b) to reliance on information given by another, that person shall not, without the leave of the court, be entitled to rely on the defence unless, not less than seven clear days before the hearing of the proceedings, he has served a notice under subsection (3) below on the person bringing the proceedings.

(3) A notice under this subsection shall give such information identifying or assisting in the identification of the person who committed the act or default or gave the information as is in the possession of the person serving the notice at the time he serves it.

(4) It is hereby declared that a person shall not be entitled to rely on the
defence provided by subsection (1) above by reason of his reliance on
information supplied by another, unless he shows that it was reasonable
in all the circumstances for him to have relied on the information,
having regard in particular –
(a) to the steps which he took, and those which might reasonably have
been taken, for the purpose of verifying the information; and
(b) to whether he had any reason to disbelieve the information.

A number of other statutes within the scope of this book include analogous
provisions. The Food Safety Act 1990 contains a comparable defence in
s.21(1).[19] The Property Misdescriptions Act 1991 provides a further
illustration,[20] and the defence also appears in the Consumer Credit Act 1974
which creates offences out of a number of objectionable practices in that
field.[21] In the realm of trade practices law beyond consumer protection as
normally conceived, the due diligence defence has a role to play. For
example, it appears in the Sunday Trading Act 1994.
    These provisions are not replicas of each other. The Consumer
Protection Act 1987 has pared down the defence from the more elaborate
requirements of the Trade Descriptions Act 1968 to focus on due diligence.
The Food Safety Act 1990 also contains the stripped down version.
Nevertheless the defences share the broad policy of offering the careful
trader a defined protection from conviction. Despite the textual differences,
their practical application is doubtless similar.[22] Blaming another person is
possible, although s.39(3) and (4) and s.24(2) attach procedural
requirements to such tactics.

14.2.3 The Practical Application of the Defences

A major argument in favour of strict liability is the flexibility conferred on
enforcement agencies by the elimination of arguments that no offence has
been committed where unsafe goods or misleading trade descriptions reach
the market. Yet the due diligence defence undermines this objective. By
protecting the innocent trader, it alters the regulatory climate and is liable to
impede vigorous enforcement. It may create the risk that unmeritorious
defences will be advanced, even encouraged. This is especially important

---

[19]   Chapter 13. This contains some special nuances, examined at 13.7.
[20]   Chapter 10.4.
[21]   Chapter 11.6.
[22]   Cf Woolf LJ in *Rotherham MBC v Raysun* [1988] BTLC 292, [1989] CCLR 1.

when account is taken of the primacy of informal enforcement and the reluctance of trading standards officers to pursue a path of formal prosecution. Although, as suggested above, it seems unjust and even pointless to impose criminal liability on traders who have truly done all they possibly could to avert the occurrence of the prohibited act, practice is rarely so clear–cut. The defence may muddy the waters sufficiently for effective enforcement to be impaired.[23]

Practice suggests a judicial awareness of the central importance of securing that the defence acts as a protection for the genuinely honest trader and not as a loophole through which the reckless, careless or even indifferent trader may escape.[24] Much will depend on the facts of individual cases before individual courts.[25] Precedent has little formal role to play here.[26] However the observations made by higher courts have confirmed the impression that the defence is not lightly to be accepted. This is demonstrated by the cases that follow, first in the area of consumer safety, then in the area of trade descriptions.

In *Taylor v Lawrence Fraser (Bristol) Ltd*[27] a company sought to rely on guarantees provided by its supplier. It carried out no tests of its own. It was held that this did not suffice to provide a defence to a charge of contravention of the Toy Safety Regulations, made under the precursor to the Consumer Protection Act 1987. Lord Widgery CJ commented that:

> 'Although every case depends on its own facts, I should think there are very few cases of this kind where reliance on certificates by itself is to be treated as sufficient when there is a possibility of professional sampling and that possibility has been deliberately rejected by the policy of the company.'

The message from this case and others is that a defendant will be able successfully to invoke the defence only where it has taken active steps to look into the safety of the items unless, very exceptionally, a small firm is prosecuted and it has done as much as can reasonably be expected. Lord

---

23   Considered further below, 14.3.

24   For an overview of policy and practice, Painter n.14 above; G. Howells, 'An Evaluation of the Role of Defences in Consumer Protection Statutes' (1988) 6 *Trading Law* 244.

25   For interesting empirical work, H. Croall, 'Mistakes, Accidents and Someone Else's Fault: the Trading Offender in Court' (1988) 15 *Jnl Law and Society* 293.

26   For a mine of practical illustrations, see O'Keeffe's *The Law Relating to Trade Descriptions* (Butterworths, loose–leaf service).

27   (1977) 121 Sol Jo 157.

Lane CJ commented in *Garrett v Boots the Chemist Ltd*[28] that '[w]hat might be reasonable for the large retailer might not be reasonable for the village shop'.

In *Riley v Webb*[29] a dangerous level of chemicals was found in pencils and a small wholesaler was prosecuted. The defence was not made out in circumstances where the traders had sought to be diligent 'on paper' alone. The defendant's order form stated:

> 'This order is placed on condition that the goods will conform with all the requirements imposed by a statute or statutory regulations or orders in force and the date of delivery of the goods and particularly of the Toys (Safety) Regulations.'

The suppliers also declared in writing that they had instructed their manufacturers and suppliers that all goods were to conform with statutory requirements. It was held that this was not enough to satisfy the requirements of the defence of due diligence. The size of the business was acknowledged as relevant, but doubt was expressed whether such 'paper' checking could ever be sufficient. Sampling would normally be required.

In *Rotherham MBC v Raysun*[30] toxic material was found in wax crayons made in Hong Kong. Checks had been performed by agents of the importers in Hong Kong. However, it was apparent that the agents' practice was to supply details only of adverse results. Specific information about the numbers of checks actually undertaken was not to hand. The importer also had the goods checked in Manchester, but in 1986 this involved no more than one packet from a batch of 10,800 dozen packets. Woolf LJ wryly described this as 'modest'; the defence was not made out and the importer was convicted.

The theme which emerges is an expectation of sampling – and effective sampling. Yet these are not rules. Small levels of sampling may suffice where, for example, it is shown that the goods are highly likely to be homogenous and that one packet could indeed be considered representative of a large batch. Moreover, sampling may not be required where the firm is small and has reliable and transparent sources.[31] However the due diligence

---

28 1980, unreported, quotation from LEXIS.

29 [1987] BTLC 65, [1987] CCLR 65.

30 [1988] BTLC 292, [1989] CCLR 1. The case is examined by S. Weatherill at [1990] JBL 36.

31 Cf acquittal in *Hurley v Martinez and Co* [1990] TLR 189, a case under the Trade Descriptions Act 1968. The decision suggests a special respect for the reliability of German sources!

defence is not readily made out and, in order to ensure that the law is capable of effective enforcement,[32] this rigour seems entirely appropriate.

A similar impression of a predominantly rigorous judicial approach to the defence is obtained from case law concerning offences under the trade descriptions legislation.

Naish v Gore[33] was a case of a clocked odometer.[34] The defendant dealer was not the clocker. He had looked over the car and judged that it had in fact done only the mileage shown. He was wrong in this assessment. He had not consulted the log book before selling the car, for it had latterly passed through the hands of a number of dealers and the log book had not yet reached him. When the consumer buyer received the log book, it was discovered that the mileage shown was inaccurate. Lord Widgery commented that '[i]t is for the defendant to prove that he took all reasonable precautions, and if he has taken none, that means he must prove that none could reasonably have been taken.' So failure to check excludes the defence where checking is possible.[35] Lord Widgery thought that, on the facts of the case, the magistrates' acquittal of the dealer should not be disturbed. However, he concluded by inviting courts before which such defences are presented 'to be meticulous in their consideration of all the courses which the seller might have adopted'.

In *Wandsworth LBC v Bentley*[36] a car dealer acquired a car at auction. He sold the car, whereupon it was discovered to have been 'clocked' in the past and the dealer was charged. The sale document stated that the previous owner was Shell UK and the dealer claimed he was entitled to assume that such a reputable firm would not be involved with clocked cars. The defence failed. He had not contacted Shell to check the car's mileage when the company had got rid of the car, nor had he even checked that it was actually Shell that was selling the car at auction. Lord Lane CJ would not entertain the argument that due diligence had been taken 'in the absence of that simple precaution'.

In *Texas Homecare Ltd v Stockport MBC* the High Court held that the Crown Court had been right to reject the defence where no system had been set up to check conformity of goods delivered to description.[37] The High

---

32   Further below, 14.3; effectiveness does not refer simply to prosecution.

33   [1971] 3 All ER 737.

34   Cf Chapter 10.2.6.

35   Cf *Sherratt v Geralds Jewellers* (1970) 114 Sol Jo 147.

36   [1980] RTR 429.

37   [1987] TLC 331.

Court also ruled that s.24(3) demanded no lower standard of care than that required under s.24(1).[38]

14.2.4 Companies and their Employees

The invocation of the defence by a legal person, a company, charged with an offence is especially sensitive when the defendant seeks to defeat the charge by blaming not a third party, as in the cases mentioned above, but instead one of its own employees. This will be uncommon in product safety cases, but has arisen with some frequency in the realm of misdescription. On the one hand, it may indeed be true that the problem has arisen because of an individual employee's foolish or even wicked conduct, in which case the stigma, however small, of violation of the criminal law should not fairly be attached to the company. On the other hand, the company might be induced to escape liability by blaming employees if permitted such a defence. It may be tempted to loosen supervision and to devolve more responsibility to lower level employees than it might otherwise prefer, simply to minimise its own chances of liability. More fundamentally, it might be pointed out that the company hires employees as part of its commercial, profit–making activities; by way of balance, it should therefore be equally subject to any detrimental effects flowing from its hiring policies.

These conflicting policy questions were addressed by the House of Lords in *Tesco Supermarkets Ltd v Nattrass*.[39] The decision offers scope for protection from conviction to the company, but on condition that serious efforts are made to ensure an effective supervisory system. The case arose out of misdescription of the price of 'Radiant' washing powder in Tesco's Northwich store. Although displayed as 2s 11d, the price marked on all packs on the shelves was 3s 11d.[40] Tesco was fined £25 with costs.

A shop assistant had put out packs marked with the higher price. The shop manager had not been told of this by the assistant, though he should have been. Nor had he checked the special offers, though he should have done. Tesco invoked the due diligence defence and blamed the manager, Mr Clement. Tesco was convicted by the local magistrates. Concern to protect its corporate image induced Tesco to pursue the matter to the House of Lords, where it was held that the firm had established the statutory defence.

---

[38] This is criticised at [1987] Crim LR 709 for overlooking distinctions between the two provisions explained in *Barker v Hargreaves* (1980) 125 Sol Jo 165.

[39] [1971] 2 All ER 128.

[40] Just under 15p; just under 20p.

The House of Lords confirmed that companies may commit regulatory offences through their employees. The key question was whether the company took all reasonable precautions and exercised all due diligence in order to bring itself within the defence. This took their Lordships into the metaphysics of how 'a company' acts. They insisted that a company has a 'directing mind'. For the purposes of this defence, it is required only that the company's directing mind establish an effective system designed to prevent the commission of offences. This it had done. Mr Clement's (in)activities were not part of the directing mind of the company. In fact his personal fault was what prevented the company's system from successfully forestalling the false price indication. The failings of a 'cog in the machine'[41] could not deprive the company of the statutory defence, provided it is shown that it (the company) diligently put in place an effective supervisory system.

It is a question of fact whether a company's system is indeed adequate. The courts appear aware of the peril for the effective application of the law that would result from an over–hasty acceptance that enough has been done. The invocation of the defence is typically scrutinised with rigour.[42] Moreover, in *McGuire v Sittingbourne Co–operative Society Ltd*[43] the importance of pinning down precisely what has led to the breach was emphasised. The defendant firm simply named all the assistants working in the shop at the time of the offence and alleged that one or more was at fault. There was no evidence of what steps had been taken to investigate how the offence had occurred or who was responsible. This was not enough to justify an acquittal.

Is the law too generous to firms in Tesco's position? The company was allowed to separate the failings of its own manager from the assessment of the operation of its overall system. It was able to convert its own employee into 'another person' for the purposes of the statutory defence. Yet it seems that the courts view such opportunity for exculpation based on a genuinely effective overall system as the essence of the statutory defence. In other areas of the law, Tesco has been distinguished precisely because of the availability there of the statutory defence. For example, in *National Rivers Authority v Alfred McAlpine Homes East Ltd*[44] the company was prosecuted for pollution of controlled waters contrary to the Water Resources Act 1991. The site agent and site manager accepted responsibility. The justices

---

41 Lord Morris 140f.
42 Cf *Denard v Smith and Dixons Ltd* [1991] Crim LR 63, where Dixons had simply not done enough. See also discussion of *Robert Gale v Dixon Stores Group Ltd* by D. Roberts at (1994) 13 *Trading Law* 50.
43 [1976] Crim LR 268.
44 [1994] 4 All ER 286.

considered that these employees were too lowly within the company structure to fix the company with criminal liability. Simon Brown LJ disagreed. He found that the justices had misinterpreted Tesco. In connection with the commission of the offence, they had wrongly used an analysis that had been presented in Tesco in relation to the statutory defence. The company had committed the offence of pollution through its employees. The separation of individual employees from the company's overall supervisory scheme could arise only in relation to the due diligence defence, as in Tesco. However, since the 1991 Act contains no equivalent defence to that in s.24 Trade Descriptions Act 1968, conviction was proper. Tesco was also distinguished in *Supply of Ready Mixed Concrete (No 2)*.[45] The House of Lords ruled that in the absence of a statutory defence of the due diligence type, the adequacy of an employer's system, set up to stop employees from acting in violation of restrictive practices law, could not shelter the company from liability for the employee's acts. Proper supervision could count in mitigation only. This seems to suggest that it is perfectly possible under English law to develop regulatory systems without the addition of the due diligence defence.[46] Be that as it may, in the consumer protection field, the defence has become a well–entrenched feature.

14.2.5 Liability of Persons Other than Principal Offender – 'Bypass'

The statutory defences envisage the possibility of acquittal where, loosely summarised, the real responsibility for the offence lies with another.[47] Whether or not the principal offender is charged, it is explicitly provided that action may be taken against that other person. This 'by–pass' procedure assists flexibility in enforcement practice.

Section 23 of the Trade Descriptions Act provides that:

> 'Where the commission by any person of an offence under this Act is due to the act or default of some other person that other person shall be guilty of the offence, and a person may be charged with and convicted of the offence by virtue of this section whether or not proceedings are taken against the first–mentioned person.'

---

[45] [1995] 1 All ER 135.

[46] And/or it suggests the lack of a clear theory of how and why companies may be held criminally liable; see J. Gobert, 'Corporate Criminality: Four Models of Fault' (1994) 14 *Legal Studies* 393.

[47] Cf D. Roberts, 'The Act or Default of Some Other Person' (1991) 8 *Trading Law* 145.

Section 40 of the Consumer Protection Act 1987 provides that:

> 'Where the commission by any person of an offence to which section 39 above applies is due to an act or default committed by some other person in the course of any business of his, the other person shall be guilty of the offence and may be proceeded against and punished by virtue of this subsection whether or not proceedings are taken against the first–mentioned person.'

And, it can be added, he can be convicted even where proceedings taken against the first–mentioned person have ended in acquittal because of the successful invocation of a statutory defence.[48]

Comparable provisions may be found in s.20 of the Food Safety Act 1990 and s.32 of the Weights and Measures Act 1985.[49]

Special rules also provide that where an offence committed by a body corporate is proved 'to have been committed with the consent and connivance of, or to be attributable to any neglect on the part of, any director, manager, secretary or other similar officer of the body corporate, or any person who was purporting to act in any such capacity, he as well as the body corporate' shall be liable to be proceeded against and punished accordingly.[50] So had Mr Clement been higher up in Tesco's organisation, he could have been liable under this section; Tesco, too, would presumably have lost the protection of the defence.

The criminal liability of Mr Clement was not in issue in *Tesco v Nattrass*.[51] By virtue of section 23 of the Trade Descriptions Act (above), presumably he could have been prosecuted ;[52] the defence of due diligence available to him would very probably not have been made out given his failure to check the shelves. However, the allocation of scarce enforcement resources to the formal prosecution of an individual employee will be relatively rare.[53]

Nonetheless, in *Warwickshire County Council v Johnson*[54] the manager of Dixons electrical goods shop in Stratford–upon–Avon was prosecuted for

---

48   This robust interpretation was adopted in *Coupe v Guyett* [1973] 1 WLR 669.
49   But not in the Consumer Credit Act 1974.
50   S.20(1) TDA; s.40(2) CPA; s.169 Consumer Credit Act 1974.
51   Note 39 above. Obiter, 'he was liable to prosecution' per Lord Reid at 135g; undecided, per Viscount Dilhorne at 143c; 'no opinion' per Lord Pearson at 147j.
52   Cf *Birkenhead and District Co–operative Society Ltd v Roberts* [1970] 3 All ER 391, 393.
53   14.3 below.
54   [1993] 1 All ER 299.

supplying a misleading price indication contrary to s.20(1) Consumer Protection Act 1987.[55] Since the offence is committed only by a person acting 'in the course of a business of his', the House of Lords was asked to rule on whether this could catch a defendant employee. It was held that the section was aimed at defendants who were either the owner or holder of a controlling interest in the business. Broadly, employers are caught, but employees are not.[56] Probably, then, the authority should have charged Dixons. But Dixons would have been able to try to show due diligence and doubtless 'the ghost of *Tesco v Nattrass* still stalks the [Warwickshire] offices'.[57]

The decision in *Warwickshire CC v Johnson* seems to confirm the impression gained from a careful reading of the provisions that s.20(1) and s.40 of the CPA are distinct from s.23 TDA. S.23 TDA (above) does not contain the proviso that by–pass proceedings may be brought only against a person acting 'in the course of any business of his' – or even a person acting 'in the course of any business'. It refers to simply 'some other person'. It therefore allows by–pass proceedings to be brought even against private individuals – and, in line with the pattern of the Act, even in the absence of *mens rea*. Such by–passing occurred in *Olgeirsson v Kitching*.[58] The defendant, acting as a private individual, misdescribed the mileage when he sold his car to a dealer. The dealer then resold the car under this misdescription. S.23 proceedings against the private seller were initiated and the High Court upheld a conviction.

On policy grounds, this is indefensible. There could be no s.1 liability because of its restriction to action in the course of a trade or business; it is irrational that s.23 liability could arise. This is a *fortiori* the case where other statutes creating regulatory offences completely exclude private liability. However, the plain words of s.23 of the 1968 Act obstruct the achievement of consistency across similar statutes. Its explicit wording supports the interpretation adopted in *Olgeirsson*, as McNeill J observed in

---

55   Chapter 10.5.

56   The case was of constitutional interest for their Lordships' reference to Parliamentary debates on the Bill that became the relevant Act; this was one of the first instances of the relaxation of the rule excluding such material accepted in *Pepper v Hart* [1992] 3 WLR 1032. The Minister had explicitly commented that the words '... of his' were designed to ensure that individual employees would not be prosecuted (All ER 305f).

57   C. Wells, 'Corporate Liability and Consumer Protection: *Tesco v Nattrass* Revisited' (1994) 57 *MLR* 817, 820. The case provoked a correspondence between drafter and enforcement officer in the pages of the *New Law Journal* that was marked by extraordinary belligerence (especially by the former); (1993) 143 NLJ 8, 228, 356.

58   [1986] 1 WLR 304.

concluding his judgment upholding conviction of the private individual in that case.[59] It is submitted that the law of theft, not the regulatory offence, is the proper place for scrutinising the conduct of the likes of Olgeirsson, but it now lies with Parliament to amend the 1968 Act to achieve that result.[60] In the meantime one would not anticipate that prosecutions would be brought against private individuals with any frequency, especially in the absence of dishonesty.[61] Enforcement practice is discussed further below at 14.3.

14.2.6 Crime and Market Failure

That cases as trivial as *Tesco v Nattrass* and *Warwickshire CC v Johnson* should find their way from Magistrates Court all the way to the House of Lords serves to demonstrate a sensitivity of commercial firms to the imposition of criminal responsibility. Plainly Tesco, as a 'repeat player' in such litigation,[62] was eager to invest resources in order to establish a favourable precedent. It succeeded in that objective. Perhaps such expensive litigation acts as a further demonstration of the advantages of formal decriminalisation of such law.[63] After all, what is at stake is repairing the market failure of deceptive marketing practices and, if that can be more readily and more cheaply achieved by other types of law, then the application of a criminal statute, generating such litigation, is simply inefficient.[64] There is a case to be made in favour of a system that allows immediate preventive action to be taken by enforcement officers, with costs incurred to be borne by the trader. This would include provision for the trader to secure compensation in the event of abusive conduct by enforcement officers.

This is not to propose the evacuation of criminal responsibility from the arena of consumer protection. Some 'regulatory offences' of the type at stake

---

59   At 311b–d. However, the defendant was dishonest in *Olgeirsson*; perhaps MacNeill J might have tried harder to avoid conviction had the defendant been innocent in mind, even though the absence of mens rea requirement means that, strictly, such issues are irrelevant.

60   Cf comment by P. Cartwright, 'Reforming the Trade Descriptions Act 1968' (1993) 3 *Consumer Policy Review* 34. See also Chapter 10.7.

61   As noted above, the defendant in *Olgeirsson* was dishonest.

62   Cf M. Galanter, 'Why the "Haves" come out ahead: Speculation on the Limits of Legal Change' (1974) 9 *Law and Society Review* 95.

63   Cf Tench n.13 above.

64   It is interesting to note that from the criminal (rather than the consumer) law perspective, such offences of differing mens rea also cause problems of coherence for commentators; cf C. Wells, *Corporations and Criminal Responsibility* (OUP, 1993).

in this book form part of what would, for most, instinctively count as 'proper' criminal law. For example, a deliberate decision to make profits quickly by selling a batch of goods known to be thoroughly dangerous is no mere administrative infraction. Nevertheless, a reduction in formal criminal laws in favour of, for example, rigorously policed licensing requirements,[65] would permit the full weight of the criminal law to be reserved for the occasional scandal.

14.2.7 The Compatibility of the Due Diligence Defence with EC Law

The use of the due diligence defence is not explicitly authorised by any EC Directive, but nor is it excluded; the UK has chosen to implement several Directives by including this defence. Supply of toys that are not safe is to be prevented by Member States under the provisions of the Toy Safety Directive. More broadly, within the scope of the Directive on General Product Safety, supply of goods that are not safe is to be suppressed by Member States. The UK has implemented these Directives: the supply of offending items prima facie constitutes a regulatory offence. However, a trader will escape conviction if able to bring him or herself within the due diligence defence, which is absent from the Directive but inserted into the UK's implementing regulations in accordance with the normal practice of the regulatory offence in the consumer protection field.[66]

Yet EC rules must be 'effectively' implemented at national level. It is arguable that the shelter of the due diligence defence – allied to the risk of incurring an obligation to pay compensation[67] – may inhibit British enforcement agencies from pursuing suspected violations of EC–derived rules. This would imperil the viability of the due diligence defence where EC rules are at issue; were the defence to be invalidated in that sphere, its continued application in other areas of domestic consumer protection law would begin to appear inconsistent.

It is submitted that this argument probably lacks sufficient weight to overturn the British predilection for inserting the due diligence defence into implementing regulations, even where this is not expressly foreseen in the Directive. Litigation would nonetheless be of interest, if only to clarify the EC notion of 'effectiveness' in this context. The European Court has declared that Article 5 EC requires Member States to take all measures necessary to guarantee the application and effectiveness of Community law and that

---

65   Cf Chapter 1.8.2.
66   14.2.1. above.
67   Chapters 12.2, 13.5 above; 14.3.3 below.

penalties, where left to national law, must be effective and dissuasive.[68] Implementation choices rest with the national system, but within a required Community framework of 'effectiveness'. The insertion of a due diligence defence is probably a permissible subtlety within a domestic enforcement regime which generally permits effective control of suspect traders and suspect goods, especially at point of first supply.[69]

14.3 ENFORCEMENT

14.3.1 The Pattern of Local Enforcement

Enforcement of the rules pertaining to the regulatory offence belongs in the hands of officers of local authorities. In practice, enforcement lies with the authority's Trading Standards Department,[70] which holds responsibility for a wide range of consumer protection and general trade practices law. The formerly common label 'weights and measures' is far too narrow to describe modern practice and is more or less redundant. The pattern of enforcement of food safety law is distinct, enforcement responsibilities being divided between trading standards officers and environmental health officers.

A feature of the British system has always been local enforcement: each trading standards authority has jurisdiction within its locality. There are 126 trading standards departments in Great Britain and some 1,500 trading standards officers.[71] Enforcement practice is not directed by central government and will vary from town to town, sometimes giving rise to oddities. For instance, a firm with a national marketing network might be subjected to differing approaches to the law. A trader in Birmingham would have some legitimate concern if the supply of the same product were to result in informal discussion with enforcement officers in Nottingham and immediate resort to prosecution in Sheffield. Administrative co–ordination has developed in order to minimise the peculiarities which can arise from local enforcement. The Home Authority principle has been developed by LACOTS, the Local Authorities' Co–ordinating Body on Food and Trading

---

68 Eg Case 68/88 *Commission v Greece* [1989] ECR 2965. Cf Cases C–382/92 and 383/93 *Commission v UK* [1994] ECR I–2435, 2479, even though these arise outside the criminal sphere.

69 14.3 below and see also 12.2, 13.5.

70 Less frequently known as the Consumer Protection Department.

71 The professional body is the Institute of Trading Standards Administration; the professional qualification is the Diploma in Trading Standards – but are they 'professionals'? cf Chapter 1.8.2.3.

Standards, a non–statutory entity established by the authorities themselves. The Home Authority principle holds that it is normally the trader's home authority which will act as the source of legal interpretation, wherever in the country the firm may be active. This is not a formally binding rule, but its advantages are such that in practice it is largely, though not uniformly, adhered to.[72] Accordingly traders are normally able to rely on a single source of interpretation of the law.

Recent statements by Government suggest that the long–established pattern of local enforcement is perceived to bring with it a risk of incoherent and costly enforcement overlap. In January 1994 Michael Heseltine, then President of the Board of Trade (DTI), announced a review into the organisation of enforcement functions of local authorities. There is an interest in reducing inconsistencies in enforcement to avoid duplication and to improve co–ordination. It seems possible that the Home Authority principle will be judged too weak to provide security for traders engaged in national and international marketing activities. This review will probably involve a close scrutiny of the 'tradition' of local enforcement and consideration of the possible merger of the functions of the trading standards officer with those of the environmental health officer. As part of the government's scrutiny process, a report was published in September 1994 in which great play was made of the benefit for business of consistency in enforcement practice.[73] It remains to be seen what specific proposals the Government will choose to translate into formal changes to law and practice.

The Deregulation and Contracting Out Act 1994 offers further scope for adjustment of the pattern of enforcement of, *inter alia*, consumer protection law. Section 5 of the Act provides 'Powers to improve enforcement procedures', powers to be exercised by order. The broad objective is the rationalisation of enforcement activity in order to reduce costs imposed on business, but here too it is necessary to await subsequent detailed implementation of this policy.

14.3.2 Local Enforcement in a European Market

Trading standards departments have worked hard for many years to establish co–operative networks that combine sensitive local level enforcement with an awareness of the reality of national marketing. The problem plainly becomes ever more challenging as European market integration progresses. There is a

---

72   Para 2.7 of the 1993 DTI review: *Review of the Implementation and Enforcement of EC Law in the UK* observes that business welcomes the Home Authority principle.

73   Report of DTI Review of Local Government Enforcement.

tension between Europe–wide marketing and local or even national enforcement. In order to build confidence among both consumers and traders in a viable internal market, it is essential to put in place strategies for even and effective law enforcement. This was a major theme in the Sutherland Report of 1992 into the future management of the internal market:

> Each authority responsible for applying and enforcing Community legislation at national and local level should accept a duty to co–operate with other such bodies, both through direct contact and via central contact points. This requires them to recognise and respond to their Community–wide responsibilities which arise from the fact that their official functions directly affect citizens of all other Member States. Their officials have Community–wide responsibilities.

Such stirring words present trading standards authorities with a major task for the future.

Developments have been most marked in the co–ordination of practice in the product safety field although, even there, an enormous range of tasks remains to be completed. Probably the immediate and direct threat of the unsafe product has stimulated a degree of willingness to act in this field which has been lacking elsewhere. Relevant developments were examined in Chapter 12.6.

Less has been achieved in developing cross–border control of trading malpractice causing prejudice to the economic interests of consumers. October 1992 saw the establishment of the International Marketing Supervision Network, whose activities roughly reflect those of the UK Office of Fair Trading (which was instrumental in its establishment). Both OFT and DTI serve as UK links in the network. Complaints are relayed through the Network, which might, in time, prove a useful forum for addressing problem areas in the operation of the internal market. The Network does not explicitly envisage harmonisation of laws, merely effective application of existing laws.

The Network is pitched at the broad policy level. In Chapter 17, attention is devoted to the scope of initiatives that are designed to help the consumer him or herself to achieve access to justice where complaints of a cross–border nature are involved.

14.3.3 Specific Enforcement Powers

The Trade Descriptions Act 1968 and the Consumer Protection Act 1987 invest trading standards authorities with powers of enforcement that are distinct in detail, but nevertheless share sufficient points of similarity to permit a common broad description.[74]

Section 27 of the Trade Descriptions Act 1968 and section 28 of the Consumer Protection Act 1987 empower the making of test purchases.

Section 28 of the Trade Descriptions Act 1968 and section 29 of the Consumer Protection Act 1987 contain powers of entry, search and related powers. These are available to a duly authorised officer of an enforcement authority at any reasonable hour. They encompass powers of inspection of goods and entry to premises (other than those occupied solely as a person's residence).

Further powers are triggered only where the officer has reasonable grounds for suspecting that an offence has been committed. Such powers cover requirements to produce records and to have them copied, and the seizure and detention of goods.[75] Officers have the opportunity to seek court orders to secure entry;[76] the statutes create offences of obstruction of an authorised officer.[77]

Under the Consumer Protection Act 1987, special powers are available in respect of goods suspected not to have been supplied in the UK since they were manufactured or imported.[78] This provision reflects a policy of targeting enforcement at point of first supply where action can be taken most efficiently, rather than waiting until batches have been split up and distributed throughout the country.[79]

The pattern of enforcement under the Food Safety Act 1990 is distinct,[80] being more closely allied with that of health and safety at work and environmental health legislation. Under these regimes, there are concerns about the condition of premises, rather than simply the nature of goods. Powers of inspection and seizure exist, but inspectors have additional powers to issue improvement notices and ultimately prohibition orders.

A number of statutes contain provisions that envisage the compensation of traders affected by the exercise of enforcement powers. We focus here on

---

[74] For more depth than is here possible, see R. Bragg, *Trade Descriptions* (OUP, 1991), Ch.9.

[75] Ss.29(5), (6) CPA 1987; s.28(1) TDA. The wording is similar but not identical.

[76] S.30 CPA; s.28(3) TDA.

[77] S.32 CPA; s.29 TDA.

[78] S.29(4) CPA 1987.

[79] This policy was first introduced by the Consumer Safety (Amendment) Act 1986. Cf the similarly motivated s.31 on detention by customs officers. For discussion, S. Weatherill, 'Consumer safety legislation in the United Kingdom' [1987/2] *E Consum LJ* 81.

[80] For an overview, see T. Hitchcock, *Food Safety* (Fourmat Publishing, 1990), Ch.5.

the Trade Descriptions Act 1968 and the Consumer Protection Act 1987.[81] Section 33 of the former provides that where an officer in the exercise of powers under s.28 seizes and detains goods and the owner –

> 'suffers loss by reason thereof or by reason that the goods, during the detention, are lost or damaged or deteriorate, then, unless the owner is convicted of an offence under this Act committed in relation to the goods, the authority or department shall be liable to compensate him for the loss so suffered.'

Section 34 of the Consumer Protection Act 1987 provides that, in cases of the exercise of powers of seizure and detention under s.29;

> 'the enforcement authority shall be liable to pay compensation to any person having an interest in the goods in respect of any loss or damage caused by reason of the exercise of the power if – (a) there has been no contravention in relation to the goods of any safety provision or any provision made by or under Part III of this Act; and (b) the exercise of the power is not attributable to any neglect or default by that person.'

The provisions may helpfully induce traders and officers to co–operate to minimise risks of loss caused through misunderstanding. In so far as such provisions spur officers to act swiftly, they seem valuable. Sums involved are usually relatively small, especially since it is frequently possible to restore goods unaltered, so the trader may suffer no loss at all. Admittedly, perishable goods will cause more problems.[82] It might also be added that protection of the innocent trader appears a justifiable objective.[83] However, such compensation provisions might deter active enforcement, especially in times of budgetary constraint at local level. For these reasons, the compensation provisions have always been controversial.[84] Parliamentary debate on what became the 1987 Act focused on the problem of striking a

---

[81] Cf generally K. Cardwell and P. Kay, 'The Consumer Protection Act 1987: Liability of the Enforcement Authorities' (1988) 6 *Trading Law* 212.

[82] Cf Chapter 13.5, dealing with these provisions in relation to food law. Consider also the hypothetical seizure 24 hours before kickoff of a large batch of specially–made souvenir items designed to be sold before Hull City played at Wembley in the FA Cup Final (SW)/FA Vase Final (GH). Release of the goods only 24 hours later after the team's glorious victory would not prevent a dramatic depreciation in value.

[83] For *obiter dicta* on their back–up role, cf Taylor LJ in *R v Birmingham City Council, ex p Ferrero Ltd* [1993] 1 All ER 530, esp 537.

[84] Cf comment by K. Cardwell, 'Consumer Protection Act 1987' (1987) 50 *MLR* 625.

balance between the interests of the individual trader and the broader issues of market failure.[85]

14.3.4 Prosecution

Ultimately formal prosecution is possible, although atypical, for reasons elaborated below. That trading standards officers are able to bring prosecutions in respect of most regulatory offences[86] explains the naming of many of the cases considered above. For example, *Kitching in Olgeirsson v Kitching*[87] was the prosecutor acting for Humberside County Council Trading Standards Department. Private prosecutions are possible but rare.[88]

R v Haesler[89] is authority for the proposition that a prison sentence is inappropriate save in cases of dishonesty. This case arose in relation to trade descriptions, but the commission of a regulatory offence will generally attract a custodial sentence only in exceptional circumstances. The imposition of a fine is typical,[90] though a compensation order made under s.35 Powers of Criminal Courts Act 1973, as amended, in favour of a consumer is also possible. The compensation order is a potentially valuable device, which offers courts the opportunity of requiring a defendant to pay compensation to a victim independently of any private suit that may be initiated by the latter. Compensation orders are made only in clear and simple cases; where complex legal issues arise they are inappropriate, and a private action should be brought by the victim wishing to obtain compensation. Although compensation orders are particularly suited to cases of assault and property damage, where both the identity of the victim and the quantification of loss suffered are frequently relatively unproblematic, orders have been made in a gradually increasing number of cases arising under consumer protection legislation.

The High Court's decision in *R v Milton Keynes' Magistrates' Court, ex parte Roberts*[91] provides an interesting glimpse into enforcement practice and resulting judicial attitudes. Buckinghamshire trading standards officers investigated suspected violations of the Trade Descriptions Act 1968 and

---

85   Eg 116 HC Debs 347–9 (13 May 1987); 485 HL Debs 919–922 (12 March 1987).
86   Cf ss.222, 223 Local Government Act 1972.
87   Note 58 above.
88   Cf policy discussion by C. Harlow and R. Rawlings, *Pressure through Law* (Routledge, 1992) Ch.5.
89   [1973] Crim LR 586.
90   D. Roberts, 'Sentencing under the Trade Descriptions Act' (1991) 8 *Trading Law* 36.
91   *The Independent* 26 October 1994.

trade mark legislation. After searching Roberts' premises, they brought criminal charges. In the background, however, was the Ford Motor Co which was concerned that widespread counterfeiting of its goods was at stake. Ford had requested the trading standards officers to act; Ford had had representatives present at the searches who were able to identify the suspect items; Ford had indemnified the authority for any compensation claims that might arise. The applicant submitted that Ford had effectively bought the authority's support in its pursuit of a civil trade mark dispute and that this amounted to an abuse of the process of the court. The application was rejected. Trading standards officers have wide discretion to enlist support for their statutory functions and, in the circumstances, they had not acted improperly.

The prosecution strategy appropriate for the regulatory offence has attracted occasional comment in the appellate courts. The prosecution in *Smedleys Ltd v Breed*[92] related to the discovery of a dead caterpillar in a tin of peas. The intruder was virtually indistinguishable from the peas and was quite harmless. The House of Lords upheld a conviction under food legislation in force at the time, but their Lordships commented on what they saw as the absence of utility in the pursuit of the prosecution in light of the manufacturer's real efforts to avoid committing the offence. In *Wings Ltd v Ellis*[93] Lord Hailsham, in common with other members of the House, explicitly declared that he did not wish to criticise the authorities who had brought the case. However, he added the observation that 'there is room for caution by prosecuting authorities in mounting proceedings against innocent defendants'.[94] Without offering any criticism of these dicta, it is submitted that there is also room for caution by appellate judges in making comments about enforcement practice. Prosecutions for regulatory offences typically form part of a nuanced strategy, attuned to particular sectors and localities, and have implications beyond the specific case at issue. Appellate courts do not see a representative diet of cases.

14.3.5 Informal Enforcement

Section 26 Trade Descriptions Act 1968 and section 27 Consumer Protection Act 1987 establish that enforcement by local authorities is a duty.[95] However, a duty to enforce is not a duty to prosecute. In practice a great deal

---

92   [1974] AC 839.
93   Note 8 above and examined at more length in Chapter 10.3.
94   Note 8 above at 585e.
95   14.3.3 above.

of enforcement work is informal;[96] there is typically no desire to adopt a policy of regular prosecution. Many trading standards officers regard prosecution as a last resort, and as ineffective in many instances. Some would even label over–rigorous prosecution policies as 'unprofessional'. Generalisations are perilous; naturally, attitudes and practices vary across the country and even among individual officers in the same department.

However, the overriding concern is typically to secure the objectives of the statute, be they elimination of unsafe food, misleading trade descriptions or unsafe goods.[97] If removal from the market is achievable by advice or gentle pressure, then that will commonly be the limits of action taken. Taking formal steps will be more costly and time–consuming – and will be no more effective than if the voluntary co–operation of the trader had been secured. Indeed, officers typically cite a co–operative relationship with 'their' traders as a cornerstone of effective enforcement practice. This would be jeopardised by formal prosecution. So if a trader is genuinely concerned to comply, prosecution will be wasteful. Enforcement in this sense involves a continuing process, not a 'one–shot' prosecution strategy. Prosecution is typically reserved for repeat offenders who exhibit high levels of careless disregard for the law and, a fortiori, for deliberate offenders.[98] The remarkably high number of cases involving 'clocked' cars that litter the law reports reveals much about the perception among trading standards officers of the practices of the second–hand car trade.[99]

In a sense, such practice reveals a *de facto* conversion of the offence into one requiring *mens rea*. Enforcement officers are naturally drawn to distinguish 'real' offenders from the unlucky or the slapdash.[100] However, the formal attachment of strict liability to the regulatory offence strengthens the power of enforcement officers. It permits a flexible approach; it allows

---

[96] For an important survey, R. Cranston, *Regulating Business – Law and Consumer Agencies* (Macmillan, 1979): the general issues have not altered radically in 15 years. For helpful overviews of the issues that arise generally in enforcement policy and practice relevant to regulatory offences, see G. Richardson, 'Strict Liability for Regulatory Crime: the Empirical Research' [1987] Crim LR 295; J. Rowan–Robinson *et al*, 'Crime and Regulation' [1988] Crim LR 211.

[97] Cf findings of B. Hutter in relation to the practices of Environmental Health Officers in *'The Reasonable Arm of the Law?'* (OUP, 1988).

[98] Cf beyond consumer law K. Hawkins, *Environment and Enforcement* (OUP, 1987); W. Carson, 'White Collar Crime and the Enforcement of Factory Legislation' (1970) 10 *Br J Criminology* 383. For an overview of the issues relevant to enforcement, cf Ogus n.7 above pp. 89–97.

[99] Chapter 10.2.6.

[100] This is a strong message in Hutter n.97 above.

guidance to be given with a strong back–up threat of recourse to law in the event of non–co–operation. It allows officers to judge the circumstances of individual cases in assessing how to achieve effective prevention.

The dilution of the practical impact of strict liability caused by the due diligence defence, examined above,[101] deserves attention. Permitting exculpation of traders able to show that responsibility for the mischief lies elsewhere brings with it the risk that the regulatory climate may change because of the defence. Effective enforcement may be deterred. In practice, of course, trading standards officers will relatively rarely pursue a formal prosecution against a trader whom they believe is not blameworthy, whether the due diligence defence is expected to operate or not. The possibility that the defence may be raised in more serious cases, however, may make the enforcement agency pause to consider the value of investing significant resources in pursuing a formal prosecution when the outcome is less certain than it would be in a system of 'pure' strict liability. This is the price paid for including a defence designed to protect the innocent trader.

The recent UK and EC preference for regulation by generally expressed standards has contributed to the interest in avoiding formal proceedings.[102] Under the general duty in Part II of the Consumer Protection Act 1987 or under the 1994 General Product Safety Regulations, the outcome in marginal cases will depend on the court's own reading of safety expectations. The legal standard is imprecise. '[T]he fewer the uncertainties which attach to the law... the stronger is the [enforcement] agency's bargaining position'.[103] The practical result has tended to be the predominance of informal controls, including guidance to traders. Although this may diminish confidence in launching formal prosecutions, the policy of informal enforcement has many benefits for both sides in terms of saved time and money.

Resource constraints are a major factor affecting enforcement practice. Trading standards departments have seen their budgets cut in real terms over recent years. Cheaper practices hold strong attraction, militating against formal action. The provisions permitting compensation to be awarded to the trader play a part in this trend. In sum, whatever changes follow in the wake of the Heseltine review,[104] the pattern of informal enforcement of the regulatory offence seems likely to endure.

---

101 14.2.

102 With special reference to health and safety law but capable of general application, see R. Baldwin, 'Why Rules Don't Work' (1990) 53 *MLR* 321. Cf Rowan–Robinson *et al.* n.96 above.

103 Richardson note 96 above.

104 14.3.1 above.

15 Competition Policy and the Consumer Interest

15.1 HOW COMPETITION POLICY FALLS WITHIN THE SCOPE OF CONSUMER LAW

15.1.1 How Producers and Suppliers May Evade the Invisible Hand

Chapter 1 of this book provides an overview of the theory of how markets could and should operate in order to benefit the consumer interest. The 'invisible hand' of the market system should ensure that producers behave in response to and in fulfilment of consumer preference. Private economic relations organise the market.

It was also noted in Chapter 1 that this model makes a number of assumptions about the market, some of which are unrealistic. Perception of this gap between theory and practice stimulates the debate about the role of law as a means of intervening in the market.

The adoption of the market system as the starting point for the protection of consumer interests draws a wide range of legal rules into the field of the law of consumer protection. This was explained in Chapter 1 and has been reflected throughout this book. Chapters 3–9 examined aspects of the private law of consumer protection, where the State supplements the market by offering legal protection for the consumer interest. This occurs in respect of both machinery guaranteeing the legal enforceability of standards agreed between the parties and, of broader general importance, the imposition of minimum standards within transactions that apply independently of the consumer's ability to negotiate them. Chapters 10–15 examined the scope of public regulation of the market in the consumer interest. A range of practices are suppressed by law, partly as a result of the perception that the market system, supported by the private law, proves inadequate to yield efficient and/or fair outcomes.

Consideration of the impact of these laws on the position of the consumer is properly regarded as the staple diet of most analysis of consumer protection law. This Chapter concentrates on the 'supply–side' – on reasons why producers and suppliers may be immunised from the discipline of competition and the need to satisfy the consumer. As a general observation one may suppose that, in the absence of effective competition between producers and suppliers, the consumer interest will be damaged. The 'invisible hand' will be ill–directed where weakness in the competitive process renders the producer and supplier insensitive to consumer wishes. The legal response to such problems on the 'supply–side' of the market is conventionally classified under the title *competition law*.

Competition law is motivated by the objective of improving the functioning of the market as a whole. The consumer on the 'demand–side' should reap the benefits of an efficiently functioning 'supply–side'. In this sense competition policy is a form of consumer protection. Like laws forbidding the supply of unsafe food or unsafe products generally, competition policy is directed at the suppression of practices on the 'supply–side' that the market system, supported by private law, cannot root out unaided. However, because competition laws are addressed at commercial parties, they are typically and comprehensibly viewed, at most, as an indirect form of consumer protection. It is explained below that in the main the competition laws of both the UK and the EC do not place an explicit emphasis on the consumer interest. Consumer policy is a concealed aspect of competition policy and vice versa!

15.1.2 Markets and their Weaknesses

It is at least a workable starting point that the consumer is potentially prejudiced by the restricted exposure of producers and suppliers to the full force of the competitive process. The obvious method of enhancing the consumer interest is to remove the muffle on the blast of competition. Thus competition law and policy should be directed at ensuring the market is reshaped into a competitive environment. The restraints which would be removed by such laws could be behavioural or they could be structural. Behavioural restrictions would include cartels agreed by producers and/or suppliers. Structural impediments would include monopolies where the pattern of the market is not competitive, irrespective of the behaviour of firms. The law could be used to prohibit cartels, to forestall the creation of monopolies (for example, by forbidding mergers) or to destroy existing monopolies (for example, by forcing large firms to sell off assets). The law would thus root out inhibitions on free competition.

Accepting that the purpose of this branch of the law is to foster 'perfect' competition is no more than a starting point, however. In some areas the purity of competition will not provide the best of all possible markets for the consumer. Limits on competition may rationally be recognised as desirable in the consumer interest. This compromise is often denoted by the comment that the law seeks 'workable' not 'perfect' competition. Desirable behavioural limitations on competition may include collaboration on research and development, where the pooling of resources may secure more effective research work carried out in common instead of duplication of superficial efforts. Desirable structural limitations may be observed in markets which are inappropriate for competition: 'natural monopolies' illustrate this phenomenon.[1] In these circumstances there is a place for competition law, but its function will not be to insist on competition. Instead, the law may be employed to permit beneficial agreements among firms. This implies a need for legal tests apt to distinguish between desirable and undesirable agreements and for institutions charged with the function of making the appropriate assessments. The law may also be used to acquiesce in monopolies, but to control their more pernicious effects.

In some circumstances the law may even be employed to provide a system which suppresses competition. If unconfined and unconfinable competition were the paramount rule of the market, there would be limited incentive for firms to invest in invention. Any new gadget would be promptly taken up by rivals who had not incurred expense in creating it. Profit would not follow investment. The long–standing response is the development of intellectual property law in the shape of rights such as copyright and patent. Such rights protect the inventor from competition by 'free–riding' rivals and, by conferring exclusive rights of exploitation, guarantee reward in the shape of profits for the duration of the right. Far from dedicating itself to foster competition, the law thus actually suppresses competition in pursuit of the greater good of innovation. 'Perfect' competition is set aside. Again, a nuanced approach will be needed to shape the detail of the law. For instance, just how long should the period of protection endure?

More generally still, the enhancement of innovation may not simply be regarded as involving the State acting to facilitate private efforts. The State may itself actively promote research and development, perhaps through its own agencies or through subsidy to private industry. The State may develop its own industrial policy, choosing to intervene in areas where the market is perceived to be performing unsatisfactorily. States themselves compete with each other and economic survival may rest on choices made about regulatory strategy.[2]

15.1.3 The Notion of Workable Competition

What emerges from this brief survey is a blend of many different policies and rationales for intervention in the market, ranging far from the notion of perfect competition. It is not simply doubtful whether perfect competition is

---

1   Further, 15.3.3 below.
2   Cf the influential work of M. Porter, *The Competitive Advantage of Nations* (Macmillan, 1990).

attainable. More fundamentally, it is doubtful whether its pursuit is desirable. As already mentioned, this drift is frequently encapsulated in the phrase workable competition, a rather vague and flexible notion which accommodates a wide range of theory and practice in assessing the operation of markets. The phrase respects that variety; just because competition is not perfect need not mean that it is imperfect in any pejorative sense. The pursuit of the compromise of workable competition is entirely rational as a policy objective. Not all departures from the model of the perfect market can be corrected; not all should be. Competition is part of the structure of the economy, but its pursuit is not an objective which suppresses all other considerations. Accordingly, competition law and policy comprise a nuanced patchwork of intervention.[3]

15.1.4 Defining Markets and Regulatory Authorities

The process of internationalisation of markets is not a recent phenomenon. Venice was the world's most powerful trading centre in the 13th century; the British Empire was economically dominant six hundred years later. For the UK market integration has accelerated since joining the European Community at the start of 1973, a process that has intensified further following the completion of the internal market at the start of 1993.[4] The internal market is defined in the EC Treaty as 'an area without internal frontiers'.[5] It is designed to create conditions within which traders may treat the territory of the Community as a single marketplace. Such liberalisation should enhance competition, leading to those improvements in quality and

---

3   The leading work on competition law and policy in the EC and UK is R. Whish, *Competition Law* (Butterworths, 1993). See also (and with US perspectives), T. Frazer, *Monopoly, Competition and the Law* (Harvester Wheatsheaf, 1992). Further overview articles by influential figures include G. Borrie, 'The Regulation of Public and Private Power' [1989] *Public Law* 552 (the author was the Director General of Fair Trading when he wrote the piece); J. Lever (QC), 'UK Economic Regulation: Use and Abuse of the Law' [1992] 2 *ECLR* 55; C–D. Ehlermann, 'The Contribution of EC Competition Policy to the Single Market' (1992) 29 *CMLRev* 257 (author an influential official in Directorate General IV [Competition] in the EC Commission). For an economist's perspective see D. Hay, 'The Assessment: Competition Policy' (1993) 9/2 *Oxford Review of Economic Policy* 1. A useful collection of materials is found in T. Frazer and M. Waterson, *Competition Law and Policy: Cases, Materials and Commentary* (Harvester Wheatsheaf, 1994).

4   Chapter 2.

5   Art.7a EC, formerly Art.8a EEC.

reductions in price which in economic theory are associated with competitive markets. Consumers stand to gain from this process. From this perspective, national frontiers have in the past served as artificial impediments to the competitive process, now swept away on a tide of economic regeneration.

This process of economic integration has two major consequences for competition law in the UK. The first is that, as a system for the regulation of the market, it must be applied with an awareness that that market no longer stops at the frontiers of the country. The British market is not isolated behind national borders and the pattern of its regulation must be adjusted accordingly. The second consequence is that transnational agencies concerned to regulate the wider market have an impact on the UK. This invites consideration of, most prominently, the institutions of the European Community. The combination of these two influences dictates that appreciation of the sources of economic law in the UK, including the law of consumer protection, demands a broad focus.

15.2 CARTELS

15.2.1 Cartels and Economic Freedom

The theory of free and competitive markets tells us that consumer choice follows from rivalry among producers. Yet producers may prefer collusion to competition. For example, instead of trying to undercut each other's prices in order to increase sales, they may prefer to arrange a common selling price. This will make life altogether more comfortable for producers, but at a cost to the consumer: price competition will be suppressed. Such cartels appear antagonistic to the fundamental notion of the competitive market.

Legal intervention may be justified as a method of correcting the imperfection introduced by producer collusion. Producers must be free to compete, but they are not free under the law to surrender that freedom. The regulatory authority charged with the supervisory task must therefore devise a legal response to the damaging effects of cartels on free competition.

It will be seen below that the modern law of cartels in the UK is a development of the second half of the 20th century. However, suspicion of anti–competitive collusion has a lengthy pedigree; legal control in several manifestations can be traced back several centuries. For example, the English common law doctrine of restraint of trade can be found in the 15th century.[6] Public policy dictates that contracts in restraint of trade are not enforceable. The doctrine is flexible in scope and application, which to some extent renders it worryingly unpredictable. However, for all the recent increase in statutory control of restrictive practices, the doctrine is still a feature of English law and retains some modern significance.[7]

In the United States, the appreciation of the need for legislative control over anti–practices came at an early stage in that country's remarkable acceleration in industrialisation. The Sherman Act of 1890 remains today a major plank of what is referred to in North America as 'antitrust law'.[8] The deep belief in the potentially pernicious effect of co–ordination of conduct among producers is vividly portrayed in the following dictum from the decision of the Supreme Court in *United States v Topco Associates*:

> Antitrust laws in general... are the Magna Carta of free enterprise. They are as important to the preservation of economic freedom and our free–enterprise system as the Bill of Rights is to the protection of our fundamental personal freedoms.[9]

Such observations locate economic law and the pursuit of free markets in the sphere of discourse about democracy and the defence of individual rights. The linkage of the consumer in the economic sphere with the citizen in the political sphere is an aspect of the law which is examined further elsewhere in this book.[10]

For the European Community too, competition law and policy have always held a high profile as part of the process of market integration and regulation. The first of the European Communities, the European Coal and Steel Community established in 1952 by the Treaty of Paris, included competition policy provisions. The European Economic Community came into existence in 1958 as the creation of the Treaty of Rome and is of much broader scope than the Coal and Steel Community. The EEC Treaty also included a Chapter entitled 'Rules on Competition', comprising three sections, 'Rules applying to Undertakings', 'Dumping' and 'Aids Granted by States'. These provisions occupy Articles 85–94. Enforcement powers were

---

6   The 'Dyer's Case' of 1414. See J.D. Heydon, *The Restraint of Trade Doctrine* (Butterworths, 1971); M. Trebilcock, *The Common Law of Restraint of Trade* (Carswell/Sweet and Maxwell, 1986).

7   Cf discussion of *Schroeder v Macaulay* [1974] 3 All ER 616 and *Panayiotou* (better known as George Michael) *v Sony Ltd* in Chapter 1.3.6.

8   For an overview, see Frazer n.3 above.

9   405 US 596 (1972) (Marshall J)

10   See especially Chapter 1.

conferred on the Commission by Regulation in 1962. Some of the common policies of the Community have emerged slowly over the last four decades, with heavy reliance on the laborious development of secondary legislation. In sharp contrast, however, the fundamental principles of competition policy have always been firmly embedded in the very fabric of the Treaty. The EEC is now properly known as the European Community (the EC) as a result of the amendments of the Treaty on European Union agreed at Maastricht.[11] However, that Treaty, which came into force on 1 November 1993, has made no significant alteration to the competition provisions. They act as a cornerstone of the activities of the EC, prominent among which remain the establishment of 'a system ensuring that competition in the internal market is not distorted'.[12]

15.2.2 Shaping a Legal Response to Cartels

As explained, for the consumer interest to be best served, legal supervision of cartels must be nuanced. In making an assessment of the appropriate scope of control over collaboration, it is helpful to distinguish horizontal from vertical agreements. Horizontal agreements are those concluded between parties at the same stage of the production or distribution process, for example, between two or more manufacturers or between two or more retailers. It is precisely these parties who, according to theory, should be competing against each other on price and quality in order to maximise consumer benefit. Accordingly the law generally tends to be hostile to horizontal agreements. Vertical deals tend to be far less pernicious and will often be ostensibly in the consumer interest. If manufacturer A agrees to supply retailer B, then a new outlet has been opened up and choice has been enhanced. Vertical agreements serve to create distribution chains, at the end of which lies the expectant consumer. Even where the deal involves an exclusive arrangement between manufacturer and retailer, the consumer interest may stand to benefit. Suppose that a supplier agrees to provide ice–cream to a retailer and provides a freezer for the shop in which those ice–creams may be displayed. There is no obvious reason for legal intervention: goods are available and the consumer has a wider choice. Suppose, additionally, that the supplier imposes an obligation that only its brand of ice–creams are to be sold by the retailer, either from that freezer or even from that shop. The arrangement benefits the supplier by removing competitors from point of supply. In some respects the arrangement benefits

---

[11]   Art.G.A TEU. See further Chapter 2.
[12]   Art.3(g) EC.

the retailer who is able to concentrate streamlined efforts on one brand only. However, one might initially suppose that there is a rationale for intervention in such a practice, drawn from the reduction in choice to the consumer. Yet this need not be so. If there are plenty of other shops in which other brands are available, choice is maintained. Even if all the competing suppliers of ice–cream set up separate exclusive arrangements with their own tied retailers, there is no significant damage to competition where there are numerous suppliers and numerous shops. Competition to buy up retailers will develop. Consumer choice will be sustained.[13]

One might go so far as to argue that even price–fixing arrangements applied vertically, between manufacturer and retailer, do not call for legal control provided the market is competitive and consumers remain free to choose between different brands, the suppliers of which are not in collusion. One cannot be dogmatic in distinguishing between vertical and horizontal deals; each requires careful assessment against the background of the market in which they operate. However, as a framework for analysis it is useful to be aware that horizontal agreements may rationally generate more rigorous scrutiny than vertical agreements.

Such critiques require further investigation against the background of specific competition law regimes. This is provided below. However, observation regarding the function of competition and competition law should sharpen awareness of the intensely political nature of debate about legal intervention in markets. The more faith one has in markets, the more sceptical one will be about the need for and desirability of legal intervention.[14] The 'Chicago School' in the US has exerted much influence in recent decades in its preference for allowing markets to organise themselves, with a concomitant insistence that the application of anti–trust law be reined in. It is in the Chicago School that one finds analysis which would leave even vertical price fixing outwith the range of legal prohibition.[15] That prescription has not been accepted by the courts in the US although other elements of Chicago analysis have affected the development of antitrust

---

13   The ice–cream supply sector has attracted the interest of both EC and UK competition authorities; EC, Decision 93/405 *Scholler* OJ 1993 L183/1, [1994] 4 CMLR 51 and Decision 93/406 *Langnese–Iglo* OJ 1993 L183/18, [1994] 4 CMLR 83; UK, MMC report, Cm. 2524, March 1994. See A. Robertson and M. Williams, 'An Ice Cream War: The Law and Economics of Freezer Exclusivity I' [1995] 1 *ECLR* 7.

14   At length, Chapter 1, esp 1.8 and 1.9.

15   Eg R. Bork, *'The Antitrust Paradox – a Policy at War with Itself'* (Basic Books, 1978).

law.[16] In Europe and in the UK, policy remains noticeably less affected by such thinking. The functioning of unsupervised markets is viewed with rather less equanimity than in some North American quarters. For Europe, it should also be borne in mind that EC competition policy operates to regulate a market which is not (yet) integrated after the fashion of a national market. This lends to it a special, interventionist flavour not found in a national system.[17]

15.2.3 United Kingdom Law of Cartels and Restrictive Practices[18]

15.2.3.1 The 'Imminent' Reform of the Restrictive Trade Practices Act 1976

In the UK, cartels and restrictive practices have been the subject of legal supervision since 1956, the year which saw the enactment of the first Restrictive Trade Practices Act. The relevant control is now exercised under the Restrictive Trade Practices Act 1976. The formal legal regime involves supervision by the Director General of Fair Trading and proceedings before the Restrictive Practices Court. Judicial proceedings are nowadays rare and control is in practice largely administrative. The Act, particularly in its early years, contributed to the expulsion of an intricate pattern of cartels which were widely believed to blight the British market.

For all its valuable early contribution to the promotion of a competitive market in the UK, the profile of the Restrictive Trade Practices Act has declined in recent years. In many respects it is a fiendishly complicated and forbidding statute. At the same time the sanctions for non–observance are weak. Both elements induce not only those subject to the Act, but also those responsible for its enforcement, to avoid rigorous adherence to its structure. This reluctant attitude is strengthened by the direct relevance in the UK since 1973 of EC competition law. The EC system is in many respects more straightforward and coherent in application than the Restrictive Trade Practices Act. The EC system is also more perilous for violators in view of the potential size of fines which may be imposed by the EC Commission. Moreover, EC law applies in preference to national law in the event of conflict between the two regimes, while compliance with the EC regime is

---

16 For a flavour of the often ferocious debate, cf R. Pitofsky, 'New Definitions of Relevant Market and the Assault on Antitrust' (1990) 90 *Columbia LR* 1806; A. Page, 'Ideological Conflict and the Origins of Antitrust Policy' (1991) 66 *Tulane Law Review* 1.

17 See especially Ehlermann n.3 above; and 15.5 below.

18 R. Whish, *Competition Law* (Butterworths, 1993) Ch.5.

commercially unavoidable for firms with interests affecting inter–State trade.[19]

Accordingly there has developed an impetus to reform the Restrictive Trade Practices Act along the model of the EC's Article 85, in part motivated by the perception that the EC system exercises more effective control. In pragmatic terms, it is recognised that it is costly for British firms to have to set up systems for ensuring compliance with two grossly divergent regimes and that therefore there are financial savings in aligning the domestic system with that of the EC.

These issues were developed in a 1988 Green Paper, 'Review of Restrictive Trade Practices Policy'.[20] Firm proposals were contained in a White Paper of July 1989 under the title, 'Opening Markets – New Policy on Restrictive Trade Practices'.[21] Reform of United Kingdom Restrictive Practices Law seemed imminent.[22] However, the law has not changed. Despite periodic observations by responsible politicians that reform along the lines indicated in the White Paper remains policy, space in a crowded Parliamentary timetable has not been found. For this reason, an awareness of the Restrictive Trade Practices Act 1976 remains important. An outline follows.

15.2.3.2 The Justiciability of Law and Economics

The Act is based on a structure of formal legal rules. In contrast to EC law, which controls agreements on the basis of their effect,[23] the Restrictive Trade Practices Act operates on the more rigid test of form. The choice was made primarily for institutional reasons. The Act contains tests for the legality of cartels which are to be applied by judges, not by administrative officials. It was therefore felt appropriate to develop rather rigid rules which could be applied by judges without obliging them to embark on the perils of economic quantification and which would (it was envisaged) provide a degree of predictability for business in calculating the impact of the Act. In

---

19 This is a low threshold; Case 8/72 *Cementhandelaren v Commission*, 15.2.5 below.
20 Cm. 331.
21 Cm. 727.
22 For comment at the time see R. Eccles, 'Transposing EEC Competition Law into UK Restrictive Trading Agreements Legislation: the Government Green Paper' [1988] *ECLR* 227; T. Frazer, 'Defects and Effects – Competition Policy for the 1990s' (1988) 51 *MLR* 493.
23 15.2.4.2 below.

1965, in *Roberts Ltd v British Railways Board*[24] Ungoed–Thomas J delivered a rather well–known comment on the unwillingness of judges to engage in economic policy making:

> Economics and trade form no part of a judge's qualifications. In general judges are not qualified to decide questions of economic policy and such questions by their nature are not justiciable.

The litigation in that case involved determination of the scope of the British Railways Board's statutory powers to manufacture rolling stock and was not concerned with restrictive practices as such. Nevertheless the judge's heartfelt comments are of broader application. This Chapter and, to some extent, this whole book should provide material for reflection on how sharp this supposed divide between law and economics really is in the application of the law to the modern market. A linked question is how separate law and economics *should* be, at least for the judiciary.

15.2.3.3 Registrable Agreements

The Act catches 'Registrable Agreements'. In line with the policy of providing a legally applicable set of rules rather than a broad discretion, this category is the subject of exhaustive and detailed definition in the statute. According to s.1(1) of the 1976 Act, 'Every agreement to which this Act applies is subject to registration under the Act'. The agreements to which the Act applies are of four types: restrictive agreements as to goods; information agreements as to goods; restrictive agreements as to services; and information agreements as to services. The precise scope of these categories is the subject of detailed definition elsewhere in the statute or in secondary legislation.

The Director General of Fair Trading bears a statutory duty to maintain a register of agreements subject to registration under the Act. The Director General also has a duty to take 'proceedings before the Restrictive Practices Court in respect of the agreements of which particulars are from time to time entered or filed in the register'.[25] This appears to be an absolute duty which deprives the system of flexibility in judging in advance of Court proceedings the merits of agreements which are registrable. However, there are exceptions to the Director General's duty to bring the registrable agreement before the Court. Of broadest significance in practice is s.21(2):

---

24   [1965] 1 WLR 396, 400.
25   S.1(2).

> If it appears to the Secretary of State, upon the Director's representation, that the restrictions...are not of such significance as to call for investigation by the Court, the Secretary of State may give directions discharging the Director from taking proceedings in the Court...

It is known that the majority of agreements are disposed of in this way. Court scrutiny is not necessary. The s.21(2) procedure permits sifting of registrable but beneficial agreements. Neither formal guidelines for the use of s.21(2) nor full details of its application in individual cases are published, although the Annual Reports of the Director General provide some relevant information.[26]

15.2.3.4 Proceedings Before the Restrictive Practices Court

Before the Restrictive Practices Court itself, the parties must satisfy the Court that the agreement should be upheld. The structure is essentially three–fold. First, because the statute operates on an presumption that the agreement is contrary to the public interest, the parties must justify it by showing that it passes through at least one of eight stipulated 'gateways' which comprise the second part of the structure. The third part amounts to a further hurdle in which the parties must demonstrate that the agreement is not unreasonable on a 'cost/benefit' analysis. This is the statutory 'tailpiece'.[27]

The gateways range from the rather general to the very specific. Gateway (b), for example, is rather broad and invites consideration of 'specific and substantial benefits or advantages' enjoyed, *inter alia*, by consumers as a result of the agreement. Gateway (a) is much more specific. It concerns agreements 'reasonably necessary ... to protect the public against injury.' There is some overlap between the several gateways. Penetration of any one will suffice for the parties, although argument will typically be presented in respect of several. The tailpiece is much broader and includes specific reference to the consumer interest. It provides that the court must be;

> 'further satisfied (in any such case) that the restriction or information provision is not unreasonable having regard to the balance between those circumstances and any detriment to the public or to persons not parties to the agreement (being purchasers, consumers or users of goods...)

---

26 See eg 1987 Annual Report of the Director General of Fair Trading p. 31. For comment see Whish *op. cit.* pp. 158–161.

27 This structure is found in s.10 in respect of goods and s.19 in respect of services.

resulting or likely to result from the operation of the restriction or the information provision.'

The Restrictive Practices Court's 1959 decision in *Yarnspinners Agreement*[28] provides a valuable illustration of how the Act operates before the Court, how and why it had a significant impact in its early years and how the consumer interest is fed into the process.

The Yarnspinners' Agreement, struck between the members of the Yarnspinners' Association, was referred to the Court. Part of the Agreement involved price fixing against a background of decline throughout the twentieth century in the British share of the world market for cotton, of which the spinners were a part. The objective of the price fixing was to guarantee the spinners a minimum return. It prevented aggressive firms from cutting prices and thereby driving weaker, smaller firms from the market, causing unemployment in the traditional spinning area of Lancashire based around Wigan, Bolton and Oldham. Such tactics were especially likely in time of recession when, were such price competition permitted, firms would be lost to the industry forever, thereby destroying capacity needed in boom times and allowing the survivors to raise prices. It was argued that the public interest favoured the stability of fixed prices.

The Court was unpersuaded. The judgment of Devlin J expressed the view that the scheme had kept prices 'higher than they would have been in a free market'. The industry was contracting, but the scheme had 'seriously retarded' the ejection of high–cost producers. Excess capacity was far beyond what it was 'prudent' to retain should demand pick up. '[T]he industry can, and ought to, be made smaller and more compact'.[29]

These observations formed the prelude to the application of the tests contained in the Act. The Court felt that the spinners had discharged the burden which lay on them to show that a gateway was penetrated. Under the legislation then in force, s.21(1)(e) (which is now s.10(1)(e) of the 1976 Act) opened a gateway where the removal of the restriction would be likely to have a serious and persistent adverse effect on the general level of unemployment in an area where a substantial portion of the trade was situated. As Devlin J commented, it is 'quite impossible to make precise calculations' about the effect of removing the agreement on levels of unemployment.[30] However he concluded that mills would close and that this would have the required serious and adverse persistent effect. Nevertheless he found against the Agreement after considering the detriment to the public

---

28   [1959] 1 All ER 299.
29   Quotations are all from the judgment of Devlin J at 314.
30   319–320.

in artificially high prices and wasted excess capacity. The industry should be left to contract as a result of competition. Those considerations outweighed the perceived benefits for the Lancashire cotton spinners.

The breadth of the statutory tailpiece invites some scepticism about whether this aspect of the legal control effectively insulates judges from economic issues, as Ungoed–Thomas J in *Roberts v British Railways Board*[31] believed appropriate. The judgment was in essence an economic calculation of the costs and benefits of stripping price competition from a market. It may also be considered from the perspective of a potential collision between regional policy and consumer policy. Devlin J felt that the effect on employment was localised and could not override the price paid nationally by consumers in general. The fundamental tone of the judgment was one of hostility to the Agreement and, for British industry in 1959, the ruling marked the need to rethink cartelisation.

At the end of the proceedings the Court makes the appropriate order, in favour of or contrary to the agreement. In practice few agreements have received the green light from the court. The statutory presumption against the permissibility of agreements which reach the Court is exceedingly difficult to rebut. In consequence few agreements have been defended before the Court in recent years, since this is widely seen as a fruitless task. Parties will endeavour to draft agreements which fall outwith the Act. They will try to persuade the authorities to invoke section 21(2) in their favour. If, however, proceedings loom, there is a considerable incentive simply to abandon the practice rather than undergo the uncertainty of legal proceedings before the Court.

15.2.3.5 Enforcement of the Act

All the comments above assume that parties will take the Act seriously, but there is some evidence that this is not always the case. This may be attributable in part to its weak enforcement structure.

The powers of investigation vested in the Director General of Fair Trading are flimsy.[32] Exhaustive analysis is inappropriate here, but they contrast starkly with the sweeping powers of entry, search and seizure enjoyed by officials of the European Commission under empowering

---

[31] Note 24 above.
[32] Practice is discussed by A. Walker Smith, 'Collusion: its Detection and Investigation' [1991] 2 *ECLR* 71.

Regulation 17/62. Sir Gordon Borrie, former Director General, complained that he had to 'fight cartels with one hand tied behind my back'.[33]

Failure to register an agreement may provide the basis for an action by a third party.[34] Litigation of this nature has been pursued very infrequently and no such award has ever been made by a court. This is in part explicable by the consideration that the obvious plaintiff, a customer of the cartel, may well have no incentive to sue, especially if dependent on the members of the cartel for supplies. Few dare bite the hand that feeds them. A consumer might in theory have a claim as the ultimate victim of the lack of competition caused by the restrictive practice. In reality, however, an individual consumer is unlikely to have the time or money to pursue such an uncertain claim. This is a clear case where institutional, rather than individual, enforcement, is appropriate.[35] Finally, quantification of such a claim would be very complex. It should be noted that this would be a claim for loss caused by failure to register the agreement, a formalistic issue. The fact of causing economic harm by pursuing an anti–competitive practice is not of itself subject to penalty under the Act. Tortious liability in areas such as conspiracy would be difficult to develop, a *fortiori* for a consumer plaintiff.[36]

Perhaps most extraordinary of all is the realisation that a finding that a registrable agreement has been practised without the Court's approval leads only to a Court Order forbidding its continuance. There is no provision for a fine to be imposed. Only if a court order is subsequently breached need the parties fear penalties, since such breach would then amount to a contempt of court. A company could be liable for the actions of its employees in such circumstances,[37] which should induce companies to put in place effective compliance systems so that employees are fully aware of the importance of scrupulously observing legal obligations. But if, despite the programme, employees act in breach, the company is not protected from liability; its efforts to secure compliance count as mitigation only.[38] However, the

---

[33]   (1988–89) HC 440 p. 19.

[34]   S.35(2).

[35]   More broadly on such questions of access to justice, Chapters 16, 17.

[36]   J. Kirkbride, 'The Private Control of Anti Competitive Practices – Some Possibilities' (1990) 11 *Company Lawyer* 134; H. Carty, 'Intentional Violation of Economic Interests: the Limits of Common Law Liability' (1988) 104 *LQR* 250.

[37]   *Re Supply of Ready Mixed Concrete No 2* [1995] 1 All ER 135, wherein the House of Lords rejected a more limited approach to company liability espoused in the Court of Appeal.

[38]   Contrast the statutory defences available in some areas to companies setting up effective supervisory systems; eg Chapter 14.2 deals with the defence of due

fundamental weakness of this structure is that colluders receive a warning in the shape of a first order before they are exposed to a real risk of financial penalty.

All these factors combine to weaken the deterrent effect of the Act. The contrast with EC law is striking and, as explained at 15.2.3.1 above, constitutes a powerful argument in favour of reform.

15.2.4 European Community Law of Cartels and Restrictive Practices

15.2.4.1 Consumer Choice in EC Trade Law

Consumer choice has played an important, though typically inexplicit, part in interpreting the application of the EC's competition rules. On occasion, however, the consumer interest in competitive markets has surfaced in explicit fashion. In *Co–operative vereniging Suiker Unie UA and others v Commission*[39] arrangements which led to the isolation of national markets from cross–border competition were condemned. The Court ruled such practices to be 'to the detriment of effective freedom of movement of the products in the common market and of the freedom of consumers to choose their suppliers'.[40] In *Zuchner v Bayerische Vereinsbank AG*,[41] concerning the market for banking services, the Court commented that Article 85 may apply where firms have abandoned their independence in favour of unlawful collusion which suppresses competition, '... thus depriving their customers of any genuine opportunity to take advantage of services on more favourable terms which would be offered to them under normal conditions of competition'.

Such statements are important because they locate competition policy in the general framework of European Community trade law which is designed to achieve an area in which national frontiers lose their economic relevance and in which consumer choice is broadened.[42] EC trade law controls State measures which fragment the European market along national lines; through

---

diligence under, *inter alia*, trade descriptions legislation. This exonerated the supermarket in *Tesco v Nattrass*, a decision distinguished on the basis of the existence there of the statutory defence by the House of Lords in *Re Supply of Ready Mixed Concrete No 2*, n.37 above.

[39] Cases 40–48, 50, 54–56, 111, 113 and 114/73 [1975] ECR 1663.
[40] Para.191 of the judgment.
[41] Case 172/80 [1981] ECR 2021.
[42] Chapter 2.

competition rules, it also controls private measures which exert a similar effect.

15.2.4.2 The Pattern of Article 85 EC[43]

In common with UK law, EC restrictive practices law is based on the overall perception that supply side collaboration carries the potential to damage the operation of the market and, ultimately and typically inexplicitly, the consumer interest. Such practices are to be controlled, but with scope left for showing justification for beneficial collaboration. However, both the nature of the substantive law and the accompanying institutional framework distance EC law from UK law.

Article 85 is the relevant provision of EC law, which reads as follows:

> 1. The following shall be prohibited as incompatible with the common market: all agreements between undertakings, decisions by associations of undertakings and concerted practices which may affect trade between Member States and which have as their object or effect the prevention, restriction or distortion of competition within the common market, and in particular those which:
>
> (a) directly or indirectly fix purchase or selling prices or any other trading conditions;
>
> (b) limit or control production, markets, technical development, or investment;
>
> (c) share markets or sources of supply;
>
> (d) apply dissimilar conditions to equivalent transactions with other trading parties, thereby placing them at a competitive disadvantage;
>
> (e) make the conclusion of contracts subject to acceptance by the other parties of supplementary obligations which, by their nature or according to commercial usage, have no connection with the subject of such contracts.
>
> 2. Any agreements or decisions prohibited pursuant to this Article shall be automatically void.
>
> 3. The provisions of paragraph 1 may, however, be declared inapplicable in the case of any agreement or category of agreements between undertakings;
>
> – any decision or category of decisions by associations of undertakings;

---

43   Whish *op. cit.* Ch.7; S. Weatherill and P. Beaumont, *EC Law* (Penguin Books, 1993), Ch.22; D. Wyatt and A. Dashwood, *European Community Law* (Sweet and Maxwell, 1993), Ch.14.

- any concerted practice or category of concerted practices;

which contributes to improving the production or distribution of goods or to promoting technical or economic progress, while allowing consumers a fair share of the resulting benefit, and which does not:

(a) impose on the undertakings concerned restrictions which are not indispensable to the attainment of these objectives;

(b) afford such undertakings the possibility of eliminating competition in respect of a substantial part of the products in question.

Article 85(1) contains the prohibition; Article 85(2) the sanction for violation of the prohibition, namely nullity; Article 85(3) the criteria for exemption of an agreement falling within Article 85(1). In stark contrast to the technical, form–based nature of the UK's Restrictive Trade Practices Act 1976, the application of Article 85 is based on the effects of an agreement. Whereas the Restrictive Trade Practices Act demands a 'registrable agreement', for EC law it does not matter what form the collaboration takes provided it has an effect which distorts trade (to summarise Article 85(1)). EC law, then, is more flexible than English law. The end result of the two systems will frequently, though not invariably,[44] be the same, but the legal criteria are shaped in fundamentally distinct ways.

The variation between EC and UK policy is in no small part attributable to institutional considerations. At the institutional level, EC law prefers the use of administrative officials over judges. The administrative application of the prohibition on anti–competitive agreements affecting trade between Member States contained in Article 85 rests with the European Commission, specifically with Directorate General IV within the Commission. A supervisory jurisdiction is exercised, initially, by the Court of First Instance, with the possibility of an appeal to the European Court of Justice.

It is the officials of Directorate General IV who investigate suspected unlawful cartels and have at their disposal powers which far exceed those vested in the Director General of Fair Trading under the Restrictive Trade Practices Act 1976.[45] Conferred by Regulation 17/62,[46] these include powers to enter and to search premises and to seize documentation. Failure to co–operate may attract financial penalties which are independent of sanctions that may be imposed should a violation of the substantive rules come to light. The Commission also rules on whether a violation of Article 85(1) has occurred and is empowered to impose fines on the participants up

---

[44]   Cf Net Book Agreement, 15.2.5 below.
[45]   15.2.3.5 above.
[46]   1959–62 OJ Sp.Ed. Whish *op. cit.* Ch.9; Weatherill and Beaumont *op. cit.* Ch.24; Wyatt and Dashwood *op. cit.* Ch.16.

to a ceiling of 10% of the firm's world–wide turnover. That has exceeded £10 million on occasion and in one celebrated case even exceeded £50 million.[47] Such investigative powers combined with potential penalties of such magnitude mean that, in contrast to the Restrictive Trade Practices Act 1976, taking EC competition law lightly is not a practical option.

15.2.4.3 Exemption

The Commission is empowered to adopt decisions exempting agreements under the third paragraph of Article 85. The Commission must therefore involve itself in the balancing of competing interests envisaged by the Article 85(3) criteria. An individual application may be made to the Commission for exemption under Article 85(3). Indeed, exemption is not available unless a request *is* made, save in the exceptional circumstances recognised under Regulation 17/62[48] or, of more practical significance, where the practice falls within a Block Exemption Regulation (below). In practice the Commission's workload is far too high for it to adopt formal Decisions in more than a handful of cases annually where it is asked to exempt an agreement. Therefore it typically responds to firms on an informal basis by issuing a 'comfort letter'. This indicates the Commission's provisional view on the permissibility of the agreement and is normally sufficient to close the matter on that basis.

Since the application of Article 85(3) solely through individual exemptions would be rather inefficient, the Commission has found it prudent to issue Block Exemptions. These are contained in Regulations which apply a Block Exemption to several categories of collaboration. Such Regulations contain a list of clauses which may or may not be included in particular types of agreement. The content of the Block Exemptions is drawn from Article 85(3); in relation to particular deals, they constitute the concrete expression of the abstract requirements of the criteria for exemption in that Article. An agreement falling within the ambit of a Block Exemption Regulation may be pursued without having to apply to the Commission. Block Exemption Regulations render the Commission's workload more manageable than would otherwise be the case and also constitute important practical frameworks for firms planning commercial collaboration. The Commission's power to issue

---

47   Dec.92/163 *Tetra Pak* OJ 1992 L72/1, upheld by the Court of First Instance in Case T–83/91 *Tetra Pak International SA v Commission* judgment of 6 October 1994. This involved a violation of Article 86, 15.3.5.1 below, although the powers to fine under Reg.17/62 are the same as in relation to Article 85.

48   Art.4(2) Reg.17/62.

such Regulations derives from Regulation 19/65; the list of Block Exemptions has expanded steadily.[49]

The officials of Directorate General IV in the Commission are placed in a powerful position to decide individual cases, subject to judicial review which is not uncommon especially in cases in which high fines have been imposed. More generally, the Commission is well placed to shape policy in this area by the development of Block Exemption Regulations which tend to dictate patterns of collaboration in those sectors which they cover. Strictly, there is no obligation to adhere to a Block Exemption Regulation: firms may draft a novel agreement and seek individual exemption. However in practical terms, it is normal to choose the convenient route of compliance with the Block Exemption.

15.2.4.4 Enforcement at National Level

The principle of the direct effect of EC law means that enforcement may be achieved through national courts in addition to activity by the Commission. In principle the victim of a cartel incompatible with EC law could initiate proceedings at national level to secure an order that the practice should terminate and perhaps to obtain damages as compensation for loss suffered. National courts must effectively protect Community law rights.[50] The action at national level may be initiated in parallel with a complaint to the Commission.[51] Private enforcement of EC competition law is a practical feature of the system. This contrasts with the UK regime, which offers no useful incentive to private litigation under the Restrictive Trade Practices Act.[52]

The Commission is eager to see an increase in 'decentralised' enforcement of EC competition law through private actions commenced

---

[49] For a comprehensive, detailed examination, see the practitioner–oriented V. Rose (ed), *Bellamy and Child's Common Market Law of Competition* (Sweet and Maxwell, 1993).

[50] The source of this obligation is Article 5 EC; for a powerful assertion see Cases C–6, C–9/90 *Francovich v Italian State* [1991] ECR I–5357 (State liability in damages for violation of EC law, in *casu* non–implementation of Directives), further examined in Chapter 2.4.2. For discussion see F. Snyder, 'The Effectiveness of European Community Law: Institutions, Processes, Tools and Techniques' (1993) 56 *MLR* 19; I. Maher, 'National Courts as European Community Courts' [1994] *Legal Studies* 226.

[51] Art.3(2)(b) Reg.17/62 confers standing for these purposes on 'natural or legal persons who claim a legitimate interest'. See 15.2.4.6 below on consumer complaints.

[52] 15.2.3.5 above.

before national courts relying on the principle of direct effect. Lately it has sought to emphasise the key role which national tribunals are able to play in the enforcement of EC competition law. It has received the support of the Court of First Instance for its policy of pursuing complaints only where there is a Community interest in doing so, leaving other matters to be pursued by the complainant at national level.[53] However, there is a gap in the capacity of national tribunals to enforce Article 85, since the Commission holds an exclusive power to exempt agreements. Accordingly national courts can and must apply Articles 85(1) and (2), which are directly effective, but may not exempt agreements under Article 85(3), which is not directly effective. This complication in enforcement practice combined with the Commission's eagerness for increased national activity dictates a need for a framework of co–operation between Commission and national courts. The Court had already commented on the existence under Community law of such an obligation to co–operate;[54] in order to provide practical substance to this obligation, the Commission issued a Notice on the matter in 1993.[55]

15.2.4.5 The Consumer Interest

In the application of the competition rules, the interest of the consumer normally remains inexplicit. Article 85 benefits the consumer in the broad sense that it forms part of the machinery for establishing the common market. A naked market–sharing agreement would violate Article 85; it would suppress competition and consumer choice. A naked price–fixing cartel would act contrary to the consumer interest for similar reasons and would be incompatible with Article 85. In this sense, consumers are envisaged as the ultimate beneficiaries of the application of the competition rules, as they are supposed to enjoy the fruits of the realisation of the internal market.[56]

However, in Article 85(3) the consumer interest is explicitly injected into the structure of Community competition policy making. Under Article 85(3), an agreement may not be exempted from the prohibition in the first paragraph of Article 85 unless it, inter alia, 'contributes to improving the production of goods or to promoting technical or economic progress, while

---

53 Case T–24/90 *Automec v Commission* [1992] ECR II–2223.
54 Case C–234/89 *Stergios Delimitis v Henninger Brau* [1991] ECR I–935. The source of the obligation is Article 5 EC.
55 OJ 1993 C39/05. See R. Whish, 'The Enforcement of EC Competition Law in the Domestic Courts of Member States' [1994] 2 *ECLR* 60.
56 Chapter 2.

allowing consumers a fair share of the resulting benefit...'. This requirement of consumer benefit must be satisfied as a precondition to a successful application to the Commission for individual exemption. The Block Exemption Regulations, which amount to formalised applications of the Article 85(3) criteria to particular types of deal, also enshrine the consumer benefit requirement.

A textual point should be taken about the notion of 'consumer' under Article 85(3). It does not simply refer to the end user, which is the normal connotation in English law. The choice in the French text of the word 'utilisateur' shows that any user is envisaged, not simply the ultimate consumer (which would normally be rendered as 'consommateur').

In formal exemption decisions which approve a practice, the Commission is always obliged to provide an explanation of how it considers that the 'consumer benefit' criterion is satisfied. However, it is common for the Commission to identify an adequate consumer benefit in the economic advantages which flow from collaboration. Only infrequently is the requirement of consumer benefit given any sharp separate identity from the insistence in Article 85(3) that the practice shall contribute to 'improving the production or distribution of goods or to promoting technical or economic progress'.

Typical is the exemption of the agreement between SOPELEM, a French company, and Rank, an English company.[57] The firms planned to collaborate on research and development, manufacture and distribution in the field of camera lenses. The Commission found that the agreement increased the range of products available to the consumer and that quality of both product and service was enhanced. It also came to the conclusion that these benefits would be maintained by virtue of the existence of efficient competition in the market. This was enough to cross the consumer benefit threshold. The Commission commonly seems prepared to assume that provided an agreement promotes efficient commercial structures and provided a sufficient level of competition endures, then the consumer will benefit in consequence.[58]

One would not expect market sharing or price fixing to benefit the consumer and therefore such agreements should not be capable of exemption. They would, however, fail to satisfy other criteria under Article 85(3), not simply that pertaining to consumer benefit.

---

[57] Decision 75/76 OJ 1975 L29/20, [1975] 1 CMLR D72.

[58] A. Evans, 'European Competition Law and Consumers: the Article 85(3) Exemption' [1981] *ECLR* 425.

15.2.4.6 Enforcement by Consumers

In theory, the consumer is able to enforce the EC competition rules as readily as any commercial party. The consumer may complain to the Commission and seek to persuade it to initiate an investigation.[59] The consumer can also rely on the direct effect of Article 85 to challenge unlawful practices at national level.

As a practical matter, the obstacles to consumer access to justice are notorious.[60] The likelihood of a consumer making effective use of national courts or tribunals to challenge a cartel is slim. The institutional support of the Commission is potentially an important means of promoting the consumer interest in controlling anti–competitive practices; indeed, there are examples of consumer complaints acting as a spur to a Commission inquiry. In *Kawasaki*[61] a Commission inquiry prompted by the representations of a frustrated Belgian consumer led to a finding that an arrangement which prevented exportation of motorcycles to Belgium from Britain, where prices were relatively low, violated Article 85.

However the Commission's shift towards prioritising only those cases with a Community interest seems capable of inhibiting this route.[62] Where the Commission chooses not to act, it is up to the consumer to pursue the matter at national level, which is often rather unlikely in practice. However, the Court of First Instance's concern to provide support for the consumer interest in effective enforcement, at least where pursued collectively, is manifested in *BEUC v Commission*.[63] In that case BEUC, a consumer representative organisation (Bureau Européen des Unions de Consommateurs), had seen its complaint about the car market rejected by the Commission. The Court of First Instance reviewed the rejection decision, found it inadequately reasoned and annulled it. At the very least this demonstrates that the Commission is obliged to take consumer complaints seriously and to provide a response even though, ultimately, a principled and properly reasoned decision to take the matter no further is probably valid.[64] The law on complaint handling is becoming clearer,[65] but absolutely clear is

---

59 Note 51 above.
60 Chapter 17.
61 Decision 79/68 OJ 1979 L16/9, [1979] 1 CMLR 448.
62 15.2.4.4 above.
63 Case T–37/92 [1994] ECR II–285, welcomed from the consumer perspective by M. Goyens, 'A Key Ruling from the ECJ' (1994) 4 *Consumer Policy Review* 221.
64 Cf. Case T–24/90 *Automec* note 53 above.
65 For elaboration, see J. Shaw, 'Competition complainants: a comprehensive system of remedies?' (1993) 18 *ELRev* 427; B. Vesterdorf, 'Complaints concerning

the Court's view that the Commission cannot be forced by a complainant to adopt a final decision on the lawfulness of the practice itself.[66]

Consumer groups may be permitted to intervene in proceedings before the Court in support of one of the parties.[67] In *Ford Werke AG and Ford of Europe Inc v Commission*[68] the President of the Court upheld the right of BEUC to intervene at the oral stage in support of the Commission's case. BEUC had complained to the Commission about Ford's practices, which involved suppression of imports into the UK. Naturally, the costs of intervention will dissuade frequent use being made of this possibility.

15.2.5 UK and EC Law Compared and Contrasted

The differences between UK and EC restrictive practices law are of interest at an academic level, where there is scope for detached assessment of which system works best. For example, the 'effects–based' approach of Article 85 has many more admirers than the form–based style of the Restrictive Trade Practices Act 1976. On the other hand, the concentration of power in the hands of the European Commission has many critics.[69] To the consternation of some who have to deal with the officials of Directorate General IV, the same individuals investigate, adjudicate and impose fines. The European Court has long defended this monolithic structure from challenge based on fundamental rights,[70] but may be forced to rethink in the light of the ruling of the European Commission on Human Rights that the similar (though not identical) structures of French competition law are incompatible with the protection afforded by the Convention.[71]

For all the 1989 White Paper's intent to propose an alignment of domestic restrictive practices law with the EC system,[72] it was not thought expedient to follow precisely the model of institutional power in Regulation 17/62. A two–tier structure is envisaged, with powers of investigation and decision spread between the Office of Fair Trading and a new Restrictive

---

Infringements of Competition Law within the Context of European Community Law' (1994) 31 *CMLRev* 77.

[66] Case 125/78 *GEMA v Commission* [1979] ECR 3173.

[67] Article 37 of the Protocol on the Statute of the Court of Justice.

[68] Case 229 and 228/82R [1982] ECR 3091.

[69] Cf discussion by Lever n.3 above.

[70] Eg Cases 100–103/80 *Musique Diffusion Francaise v Commission* [1983] ECR 1825.

[71] *Societe Stenuit v France* (1992) 14 EHRR 509. See further Weatherill and Beaumont *op. cit.* Ch.24.

[72] 15.2.3.1 above.

Practices Tribunal. Private enforcement on the EC model *is*, however, proposed.

At the practical level, the discrepancies between the two existing systems are commercially unsettling. Overlap and conflict arises not just in theory, but also in practice. The saga of the Net Book Agreement provides a case study in different choices. The Agreement has been in place for most of this century and is at heart a price–fixing arrangement. Its supporters justify such restrictions on competition by appealing to the notion that, where books are concerned, more is not necessarily better. Unconfined price competition would lead to cheaper 'popular'[73] books ousting higher price specialist volumes from the shelves.

In 1962, the Restrictive Practices Court found the agreement to be in the public interest.[74] In 1968 the same verdict was delivered.[75] However the European Commission came to the opposite conclusion on the lawfulness of the agreement after testing it against Article 85.[76] The Commission's Decision was suspended on application by the Publishers' Association which permitted the agreement to remain in force pending a final ruling.[77] The ruling by the Court of First Instance upheld the view of the Commission.[78] At this stage in the litigation, the outcome in law for the future of the agreement could be easily stated. The Agreement in its traditional form could not be enforced in deals which affected cross–border trade in books. EC law applied. It is supreme. In purely domestic deals, by contrast, the agreement remained enforceable. The EC is not omnicompetent. In a purely internal matter, the writ of EC competition law does not run. Supervision of deals which do not affect inter–State trade is the province of national law. The legal treatment of deals within the Agreement was therefore split into two, varying according to whether they had an impact on cross–border trade. This legal dichotomy made little commercial sense, especially in an integrating market. Partly as a result, but also in the face of the growth of aggressive competition in the book trade, the Agreement begun to crumble as traders opted out. There was a remarkable further twist in January 1995 when the matter reached the European Court. It overturned the ruling of the Court of

---

73 Meant descriptively and pejoratively!

74 [1962] 3 All ER 751.

75 Unreported.

76 Commission Dec. 89/44 *Net Book Agreement* OJ 1989 L22/12, [1989] 4 CMLR 825

77 Case 56/89R *Publishers Association v Commission* [1989] ECR 1693, [1989] 4 CMLR 816, [1989] 2 All ER 1059.

78 Case T–66/89 *Publishers Association v Commission* judgment of 9 July 1992 [1992] 5 CMLR 120, noted by Bright, 'The Court of First Instance and the Net Book Agreements' [1992] 6 *ECLR* 266.

First Instance and annulled the Commission Decision that had declared the Agreement in breach of Article 85 in the first place.[79] The Court found aspects of the Commission's analysis to be inadequately reasoned. For the time being, then, the Net Book Agreement survives in law, although whether it has any commercial future seems doubtful.

The major point to draw from this saga is that the two competition law systems are distinct in substance and procedure. It is apparent that the Commission did not completely rule out the possibility of special arrangements in the book trade, but it was unpersuaded that the objectives of the agreement could be achieved only through such a tight cartel. The domestic approach was more permissive of the book trade's practices. The European Court's 1995 annulment of the Commission Decision does not in any way preclude future divergence in the application of cartel law to other matters. The systems have quite different pedigrees and it is not 'wrong' that they should be capable of producing different outcomes.

This is a problem for traders in the internal market who are forced to comply with two different systems. A further complexity for commercial parties is that the jurisdictional divide between Community law and national law in the control of cartels is in any event rather blurred and frequently both systems will be applicable. Although only deals with an effect on inter–State trade are capable of falling within Article 85, that threshold is low. In *Cementhandelaren v Commission*[80] an agreement involving the practices of Dutch firms on the Dutch market was found to fall within EC jurisdiction because it tended to cause the isolation of the Dutch market from the rest of the territory of the Community. In practice, few deals are 'purely' national in impact and therefore subject to domestic regulation alone without taking account of the Community dimension. Firms must 'shop' for their regulation at two or more outlets, in Brussels and in one or more national capitals. This increases the compliance costs of business, a fortiori where the systems diverge in their substance.

This discussion of the discrepancies between the EC and UK regimes should be placed in context. For all the differences in substance between the regimes and the remarkable gulf between enforcement mechanisms, whether pursued by specialist institutions or private individuals, the two regimes ought to lead to the same outcome in most circumstances. Both, after all, are designed to achieve a competitive market structure in the interest of the consumer. However, the fact that different outcomes cannot be discounted[81] might suggest that the case for reform is overwhelming. As explained at

---

[79] Case C–360/92P *Publishers Association v Commission* judgment of 17 January 1995.
[80] Case 8/72 [1972] ECR 977.
[81] See 15.5 below on the distinctive market integrationist flavour of EC law.

15.2.3.1 above, the 1989 White Paper proposes the adoption of a model analogous to the EC's system. This is motivated by the perceived superiority of the EC control mechanism and by the practical aim of lifting from business the burden of achieving compliance with two quite distinct regimes. Aligning the UK system in most[82] respects would still require business to operate in the shadow of two regulatory regimes, but the substance of the two would be brought into line.[83] There would be less risk of divergence, especially if, as the White Paper suggests, reformed UK law were to be interpreted to conform to EC law as far as possible and if a new specialist tribunal were to be established to deal with all competition cases under both domestic and EC law. It seems, however, that the UK must wait longer for reform of its law of cartels and restrictive practices.

15.3 MONOPOLY LAW

15.3.1 The Phenomenon of the Monopoly and Related Market Structures

Discussion of cartels is concerned with situations where the behaviour of producers and suppliers impedes the operation of the market. The structure of the market may also impede the operation of the invisible hand. Consumer choice in conditions of perfect competition assumes the availability of a sufficient number of suppliers to ensure genuine variety. Yet this may not always be the case. Where there are a few producers only, the invisible hand is weakened. Monopolies provide the most extreme example: where the supplier holds a monopoly, the consumer is no longer sovereign. In consequence, the price and quality of what is produced are dictated by the choice of the producer, not the consumer.

Naturally, any control system must devote careful attention to the proper definition of a monopoly. Products may be interchangeable. The sole producer of widgets is not in a monopoly in economically meaningful terms if there are available sources of gizmos, a product that is readily interchangeable with widgets. If the widget producer hoists prices, consumers can switch to gizmos. There is no rationale for treating the market as a monopoly enjoyed by the widget producer. More subtly, even where a producer is the single source of widgets, for which there is no other interchangeable product, there is no monopoly if other producers are capable of altering their techniques in order to enter the market for widget production. In such circumstances, consumers have no immediate alternative

---

[82] But not all; see text at n.72 above on enforcement machinery.

[83] See comment by Whish, *Competition Law* (Butterworths, 1993) pp. 730–38.

supply source, but prices should nevertheless be held down to competitive levels because the sole active producer knows that price rises will attract new firms into the market, offering lower prices and consumer choice. Markets should therefore not be assessed as static. They should not be treated as monopolistic where they are in fact 'contestable'.[84] The need to define markets with care applies equally to geography as to product. The only British producer has no monopoly if the British market is open to external competition from sources of supply based in other countries. Monopoly law, like competition law generally, deals with the state of markets, so that where those markets change shape, the application of the law too must adjust.[85]

These issues of market definition are critical in any policy of monopoly control. An underestimation of actual or potential competition will lead to an overestimation of market power. This in turn may prompt an intervention in the name of monopoly control where there is no monopoly. However, if a monopoly *is* identified, control may be judged appropriate in light of the potential damage caused by the absence of competition, ultimately to the detriment of the consumer.

15.3.2 Shaping a Legal Response to the Monopoly

The law may address the pernicious effects of monopolies in several ways. It may attempt to prevent them coming into being by exercising controls over mergers and acquisitions. It may be possible to preserve a competitive market by creating a regulatory agency for that market which is competent to forbid mergers between competitors where the result would be an undue diminution in the number of rival suppliers. The law of merger control is in this sense an aspect of both monopoly law and consumer law. Merger law is examined below.[86]

A related set of legal techniques concentrates on entry barriers which impede the creation of efficient competition. A theory based on the desirability of fostering markets which are contestable would direct legal instruments to the improvement of market flexibility, rather than treating markets as static and in need of regulation.[87] So attention may be paid to removing legal or economic obstacles to firms which wish to enter markets

---

84   Eg W. Baumol and R. Willig in D.J. Morris (ed), *Strategic Behaviour and International Competition* (OUP, 1986).

85   Further, see Part 4.4 of this Chapter below.

86   15.4 below.

87   Cf *Barriers to Entry and Exit in UK Competition Policy* (OFT Research Paper 2, March 1994).

or, stronger, to providing positive inducements to would–be new firms. Economic obstacles to entry may comprise the difficulty in obtaining the investment needed, especially (and on some views only[88]) where a new entrant will not obtain economies of scale already claimed by existing market participants. Legal obstacles may take the form of governmental regulation. Quality standards set by the State may have the benefit of preventing unsafe or unacceptable goods or services reaching the market; equally, they carry a cost in reducing choice by keeping out firms unwilling or unable to meet those standards. Chapter 1 provides an amplified discussion of these key issues in shaping regulation.[89] It is not unknown for firms already active in a market to arrange their own self–regulation and/or to seek public regulation which reflects their existing practices in order to protect themselves from the threat of being undercut by competitors. Whether competition is fair or unfair may be in the eye of the beholder: trader, would–be trader and consumer may have very different perspectives. In any event, the pursuit of market flexibility involves some difficult questions about the desirability of public intervention.

More radically still, the law may address the problem of existing monopolies by forcing the monopolistic firm to be broken up into constituent parts and sold off in order to (re)create competition. In practice this route is rarely chosen, although it was in vogue for a short period in the US. This technique should be sharply distinguished from a governmental policy of privatisation of monopolies. Privatisation connotes the transfer of assets from public to private sector and *of itself* it exerts a neutral effect on competition. A monopoly is a monopoly whoever owns it. It is a different matter where privatisation of monopolies is combined with an attempt to inject competition into the market by, for example, splitting up the monopoly into constituent, potentially rival, elements prior to selling it off.

There is a middle way between preventing monopoly power from coming into existence and destroying it once it has: to accept the existence of dominant economic power but to regulate the firm so that it cannot behave independently of the market and of consumer preference. This approach is the norm in the UK and the EC. For example, the firm may be subjected to price control or quality standards; it may be obliged to deal equitably with customers, existing or prospective. The essential point is that, once a firm has crossed a threshold of economic power which renders it in part immune

---

88 Many of the issues are helpfully raised in the EC context by R. Baden Fuller, 'Article 86 EEC: Economic Analysis of the Existence of a Dominant Position' (1979) 4 *ELRev* 423; L. Gyselen and A. Kyriazis, 'Article 86: Monopoly Power Measurement Issue Revisited' (1986) 11 *ELRev* 134. In the US context, see Pitofsky n.16 above.

89 Especially Chapter 1.8.

from the pressure of competition, it becomes liable to act inefficiently and/or unfairly. There is then a rationale for exercising regulatory control which would not apply if it were economically weaker. So, whereas in a competitive market one might accept that ice–cream suppliers could install freezers from which their goods and no others could be sold, one might take a very different view of such activities by a firm which dominates a market.[90] A strong firm can tie up the market by exercising its economic clout to conclude deals with retailers. Such practices will reduce or even eliminate opportunities for smaller suppliers to compete in even a limited way. Consumer choice will shrink. The pursuit of exclusive ties in a market which is not fully competitive may be a cause for concern which would not arise in the presence of effective competition.[91]

Decisions have to be made about the type of institution which should be established to wield regulatory power, including appropriate appeal and review machinery. Such controls in one sense mimic the results which would obtain were a competitive market in operation. In that case, an individual firm's prices would be controlled by reference to those set by rivals, but in a monopoly a regulatory authority may assume that function. The question of the precise level at which prices should be set (in the absence of guidance from the operation of the market) then becomes a point of detail, but one which is itself likely to be controversial.[92]

The need for regulatory agencies is very evident in the policy of privatisation of publicly–owned monopolies pursued over the last 15 years in the UK. The simple transfer of public assets into the unregulated private sector has not been considered feasible where a monopoly is concerned, because of the power thereby handed to a private monopolist.[93] It has accordingly been thought necessary to establish legal controls over the newly–created private sector. This perception explains the rise of (a bewildering variety of) regulatory agencies charged with the task of overseeing the performance of nominally privatised industries.[94]

---

[90] Cf note 13 and accompanying text above.

[91] The European Court's ruling in Case C–234/89 *Stergios Delimitis v Henninger Brau* [1991] ECR I–935 serves as an example of an attempt to reflect such nuances in the application of legal rules (specifically Art.85 EC in relation to the market for beer supply).

[92] On capture theory and, still broader, public choice analysis, see Chapter 1.9.

[93] In some instances it was this perception that had prompted the State in the past to take the sector into public ownership; cf A. Ogus, *Regulation* (OUP, 1994), Ch.13.

[94] See 15.3.4.2 below and discussion in Chapter 1.9.3.

Looking briefly beyond competition policy as an economic instrument, it has been explained that price fixing by firms in a competitive market is almost invariably unlawful, whereas price fixing by a public authority in a non–competitive market can be justified for economic reasons. It might additionally be noted that price fixing by a public authority even in a competitive market may be justified, albeit not from the perspective of wealth maximisation. Legislation permitting the fixing of fair rents provides a good example, where the law may intervene to fix prices below the level at which the market would settle.[95] Political choices about wealth distribution and social justice may thus intrude into the shaping of economic law. In other sectors, the law may intervene to fix prices *above* the market price, typically to maintain capacity in the industry concerned. Such intervention has often been connected with a desire for national self–sufficiency, for example in food and energy, although where national markets are integrated into a wider market, such intervention can work only if undertaken at the transnational level.

15.3.3 Desirable Monopolies

In monopoly control, the wrinkle that should be taken into account is that monopolies are not always undesirable. In some sectors a monopoly may be the most effective and 'natural' method of structuring the market. For example, there are obvious limits to the potential for a competitive market for the supply of water from reservoirs or the operation of different train routes from London to Paris. There may conceivably be more than one supplier, but there is only one set of pipes or rails. The competitive market has its limits. The appropriate legal response to the true natural monopoly cannot be to forbid its coming into existence nor to break it up, but instead to regulate its operation. For the supply of water and energy there has been long–standing public concern to impose, for example, price controls and obligations of equitable supply to all consumers irrespective of geography.

However the term 'natural monopoly' demands careful attention, since it may cloak situations requiring more nuanced study. Transport markets are especially telling. Train travel seems to be a natural monopoly, yet the market may be competitive if defined to include a variety of forms of transport. There is only one train line between London and Birmingham, but a train is not the only means of travelling between the two cities. Such

---

95   Further, Chapter 1.9.3, where it is explained that recent UK policy preference has moved in precisely the opposite direction.

questions of market definition are essential prerequisites to the choice of legal control.

In the UK, perceptions of the limits of natural monopolies have recently sharpened. Attention has been paid to the possibility of paring down monopolies to a smaller core than had previously existed. Such activity has frequently accompanied decisions about the transfer of assets from public into private hands.[96] For example, the collection of water in reservoirs may be a natural monopoly, but retailing water may not. Competition may be injected into the retail sector. Similarly, a proliferation of railway track may not be desirable, but competition between operators wishing to use that track may be feasible.

15.3.4 United Kingdom Monopoly Law[97]

15.3.4.1 The Fair Trading Act 1973 and the Competition Act 1980

The structure of the Fair Trading Act 1973 involves three distinct players: the Director General of Fair Trading, supported by his staff at the Office of Fair Trading (OFT), the Secretary of State for Trade and Industry, and the Monopolies and Mergers Commission (MMC).

The first two named, the Director General and the Secretary of State, are empowered to refer monopoly situations to the MMC, which investigates and reports. Then the Secretary of State takes action. This three–stage structure has nothing of note in common with the UK's restrictive practices regime.[98] However, it is comparable to that used in UK merger control, examined at 15.4.2 below, although there are differences of detail.

Both Director General and Minister have flexibility in choosing whether to make references of possible monopoly situations, as defined in the Act.[99] This is a discretionary statutory power.[100] It offers scope for filtering cases according to their perceived seriousness, thereby avoiding the investment of time and money inherent in an MMC inquiry. As part of a policy of speeding up the regulatory process in order to reduce costs for business, the Deregulation and Contracting Out Act 1994 introduced procedures that allow firms to give undertakings as to conduct in lieu of a reference to the

---

[96] Cf Chapter 1.9.3.
[97] R. Whish, *Competition Law* (Butterworths, 1993), Chs.3,4; T. Frazer, *Monopoly, Competition and the Law* (Harvester Wheatsheaf, 2nd ed, 1992), Ch.2.
[98] 15.2.3 above.
[99] Ss.6–9 FTA 1973.
[100] Ss.50, 51 FTA 1973.

MMC.[101] Formally, the undertaking is made to the Secretary of State, although in practice the Director General plays the lead role.

If a decision is made to refer the situation to the MMC, the Fair Trading Act 1973 provides that the terms of the reference may be general or may be tied to particular aspects of the perceived monopoly situation.[102] The core of the MMC investigation is an examination of the effect of the monopoly situation on the public interest. For both monopolies and mergers[103] the MMC's elaboration of the public interest is guided, but not exhaustively defined, by the Fair Trading Act 1973. This provides that 'the Commission shall take into account all matters which appear to them in the particular circumstances to be relevant'.[104] Five matters are specifically referred to, but the MMC's inquiry is not confined to them. For example, the second refers to the promotion of 'the interests of consumers, purchasers and other users of goods and services in the United Kingdom in respect of the prices charged for them and in respect of their quality and the variety of goods and services supplied'. This could be construed as a simple expression of the consumer interest in a competitive market, but it is entirely open to the MMC to report in a spirit of social justice and consumer welfare. Since the statute permits the MMC to develop its own conception of the public interest, much can depend on the composition of particular panels.[105]

The MMC's report is required to provide definite conclusions on questions referred to it, adequately supported by reasons.[106] In the case of references not tied to particular facts which condemn a monopoly as contrary to the public interest, the MMC must explain what factors contribute to the finding and, additionally, suggest appropriate remedial action. This might involve, for example, a recommendation that price controls be introduced.[107] Forced sale of assets has also been recommended on occasion.[108]

Findings are reported to the Secretary of State, who can do nothing if no adverse view is taken. If the report concludes that the situation operates contrary to the public interest, the politician can still decide to take no action. But if action is decided upon, the Director General may be instructed to seek

---

[101] S.7 of the 1994 Act, inserting new ss.56A *et seq* into the Fair Trading Act 1973.
[102] Ss.47–49 FTA 1973.
[103] 15.4.2.4 below.
[104] S.84(1).
[105] S. Lipworth, former Chair of the MMC, 'The Work of the Monopolies and Mergers Commission' [1992] *CLP* 99.
[106] S.54 FTA 1973.
[107] Eg report on *Contraceptive Sheaths* HC 1974–5 135.
[108] Eg report on *Domestic Gas Appliances* HC 1979–80 703.

undertakings from the firm; failing a satisfactory outcome, an order controlling the activities of the monopoly may be made.

The other statute of relevance in this area is the Competition Act 1980. This allows a more focused investigation of anti–competitive practices by single firms or corporate groups and may be used even in the absence of monopoly power. The structure of the 1980 Act is close to that of the Fair Trading Act 1973's monopoly provisions. The Director General investigates. Where he finds an anti–competitive practice, he is empowered to conclude the matter if in receipt of satisfactory undertakings by the firm concerned as to its future conduct. This power, which avoids the need for further costly investigation, has been extended by the Deregulation and Contracting Out Act 1994.[109] If the matter is not resolved in this way, a reference to the MMC will follow. The MMC inquiry is based on the notion of impact on the public interest. For amplification of this notion, the Competition Act refers to the Fair Trading Act 1973.[110] The same open–ended inquiry is envisaged and consequences are analogous, with findings reported to the Secretary of State. Where it is decided to take action, either undertakings from the firm are extracted or an order will be made.

Reform was mooted in a Green Paper of 1992 entitled 'Abuse of Market Power'.[111] This was to some extent a parallel in the monopoly field to the proposals already made (but still unimplemented) in the area of restrictive practices.[112] The Green Paper raises the question of whether the UK would benefit from a general prohibition against abuse of market power, comparable to Article 86 EC, the EC's monopoly control provision (examined below). This change would provide the opportunity to introduce a more effective enforcement regime, including the presently unavailable possibility of private enforcement. The current system has a limited deterrent effect, for there is no scope for imposing penalties for past abusive conduct by a monopolist. Reform would also yield the general advantage of clarity flowing from alignment between domestic and European laws. However, the Green Paper has not been translated into firm proposals for an Article 86– style prohibition. Instead the government has declared that it has no current plans for radical reshaping of the current regime.

---

[109]   S.12 of the 1994 Act, amending s.5 CA 1980.

[110]   S.7(6) CA 1980.

[111]   Cm.2100 (1992). See J. Goh, 'Competition Law Reform: A Comment' (1993) 44 *NILQ* 291; R. Taylor, 'Abuse of Market Power: The Green Paper Proposals' [1993] 4 *ECLR* 169.

[112]   15.2.3.1 above.

15.3.4.2 Privatisation and Monopolies

It was explained in Chapter 1 that UK policy has pursued the path of privatisation in its several forms.[113] This is part of a process of withdrawal of State participation from the market, driven by a political choice in favour of the private ordering of the market as the preferred means of providing for the consumer interest, even in respect of 'public services' as traditionally conceived. But simply moving a monopoly from the public to the private sector has no effect on the structure of the market, which remains equally likely to operate inefficiently and unfairly. In some areas privatisation of monopolies was accompanied by an injection of competition. Where it was not, there was a perceived need to set up regulatory agencies. The loosening of direct State control over the supply of services of such vital importance to the consumer as gas, water and electricity has raised the profile of regulatory control of private monopolists. Several different regulators appeared – OFFER, OFTEL, OFWAT and so on.[114] This pattern of control is still taking shape.

Disputes between regulator and regulated industry about the appropriate level of control have become fairly common. Regulated industries have also looked beyond 'their' regulator to press the Government to lift, or at least relax, the control exercised. The process is dynamic. In some sectors the Government was initially reticent to alter the monopolistic structure when it transferred assets from the public to the private sphere.[115] It has subsequently pursued a policy of trying to inject competition.[116] The Competition and Service (Utilities) Act 1992 provided for the introduction of further competition into privatised, regulated sectors, most notably gas and water. The electricity industry was restructured on a more competitive pattern at the time of privatisation.

The Competition and Service (Utilities) Act 1992 was a major practical manifestation of the Citizens Charter programme.[117] Apart from its role in adjusting patterns of competition, it was also important for its contribution to placing the 'new' regulators of privatised monopolies/quasi–monopolies on a more standardised footing and aligning them more closely with the normal structure of monopoly control. Although precise details vary sector by sector

---

113 Chapter 1.9.3 above.
114 Chapter 1.9.3.
115 A reticence criticised in some quarters; cf Chapter 1.9.3, esp text at n.225.
116 Note also the role of Article 90 EC, 15.3.5.2 below, in obliging the government to take such a course.
117 Chapter 1.9.3. On the Act, see A. McHarg [1992] *Public Law* 385.

and regulator by regulator, the possibility of referral of practices to the MMC for investigation is now widespread.[118]

The regulated industries typically demand that the shift in market structure be accompanied by a change in regulatory climate. Calls for the lifting of price caps, for example, are heard with increasing regularity. Where markets are becoming truly competitive, these requests are justified from the perspective of the theory of free markets, whereby prices ought to be controlled by the forces of competition. However, this is dependent on the markets assuming a genuinely competitive shape, which some critics doubt is either feasible or desirable in sectors formerly viewed as 'public services'. The process remains dynamic and the to–and–fro between regulated industry, regulator and government will continue. Direct input by the consumer seems rather neglected.

15.3.5 European Community Monopoly Law

15.3.5.1 Article 86 EC

Article 86 acts as the EC monopoly control provision, although the terminology used is prohibition of 'abuse of a dominant position'.

> Any abuse by one or more undertakings of a dominant position within the common market or in a substantial part of it shall be prohibited as incompatible with the common market in so far as it may affect trade between Member States. Such abuse may, in particular, consist in:
> (a) directly or indirectly imposing unfair purchase or selling prices or unfair trading conditions:
> (b) limiting production, markets or technical development to the prejudice of consumers;
> (c) applying dissimilar conditions to equivalent transactions with other trading parties, thereby placing them at a competitive disadvantage;
> (d) making the conclusion of contracts subject to acceptance by the other parties of supplementary obligations which, by their nature or according to commercial usage, have no connection with the subject of such contracts.

---

[118]   Cf for more detailed references, Chapter 1.9.3. The *Utilities Law Review* provides a useful source of current comment.

Indirectly, Article 86 is a consumer policy instrument in its capacity to suppress inefficient practices such as high prices which are not adequately controlled by the market in the absence of effective competition. It will be seen that (b) in the non–exhaustive list of abusive practices attached to Article 86 contains an explicit reference to the position of the consumer. This is rare. In the original Treaty of Rome, which entered into force in 1958, there were only four references to the 'consumer', all of them tangential.[119]

The chief relevant piece of evidence that a firm has sufficient economic strength to render it subject to the Article 86 obligation not to abuse a dominant position is its ability to act in the market independently of normal competitive pressures. Article 86 applies to firms able to ignore the demands of 'competitors and customers and ultimately of consumers'.[120]

It was explained above at 15.3.2 that monopoly law may be structured to tolerate the existence of monopolies while regulating the exercise of monopoly power. Article 86 bears this stamp. Abuse is unlawful, not dominance per se. Dominant firms may not set unfair prices or act to segregate the market. Article 86 may be applied in order to require a reluctant dominant firm to respond to consumer demand. In this vein, the Commission found a violation of Article 86 in *ITP, RTE, BBC*.[121] The three television companies printed separate guides to future programmes, using copyright which they held over their own listings to prevent the appearance of a single, integrated publication. A consumer of the information was thus forced to buy three separate guides. The Court of First Instance upheld the Commission finding that an abuse had occurred in *RTE, BBC, ITP v Commission*[122] and the European Court subsequently dismissed appeals by two of the television companies.[123] The firms were obliged to make their listings available to third parties, subject to payment of a reasonable fee. The protection of the consumer interest is explicit in this decision, which imposes consumer choice on unwilling firms. Both courts observed that the companies had abused the economic power they enjoyed under their copyright by unjustifiably preventing the appearance of a new product for which there was potential consumer demand.

---

119 Arts. 39, 40, 85, 86. The well–known Art.100a(3) was an addition of the Single European Act in 1987. See Chapter 2 on this and on the significant adjustments effected by the Treaty on European Union from 1 November 1993.

120 Case 322/81 *Michelin v Commission* [1983] ECR 3461.

121 Decision 89/205 OJ 1989 L78/43, [1989] 4 CMLR 757.

122 Cases T–69, T–70, T–76/89 [1991] ECR II–485, 535, 575.

123 Joined Cases C–241/91P and C–242/91P *RTE and ITP v Commission* judgment of 6 April, 1995, The Times 17 April, 1995.

Enforcement of Article 86 lies in the hands of the Commission. Much of the comment relating to Article 85 may be applied *mutatis mutandis* to Article 86,[124] which is directly effective and may consequently be enforced at national level at the suit of private individuals.

15.3.5.2 Article 90 EC

State monopolies have been a common feature of the economies of most EC Member States. They are typically part of the patchwork of public and private participation in the modern mixed economy. One of the most high-profile developments in EC law in recent years is found in the increasing threat to State monopolies posed by the application of Article 90 EC.

Article 86, examined above, controls existing monopolies. There are also trends in EC law directed at dismantling monopolies where the monopolistic market structure is created or sustained by State restrictions. In this vein, Article 90(1) provides that:

> 'In the case of public undertakings and undertakings to which Member States grant special or exclusive rights, Member States shall neither enact nor maintain in force any measure contrary to the rules contained in this Treaty, in particular to those rules provided for in Article 6 and Articles 85 to 94.'

Article 90(3) concerns enforcement. It provides that the Commission 'shall ensure the application of the provisions of this Article and shall, where necessary, address appropriate directives or decisions to Member States'. The fact that the Commission has become very vigorous in its determination to exercise these powers over the last ten years is a major policy development. For many years, Article 90 was regarded as relatively peripheral in practical terms. This perception has completely changed.

Read with Article 86, Article 90 has been used to forbid State measures which place an undertaking in a position where its isolation from competition will inevitably lead it to act abusively. For example, in *Höfner and Elsner v Macrotron*[125] Höfner and Elsner had provided Macrotron with a candidate for the post of sales director. Despite his suitability, Macrotron did not appoint the person and refused to pay Höfner and Elsner. Since German law granted exclusive rights for employee recruitment to a public agency, the contract on which Höfner and Elsner sued Macrotron was void. Höfner and

---

124   15.2.4 above.

125   Case C–41/90 [1991] ECR I–1979.

Elsner relied on Community law to challenge the German law which excluded them from the market for supplying staff. The Court ruled that Articles 86 and 90 imposed an obligation on the State not to sustain a market which was uncompetitive. Here, the State prevented supply from meeting demand. This was incompatible with EC law. The decision amounts to a strong message in favour of liberalisation through which the structure of the market should be determined by private market decisions (supply and demand) and not by State regulation.

Article 90(2) provides an exception to the basic prohibition. It offers leeway to a State to pursue goals other than free competition:

> Undertakings entrusted with the operation of services of general economic interest or having the character of a revenue–producing monopoly shall be subject to the rules contained in this Treaty, in particular to the rules on competition, in so far as the application of such rules does not obstruct the performance, in law or in fact, of the particular tasks assigned to them. The development of trade must not be affected to such an extent as would be contrary to the interests of the Community.

Article 90(2) has been interpreted restrictively.[126] The European Court has ruled against its application much more frequently than it has ruled in favour. This has tended to give primacy to the ethos of free competition in the first paragraph of Article 90 over the receptivity to public service provision in its second paragraph.

However, Article 90(2) remains potentially important as a forum in which development of a Community law notion of social and consumer policy provision within the free market could occur. Indeed, the wider the scope of Article 90(1) in challenging State market regulation, the brighter the spotlight on the role Article 90(2) may play in justifying intervention. Article 90(2) may be read as an invitation to elaborate a theory of the social market under EC law. The invitation has not yet received a firm reply.[127]

Paul Corbeau concerned the State–conferred monopoly over postal services in Belgium.[128] The European Court accepted that, if the core

---

[126] Eg Case 66/86 *Ahmed Saeed Flugreisen and Silver Line Reiseburo GmbH v Zentrale zur Bekampfung unlauteren Wettbewerbs e.V.* [1989] ECR 803.

[127] For deeper discussion, see C.–D. Ehlermann, 'Managing Monopolies: the Role of the State in Controlling Market Dominance in the European Community' [1993] 2 *ECLR* 61; C. Bright, 'Article 90, Economic Policy and the Duties of Member States' [1993] 6 *ECLR* 263; N. Reich, 'The "November Revolution" of the European Court of Justice: Keck, Meng and Audi Revisited' (1994) 31 *CMLRev* 459.

[128] Case C–320/91 judgment of 19 May 1993.

monopoly over letter delivery were lost, the social function of the service would be jeopardised. Private firms would have no interest in maintaining a national system; their preference would be to 'cherry–pick' profitable parts of the service, leaving rural consumers under provided. In *Corbeau* the Court recognised the role of cross–subsidy as a means of maintaining the viability of loss–making but socially worthwhile services. Article 90(2) is capable of justifying restrictions on competition in such circumstances. However, the Court *was* prepared to apply Article 90 read with Article 86 in order to lop off ancillary rights reserved to State monopolies and to open them up to competition. The case was an Article 177 preliminary ruling, so the Court did not have the task of deciding the case, but merely of interpreting Community law. The ruling expresses an (as yet) undefined role for Article 90(2) in insulating core elements of socially valuable State monopolies from the blast of free competition.

It remains controversial whether EC practice takes sufficient account of the importance of maintaining social obligations to all consumers which is a characteristic feature of State monopolies. The benefit of increased competition may have to be weighed against the cost of diminished social justice and consumer protection.

15.4 MERGER LAW

15.4.1 Rationales for Merger Control[129]

A merger or take–over occurs where two or more previously independent firms come under common control. For legal purposes the constituent elements of the merged entity may remain separate, but in economic terms what counts is the reduction in competition consequent on surrender of commercial independence.[130]

Mergers between firms may be seen as the expression of commercial free will. They can serve a valuable function of restructuring the market. Economic theory tells us that big firms should be able to produce goods and services more cheaply than small ones and that, in a competitive market, price savings should be passed on to consumers. Such mergers should serve the consumer interest. In Europe, mergers between firms in different countries can be especially important in the process of market integration.

---

129 J.A. Fairburn and J.A. Kay (eds), *Mergers and Merger Policy* (OUP, 1989); B. Chiplin and M. Wright, *The Logic of Mergers* (IEA, 1988).

130 Reflected in UK law in s.64 Fair Trading Act and in EC law in Art.3(3) Merger Regulation, in more detail below.

However, mergers may lead to a restriction of competition. The fewer the firms active or potentially active in a market, the more sceptical the law is likely to be about a 'horizontal' merger between rivals. Mergers may need to be controlled because they damage the competitive structure of the market by increasing concentration of economic power above acceptable levels. The ultimate loser in such circumstances is the consumer.

Economic considerations may not be the sole motivation for merger law. It may also seem important to subject mergers to control for social reasons. For example, they may rob a region of a firm and its associated jobs. It will be appreciated that a merger policy informed by such concerns will be rather interventionist. Whatever the political and economic motivations for merger control, the associated question arises of the appropriate institutional machinery. An agency of some type, accountable for its choices, must be established which will rule on the tricky economic and political aspects of merger control.

15.4.2 United Kingdom Merger Law[131]

15.4.2.1 The Pattern of Control

UK merger law is contained in Part V of the Fair Trading Act 1973.[132] The nature of the statutory controls is well summarised by Whish: 'The system of control is benign and is essentially predisposed in favour of mergers'.[133] The choice in the UK has been to regard mergers as elements in maintaining flexible market structures. They are normally permitted in the absence of rather strong evidence of anti-competitive effect.

Merger control under the statute has three distinct steps. This framework is comparable with, though not identical to, monopoly control in the UK.[134] First, a discretion is vested in the Minister to refer a merger to the Monopolies and Mergers Commission (MMC). Second, the MMC reports on the merger, but its views are not necessarily conclusive. Stage three involves final disposal of the case by the Minister, who may confirm the MMC's

---

131 R. Whish, *Competition Law* (Butterworths, 1993) pp. 671–702; T. Soames, 'Merger Policy: As Clear As Mud?' [1991] 2 *ECLR* 53; J. Fairburn, 'The Evolution of Merger Policy in Britain' in M. Bishop and J. Kay, *European Mergers and Merger Policy* (OUP, 1993).

132 A special regime is applied to newspaper mergers by ss.57–62 FTA 1973, but this lies beyond the scope of the present survey.

133 *Op. cit.* p.679.

134 15.3.4 above.

views, but who may give a green light even to a merger viewed unfavourably by the MMC. The central role of the Minister – the Secretary of State for Trade and Industry, though Michael Heseltine preferred the title of President of the Board of Trade – shows that in the UK it is perceived that merger policy is firmly located in the political arena. This contrasts with domestic Restrictive Practices law and contrasts with EC merger policy.

15.4.2.2 Referral – the Statutory Discretion

At stage one of this three–stage process, mergers, as defined under the Fair Trading Act 1973, may be referred by the Minister to the Monopolies and Mergers Commission.[135] In practice the Office of Fair Trading plays a significant part in merger control.[136] A great deal of the investigation and preparatory work is carried out by the Director General of Fair Trading and his or her officials.[137] His or her advice to the Minister is highly influential, although the politician retains the formal statutory discretion on referral. The political environment in which decisions are taken is emphasised by the shadowy input of the Mergers Panel, a committee in which the views of different governmental departments are advanced. It has no formal statutory recognition, nor are its deliberations made public, but it seems plain that political pressure is brought to bear through it and other sources when the Minister is considering the exercise of his or her discretion.

There is no obligation on firms to notify a merger. However, it is common practice for firms to clarify their position in advance as far as possible. This is commercially helpful, not least because of the possibility that firms may complete a merger only subsequently to find that the deal is investigated and must be unscrambled. The practice of 'informal notification' involves contact between firms and the Director General in which plans are put forward and reaction sought. The limits of the statutory role of the Director General means that he or she cannot supply a definitive legal response, but, given the Director General's influence, his or her comments are usually a reliable guide. The Companies Act 1989 introduced a more formal structure of pre–notification which is capable of leading to protection

---

[135] S.64.
[136] For comment by an official of the OFT see M. Howe, 'UK Merger Control: How Does the System reach decisions? A note on the Role of the Office of Fair Trading' [1990] 1 *ECLR* 3.
[137] Section 76.

from the possibility of a reference to the MMC.[138] This remains voluntary; obligatory pre–notification is not a feature of the British system. The 1989 Act also established a procedure whereby firms may give an undertaking in lieu of a reference. This type of 'plea bargaining' allows circumvention of the full formal procedure and provides flexibility in the control of mergers. The Deregulation and Contracting Out Act 1994 provides the possibility to make wider use of this strategy.[139]

It is rather important to appreciate the practical point that a reference to the MMC slows up the commercial process and costs the firms involved time and money. Firms wishing to conclude a merger will typically be desperate to avoid a reference and, indeed, they will frequently simply abandon the plan if a decision to refer is made. As a corollary, a firm which is the unwelcome target of a take–over bid will be eager for a reference to be made in order to provide it with breathing space in which to marshal its defences or at least to find a 'white knight' to act on its behalf. In view of these tactical considerations, the process whereby the Minister exercises statutory discretion under the guidance of the Director General is highly politicised and commonly characterised by high–pressure lobbying.

The fact that the Minister has a discretion, not a duty, to refer lends flexibility to the process of merger control under the Fair Trading Act 1973. This point was firmly emphasised by the House of Lords in *R v Secretary of State for Trade and Industry, ex parte Lonrho*.[140] This was an unsuccessful application by Lonrho for judicial review of a decision not to refer a merger involving, *inter alia*, the acquisition of Harrods by the Al–Fayeds. (The Fair Trading Act 1973 had previously been used to frustrate Lonrho's own attempts to obtain Harrods.[141]) In rejecting the application, their Lordships even declined to impose a duty to give reasons for non–referral.[142] The key to this decision lies in their Lordships' perception of the deliberate politicisation of merger control under the statute. Lord Keith observed that;

---

138   Inserted as ss.75A–75F Fair Trading Act. Tightened up in the Fair Trading Act (Amendment) (Merger Prenotification) Regulations 1994 No 1934.

139   S.9 of the 1994 Act. Cf 15.3.4.1 above on this technique in the area of monopoly control.

140   [1989] 2 All ER 609, [1989] 1 WLR 525.

141   The Lonrho/Fayed acrimony, of which this litigation was but a part, was settled only in October 1993.

142   For comments of the Director General see Borrie, 'The Regulation of Public and Private Power' [1989] *Public Law* 552, 557–8. Cf S. Weatherill, 'The Changing Law and Practice of UK and EEC Merger Control' (1991) 11 *Oxford JLS* 520.

'whether or not a particular commercial activity is or is not in the public interest is very much a matter of political judgment and the Act is structured to bring under direct Parliamentary scrutiny any action proposed by the Secretary of State to interfere with commercial activity which he considers to be against the public interest.'[143]

15.4.2.3 Referral – the Tebbit Guidelines

The conferral of discretion on the politician provides flexibility, but also renders the process unpredictable. A firm planning a take–over or firms planning a merger may lose confidence if the law is haphazard in application. This may deter merger activity. In so far as mergers act as beneficial means of adjusting market structure, such deterrence is harmful to the public interest. The processes of negotiation involving the Director General mentioned above serve in part to clarify the system for those subject to it. At a much more general level, Ministers have declared their hand by stating the policy that will guide them in exercising their discretion to refer. Norman Tebbit, then Secretary of State, said in 1984:

'I regard mergers policy as an important part of the Government's general policy of promoting competition within the economy in the interests of the customer and of efficiency and hence of growth and jobs. Accordingly, my policy has been and will continue to be to make references primarily on competition grounds.'

These 'Tebbit guidelines' are not binding legal rules. Moreover, it should be appreciated that references are to be made 'primarily', not exclusively, on competition grounds. This allows some leeway. However, the tenor of these guidelines is that merger law will be activated only where a deal threatens the competitive structure of the market. It will not normally be used as an instrument of social or regional policy, for example to protect a firm in one area from losing its identity through merger with a bigger national or international rival. Tebbit espoused a 'hands–off' approach by Government towards mergers. As the first sentence of the quotation shows, he perceives that competitive markets best serve the public interest, including that of the consumer.

---

143   For critical Parliamentary scrutiny of merger control in this instance and more broadly, see House of Commons Trade and Industry Committee (1989–90) HC 36 paras.118–140.

The identity of the responsible Minister in the Department of Trade and Industry changed with bewildering frequency through the 1980s and early 1990s, but policy on mergers did not. The Tebbit guidelines and their emphasis on competition were adhered to. In 1990 Peter Lilley commented that he would be particularly mistrustful of mergers involving acquisition by State–owned firms, claiming that 'State–controlled companies are not subject to the same disciplines as those in the private sector'. In so far as this was simply an application of the Tebbit competition guidelines, it was not radical; however, there was considerable speculation that Lilley was in fact aiming to halt the acquisitive activities of non–British State–owned firms.[144] Such possible discrimination attracted the attention of the European Commission and in 1991 Lilley issued a 'clarification' that no discrimination based on nationality was intended. The special concern to scrutinise mergers involving State–owned firms appears to have faded from view.

Michael Heseltine, responsible for merger policy between 1992 and 1995, preferred to avoid wide–ranging policy statements on merger policy. Although some commentators wondered initially whether Mr Heseltine might prove more interventionist than his predecessors, there was no apparent trend away from Tebbit. In fact, the general impression is that Mr Heseltine was, if anything, more laissez–faire than his predecessors. As a result of the Cabinet reshuffle that followed John Major's re–election as leader of the Conservative Party in July 1995, the responsible Minister is Ian Lang.

15.4.2.4 The Report of the Monopolies and Mergers Commission

The MMC must report within a maximum period of six months[145] and is frequently required to respond more promptly than that. Commercial certainty dictates a need for quick decisions.

The MMC is required to report on whether 'the creation of that [merger] situation operates or may be expected to operate against the public interest'.[146] It bears a statutory duty to provide reasons for its conclusion,[147] rather oddly, perhaps, given that the Minister, the formal decision maker under the statute, is under no such obligation.[148]

---

144 R. Taylor, R. Bointon, A. Collinson, 'UK Merger Control and State–controlled Companies' [1991] 4 *ECLR* 133.
145 S.70 FTA.
146 S.69(1).
147 S.72.
148 *Ex parte Lonrho* note 140 above.

The framework within which assessment of the 'public interest' is performed has the same statutory basis in merger control as in relation to monopolies. The Fair Trading Act 1973 provides that 'the Commission shall take into account all matters which appear to them in the particular circumstances to be relevant'.[149] Five matters are specifically referred to, though this is a non–exhaustive list.

The first matter on the list is 'maintaining and promoting effective competition between persons supplying goods and services in the United Kingdom...'. This conforms to the focus on merger policy as an instrument for ensuring competitive markets which informs Ministerial policy on referral to the MMC. However, the MMC is not confined to such matters. For example, the second refers to the promotion of 'the interests of consumers, purchasers and other users of goods and services in the United Kingdom in respect of the prices charged for them and in respect of their quality and the variety of goods and services supplied'. As already suggested above in relation to monopoly control,[150] this can be interpreted as no more than an expression of the consumer interest in a competitive market, but the MMC is not precluded from preferring a more interventionist view flavoured by a spirit of social justice and consumer welfare. Much hinges on the composition of individual panels, as the MMC is rather heterogeneous.

In the current political climate it may not be thought worthwhile for an MMC report to propose blockage of mergers on grounds other than their competitive implications, given that it is open to the Minister to permit a merger despite an unfavourable MMC report.[151] In fact recent developments in the MMC suggest that it is moving ever closer to the competition focus espoused by the government. Graham Odgers, who took over as Chair in 1993, has attracted political criticism for his perceived close association with government policy.[152] Sir Brian Carsberg's resignation from the post of Director General of Fair Trading in 1994, effective in 1995, appears to have been motivated, in part at least, by frustration at the unwillingness of the MMC to pursue matters that he, Carsberg, had judged in need of investigation and/or for finding criticised practices (in sectors including perfumes and compact discs) to be compatible with the public interest.[153] In 1994 and 1995 the Office of Fair Trading has seemed increasingly at odds

---

[149]   S.84(1).

[150]   15.3.4.1 above.

[151]   *Ex parte Anderson Strathclyde* n.154 below.

[152]   For criticism, S. Locke, 'A New Approach to Competition Policy' (1994) 4 *Consumer Policy Review* 159.

[153]   Cf *The Independent on Sunday*, 4 December 1994, Business p. 3.

with an MMC and a Minister both distinctly less prone to favour intervention.

15.4.2.5 The Minister's Decision

If the MMC finds that the merger will not operate against the public interest, the deal may proceed. Where, by contrast, the MMC finds that it will do so, the Minister may make an order forbidding it or, if necessary, requiring it to be unscrambled. Typically no formal order is needed: firms simply abandon their plans or devote attention to their amendment, and the situation is monitored by the Director General.

The Minister is not obliged to confirm an MMC finding that the merger will operate against the public interest, but can allow it to proceed notwithstanding an adverse report. This reinforces the point that the statute places decision making squarely in the political arena and casts the MMC in an advisory capacity. The Minister's power to go against an MMC report was confirmed by the Court of Appeal in *R v Secretary of State for Trade, ex parte Anderson Strathclyde*.[154] As observed above, this undermines the practical muscle of an interventionist MMC in a political climate favourably disposed to mergers.

The House of Commons Trade and Industry Committee has proposed institutional adjustment of merger control.[155] The functions of both MMC and OFT would be assumed by a new Competition and Mergers Authority (CMA). However the Committee does not believe that there should be any change in the basic structure of political accountability for merger control. The Minister could still overrule the CMA's view, although he or she would have to provide reasons. These proposals have not yet been accepted.

---

[154] [1983] 2 All ER 233.

[155] First Report on Takeovers and Mergers, 27 November 1991, HC (1991–92). Discussed by S. Lipworth, then Chair of the MMC, 'Developments in UK Competition Policy' (1992) 2 *Consumer Policy Review* 132.

15.4.3 European Community Merger Law[156]

15.4.3.1 The Pattern of Control

In view of the significance of mergers in the economy, it is extraordinary to realise that the Treaty of Rome failed to put in place any specialist merger control machinery. Political disagreement about the proper structure of merger policy led to this gap. In the late 1980s a burst of merger activity, driven by firms preparing for the completion of the internal market at the end of 1992, created a political environment conducive to the adoption of legislation to fill the gap. This was the Merger Regulation – more properly Regulation 4064/89[157] on the control of concentrations between undertakings. Since September 1990 mergers, or, in Community parlance, 'concentrations', have been controlled in the EC under the Merger Regulation by the Merger Task Force (MTF), a specialist unit within the European Commission's Directorate General IV. The heart of the control exercised involves an assessment of the impact of the merger on competition within the EC. This is comparable to the UK approach to merger control under the Tebbit guidelines, although institutionally the systems are far apart. The Regulation also contains an attempt to demarcate the respective jurisdictions of national and EC authorities in a more clean–cut fashion than is available under Articles 85 and 86 EC. It thus goes some way in helping business to shop at one stop only.[158]

The Regulation controls mergers or concentrations, as defined.[159] In contrast with the formal position under the Fair Trading Act in UK law,

---

156   R. Whish, *Competition Law* (Butterworths, 1993) pp. 702–29; D. Goyder, *EC Competition Law* (OUP, 1993) Ch.20; T.A. Downes and J. Ellison, *The Legal Control of Mergers in the European Communities* (Blackstone, 1991); J. Cook and C. Kerse, *EEC Merger Control*, (Sweet and Maxwell, 1991); C. Jones and Gonzalez Diaz, *The EEC Merger Regulation* (Sweet and Maxwell, 1992).

157   OJ 1989 L395/1, corrected version published OJ 1990 L257/14.

158   The Regulation provides that *only* the Commission will examine mergers with a 'Community dimension' within Art.1; *only* national authorities will examine other mergers. However this division is in part undermined by Arts. 9 and 21 Reg. where the merger has a Community dimension and by Art.22(3)–(6) where there is no Community dimension; cf C. Bright, 'The European Merger Control Regulation: Do Member States still have an independent role in Merger Control?' Part One: [1991] 4 *ECLR* 139 and Part Two [1991] 5 *ECLR* 184.

159   Art. 3(1) Reg. provides that a concentration arises where
      (a) two or more previously independent undertakings merge, or

there is under the EC Regulation an obligation to notify qualifying mergers to the Merger Task Force *in advance*. Procedures then impose tight time limits on the MTF. The officials have one month to dispose of each case ('Phase I'), although they may take a further four months where serious issues are identified ('Phase II'). In practice most deals have been scrutinised and cleared within the first month. The MTF has gained a good reputation for speed and efficiency in coping with a workload of some 50 to 75 referrals annually in the Regulation's early years.

The EC institutional pattern is distinct from that of the UK in its concentration of power in the hands of administrative officials. Political accountability is not a feature of the EC system. Judicial review of decisions by, initially, the Court of First Instance is available, but this does not amount to a rehearing of the merits of the case.

15.4.3.2 The criterion of control

The Regulation provides that:

> 'A concentration which creates or strengthens a dominant position as a result of which effective competition would be significantly impeded in the common market or in a substantial part of it shall be declared incompatible with the common market.'[160]

The emphasis of this test is on competition and as such has much in common with the UK's Tebbit guidelines.[161] Merger law in both the EC and the UK assumes that the number of rivals in a market cannot be reduced below a level which permits adequate competition. Practical experience of the Merger Task Force's handling of the Regulation is accumulating steadily.[162] The

---

(b) one or more undertakings (or one or more persons already controlling at least one undertaking) acquire, whether by purchase of securities or assets, by contract or by any other means, direct or indirect control of the whole or parts of one or more other undertakings.

[160] Art.2(3) Reg.

[161] 15.4.2.3 above.

[162] For discussion see J. Venit, 'The Merger Control Regulation: Europe Comes of Age...or Caliban's Dinner' (1990) 27 *CMLRev* 7; M. Siragusa and A. Subiotto, 'The EEC Merger Control Regulation: the Commission's Evolving Case Law' (1991) 28 *CMLRev* 877; A. Pathak, 'EEC Merger Regulation Enforcement during 1992' *ELRev* Competition Checklist 1992, CC132; M. Picat and J. Zachmann, 'Community Monitoring of Concentration Operations: Evaluation after over two years' application

impression is that few mergers will be blocked. This too accords with British practice. In the first four years of the application of the Regulation, only one merger was held incompatible with the test in the Regulation and blocked by the Commission, that contemplated by Aerospatiale Alenia, a French/Italian company, and De Havilland of Canada.[163] The merged group would have acquired a large slice of the market for short haul commuter aircraft and the Merger Task Force considered that the anti–competitive consequences took the deal beyond the realms of permissibility under the Regulation. This was confirmed in a formal Decision of the full Commission.

A small number of other mergers were permitted only after firms agreed to modify their plans.[164] In one instance the full Commission voted to clear a merger of which the Merger Task Force had disapproved.[165] In the overwhelming majority of cases, deals have been cleared, usually after the one–month 'Phase I' inquiry.

15.4.3.3 Social and Consumer Policy Under the Regulation

Although the focus of the test in Article 2 of the Regulation (above) appears to be on the competitive implications of a merger, there is a whiff of ambiguity in the Regulation. It is provided that the Commission shall take into account *inter alia* 'the interests of the intermediate and ultimate consumers, and the development of technical and economic progress provided that it is to consumers' advantage and does not form an obstacle to competition'.[166]   It cannot be completely excluded that this could be interpreted as a window through which the Commission could introduce into merger policy an element of consumer and social policy making.[167]

---

of Regulation 4064/89' [1993] 6 *ECLR* 240; A. Pathak, 'Market Definitions, "Compatibility with the Common Market" and Appeals from Commission Decisions under the Merger Regulation during 1993' *ELRev* Competition Law Checklist 1993, CC166; T.A. Downes and D. MacDougall, 'Significantly Impeding Effective Competition: Substantive Appraisal under the Merger Regulation' (1994) 19 *ELRev* 286. On evolving practice, largely from the economic perspective, D. Neven, R. Nuttall and P. Seabright, *Merger in Daylight* (CEPR, 1993).

163   OJ 1991 L334/42, [1992] 4 CMLR M2 noted by Hawkes [1992] 1 *ECLR* 34.

164   Eg *Nestle/Perrier* OJ 1992 L356/1, [1993] 4 CMLR M17.

165   *Mannesmann/Vallourec/Ilva* OJ 1994 L102/15.

166   Art. 2(1)(b) Reg.

167   Cf F. Fine, 'The Appraisal Criteria of the EC Merger Control Regulation' [1991] 4 *ECLR* 148, esp 150–151.

Sir Leon Brittan, Competition Commissioner in the early years of the Regulation, declared his view that this formulation does not deflect the Regulation from its paramount concern to secure a competitive market:[168]

> 'The technical and economic progress which a merger may bring about will certainly form part of the Commission's analysis of the reasons for a merger. However, this does not mean that such progress is a legitimate defence for a merger which creates a dominant position.'[169]

This is firmly in line with British political choices and of course Brittan himself was a member of the British government when the Tebbit guidelines were announced.[170] It remains to be seen whether this approach may alter in the hands of a Commissioner more disposed to using merger policy for objectives which are broader than securing a competitive economy in Europe. Karel van Miert, a Belgian, has held the competition portfolio since 1993, but there has been no apparent shift in policy in this area.

The only blocked merger, that between Aerospatiale Alenia and De Havilland,[171] attracted two distinct levels of criticism from commentators who would have preferred the deal cleared. Some thought the MTF's market definition unduly narrow and that therefore the power of the merger firm was rather exaggerated by the exclusion of potential competitors in neighbouring markets. This turns on an essentially technical point of economic analysis of markets. The second criticism was broader. It was said that the MTF, led by Brittan, had failed to use merger policy as an instrument of industrial policy. The deal, it was said, would have created a strong European firm capable of competing effectively in world markets and that this should have motivated support for the merger, even where there were anti–competitive implications internal to Europe. Such belief in the virtue of a policy of developing 'European Champions' appears especially firmly held in France, though much less popular in Britain or Germany.[172] In any event, the Community

---

168   Sir Leon Brittan, 'The Law and Policy of Merger Control in the EEC' (1990) 15 *ELRev* 351 and, more fully, *Competition Policy and Merger Control in the Single European Market* (Grotius, 1991). See also C. Overbury (first head of the MTF), 'First Experiences of European Merger Control' (1990) *ELRev* Competition Law Checklist 79.

169   P.35 in *Competition Policy and Merger Control in the Single European Market*, note 168 above.

170   15.4.2.3 above.

171   Note 163.

172   For discussion see J. Halverson, 'EC Merger Control: Competition Policy or Industrial Policy? Views of a US practitioner' [1992/2] *LIEI* 49.

regulatory authorities under Sir Leon Brittan declined to use the Regulation in this way and it remains a moot point whether the Regulation, as presently drafted, *could* be interpreted as an industrial policy instrument of this type. Shortly after the affair, the European Parliament adopted a resolution which proposed a revision of the Regulation to take account of industrial, social, regional and environmental factors. This has not been accepted, nor are such notions likely to find favour in the current political climate where Britain and Germany, in particular, are firmly wedded to using merger policy solely to protect competitive markets.[173]

In common with most competition law, merger law assumes that consumers stand to benefit indirectly. Explicit reference to the consumer is relatively rare and participation of consumers in decision making rarer still. However, it might be noted that in *Comité Central d'Entreprise de la SA Vittel v Commission*[174] workers in a firm affected by a merger which the Commission had cleared were considered to have standing to challenge the Decision before the European Court, although on the facts no interim measures were granted. It is possible that a consumer organisation could be sufficiently involved in a merger to have similar standing before the European Court in the event that a decision is taken which it considers contrary to the consumer interest. By analogy, the decision in *BEUC v Commission*[175] provides support for this view.[176]

15.4.4 Merger Control and the Internationalisation of Markets

As systems for the regulation of the market, competition policy in general and merger law in particular must be applied with an awareness that markets are increasingly international. Issues of market definition in an international environment confront both the UK and the EC authorities. They are of prime importance in shaping a legal response and in selecting appropriate regulatory agencies.

Assessment of the competitive implications of a merger with reference to the UK market is economically flawed where that market is European.

---

[173] The Treaty on European Union introduced a new Title XIII on Industry: Art.130 EC. The potential for developing industrial policy under this provision remains to be seen.

[174] Case T–12/93 R judgment of 6 July 1993.

[175] Note 63 above.

[176] Contra, however Case T–83/92 *Zunis Holdings SA and others v Commission* judgment of 28 October 1993; no standing was granted to shareholders in an affected firm, although it should be noted that the application was on behalf of only 0.5% of them. On appeal to the European Court, Case C–480/93.

Similarly, assessment of a merger with reference to the EC market is economically flawed where that market is international. The necessary awareness that regulation of the UK or the EC market is pointless, perhaps even damaging, where such markets lack an economically distinct identity can be identified in the recent practice of the relevant authorities. For example, in the field of merger control, Lord Young, as Secretary of State for Trade and Industry, declared in 1988 that 'Effective competition in the market is the main test, not some geographical limit'.[177] In accordance with this policy, a proposed merger between *Glynwed International and JB & S Lees*[178] was cleared even though the firms would thereby gain 64% of the UK market for hardened and tempered steel strip. The fact that the deal would yield a new British firm larger than any other British competitor was not a rational economic basis for intervention once it was established that competitors based outside the UK were capable of invading the British market. Competition would prevail despite the merger.

A parallel may be found in the Merger Task Force's decision to clear a merger between *Aerospatiale*, a French firm, and *MBB*, a German firm[179] in so far as it concerned the manufacture of civil helicopters. The product was of standardised design and there was open purchasing across borders. With European firms active in North America and vice versa, the market was held to be global. The new merged firm would acquire 50% of the EC market, but the deal was held compatible with the Regulation because, world–wide, the merged group would not be independent of competitive pressures. This should be contrasted with the finding that the *Alenia/De Havilland* merger was incompatible with the Regulation[180] since it was considered likely to obtain too much power even in a market judged to be international in scope.[181]

Nonetheless, a balanced appraisal of markets remains important. In some markets a purely national or even local assessment will remain appropriate to the application of the law. As Colin Overbury, the first Head of the Commission's Merger Task Force, has written:

> 'One of the questions raised most frequently is the approach that the Commission will take in relation to the definition of the geographic

---

[177] Speech of 10 June 1988.
[178] Cm. 781 (1989).
[179] [1992] 4 CMLR M70.
[180] Note 163 above.
[181] Cf *Vallourec* n.165 above on this point; the full Commission was more receptive to the argument that the market was open to potential competition from outside Europe than was the Merger Task Force.

market – local, national or Community–wide? There can be no standard answer to this question, except that each case must be considered on its own merits. It is important, however, that the Commission's examination is not undertaken with political or ideological preferences that markets should be European. If they are, as a question of fact, local or national markets, they must be considered to be so.'[182]

Critically, the application of British and EC competition policy depends on a realistic assessment of the scope of the market. If the market is, say, British, the impact of the deal on the British market is the appropriate basis for assessment, but if the true market is wider, the authorities should not adopt an artificially narrow perspective. It should finally be remembered that market structures are not static. Colin Overbury added that '... it would be wrong for the Commission to ignore the fact that markets in Europe are integrating rapidly...'. The same caveat applies to domestic competition authorities.

The Merger Regulation provides that the Commission may surrender its jurisdiction over mergers with a Community dimension, as defined,[183] where it is satisfied that a distinct local market exists.[184] This may be seen as a flexible arrangement which permits the Commission to choose the appropriate regulatory level with reference to any peculiarities in the market in question which render control from Brussels undesirable.[185] This power to transfer jurisdiction was exercised for the first time in *Steetley/Tarmac*.[186] Because of the high cost of transportation of the products in question, building bricks and tiles, the market was limited to parts of the UK. That was probably sufficient on its own to persuade the Commission to return the (Community–dimension) merger to the British authorities, but the case was strengthened by the existence of a second bidder for Tarmac, in respect of which any ensuing merger would have lacked a Community dimension for want of sufficient turnover. The Commission was pragmatically prepared to accept that, in such circumstances, the two deals should be regulated by a single authority. In practice the power to refer mergers back to national authorities has been little used. The Commission has rejected requests for a reference back where it is of the view that the market is truly cross–border. One might expect this reluctance to become more pronounced as the

---

182   Note 168 above, 81–82.
183   Art.1 Reg., n.158 above.
184   Art.9 Reg., note 158 above.
185   In this vein, Overbury note 168 above.
186   OJ 1992 C50/25, [11992] 4 CMLR 337.

integrative process in Europe accelerates.[187] The Commission seems to anticipate that market integration will lead to a gradual seepage of regulatory power into its hands at the expense of national authorities. In fact, it had hoped that, as a result of a 1993 review, the 'Community dimension' threshold figures would be lowered and its own jurisdiction consequently increased. However, with no consensus among the Member States, the figures remain unaltered.[188]

15.5 THE PURSUIT OF MARKET INTEGRATION IN EC LAW

The differences between EC and UK competition law are in several respects more striking than the similarities. This is especially marked at the institutional level, where UK competition policy suffers from fragmentation. The Director General of Fair Trading and the OFT, the MMC, the Secretary of State for Trade and Industry and the Restrictive Practices Court combine to produce an incoherent pattern. Discrete reform proposals have stalled in the areas of the law of restrictive practices, monopolies and mergers. Perhaps this is for the good. To reform one area alone would leave in place the basic problem of lack of coherence across the whole spread of competition policy. The ideal may lie in an overall restructuring of UK policy directed at institutional streamlining and, inter alia, a more explicit input of the consumer interest.

Reform of UK law along the lines of the EC model is mooted in some, but not all, areas. The use of the EC model is desirable and should help in the construction of a coherent system.[189] The EC pattern has advantages, especially in the area of restrictive practices law and in relation to the general structure of enforcement powers and private rights. Moreover, alignment ought to cut compliance costs for business in the medium– and long–term.

However, it seems probable that the short–term costs incurred in effecting such radical changes militate against a commitment to reform. There appears to be little impetus in Government. One of several factors contributing to Sir Brian Carsberg's decision to resign the post of Director General of Fair Trading in 1994 appears to have been frustration at the absence of political commitment to renovate UK competition policy. Carsberg subsequently argued publicly in favour of the creation of a unitary competition authority equipped with powers modelled on the EC's prohibitive

---

[187] Cf Overbury n.168 above.

[188] COM (93) 385.

[189] Cf comment by Lever n.3 above; J. Pratt, 'Changes in UK Competition Law: a Wasted Opportunity' [1994] 2 *ECLR* 89.

system combined with the availability of heavy fines.[190] In what was widely regarded as a riposte to Carsberg, Graham Odgers, Chair of the MMC, proclaimed his view of the basic soundness of the system.[191] Although Odgers favoured some reform (in the area of restrictive practices and enhanced powers of the OFT), he argued in favour of the maintenance of the tripartite arrangements involving the OFT, the MMC and the Secretary of State. A report on competition policy prepared by the House of Commons Select Committee on Trade and Industry will be published during 1995. However, even while we patiently await the possibility of reform, burgeoning administrative co–operation has a role to play in avoiding wide divergence between UK and EC practice. It is also important to remember that one would expect UK and EC law frequently to reach the same result in assessing the lawfulness of a particular deal or practice, even though their institutional routes are quite distinct.

However, there is a key element in EC competition policy which distinguishes it from the majority of national regimes. This is the *objective of market integration*. The EC is founded on the pursuit of market integration between its States, which should invigorate competition and stimulate consumer choice. The process is well advanced but, for all the advantages of the post–1992 market, not yet complete. The European Court itself observed in *Metro v Commission*[192] that among the Treaty's objectives is 'the creation of a single market achieving conditions similar to those of a domestic market'. Competition policy has its part to play.[193] Commercial practices liable to obstruct the process of market integration are hostile to the core aims of the EC and for decades have been consistently condemned under the competition rules. A cartel which attempts to divide up national territories among its members violates Article 85 and exposes itself to the likelihood of heavy fines. Firms ought to compete and they ought to compete Community–wide, irrespective of national borders. Similarly a firm which uses dominant economic power to achieve segregation of the market along national lines infringes Article 86. Accordingly EC competition policy shares with typical national systems the objective of regulating the competitive process but, additionally, it pursues the dynamic objective of securing integration between long–isolated national markets.

A practical example of how the objective of market integration may induce EC competition policy to adopt a more interventionist approach to

---

190   Cf 'Carsberg seeks tougher line on competition', *The Independent*, 23 February 1995.
191   Cf 'The future of competition policy' *Financial Times*, 18 May 1995.
192   Case 26/76 [1977] ECR 1875, 1904.
193   C–D. Ehlermann, 'The Contribution of EC Competition Policy to the Single Market' (1992) 29 *CMLRev* 257.

private contractual freedom than would be necessary in a fully integrated market was the ground–breaking decision of the European Court thirty years ago in *Consten and Grundig v Commission.*[194]

Under the agreement, Consten undertook to act as the French distributor for Grundig's German–made electrical products. Consten was allowed to register Grundig's trademark under French law. Consten also undertook not to deal in competing brands of electrical products. Grundig agreed to supply Consten and no one else in France. Grundig also agreed that it would take steps to prevent its appointed dealers in other Member States from reselling Grundig products in France or to a French customer. The plan was designed to confer on Consten exclusive control over the supply of Grundig's products in France.

If one assumes that competition policy is designed to maintain consumer choice within a competitive environment, then it is possible to argue that this deal, as described, should have been permitted, even encouraged. True, Consten was the only supplier of Grundig goods to French consumers but, assuming that other brands of electrical goods were readily available in France, consumer choice would have been enhanced by the appearance of a German–made product on the French market. Consten could not exploit consumers because of their obvious ability to buy a different brand. Yet the EC Commission ruled this deal incompatible with Article 85. The Court agreed and even today this remains the state of EC law. The objection was directed at the perpetuation of existing national boundaries consequent on the deal. Interbrand competition between suppliers of electrical goods might indeed have been sufficient to protect the French consumer in the context of this particular deal. However the Community authorities took a broader view, insisted on the importance of maintaining cross–border trade even in goods of the same brand. They were not prepared to accept the complete isolation of the French market for Grundig goods from the rest of the territory of the Community. In this way, the policy of market integration informed the development of competition policy.

The simple conferral of exclusivity on Consten would have been permitted. Indeed Consten needed the inducement of exclusivity to lure it to take on the deal in the first place. Otherwise, it might have made an investment in raising consumer awareness of Grundig products through advertising, only to see a free–riding supplier reap profits without having incurred corresponding expense. However, the parties could not suppress traders based outside France from supplying French customers – 'parallel trade'.

---

[194] Cases 56 and 58/64 [1966] ECR 299, [1966] CMLR 418.

Since this seminal decision, the willingness of the EC's competition authorities to intervene in distribution deals in apparently competitive markets has ebbed and flowed. Exclusive dealing agreements are now measured against relevant Block Exemption Regulations.[195] However the determination to abolish absolute territorial protection has remained unwavering. The Court is a firm supporter of parallel trade as the motor of market integration. For the consumer, the perception is that choice is best guaranteed in an integrated market. This long–term goal can be achieved only through medium–term legal intervention which insists on the availability to the consumer of not simply inter–brand competition, but also cross–border inter–brand competition.[196]

15.6 COMPETITION POLICY AND THE CONSUMER INTEREST REASSERTED

Competition policy suffers from an obscurity born of the unavoidable imprecision of economic analysis and the thoroughly avoidable confusion inflicted by institutional fragmentation. In the UK, ineffective powers of enforcement act as an additional major obstacle to effective policy implementation. For all these shortcomings, competition policy is a significant element in shaping the operation of the market in the consumer interest. Competition policy is, admittedly, an indirect expression of consumer policy. However, the deterrence of anti–competitive cartels, the control of abusive practices by monopolists and the supervision of firms proposing to merge are all elements in promoting free and fair market structures. The consumer stands to benefit from effective implementation of such policies.

The next Chapter returns to matters that are more explicitly presented by the law in the language of consumer policy. The linking thread is supplied by the activities of the Office of Fair Trading.

---

[195] On such Regs., 15.2.4.3 above. In depth on the detail of the law, Bellamy and Child n.49 above.

[196] Once the long–term goal of integration is achieved, it may be possible to consider readjusting the policy thrust of EC competition policy. See discussion by Ehlermann, n.193 above; T. Frazer, 'Competition Law after 1992: the Next Step', (1990) 53 *MLR* 609.

16 Office of Fair Trading

16.1 BACKGROUND

In the last chapter we considered the role of the Office of Fair Trading as a competition authority; a role which concerns, perhaps sometimes indirectly, consumer affairs. In this chapter we consider its more expressly consumer affairs functions. As a national agency, it should be distinguished from local trading standards officers, although there is clearly a need for co–ordination between national and local levels and debate about the appropriate allocation or sharing of powers between the two levels.[1] The Office of Fair Trading should also be distinguished from the National Consumer Council which is also a national body, but one which has the avowed objective of representing the consumer interest, particularly vulnerable consumers. In contrast to the partisan brief of the National Consumer Council, the Office of Fair Trading was created 'to remove the regulation of competition and consumer policy from the political arena, permitting continuity and expertise in the development of consumer policy'.[2] Whether an area so closely connected to the regulation of the marketplace can be depoliticised and deideologised in this way is a matter for debate.

The post of Director General of Fair Trading (hereafter Director General) was created following reform to the role of the Registrar of Restrictive Trading Agreements, whose functions the Director General took on. The Director General's fair trading responsibilities were added to give the reforms more consumer appeal and to make amends for the abolition of the Consumer Council in 1970.[3] The Fair Trading Act 1973, which established the office of Director General, makes no mention of an Office of Fair

---

1   See Chapter 14.
2   I. Ramsay, *Consumer Protection*, (Weidenfeld and Nicolson, 1989) at p. 262. See generally I. Ramsay 'The Office of Fair Trading: Policing the Consumer Market–Place' in *Regulation and Public Law*, R. Baldwin and C. McCrudden (eds), (Weidenfeld & Nicolson, 1987).
3   Apparently the Consumer Council was axed because the Conservative Government opposed the use of public money for functions which could be performed by private enterprise concerns using private money. It noted, for instance, the development of voluntary consumer organisations. In his final Report, the Chairman of the Consumer Council noted that 'Some day someone will have to invent a new, publicly financed body to promote and protect the consumer's interests'. He clearly did not have to wait long to be proven right.

Trading, but it does permit him to appoint staff and these in fact comprise the Office of Fair Trading. It was thought that the Director General would bring in outside experts on a regular basis, but pressure from civil service unions has meant that the Office is almost entirely staffed by career civil servants. Interestingly, their distance from direct political control may isolate them to some extent from political fashions, as is perhaps illustrated by their constructive response to the deregulation initiative in the form of their report *Consumer Credit Deregulation.*[4]

The notion of an agency combining both consumer protection and competition functions is one borrowed from the US Federal Trade Commission. The combination of these functions is not unproblematic. The competition functions can easily be seen as more high profile and glamorous than the more humdrum consumer protection functions. This can lead to energy, resources and the best qualified staff being diverted away from the agency's consumer protection functions. More fundamentally, the competition philosophy can influence the consumer protection function so that remedying market failure is viewed as – if not the sole – then at least the most significant objective of consumer protection. Certainly the Office's brief does not see consumer protection as having redistributive functions.

There have been three Director Generals – Sir John Methven, Sir Gordon Borrie and Sir Bryan Carsberg. Sir Gordon Borrie held the post for a substantial portion of the Office's existence. Whilst he was in charge, consumer protection was given a fairly high profile and those who knew of his past work as a professor of commercial law, specialising in consumer protection matters, felt confident that the consumer interest would not be neglected. His successor, Sir Bryan Carsberg, had a different background, having been formerly Director General of OFTEL, the telecommunications regulator. His experience in the competition regulation field and his public commitment to competition and deregulation placed some (perhaps unfounded) fears in the minds of consumer activists about the strength of the Office's continued commitment to consumer protection. In the event he apparently became disillusioned with the Monopoly and Mergers Commission's lack of sympathy for matters he referred to them and has announced his resignation, but at the time of writing no successor has been appointed.

Apart from the US, the other overseas experience which inspired the concept of the Office of Fair Trading was that of the Scandinavian Consumer Ombudsman. The Scandinavian experience has encouraged reliance on 'soft law', ie non–legally binding law, as a method of consumer protection. We shall see that there is an increased emphasis placed by the Office of Fair Trading on the role of soft law, especially the development of

---

4   See Chapters 7 and 11.

trade association codes of practice. Although not doubting that there are instances when soft law is useful and even essential, some reservations might be made as to its appropriateness to all legal cultures. In Scandinavia soft law is used to clarify and amplify more broadly–framed legal duties. In the UK, soft law often stands alone, outside the area of advertising where the Director General has injunctive powers to back up self regulation and apart from the general regulatory or licensing controls the Director General has available to him.

In this chapter some of the functions of the Office of Fair Trading will be discussed, namely (i) its powers to propose legislative changes, (ii) its role in promoting codes of practice and (iii) its controls over rogue traders. Finally, the proposal that the Office should have increased powers to deal with trading malpractices will be discussed. To have a complete picture of its functions, the reader ought also to consult the material on the Office's competition function,[5] its role as a licensing authority[6] and its powers to seek injunctions against misleading advertising[7] and unfair terms.[8] It should also be mentioned that s.2, Fair Trading Act 1973 places a general function on the Director General to keep under review and to receive and collate evidence on commercial activities which affect consumers; moreover it allows him to recommend reforms to the Secretary of State. As we shall see, the rule-making powers under Part II have become moribund, so that this ability to suggest reforms directly to the Secretary of State has taken on an increased significance.[9] The Office of Fair Trading undertakes a certain amount of empirical research and also publishes some very useful discussion papers on problem areas of law and practice, many of which are referred to at appropriate points in this book. The Office of Fair Trading also has a consumer information function, being authorised to produce materials giving information and advice to consumers.[10] In fact the Office produces a wide range of booklets, many of them explaining and promoting the codes of practice it recognises in different industry sectors. The Office also publishes a useful free quarterly magazine entitled *Fair Trading*, which informs the

---

5   See Chapter 15.

6   See 11.1.

7   See 10.6.

8   See 9.8

9   For instance, anticipated difficulties in using the Part II procedure caused the Director General to make a recommendation directly to the Secretary of State which led to the Price Marking (Bargain Offers) Order 1979, S.I. 1979/364.

10   S.124, Fair Trading Act 1973.

readers of the Office's activities in relation to consumer protection and competition policy.[11]

The Director General clearly has a wide range of powers. It should be noted, however, that primary enforcement is left to local officials, that the Office has no powers to seek damages for individual consumers and no powers to act swiftly to ban practices or rogue traders. The Office's role is viewed mainly as a 'long stop' control on rogue traders combined with a monitoring and law reform function. In the words of a Director General, he is required to be 'a *regulator* of business, a *monitor* of markets and laws, a *proposer* of policies, an *educator* of the public and a *promoter* of high trading standards.'[12]

Some political science theorists suggest that regulatory agencies typically have a life cycle. In their youthful stage they are vigorous and lively and eager to solve the problems or promote the interest of the groups they were established to oversee. Over time they become tired and their enthusiasm wanes as they settle into a cosy relationship with (some might suggest they become captured by) those they were created to regulate. Superficially this might appear to represent the experience of the Office of Fair Trading. In its early years it sought legislative solutions to problems, whereas in recent times it has preferred to allow business to exercise self-regulation. It may, however, be too simple to claim that the Office has been captured by industry. First, one naturally expects an agency to be most energetic in its first years as it deals with the main problems in its field. Second, the agency cannot act in isolation from the current political environment, in which Government now sets its face against regulatory solutions. Third, the touchstone will not be whether the Office supports self-regulation, but rather what it does if, and when, that approach fails. The self-regulation movement is in too early a stage of development to draw any answers to this final question.

16.2   RULE–MAKING UNDER PART II OF THE FAIR TRADING ACT 1973[13]

When the Fair Trading Bill was progressing through Parliament, pyramid-selling practices were causing such concern that special provisions were

---

[11]   It was previously known as *Bee Line* and dealt exclusively with consumer protection matters.

[12]   *Annual Report of the Director General of Fair Trading 1986*, at p. 10.

[13]   Ss.13–33, Fair Trading Act 1973.

included in the Act to deal with this problem.[14] Recognising the need for powers to react to other unfair trading practices which might arise in the future, Part II of the Act introduced a scheme whereby the Director General could propose amendments to the law where the consumer's economic interests were threatened. This is to be contrasted with Part III of the Act which seeks to control individual rogue traders, not unfair practices in general. Unfortunately the Part II procedure has been widely viewed as a failure. One former Director General has described it as 'an example of a bold idea smothered by an excess of nervous caution so that the resulting provisions have inevitably been a disappointment'.[15]

16.2.1 Reasons for Failure

16.2.1.1 Legal Powers Too Narrow

The reasons for this failure lie both in the formulation of the rule making powers and the structures put in place. The Director General's powers to invoke the rule making procedure are limited, relating only to 'consumer trade practices' as defined in s.13. Thus a former Director General has noted that he would have liked to use the powers to deal with the problem of property misdescriptions, but the term 'consumer trade practice' covered goods and services, but not houses.

The consumer trade practice in question must be shown to mislead or confuse consumers, subject them to undue pressure or cause the transaction to be so adverse as to be inequitable.[16] A fundamental flaw of the regulatory scheme was the requirement that the Director General had to show that the practice 'may adversely affect the economic interests of consumers in the United Kingdom'.[17] A minor objection is the limitation to economic interests – are health and safety matters not deserving of similar rule making powers?[18] More significant is the criticism that there is no standard against which to judge the consumer's economic interest, since the legislation was not based on, nor had Government established, a clear economic theory for

---

14 Ss.118–122 Fair Trading Act 1973 and Pyramid Selling Schemes Regulations 1989 S.I. 1989/2195 (as amended).
15 G. Borrie, *The Development of Consumer Law and Policy*, (Stevens, 1984) at p. 127.
16 S.17, Fair Trading Act 1973.
17 S.19(1), Fair Trading Act 1973.
18 See R. Cranston, *Consumers and the Law*, (Weidenfeld and Nicolson, 1984) at p. 338.

consumer protection.[19] This threshold test could have been treated as either (i) a fairly formal easily establishable requirement or (ii) a demanding standard, with the Office of Fair Trading being given the resources to establish the case for intervention. The fact that it was treated as a demanding standard, but without the resources being available to satisfy demands for statistical proof, meant that Part II became a quagmire rather than a fast route to legislative change. The Office of Fair Trading diverted its limited resources to other techniques of improving trading standards, for example influencing trade associations to develop codes of practice, using licensing powers, Part III orders and lobbying Government directly for legislative intervention.

16.2.1.2 Procedure Too Restrictive

The process by which Part II orders could be made involved the Director General referring a consumer trade practice, together with his proposal for an Order to a Consumer Protection Advisory Committee which comprised between ten and fifteen members appointed by the Secretary of State. The Committee could agree to the proposal, agree to it subject to modification or reject it. If rejected, no action could be taken; in other cases, the Secretary of State could choose to legislate. However, a fundamental weakness was that, having decided to act, the Secretary of State's options were restricted to choosing between the Director General's order and that proposed by the Committee. He had no room to negotiate or amend; if he was not prepared to accept either version, the process would have to be recommenced by the Director General making a fresh referral.

The Committee was intended to perform the function of a jury on proposals made by the Director General. However, it demanded too much evidence of the need for legislation for the procedure to function effectively. The lesson of what happened in practice indicates the need to make future procedures simpler so that reforms can be speedily implemented.[20] This does not mean that law–making procedures should not allow opportunities for consultation. The problem with the Part II procedure was that the reference to the Committee simply added an additional layer of consultation. For

---

19 See *Ramsay, op. cit.,* at p. 281 who says 'All it had, perhaps, was a muted "exploitation theory"'.

20 Ironically this is a lesson which appears to have been (too) well learnt when it comes to the powers to deregulate! See Deregulation and Contracting Out Act 1994 which allows consumer protection measures to be removed by ministerial order. Thus instead of merely simplifying the law–making process many of the usual safeguards have been swept away.

example, although the Committee had to consider representations by interested parties and normally permit such persons oral hearings, civil servants nevertheless felt they could not adequately advise the Secretary of State unless they undertook their own consultations to be 'in touch' with the views of interested parties.[21]

In part the failure of the Part II procedure should be laid at the feet of those who implemented the legislation as much as at those who drafted it. One certainly gains the impression that the Consumer Protection Advisory Committee was rather pedantic in the four reports it issued.[22] This might be partly explained by the fact that the resulting legislation had to create a criminal offence, and so obviously great care had to be taken. The criminal law can be a fairly blunt instrument of consumer protection and the caution of the legal system in applying criminal sanctions often frustrates the aim of such legislation, which, essentially, is not to impose penal sanctions but rather to raise the standard of business conduct. Rather bizarrely Governments have admitted the need to support contract formation by the use of criminal law, such as trade descriptions legislation, but have been reluctant to provide criminal sanctions for breach of contract.[23] The ability to legislate for civil or administrative sanctions might have been more appropriate in some contexts and have made the legislation easier to enact.

16.2.2 Results Under Part II

The first three referrals resulted in Orders being made. The first reference concerned (i) the continued use of notices which restricted consumer rights in a way not permitted by the Supply of Goods (Implied Terms) Act 1973 and (ii) guarantees which did not refer to consumers' inalienable rights. The use of such notices or the failure to mention that guarantees do not affect a customer's statutory rights were made a criminal offence by the Consumer Transactions (Restrictions on Statements) Order 1976.[24] The failings of such specific interventions are shown up by the anomaly that the Order does not apply to the wider range of terms made void by the Unfair Contract Terms Act 1977. It is interesting to note that the Director General preferred to tackle this new problem by voluntary persuasion and the use of his other

---

[21] See *Ramsay, op. cit.,* at p. 279.

[22] *Rights of Consumers* (HC 6, 1974), *Prepayment for Goods* (HC 285, 1976), *Disguised Business Sales* (HC 355, 1976) and *VAT – Exclusive Prices* (HC 416, 1977).

[23] See the comments of John Frazer, Consumer Affairs Minister on the mail order prepayments referral: 30 July, 1976 HC Vol 916 Col 1172.

[24] S.I. 1976/1813.

regulatory powers, such as his licensing powers, rather than invoke the Part II procedure again.[25]

The second reference concerned mail order suppliers (i) who advertised without disclosing their name or address, for example by using a P.O. Box, and (ii) who took pre-payments without undertaking to return the money if goods were not supplied within a reasonable time. The resulting Mail Order Transactions (Information) Order 1976[26] only dealt with the first of these problems. The Director General returned to the second issue in a Consultation Paper in 1979,[27] but opposition meant he had to abandon legislative change and rely on codes of practice.[28]

The third reference resulted in the Business Advertisements (Disclosure) Order 1977,[29] which made it an offence for a trader to advertise goods for sale to the public without making it reasonably obvious that such goods were being sold in the course of a business.

The fourth and final reference concerned businesses advertising prices without including VAT. No order resulted from this reference. The Price Marking (Food and Drink on Premises) Order 1979[30] dealt with the problem in a restricted sector and now the matter has been dealt with in the Code of Practice for Traders on Price Indications issued under s.25, Consumer Protection Act 1979.

The Director General has thus abandoned the Part II procedures in favour of direct lobbying of Government and the use of his other powers. In 1982 the Government announced it would not be reappointing members to the Committee until such time as a reference was made. One can speculate with some certainty that none will be made. Thus this section might be viewed as of historic interest only, and serve as a guide of how not to regulate for consumer protection. That may, however, be too severe a judgement. Even though the process was slow, the Director General noted that the fact that a reference was made at all generated publicity and debate about the relevant problem which caused some voluntary changes in practice.[31] Also the references may have had an important symbolic role through which the Office of Fair Trading gained the respect of consumers

---

25 See G. Vaughan–Davies, 'Void Terms in Consumer Contracts: Should Their Use be a Criminal Offence?' (1983) 88, 30 *LSGaz* 1978–9.

26 S.I. 1976/1812.

27 See R. Cranston, *op. cit.* at p. 340.

28 The Association of Mail Order Publishers Code of Practice states that goods should normally be despatched with 28 days of the receipt of an order; if they are not, an offer must be made to refund any pre-payment.

29 S.I. 1977/1918.

30 S.I. 1979/361.

31 *Annual Report of the Director General of Fair Trading 1975* at p. 9.

and industry. Now that the Office is a mature institution, it is perhaps difficult to imagine it as a fledgling body seeking a role for itself. It could easily have been viewed as little more than a weak monitoring body. The fact it could propose changes in the law seems to have forced industry to realise it was dealing with a regulator with teeth. Having gained its feet, it perhaps does not need the Part II procedure so much for it can lobby Government directly for reforms and use its other powers (such as licensing powers, powers under restrictive practices legislation and its role in encouraging the development of codes of practice) to promote business standards. Yet one suspects consumer protection would be well served if the Office retained some device to pressure Government to act, or at least publicly decline to act, with regard to consumer problems. It has also been suggested that, once the threat of legislation was removed, it became more difficult for the Director General to persuade trade associations to adopt rigorous codes of practice.

16.3 CODES OF PRACTICE

S.124(3), Fair Trading Act 1973 imposes a duty on the Director General 'to encourage associations to prepare and to disseminate to their members, codes of practice for guidance in safeguarding and promoting the interests of consumers in the United Kingdom'. This provision was very much a legislative afterthought, being introduced during the passage of the Bill. In hindsight, this is ironic for the development of codes of practice has been one of the major contributions of the Office of Fair Trading.[32] The explanation for the emphasis placed by the Office on codes of practice as a means of consumer protection has traditionally been seen as the failure of the Part II order–making procedure, which caused the Office to invest its resources in voluntary codes of practice. However, this is not the whole picture for as early as 1976, when Part II orders still had some life in them, the Director General said:

> 'I believe that proposals to change the law should be made only when absolutely necessary because I have increasingly realised that extension of the law is no automatic panacea for consumer problems. I have always

---

[32] One leading consumer law textbook describes the codes of practice 'as the most significant contribution which the Fair Trading Act has made to the protection of individual consumers' (R. Lowe and G. Woodroffe, *Consumer Law and Practice* 3rd ed. (Sweet & Maxwell, 1991), but this may be overstating the point given the doubts of some officials within the Office of Fair Trading about the value of codes to consumers: see *Ramsay, op. cit.* at p. 287.

considered one of my most important functions is the duty to encourage voluntary codes of practice.'[33]

16.3.1 The Extent of Coverage by Codes of Practice

The general debate about the value of codes of practice is analysed elsewhere.[34] What is clear is that self–regulation has become a distinctive feature of UK consumer protection law. Twenty–eight codes have so far been promulgated by trade associations and endorsed by the Office of Fair Trading; self–regulation also plays an important role in other areas, notably in relation to advertising.[35] With some legitimacy the British Government can claim to have exported this soft law approach to Europe where an increasing number of measures are framed in terms of non–binding recommendations or else foresee voluntary standards as a means of implementing legislation.

The codes sponsored by the Office of Fair Trading cover a wide variety of sectors including many of those which have given rise to high levels of consumer complaints. Thus sectors covered include holidays, double glazing, motor vehicles, footwear, consumer credit, photography and funerals. In addition to codes covering specific products or service sectors, there are also others governing mail order and other forms of distant selling. The first code issued in 1974 was the Association of Manufacturers of Domestic Electrical Appliances' *Principles for Domestic Electric Appliance Servicing*. Many of the codes were passed in the 1970's when the Office was in its youthful and vigorous stage and was keen to solve the more obvious problems. Clearly codes could not continue to be produced at the same rate year after year. However, Sir Gordon Borrie, the former Director General has noted that, paradoxically as the political climate became less favourable to consumer legislation, so too it became more difficult to negotiate codes of practice.[36] This indicates that perhaps there is some credence in the cynic's viewpoint that voluntary codes are frequently a means of 'buying–off' regulatory control.

---

33   *Annual Report of the Director General of Fair Trading 1975* at pp. 9–10.

34   See 1.8.4. To summarise, codes are seen either (i) as a flexible, easily amendable tool by which industry can be encouraged to regulate beyond the limits of the existing law and about matters which are difficult to codify in legal rules, or (ii) as a second–best solution which gives industry control over what standards are set, but does little to secure the legal position of the consumer.

35   See 10.6.

36   See *Ramsay, op. cit.* at p. 287.

16.3.2 Regulating the Content of Codes of Practice

One lever which the Director General retains over the content of codes of practice is provided for by the Restrictive Trade Practices Act 1976 which equates such agreements with those registerable with the Director General. If the Director General is not happy with the form of the code, he can threaten to refer the agreement to the Restrictive Practices Court for a determination that it is against the public interest and hence void.[37]

From the start the Director General realised that:

> 'Codes, to be effective, must be carefully constructed and precise. General expressions of goodwill towards the customer, or declarations of good intent, are not nearly enough. Once a code has been negotiated and publicised it cannot stop there. It must be kept up to date in the light of changing expectations and events, and it must be monitored to see if it is working effectively.'[38]

There is an obvious danger that once an agency begins negotiating with industry, it will be captured and the industry will be able to imbue its values into the officials. In their study of codes of practice, published in 1980, Pickering and Cousins were unable to ascertain whether the capture theory applied to the Office of Fair Trading and its development of codes of practice. Whilst some traders argued that the process had helped foster a greater understanding of each other's viewpoints, another admitted that 'the trade quickly learned how to handle officials.'[39] In 1991 the Office of Fair Trading adopted a new approach to the development of codes:[40] instead of negotiating their detailed wording, the Office would instead endorse codes which met a series of 'best practice' criteria. These required:

(i)   the trade association to have a significant influence on the sector;[41]
(ii) compliance with the code to be mandatory for members;
(iii) consultation during the preparation of the code with consumer organisations and enforcement bodies and with the Office of Fair Trading on competition aspects;

---

[37] See 15.2.
[38] *Annual Report of the Director General of Fair Trading 1975* at p. 10.
[39] J.F. Pickering and D.C. Cousins, *The Economic Implications of Codes of Practice*, (UMIST, 1980).
[40] *Bee Line* No 91/1, pp. 3 and 24–25.
[41] In practice the influence of trade associations varies greatly, with some industries being fragmented into several trade associations.

(iv) the code to give consumers genuine benefits above legal requirements, to set high standards and remove undesirable practices;

(v) information to be provided to consumers, publicity to be given for the code and those who comply with it and copies of the code to be made available;

(vi) adequate complaints–handling machinery, a conciliation service and a low–cost independent arbitration scheme;

(vii) monitoring, with annual reports; and

(viii) provision for penalties and mechanisms to ensure that judgments can be enforced against defaulting members.

16.3.3 Enforceability of Codes of Practice

The enforceability of codes of practice is a major problem. In some sectors, codes of practice, such as the ABTA code for the travel industry, have such a high status that membership of the trade association is viewed by many in the industry as essential for trading. In these circumstances expulsion from the association is a real threat, helping to ensure that members adhere to the code and abide by any penalties imposed for breaching it. Other codes are less well known, and even if trade associations can rely on a contract with its members to enforce a particular penalty, this may be a rather Pyrrhic victory since the member can simply leave the trade association. One aspect of the Director General's proposals for a general duty to trade fairly, discussed below, was the extension of the standards set in the codes to non–members.[42]

It is a moot point whether consumers can enforce provisions in a code of practice. For consumers to be able to rely on the code, it must have been incorporated into the consumer's contract. Traditionally the courts have been reluctant to imply terms into consumer contracts, only doing so on a 'business efficacy' standard; they still continue to demand that the term be necessary to make the contract work.[43] This approach rejected the view of Lord Denning that the courts should be free to imply terms to make the contract reasonable.[44] However, Lord Denning returned to the point by arguing, with some success, that in common contractual settings, the law can define obligations which are reasonable in the common run of cases.[45]

---

[42] Sir Gordon Borrie, a former Director General, has commented that the Motor Agents Association stressed many times the unfairness of imposing higher standards on members than non–members: *The Development of Consumer Law and Policy, op.cit.*, at p. 76.

[43] *Liverpool City Council v Irwin* [1976] 2 All ER 39.

[44] *Liverpool City Council v Irwin* [1975] 3 All ER 658.

[45] See, for instance, *Shell UK Ltd v Lostock Garages Ltd* [1977] 1 All ER 481.

Optimistically, it might be possible to argue that when members of trade associations contract with consumers, the terms of any relevant codes of practice would be implied as part of the normal incidents associated with that type of contract. It might even be possible to argue that some of the standards, if not the redress mechanisms, could be viewed as the normal incidents of contracts with non–members. It would be a useful clarification if the law were amended to make it clear that the code of practice forms a term of any contract between a consumer and member of a trade association.

The criminal law may be of some assistance. In *Re VG Vehicles (Telford) Ltd*[46] a motor dealer was found to have breached s.14, Trade Descriptions Act 1968 for falsely claiming that he complied with the Motor Industry Code of Practice. Breaches of codes of practice can also be taken into account by the Director General when exercising his licensing function under the Consumer Credit Act 1974. However, unless the code is incorporated as a contract term, then breach cannot be used as a ground for acting against a rogue trader under Part III of the Fair Trading Act 1973, since that requires a breach of law to have been committed. Nevertheless, the requirement that a trader comply with codes of practice has been made a clause of assurances given by traders under Part III.[47]

16.4 PART III, FAIR TRADING ACT 1973[48]

Part II, Fair Trading Act 1973 and codes of practice both seek to promote general business standards. By contrast Part III, Fair Trading Act 1973 provides a mechanism by which the Director General[49] can seek assurances from individual rogue traders or as a last resort (where a trader has persisted in a course of conduct which is unfair and detrimental to consumers) go to court to obtain an undertaking or order.[50] The rationale for such a power is

---

[46] (1981) 89 *ITSA Monthly Review* 91.

[47] *Annual Report of the Director General of Fair Trading 1980* at p. 73.

[48] Ss.34–42, Fair Trading Act 1973.

[49] Local authority trading standards officers sometimes believe that they have greater information and expertise to use such powers. The Director General in his 1982 Annual Report seemed keen to hold on to his exclusive power in this area, believing this would allow for the 'consistent application of principle'. On the other hand more recently in his proposals for a general duty to trade fairly and to reform part III (see 16.5), he seemed to be arguing for a greater role for local enforcement authorities. This was resisted by industry which feared inconsistent application of laws.

[50] This is a development out of the Attorney General's power to seek an injunction in the civil courts to prevent the commission of further offences by those flouting the law: see *Attorney General v Harris* [1960] 3 All ER 207.

that few consumers bring civil cases and that even the occasional civil or criminal sanction may not deter traders who find it more rewarding to continue the unfair practice. There is no provision for compensation to be sought under this procedure; instead as one Director General has stated, the aim of the provisions is 'not to punish, but rather to bring about, whenever possible, improvements in trading standards'.[51] Ison has criticised this function, arguing that 'it is no deterrent against a predatory course of trade to show that what happens to the trader concerned at the end of the line is that he is to stop'.[52]

In a 1983 report, the Director General published the following results of a study of 120 businesses which had given 273 assurances:

(i)   the traders responsible for 100 assurances had subsequently traded satisfactorily,
(ii)   those responsible for 145 assurances had ceased to trade, and
(iii) with respect to 28 assurances further court action by the Office of Fair Trading had been required.[53]

This seems to suggest three categories of traders: those who can be educated by Part III to improve their standards, those for whom Part III proceedings are the end of the line and who simply exit the market, and the rump of disreputable traders who need court action. Thus, ironically, Part III may fulfil both reformist and deterrent functions and thereby satisfy both the Director General and those who take Ison's more hawkish stance.

The Director General's powers arise when persons carrying on a business persist in a course of conduct which is both detrimental to the economic, health, safety or other interests of consumers in the UK and is unfair to consumers according to the Act's criteria.[54] These powers are wider than those of Part II since they extend protection beyond economic interests. However, being limited to protecting against conduct which is detrimental to consumers in the UK poses some problems in the European context. If firms trading in Britain use unfair trade practices, but direct them only against consumers in other Member States, then the Director General has no powers

---

51   *Annual Report of the Director General of Fair Trading 1982* at p. 10: this approach was judicially approved by Donaldson LJ in *R v Director General of Fair Trading, ex parte F.H.Taylor & Co Ltd* (1981) ICR 292.
52   T. Ison, *Credit Marketing and Consumer Protection*, (Croom Helm, 1979) at p. 396.
53   *1983 Report to the Consumer Affairs Minister* quoted in *Ramsay, op. cit.* at 294.
54   S.34 (1), Fair Trading Act 1973.

and little incentive to act. Equally the Director General is powerless to act against overseas companies who send unsolicited mail into the UK.[55]

Unfairness for these purposes includes contraventions of any enactment which imposes duties, prohibitions or restrictions enforceable by criminal proceedings, whether or not that enactment was an explicitly consumer protection measure and irrespective of whether there has been an actual conviction.[56] Additionally unfairness also includes breaches of contractual or other duties enforceable in civil proceedings which arise in the course of business.[57] There must therefore have been a breach of the civil or criminal law, though this need not have been established by a court. This contrasts with the position in relation to consumer credit licensing[58] where power does exist to act against 'unfair', but not necessarily unlawful practices. This gap is a major weakness in the protection offered by Part III, Fair Trading Act 1973. Not only does it shield those traders who manage to stay one step ahead of the law, but it also increases the burden of data collection by requiring that data be clearly linked to specific breaches of the law.

A criticism of the procedures is that they are long–winded and that, even if an assurance or court action eventually results, the practice will meanwhile have continued – to the consumer detriment – for a long time whilst evidence is collected and the procedures gone through. A major problem is the requirement to show that the business has 'persisted in a course of conduct'. The Act directs the Director General to take into account complaints that he receives from consumers and others and any other information collected by or furnished to him. In advice to Trading Standards Officers, the Director General has noted that persistence involves an element of deliberation. In determining 'persistence' he will take into account the number of complaints, the seriousness of individual complaints within the total, the period covered by the complaints and the volume of complaints in relation to the trader's business. Persistence might be shown by the fact that a trader had ignored a trading standard officer's warning.[59] In the past it appears that ten to fifteen well–documented complaints (more in relation to large concerns) about a similar kind of misconduct over about a year were usually needed to demonstrate a persistent course of conduct.[60] In March 1993 the Office of Fair Trading adopted a more streamlined approach to Part III assurances,

---

[55] The *Sutherland* Report (*The Internal Market After 1992 – Meeting the Challenge*) commented on the need for co–ordination between administrative authorities to ensure the good functioning of the internal market.

[56] S.34(2), Fair Trading Act 1973.

[57] Ss.34(3), Fair Trading Act 1973.

[58] See 11.1.

[59] See *Assurances by Traders* (Office of Fair Trading, 1985).

[60] *Trading Malpractices* (Office of Fair Trading, 1990) at p. 30.

which in part concentrated on improving the quality of evidence collected by trading standards officers.[61] There it is stated that if the evidence is clear and precise, six to ten complaints about a single trading practice or related practice should be sufficient, though more might be needed if they relate to a wider range of civil or criminal breaches.

Even once a persistently unfair course of conduct has been established, before taking court action the Director General has first to use his best endeavours to obtain a written assurance from the trader that he or she will refrain from that or any similar conduct in the course of that business. This procedure further lengthens the process of bringing the unfair conduct to an end and moreover gives the trader the opportunity to prevaricate. In one instance it took the Director General eighteen months to exhaust his best endeavours when a trader argued minor points on forty–four complaints of breach of contract.[62] In its recent document on streamlining the Part III assurances procedure, the Office of Fair Trading has stated that, in future, 'best endeavours' will usually be confined to an initial request and one reminder sent four weeks later.

If a trader refuses to give an assurance, or an assurance is given but the Director General believes it has not been observed, he may, at his discretion, bring proceedings against the trader in the Restrictive Practices Court or, in smaller cases, in the county court for the district in which the practice is carried on.[63] If the court finds that the trader has persisted in a course of conduct which is unfair to consumers, two things can happen. If the trader is prepared to give an undertaking that he or she will refrain from continuing that or similar conduct in the course of his or her business, the court may accept such an undertaking. Alternatively, if no undertaking is offered or at least none acceptable to the court, an order can be made in similar terms. An order refraining the continuance of that (or a similar) course of conduct can be made if the court considers that unless the order is made it is likely the trader will continue with that or similar conduct. Such a finding will usually require evidence of recent malpractices – which gives traders the opportunity to lie low or improve their behaviour in the short term. All these delays in the procedure often mean that, when cases eventually reach the courts, the facts are 'cold'. As already noted, the Office of Fair Trading is seeking to address this problem by adopting new streamlined procedures, but whether these will be sufficient to meet the increasing need for speedy enforcement action in an ever faster moving trading environment is uncertain.

Presumably in an attempt to ameliorate some of the inherent weaknesses of the Part III procedure, the recent Office of Fair Trading document which

---

[61]   See *Part III Assurances – a New Approach* (Office of Fair Trading 1993).
[62]   See *Trading Malpractices, op. cit.,* at p. 32.
[63]   Ss.35 and 41, Fair Trading Act 1973.

attempts to streamline the procedure has called for greater use of warnings. When issued at a local level by trading standards officers, warnings may be appropriate to deal with local problems, though they also have an important role to play in the Office's own administrative armoury. A warning can be issued when an assurance cannot be obtained, for example where a trader has ceased trading or where there is insufficient evidence. In these circumstances a warning puts the trader on guard that his future behaviour will be monitored. Warnings can also be used if the level of complaints is not high enough to support an approach for an assurance or even if six or more convictions are documented, but the home or prosecuting authority does not consider that a formal approach for an assurance is needed. Warnings can also be used against national companies whose actions give rise to a significant number of complaints, but not enough to warrant a formal approach. A useful by–product of issuing a warning is that if it is ignored this can itself be used as evidence of persistence in an unfair course of conduct.

A potential loophole would have arisen if assurances, undertakings or orders could be made solely in respect of businesses, for then it would be easy to circumvent them by the business simply starting to trade under a different name or corporate form – a practice not unfamiliar to those who hide in the shadier reaches of the business community. However, this potential loophole is plugged by allowing action to be taken against directors, managers, secretaries and similar officers and persons with a controlling interest (one–half of votes) who have consented or connived in the course of conduct.[64] The courts can also act against other members of an interconnected group of companies, including those formed after the original order was made. This prevents new subsidiaries being created to circumvent the measures taken by the Office of Fair Trading.

Adverse publicity is one of the biggest fears of trading companies. Publicising the assurances given by traders can thus be an effective way of alerting the general public to past errors and thereby enlisting its co–operation in monitoring the firm's future performance. To a firm subjected to this unwanted publicity, it can, however, appear to be a sanction, which in its financial impact may well exceed the typical county court order. Thus when the Director General issued a press release stating, *inter alia*, that F.H. Taylor Ltd had only given an assurance after being threatened with proceedings and listing the number and nature of its convictions, the company complained that the Director General had abused his powers to publish information and advice[65] and had breached the Act's restrictions on

---

[64] S.38, Fair Trading Act 1973.
[65] S.124, Fair Trading Act 1973.

disclosure of information.[66] The legality of the press release was upheld since the company had not been misled into giving the assurance and had even had the opportunity to make amendments to a draft, but the court did raise some questions for the Director General to consider when issuing press releases in the future.[67] Subsequently little publicity was given to assurances for a while, but since 1989 almost all assurances have again been publicised through press notices and paid advertisements in selected newspapers and magazines.

Breach of an undertaking or court order amounts to a contempt of court and leaves the trader subject to an unlimited fine or imprisonment. The first person to be sent to prison under these provisions was a double glazing salesman, who was jailed for fourteen days at Weston–Super–Mare county court in August 1983.

16.5 REFORMS

16.5.1 The Need for Reform

Proceedings under Part III, Fair Trading Act 1974 were intended to provide a means of pulling aberrant traders into line. However, we have noted the limitations of these procedures, both because of the narrow range of activities which can be condemned under these provisions (the practice must be unlawful, not simply objectionable) and because of the complex formalities which need to be invoked before the Director General can use his powers. Licensing powers are also useful but limited to certain sectors, such as consumer credit and estate agencies. Therefore on several occasions, the Director General has suggested the addition of a fall–back power to catch rogue traders more effectively than under the present law. This idea was first mooted in the context of the Office's study of the home improvements sector.[68] An ambitious discussion paper was put out in 1986[69] followed by a more pragmatic report in 1990.[70] The Department of Trade and Industry has recently issued a consultation paper on the topic (discussed below).

The reasons for such reforms are evident throughout this book. Private law is unable to escape sufficiently from its *laissez–faire* and commercial

---

66   S.133, Fair Trading Act 1973.

67   *R v Director General of Fair Trading, ex parte FH Taylor & Co Ltd* [1981] ICR 292.

68   See *Home Improvements: a Discussion Paper* (Office of Fair Trading, 1982) and *Home Improvements: Report by the Director General of Fair Trading* (Office of Fair Trading, 1983).

69   *A General Duty to Trade Fairly: a Discussion Paper* (Office of Fair Trading, 1986).

70   *Trading Malpractices, op. cit.*

origins to respond to consumer problems; in any event private law is difficult to enforce and often inappropriate for the small individual amounts involved in consumer claims. The criminal law can be too rigid a tool to protect consumers, given the boundless ingenuity of entrepreneurs to circumvent legal controls. Whilst the modern vogue for self–regulation gives flexibility, it can be seen as lacking 'bite' when it comes to enforcement; questions might also be raised as to whether an industry is able to impose adequate standards of consumer protection on itself. Thus the call has come for a general requirement that businesses trade fairly, with enforcement powers given to public authorities to step in with corrective control where necessary. Although there will still be enforcement problems, it is hoped that the existence of this general duty will at least prevent disreputable traders from hiding behind legal technicalities.

16.5.2 General Standards[71]

The use of general standards is becoming an increasingly familiar aspect of modern legislation. One only has to look at labour law to see the very widespread use of the broad 'unfair' dismissal standard. In the consumer law field, one could consider the reasonableness standard under the Unfair Contract Terms Act 1977, the unfairness/good faith standard under the Unfair Terms in Consumer Contract Regulations 1994, the defectiveness standard in Part 1, Consumer Protection Act 1987, the general prohibition on misleading advertisements in the Misleading Advertisement Regulations 1987, the general product safety standard under Part II of the Consumer Protection Act 1987 and the General Product Safety Regulations 1984, and the food safety requirements in the Food Safety Act 1990. All these demonstrate the familiarity of English consumer law with duties couched in general terms.

16.5.3 Overseas Experience

The Office of Fair Trading was also much influenced by overseas experience where it is common to set a general trading standard which the consumer protection authorities can invoke in order to stamp out objectionable practices. The overseas models differ slightly in the range of conduct they cover, how the content of the general duty is fleshed out, who does the enforcing and what the methods of enforcement are. The most obvious models were from the Commonwealth countries of Australia and Canada,

---

71   See 1.8.1.

which inherited and have stayed relatively faithful to the common law tradition.

16.5.3.1 Australia

In Australia s.52, Trade Practices Act 1974 contains a general prohibition against misleading or deceptive practices. Subsequent ss.53–64 then provide a non–exhaustive list of specific prohibitions which seem to extend beyond practices ordinarily described as 'misleading or deceptive' conduct to embrace 'unfair' practices, such as the sending of unsolicited credit cards. Breach of a specific prohibition is a criminal offence, but there is no criminal sanction for breaching the general prohibition. Other remedies are injunctions which can be sought by anyone, including the Federal Trade Practices Commission, and compensation which can be awarded to anyone who has suffered loss as a result of conduct which contravened the general prohibition.

In 1986 a new s.52A was added to the Trade Practices Act governing unconscionable conduct. The term unconscionable is not defined in the Act but various criteria for judging the conscionability of a transaction are suggested. These include the relative bargaining strength of the parties, whether conditions were not reasonably necessary for the protection of the corporation's legitimate interest, whether any documentation was understandable, whether any undue influence or pressure was exerted or unfair tactics were used, and whether other available supplies of the product were available. In its guidance notes to this section, the Federal Trade Commission cites four examples of situations where the risk of unconscionable conduct was high, namely:

(i)   where the sales techniques by their very nature produce a disadvantage to the other party,
(ii) where the supplier knew or ought to have known that the consumer did not fully understand the transaction,
(iii) where there is no real opportunity for the weaker party to bargain,
(iv) where the contract is extremely one–sided.

Breach of s.52A does not give rise to criminal liability nor a right to damages as such. Instead individuals may seek an injunction and/or certain orders for compensation, specific performance, refund of money or return of property, variation of a contract or a declaration that a contract is void. It may also be used as a defence in state courts where a tainted contract is being enforced against a consumer.

16.5.3.2 Canada

Similar trade practices legislation is to be found in the Canadian Provinces of British Columbia (Trade Practices Act 1979), Ontario (Business Practices Act 1974) and Alberta (Unfair Trade Practices Act 1975). The British Columbia and Ontario legislation contain general prohibitions[72] supported by a list of specific prohibited practices. In British Columbia this list of practices can be added to by regulations. The Alberta legislation simply lists acts which are to be treated as unfair. In British Columbia and Alberta enforcement authorities can seek assurances and failing success in obtaining such an assurance they (and indeed any other person) can seek a declaration or injunction. Consumers can bring an action for damages and, irrespective of whether the consumer has suffered loss, the courts have the discretion to cancel the contract. In Ontario the enforcement authorities have similar powers, but in addition they can order a trader to cease engaging in unfair practices, with the trader having a right of appeal, in the first instance, to the Commercial Registration Appeal Tribunal. In Ontario consumers do not seem to have the right to bring an action for an injunction, although the administrative tribunal can join them as parties to an action. Consumers can rescind a contract induced by deceptive or unconscionable conduct within six months, but for damages they must rely on the general law .

16.5.3.3 United States

Since 1914 the US Federal Trade Commission Act has given the Federal Trade Commission the power to act against unfair methods of competition and unfair or deceptive methods of commercial practice. In 1938 the Act was amended so as to permit the Commission to consider the impact of deceptive and unfair practices on consumers as well as competitors. Unlike the Australian and Canadian laws, there is no attempt to list specific prohibited practices since this was felt to be an impossible task. Instead these are worked out in decisions of the Federal Trade Commission and by the courts on appeal. The Federal Trade Commission deals with complaints of violation through a series of formal and informal means. A voluntary written assurance can be obtained; however, if the Commission wants the matter to be placed on a more formal footing, it can serve notice that it is going to issue a complaint. The violator may agree to a consent order, which has the same force as if the matter had gone to a full hearing. The most serious

---

[72] In the case of British Columbia, against deceptive and unconscionable practices and, in Ontario, against unfair practices.

disputed cases are heard before an administrative law judge. The most usual order is a 'cease and desist' order.

16.5.3.4 Scandinavia

Scandinavia has a very well developed system of public regulation of business practices centred around the Consumer Ombudsman's offices. Part of the Ombudsman's function is to develop guidelines on good business practice to supplement statutory consumer protection, and this is normally undertaken in consultation with trade associations and businesses. The authority of the Ombudsman is, however, enhanced by his power to seek injunctions against traders who operate poor business practices. It might be noted that these powers are very wide; also such cases are not heard by the ordinary courts, but rather by a special Market Court. S.2 of the Swedish Marketing Practices Act 1971 aims to prevent improper marketing practices which adversely affect the interests of consumers (and other businesses) by providing that:

> 'If a merchant, in the marketing of a product, service or anything else of value, advertises or takes other action which by conflicting with good commercial standards or otherwise, adversely affects consumers or merchants, the Market Court may enjoin him from continuing therewith or undertaking any similar action.'

Traders can also be enjoined to give consumers information of significant interest which they had neglected to give or be prohibited from offering for sale goods posing a special risk of personal injury or damage to property or which are manifestly unfit for their main purpose. The Ombudsman is required to bring cases before the Market Court where he considers this to be in the public interest. If he decides not to act, consumers' organisations can apply to the court. The Court can issue an injunction. The Marketing Practices Act allows for an action for damages by business competitors who are harmed by breach of injunctions or criminal provisions. There is no similar provision for consumers, but there is a simplified redress procedure whereby consumers can complain to the Consumer Complaints Board which hands down non-binding Recommendations, which are however usually accepted by business and are highly persuasive on the courts.

16.5.3.5 France and Germany

France and Germany have general provisions which can be used to control business practices not caught by specific controls. Thus in the recently consolidated French consumer code, there are general controls on misleading information and product and service safety. In the enforcement of consumer protection laws, the Direction Générale de la Concurrence, de la Consommation et de la Répression des Fraudes plays a central role.

More broadly s.1 of the German Law Against Unfair Competition provides that:

> 'A person who in the course of business and for the purposes of competition conducts himself in a manner which offends against good morals may be enjoined and held liable in damages.'

There is, however, no central enforcement authority. Instead it is left to individuals (or more likely consumer organisations) to bring actions. Indeed, for a long time after its enactment in 1909, the Act was used to protect traders against unfair competition. Its modern use as a means of consumer protection is of fairly recent origin, albeit one which has been used to control a wide range of undesirable practices.

Both France and Germany place far greater emphasis than the UK on enforcement by actions taken by consumer associations. We shall note later on that this difference in control technique causes some problems in the European context when attempts are made to put in place common procedures for acting against unfair business practices which transcend national boundaries.[73]

16.5.4 A General Duty to Trade Fairly?

In its 1986 discussion paper *A General Duty to Trade Fairly* the Office of Fair Trading set out proposals for a general duty to trade fairly. It later drew back, believing that it had been too ambitious in attempting to use the general duty as the mechanism to achieve all the objectives of (i) raising trading standards, (ii) stamping out errant traders, and (iii) improving consumer redress.

Those proposals would have introduced a general duty to trade fairly, enforced by local trading standards officers, with the Office of Fair Trading having the power to intervene in cases of general importance or which involved difficult questions of law or fact. In the first instance, informal

---

73   See 17.9.3.

approaches would be relied upon to try to ensure that the unfair practice was desisted from and adequate redress provided, but in the final resort court action could be taken to seek an injunction and redress. There are some difficulties with giving officials the power to seek compensation for citizens. For instance, with only limited resources, whom do the officials decide to assist? However, this anomaly already exists. Where a prosecution is successful an application can be made for a compensation order under s.35, Powers of Criminal Courts Act 1973.[74] Extending compensation orders to cases which are settled before the civil courts might be viewed as a way of enhancing the principle that the victim should be given redress. Certainly, given the access to justice problems faced by consumers, this might have been an avenue worth exploring further. It would also have encouraged consumers to bring matters to the attention of the enforcement authorities. However, we shall see that subsequently the Director General felt unable to continue to advocate the availability of individual remedies when his Office was bringing an action against a rogue trader.

The traditional UK inclination to self–regulation was reflected in the significant role envisaged for codes of practice in fleshing out the general duty to trade fairly and also by the hope that a side effect of the introduction of the general duty (supported by administrative powers) would be the decriminalisation of regulatory consumer protection legislation. It was proposed that the content of the general duty be spelt out in codes of practice, both of a horizontal nature (like the advertising codes) and of a vertical sectoral nature. It left open such questions as whether the duty should only apply where a code existed or whether in other areas court practice could fill the gaps, and whether, in addition, specific unfair or deceptive practices should be prohibited. Once codes had been approved by Parliament, they would have been given statutory backing and apply to all traders not only those covered by the relevant trade associations. Non-observance of a Code could have been cited as evidence by a plaintiff, although a defendant could show he had given equivalent protection, whilst observance of a code would have been a defence.[75]

---

[74]   See 14.3.4.
[75]   As it was a discussion paper, the question of the exact evidential status of the Code was left somewhat vague. However, one can see signs of this approach in relation to the Code of Practice on Price Indications which is given evidential status by virtue of s.25, Consumer Protection Act 1987: see 10.5.

16.5.5 Trading Malpractices

The Office of Fair Trading's 1990 *Trading Malpractices* report adopted, perhaps regrettably, a far more pragmatic approach. It did not seek to use the occasion to enhance consumer redress, but instead sought to tackle the problems of trading malpractices through a proposed overhaul of Part III of the Fair Trading Act 1973.

Action under the proposed powers would be possible where the enforcement authorities could show that the trader had carried on a course of conduct which was unfair and detrimental to the interests of consumers in the UK. This would be a far easier requirement than that under Part III of the Fair Trading Act 1973 which requires that the trader be shown to have *persisted* in such a course of conduct.

The definition of unfairness would be extended beyond conduct which breaches the criminal and civil law. It would also cover 'deceptive or misleading' and 'unconscionable' practices. The 'deceptive or misleading' standard would be supported by a non–exhaustive list of illustrative acts or practices. 'Unconscionable' practices refers to those practices which are considered indefensible or objectionable by virtue of their oppressive or exploitative nature; this standard would be backed up by a set of factors or circumstances to be taken into account in individual cases. This approach was expressly said to mirror the Australian/Canadian legislation. Ironically its style is far more interventionist and regulatory and based on formal adjudication by the courts than the previous proposal which would have built on the UK's self–regulatory tradition. One might wonder whether the rather conservative British judiciary would be as at ease handling a concept such as unconscionability as their Commonwealth counterparts. Certainly one suspects that they would not be as innovative.

Action by the authorities would be more direct than under the present procedures. Instead of having to seek assurances, under the new powers enforcement authorities would be able to serve a caution on a trader seeking the discontinuation of a course of conduct and where appropriate the modification of trading practices. Traders would be able to challenge the caution in court. Enforcement authorities would be able to seek a court order if the caution were breached or if there were a risk of the conduct being repeated. An application could be made directly to court, by–passing the caution procedure, where the likelihood existed of substantial detriment to the health, safety or economic interests of consumers. Breach of a court order would be contempt of court. It was proposed that the power be available to both trading standards officers and the Director General. The Office of Fair Trading was keen that power be given to local trading standards authorities to act, as often they spot the rogue traders at a local level, but the current procedures under Part III, Fair Trading Act 1973 (which gives the Office a monopoly power to act against rogue traders) involves an unwieldy paper chain from local to central government. The business community was concerned at powers being given to trading standards officers, however, fearing there would be variations in approaches and dangers from overzealous individual officers.   The Office of Fair Trading, however, believed these fears could be allayed by the supervisory powers of the court and by giving itself powers to monitor actions taken at a local level.

16.5.6 Subsequent Developments

In July 1991 the Government announced its acceptance in principle of the need to reform Part III, Fair Trading Act; the Conservative party also included a commitment to deal with rogue traders in its 1992 election manifesto. The Director General, Sir Bryan Carsberg, then suggested some amendments to the reform proposals set out in *Trading Malpractices* 'to reflect sensitivities regarding enforcement matters generally and the realities of the process of legislative change'.[76] The main points of change were that enforcement powers would be retained exclusively by the Office of Fair Trading and not shared with trading standards officers; the reference to unconscionable practices would be dropped (instead conduct detrimental to the consumer would mean 'deceptive, misleading or oppressive' conduct); there would be no illustrative list of deceptive or misleading practices, and the caution procedure would be restyled as a 'warning notice'.

The Department of Trade and Industry issued a consultation paper in December 1994.[77] It acknowledged the need for reform, but still raised some doubts about even the more moderate proposals put forward by Sir Bryan Carsberg. In particular it queried whether the concepts of misleading, deceptive and oppressive were not unduly subjective. There is clearly nervousness about crossing the line between condemning unlawful and simply immoral practices. There are also some fears that the warning notice (caution) procedure would put too much power in the hands of the Director General. This timid approach to what are by international standards moderate reforms demonstrates a lack of commitment to a positive approach to consumer protection which would seek to use the law to promote best practice.

---

[76]   *Revision of Part III, Fair Trading Act 1973* (Office of Fair Trading, 1993).

[77]   *Reform of Part III of the Fair Trading Act 1973* (Department of Trade and Industry, 1994).

16.6 REFLECTIONS ON THE FUNCTION OF THE OFFICE OF FAIR TRADING

Any assessment of the Office of Fair Trading will depend upon the expectations one judges it against. Account should also be taken of the fact that, for the majority of its life, the Office has operated against a political background of a Government whose instincts favoured a hands–off regulatory approach. Nevertheless the Office has managed to achieve widespread acceptance of its consumer protection regulatory functions, for instance those relating to consumer credit. It has also been able to highlight consumer problems which have either been addressed by legislation, codes of practice or are on the agenda for future reform. Indeed the fact that potentially contentious reform proposals – such as those on *Unjust Credit Transactions* and *Trading Malpractices* – have gained a measure of support from a Government instinctively opposed to greater legislative intervention in the functioning of the marketplace says a lot for the political astuteness of the Office's staff and in particular, Sir Gordon Borrie, who was for many years the Director General.

One of the most useful contributions of the Office may be as a body in which both consumers and industry have confidence and which can therefore enter into a dialogue with interested parties to resolve problems. Consumer groups may sometimes consider the Office too timid; business may sometimes think it too interventionist. Both sides, however, seem to believe that the Office acts in good faith. Perhaps at times one might wish to discern a clearer impression of the Office's consumer philosophy, but this might run the risk of threatening the relationships of confidence which it has built up by adopting a pragmatic approach to problem solving.

What is clear from the next chapter, where we look at problems of access to justice, is that consumer protection cannot depend on individuals taking the initiative to invoke the law. Even groups of individuals may not be able to function effectively in the legal system. Public authorities, such as the Office of Fair Trading and Trading Standards Departments, are needed to regulate the consumer market. Partly this is because of the resources they have at their disposal, but also because they can take a dispassionate long–term view of the problem and thus counter the tactical advantages businesses enjoy as 'repeat players' over the 'one–shot' consumer.[78] Moreover, consumer law is not simply about protecting the individual interests of consumers, but also should require respect to be paid to the collective interests of society. The Office of Fair Trading can represent those collective interests.

---

[78] See 17.2.3.

17 Access to Justice

In the last chapter we discussed the role of the Office of Fair Trading in protecting consumers and we have also considered the important role played by trading standards officers.[1] Public enforcement helps to promote standards and thereby indirectly benefits consumers, though it can rarely provide the individual aggrieved consumer with a remedy. In this chapter we concentrate on ways in which the individual consumer can seek redress. This should not blind us to the debate as to whether resources are best used to improve public enforcement of regulatory laws or to establish consumer rights in the court system. Thus debate largely centres on one's belief in the effectiveness of public law regulation and regulatory agencies as opposed to the value in allowing the citizen the right to protect his own interests by litigation. We return to the choice between private and public enforcement briefly when we consider whether the collective redress of consumer grievances is best achieved by a group or class action brought by individuals joining together or by actions brought by consumer organisations or public agencies.

17.1 IS THERE AN ACCESS TO JUSTICE PROBLEM?

At many points in this book lacunae in the protection afforded to consumers by the private law have been noted. However, the most damning criticisms of private law as a method of consumer protection relate to the inability of legal institutions to deal with consumer complaints.[2] Critics claim that, even if the substantive law were framed in the most pro–consumer terms, the rights granted to consumers would not be effective because the amounts of money involved are generally too small to be worth litigating; because the legal system and lawyers appear alien to the average consumer and only the more educated consumers are aware of and can articulate their complaints in terms which allow them to take advantage of the law. These criticisms have been well made and have encouraged responses seeking to question the way legal services are delivered to consumers and to re–examine dispute resolution procedures.[3] These issues will be considered below.

---

[1]   See 14.3.
[2]   See 1.6.
[3]   See generally I. Ramsay, 'Consumer Redress Mechanisms for Poor Quality and Defective Products' (1981) 31 *UTLJ* 117.

Many reforms have still been based on a paradigm which involves an individual consumer in dispute with an individual business. Attempts have been made to even up this relationship by providing or subsidising the advice costs of the consumer or making legal action less expensive, less intimidating, less risky and more convenient.[4] However, legal reforms which continue to view consumer problems as individual problems are going to lead to a continuation of many of the present difficulties. Consumer law will continue to be viewed as 'middle class' law, for it will only be worth litigating disputes involving high-cost goods and services (although many middle–class consumers will themselves be excluded by the high cost of lawyers). Equally consumers will not be allowed to claim the organisational advantages which are automatically available to all but the smallest businesses. One response is to recognise the collective dimension by increasing the public law protection of consumers. Alternatively, consumers can be permitted to aggregate individual claims in group or class actions, or consumer organisations can be allowed to invoke private law rights on behalf of consumers generally.

Sometimes it is suggested that too much is made of the problem of lack of consumer redress. Susan Silbey reminds us that consumers do not always expect their purchases to satisfy their expectations 100 per cent. She impliedly questions whether consumers benefit from attempts to remedy every minor harm: 'Are we engaged in an ever escalating cycle of increasing expectations, the major beneficiaries of which are those whose occupation it is to provide remedies and services for the victims of failed expectations?'[5]

Whilst it is right that care should be taken to ensure that reforms benefit consumers and not their advisers, it would be wrong to suggest that society wastes its resources when it allows litigation to proceed over minor disputes. First, litigation has two functions – resolving the dispute and giving the parties the opportunity to air their grievances in front of an impartial third party.[6] Second, society has a wider interest in the outcome of the dispute than the actual decision, for the rules established can affect supplier behaviour in the future. Other forms of enforcement may be more efficient than private redress. Nevertheless allowing individuals to enforce their own rights corresponds to the notion of the rule of law. It is also an important safeguard, at times when public authorities are not able to enforce laws as

---

4   See W. Whitford, 'Structuring Consumer Protection Legislation to Maximise Effectiveness' [1981] *Wisc LR* 1018.

5   S. Silbey, 'Who Speaks for the Consumer? [1984] *Am Bar Foundation RJ* 429.

6   Although only a few high–income consumers are likely to be motivated solely by altruism in bringing complaints, nevertheless most complainants welcome the opportunity to get the grievance off their chest; see E. Steele, 'Fraud, Disputes and the Consumer; Responding to Consumer Complaints' (1975) 123 *UPaLR* 1107.

effectively as they might wish (be that for reasons of lack of resources or political dictate).

This chapter starts by discussing the availability of legal services for consumers, which inevitably involves such topics as legal aid and the system for awarding costs in the legal system. We then consider alternative ways of advising consumers, bearing in mind criticisms made of the performance of lawyers in consumer protection matters. Most of the rest of the chapter is concerned with innovations whose object is to increase access to justice for consumers – class actions, small claims courts, Ombudsmen and arbitration schemes – before we remind ourselves that most consumer disputes are resolved in direct negotiations between the consumer and supplier. We then simply note the particular issues relating to utilities, before contemplating the European dimensions of the problem.

17.2 CONSUMERS AND LAWYERS

17.2.1 Funding Lawyers

17.2.1.1 Fees and Costs

It is commonly assumed that consumers are disadvantaged by not having the same access to lawyers as the business community. In the US this is addressed to some extent by giving lawyers economic incentives to take on consumer cases – either by allowing contingent fees[7] or specifically permitting reasonable attorney fees to be recovered.[8]

In the UK a victorious consumer has always been able to recover costs. The problem has been that lawyers have not been able to take cases on a 'no win, no fee' basis for then the other side would not have been liable to pay any costs. S.58, Courts and Legal Services Act 1990 now permits lawyers to take cases on a contingent basis. Controversy surrounded the amount of 'uplift' lawyers would be allowed to charge in successful cases. The Lord Chancellor's department had at first suggested a modest 'uplift' of up to 10 per cent to take account of the risk the lawyer had taken on. The Law Society

---

7   This involves allowing lawyers to take cases on a 'no win no fee' basis with the fee usually being a percentage of the damages recovered. The limitation of this approach is that lawyers will only take on cases worth a reasonable sum since their payment is linked to the amount at stake. Also they will not take on marginal cases unless they can claim a sizeable portion of any amounts recovered: most US states operate a cap at around 30–40 per cent.

8   See for example 15 USC S. 1692 (Supp.IV 1980) (Fair Debt Collection Practices Act).

had suggested a 20 per cent figure, but said a case could be made out for a 100 per cent uplift on the basis that a lawyer would only break even if he or she won half the cases brought on a conditional fee basis. In the end the Government decided to allow an uplift of 100 per cent. This should encourage lawyers to be more adventurous in the cases they take on, but it could simply mean an increase in fee income.[9]

The rule that consumers are normally liable for the other side's costs should they lose remains likely to act as a significant deterrent to consumers bringing cases; however, the 'costs following the action' rule does not normally apply in the small claims court.

17.2.1.2 Legal Aid

In the UK, the main means of providing legal advice to consumers is through the Legal Aid scheme. Although much practical help is also available through the nationwide network of citizens advice bureaux and the few remaining Law Centres.

The Legal Aid Act 1988 provides for two forms of legal aid of use to consumers. Legal advice and assistance is available under the 'green form' scheme. This allows lawyers to give up to two hours of advice without having to ask for an extension from the Legal Aid Board (more if the lawyer is a legal aid franchisee approved by the Law Society). This would allow a lawyer to give advice, write a letter, negotiate or if necessary obtain counsel's opinion. In other words most of the things which are necessary to resolve the majority of consumer disputes. If the matter needs to be taken further, then civil legal aid can be applied for. Both the green form scheme and civil legal aid are means tested, but in addition the latter has a merits test[10] and a reasonableness test.[11] The merits test requires that the applicant has reasonable grounds for taking, defending or being a party to proceedings. Here the authorities must strike a balance between being over cautious and granting legal aid in hopeless cases. The applicant will be taken as having reasonable grounds if:

(i)   there is an issue of fact or law which should be submitted to the court;
(ii) the solicitor would advise a private client to take or defend the proceedings (the private individual is assumed to be someone who could

---

9   See C. Hodges, 'European Product Liability: Factors which in Practice Remain Unharmonised' (1993) 1 *Consum LJ* 127.
10   S.15(2) of the Legal Aid Act 1988.
11   S.15(3) of the Legal Aid Act 1988.

meet the costs if necessary, though paying them would be something of a sacrifice);

(iii) the applicant shows that as a matter of law he has reasonable grounds for taking or defending proceedings (for instance, he has a case or defence which has a reasonable prospect of success, if he can prove the relevant facts).

Even if an applicant can satisfy this merits test, the reasonableness test must also be satisfied; that is, is it reasonable in the particular circumstances of the case for the applicant to be granted civil legal aid? The *Legal Aid Handbook* cites several reasons why legal aid is likely to be refused as being unreasonable, including the fact that the amount of the claim is small or that the likely costs will exceed the benefit to the client.[12] Also legal aid is not appropriate where the consumer has a reasonable expectation of help from another body. The handbook cites the AA/RAC as such bodies, but it is to be hoped that this reference is only to assistance regarding accidents and not general claims about the poor quality of cars, otherwise members of organisations such as the Consumers' Association would be ruled out of legal aid for consumer claims simply by virtue of their membership. Citizens should not be penalised for their foresight in joining consumer protection organisations.

The means test has been tightened in recent years. When the scheme was established in 1950 it covered 80 per cent of the population. In 1987 the Government estimated that 70 per cent of the population was still covered,[13] but the National Consumer Council is rightly sceptical about this.[14] Legal aid has eligibility rules which provide upper and lower limits for income and capital for both the green form scheme and civil legal aid. For instance in 1993 single persons were ineligible under the green form scheme if they had capital exceeding £1,000 or more than £61 weekly disposable income. Civil legal aid had an annual lower income limit of £2,294 and an upper limit of £6,800 (£7,5000 for personal injury cases); also a lower capital limit of £3,000 and an upper capital limit of £6,750 ((£8,560). Those below the limits obtain free legal aid; those falling above the limits are ineligible, whilst those in between obtain legal aid subject to contributions.[15] It is often said

---

12   Even though the other party will be liable for costs if the consumer wins, this may not cover everything; for example, where costs are awarded against the consumer at interlocutory hearings.

13   Sir Patrick Mayhew, Attorney General, Hansard, 13 July 1987, Vol. 119, Col 316.

14   National Consumer Council, *Ordinary Justice*, (HMSO, 1989) at p. 88.

15   In fact one in five applicants refuses the offer of contributory legal aid: Lord Chancellor's Department, *Legal Aid Efficiency Scrutiny*, 2 vols, June 1986, quoted in *Ordinary Justice, op. cit.*

that the law can only assist the very rich and the very poor and this appears to be true here as the middle classes are excluded from legal aid.

An advantage of being legally aided is that costs are usually not awarded against legally aided litigants. However, the rules are not so generous to successful litigants. While losers can normally walk away from litigation with no costs liabilities, winners have a statutory charge imposed on them. The statutory charge means that any damages are paid to the Legal Aid Board which deducts any outstanding amounts in respect of money advanced to fight the case before paying the remainder over to the legally aided party. To a winner, civil legal aid is merely a loan. Although the losing party will usually be liable for costs, this will not help the successful party if the loser is unable to pay them. The legally aided party may also be held liable for costs incurred during interlocutory proceedings or if the costs awarded on taxation do not cover the full amount.

In one type of consumer case – large–scale personal injury cases – the Legal Aid Board has put in place arrangements for the contracting out of services. This system may limit the freedom of the consumer to select his own legal representative, although empirical research suggests that plaintiffs fare decidedly better when their cases are handled by specialists.[16] This raises a general point about whether simply providing consumers with access to traditional lawyers will provide them with adequate legal services.

17.2.2 How Good are Lawyers at Consumer Law?

Macaulay suggests that consumers may be given a raw deal by the legal profession.[17] His study found a wide degree of ignorance on consumer law matters amongst lawyers who do not come into contact with them on a regular basis. Lawyers are also less likely to empathise with consumers and the problems they face. Lawyers tend to be able to understand the consumer contracts they sign personally and may not appreciate the problems experienced by some consumers with legal technicalities. As small businessmen themselves, lawyers are likely to appreciate the position of the businesses involved and view consumers who complain as 'freaks'. Lawyers who acted aggressively to protect consumer rights were viewed as 'members of the "rag tag bar"'. The respectable role for the lawyer was seen merely as a mediator, putting the consumer in touch with the right person in the relevant organisation to deal with the complaint. Whilst there is clearly a role

---

16　S. Fennell, 'Funding Personal Injury Litigation' in *The Changing Shape of the Legal Profession*, J. Shapland and R. Le Grys (eds), (Sheffield Institute for the Study of the Legal Profession, 1994).

17　S. Macaulay, 'Lawyers and Consumer Protection Laws' (1979) 14 *Law and Soc R* 115.

for conciliation, the danger is that consumer claims can be too easily compromised and that settlements fail to establish positive legal principles which other consumers can rely on in future cases.

17.2.3 Repeat Players

The consumer's position in the legal system is structurally weak. In the terminology of Galanter, the consumer is a 'one–shotter' as opposed to business which is a 'repeat player'.[18] The problem is not merely that the repeat player may be a better lawyer, or at least one more conversant with consumer law. Rather business has the advantage of being only marginally concerned with the instant case and more interested in the development of the law. Thus repeat players have 'the ability to play for rules as well as for immediate gain. It pays a recurrent litigant to expend resources in influencing the making of the relevant rules and avoiding unfavourable outcomes through settlements'. Thus Ramsay astutely defines the disparity in legal services as being not so much between rich and poor, but rather as between individuals and organisations.[19]

Drawing on the work of Wexler[20] in the area of poverty law, Ramsay[21] argues that consumers may need a different type of lawyer from that traditionally found in High Street offices. Just as an army of poverty lawyers could not deal with all the legal problems of the poor which were recognised, yet alone those which remain unrecognised, so consumer problems are too numerous to be dealt with effectively through traditional lawyer/client relationships. Consumer lawyers may need to have skills such as the ability to mobilise consumers, teach consumers how to help themselves and act as lobbyists and strategists for the consumer movement.

Part of the difficulty in developing a strategy for the enforcement of consumer rights is to decide which is more important: the resolution of an individual dispute or the proper development of the law. The first technique we shall look at – class actions – views consumer problems as public problems, albeit ones in which individual litigants have an important interest. The other techniques of improving redress tend to view the problems in a more individualistic manner, a tendency which increases the more private the

---

18   M. Galanter, 'Why the "Haves" Come out Ahead: Speculations on the Limits of Legal Change' (1974) 9 *Law and Soc R* 95.

19   I. Ramsay, *op. cit.*, at p. 136.

20   S. Wexler, 'Practising Law for Poor People', (1970) 79 *Yale LJ* 1049.

21   Ramsay, *op. cit.*, at pp. 138-9.

redress mechanism.[22] It is important, however, that even where private out–of–court schemes are developed, the public interest in using complaints as a way of forcing businesses to improve practices is not overlooked.

17.3 GROUP OR CLASS ACTIONS

Consumer complaints can either be viewed as isolated one–on–one disputes, or they can be considered as social problems calling for collective solutions. Clearly some consumer complaints affect only individuals, who have been unfortunate enough to buy a rogue product or have suffered poor service in a one–off situation. Frequently, however, consumers suffer collective grievances which affect all, or a large proportion, of the users of a certain product or service. Consumers may find particular difficulty in litigating such claims. The loss to the individual consumer may be so small that it is simply not viable for the consumer to litigate. Even if the loss is substantial, consumers may be deterred from going to court because the cost of litigating, and in particular the cost of losing, may be too high. The expense of producing the required scientific and technical evidence, in product liability cases for instance, can be enormous. Only recently have lawyers in the UK been allowed to act on a 'no win, no fee' basis (see above) and it is not clear how popular this will be with plaintiff lawyers. Few are likely to be able to afford to fund complex litigation where the outcome is uncertain.[23] Even if plaintiffs can afford to commence litigation, they may still be reluctant to do so, because of the rule in the UK that an unsuccessful plaintiff normally has to pay the defendant's costs.[24]

One obvious solution is for a 'group or class' action to be brought on behalf of all affected consumers. This allows the consumers to have a better chance of access to resources with which to take on the defendants, who are frequently wealthy corporations. Hopefully, this would make possible the satisfactory out of court resolution of these types of disputes. For whilst it is unfair that traditional rules *de facto* bar consumers from taking legal action, equally the court system could not function if it had to adjudicate individually on all consumer claims. However, class action procedures do

---

22 Although there are dangers in viewing the matter in this way. For example, to varying degrees the Ombudsmen see promoting good practice as part of their function: see 17.5.5.

23 See M. Mildred, 'Representing the Plaintiff in Drug Product Liability Cases' in *Product Liability, Insurance and the Pharmaceutical Industry*, G. Howells (ed), (MUP, 1991).

24 We have already noted that this does not usually apply where the plaintiff was legally aided or in the small claims court.

raise important issues about who has the right to act for the class and whether members of the class should be able to dissociate themselves from the class action. Class actions may also call for novel remedies, if the individual members of the class cannot be identified or if individual damages are not appropriate. Also if one assumes that society has tailored its regulatory and liability rules with regard to their impact in terms of the present degree of enforcement, any increased enforcement may eventually require a re–evaluation of the impact of the substantive law of consumer protection.

Three ways of protecting the collective interests of consumers have been identified.[25] We shall call these:

(i)   The *private initiative* model, where the case is brought by the individual consumers affected. This is what is traditionally thought of as a class or group action.
(ii) The *consumer organisation* model, where consumer organisations are given standing to represent consumers.
(iii) The *public agency* model, where public bodies can act to protect the consumer interest.

Whilst we shall largely concentrate on the first of these models, readers should not underestimate the value of the other two, both of which have received detailed scrutiny in recent times and have been increasingly utilised. To some extent the choice of model depends upon the outcome to be achieved. Litigation led by individual consumers appears more appropriate where damages are sought, whereas organisation or agency involvement seems appropriate for claims for injunctive relief. Although one should not be too quick to restrict consumer organisations or public agencies to simply seeking injunctive relief.

Later in the chapter we shall consider other reforms which are intended to make it easier for consumers to have access to justice to resolve their individual disputes. Class actions can, however, be viewed as having a greater impact on the moulding of future behaviour, partly because of the large amounts of money at stake and partly because of the publicity which

---

25   See Th. Bourgoignie's Preface to his edited work *Group Actions and Consumer Protection* (Story Scienta, 1992). Here we are concerned with protection through some kind of court procedure: obviously it is possible to rely on stronger administrative regulation, but that is another debate taken up elsewhere: see Chapter 14.

typically surrounds them. Class actions can also be a vehicle for promoting consumerism as part of a social action agenda.[26]

17.3.1 Private Initiative Model

In the context of private initiative strategies for collective consumer redress some definitions need to be established.[27] A distinction can be drawn between a 'group' and a 'class' action. A group action involves a co–ordinated litigation strategy by a group of consumers with a common or similar grievance through traditional court procedures. Class actions, on the other hand, involve consumers using a dedicated procedure for class litigation. Generally the class action will be more coercive on dissenting or absent members of the class, although this need not be the case. A group action may be more closely associated with a 'test case' strategy, under which 'lead' cases are selected to test certain points of principle in the hope that, once the courts have ruled on the disputed issues, similar cases can be settled by negotiation. Such cases do not typically bind future litigants, at least so far as issues of fact are concerned. However, this is not true of all group actions; representative actions can bind all those represented even if they were not aware of the litigation.

17.3.1.1 History

The history of the group/class action goes back to chancery procedures on the eve of the agricultural revolution when it was used as a means of establishing and modernising villager rights based on manorial or parochial relationships.[28] During the industrial revolution it was used as a means of testing the rights of parties in organisations which were not yet properly recognised in law, such as friendly societies and joint stock companies. It was only in the late twentieth century that the concept of group action was adopted by social activists fighting for the rights, *inter alia*, of tenants, the environment and of course consumers.

The UK has not yet established a formal class action procedure, preferring instead to continue with either test case strategies or the

---

26   See I. Ramsay, 'Consumerism, Citizenship and Democratic Politics: Class and Group Actions' in Th. Bourgoignie (ed), *op. cit.*

27   Care needs to be exercised when reading other works, as our definitions are not used consistently in the same sense by other authors.

28   S. Yeazall, 'Group Litigation and Social Context: Towards a History of the Class Action.' (1977) 77 *Colum L Rev* 866.

representative action. However, the *Opren* case has focused attention on the need for reforms.

17.3.1.2 Overseas experiences[29]

17.3.1.2.1 United States and Commonwealth: The US and Commonwealth inherited the English legal tradition, but have developed distinctive class action procedures. It is in the US that the class action has gained the most prominence – even notoriety – and where it represents about 0.4 per cent of all civil cases at the Federal level (there are also state procedures).[30] At the Federal level the class action procedure is only available for damages in excess of $50,000; however, certain statutes, including consumer protection statutes, provide for class action procedures which cover both the granting of injunctions and the awards of small amounts of individual compensation. There are seven pre–requisites which an action must satisfy before the courts will certificate it as suitable for the class action procedure:

(i)   there must be a class,
(ii)   the plaintiff must be a member of the class,
(iii)   the number of members of the class must be numerous enough,
(iv)   there must be common questions of law or fact,
(v)   the claim must be representative of the group members' claims,
(vi)   the plaintiff and representative must be adequate to represent the class, and
(vii)   the claim must fit into one of the three categories set out in Rule 23(b) of the Rules of the Federal Supreme Court.

These are that:

(i)   separate actions would be likely to cause the defendant to face inconsistent standards or would as a practical matter dispose of the case with respect to other members of the class;

---

29   A good comparative survey is given in Scottish Law Commission, Discussion Paper 98, *Multi–Party Actions: Court Proceedings and Funding* (Scottish Law Commission, 1994).

30   For further reading see J. Fleming, *The American Tort Process* (Clarendon Press, 1988); Note, 'Developments in the Law: Class Actions' (1976) 89 *Harv L Rev* 1318; K. Dam, 'Class Actions: Efficiency, Compensation, Deterrence and Conflict of Interest' (1975) 4 *J Leg Stud* 47 and P.H. Lindblom, 'Group Actions: A Study of the Anglo–American Class Action from a Swedish Perspective' in Th. Bourgoignie (ed), *op. cit.*

(ii)   the defendant has acted or refused to act on grounds generally applicable to the class which make injunctive or declaratory relief appropriate;

(iii) questions of law or fact common to members of the class *predominate* over any questions affecting only individual members and a class action is *superior* to other available methods for the fair and efficient adjudication of the controversy.

A great deal of unwarranted litigation has taken place considering whether the common issues predominate and whether the class action is superior. By focusing on such technical points, defendants (who fear the potentially devastating impact of class actions, particularly in mass tort cases where punitive damages are claimed) have tried to fight a rearguard action against the advance of the class action.

In Canada, the French law province of Quebec has known a class action procedure since 1979,[31] and Ontario adopted a class action procedure in 1992.[32] In Australia, Victoria and South Australia led the way by introducing class action procedures at the state level, though recently they have also been introduced at the Federal level.[33]

17.3.1.2.2 Europe: European reforms may be of greater significance given the single market and the European Commission's interest in consumer access to justice, as witnessed in a recently published Green Paper on the subject.[34] In France the 'Commission de Refonte de Droit de la Consommation' proposed a class action procedure. Though not introduced, there has been established an 'action d'intérêt collectif' which is considered below under the consumer agency model. Holland has recently established a class action procedure,[35] and in Scandinavia there are proposals to introduce such schemes. In Scandinavia collective redress is generally achieved through the ombudsman system (a public agency model).

---

31   N. L'Heureux, 'L'action Collective au Quebec' in Th. Bourgoignie (ed), *op. cit.*

32   I. Ramsay, 'Class Action: Class Proceedings Act 1992' (1993) 1 *Consum LJ* CS 39.

33   J. Goldring, L. Maher, J. McKeough, *Consumer Protection Law* (4th ed. (Federation Press, 1993) at pp. 440–6.

34   Com (93) 576: see 17.9.3.

35   See N. Frenk and E. Hondius, 'Collective Action in Consumer Affairs: Towards Law Reform in the Netherlands' [1991] *EConsum LJ* 17.

13.3.1.3 Opren:[36]

The English legal system knows of no specific class action procedure. Instead, until recently, it muddled through in good common law fashion by using a test case strategy, perhaps combined with some sort of 'group action'.[37] This system worked well so long as the costs of the group/class action were borne either by a trade union or the legal aid fund. Whilst trade unions will continue to underwrite the costs of test cases, the tacit consensus over the use of the legal aid fund to finance group actions was smashed by the *Opren* case.[38]

Opren involved almost 1,500 plaintiffs who were suffering side–effects after having taken Opren, an anti–arthritis drug. Two–thirds were eligible for legal aid, which is granted to applicants who pass both a merits test and a means test judged against both income and capital (see above). Of the 500 or so plaintiffs who failed to obtain legal aid, most failed on the capital means test as the majority of the victims were old people whose savings were above the permitted capital (£4,850). Prior to the *Opren* case, such plaintiffs had in effect been provided with a free ride on the back of legally aided plaintiffs, who were selected to be the test cases. Defendants had never seen fit to question this – perhaps fearing adverse publicity if they were seen to be intimidating hapless victims. In *Opren* the Government was joined as a defendant. The Treasury Solicitor, representing the Committee on Safety of Medicines and the Medicine Act Licensing Authority, was not shy of seeking guidance on the question of liability for costs. In the High Court, Mr Justice Hirst concluded that the 500 non–legally aided plaintiffs could not have a free ride on the back of the legal aid fund and that the costs should be borne equally by all plaintiffs. This decision was upheld by the Court of Appeal.[39] In the event the non–legally aided Opren victims were only able to continue with their claims because a millionaire benefactor, Mr Godfrey Bradman, underwrote their costs. The reason why the plaintiff lawyers were so keen to

---

36 The following discussion draws on the paper by G. Howells 'Mass Tort Litigation in the English Legal System – Have the Lessons from Opren been Learned?' in *United Kingdom Law in the Mid–1990s* J. Bridge *et al.* (eds) (UKNCCL, 1994).

37 But note that in *Horrocks v Ford Motor Company, The Times,* 15 February 1990, Lord Donaldson, the Master of the Rolls, said: 'Standard court procedures were designed for the determination of the general run of claims coming before the Courts. But, if the Courts were presented with large numbers of claims with special features in common they would devise new procedures specially adapted to such cases.' This represents a flexible attitude on the part of the judiciary towards group litigation. The major problem has been the financing of such litigation and the liability for costs.

38 *Davies v Eli Lilley & Co* [1987] 1 WLR 1136.

39 *Ibid.*

use legally aided plaintiffs for the test cases was because, if they lost, the normal rule that 'costs follow the event' does not apply. Making non–legally aided plaintiffs liable for a proportion of the costs was effectively pricing justice out of their reach. Even if they could have afforded to risk their money on a legal battle, this might not have been sensible given that the damages involved were relatively modest[40] and that, even if the case were won, costs could easily be incurred due to unsuccessful interlocutory or preliminary applications.

In the light of the *Opren* case there have been several calls for the law to be reformed. However, the Legal Aid Board had cautioned against abandoning too quickly a test case strategy in favour of a formal 'group or class action' procedure and had pointed out that the risks could be overcome by establishing a cost–sharing regime or pursuing the case under the new Multi–Party Action Arrangements.[41] Some experience of the new regime – particularly the litigations concerning the drug Benzodiazepine – seems to have changed the Board's opinion, for it has recently called for an overhaul of how legal aid is granted in such cases, the court procedures adopted and even suggested that some cases might be better dealt with by alternatives to the courts, such as a Drugs Compensation Tribunal.[42]

17.3.1.4 Guide For Use in Group Actions

As a response to the *Opren* case the Supreme Court Procedure Committee issued a *Guide For Use in Group Actions* in May 1991. This document does not comment on the law or proposed reforms, but instead provides practical advice about how group actions can be brought under the present rules. As the law presently stands, there are several forms of procedure a group action can rely on.

17.3.1.4.1 The Representative Action: The Rules of the Supreme Court provide a mechanism for a representative action to be brought 'where numerous persons have the same interest in any proceedings'.[43] The class

---

40   It has been suggested that few of the claims were worth more than £10,000 with many worth only around £1,000, the reason for the low damage levels being the old age of many of the victims: see G. Dehn, 'Opren – Problems, Solutions, and More Problems' (1989) 12 *JCP* 397.

41   See *infra*.

42   See *Issues Arising for the Legal Aid Board and the Lord Chancellor's Department from Multi–Party Actions,* (Legal Aid Board, 1994).

43   RSC Order 15, rule 12(1).

being represented must be clearly defined and the party must be able to claim to represent all of the class. The procedure would allow a claim to be brought or defended by a representative of the class.

There are, however, some hurdles to be overcome before this procedure can be invoked. It is not at all clear whether parties in mass tort actions will 'have the same interest in any proceedings'. There is some authority that claims for damages (or debt) can never involve parties with the same interest. It is contended that the parties will not have the same interest if, in spite of some common ground, there are also peculiarities in the individual cases, for example defences or counterclaims not applicable to the class as a whole. The action also imposes the onerous procedural requirement that, in cases of doubt, the names of members of a class should be annexed to the writ. This is at best likely to be highly inconvenient in consumer cases.

Where claims involve a large number of plaintiffs suing a known defendant, or at most a limited number of defendants joined in the action, a representative action may be feasible. However, where there are also numerous defendants it would not seem appropriate to bind them by a representative action to which they were not a party, unless they could be considered bound by a contractual arrangement to accept such a decision.

The tendency, however, is to be more generous in allowing the representative action. The consequences of a representative action can be quite draconian for Ord. 15 rule 12(3) states that the judgement or order is binding on all parties who are considered to have been present by representation, even if they had not been informed of the court action (although it can only be enforced against persons who were not party to the action by leave of the court). A defendant with a specific defence (or a plaintiff who did not want to be a party to the action) would have to apply to be excluded from the action under Order 15, Rule 12(1) 'by reason of facts and matters particular to his case'.[44] This would not seem possible once judgement was entered; thus although the judgement might not be enforced against that member, he or she would still be bound by the decision.

The representative action is in the control of the representee. This means that the representee and not the represented parties is liable for costs. It also means that the representee has power to settle the case on such terms as he or she thinks fit, although then it would be possible for the others in the class to bring an action on their own count; equally the court has power to add or substitute a new representee. The choice of representee is therefore crucial. If there is a dispute as to who this should be, then the court has discretion under Ord. 15, Rule 12(1) to select the representee or possibly to decide that the action is not appropriate for a representative action.

---

[44]   RSC Ord. 15, rule 12 (5).

17.3.1.4.2 Joint Plaintiffs: The Court rules allow one solicitor, who either represents a large number of plaintiffs or has powers delegated to him or her through a committee of instructed solicitors, to issue one writ covering all the actions.[45] It has been estimated that serving one writ on behalf of 1001 plaintiffs instead of individual writs would save £70,000 in court fees for the writ alone and £10,000 for each interlocutory summons.[46]

The court also has powers to consolidate actions started independently on such terms as it thinks just.[47] Normally, one firm of solicitors will be given conduct of the consolidated action, usually guided by a co–ordinating committee. Once issues of liability have been sorted out, the matter may be referred back to the original solicitors to deal with matters relating to damages.

The court is given power to select certain test cases or lead actions – a useful approach if all parties co–operate.[48] Once selected, plaintiffs in lead cases should pursue to judgment; equally, defendants should not seek to 'buy off' actions which have been selected as lead actions. This advice from the Supreme Court Procedure Committee reflects a serious problem with the test case strategy – defendants may try to settle the strongest cases in the hope of avoiding liability in weaker cases.

Thus the English legal system does not have a class action procedure, though it does have mechanisms for both representative actions and test cases. These, however, are not geared up to deal with the problem posed by mass tort claims. Funding has been a particular problem, but is not the only weakness of the present system.

17.3.1.5 Multi–Party Action Arrangements

The Legal Aid Act 1988 allowed for the possibility of contracting out legal aid services. This was followed up in the context of 'multi–party actions' (actions with ten or more assisted persons) in personal injury cases by provisions being made for representation by means of contracts under reg. 152 of the Civil Legal Aid (General) Regulations 1989.[49] The actual procedures are set out in the Legal Aid Board Multi–Party Action Arrangements 1992. Under the procedures, when ten legal aid certificates have been issued in respect of an action, the Area Director nominated to

---

45   RSC Ord. 15, rules 4, 5 and 6.
46   *Guide For Use in Group Actions*, at p. 18.
47   RSC Ord. 4, rule 9.
48   RSC Ord. 4, rule 9(1).
49   S.I. 1989/339; see also *Legal Aid Handbook 1993* prepared by the Legal Aid Board (Sweet & Maxwell, 1993).

receive all applications concerning the action in question will make a report to the Multi–Party Action Committee. That committee will decide whether to invoke the contracting procedures based on, *inter alia*, whether common issues of fact and law arise out of the cause and event in question and whether the action involves significant complexity in terms of assembling statements, undertaking research, obtaining expert evidence, examining and processing large volumes of documents or otherwise. If it is decided to invoke the contracting procedures, tenders will be invited from firms alone or in conjunction with others, perhaps as part of a consortium or steering committee. The selection of firms is based on criteria contained in the Arrangements, with the successful firm being granted a standard contract incorporating the terms laid down in the Arrangements.

The contracting out of legal aid services in multi–party actions was driven by two sets of considerations. First, experience shows that costs in such cases can soon escalate to the extent that they far exceed the sums being claimed; moreover, costs are often duplicated with different firms doing the same work. Second, there is concern over the quality of work in large scale personal injury cases. Handling not only the legal aspects but also the public relations side of such litigation requires both expertise and also a large infrastructure which can only be found in a limited number of firms. There is an obvious danger that these rules, which are aimed at protecting the consumer, could instead end up benefiting the small circle of law firms which have been quick to develop experience in this type of work. To some extent this danger has been recognised, which explains why only the generic work is expected be subject to the multi–party action arrangements, with clients being able to retain their own solicitors for matters such as assessment of damages. This also goes some way to strike a balance between the desire to allow clients their choice of representation and the need to ensure efficient and effective delivery of legal services. The procedures permit firms to bid in groups, though the Committee can invite firms to agree to smaller, larger or different groups of firms being selected. This power could be used innovatively to ensure that smaller firms and firms just moving into this area are included in a group given the contract for generic work so that they can gain the necessary expertise in mass tort litigation and prevent a monopoly situation from arising.

A major problem remains, however. Private clients must bear a fair proportion of the costs of the actions. Contracting firms must state in their tender reports how they propose private clients will contribute to the costs. As in the *Opren* litigation, the fear of costs may well force private litigants to drop their legal claim. Even legally aided claimants may not consider litigation worthwhile if the damages recoverable are likely to be wholly or significantly subject to a statutory charge.

The merits and means tests for civil legal aid in multi-party litigation remain the same as for other civil cases, although the *Legal Aid Handbook* does note that the strength and viability of such actions should be considered globally. The delivery of legal services should be streamlined, but the costs of proceedings will continue to be borne by the group of litigants as a whole. Several suggestions have been made for more fundamental reforms to the funding of class actions; the Lord Chancellor commented during the debates to the Legal Aid Bill 1988 that such changes could be introduced under that legislation.

17.3.1.6 Reform

17.3.1.6.1 Funding: During the course of the passage of the Legal Aid Bill 1988, the Law Society had argued that, in complex and lengthy group actions, a High Court judge should be allowed to issue a certificate if the court was satisfied that injustice would occur if the claims were dealt with individually. The Legal Aid Board would then grant representation, without contribution, to all those covered by the certificate and the statutory charge would not apply. The only consolation for defendants would be that, if successful in defending the case, they would be able to recover their costs from the Legal Aid Board, without having to show that they would suffer severe financial hardship (which is the test usually applied). Lord Ackner also proposed that the statutory charge should not apply, whilst the National Consumer Council proposed a more limited scheme, which would have been restricted to plaintiffs challenging the development risks defence in product liability actions, who it was argued should be granted non–means tested legal aid. Recently the National Consumer Council has, whilst retaining its proposal relating to the development risks defence, also called for non–means tested legal aid to be extended to all plaintiffs in group actions, with a maximum contribution from capital/income or by way of a statutory charge of £1,000.[50] Alternatively it suggests that the costs of the successful plaintiff should be paid by the defendant(s) on an indemnity basis. This would prevent any statutory charge from arising and allow for the full recovery of damages.

The Law Society proposed that there should be no statutory charge; the National Consumer Council suggested either a £1,000 limit or an indemnity from the defendant for all plaintiff costs. At first consideration an indemnity might appear to be the fairest solution – after all, why should a successful plaintiff have to pay any costs, unless costs were incurred by the case being mishandled? However, this raises general questions of equity in the cost system which are not peculiar to this type of litigation. Thus, limiting the

---

50   See National Consumer Council, *Group Actions,* (NCC, 1988) and National Consumer Council, *Ordinary Justice,* (NCC, 1989) at pp. 327–35.

contribution to, say, £1,000 appears a sensible compromise.[51] Consideration might be given to holding the defendants liable to the Legal Aid Fund for any shortfall, perhaps in return for the right to recover damages from the Legal Aid Fund if they successfully defend the case. In this way all parties are given an incentive to ensure costs are minimised.

Some more radical proposals to the funding problem have emerged. In 1982 the Scottish Consumer Council issued a report proposing a class action procedure for Scottish courts.[52] This suggested the establishment of an independently administered Class Action Fund to finance class actions. Successful litigants would be required to pay a percentage of any damages recovered to the Fund, so that, in time, it would be self–financing. Such a model has much to commend it, especially as its funds could be further enhanced by paying over to it the damages of any members of a class who cannot be traced. However, the need for an initial outlay of cash would seem to make this option politically unacceptable in the present climate.

The Courts and Legal Services Act 1990 now allows solicitors to take on cases on a 'no win, no fee' basis, with successful lawyers being able to claim normal costs. Class actions may be one area where this power could be invoked. However, it is difficult to see many firms being able to underwrite complex litigation; whilst on the other hand it is difficult to see why, in straightforward cases, firms should take a slice of the plaintiff's damages.[53]

17.3.1.6.2 Procedure: During the Parliamentary debates on the Legal Aid Act 1988, the Lord Chancellor raised the prospect of procedural reforms. The Legal Aid Board has since put forward some proposals for a designated group action procedure. This essentially involves the creation of a register which potential plaintiffs can join. Costs would then be on the basis of the multi–party action arrangements and procedures would be streamlined, with any similar proceedings started independently being transferred to the group action, save in exceptional circumstances.[54] However, these proposals are limited in scope and do not deal with the complex questions, which need to be resolved if a group/class action procedure is to be established. The best discussion to date is to be found in the National Consumer Council's *Group*

---

51   Possibly the judge could be given a discretion to reduce this contribution if it amounted to too large a proportion of the damages recoverable.

52   Scottish Consumer Council, *Class Actions in the Scottish Court* (1982); this proposal has recently been placed back on the reform agenda by the Scottish Law Commission *op. cit.*

53   M. Mildred, *op. cit.*

54   Although note that the Legal Aid Board has recently called for a more thorough overhaul of multi–party action arrangements, *Legal Aid Board, op. cit.*

Action document. The National Consumer Council favoured a formalised group/class action procedure along the following lines.

(i) Certification

Group actions would be based on certification by the courts that a particular action was suited to the procedure. The following criteria were suggested as being relevant:

(i)   The group must be numerous.
(ii)   Substantial questions of fact or law must be common to the group. The National Consumer Council quite rightly rejected the idea that such group questions must predominate over questions affecting individual members of the group. Such a test is included in the US Federal Rule 23(b)(3) and has been found to exclude mass tort claims from the class action procedure, because claims for damages turn on unique features concerning questions of causation and quantum of damages.
(iii)   The named representative plaintiff must fairly and adequately represent the group.
(iv)   The action must be manageable given the size of the group and the issues raised.
(v)   The group action must be superior to the alternatives available for the fair and efficient resolution of the issues.
(vi)   There must be a reasonable possibility of success. This was intended to parallel the merits test in legal aid. The standard of reasonable possibility was sensibly preferred to a test related to any degree of probability, given the need for certification to occur earlier in the proceedings.
(vii)   The action must not be frivolous, vexatious or abusive.

These proposals seem to strike a good balance between invoking group/class action procedures where desirable, with the minimum of procedural technicalities, whilst ensuring that the procedure is not abused.

(ii) Opting in or out and notice requirements

There is an important question as to whether it should be the plaintiff's choice to join a group/class action or whether the action should bind all members of the group, possibly with some members being allowed to opt out in specific circumstances. Indeed the debate as to whether opt outs should be available at all raises questions about the relative weight to be given to the right of individuals to control the prosecution of their legal claims versus the efficiency gains of collective litigation. In the US class actions are available for mass tort claims on two bases: either because the class has common issues in dispute or to prevent a scramble for limited funds. Whilst opting out is possible in the former scenario, although the courts have been reluctant to allow it, it is not possible where there are limited funds available for distribution; in such a case absent members of the class need not even be notified of the action.

It is on the opt–out/opt–in choice that the National Consumer Council proposals are the most vague. The report seems to draw a distinction between on the one hand consumer claims and on the other product liability/disaster claims. The latter would be subject to the traditional opt–in principle, whereas for the former consumers would be treated as part of the group unless they opted out. This draws a sensible distinction between claims where the victims are more easily identifiable, such as users of a defective product or victims of a disaster, and those cases where the damage is spread over a wide non–identifiable mass of the population, such as the victims of an overpricing policy by taxi drivers. In practice, however, it may be difficult to draw such a distinction in terms which the courts can readily recognise and apply. Notice would be required to be given in both types of action. Sensibly, it is suggested that when it is not possible to identify members of the class, the judge should have the discretion to order an appropriate method of giving notice, for example by using local and/or national newspaper advertisements. The National Consumer Council report emphasises the importance of notice in product liability/disaster type cases to avoid problems of *res judicata*. Yet if group/class actions are to be available to such litigants on an opt–in basis there should be no issue of *res judicata*, for parties who have not positively opted–in should not be bound by the action.

The advantages of having all the issues tried at once in a class action would seem to justify compelling all plaintiffs to join in one action, save in wholly exceptional circumstances. The advantages relate both to efficiency in court administration, savings in lawyers' fees and also the greater chance of an improved and more coherent case being made out by the plaintiffs if all parties act in a co–ordinated manner. There may, however, be a case for allowing individual plaintiffs, or groups of plaintiffs, to be separately represented; in addition the judge should be given the role of protecting the interests of absent class members.

(iii) Damages

The National Consumer Council's report recognises the need for flexibility in the remedies available in class actions. Sometimes damages should be assessed individually, even if liability is to be determined communally; in other cases a rough and ready apportionment of damages may be the only practicable course. In some instances damages may be more appropriately paid to collective organisations representing the interests of the victims than to individuals directly. Thus in the *Agent Orange* case brought in the US courts by Vietnam veterans who claimed to have suffered injury as a result of a chemical defoliant used in the jungle war, a substantial proportion of the damages was paid to veterans' associations rather than to individuals. Other cases may call for still more innovative remedies. For instance, in the *New York Yellow Cab* case, when overcharging was proven in a class action, the company was ordered to reduce its costs until the damages suffered generally had been returned to the public. The car company Rover has agreed to pay the Consumers' Association £1M for breaches of competition law involving limiting the discounts available from dealers.[55] Since it would be impossible to trace the customers affected, it was thought best to provide money for the benefit of all British car buyers. Such innovation is to be commended.

17.3.2 Consumer Organisation Model

The private initiative model essentially continues to see the complaint in terms of an aggregation of individual grievances, albeit having wider implications which justify modifying certain rules of procedure and remedies. Continued reliance on private initiative alone would mean that many consumer complaints would still not reach the courts, due to the remaining problems of funding litigation and/or a lack of motivation on the part of consumers to bring claims. Consumers may be uninterested in taking action if the damages are only minor; in some cases, there might also be difficulty in showing individual damage. One response is to allow consumer organisations to bring claims on behalf of consumers generally.[56] Usually this would be for injunctive relief, although one might wish the court to be able to award damages to redress a wrong suffered by specific consumers if this is practicable. The £1M payment by Rover to the Consumers' Association for breach of competition law illustrates the sort of order which could be possible even if individual losses cannot be traced. In France consumer organisations are allowed to bring actions representing the consumer interest where there has been a criminal infraction or an unfair contract term has been used. Furthermore, consumer organisations can participate in civil

---

55 See *The Independent*, 17, November 1993 at p. 2.
56 There are of course important questions about the legitimacy of consumer groups representing the consumer interest. See G. Howells, 'Consumer Representation' (1993) 1 *Consum LJ* 17.

cases started by individuals and seek the cessation of illegal acts which damage the consumers' collective interest. There is also a class action procedure in France, but individuals cannot bring it themselves, instead the action must be brought by a consumers' association.[57]

Certain European directives have allowed for the possibility of injunctive relief being sought by consumer organisations. Thus the Misleading Advertisements Directive provides that 'persons or organisations regarded under national law as having a legitimate interest in prohibiting misleading advertisement' may take action against such advertisements.[58] The Unfair Terms in Consumer Contracts Directive is even more explicit that this right extends to consumer groups, claiming 'persons or organisations, having a legitimate interest under national law in protecting consumers' should have the right to take action to prevent the continued use of unfair terms in consumer contracts.[59] However, perhaps the key words in the two provisions cited are 'under national law', for the UK Government has seen fit to limit the persons or organisations given such powers to just the Director General of Fair Trading (hereafter Director General).[60] Whilst this extension of the Director General's functions is to be welcomed, it nevertheless represents a missed opportunity to allow consumer organisations to take on a more activist role if they so chose, although it is unlikely (for financial reasons) that the powers would be widely used by them. The Government is in truth not so much concerned about the possibility of actions by consumer groups, but rather fears environmental groups seeking similar powers.

17.3.3 Public Agency

The Scandinavian consumer ombudsman model is perhaps the most developed public agency model.[61] Although many countries have powerful public agencies to supervise consumer matters, notably the US which has a very powerful Federal Trade Commission and Food and Drug Administration. In the UK the most influential public agency for consumer

---

57   See J. Calais–Auloy, 'Settlement of Disputes by Judicial Means: Situation in France' in *III European Conference on Consumer Access to Justice* (Instituto do Consumidor, 1992).
58   Art.4, Directive 84/450: OJ 1984 L250/17.
59   Art.7(2), Directive 93/13: OJ 1993 L95/29.
60   See Control of Misleading Advertisements Regulations 1988, S.I. 1988/915 and the Unfair Terms in Consumer Contract Regulations 1994, S.I. 1994/3159. The Consumers' Association are seeking judicial review of the UK goverment's decision not to give them standing to challenge unfair terms.
61   See 17.5.

affairs is the Office of Fair Trading.[62] The powers of the Office of Fair Trading to intervene under the misleading advertisements regulations have already been mentioned. This power was scrutinised by the courts in *Director General of Fair Trading v Tobyward*[63] where Hoffmann J, as he then was, endorsed the use of injunctive powers to support the self–regulatory controls on advertising.[64] We have also seen that the Director General has various other means by which he can control undesirable practices. For example, he can invoke his powers as a licensing authority for consumer credit[65] or make orders under Part III of the Fair Trading Act 1973 against persistently unfair traders.[66] Proposals to extend these powers have been considered elsewhere.[67]

Public agencies are well placed to perform a policing role on behalf of consumers. Organisations such as the Office of Fair Trading build up a lot of experience of trading practices and are sufficiently aware of commercial reality to arrive at sensible judgements about what is reasonable business conduct.[68] The justification for public agencies taking on this role is self–evidently the inability of consumers to protect their diffuse interests. A distinction may perhaps be drawn between the desirability of public agencies seeking injunctive relief and litigating claims for damages. Questions may be raised as to whether litigation to help individual consumers obtain damages is a proper role for a public agency and the most effective way of using limited public resources. But this perhaps relates more to the question of how the powers should be exercised, not whether they should theoretically be available.

17.4 SMALL CLAIMS

In 1970 the now defunct Consumer Council published a document, *Justice Out of Reach: A Case for Small Claims Courts*, which showed that consumers were not using lawyers or the courts to settle their disputes. In fact the study did not reveal a single instance of a consumer suing a business. The county court system was castigated as little more than a debt collection

---

62 See Chapter 16.
63 [1989] 2 All ER 266.
64 See 10.6.
65 See 11.1.
66 See 16.4.
67 See 16.5.
68 It should be noted that the business community is more concerned that such powers do not come into the hands of local trading standards officers, who they suspect lack consistency and can sometimes be too zealous: see 14.3.1 and 14.3.4.

agency for business. The Government's response was to introduce an arbitration procedure for small claims in the county court (the so–called small claims court), which would aim to be more informal and not apply the usual rule that costs follow the event. This procedure was further refined following the National Consumer Council's report *Simple Justice:*[69] higher ceilings were placed on claims which could be arbitrated and cases where a defence was filed would automatically be referred to arbitration. Recently further changes have been effected following the recommendations of the *Civil Justice Review*[70] The rules of the small claims court will first be summarised, then some evidence of its actual operation will be considered, before addressing some questions about its effectiveness.

17.4.1 Procedure

The small claims arbitration procedure was established by the Administration of Justice Act 1973.[71] Since 1991 all claims for £1,000 or less are automatically referred to the arbitration procedure; claims for more than £1,000 *may* be referred to arbitration if both parties agree. Originally a preliminary hearing was introduced into the procedure in the belief that this would help the parties resolve their disputes, or at least speed matters up and make the actual trial more effective. However, experience showed that these advantages did not accrue. Following the recommendations of the *Civil Justice Review* there is now normally no preliminary hearing, although the Government preferred not to remove the possibility of one in the most complex cases.

An important rule in arbitration is that the losing party is not normally liable for the other party's lawyers' fees, except for costs incurred 'through the unreasonable conduct' of the case and a small sum in respect of the issuing of the summons.

Where a matter is referred to arbitration, the district judge who hears the

---

[69] (NCC, 1979).

[70] (Cm 394, 1988).

[71] See now s.64, County Courts Act 1984, as amended by the Courts and Legal Services Act 1990. For a good history of small claims procedures see C. Whelan, 'Small Claims in England and Wales: Redefining Justice' in C. Whelan (ed), *Small Claims Court: A Comparative Study* (Clarendon Press, 1990). He is especially interesting on the independent small claims courts which were set up in Manchester in 1971 and in London in 1973. Both eventually failed due to funding problems, but the procedure of the London scheme in particular was markedly different from that of county court small claims, being far more informal and for the most part eschewing legal representation.

case may rescind the referral and send the matter for trial in the ordinary county court in the following circumstances:

(i) if a difficult question of law or a question of fact of exceptional complexity is involved:
(ii) if there is a charge of fraud;
(iii) if the parties agree that the dispute should be tried in court;
(iv) if it would be unreasonable for the claim to proceed to arbitration having regard to its subject matter, the circumstances of the parties or the interests of any other person likely to be affected by the award.[72] (In *Pepper v Healey*[73] this exception was applied where the defendant had legal representation financed by an insurance company. It was felt unfair on the plaintiff to allow the matter to be dealt with by arbitration as, if she won, she would not be able to recover her costs.)[74]

Arbitration proceedings are commenced by the plaintiff filing a 'particulars of claim' and a 'request' for the court to issue a summons against the defendant. The costs of issuing a summons are modest. The litigants are assisted by a free booklet published by the Lord Chancellor's Department entitled *Small Claims in the County Court: How to Sue and Defend Actions Without a Solicitor*, which, amongst other things, contains specimen particulars of claim. The case is usually heard by a district judge.[75]

The county court rules provide that 'Any hearing shall be informal and the strict rules of evidence shall not apply'; moreover 'the arbitrator may adopt any method of procedure which he may consider to be convenient and to afford a fair and equal opportunity to each party to present his case'. However, in *Chilton v Saga Holidays Plc*[76] this was not held to go so far as challenging the adversarial system and the Court of Appeal overruled the registrar's[77] opinion that, where one party was unrepresented, he could prohibit cross–examination and require all questions to be put through the

---

[72] County Court Rules, Ord. 19, rule 1(4).
[73] [1982] RTR 411.
[74] However, it is not of itself unreasonable to proceed by way of arbitration where both parties are insured and can therefore be legally represented, even if this means that the insurers cannot recover their costs; cf *Russell v Wilson, The Independent*, 2 June 1989.
[75] The district judge may refer the matter to a circuit judge, who will normally deal with arbitrations for more than £1,000, or, if the parties agree, to an outsider. Of the 52,360 arbitrations heard by the county courts in 1990, 99 per cent were conducted by a district judge: see *Judicial Statistics 1990*, (Cm 1573, 1991).
[76] [1986] 1 All ER 841.
[77] Registrars are now known as district judges.

chair. The Civil Justice Review found a wide variation in the way arbitrators handled proceedings, but thought that the registrar should, according to the circumstances of the case, 'adopt an interventionist role, dispensing with the rules of evidence and procedure and assuming control of the questioning of the parties and their witnesses'. This recommendation has been followed (with the intention of circumventing *Chilton v Saga Holidays*) in s.6, Courts and Legal Services Act 1990, which provides that the County Court Rules may prescribe the procedure and rules for small claims arbitrations; in particular such rules may 'make provision with respect to the manner of taking and questioning evidence'.

17.4.2 Empirical Evidence

As part of the *Civil Justice Review* the Lord Chancellor's Department commissioned management consultants *Touche Ross* to undertake an empirical study of the operation of the small claims court.[78] Several criticisms have been made of this study's methodology. For example, it only studied defended cases set down for an arbitration hearing[79] and did not treat private litigants as a separate category. Rather, it recategorised litigants into 'small' and 'large' litigants, with 'small' litigants also including groups such as small businesses, shops and local professionals (eg solicitors, accountants and estate agents).[80] Nevertheless, read with care, the study gives some insights into how the scheme operates.

Of the sample of 876 defended cases, the *Touche Ross* study found that private citizens were plaintiffs in 21 per cent of cases against small business or local professionals and in 20 per cent of cases against fellow private citizens; 7 per cent of cases were brought by the combined force of small businesses, local professionals or private citizens against large defendants. Small litigants accounted for about 88 per cent of all defendants. Whilst it could be shown that in 20 per cent of cases private citizens were defending cases brought by fellow private citizens and 14 per cent were defended by private citizens against large litigants it is not possible to know how many

---

[78] Touche Ross, *Civil Justice Review: Study of the Small Claims Procedure* (Touche Ross, 1986).

[79] A subsequent study found that 85 per cent of such cases never proceeded to an arbitration hearing and that private individuals dropped out of litigation at a faster rate than companies: see R. Bowles, 'The County Court Small Claims Procedure: Preliminary Findings from a Small Survey' quoted in Whelan, *op. cit.* at 119.

[80] See C. Whelan, *op. cit.* at pp. 111–119 and C. Whelan, 'The Role of Research in Civil Justice Reform: Small Claims in the County Court' (1987) 6 *CJQ* 237. See 1.1.3 where we consider the 'fuzzy edges' of consumer protection.

cases involved private citizens defending cases against small businesses. In a subsequent study, Bowles has shown that these figures give a misleading impression because they concentrate on defended cases. Private individuals are less likely to defend claims and more likely to have their claims defended. Thus in Bowles' sample, individuals were defendants in 59 per cent of the cases but only entered a defence in 14 per cent; although individuals only brought 12 per cent of cases, they accounted for 29 per cent of those cases in which a defence was filed.

60 per cent of claims in the Touche Ross study involved claims for money owed for goods sold or work done; 13 per cent sought the refund of money for unsatisfactory goods or services or claims for related damages, and 5 per cent related to repayment of loans, overdrafts, hire purchase instalments and the like. The study states that 67 per cent of cases were won by the plaintiff. Yet this fails to recognise that a paper victory for the plaintiff may well disguise an actual victory for the defendant if the plaintiff recovered or settled for less than the amount claimed.

The Touche Ross data on legal representation does not break the information down into detailed categories. Nevertheless in 39 per cent of cases one party was represented by a solicitor (12 per cent the plaintiff and 27 per cent the defendant) while in 9 per cent both parties were represented. (Bowles found that solicitors filed only 2 of the 12 cases brought by private individuals in his sample, whereas of the 59 claims filed against private individuals 21 were filed by solicitors.) The likelihood of representation increased with the size of the claim and also the size of the litigant. Solicitors were by far and away the most likely source of advice. However, the study claimed that whether or not the parties were legally represented made little difference to the outcome.[81]

17.4.3 Perennial Questions

Certain perennial questions are raised about the role and functions of small claims courts.[82] At the root of these lie debates about the need for the civil justice system to balance two factors:

---

[81] Despite flaws in the study's methodology this finding mirrors the results of US studies: see J. Ruhnka and S. Weller, *Small Claims Courts*, (National Center for State Courts, 1978).

[82] The issues discussed here are dealt with more fully in Consumer Council, *Justice Out of Reach*, (HMSO, 1970), *Civil Justice Review, op. cit., Ordinary Justice, op. cit.*, and C. Whelan, *Small Claims Courts: A Comparative Study, op. cit.*, which has a useful concluding chapter dealing with these issues entitled 'Small Claims Courts: Heritage and Adjustment'.

(i)   the desire to have a quick, cheap, accessible system of delivering justice which provides common sense solutions to consumers' problems, against

(ii) the need to ensure that the parties are given an adequate opportunity to present their case and have it decided by an impartial adjudicator on the basis of established legal principles.

The 'smallness'[83] of consumer claims and the fact that consumers are not used to dealing with legal formalities have tended to militate in favour of the former considerations in recent years. However, there is an ongoing debate as to how the balance can best be struck.

17.4.3.1 Business Plaintiffs

A frequently raised issue is whether businesses should be allowed to bring claims in small claims courts: in other words, should the court be a small claims court or simply a consumer court? The argument against allowing access to businesses is that their cases can clog up the system and also create an atmosphere of business values and formalism which may prevent the courts being viewed as 'people's courts'. The answer is, however, surely not to ban businesses but rather to make sure that the presence of business plaintiffs is not allowed to tarnish the image and reality of the small claims courts as a consumer friendly forum for resolving disputes. To ban them from using this cheap form of justice may indeed have adverse effects on consumers. After all, it is consumers who normally have to pay for the enforcement costs of businesses – either directly by costs being added to debts or indirectly through the price of commodities.

17.4.3.2 Legal Representation

A further suggestion for making small claims courts more user–friendly is the prohibition of legal representation. Allowing legal representation may seem unfair to consumers since businesses are more likely to have access to lawyers. Even if a consumer employed a lawyer and won the case, he or she would be unable to recover their costs because of the no costs rule. Removing the right to legal representation is, however, a step not to be taken

---

83   There is of course a debate as to what constitutes a small claim. Recent years have seen the small claims limit raised by more than the rate of inflation. In addition, claims of small monetary value may have a high symbolic or moral value and, to a low–income consumer, may be of considerable significance.

lightly in a society based on the rule of law. It is also doubtful whether to do so would assist consumers greatly. For instance, there is no way to prevent parties from taking legal advice prior to court action or from being coached for the trial. Also the result is likely to be that consumers will find themselves up against company officials more experienced in court proceedings than themselves. With evidence that legal representation has little impact on the outcome of cases, the emphasis should perhaps be placed on creating an atmosphere in which legal representation is not viewed as necessary in small claims cases.

17.4.3.3 Making the Courts More Consumer–Friendly

Much more can perhaps be done to make the prospect of taking or defending a case less formidable and thereby hopefully to increase the number of consumers who use the court system to resolve their consumer disputes.[84] Court staff can be encouraged to assist litigants in filling in the various forms and can advise the parties on the workings of the system. Advice agencies, like citizens' advice bureaux, can be given a clear role in advising parties of their legal position. The information available on the small claims system can be improved. Legal jargon can be avoided. Perhaps most importantly, the judge can be given a far more interventionist role in the process of establishing the facts. The judge should not simply rely on the parties to present salient evidence. In appropriate cases, judges should be allowed to seek their own expert evidence and, where reasonable, charge this to the business party to the litigation, or, alternatively, pay for it out of a contingent fund, perhaps financed by a levy on the summons fee. Courts could be encouraged to make access easier by dealing with some matters purely by way of written papers so that individuals do not need to take time off work. Experiments with evening sessions should be encouraged.[85]

17.4.3.4 Law or Justice?

The current system is described as a 'small claims arbitration' procedure. The *Civil Justice Review* recommended that cases be renamed as 'small claims cases'. This is probably more accurate for the role of the judge is akin to that

---

84 It is not encouraging to note that a 1985 Office of Fair Trading survey found that less than 2 per cent of consumers who took further action in respect of a consumer dispute threatened court action, and that an even smaller number actually took their case to court: quoted in *Ordinary Justice, op. cit.*, at p. 283.

85 Both of these last two matters were suggested by the *Civil Justice Review, op. cit.*

of a judge in the normal court system rather than someone who acts as an arbitrator, mediator or conciliator.[86] This is his or her proper role, for any attempt at conciliation is likely to mean the loss of part of a valid claim by consumers with genuine grievances; it is also likely' that industry would use every opportunity to seek attractive settlements.

However, whilst the judge should be a judge and not an arbitrator, mediator or conciliator, there is still a debate about what laws should be applied. Earlier chapters illustrated how many traditional legal concepts could be inappropriate in the consumer context and require modification. In small claims cases, an argument can be made for allowing cases to be decided on their merits and for not allowing technical legal defences to be raised. Thus s.15(4), New Zealand Small Claims Tribunals Act 1976 provides that:

> 'The Tribunal shall determine the dispute according to the substantial merits and justice of the case, and in doing so shall have regard to the law but shall not be bound to give effect to strict legal rights and obligations or to legal forms or technicalities.'[87]

Similar rules requiring fairness and equity to override strict legal concerns are to be found in Australia,[88] while in Scandinavia the Consumer Complaints Boards take an openly pro–consumer interpretation of the law.[89] Objections that such provisions undermine the certainty of the law can be countered by pointing out that the courts are unlikely to use this power extravagantly and that, since the amounts involved are small, so the effects will only be minor. Of course, as the small claims limit increases, so may the validity of the objection. Indeed, many of the issues relating to informality may have to be reconsidered if the system is asked to deal with more than truly 'small' claims.

---

[86] Although doubtless all judges perform these tasks, as well as adjudication, to various degrees at various times. The pre–hearing assessment provides a good opportunity for judges so inclined to attempt to mediate a solution.

[87] See A. Frame, 'Fundamental Elements of the Small Claims Tribunal System in New Zealand' in C. Whelan, *op. cit.*

[88] See C. Yin and R. Cranston, 'Small Claims Tribunals in Australia' in C. Whelan, *op. cit.*

[89] The decisions of the boards are not binding, but are persuasive on the ordinary courts. K. Vitaanen, 'Consumers Access to Justice in Finland' in *Consumer Protection in Czechoslovakia and Finland*, T. Wilhelmsson and J. Svestka (eds), (Institute for Private Law, 1989).

17.4.3.5 Appeals

There are only limited rights of appeal on points of law from small claims courts. In *Ordinary Justice* the National Consumer Council recommended that the right of appeal be extended, especially as the claims limit increases. In its opinion, simple justice need not be rough justice. However in small claims, which have no or little precedent value, most people would be happy to accept the determination of an independent third party. In any event the right of appeal would probably be used far more by businesses than consumers. Thus the present position seems to reflect a fair compromise between the various objectives of a small claims system.

Small claims tribunals represent a step away from formal court-provided justice towards informal justice. Recent years have seen a growth in the number of Ombudsmen, who represent a further stage in the 'delegalisation' of consumer disputes.

17.5 OMBUDSMEN

The Scandinavian Ombudsman model, which allows the complaints of individuals against the state to be investigated by an independent person, was imported into the United Kingdom in 1967 by the establishment of a Parliamentary Commissioner for Administration. This was subsequently extended to local government and to other areas which were, at least at that time, the responsibility of Government, such as the health service. The Scandinavian countries also have a Consumer Ombudsman,[90] who has proved very successful, not so much in resolving individual disputes, but rather in monitoring market practices.[91] The UK has no equivalent public institution, although the Office of Fair Trading might be viewed as fulfilling some of the functions of the Scandinavian Ombudsmen.

There has, however, been a trend in the UK to establish private sector Ombudsmen to deal with complaints from the public. Since this has been most apparent in the financial service sector,[92] subsequent discussions will concentrate on the insurance, banking and building society ombudsmen

---

[90]   Known as 'Ombud' in politically correct Norway.

[91]   See T. Wilhemsson, 'Administrative Procedures for the Control of Marketing Practices – Theoretical Rationales and Perspectives' (1992) 15 *JCP* 159.

[92]   Note that whilst the Securities and Investment Board's (SIB) proposal to establish an Ombudsman to cover all the self-regulatory organisations (SROs) it controls has not materialised, in practice the SROs have developed Ombudsman–style grievance resolution procedures: see J. Birds and C. Graham, 'Complaints Mechanisms in the Financial Services Industry' (1988) 7 *CJQ* 313 at 324.

schemes.[93] But other Ombudsmen have been spawned too, covering such matters as estate agents, pensions, legal services and complaints against newspapers; and a personal investment authority ombudsman scheme (taking on some of the work previously done by the Insurance Ombudsman) has also recently been established. This proliferation of Ombudsmen, many of them set up on a private basis, has caused the Ombudsmen to come together to question whether institutions should meet certain criteria before they can designate themselves as Ombudsmen. This has also been suggested by the European Commission in their Green Paper on Access to Justice. There are sometimes problems in identifying which Ombudsman has jurisdiction (for example Abbey National changed from a building society into a bank and thus changed Ombudsman); indeed a house purchase may give rise to complaints which must be taken to several different Ombudsmen. Thus one might question whether the sectoral approach is the best choice, although it seems likely to be maintained, not least because there are too many entrenched interests in the 'Ombudsman industry'.

From the industry perspective, Ombudsmen are viewed essentially as providing a dispute resolution machinery. Industries with Ombudsmen gain good public relations advantages by being perceived as offering their customers open and fair consumer redress mechanisms. Ombudsmen schemes also provide business with other advantages over the ordinary courts. These include their greater speed, lower costs and the decision-maker's specialist knowledge of the industry which hopefully results in higher quality decisions. Another important advantage to industry is that the Ombudsman is a private grievance resolution mechanism, which prevents it from having to hang its dirty washing in public. In most instances indications of a likely adverse determination by the Ombudsman will cause the company to settle a dispute. Even when an adverse determination is made, no formal decision is published. Nor do the decisions of the Ombudsmen create binding precedents, although they are likely to be followed by the Ombudsman in the future. Although consumers individually may be satisfied with a system which resolves cheaply and expeditiously their particular dispute, in a broader perspective consumers need a grievance system which also promotes standards and encourages good practice. Thus in the following description of

---

93   See J. Birds and C. Graham, *op. cit.* and 'Complaints against Insurance Companies' (1993) 1 *Consum LJ* 92; National Consumer Council, *Ombudsman Schemes in the Private Sector: A Comparison and Assessment*, (NCC, 1988) and *Ombudsmen Services* (NCC, 1993); P. Morris, 'The Banking Ombudsman' [1987] *JBL* 131 and 199 and 'The Banking Ombudsman – Five Years On' [1992] *LMCLQ* 227; R. James and M. Seneviratne, 'The Building Societies Ombudsman Scheme' (1992) 11 *CJQ* 157 and M. Seneviratne, R. James and C. Graham, 'The Banks, The Ombudsman and Complaints Procedures' (1994) 13 *CJQ* 253.

the insurance, banking and building society ombudsmen schemes, attention will be paid to the extent to which Ombudsmen view their function as promoting good practice. Consideration will be given to the publicity or lack of publicity which attend their decisions. This publicity may not be on an individual case basis, but rather may take the form of statements of the position adopted by the Ombudsman on particular issues, which might for instance appear in annual reports.

17.5.1 History

The origins of the insurance, banking and building society ombudsmen schemes are quite different. In 1981 five major insurance companies came together to form the Insurance Ombudsman Bureau (IOB). It now has 336 company members (90 per cent + of its potential membership)[94] although the Co–operative Insurance Society remains a notable absentee. It took over the functions of the Unit Trust ombudsman, which was found to have an insufficient workload to merit its continued existence. However, recently part of its workload had been lost to the Personal Investment Authority. It has been alleged that the impetus for the voluntary creation of the IOB was to stave off further Government regulation of the insurance industry, though whether this is true may perhaps never be known for certain.

The establishment of the Banking Ombudsman, however, did originate as a response to the threat of having a solution imposed on the industry from outside. This followed the publication by the National Consumer Council of their report, *Banking Services and the Consumer*,[95] which recommended that an Ombudsman, modelled on the IOB, be created for both bank and building society customers. The banking ombudsman came into operation in 1986.[96]

With hindsight, the Building Societies' Association had, perhaps, rather too rashly rejected the idea of an Ombudsman. Faced with this opposition, the Government accepted an amendment to the Building Societies Bill, put

---

94 The potential always exists for voluntary schemes not to cover the whole of an industry. One possibility might be for the Ombudsman to give an opinion on issues of principle (opinion on the facts could not be given as only one version of events would be available to the Ombudsman) – even if a case concerned a non–member – which might then be used to reach a settlement. There are, however, dangers with this approach since it may antagonise non–members, making them less willing to consider joining the scheme.

95 (HMSO, 1983).

96 Jack (Cmnd 622, 1989) para.15.15 criticised the voluntary nature of the Banking Ombudsman scheme, but the Government rejected these criticisms.

forward by Conservative MPs, for the creation of a statutory Ombudsman scheme which came into effect on 1 July 1987.[97] The consequences of having a statutory scheme foisted upon them are (i) that the scheme is less flexible than the voluntary schemes, (ii) that the Building Society Ombudsman has greater powers than his counterparts, and (iii) that there is a degree of external control of the scheme due to the supervisory role of the Building Societies' Commission.

17.5.2 Constitutions

All three ombudsmen schemes are set up as companies limited by guarantee and share a similar constitution, with power and functions being divided between the ombudsman, a board of directors and a council. For building societies, the legislation provides the scheme must be approved by the Building Societies Commission.[98] The board of directors are appointed by the industry and are responsible for the financing of the schemes. Crucial questions concerning the independence of each scheme therefore relate to the independence of the council and the control it can exert on such matters as the appointment of the Ombudsman and his terms of reference.

The IOB constitution permits 12 council members (there are currently 11) of whom three are board nominees, with the remainder being appointed by the council, subject to board approval which is not to be unreasonably withheld. Four of the council nominees are to be representatives of the public and consumer interest. The council of the Banking Ombudsman Bureau (BOB) has seven members of whom four, including the chairman, must represent the consumer interest. The Building Society Ombudsman Scheme (BSOS) has an eight–strong council comprising three board members and five lay members including a lay chairman. Thus in each case, board members are in a minority, but consumers are only just in the majority under the banking ombudsman scheme and are not even assured of such a majority under the other schemes. Each of the councils appoints the Ombudsman. It is noteworthy that the boards of the BOB and BSOB can veto such an appointment, but the board of the IOB has no such blocking power.

As regards the terms of reference given to the Ombudsmen, the BSOS is the most obviously independent. Statute prescribes certain minimum standards and the scheme has to be approved by the Building Societies Commission. The council then monitors the functioning of the scheme and recommends amendments although, given its power to withdraw approval

---

97   Ss.83–85 and Scheds 12–13, Building Societies Act 1986.
98   S.83(8), Building Societies Act 1986: only one scheme, that proposed by the Building Societies' Association, has been approved.

from a scheme, the Building Societies Commission would surely be consulted on any such amendments. The Insurance Ombudsman's terms of reference are determined by the council, subject to the board's approval. Formally at least the Banking Ombudsman's board of directors has the greatest formal powers over the terms of reference, which it determines and may amend. The council merely monitors the terms of reference and can only recommend amendments to the scheme. Under all three schemes the councils submit budgets to the boards, who may accept, reject or amend them.

17.5.3 Jurisdiction

The IOB's terms of reference provide for the Insurance Ombudsman to receive complaints in connection with or arising out of a policy (or proposed policy) of insurance. There are several exclusions from this jurisdiction, the most notable being that the Ombudsman cannot take into account matters of actuarial judgement. However, some complaints which might appear to involve actuarial judgments, for example calculation of surrender values, may in fact be instances of mis–selling which are within the Ombudsman's jurisdiction. This is similar to the 'commercial' decision exclusion which applies to banks and building societies. The Insurance Ombudsman's awards of up to £100,000 are binding on companies; above £100,000 the Ombudsman can merely make a recommendation.

Both the BOB and BSOS have a limit of £100,000 on binding awards, with no apparent power even to make recommendations above this ceiling. The BOB covers all banking services which are widely defined in the terms of reference as all such services provided by banks in the ordinary course of their business, (including credit card services, executor and trustee work and advice services relating to taxation, insurance and investments). There are several limitations imposed on this jurisdiction, only the most significant of which will be discussed here. An important exclusion, also present in the BSOS, is the 'commercial decision' exclusion which, understandably, seeks to prevent the Ombudsman from interfering in a bank's 'judgment of risk and other financial or commercial criteria (including assessments of character)'. Concern has been expressed that the exclusion is too widely drawn, for it precludes the Ombudsman from giving a formal ruling even where such decisions are based on gross maladministration. Although the Ombudsman would no doubt ask the bank to reconsider the case, it might be better if the same approach were taken as under the BSOS which requires a building society (which has made a commercial decision in the wake of a serious procedural error) to 'take its decision again and reach it by proper procedures.'[99] In similar vein the Banking Ombudsman cannot take into account 'a practice or policy of a bank which does not itself give rise to a breach of any obligation or duty owed by the bank to the applicant'. Again this needs to be flexibly interpreted so that, whilst the banks should be free to set their own policies, these should not cause injustice to individuals. Instances where this occurs might be caught by giving a wide definition to 'maladministration', but again the BSOS seems to cover the position more clearly by including decisions involving unfair treatment.

The BOB scheme has one unique feature which allows members to require the Ombudsman to terminate his inquiries if the bank considers that the complaint raises a point of important consequence for the bank or banks generally or raises an important or novel point of law. The matter will then be considered by the normal courts with the bank undertaking to pay the complainant's legal costs. Whilst the consumer may benefit from a test case strategy in which the courts give authoritative rulings on controversial points of law, there must be some concern over a scheme which gives the power of selecting cases to the industry defendant. A useful development might be for the Ombudsman to order that cases raising difficult or novel points of law be referred to the normal courts at the industry's expense.

The BSOS terms of reference comply with those laid down in sched. 12, part II, Building Societies Act 1986 which limit jurisdiction to complaints relating to share and deposit accounts, borrowing of any kind, banking services, and trustee and executorships. A controversial exclusion is that of negligent valuation and surveys carried out by building society employees. A proposal by the council to extend the Ombudsman's terms of reference to cover such situations was not accepted by the Building Society Commission.[100]

Certain limitations are common to all three schemes, namely that the Ombudsmen cannot take on a case:

(i) if it is the subject of legal proceedings,
(ii) until the defendant company's internal complaints procedures have been exhausted,
(iii) if it has been previously heard by him unless new evidence is produced, and:

---

[99] Sched.12, para.4(4) of the Building Societies Act 1986; see P. Morris (1987), *op. cit.* at 202. Such a provision could also usefully be included in the Insurance Ombudsman's terms of reference where an actuarial judgement was based on a procedural error. The Insurance Ombudsman takes the view that, where details on the calculation of surrender values are contained in the policy, he can ask whether the actuary calculated the surrender value in accordance with that policy.

[100] Building Society Ombudsman Annual Report 1989–90 at 23.

(iv) if more than six months have elapsed from the time the company refused to satisfy the complainant's claim.

Both the BOB and BSOS terms of reference allow their Ombudsmen to refuse a complaint on the ground that it is frivolous or vexatious. This power has been used sparingly: the Insurance Ombudsman has no such power.

17.5.4 Procedure

The procedures adopted by the Ombudsmen differ markedly from those followed by the courts. Although the Ombudsmen have a broad discretion as to the conduct of cases, the vast majority are dealt with by written correspondence which should make the proceedings cheaper and speedier. There may be a danger that consumers are unable to express themselves clearly in written form, but this is countered by the more central investigative role played by the Ombudsmen.

Central to their function is the need for access to information, However, whilst the Building Society Ombudsman can require information to be disclosed,[101] the Banking and Insurance Ombudsmen can only request information and have to rely on the threat of reporting non–compliance to the council to ensure that members co–operate with their requests. This difference would seem to result from the building society scheme being statutory, which perhaps also explains why the Banking and Insurance Ombudsmen place importance on trying to conciliate cases. This is most clearly seen under the BOB scheme where the process incorporates a specific stage at which the Ombudsman tries to help the parties reach agreement. Failing this, the Ombudsman will make an informal assessment with written reasons. This is usually accepted by the bank but, if not, the Ombudsman then makes a 'formal recommendation' with written reasons which is binding on the bank. The complainant cannot appeal this decision although he or she remains free to bring an action in the normal court. The Insurance Ombudsman works in a similar way, except that the process of conciliation is less formal.

Although in many ways the statutory nature of the BSOB has endowed it with stronger powers than those enjoyed by the voluntary schemes, nevertheless it was felt unfair to bind societies to implement the Ombudsman's decisions. Thus s.84(4), Building Societies Act 1986 gives a society which does not accept a ruling of the Ombudsman the option of publishing the fact of its non–compliance together with their reasons, in a manner deemed suitable by the Ombudsman. This option has in fact been

---

101   Sched.12, para. 3(e), Building Societies Act 1986.

invoked by the Cheshunt Building Society and is obviously a weakness in the scheme's functioning as a grievance redress mechanism for consumers.

17.5.5 Outcomes

A survey of the most recent annual reports from the ombudsmen reveals the following information on how complainants fared. Under the BOB 8,691 complaints were received in 1994 of which 1,033 are known to have been settled by the bank at an early stage after referral; 345 were settled (in the sense of the complainant having gained something) by the time a preliminary assessment had been made. Of the 1,095 complaints fully investigated, decisions were favourable to the complainant in 44.3 per cent of cases.[102] The BSOB received 8,407 cases in 1994 of which 280 were resolved through internal complaints procedures and 444 settled by the time the provisional assessment had been made; of the 589 which went to a formal decision, the complainant was wholly or partly successful in 338 cases (57 per cent).[103] IOB had 8,500 new cases referred to it in 1994 and, of the cases decided, 60 per cent upheld the insurer's decision. The insurer's decision was revised in favour of the policyholder in 36 per cent of cases and the complaint was withdrawn in 4 per cent.[104]

The Ombudsmen should not be judged solely by how well they perform the essentially private function of resolving disputes. Ombudsmen should also play a public function by raising standards generally. To some extent it could be argued that the mere fact the industry now knows that its decisions will be subject to an easily accessible independent review should itself help promote standards. This of course depends upon how effective the Ombudsmen are at modifying the behaviour of the businesses they supervise. The low public awareness of the schemes[105] may mean that banks can ignore the Ombudsmen, especially if their determinations are viewed as relating to individual problems which can be bought off. For the decisions to affect standards, they must be universalisable. This requires, first, that they must be in the public domain. The Insurance Ombudsman has just started to publish anonymous case reports. None of the other Ombudsmen publishes reports of cases, though cases are reported anonymously in annual reports which also discuss general principles. It is important that these decisions and

---

102   BOS, *Annual Report 1993–94.*
103   BOB, *Annual Report 1993–94.*
104   IOB, *Annual Report 1994.*
105   R. James and M. Seneviratne, *op. cit.* at 172 show public awareness as being 22 per cent for the Building Society Ombudsman and only slightly better, at 24 per cent, for his banking and 27 per cent for his insurance counterpart.

principles have some authority. It is significant in this respect that, whilst the Ombudsmen do not operate a system of binding precedent, they nevertheless view the principles which emerge from the annual reports as indicating how future cases are likely to be decided.

Whether Ombudsmen help to raise industry standards is likely to depend upon the rules and principles ombudsmen use to judge their industries by – in other words, are they prepared to go beyond the strict legal position in order to censure bad practice. The terms of reference of all three require that they have regard to principles of good commercial practice. The extent to which they are prepared to use this power to develop general principles depends upon the conception each Ombudsman has of his role. Thus whilst the first Insurance Ombudsman did not see this as part of his function, his successor, Julian Farrand, a former law professor, clearly did. However, Farrand's approach was markedly more assertive than most other Ombudsmen have dared to be. Thus the Building Society Ombudsman has said he does not see it as part of his task to issue codes of good practice, because he does not believe he should tell societies how to run their businesses. In his 1986–87 annual report, the Banking Ombudsman explained the failure to publish decisions on the basis that he had 'merely applied existing authorities to the facts of particular cases'. However, one ought not to be too critical of the Ombudsman's ability to raise standards, for the institutions have only relatively recently been established. It is perhaps understandable that they want to win the confidence of the industry and may only begin to demand higher standards after their adjudicative role has been accepted. As noted, the Insurance Ombudsman has begun to show his teeth. It will be interesting to see if Mr Farrand's successor, who was his previous Deputy, will continue in the same vein. If he does, the reactions of the industry will be interesting to monitor.

17.6 ARBITRATION

17.6.1 Legal Status

Ombudsmen's decisions are not binding on the consumer and Ombudsmen are not bound by the strict letter of the law. By contrast, arbitration involves referring the complaint to an independent arbitrator who will hand down a binding decision in respect of the case according to strict legal rules.[106] Arbitrations are governed by the Arbitration Acts 1950, 1975 and 1979,

---

[106] One disturbing feature of the British Telecom arbitration's scheme is that it excludes 'complicated issues of law', which prevents consumers challenging BTs conditions of contract.

which give only limited rights of appeal – from an arbitrator's decision to the ordinary courts – on points of law. Arbitration is an alternative to the county court system and is viewed as beneficial to consumers because it is meant to be quicker, cheaper and more informal than the courts. However, where the claim is within the county court limit, the Consumer Arbitration Agreements Act 1988 prevents the consumer being bound to take disputes to arbitration; where the claim exceeds the small claims limit the court can enforce such a term if it finds no detriment to the consumer in doing so.[107]

Under s.124(3), Fair Trading Act 1973 the Director General is under a duty 'to encourage relevant trade associations to prepare, and to disseminate to their members, codes of practice for guidance in safeguarding and promoting the interests of consumers'.[108] Most of the Codes of Practice contain low–cost arbitration schemes. However, there is no such scheme for electrical appliances operated by the Radio, Electrical and Television Retailers' Association; the arbitration scheme operated by the Association of Mail Order Publishers is not a specially established low cost scheme and there is no arbitration scheme under the footwear codes, but footwear can be tested at a reduced rate at the Footwear Testing Centre: the shop is bound by its findings and must pay two–thirds of the cost, with the consumer paying the other third. Most of the schemes are operated by the Chartered Institute of Arbitrators, although the motor trade makes separate arrangements and use an independent panel of arbitrators.

In addition there are several other consumer arbitration schemes which are not part of an Office of Fair Trading sponsored code. These cover British Rail, British Telecom, the Personal Insurance Arbitration Service (set up to cover those insurance companies which do not belong to the Insurance Ombudsman scheme), the Royal Institution of Chartered Surveyors and the Law Society. The Law Society scheme covers claims of negligence against solicitors and is entirely separate from the Solicitors' Complaints Bureau. Solicitors can refuse to be taken to arbitration under the scheme. The National House Building Council (which provides a warranty for new houses) also has an arbitration scheme, but this is not run on a low cost basis. All of these are administered by the Chartered Institute of Arbitrators.

The Office of Fair Trading has established model procedures for handling consumer complaints to which most trade association schemes roughly conform. Consumers first take up their complaint with the trader. If this fails the matter should be referred to the trade association which will attempt conciliation. If this too is unsuccessful, the consumer can opt for arbitration; both sides will sign an arbitration agreement accepting to be bound by the arbitrator's decision. The consumer is then precluded from

---

[107] See G. Howells (1988) *Co Law* 20.
[108] See 16.3.

taking the matter to court, save for the instances where there are limited rights of appeal from the arbitrator's decision. Given the importance of this point to consumers, it is obvious that they should be informed about their choice as to the forum in which the case should proceed and also about the pros and cons of the two options. In its study of three low cost trade arbitration schemes (run by the Association of British Travel Agents (ABTA), the Glass and Glazing Federation (GGF) and British Telecom (BT)) the National Consumer Council preferred the fuller explanation of the alternatives which ABTA provided to its complainants.[109]

17.6.2 Procedure

Although arbitration prevents the consumer from having access to the courts it does not mean that he or she is barred from taking legal advice. In fact, the National Consumer Council found that only 15 per cent of complainants had legal advice in preparing their cases for arbitration.[110] The parties submit written evidence to the arbitrator. Most arbitrations are based simply on the written papers, although the GGF code does provide for arbitrators to make site visits where necessary. The consumer will pay a registration fee (usually less that £40) which is returnable if he or she wins; there is no extra charge for a site visit under the GGF scheme. If the consumer loses, he or she is only liable for an amount up to the cost of the registration fee. The rest of the costs are borne either by the trader or trade association and also indirectly by the arbitrators, who seeing this work as a kind of social service, charge well below their normal rates. Some schemes also offer cheap testing facilities: thus for £5 shoes can be tested at the Footwear Testing Centre and for £22.50 the British Shops and Stores Association will send an inspector to report on furniture faults. The arbitrator will give reasons for his decisions,[111] which can be enforced through the court system.

17.6.3 Conciliation

The controversial features of the arbitration procedure are the inclusion of a conciliation stage and the reliance on paper only hearings. In its *Out of Court* report, the National Consumer Council noted that little is known about the

---

[109]   *Out of Court*, (HMSO, 1991) at 62.

[110]   *Ibid.* at 33.

[111]   This follows on from a recommendation to that effect contained in the Office of Fair Trading's report *Redress Procedures under Codes of Practice: Conclusions Following a Review by the Office of Fair Trading* (1981).

conciliation stage. However, many of the consumers who responded to its survey on arbitration felt that conciliation had been a waste of time.[112] Adding in a conciliation stage certainly prolongs proceedings and speed was not found to be one of the best features of the arbitration schemes. There were in fact allegations that traders deliberately delayed matters during the conciliation process. In its 1981 report, *Redress Procedures under Codes of Practice*, the Office of Fair Trading had recommended that trade bodies should set targets of not more than three months for the conclusion of the conciliation stage. In 1991 the Office was forced to concede that, where conciliation was used to any great extent, this target was often not met.[113] Consumerists tend to be wary of any attempt to conciliate, especially when undertaken by a trade association for, by definition, conciliation involves the two parties finding a compromise solution. If the consumer has a valid claim, this inevitably means that he or she recovers less than is due.

The National Consumer Council found that consumers mistrusted the evidence provided by traders and were concerned that, whilst their evidence was passed on to the trader, they did not receive copies of the trader's replies. The Office of Fair Trading has therefore recommended that trade bodies give serious consideration to having the conciliation process conducted by independent people and have promised to undertake further research into the conciliation process.

17.6.4 Paper Only Proceedings

The National Consumer Council found that two–fifths of the consumers surveyed would have liked to have met the arbitrator face to face, and that complainants to the GGF were more likely to consider the result fair if a site visit had occurred. They also noted that arbitrators were reluctant to keep going back to the parties for further information as this meant postponing the decision. It was recommended that personal hearings ought to be allowed where the claim exceeded the small claims limit, with the additional cost (estimated to be £150) being paid by the consumer but being returnable if the case was won. The National Consumer Council thought this could benefit complainants from lower socio–economic groups with whom personal hearings were particularly popular, although the requirement to pay a fee would obviously deter them. The Office of Fair Trading had recommended, in its 1981 report, that arbitrations be conducted on a documents only

---

112 *Out of Court op. cit.* at 26; but note the National Consumer Council's sample was biased as it only covered persons for whom conciliation had failed and who had proceeded to arbitration.

113 *Consumer Redress Mechanisms*, (Office of Fair Trading, 1991).

basis[114] and has continued to maintain this position, arguing that personal hearings, when available, have been little used and add to costs and delay. It points out that consumers who want their day in court can use the county courts which now have higher financial limits on the claims they hear. This would seem to go to the crux of the matter, for if arbitrations start to replicate court procedures, then the advantages of cost and speed which they ought to provide to the consumer are diminished.

17.6.5 Awareness and Use of Arbitration

One of the most disturbing features of the arbitration schemes is the lack of use made of them. Most are hardly ever used. Indeed the National Consumer Council found that the funeral scheme had never been used, the photography scheme had been used only once and, whilst a referral had been made under the caravan scheme, no arbitrator had been appointed at the time its report was prepared. On the other hand, ABTA received 14,200 complaints in 1989, 756 (5.3 per cent) of which resulted in an arbitration application being submitted. One explanation for the lack of use of arbitration schemes is a lack of awareness of the existence of the codes. Whilst more people were aware of the ABTA scheme than knew of the existence of the small claims courts,[115] the lack of awareness of lower-profile codes is dramatic. Thus only 11 per cent of those buying furniture had heard of the furniture code and only 4 per cent recalled the symbol of the trade association.[116] There is a clear need for the schemes to be given increased publicity, both to the general public and more particularly to consumer advisers.

17.6.6 Comparison with the Small Claims Court

It is interesting to note the comparisons made in the National Consumer Council's *Out of Court* report[117] between their present survey and that made in their 1979 report *Simple Justice* of small claims procedures in the county

---

[114]   *Redress Procedures under Codes of Practice, op. cit.* This report followed some reported instances where consumers had been held liable for substantial legal costs incurred following the holding of personal hearings.

[115]   *Consumer Redress Mechanisms, op. cit.* at 32.

[116]   Office of Fair Trading, *Furniture and Carpets: a Report by the Director General of Fair Trading*, (Office of Fair Trading, 1990).

[117]   *Op. cit.* table 4.1 at 39.

court.[118] Respondents rated arbitration and the county courts on a scale of 1–4, with 4 being the highest rating.

	Court	Arbitration
Approachable	2.68	2.90
Simple forms	3.04	3.25
Fair decisions	3.15	2.55
Informal procedure	2.95	3.00
Low costs	2.68	3.20
Speedy settlement of claims	2.36	2.37
Easily enforceable judgments	2.34	3.00
Base (nos. of respondents)	248	127

It will be seen that arbitration fares particularly well on cost and the ease with which judgements can be enforced, although rating of the latter varied between the different schemes. ABTA scored an impressive 3.19 on this count, but the GGF scored marginally less well than the county courts (2.33). The ABTA score may reflect the fact that failure to comply will lead to expulsion of the trader from ABTA and *de facto* from the UK travel industry. Concern must, however, be expressed at the low regard users of the arbitration schemes had for the fairness of the decisions. Most of the criticisms seemed to concern the size of the awards made. Earlier research by the Consumers' Association also suggested that arbitrators would award on average only between 58–64 per cent of the amount a registrar (as they were then called) in a county court would award.[119] It must also be disturbing to see that arbitration has not improved upon the speed at which cases are disposed of. Whilst the arbitration stage itself normally averages 20 weeks (compared to the 26 weeks which *Simple Justice* found it took for the county court to dispose of a case), when the conciliation stage is taken into account, the disposal time rises to 54 weeks for the GGF scheme and 45 weeks for ABTA.

17.6.7 Raising Standards by Publishing Information on Arbitration Practice

At present arbitration and conciliation are purely private affairs. Currently arbitrators meet informally to discuss the schemes. The National Consumer

---

[118] *Op. cit.*

[119] Consumers' Association, 'Package Holiday Disasters', *Holiday Which?* September 1986, p. 194.

Council has recommended that this be formalised and that the Chartered Institute for Arbitrators be responsible for publishing annual reports giving statistical breakdowns of the cases heard, a summary of what the arbitrators perceive to be the main issues arising during the year and anonymous reports of cases. It has also proposed that there should be similar reports for the large conciliation schemes.[120] These reports would help publicise the schemes, raise awareness of the approach arbitrators are taking and enable industry to develop good practice. This public accountability is needed if arbitration is going to raise standards as well as efficiently resolve individual disputes.

17.7 COMPLAINING

It is perhaps understandable that lawyers concentrate predominantly on formal legal rules and legal dispute resolution fora. In the consumer context, however, a broader view of dispute resolution is needed. Yet even some of the most liberal thinkers still view consumer redress mechanisms as involving third parties as negotiators, mediators, conciliators, arbitrators or adjudicators. The evidence suggests that this is not how most complaints are resolved. Thus Best and Andreasen's survey based on 2419 telephone calls with consumers in 34 cities in the US found that only 1.2 per cent of consumers who perceived a complaint 'voiced' this to a third party.[121] This would seem to support the Office of Fair Trading's research which showed that less than 2 per cent of those taking some form of action threatened court action.[122]

Best and Andreasen found that only 39.7 per cent of consumers who perceived a problem took any action to obtain redress. This does not mean that the remaining consumers were inactive in an economic sense; they may simply have decided to 'exit' (that is not purchase that product in the future, at least not from that supplier). Interestingly, complaining to the supplier directly was found to be fairly effective, with a 'satisfactory' solution being reached in 56.5 per cent of cases.[123] The study found that complaints were

---

120   *Out of Court, op. cit.*, at 60—1. This approach is broadly followed by the Office of Fair Trading in *Consumer Redress Mechanisms, op. cit.* at 53.

121   A. Best and A. Andreasen, 'Consumer Response to Unsatisfactory Products: A Survey of Perceiving Defects, Voicing Complaints and Obtaining Redress', (1976–7) 11 *Law and Soc R* 701.

122   See note 84.

123   This is in line with the results found in relation to the outcome of consumer complaints to UK insurance companies: in 39.6 per cent of cases the company gave

more likely to be voiced if they involved high price items and if the complainant had a high socio–economic status. Interestingly voiced complaints overrepresented simple objective problems, such as where the product was broken or the wrong product supplied, whilst there was a reluctance to voice judgmental complaints. Judgmental matters clearly covers questions of product design or durability, but could also include complaints about dubious selling methods.

From their study of complaint–handling by a major store in Denver (Colorado), Ross and Littlefield also concluded that complaining directly to retailers was a cheap and effective means of consumer redress.[124] In fact they found retailers were prepared to go beyond their strict legal obligation under the Uniform Commercial Code, for example by accepting goods back where the decision to return them was quite arbitrary. Again, complaining was seen to be a greater advantage to the middle classes, who were more confident and better able to articulate their problem. It was suggested that the generous policy adopted may be explained by the fact the study was based on a large store for whom the complaints represented a small proportion of their turnover. It might be conjectured that small retailers faced with complaints about expensive goods would be less liberal in their complaints handling policy. Smaller retailers may also find it less easy to return goods to suppliers as they have less bargaining power than large retailers.

A study by Ramsay and Enzle[125] confirmed that businesses usually allowed consumers rights which went beyond their strict legal entitlement. The reasons for doing so were to encourage repeat business and to engender good publicity. As the estimated cost of providing services to dissatisfied customers was less than 1 per cent, this could be viewed as money well spent. However, Ramsay 'obtained the impression that it might be easier for a consumer to obtain a refund or replacement where he was returning goods on arbitrary grounds for which their was no legal justification than if goods were being returned for judgmental problems ... for which there might be legal justification'. Presumably this can partly be explained by the fact that goods returned for arbitrary reasons (the wrong colour) can be easily resold and the consumer can often be persuaded to take a substitute product, whereas a claim that the product is defective may involve the retailer incurring costs. Also suppliers may become more defensive when the quality of their product or service is being questioned.

The practical value of complaining should not be under estimated.

---

the complainant everything asked for and in 25.4 per cent of cases the complainant was given something: see J. Birds and C. Graham (1993), *op. cit.* at 104.

124 L. Ross and N. Littlefield, 'Complaint as a Problem Solving Mechanism' (1978) 12 *Law and Soc R* 199.

125 Described in I. Ramsay, *op. cit.* at 126–130.

Complaining can be encouraged by increasing consumer awareness of their rights. However, there are also warning signs which should alert us to the limits of this approach to consumer protection. First, members of lower socio–economic groups appear less willing to complain. Of course they are also less likely to invoke the law. The difference is that, if the law is strengthened and made more accessible, they will benefit. If, however, lower status consumers are simply encouraged to complain and perhaps even given increased access to consumer advisers, they may still not improve their success rate. This is because much of the high success rate of complaining is due to retailers' goodwill, which is extended in the hope of retaining consumer loyalty. Retailers may be less concerned to retain the custom of low–income consumers. Second, retailers are less willing to accept complaints of a judgmental nature. Yet, matters such as the durability of goods, their quality, misrepresentations and bad selling practices are the very problems which consumer protection laws seek to redress. Third, there is a danger that voluntary settlement by traders may mask problems which continue to affect the sizeable number of consumers who take no action when confronted with a similar problem.

There is little research into the extent to which businesses monitor consumer complaints and use them to improve standards. Ross and Littlefield suggested that consumer complaints had an important role in quality control and that retailers passed on complaints to manufacturers.[126] In their study of insurance companies, Birds and Graham[127] found that all except the smallest stressed the importance of learning from complaints. One suspects that that exception is quite significant and that the extent to which companies attempt to learn from complaints varies greatly and often correlates to size. Even if smaller companies want to learn from complaints, they may not have the expertise, resources or even volume of complaints to be able to put this aspiration into practice. In this respect it is significant that, in the Birds and Graham study, the large companies had well established processes for monitoring complaints, but smaller companies' practices were often less well organised.

17.8 UTILITIES[128]

Limitations of space prevent us from looking in detail at consumer protection and access to justice within the privatised utilities such as gas, electricity, water and telecommunications, as well as those still in the public sector such

---

[126] L. Ross and N. Littlefield, *op. cit.*
[127] (1993), *op. cit.*
[128] See 1.9.3.

as British Rail. These industries do have unique features and we would like to stress the need for proper control of these sectors and adequate redress for consumers, especially as the action of utilities can affect in a very real way the standard of living of the poorer sections of the community who rely on these basic services. The privatised utilities are regulated by regulators under complex schemes, many of which provide for consumer committees. These committees and the regulators' offices provide channels through which complaints can be made.[129] Increasing these powers and providing a role for compensation to consumers who suffer unsatisfactory services have been central to John Major's Citizen's Charter initiative and are reflected in the strengthening of standards which seem to be behind the Competition and Services (Utilities) Act 1992.[130] The value of the Citizen's Charter programme and the real amount of influence the regulators have are matters of contention.

17.9 ACCESS TO JUSTICE - THE EUROPEAN DIMENSION

17.9.1 The Nature of the Problem

The creation of a single market within Europe requires consumer law to take account of the European dimension of consumer problems. These problems are likely to increase as cross-border transactions become more frequent in the future. There are several variants of cross–border problems which can affect consumers. UK consumers may be sold products and services in the United Kingdom by firms based in other Member States. These sales may be effected at a distance or be made through local retail outlets in the UK, which may, or may not, be branches of the foreign company. Traditionally the overseas firms have been manufacturers, but recently several foreign companies have entered the UK retail sector (eg Aldi, Ikea, Netto). Foreign manufacturers may or may not have set up local branches or subsidiaries.

However, as business and tourist travel increases within the European Union, another dimension of the cross–border problem will increase in significance: namely, that of the consumer who purchases goods and services abroad. Consumers on holiday in Italy may well avail themselves of local services such as hairdressers and almost certainly will have to use hotels and restaurants. They may also want to take advantage of differential pricing

---

129 See B. Harvey and D. Parry, *The Law of Consumer Protection and Fair Trading*, 4th ed. (Butterworths, 1992) at pp. 64–72.

130 See A. Barron and C. Scott, 'The Citizen's Charter Programme' (1992) 55 *MLR* 526 and P. Rawlings and C. Willett, 'Consumerism and the citizen's charter' (1994) 2 *Consum LJ* 3.

within the Union to buy local bargains; for example, many Danish consumers buy televisions from Germany where they are a lot cheaper, while many UK consumers would be happy to pay the lower prices for cars which apply in many European countries. New technology and the increased use of distant selling mean that consumers can make purchases overseas from the comfort of their own home. These cross–border transactions inevitably give rise to consumer complaints, which are even more difficult to resolve than domestic disputes.

17.9.2 Jurisdiction, Choice of Laws and Enforcement

17.9.2.1 Jurisdiction and Enforcement

There are several European Conventions aimed at making litigating within Europe simpler and more effective. Although many of these have special provisions governing consumer transactions, the coverage of the Conventions remains incomplete. In practice the additional costs of cross–border litigation make it impracticable for consumer complaints of relatively low monetary value.

The Brussels Convention on Jurisdiction and the Enforcement of Judgements in Civil and Commercial Matters 1968 was implemented in the UK by the Civil Jurisdiction and Judgements Act 1982. The Act provides that the Convention is to have the force of law and attaches it as a schedule to the Act. The basic principle behind the Convention is that defendants domiciled in a Contracting State should be sued in the courts of that State (art.2). The convention then goes on to make certain exceptions to this basic rule which allows defendants to be sued in courts in other contracting States. Those of particular relevance to consumers allow actions to be taken:

(i)   in matters relating to a contract, in the courts for the place of performance of the obligation in question (art.5(1));
(ii) in matters relating to tort, in the courts where the harmful event occurred (art.5(3)); and
(iii) as regards a dispute arising out of the operation of a branch, agency or other establishment, in the courts for the place in which the branch, agency or other establishment is situated.

There is another set of provisions which are specifically consumer protectionist (arts.13–5). These allow a consumer in specific situations to bring an action in either the state where the defendant is domiciled or in the courts of a Contracting State in which he or she is domiciled. This applies where the consumer made:

(i)   a contract for the sale of goods on instalment credit terms, or

(ii) a contract for a loan repayable by instalments, or any other form of credit, made to finance the sale of goods, or

(iii) any other contract for the supply of goods or services, where

(a) in the state of the consumer's domicile the conclusion of the contract was preceded by a specific invitation addressed to him or by advertising, and

(b) the consumer took in that state the steps necessary for the conclusion of the contract.[131]

Actions can only be brought against consumers in the courts of the Contracting State in which the consumer is domiciled.

However, despite these provisions there may still be occasions when consumers are left to litigate in foreign legal systems – a daunting prospect for the average consumer! Art.31 of the Convention does permit the enforcement of judgements made in one Contracting State by courts in another Contracting State on application by an interested party. However, the Sutherland Report on meeting the challenge of the internal market expressed doubts about the effectiveness of the Convention as in practice it seemed courts in Member States refused to execute orders made in other states on public interest grounds. Another weakness was seen as being that it did not apply to decisions taken by administrative bodies rather than courts of law.

17.9.2.2 Choice of Law

17.9.2.2.1 Contract: As well as the question of jurisdiction there is also the matter of which law applies. In contract, this matter is governed by the Rome Convention on the Law Applicable to Contractual Obligations 1980, which was implemented in the UK by the Contracts (Applicable Law) Act 1990. This convention sets out two basic principles. First, where the parties have made a choice of law, this will generally be respected (art.3(1)). Where no choice of law has been made, the contract will be governed by the country with which it is most closely connected (art.4(1)). Art.4(2) presumes that the contract is most closely connected:

> 'with the country where the party who is to effect the performance which is characteristic of the contract has, at the time of the conclusion of the contract, his habitual residence, or in the case of a body corporate or unincorporate, its central administration. However, if the contract is

---

131   Transport contracts are excluded from this provision.

entered into in the course of that party's trade or profession, that country shall be the country in which the principal place of business is situated or, where under the terms of the contract the performance is to be effected through a place of business other than the principal place of business, the country in which that other place of business is situated.'

As the characteristic of a consumer contract is the supply of goods and services then in most cases the governing law will be that of the supplier's country, unless the performance is effected through another place of business, which may or may not be in the same jurisdiction as the consumer.

Art.5, however, gives some special protection to consumers, the problem being that this is limited to certain consumer contracts defined in a limited manner. The consumer contracts to which art.5 applies are 'contracts the object of which is the supply of goods or services to a person ("the consumer") for a purpose which can be regarded as being outside his trade or profession, or a contract for the provision of credit for that object' (art.5(1)). In addition one of the three conditions outlined in art.5(2) must be satisfied, namely:

(i)   in the country of the consumer's habitual residence, the conclusion of the contract was preceded by a specific invitation or by advertising and the consumer had taken in that country all the steps necessary on his part for the conclusion of the contract (this parallels the exception provided under the Brussels Convention discussed above);

(ii) the other party or his agent received the consumer's order in the country where the consumer is habitually resident;

(iii) in the case of sale of goods contracts, the consumer travelled from the country of his habitual residence to another country and the consumer's journey was arranged by the seller for the purpose of inducing the consumer to buy (this will be more common on the continent, but could apply for instance to a trip specially arranged by a French retailer or vineyard for English consumers with the intention that they would buy wine in France).

For consumer contracts which fall within this definition a choice of law clause in a consumer contract cannot deprive the consumer of 'mandatory rules'. These are defined as rules of law in the consumer's country which cannot be derogated from by contract (article 3(3)), such as the implied quality conditions in consumer sale of goods contracts. Also for this limited range of consumer contracts where there is no choice of law clause, the contract will be governed by the law of the country in which the consumer has his or her habitual residence.

17.9.2.2.2 Tort: There is no equivalent of the Rome Convention governing choice of law in tort law.[132] Instead each state has its own rules of private international law. In the UK the position is currently governed by the double actionability rule in *Phillips v Eyre*.[133] This requires that the tort must be actionable both in the English legal system (*lex fori*) and in the foreign country in which it is alleged that the tort occurred (*lex loci delicti*). It now appears that the action need not attract tortious liability in the foreign country: contractual liability would suffice. But it must attract some form of civil liability and criminal liability would not be sufficient.[134] In *Boys v Chaplin*[135] some flexibility was given to the rule in *Phillips v Eyre* by stating that, on policy grounds and considering the various interests, it could be displaced in favour of the most appropriate law . Some of their Lordships favoured a test along the lines of the American Restatement so that the court could refer to the law which has 'the most significant relationship with the occurrence and the parties'. *Boys v Chaplin* itself concerned an accident between an English plaintiff and English defendant in Malta; the House of Lords applied English law, which allowed for damages for pain and suffering, since the parties were only in Malta temporarily.

17.9.3 Green Paper on Access to Justice

In a Green Paper entitled *Access of Consumers to Justice and the Settlement of Consumer Disputes in the Single Market*,[136] the European Commission has tried to encourage debate on consumers' access to justice. As early as 1975 the Council of Europe had recognised the right of consumers to proper redress by means of swift, effective and inexpensive procedures as one of

---

132 There is the Hague Convention on the Law Applicable to Products Liability 1973, but this has only been ratified by four member states.

133 (1870) LR 16 QB 1. It is likely that this rule will be reformed in the near future by the Private International Law (Miscellaneous Provisions) Bill currently before Parliament. This would as a general rule make the applicable law that of the country in which the events constituting the tort occured, but this could be displaced where factors make the laws of another country substantially more appropriate.

134 This appears to be the conclusion of *Boys v Chaplin* [1971] AC 356.

135 [1971] AC 356.

136 Com (93) 576: see discussion of the Green Paper in the special issue of the *Consumer Law Journal* devoted to Access to Justice in the light of the Green Paper (1995) 3 *Consum LJ* 1–39.

five categories of fundamental rights.[137] The Green Paper sees access to justice as a way of ensuring that the rhetoric of a 'People's Europe' is made a reality for consumers. The Sutherland Committee on meeting the challenge of the internal market had also recommended that the effective protection of consumers' rights be given 'rapid consideration'.[138]

After a useful survey of the position in Member States, the Green Paper notes the general trends towards (i) simplified procedures in small claims (although it notes the variance in the financial ceilings in different countries and different role conciliation plays in each system)[139] and (ii) out–of–court procedures. It comments that the independence (or at least impartiality) of the new 'judges' in out–of–court procedures might be questioned. It also makes the interesting suggestion of establishing minimum conditions which a body must satisfy before it can label itself as an 'Ombudsman'. The result should be to give consumers confidence in using such bodies in other Member States.

As regards the resolution of cross–border consumer claims by courts, the Green Paper recognises the problems, but before considering further powers suggests a period of study to identify the problems which are causing practical difficulties. The issue of legal aid has been the subject of a separate report by the Conseil des barreaux de la Communauté Européene.

We have already noted the suggestion concerning minimum standards for Ombudsmen; another interesting self–regulatory approach is to find sectoral solutions to problems. This could build on the Recommendation on transfrontier money transfers[140] which requires institutions participating in such transactions to be capable of dealing with complaints. If the matter is not dealt with within three months the consumer should be free to refer the matter to one of the national bodies in Member States competent to deal with complaints. Distance selling, motor car sales and package holidays have been identified as sectors to which this approach might be extended.

The Commission also suggests developing existing transfrontier co-

---

137 Council resolution of 14 April 1975 on a preliminary programme of the European Economic Community for a consumer protection and information policy: OJ 1975 C92/1.

138 Recommendation No. 22,

139 The Green Paper (at p. 56) appears to prefer conciliation by the judge who may eventually hand down the judgment, arguing that his credibility is underpinned by his independent and impartial status. It could, however, be said that his involvement in conciliation might make it inappropriate for him to decide the case if he learns too much about it during the negotiation process. It may be that if the conciliator is also to decide the case eventually then the parties may not be truly open with him or her at the conciliation stage for fear of revealing too much of their hand.

140 OJ 1990 L67/39.

operation. For example the 'International Marketing Supervision Network' promotes co–operation between national authorities responsible for consumer protection in the 20 OECD countries, while the European Advertising Standards Alliance was created to promote self–regulation of advertising at the European level. The Commission has also supported co–operation between consumer organisations in frontier regions. This might take the form of seminars on the most common legal problems or the creation of software packages for debt advisers which can be exchanged between organisations from different countries.[141]

Consumer justice involves not only the settlement of individual disputes but also the resolution of general problems. To some extent this can be done through private law mechanisms, such as the class or representative action. However, the Green Paper notes that these mechanisms suffer many of the transfrontier barriers which individuals face when seeking to exercise legal rights. Instead the Green Paper preferred to concentrate on the means available to seek injunctions against unlawful acts. It noted a paradox which makes many of these supervisory powers (such as those of the Director General under Part III of the Fair Trading Act 1974)[142] irrelevant in cross–border problems. If a UK company is pursuing an unfair trade practice which only affects consumers in, say, Denmark, then the Danish authorities will not have any standing in the UK courts while the UK authorities will have no interest (or legal power) to take action to stop the unfair practice.

After rejecting the idea of a Community regulator, the Commission proposed either (i) mutual recognition of the right to bring actions by bodies in other Member States representing the injured interest, or (ii) harmonisation setting the minimum circumstances when bodies representing those injured by unfair commercial practices can seek injunctions. Certainly if confidence is to be instilled and a level playing field achieved, then a minimum level of protection should be set; above this, bodies from other states should have the same rights as national entities. This does not interfere with Member States' rights to organise their own affairs, but simply prevents the exportation of trading practices which would be unlawful in the recipient country.

One problem may be the issue of standing. The Green Paper states that the subsidiarity principle requires Member States to define the criteria for capacity to bring such actions. It then, however, goes on to suggest that this does not so much mean actually setting the criteria (which is presumably 'bodies representing the interest injured by an unlawful commercial

---

141 Although raising the awareness of consumer groups and consumer advisers about the laws in other Member States may be desirable, there are the dangers: (i) a little knowledge can be a dangerous thing and (ii) legal knowledge can soon become dated.

142 See 16.4.

practice'), but rather the means by which these criteria are established (for example administrative procedure or court practice). Thus foreign entities would presumably have to be registered or satisfy the court that they comply with the same criteria as are applied to national bodies. However, there are a wide variety of approaches to the question of whom should have the right to bring injunctive procedures. For instance, France recognises ten consumer organisations as having this right; in Germany the matter is determined by the courts, whereas in the UK only the Director General is given these powers. If the Government does not want the Consumers' Association to have standing one suspects they will be even less enthusiastic at the prospect of foreign consumer organisations having the power to litigate in the UK courts. Thus mutual recognition may run into problems if the various countries do not recognise the same sort of organisations (for example, private bodies versus Government agencies). It is understood the European Commission is contemplating a directive on this topic of mutual recognition, but any legislation is likely to respect national traditions. An alternative approach might be to give national bodies responsibility for protecting all European consumers from unfair trading practices originating within their jurisdiction.

17.10 SOME FINAL REMARKS ON ACCESS TO JUSTICE

Consumer rights are only as effective as their enforcement, be that through individual initiative as discussed in this chapter or by public authorities as discussed in Chapters 14 and 16. It is sometimes less well appreciated that access to justice should not only solve individual problems, but also provide information on complaints which business can use to improve standards and which law reformers can draw on to inform debate about the future direction of the law.

17.11 SOME FINAL REMARKS TO THE READER

The reader who has stayed with us this far will know that consumer lawyers need a wide range of legal knowledge, covering, *inter alia*, competition law, common law, criminal law, administrative law, European law, soft law and procedural law. The list does not end there for they must also be conversant with economics, sociology and psychology. All these skills are needed because consumer problems are on the borderline of private/public and social/commercial problems. Consumer law forces one to consider the position of the individual in the complex modern world, a world which is becoming more complicated with the increased internationalisation of trade and the use of new technologies. The future offers great opportunities for consumers, but consumer law must ensure them the freedom to choose how to exploit these possibilities without danger to themselves, their fellow citizens or their environment. We hope the reader will feel better able to engage in these debates for having read or consulted this book.

Index